Cape of Good Hope Education Commision

Second Report and Proceedings

With Appendices, of a Commission Appointed to Enquire Into and Report Upon

Certain Matters Connected with the Educational System of the Colony

Cape of Good Hope Education Commision

Second Report and Proceedings
With Appendices, of a Commission Appointed to Enquire Into and Report Upon Certain Matters Connected with the Educational System of the Colony

ISBN/EAN: 9783337161200

Printed in Europe, USA, Canada, Australia, Japan

Cover: Foto ©Andreas Hilbeck / pixelio.de

More available books at **www.hansebooks.com**

CAPE OF GOOD HOPE.

SECOND REPORT AND PROCEEDINGS, WITH APPENDICES,

OF A

COMMISSION

APPOINTED TO ENQUIRE INTO AND REPORT UPON CERTAIN
MATTERS CONNECTED WITH THE

EDUCATIONAL SYSTEM

OF THE COLONY.

Presented to both Houses of Parliament by command of His Excellency the Governor.
1892.

CAPE TOWN:
W. A. RICHARDS & SONS, GOVERNMENT PRINTERS, CASTLE STREET.
1892.

[G 3—'92.]

CONTENTS.

REPORT

To His Excellency Sir HENRY BROUGHAM LOCH, Knight Grand Cross of the Most Distinguished Order of Saint Michael and Saint George, Knight Commander of the Most Honourable Order of the Bath, Governor and Commander-in-Chief of Her Majesty's Colony of the Cape of Good Hope in South Africa, and of the Territories and Dependencies thereof, and Her Majesty's High Commissioner, &c., &c., &c.

MAY IT PLEASE YOUR EXCELLENCY,—

Your Commissioners beg to submit further Minutes of Evidence taken in the prosecution of the enquiry, and additional answers to their Circular, received since the printing of the first report.

J. D. BARRY,

President.

EDUCATION COMMISSION.

MINUTES OF PROCEEDINGS.

EDUCATION COMMISSION.

MINUTES OF PROCEEDINGS.

Graham's Town, Thursday, September 3rd, 1891.

The Commission assembled, pursuant to adjournment, in the Library of the Eastern Districts Court, at 10 a.m.

PRESENT:

Sir J. D. BARRY, Kt. (President),

T. P. THERON, Esq., M.L.A.,   A. N. ROWAN, Esq.,
Rev. M. P. A. COETZEE, jun.,   The Very Rev. J. G. HOLMES,
Rev. A. MOORREES,   Dr. W. B. BERRY.

The Secretary submitted replies received to the General Circular issued by the Commission.
The Secretary laid before the Commission the following documents :—

Natal Education Reports, 1888-89.
Reports of the Royal Commission on Elementary Education Acts (England and Wales), 1886-87-88.
Report and Evidence of Commission on Education (Natal), 1891.
Reports of Committees of County Councils and other schemes and proposals for utilisation of new fund under the Local Taxation Act, 1890, for educational purposes.
Report of proceedings of Conference *re* working of Education clauses of the Local Taxation Act, 1890.
Austrian Educational Statistics.
Belgian Education Reports.
Reports relative to various English Educational Institutions and Night Schools.
Extracts from various colonial newspapers bearing on the question of Education.
Return, compiled from the last Census, showing the population of all towns with 2,000 inhabitants and upwards.
The Secretary read a letter from the Under Colonial Secretary, dated July 4th, 1891, forwarding a resolution adopted by the Hon. the House of Assembly on the 26th June, to the following effect :—" This House is of opinion that it is desirable that the question of establishing night schools in the leading towns of the Colony be referred to the Education Commission now sitting for enquiry and report."

The Rev. J. Roos, the Rev. J. C. Reyneke, the Rev. T. Chubb, and the Lord Bishop of Graham's Town were examined.
The Commission deliberated.
Resolved,—That the Commission, upon rising at Graham's Town, proceed to Port Elizabeth. Also that Mr. Theron and the Rev. Mr. Moorrees bring up a recommendation as to what places should be visited, and what witnesses called for the purpose of ascertaining the views of the farmer class on the various questions referred to the Commission.
Adjourned till the following day at 10·15 a.m.

Graham's Town, Friday, September 4th, 1891.

PRESENT:

Sir J. D. BARRY (President),

Mr. THERON,   Dr. BERRY,
Rev. COETZEE,   Dean HOLMES,
,, MOORREES,   Mr. ROWAN.

The minutes of the last meeting were read and confirmed.
The Commission deliberated.

Resolved,—That the Secretary be directed to apply to the Superintendent of the Census for information on the following points :—

1. The gross number of children in the Colony under the age of 15, distinguishing the sexes and colour.

        A. In Towns.   B. In the Country.

2. The number of children under the age of 15 who are now under education in all Colonial Schools whether Government Aided or Private, the numbers in each of these classes of schools respectively, distinguishing the sexes and colour.

        A. In Towns.   B. In the Country.

3. The gross number of children under education of an age not exceeding 7 years; how many are between 7 and 10 years, how many above 10 and under 15 ; and how many are over 15, distinguishing the colour and sexes.

The Secretary read the following letter from the Colonial Secretary, dated the 31st August, 1891 :—

Colonial Secretary's Office,
Cape Town, Cape of Good Hope,
31st August, 1891.

Sir,—With reference to certain enquiries made on your behalf by the Secretary to the Education Commission, I have the honour to inform you that the Government does not contemplate an enquiry by the Commission into a general plan of compulsory education for the Colony, but only into the question of truancy and irregular attendance in the larger centres of population.

With regard to the extension of the present plan of industrial training among aborigines, the Government does not wish to encourage among the aborigines any expectation of large additional subsidies for their Institutions and Schools; the consideration of the question need not therefore involve a lengthy enquiry into the general system of Education amongst the natives.

I have the honour to be,
Sir,
Your obedient Servant,
J. W. SAUER.

The Honourable Sir Jacob D. Barry,
    Graham's Town.

Mr. J. Slater, Sister Cecile, the Rev. Father Simeon, the Rev. Canon Mullins, Mr. F. M. de Vries van Heijst, and Mr. W. C. Meredith were examined.

Adjourned till the following day at 10·15 a.m.

Graham's Town, Saturday, September 5th, 1891.

PRESENT :

Sir J. D. Barry (President),

Mr. Theron,	Dr. Berry,
Rev. Coetzee,	Dean Holmes.
,, Moorrees,	

The minutes of the last meeting were read and confirmed.

Resolved,—That the Government be requested to sanction the payment of reasonable expenses of such non-official witnesses as the Commission may consider it necessary to summon from a distance, and that all such payments as the Commission may deem proper to be incurred shall be approved under the certificate of the Secretary.

The Rev. C. Taberer, Rev. Gana Kakaza, and the Rev. Father Fitz Henry were examined.

Adjourned till Monday, the 7th inst., at 10 o'clock a.m.

Graham's Town, Monday, September 7th, 1891.

PRESENT :

Sir J. D. Barry (President),

Mr. Theron,	Dean Holmes,
Rev. Coetzee,	Dr. Berry,
,, Moorrees,	Mr. Rowan.

The minutes of the last meeting were read and confirmed.

The Rev. Father Fitz Henry was further examined.

Rev. Father Berghegge, Rev Father Daignault, Rev. Canon Espin were examined.

Adjourned till the following day at 10 o'clock a.m.

Graham's Town, Tuesday, September 8th, 1891.

Sir J. D. BARRY (President),

Mr. THERON,   Dean HOLMES,
Rev. COETZEE,   Dr. BERRY,
„ MOORREES,   Mr. ROWAN,

The minutes of the last meeting were read and confirmed.
Mr. F. Howe Ely, the Rev. G. W. Cross, Mr. A. C. McDonald were examined.
The Secretary read the following letter from the Colonial Secretary, dated the 5th
September, 1891 :—

Colonial Secretary's Office,
Cape Town, Cape of Good Hope,
5th September, 1891.

SIR,—With reference to a letter dated 15th July last from the Secretary to the
Education Commission, and in continuation of my letter of the 31st ultimo, I have the
honour to inform you that the Government consider it advisable that the attention of the
Commission should be directed to the question of technical instruction in connection with
Undenominational Public Schools.

I have the honour to be,
Sir,
Your obedient Servant,
J. W. SAUER,
Colonial Secretary.

The Honourable Sir JACOB D. BARRY, Kt.,
Graham's Town.

The Commission deliberated.
The Rev. Moorrees brought up the following report :—
"That two or more sub-committees be appointed before the adjournment of the
present sitting, who shall further investigate as far as possible the educational
wants of the agricultural population, and submit a report to the Commission
at its next sitting."
After discussion, the further consideration of the subject was adjourned.
The Commission resolved to hold its next sitting at Port Elizabeth, and adjourned till the
following day at 10 o'clock a.m.

Port Elizabeth, Wednesday, September 9th, 1891.

PRESENT:

Sir J. D. BARRY (President),

Mr. THERON,   Dean HOLMES,
Rev. MOORREES,   Dr. BERRY.
„ COETZEE,

The minutes of the last meeting were read and confirmed.
Mr. E. Noaks and Mr. R. H. Hammersley Heenan were examined.
The Commission deliberated.
Mr. Moorrees requested that the report brought up by him the preceding day might be
withdrawn.
Agreed to.
Resolved,—That the following centres be visited by the Commission, viz. :—Somerset East
and Middelburg, principally to get information regarding the educational wants of
the agricultural population.
Resolved,—That the Commission assemble at Somerset East on Monday, the 14th inst.
Adjourned till the following day at 10 o'clock a.m.

Port Elizabeth, Thursday, September 10*th,* 1891.

PRESENT :

Sir J. D. BARRY (President),

Mr. THERON,	Dean HOLMES,
Rev. MOORREES,	Dr. BERRY,
„ COETZEE,	Mr. ROWAN.

The minutes of the last meeting were read and confirmed.
The Rev. Dr. Wirgman, Mr. A. S. Marshall-Hall, Rev. Father Strobino, Rev. S. Brook, Rev. C. E. Mayo, Mr. R. W. Clarry, Hon. H. W. Pearson, M.L.A., and Mr. McIlwraith were examined.
Adjourned till the following day at 10 o'clock a.m.

Port Elizabeth, Friday, September 11*th,* 1891.

PRESENT :

Sir J. D. BARRY (President),

Mr. ROWAN,	Rev. MOORREES,
Mr. THERON,	Dr. BERRY.
Dean HOLMES,	

The minutes of the last meeting were read and confirmed.
Rev. Dr. Hewitt, Rev. D. J. Pienaar, Mr. A. MacQuaig, Mr. J. M. Thornton, Dr. A. Vanes, and Mr. J. Buckley were examined.
Adjourned till the following day at 10 o'clock a.m.

Port Elizabeth, Saturday, September 12*th,* 1891.

PRESENT :

Sir J. D. BARRY (President),

Mr. ROWAN,	Rev. MOORREES,
„ THERON,	Dr. BERRY.
Dean HOLMES,	

The minutes of the last meeting were read and confirmed.
Rev. J. Pritchard, Mr. D. Lumsden, Mr. J. Brister, and Rev. G. Smith were examined.
The Commission deliberated.
The Secretary read a letter from Mr. H. W. Bidwell, of Uitenhage, dated the 9th inst. suggesting the names of certain witnesses who wished to give evidence at that place.
Resolved,—That the circular of questions be sent to the several gentlemen named in Mr. Bidwell's letter, only received this day ; and that Mr. Bidwell be informed that the Commission will be pleased to have the written evidence of the gentlemen, but that arrangements which have been fixed by the Commission for sittings at other places, preclude a visit to Uitenhage at the last moment.
The Commission resolved to hold its next sitting at Cookhouse on Monday, the 14th inst., and subsequently proceed to Somerset East.
Adjourned until Monday, the 14th inst.

Cookhouse, Monday, September 14*th,* 1891.

PRESENT :

Sir J. D. BARRY (President),

Dean HOLMES,	Dr. BERRY.

Mr. H. Veary and R. T. Pearce were examined.
Resolved,—That the Commission meet at Somerset East at 2 o'clock p.m.

Somerset East, Monday, September 14th, 1891.

PRESENT :

Sir J. D. BARRY (President),

Dean HOLMES, | Dr. BERRY.

The minutes of the last meeting were read and confirmed.
Professor MacWilliam and the Rev. N. Abraham were examined.
Adjourned till the following day at ten o'clock a.m.

Somerset East, Tuesday, September 15th, 1891.

PRESENT :

Sir J. D. BARRY (President),

Dr. BERRY, | Rev. MOORREES
Mr. THERON | Dean Holmes

The minutes of the last meeting were read and confirm
Professor MacWilliam further examined.
Miss M. Houliston, Mr. P. Botha, Mr. J. S. B. Holden, Mr. A. Louw, Mr. J. H. Overman,
Rev. J. H. Hofmeyr, and Mr. F. A. Brailsford were examined.
The Commission resolved to hold its next sitting at Middelburg, Wednesday, the 16th inst.,
at two o'clock p.m.

Middelburg, Wednesday, September 16th, 1891.

PRESENT :

Sir J. D. BARRY (President),

Dean HOLMES, | Dr. BERRY.
Mr. THERON, |

The minutes of the last meeting were read and confirmed.
The Commission deliberated.
Adjourned until the following day at nine o'clock am.

Middelburg, Thursday, September 17th, 1891.

Sir J. D. BARRY (President),

PRESENT :

Dean HOLMES, | Dr. BERRY,
Mr. THERON, | Rev. COETZEE.

The minutes of the last meeting were read and confirmed.
Mr. J. Joubert, M.L.A., Mr. J. R. Cuthbert, Mr. G. J. Steenekamp, Mr. P. J. Grobler, Mr. N.
Kruger, Rev. H. J. Withers, Rev. A. F. Weich, Rev. G. van Niekerk were
examined.
Adjourned until the following day at nine o'clock am.

Middelburg, Friday, September 18th, 1891.

PRESENT :

Sir J. D. BARRY (President),

Rev. COETZEE, | Dean HOLMES,
Mr. THERON, | Dr. BERRY.

The minutes of the last meeting were read and confirmed.
Mr. N. F. de Waal, Rev. M. Postma, Mr. N. Duvenage, Mr. S. Buis, Mr. D. K. Theron
were examined.
Resolved,—That the Commission, after taking such evidence as is obtainable at Kimberley,
set apart one day for deliberation on the questions referred to it.
Adjourned until Monday, the 21st inst.

Vryburg, Monday, September 21st, 1891.

PRESENT :

Sir J. D. BARRY (President),
Dr. BERRY.

Mr. Howarth and Mrs. Chiddy were examined.
Adjourned until the following day at 10 o'clock.

Kimberley, Tuesday, September 22nd, 1891.

PRESENT :

Sir J. D. BARRY (President),

| Dr. BERRY, | Dean HOLMES, |
| Mr. THERON, | Rev. MOORREES. |

The minutes of the last meeting were read and confirmed.
Von. Archdeacon Gaul, Mr. W. Norrie, Mr. E. A. Judge, Rev. D. D. Fraser were examined.
Adjourned till the following day at 10 o'clock a.m.

Kimberley, Wednesday, September 23rd, 1891.

PRESENT :

SIR J. D. BARRY (President),

| Dr. BERRY, | Mr. THERON, |
| Dean HOLMES, | Rev. MOORREES. |

The minutes of the last meeting were read and confirmed.
Mr. A. H. Bleksley. Rev. W. Loith, Mr. J. S. Cowie, Mr. C. A. Blackbeard, Rev. G. Mitchell, Dr. Watkins, Mr. Gardner Williams, Rev. W. Pescod, and His Lordship Bishop Gaughran were examined.
The Secretary read the following telegram from the Hon. Mr. Dolley, M.L.C., Uitenhage :
—"Newspaper states Thornton, Pienaar and Vanes were summoned as witnesses before the Commission. Please wire if correct, as statement gives dissatisfaction ; others b.ing passed over."
Resolved,—That the Secretary be instructed to forward to the Hon. Mr. Dolley a copy of the Resolution adopted on the 12th inst., and inform him further that Mr. Thornton and Dr. Vanes were requested to give evidence in regard to the subject of technical education, and that the Rev. Mr. Pienaar happened to be in Port Elizabeth at the time the Commission was sitting there.
The Commission deliberated.
Adjourned until the following day at 10 o'clock a.m.

Kimberley, Thursday, September 24th, 1891.

Sir J. D. BARRY (President),

PRESENT :

| Dr. BERRY, | Mr. THERON, |
| Dean HOLMES, | Rev. MOORREES. |

The minutes of the last meeting were read and confirmed.
Mr. F. L. Dwyer and the Hon. Mr. Justice Solomon were examined.
The Commission deliberated.
Resolved,—That on its rising at Kimberley, the Commission adjourn until Thursday, the 21st of January next, to meet in Cape Town.

EDUCATION COMMISSION.

MINUTES OF EVIDENCE.

CAPE OF GOOD HOPE.

EDUCATION COMMISSION.

MINUTES OF EVIDENCE.

Presented to both Houses of Parliament by command of His Excellency the Governor.

1892.

Graham's Town, Thursday, 3rd September, 1891.

PRESENT :

Sir JACOB DIRK BARRY, Knight (President),

T. P. Theron, Esq., M.L.A.,
Rev. M. P. A. Coetzee. Jr..
Rev. A. Moorrees,

A. N. Rowan, Esq.,
The Very Rev. J. G. Holmes,
Dr. W. B. Berry.

Rev. Johannes Roos examined.

Rev.
Johannes Roos.

Sept. 3rd, 1891.

2616. *President.*] I believe you live at Alexandria ?—Yes.

2617. And you are a minister of the Dutch Reformed Church ?—Yes.

2618. Have you any schools ?—Yes. At one time I was the chairman and secretary of four aided schools.

2619. What are you now ?—At present I am the chairman and secretary of two Government undenominational schools—the second class girls' school and a third class country mixed school.

2620. In the district or town ?—In the district.

2621. Is there any und-nominational public school in the town itself ?—Not for boys at present. There is a private boys' school.

2622. Have you any guarantors ?—Yes, in connection with the girls' school.

2623. Do you find that the system of guarantors works well ?—Not very well. We find as a rule that the guarantors have to pay in at the end of the year.

2624. Have the schools which you refer to any property now ?—No. The building in which the girls' school is held belongs to the Dutch Reformed Church. It is given free of any rent, which of course helps.

2625. Are the guarantors principally members of the Dutch Reformed Church ?—At present they are altogether.

2626. Is there anything which you would substitute for the system of guarantors? I think a permanent Board will be a good thing.

2627. How do you think such a Board should be created ?—By the ratepayers or the voters.

2628. By the voters for the Divisional Council or by the Parliamentary electors? —By the former, I think.

2629. You would have a Board established ?—Yes.

2630. And vest in the Board any property belonging to the school ?—Yes.

2631. Would you force the Board to start schools of its own. or should it work with the schools that are in existence ?—I would prefer that it worked with existing schools.

2632. And if it found them insufficient, start others ?—Quite so.

2633. And if there is a deficiency, come upon the rates ?—Yes.

2634. What could you work a school at per head, independent of what the Government gives, including rent, provisions, lighting, books, and so on ?—It would all depend on the number of teachers and number of pupils.

2635. What would it be fair for the Government to contribute per head if there was such a Board in existence ?—About five shillings per head a month.

2636. Would that be enough ?—Yes.

2637. That is for white children ?—Yes.

2638. Are they all white children coming to your school ?—Yes.

[G. 3—'92.]

B

Rev.
Johannes Roos.

Sept. 3rd, 1891.

2639. Are there many blacks also to be provided for ?—There is a mission school for them.

2640. Are there many white children who do not go to a school at all ?—Yes ; a good number, not in the town but in the country.

2641. What proportion do you think in the country ?—At least one-tenth of the children of school-going age are not going to school.

2642. That is under the age of fifteen ?—Yes.

2643. And in the town ?—They pretty well all go to school.

2644. Do you see any way of getting all the children in the country into school ? —To some extent, by making education as cheap as possible for them. We have had to close the country school, as the people were very poor, and we were unable to get a sufficient grant. It was in existence for a couple of years. I applied for a circuit grant, but Sir Langham Dale did not see his way clear to give it.

2645. With regard to coloured children, do they all go to school ?—No.

2646. Do you see your way to starting a school which would suit coloured children ?—I have one in the town. It is not in connection with our Church ; but there is no minister for the native congregation there, and I have taken it in hand and got a small grant from Sir Langham Dale for it.

2647. Do you think that an industrial department in connection with these schools would answer ?—It would hardly be necessary at present in a small place like ours.

2648. Would it not be a good thing ?—It would be a very good thing.

2649. What industry can you think of that would be suitable ?—Farm work would be the chief thing.

2650. Could you have farm work, gardening, and so on, taught in schools in town ? Yes.

2651. Could it be done inexpensively ?—It would be very little expense.

2652. Could the same management that now undertakes the native school manage the industrial department ?—Yes, I think so.

2653. *Dean Holmes.*] What is the percentage of attendance of children in your school to the number on the roll ?—We have two teachers at present with about 27 children, girls, and a few small boys, and the attendance is very fair, about 24 out of 27.

2654. Then you have no complaint to make about the irregularity of attendance ? —No. There is no irregularity of attendance in our school, nor in the country school either, as far as I know.

2654A. *Mr. Rowan.*] You said there were some children not attending any school. Could you tell us what children they are, taking the white children first ?—The children of tenants living on the farms, very poor people, bywoners. With regard to the blacks, they are the children of people who live with the farmers.

2655. Is there any way of reaching the children of these bywoners ?—Yes. The circuit schools to a certain extent would reach them.

2656. Do they take advantage of these schools ?—They would take advantage of them, only there is the difficulty about boarding accommodation. We cannot get a grant for these children, because there is only one centre.

2657. You spoke of the guarantee system ; have you ever had any difficulty in making up deficiencies that have arisen ?—I have always tried to avoid the difficulty by paying the deficiency out of my own pocket. A school always suffers. You will not get people to guarantee again if they find they have to pay in. That has been my experience at least.

2658. Are both English and Dutch taught in your school ?—Yes.

2659. Do you think that further facilities should be afforded for the acquisition of the Dutch language ?—Yes ; I think so in regard to the examinations.

2660. To what examination do you allude specially ?—All the examinations, beginning with the elementary.

2661. You think that Dutch should be given equal rights with English ?—Yes.

2662. Has there been more activity as regards the teaching of Dutch of late than there was formerly ?—I think so. I think people are now taking more interest in Dutch education.

2663. *Rev. Moorrees.*] Can you always get sufficient children to make up the number required for circuit schools ?—I do not know exactly what the number is. I think it is 20 ; and I believe we would be able to get that number. The farms are pretty close together, and the tenants live pretty much on one farm. It is not like many other districts.

2664. If you had a School Board, would you give to that Board the direction of the education of the district ?—Yes.

2665. If Dutch were introduced into the Elementary examination would you give special marks to a boy who took Dutch ?—I would have the marks equal. Dutch would count as well as English.

2666. Do you think in the School Higher examination and the Matriculation, the two languages of the country, Dutch and English, should get higher marks than foreign languages, such as German and French?—Yes; I think they should.

Rev.
Johannes Roos.

Sept. 3rd, 1891.

2667. *Rev. Coetzee.*] Would you make Dutch compulsory in the Elementary examination like English?—I would hardly go that length.

2668. How would you fix the marks then?—I would make them equal.

2669. Suppose half the candidates took Dutch as well as the other subjects, and half only took English, how would you fix the marks?—They would have to be divided.

2670. *Dean Holmes.*] You would be content to have the whole examination set in either Dutch or English?—Yes.

2671. *Rev. Coetzee.*] Would that be practicable as the schools are constituted at present?—I do not know whether it would be practicable. It might be in some places. I cannot say as a rule. I do not think it would be very much followed up. We must have both languages; we cannot dispense with one.

2672. You think that that is the only means of meeting the difficulty, by having two sets of papers?—Yes, I think so; but then the marks ought to be divided, as I said before.

2673. *Rev. Moorrees.*] If a child takes Dutch and English, ought it to get more marks than the one who takes English only?—Yes.

2674. *Dean Holmes.*] You would give an alternate subject to the other boys to make it fair in the aggregate, would you not?—Yes.

2675. *President.*] Your district is an agricultural district, is it not?—Yes.

2676. You told us that about fifty per cent. of the children of European parentage do not go to school?—Yes.

2677. Do they work on the farms?—Yes.

2678. What would be the age, as a rule, at which they begin to work?—They commence very young.

2679. Would you call the parents an illiterate class?—To a certain extent.

2680. Do they teach their children at home?—They give them a little teaching.

2681. How do they arrange for such education as is necessary for church purposes?—They give the children schooling before confirmation.

2782. How is that schooling procured?—They either have to get a teacher for the time being, or else send them to the nearest school.

2683. Do they pay the teacher?—Yes.

2684. Are there many private farm schools in your division?—Not so many. I daresay there are about half-a-dozen at present.

2685. Would the farmers take the children of bywoners into a private farm school?—Yes.

2686. Is the Government grant available for those children too. I mean the capitation grant?—I do not think so. There are no cases that I know of where they get that grant. Of course the farmer gets the grant for aided farm schools, and a teacher.

2687. If the child of a bywoner comes to the private farm school, could not the capitation grant be obtained for him?—It could, but I do not know of any case.

2688. What is the reason, is it dislike on the part of the farmer?—I do not think so. Perhaps the children do not attend so regularly that they think they could get the grant. I know of only one aided school on a farm. I have tried to establish more, but as a rule, they have to exist for a year before they can get a grant, and sometimes, after the school has been there a year, the teacher has left, and they have not been able to continue the school. I know of one school where such a grant is made. They get a certain sum according to the Standard passed. Personally I have nothing to do with the school, and I do not know whether they get a capitation grant. It is just possible.

2689. As far as you know, would there be any objection on the part of the better class of farmers who might have private farm schools, to take the bywoner class into those schools?—No objection whatever. The bywoners will only be too glad to get the grant.

2690. Then the reason why these grants are not taken advantage of is because they are not applied for?—Yes.

2691. And there are no such schools hardly in the district?—I know of only one Dutch school. There may be English schools where they do get a capitation grant.

2692. You are not aware that the capitation grant for indigent boarders has been applied for in your district?—I am not aware. There is only one school where they could have anything of the kind. They have two or three children coming from a distance, and boarding there. I am not aware whether they get a capitation grant. I know they get the grant for farm schools.

B 2

Rev.
Johannes Roos.

Sept. 3rd, 1881.

2693. You said that you would be in favour of the establishment of local Boards, and that you would give to those Boards the direction of the education of the district; do you mean subject to the general control of the Education Department?—**As far as practicable.**

2694. Would you give the local Board the power to direct the whole method and plan of education in the district, the quality of the education and the subjects?—I should like to see the inspection varied according to circumstances. I have always found fault with the system of inspection, whereby you must work children up for certain standards and get into a certain routine of instruction, without being able to deviate from it. In country schools you want the children to be well up in the three r's, and things that they need every day. A boy, for instance, works up for a certain standard, and he would do very well in everything else except arithmetic, but for lack of that he fails. I think it would therefore be a very good thing if the system of inspection could be suited to the requirements of the various localities.

2695. *Dr. Berry.*] With reference to the question of Dutch in the Elementary examination, if there is a large number of children coming forward for that examination who have no means of acquainting themselves with Dutch at all, would it not be rather unfair that those who know a little Dutch should get marks for that little knowledge over and above boys and girls who have no such advantage at all?—It would certainly seem not very fair.

2696. Would it not be better for all classes and all interests, if a separate list was prepared in connection with the examination for such boys and girls as were willing to be examined in Dutch?—If it could be done.

2697. Suppose that we were to have in connection with the Elementary examination a separate list of candidates for examination in Dutch, and you were to encourage such candidates by saying that such and such number of them as were at the top of the list might get a bursary. Would not that encourage the study of Dutch?—I think it would.

2698. *President.*] Suppose such a system were to be established, would it not be necessary to say also that pupils who were to get the bursary would require to come up to a certain standard in other subjects. You would not, for instance, give a boy a bursary who knew Dutch and very little else?—No.

2699. He should come up to a certain standard as far as other subjects are concerned?—Yes.

2700. Suppose you had a separate list for examinees in Dutch, and the University were to value the total paper say at 1,000 marks, would it be fair for them to say that no boy should get a bursary for Dutch alone, who did not attain 500 marks on the general list, just one half?—I think that would do.

2701. Reverting to the question of local Boards, would you be in favour generally of giving such Boards power to levy rates or get assistance from the rates over and above what was found to be a deficiency in the funds of a school?—If the deficiency could be made up in that way, then of course we might retain the present system, but I think it would be better to have Boards altogether and do away with the present system.

2702. Would you give them power to increase the school revenue by rates, or simply limit their powers to getting money to the extent of any deficiency that might arise?—I think the latter course would be sufficient.

2703. Would you be willing that they should thereby extend the system of education locally?—Yes, according to the requirements.

2704. You would approve of this rating for deficiencies being levied quite in view of any prospective increase in the local expenses of the school?—Just so.

2705. *Mr. Theron.*] With regard to these School Boards, would you have one central Board stationed say in Cape Town, or some other large centre, or would you have a Board for every district?—I think local Boards would be better; every district have its own Board.

2706. And that Board would have to provide for the education of all children in the district?—Yes.

2707. Whites as well as blacks?—I do not know about blacks. I would say for all white children at present.

2708. Then are you going to draw a line?—There are no coloured people paying rates, and the mission schools might exist all the same. I think there would be a difficulty with regard to Boards if that question enters.

2709. At present, according to the report of the Superintendent-General of Education, our expenses are £3 16s. 5¼d. for every child. According to your idea, the Government contributing five shillings per head, would virtually be £3 per annum, so that by doing that, you would decrease the support to the white population and increase that to the native population?—It would not be the case in our district. We do not get five shillings out of the Government for every child educated.

Rev
Johannes Jous.

Sept. 3rd, 1891.

2710. Virtually it comes to this, you advocate free education to a certain extent, Government paying for the same?—Not altogether free; 7s. 6d. a month per child would suit our purposes, but there are other higher schools where it is 10s. or 12s. a month, and that of course would make the expenditure on the part of the Government so much greater, and we would not benefit by it. Government at present contributes a little less than half (not counting mission schools), and I would say that the Government ought to contribute two-thirds or at least fully one-half. Now, the local Board has to supply the buildings, find board and lodging for the principal teacher, and so on, therefore we pay considerably more than half; I want the Government to pay at the very least one-half, and if possible two-thirds. We do not get £3 a year from Government for every child that is educated in our district. If we got 5s. a month per child we would be satisfied.

2711. With regard to the children of bywoners generally, you said that they were compelled to work when very young; can you give us a reason for that?—Poverty on the part of the parents is one reason, and the difficulty of getting servants sometimes.

2712. What time would you allow these children for schooling, to suit their station in life?—They ought not to have less than four years' schooling, I should think.

2713. Do you require any industrial schools for those children, or should there only be literary teaching?—I am speaking about literary training.

2714. Do you require a school in order to teach them to work with a spade?—Not the whites.

2715. As far as the native population is concerned, are such schools required to teach them to work?—In some of the large places I daresay it might be required. It all depends upon whether these children live on the farm. Where they live on the farm, they are taught to work, and in that case it would not be required. Where they live in towns, it would be some advantage, and they would be better able to serve the farmer afterwards when they went out into service. They would leave school able to do some work.

2716. What kind of work?—Agricultural work.

2717. Do you require a school to teach the natives to work?—It all depends on the class of boy. A white boy would learn at once to work, but a Kafir boy who lies about in his location would require to have his lazy habits taken out of him so that he might be of some use in after life.

2718. Can that be done in a school?—It all depends. If you have a plot of ground attached to the school, it could be done to some extent.

2719. Do you think industrial schools are required to teach those boys to work?—If you only teach them habits of industry it would be a help to the farmers; I allude more to those in the towns. Children living on the farms are compelled to work.

2720. Suppose you started such an institution in a town, would it not be a place of attraction for children?—In our little town it would have to be a very simple sort of thing. They might learn how to plant out things properly and so on.

2721. Is it not your experience that very often in the case of mission schools, farm labourers leave their master to come and settle in town to have their children educated?—I cannot speak from any experience. We have not a very large black population. The number of native children going to school varies from 20 to 30. I do not think it has ever been higher than that. They cannot all get employment on farms. At some seasons their services are not needed, and they come into town to seek work. We have no location, so there is hardly any facility for them to come and live there.

2722. You said that there was a want of labour, because the white people have to employ their children. Are you not afraid that the placing of such schools in towns would to some extent create a worse condition of things than exists at present?—They can do no harm whatever. I admit that a farmer who trains his own servants can train them as well as anybody else, and perhaps better than they would be trained in schools. At the same time, I believe it would be a good thing to train all these people in habits of industry. If they are taught to work when they are young, they are more useful in after life.

2723. Rev. Coetzee.] I understood you to say in reply to a question by Dr. Berry that by allowing a Dutch boy to take a Dutch paper and by adding these marks to the marks he gained in other subjects, it would put an English boy who does not understand a word of Dutch, at a disadvantage. Is it not the fact that many Dutch boys, when they enter school, do not understand a word of English?—Yes.

2724. And they get all their instruction through the medium of the English language, and they have to do their examination in English?—Just so.

2725. Does not that put a Dutch boy at some disadvantage over against an English boy?—Yes, I must admit that.

Rev.
Johannes Roos.
—
Sept. 3rd, 1891.

2726. Can you suggest anything to solve this difficulty?—The marks should be counted, and a separate certificate given. I think if a certain percentage of marks could be added, it would be fair. I admit that a Dutch boy has to contend with certain disadvantages when he has to take an English paper, which an English boy has not got if a Dutch paper is given. If the whole of the marks for the Dutch paper should count with the English, I think it would be a little unfair, because the Dutch boy takes up the English paper also, and he may do that paper as well as the English boy.

2727. *Mr. Rowan.*] Would you make it compulsory that boys should take both papers, or only one?—We do not believe in education that is altogether Dutch. You cannot get on without English, and they would be very glad to take up English as well as Dutch, but of course there is the loss of time to be considered. We say, give them a certain number of marks for the Dutch paper, and if their English paper does not come up to the mark altogether, let a certain percentage of the marks they get for the Dutch paper count and be added to the aggregate.

2728. *President.*] Suppose another boy learns Latin or French, he also loses time so far as the Elementary examination is concerned, so would it not be a good thing to have three papers, Latin, French and Dutch, and give a boy an opportunity of displaying his knowledge in either, and then add the marks to the total?—I would not say Latin; I would stick to modern languages. With regard to circuit school grants, I certainly think under the present system they do not work well. In the poorer neighbourhoods you are obliged to have two or more centres. You find perhaps that a neighbourhood is a very poor one, and at the same time a very suitable one to be a centre. You establish a school, but if you cannot prove to the satisfaction of the Superintendent-General of Education that you have more than one centre, he tells you that it is not a case for a circuit grant, although the minister conscientiously certifies that the people are not able to pay. The difficulty could be done away with, if they would say, let there be one centre, but let the grant be given for not longer than two years at a time. At present, according to circuit grant regulations, a teacher has to remain six months on a particular farm. Perhaps by correspondence with Sir Langham Dale, he may extend the time a little longer, but they are not supposed to remain longer than a year at the outside in one centre. Let there be one centre, but let the grant be given for two years instead of six months. That would considerably help poorer neighbourhoods. We had a third class aided school, and we managed by getting help from outsiders for two or three years to keep it going, but owing to bad seasons and people being short of money, we were obliged to close the school; we were not able to raise the guarantee, and I wrote to Sir Langham Dale, asking him whether he could give us even temporarily a circuit grant, but he did not see his way to comply with the request. We were at one time an aided school, and made up our part of the guarantee. Now, the Superintendent-General of Education is under the impression that we ought to stick to that arrangement.

Rev.
J. C. Reyneke.
—
Sept. 3rd, 1891.

Rev. J. C. Reyneke examined.

2729. *President.*] I believe you are a minister of the Dutch Reformed Church at Cradock?—Yes.

2730. Do you know anything of the undenominational public schools there?—Yes; I know a little.

2731. Are they under the guarantor system, generally speaking?—Yes.

2732. Does that system work well in Cradock?—Yes, but not in the way intended by Government. I understand that by that system certain guarantors put down their names as subscribers.

2733. How is it worked at Cradock?—In the town the boys' public school is under the municipality, and the girls' public school is under the Dutch Reformed Church.

2734. Does that work well?—Yes, very well.

2735. Is there a deficiency at all in the boys' school; has the municipality ever been called upon to pay?—No. There has always been a balance in favour of the school.

2736. Do both schools work at a profit?—Yes. The guarantor system is adopted in the district. The third class schools generally have three or five guarantors.

2737. Does that work well too?—Yes, as far as I know.

2738. Do you think that system ought to be superseded by some other system, such as School Boards?—If something could be done to assist the boarding it would be a good thing. The great difficulty with the poorer classes is that they cannot afford the boarding. Sometimes there are very good schools in the neighbourhood five or six miles away, but children cannot make use of them on this account.

2739. How would you propose to meet that difficulty?—I have thought about it a good deal, but I can hardly say. It is a difficult question.

2740. Do you think it would be a good thing if the ratepayers were to elect a Board, whose duty it should be to see that there were sufficient schools adequate for the wants of the community?—I think it would be a good thing, but the question of money is the difficulty.

2741. If there is a deficiency, would you call upon the ratepayers to pay it out of the taxes?—I am afraid that will not answer in every respect, because in the large districts you may have very good schools in the town, but there are so many children far away from the town, and they will have to pay too much if all the wants have to be met.

2742. Why would they have to pay too much. Would the deficiency be so great as to make it a burden?—In towns it is always easy to get boarding. Where children are near a school there is no difficulty about it. The Cradock schools are mostly fed by the town; there are very few children from the district, and for this reason the day school is in a flourishing condition, there is always a balance to the good, but the country schools are not at all in a flourishing condition, for the simple reason that they cannot keep up the number of pupils. We get a grant from Government if there are ten pupils, but very often we can only get about eight. The poor children are four, five or six miles away, and they cannot attend because of the boarding.

2743. Can you suggest any solution of that difficulty at all?—The Government might increase the capitation grant so as to meet the case of the poorer people.

2744. Increase it beyond £6?—If a parent has five or six children, and lives several miles away from the school, even if all the children go to school gratis, there is always the difficulty about boarding.

2745. Dr. Berry.] Would not all these questions be better managed by a local Board created to make provision for the wants of the district than by any other agency. Why should not a Board manage the educational wants of a district just as well as another Board manages the roads of a district?—The Divisional Council has an income, and as long as they have money they can work.

2746. But a School Board could have money in the same way. Let them have power either themselves to rate, or power to call upon the Divisional Council to rate for them?—I think as far as I can see, that would be the only way to meet the difficulty. I would go with that plan. Then the poor man would pay according to his circumstance and the rich man according to his.

2747. Mr. Rowan.] Is the attendance at the schools in Cradock pretty regular?—I do not think we have any reason to complain either in town or country.

2748. Dean Holmes.] Could you give us the percentage?—No.

2749. Would it be over 70 per cent.?—Yes.

2750. Rev. Moorrees.] Have you any circuit schools in your district?—No; we have several third-class schools—schools getting £30 a year from Government, on condition that there are ten children.

2751. Dean Holmes.] Have you any knowledge whether there is a large number of children in Cradock who do not go to school at all?—Yes; in the district very many.

2752. And in the town?—In the town not many.

2753. Have you considered the question of compulsory attendance?—No.

2754. Rev. Moorrees.] I understand you to say that you have no circuit schools; is there no necessity for them, or is it difficult to establish them?—It would be a very good thing if we could have say three. There are three places where there are many poor people, but there is nowhere for the teacher to board. That is always the difficulty in trying to establish a circuit school.

2755. Dr. Berry.] Is the Cradock boys' school managed by the Town Council?—Yes.

2756. Do discussions crop up in the Town Council about school matters at any time?—No. There is a sub-committee which manages the school and discusses its interests, and they appoint the teachers. The sub-committee is under the Town Council, whose sanction is obtained.

2757. Are the reports of the committee laid before the Town Council?—I believe so.

2758. Have you noticed anything like party or sectarian feeling arise in regard to school matters?—Not as far as I know.

2759. They are all good friends on school matters?—Yes.

2760. As far as the denominational element is concerned in Cradock, is there a great predominance of any one denomination, or are they evenly balanced?—The Dutch Reformed Church is by far the strongest in the district. In the town it lies between the English Church and the Wesleyans. Perhaps the Wesleyans are a little stronger, but I cannot say for certain.

2761. President.] Is not the Dutch Reformed Church strong in the town?—Not so strong as the other churches.

Rev.
J. C. Reyncke.

Sept. 3rd, 1889

Rev.
J. C. *Reyneke.*

Sept. 3rd. 1891.

2762. *Dr. Berry.*] Have the Wesleyans any denominational school in the town?—Yes, under Mr. Lightfoot. I do not think the school has any grant from Government. It is a private school, I believe.

2763. Is it well attended?—Yes There are boys belonging to my church who go there.

2764. And the church of England?—I cannot say for certain; I think so. Mr. Lightfoot's school is more a preparatory school for smaller children. Some people send their children to that school as they say it is nearer to their houses. That is their only reason. The boys' public school is about three-quarters of a mile away. Mr. Lightfoot's is a very flourishing school.

2765. *Rev. Moorrees.*] There was formerly a church school in connection with the Dutch Reformed Church; do you know why there was an opposition school?—When I came to Cradock, that school was in existence, but it was about to die, and I used all my influence to amalgamate the two schools. Now the two are amalgamated, and they have been for about six years, and work very nicely together.

2766. Have you thought about introducing the Dutch language into the Elementary examination?—Yes.

2767. Would you be in favour of introducing it as an optional subject?—Optional in a certain sense, that is to say, I think that English ought to be compulsory in this country. That is my private opinion. It would not do to make Dutch compulsory. Let there be one other language for the candidate to select from; Dutch, German, French, or Kafir.

2768. *Mr. Theron.*] Why would it not do to make Dutch compulsory?—It would only create unpleasantness and opposition. It is best to let things go on peaceably.

2769. *Rev. Moorrees.*] Do you think by rights it ought to have some favour shown it. I do not say make it compulsory, but it is one of the languages of the country?—I think it is entitled to some favour. It is the language spoken by the majority of South African people, born and bred here.

2770. If Dutch is one of the languages of the country spoken by the majority of the people, do you think it should be classed with French or German on equal terms?—Speaking as a minister of the Dutch Reformed Church, I do not think it is right. It is entitled to the same place as English. English and Dutch are certainly the languages of South Africa, and I think it is very necessary for every educated man to know the two languages. I have spoken to several English ministers, and I have not yet met one who did not regret not knowing Dutch. I think the two languages ought to go side by side, but I see a difficulty in making Dutch compulsory at present. I can feel for any English parent who does not care to have his child taught Dutch, and therefore to make it compulsory would be very difficult. For that simple reason I should be in favour of letting it be at the option of the candidate to choose either Dutch or some other language, French, German or even Latin or Greek.

2771. In the case of a Dutch child coming to one of our public schools, is he not at a disadvantage because he is taught through the medium of a language which he does not fully understand?—I think he is at a disadvantage. Speaking for myself, when I left my father's house, I was a Dutch boy, and did not understand a word of English. I could read Dutch very well, but before I could do anything at my studies, I had to learn English. The school I went to was an English school, and there I was at a disadvantage. If I could have been educated at once in the Dutch language, I would have learned much more.

2772. So that in the first years of his schooling a Dutch child is handicapped as over against an English child?—I certainly think so.

2773. *Mr. Rowan.*] Can you tell us whether more attention is paid to Dutch now than was the case formerly in your district, say five years ago?—I think that more attention is being paid to it in the boys' public school in the town. We have had a good Dutch teacher for some years, and they have always had Dutch. At the Rocklands Seminary in Cradock I am sure that for the last few years much more attention has been paid to Dutch.

2774. To what do you ascribe that. Is it on account of the additional interest taken in Dutch?—In the first place I would ascribe it to the teacher, who is a lady from Holland, and does her best to encourage the pupils. Another thing is that the parents like their children to know something about their own language.

2775. And in the country schools has there been any advance, or is it just the same?—It is about the same in the country schools.

2776. That is to say, attention is paid both to English and Dutch?—Yes.

2777. *President.*] Do I understand you to say that although you would like to see Dutch and English placed on equal terms, under the circumstances it would better meet the difficulty if a paper were set in two or three languages and the candidate had the option of choosing which he pleased, and answering any one of the papers, the marks being added to the sum total?—Yes. That would be perfectly just to the Dutch community.

Rev.
J. C. Reyneke.

Sept. 3rd, 1891.

2778. *Dean Holmes.*] How would it do to have all the papers set either in Dutch or English, and allow the candidates to answer in which they liked?—There is one difficulty. I fear that that will not meet the wants of those who are fighting for Dutch and take an interest in it. If I were to go to school and be taught English history, Geography or Euclid, I would prefer to answer in the language I was taught in.

2779. *President.*] Suppose they teach you in Dutch?—I should not like to lose the advantage of knowing English.

2780. The Dutch boy wants to learn English, and the English boy does not always want to learn Dutch; don't you force him to a certain extent to do what he does not want to?—In that way I should be in favour of having two or three optional languages with Dutch.

2781. *Mr. Theron.*] Do you mean to say that Dutch is a foreign language in this country?—No.

2782. Are you in a Dutch or an English Colony?—I fear at present, if Dutch were made compulsory, what we would gain in one respect we should lose in another. We might gain our point as a Dutch community, but we should not be on the same terms with our English friends.

2783. You advocate equal rights. You take an English child doing his four subjects in the Elementary examination, and you compel a Dutch child to do the same four subjects. Is that equal?—It is not equal, but if you cannot get the whole loaf, you must be satisfied with half.

2784. What right have you to expect half when you can get the whole. You advocate equal rights. Suppose an English child, after having finished his four subjects, says I will take the Dutch language too, and he passes in that, would you give him extra marks?—I have already said I would have optional subjects.

2785. Suppose an English boy takes Latin, would that be of any use to him in the future if he proceeds with his studies?—That I would leave for the parents to judge.

2786. *Rev. Moorrees.*] Would not an English boy have a certain advantage over a Dutch boy, because he can select his Latin before passing the Elementary examination. A Dutch boy also wants Latin for the School Higher examination, but he can only take it up after having passed the Elementary examination, because he has to pass in Dutch. Does not that give a second advantage to the English boy?—It may give him an advantage in the School Higher examination.

2787. At all events, in the Elementary examination, you acknowledge that an English boy has an advantage over the Dutch boy at present?—Yes.

2788. And if you allow the English boy to take Latin instead of Dutch, you give him a second advantage in the School Higher examination, do you not?—Under the present arrangement, he certainly has an advantage, but my point would be not only to have a change in the Elementary examination, but a change all through.

2789. *Dr. Berry.*] Do you know whether the result of the examinations already held by the University in these elementary subjects shows that a Dutch boy is at a disadvantage. Have not the Dutch boys been every year as high as the English boys as a rule?—I believe so.

2790. Where can this advantage be then?—Before one can decide that, we must see whether he would not be much higher.

2791. Suppose you give the advantage that is claimed, will not you disadvantage English boys so much the other way?—I do not think it is a disadvantage for an English boy if what I suggest is carried out, namely, have alternative subjects. If Dutch were made compulsory, the scale would turn the other way.

2792. Would not a better way to remedy the difficulty be to have a paper in Dutch set so that the marks should count on an extra list altogether, and have an endorsement on the certificate?—I am afraid that will not meet the requirements of the Dutch, because a boy does not care about having a separate certificate. He likes to have his name high up on the pass or honours list.

2793. There are the interests of Education and the interests of the individual?—Yes, so I would not make it compulsory, although I think it has rights as being the language spoken by the great majority. I do not think it would be advisable, under the circumstances, to make it compulsory.

Rev. Theophilus Chubb examined.

2794. *President.*] I believe you are head of the Wesleyan body here?—Yes; I am chairman of our Church in this part.

Rev.
Theophilus Chubb.

Sept. 3rd, 1891.

c

2795. Are you connected with the undenominational public school ?—I am a member of the committee, and I am chairman of the Board of Trustees for our girls' high school here. I am also manager of the mission school in the Shaw Hall.

2796. How many children are there in the mission school in the Shaw Hall ?—It is a European school. There were 202 present last Monday. Last quarter we had 230 on the roll, and at the present moment there are about 248.

2797. Is the attendance regular or irregular ?—It is very fairly regular for such a school. It would not compare favourably with the higher school. If the first and second days of the week are wet, for instance, the parents often keep a child at home, and then it is not sent the remaining days.

2798. Can you suggest anything to remedy irregular attendance in this town ?—I should like to see many children in school who now do not go anywhere, and I would compel them to attend some school.

2799. How would you propose to do that ?—I believe in utilizing existing schools as far as possible. I should try that plan and see if it would answer. Children might attend any school, public or private, provided they were being educated.

2800. Under the present system there is no power of bringing into existence or perpetuating any school that is in existence except by voluntary effort. Is not that so ? —I should think the Government must either start schools of its own or devise some scheme for paying the fees, if they are perfectly satisfied that the parents cannot pay, but I think in this country nearly all the parents can pay. Government should compel them to send their children to school.

2801. You recognise that under the present system there is no power to initiate a school; no duty is imposed on anyone; it is only done by voluntary effort ?—Yes.

2802. Do you think that is a defect in the present system ?—No ; I am not sure that it is. In towns and villages I believe it is better managed on the present plan than it could be by any other plan I can think of.

2803. Do not you think if a Board were started, upon whom the duty was imposed of satisfying the central Government or the Superintendent-General of Education, that such Board would be able to initiate schools, and that would remove the defect ?—It would entirely depend upon the way the Government go about it. It is in the power of the Government to start schools, and compel every one to attend. I mean they can pass a law to that effect. It is a weak point at present.

2804. Would it not be a good thing to have a Board elected by the ratepayers, whose duty it should be to satisfy the Superintendent-General of Education that there were sufficient schools for Europeans, and find them if there were not enough ?—I am afraid the working of such a system would not be so satisfactory as the present one. I am not in favour of such a Board levying a rate for any particular locality. I would prefer its being done through the Government. I am afraid in a town like this the Board would consider it one of their first duties to have no school rate at all, or at all events as small a one as possible. I should like to know also how far schools, if started, would interfere with present schools. I believe in compelling Europeans to send their children to some school or other, and the Government must somehow see that there are schools for them to be sent to.

2805. I believe your undenominational public school gets £700 or £800 from Government, does it not ?—About that.

2806. And there are about 100 boys ?—Yes.

2807. And how much does your mission school get in the way of aid from Government ?—£75, and also an amount that varies for pupil teachers. We have two or three, who are paid according to the usual rates.

2808. And in the mission school you have about 200 children ?—Yes ; 202, boys and girls.

2809. The mission schools are for the poorer classes, are they not ?—Yes.

2810. Then the Government is really helping by greater aid those who can best help themselves ?—When I say that there is the poorer class in the mission school, I should add that the parents would send their children perhaps to a little better school, but they cannot afford to pay the fees in the first-class school, and there is very little that is intermediate.

2811. Have you anything to propose with regard to mission schools ?—I think the term "mission school," as they exist in a town of this sort, is a misnomer. They work satisfactorily and do a great deal of good work, but they are not helped as they ought to be in proportion to the general rate of help given by the Government to schools.

2812. What rate of help do you think they ought to get ?—Such a school as the Shaw Hall school ought to get practically double what it receives.

2813. Taking the average attendance, what do you think would be a fair contribution per head from Government ?—I could scarcely say. Some of the children are very small. Perhaps 15s. to 20s. a head.

Rev.
Theophilus Chubb.

Sept. 3rd, 1891.

2814. You think if the Government gave that it would enable you fairly to work the school with competent teachers?—If they gave 20s. it would. At present the school has to be subsidized by voluntary contributions to some extent.

2815. That really falls upon your church, does it not?—Yes. We provide the building free, and we make collections in our church, and there are a few gentlemen who give money. If we received aid for pupil teachers as we do now, 20s. a head would do.

2816. If this Board were brought into existence, it might be a condition that existing schools remained, and if recommended that they should receive further aid, give it them?—I would much rather take the report furnished by the Inspectors to the Government. The present system of inspection by the Government to test the efficiency of a school is very satisfactory.

2817. That would remain. The Government officer would come and see if he was satisfied with the school, but the Government in no instance to increase the aid except through the recommendation of the Board; the Board having also the power to start any other school where it was found necessary for the wants of the people?—I do not think there is any necessity to bring in a Board at all. I think the present arrangement is adequate. You have so many children, and the Government Inspector reports that the school is satisfactory.

2818. A school might in itself be sufficient, but those outside require to be educated, and the Board must have power to supply the schools for them. It would scarcely be fair to allow an increase of aid to be given to schools that are in existence and doing good work, when by giving it you may interfere with new schools that necessarily have to come into existence for the poorer classes?—I am not sure that such schools would in all cases have to come into existence. Those who manage the present schools in many cases would scarcely consider the Board that might be chosen satisfactory. The Divisional Council, for instance, would not be a satisfactory Board.

2819. But if the Board were elected for educational purposes entirely?—I do not see the necessity for it. Government knows very well the condition of these schools.

2820. But Government has no power to bring another school into existence, and if they do, and a tax is imposed, the ratepayers will oppose it?—Those who contribute now to a satisfactory school would resent being taxed for another. The educational wants of all Europeans can be met in Graham's Town. They would find some school, and if they are not satisfied with the existing schools, I do not think they would be satisfied with anything the Government might propose. No doubt a readjustment is wanted, but I am not prepared to say that the wealthy classes ought to be helped the same as the poorer classes.

2821. Is it advisable in your opinion that a Board of some sort should come into existence?—Who is to choose it?

2822. The ratepayers?—I have no confidence in the ratepayers for such a purpose. On our committee in this town, there are a few laymen who are pretty regular in their attendance, but the others it is a rare thing to see from the beginning to the end of the year. I should be afraid that a School Board would consist of men taking no great interest in education.

2823. You find in England that the ratepayers elect men who take a vast amount of interest, and there is almost as much competition sometimes to get a seat on a School Board as to get into Parliament. How would you remedy the defect that there is nobody charged with the duty of bringing into existence schools to meet the wants of the poorer communities. Government cannot do it of themselves?—Is it not a fact that schools do exist in towns and villages, and might not the present system be improved?

2824. How would you improve it?—I am inclined to think that something may be done in helping what are called mission schools. Take a town like this. I doubt very much whether it would be wise to start a school under a Board which should carry pupils forward to say St. Andrew's College.

2825. This Board would be limited to elementary education, up to the sixth standard?—I do not believe that in this town there is any need for such a Board, and I can say with regard to a good many other towns that there is no need for it as far as I know.

2826. And you think there is no need for further schools here?—No; I think the present system is a very good one indeed.

2827. How is it then that Sir Langham Dale has suggested that there is a large section of the white children unprovided for. He suggests the establishment of fourth class undenominational public schools?—I think it would be a great mistake if you were to start and close up such schools as exist in the town at present.

2828. Then you are opposed to these fourth class undenominational public schools?—I do not say that. I am opposed to Government coming into competition with existing schools.

c 2

Rev.
Theophilus Chubb.
——
Sept. 3rd, 1891.

2829. The Government would have to be satisfied that there is a necessity for futher schools before it gives a grant, and would bind itself not to give a grant till it is satisfied through the medium of the Board, so the Board is the recommending body and the Government is the deciding body, and thus all interested would be heard?—So much depends upon what is the constitution of the Board. As to the Shaw Hall school, we have a small committee, every member of which is greatly interested in the school. If it had not been for that, that school would never have attained its present position. If you get a Board composed of those who are not thoroughly interested, I am afraid it would not work so satisfactorily as the present system. I would rather give additional aid to existing schools than strike out altogether on new lines.

2830. How would you propose this aid to existing schools should be given?—You might say, when there are so many children in a school, certain aid should be given, and increase that aid according to the numbers attending. At present a school gets no more help, whether it has 150 or 200 children. It cannot go beyond £75 a year. The limit is placed too low, and I would raise it.

2831. Would you compel children to be forced into that particular school?—No; so long as they get education, they might go to a public or a private school.

2832. Into what school are they to be forced?—The parents can choose.

2833. Suppose there are no parents to choose?—The Government now has certain rights in the matter, and they might claim other rights with regard to sending free scholars to schools.

2834. Rev. Moorrees.] Have you followed Sir Langham Dale's plan with reference to fourth-class undenominational public schools?—Yes; I understand it.

2835. Are you in favour of it?—I am in favour of something being done in that direction. I do not bind myself exactly to his plan. I should not care for instance to start a fourth class undenominational public school in a town like this, in addition to the first class school, but I would give help in some way to such schools as are in existence.

2836. If these fourth class undenominational public schools are started at all, would you like them to be under the management of the present religious bodies, or under an undenominational Board?—I should prefer that they remain under the committees of existing schools, because I believe, as a rule, those who take such a deep interest are far more likely to work them satisfactorily, and they have the premises, but I would give greater help. I am not wedded to the phrase "fourth class schools," and I should see a difficulty in having a first and a fourth class undenominational public school in a place like Grahamstown, where you have both a preparatory and a branch school in connection with the first-class school.

2837. It would be understood that these fourth class schools would only be to help the poorer class of children?—I do not think they would draw a large amount from Government. As a matter of fact, our fees in the Shaw Hill school are larger than what we get from Government.

2838. They would draw a larger amount than the present mission schools?—Yes. Having spent so many years among natives and in connection with native mission institutions, and watched their working, it was surprising to me to find that this school here, the Shaw Hall school, went by the name of a mission school.

2839. Mr. Theron.] Are there so many white children there?—They are all white, the 200.

2840. Rev. Moorrees.] Would not the idea of the fourth class undenominational public schools be to help such schools as yours?—Yes. Of course the help could be given without calling them fourth class undenominational public schools, by raising the minimum of £75, and making the grant proportionate to the number in actual attendance in the school, and making the grant for an extra teacher.

2841. Dean Holmes.] Would you like Sir Langham Dale's scheme as suggested for fourth class schools to be applied to mission schools, leaving the mission schools under their own management?—Yes.

2842. Rev. Coetzee.] As far as your experience goes, are there any defects in the working of the present system of education. Take the guarantor system for instance, does that answer well?—I think it answers. It is not a perfect system in some cases.

2843. Can you suggest something instead of that system, so as to make it easier for people to start schools and keep them going?—I cannot suggest anything which on the whole would be an improvement I am afraid. I do not think that Boards under the Divisional Council would be an improvement.

2844. Did I understand you to say that you would not be in favour of direct taxation for school purposes?—I would rather that the Government supplied the money out of the general revenue than that there was direct taxation by way of a school rate, but if we cannot get the first. I am not prepared to say I am not in favour of a school rate.

Rev.
Theophilus Chubb.

Sept. 3rd, 1891.

2845. *In re Holmes.*] Would you object to money being taken out of the Divisional Council rate for the purpose?—The margin of funds is so very slight, and if there is a margin there would always be an outcry and practically they would do nothing. I am afraid that it would not work.

2846. *Rev. Coetzee.*] Would you be in favour of the Government contributing two-thirds of all the expenses of working the school, and the local bodies contributing one-third?—Then the local Board would want to have a considerable say in the management of the school.

2847. I mean under the present system?—I am inclined to think the present rate of payment by Government in the case of undenominational public schools, namely one-half, is fair, because our people are not so poor here as they are in England.

2848. *Mr. Rowan.*] Under the present system, how are schools to be started?—I do not know whether the difficulty is very great in that line. A great many come to our school who do not belong to our church, and indeed belong to no church at all.

2849. *Dr. Berry.*] You are opposed to a public school out and out; you prefer the denominational system?—No; I thoroughly approve of the public school system.

2850. You are aware that mission schools were established for the children of coloured people, and if we find a school with 202 white children in it, does not that seem to be robbing other people of their just rights?—We have coloured schools also. I do not see that we rob anyone. We take what we can get, and we think we ought to get a little more under some other head.

2851. Are all the children in Graham's Town provided with schools?—There are a good many schools, and I think there is accommodation for all who choose to attend.

2852. For coloured children also?—Yes.

2853. *Dean Holmes.*] Is there accommodation for many more children in the coloured schools: are not they all full?—If we found that we were overburdened, we could make more room ourselves.

2854. *Dr. Berry*] Do you propose a modification in the present system?—Yes.

2855. I understand that the Wesleyan body in England say, if there is any modification of the system of education, it should be in the direction of public School Boards everywhere; why should we differ here. The committee of privileges published their report in May last, and it was resolved that the policy should be in the direction of the establishment of School Boards everywhere; a complete system of national schools?—That may have been published in England, but they have been in a very uncertain frame of mind. There have been two parties.

2857. There are two parties here also, and the strongest party is in favour of enlarging the public school system. You want to enlarge the mission school system?—The mission schools occupy a very anomalous position. They are called mission schools, but they are practically something else.

2858. Why should not the schools in a place like this be put on the same footing as the other institutions of the country. Why should education be established on different principles to those which govern other matters connected with local government?—That is a very broad question. As men are constituted, I am afraid it will be some time before we all see alike. The question of religion enters a good deal into the matter. Religious people are more charitable than those who are not religious, and therefore more anxious to promote education.

2859. We are very anxious to give education. The public are now proposing to double the grants for the lower class of schools: all the public say is, give us the control of them?—When you come to elect a Board by the ratepayers, I have not the same confidence in it in the matter of education.

2860. Why not?—Because of stern facts.

2861. Could not people be educated up to the system as in other matters, and if so, why should we not make a beginning?—I have not the slightest objection to make a beginning, but you must not destroy what exists at present.

2862. No one proposes to destroy what exists at present?—I say we must be careful not to do it. If the Boards are to take the control of education, as some suggest, I consider that a very radical change indeed.

2863. They would not take control of education; they would only administer. The State would really direct education. All the Board would do would be to provide for local wants, and adapt the general system to local requirements?—I am afraid that it would work in this way. In the different churches, those who already have existing schools would perhaps not be willing to give them up, but wish to carry them on; I am afraid in many places you would scarcely get a School Board elected by ratepayers who would devote sufficient time and interest to the subject. If that could be insured I might be in favour of it; but I do not think it can be, therefore I am not in favour of it.

Rev.
Theophilus Chubb.

Sept. 3rd, 1891.

2864. *Mr. Theron.*] You said that you had 202 children in your school last Monday ; were they all whites ?—Yes.

2865. Are there first, second and third class schools besides this school ?—Yes ; in the town.

2866. You are also a member of the Undenominational Public School Committee, I believe. Is there a preparatory and a branch school ?—Yes.

2867. Suppose your so-called mission school came under the fourth class school head, you would get a greater allowance ; would you have any objection to adopting the latter name ?—I do not cling at all to the word "mission school." I rather dislike it personally. I should call it the Shaw Hall School.

2868. The children attending that school are children of the poorer classes, are they not ?—Yes ; speaking generally they are ; and a great many of the parents say they wish there was some school intermediate between this and the Wesleyan High School.

2869. Do these children pay any fees ?—Twopence, fourpence, and sixpence a week.

2870. That is less than in the other schools ?—Yes.

2871. Is that the reason why more children attend than otherwise would ?—No doubt the lowness of the fee helps to draw a number of children, especially in the case of those parents who have several children and who cannot afford to pay a great deal.

2872. Do any of the better classes attend that school ?—I would not say the better class exactly, but people comfortably off. The children really get a first class education and cheap. You can see from the returns the number that have passed Standard 4.

2873. *Dr. Berry.*] Does not the fact that a large number of the children who attend this particular school, all of them not children of parents belonging to your body, indicate that the parents are more anxious to have a good secular education than so-called religious or denominational education ?—The parents are connected with churches that think alike with us in so many respects. We can work together as ministers, just as we have a ministers' union, and all meet and talk about many things in common.

2874. Suppose the Roman Catholic mission schools were attended by as many Protestants as Roman Catholics, would you say there that ministers of one congregation mix and mingle freely with others?—There is a very radical distinction. It is not simply the question of doctrine. Parents know very well that we shall not attempt in any way to interfere with their children.

2875. Would not the same thing hold good with regard to public board schools in this country ?—There are a good many parents who would be perfectly satisfied to send their children to a public school. We have on our committee men who devote their time and who are interested in education, and who will put their hand in their pocket to supply any deficiency.

2876. Why does that committee belong to the Shaw Hall School and not to the undenominational public school ?—I have a great interest in the undenominational public school, and there are those on one committee who are on the other.

2877. Will they put their hands in their pocket to aid in any deficiency ?—They have got Government to fall back upon. It is very little that is required.

2878. *President.*] Is there any Dutch taught in your school ?—I do not think so.

2879. Is there any facility you would suggest for acquiring it ?—We do not require it at all.

2880. Parents do not require it, and you do not think it necessary to have it ?—No. There are no further facilities required here.

2881. With regard to the Elementary examination, do many of the children in the schools you are connected with go up for it ?—Yes ; quite a number passed this year from the girls' school. Eight or nine passed in the first class.

2882. Does the same thing apply in regard to that school, that you do not want the Dutch language ?—It is not taught at all.

2883. You are aware that in the Elementary examination there are four subjects, and it has been suggested that there should be a fifth, a paper in Dutch, and those taking it up have the benefit of additional marks ; do you approve of that ?—I cannot say I do. I have no objection to having a Dutch paper, but then you must make it optional with others. I think it is a very good thing for any one to learn some language besides his own, therefore I would be in favour of an alternative paper in French, German, or Kafir, as the case may be, but it would be very hard indeed to make a Kafir who has to pass the examination learn Dutch. I have sent up a great many natives, and they are handicapped by having to learn English. If you make them learn Dutch too, it would shut them all out at once.

Rev.
Theophilus Chubb.
Sept. 3rd, 1591

2884. *Mr. Theron.*] Suppose the Kafir takes the Dutch language as well as his own, would you give him something extra ?—Not unless you allowed others to have something extra for something else also.

2885. *Rev. Moorrees.*] I understood you to say that a Kafir would be handicapped because he had to learn the Dutch language ?—As a matter of necessity, he must learn the English language.

2886. Do not you think a Dutch boy going up for the Elementary examination is handicapped in the same way ?—No ; he is handicapped, but not to the same extent. It is very much easier for a Dutch boy to learn English than it is for a Kafir to learn English.

2887. *President.*] How would you get over the difficulty ; would you have two or three alternative papers ?—If you do anything at all, and there is to be another language, I would simply give the choice of several languages and let the candidate take anyone he chose.

2888. Would you include Latin as an alternative language ?—I am not sure about the advisability of including Latin as an alternative. You would require a much higher knowledge of Dutch or English or French than you would of Latin as a rule. I am not sure that it is wise to bring in a language that is not spoken. It would be a great mistake if our boys thought that they were not to take up other subjects beyond what are set apart for the Elementary examination.

2889. *Rev. Moorrees.*] Do not you think that in a bi-lingual country like this, it is of the greatest advantage to know the two languages. I can at the same time conceive of the case of an English parent saying my boys or girls will find it an advantage to know French or German, but Dutch will help them very little, though very much depends upon whether they learn the high Dutch or common Dutch that is spoken. For the greater proportion of children born in this Colony, however, is it not a greater advantage for them to know Dutch rather than French or German, I mean for practical purposes ?—It is for most no doubt.

2890. *Dr. Berry.*] Would you be in favour of having a separate list for those who take Dutch in the Elementary examination ?—I should make it an entirely separate examination. If Dutch parents insist on the examination in Dutch, there is no alternative.

2891. Would you attach bursaries to those highest in such list ?—There can be no objection to that. I think it would be wise to test Dutch boys in their own language and to encourage it by prizes.

2892. Would you encourage it by giving boys who attain a high position some bursary to compete for ?—I think I would ; I would certainly encourage them in some way ; it would be only fair.

2893. Before you gave a boy a bursary, would you say he must attain a certain position in other subjects ?—I should let it depend not simply on Dutch alone, but upon his knowledge of other subjects also.

2894. *Rev. Coetzee.*] What would you think of abolishing the Elementary examination altogether ?—I would not say abolish it until you get something better.

2895. It is equivalent to Standard 5, is it not ?—I think the Elementary examination has a very good influence upon the different schools, and it very often stimulates the pupils. Sometimes it proves that pupils are not so forward as they were thought to be, especially as the examiners will always let candidates know where they fail.

2896. Does it not interfere with the thoroughness of the school work ?—It is considered in some schools rather an interruption when the teachers wish to carry the children on in other subjects.

2897. *Mr. Theron.*] With regard to getting the waifs and strays into school, how are you going to compel them ?—I suppose there would be an Act of Parliament which would render parents liable if their children were not sent to some school.

2898. Would you pass such an Act ?—I do not see any other way of doing it, except by having truancy and attendance officers.

2899. You would apply that system to towns ?—Yes, I think so ; towns and villages. I speak of the European population.

2900. *Dr. Berry.*] Why would you not apply it to the native population in towns ? —That is a very broad question. I would do it in towns perhaps, but not outside. You cannot do it in Kafirland at present. If the parents of native children come within the range of European influence and choose to reside in our towns, then I would say do it.

2901. It practically comes to this, you are in favour of compulsory education for all classes in towns ?—Yes, and I am in favour of it also in the country. I would appoint in certain parts two of the headmen to collect the money. These headmen are already paid by Government. I would make every parent who has children pay so

Rev.
Theophilus Chubb.

ept. 3rd, 1891.

much a year. At present there are on the location here some twenty children of Christian natives who send their children to school. The reason why the others do not do so is because they think they will be asked to contribute to the school.

2902. *President.*] Ought they to be forced to contribute?—Yes, where a school exists.

2903. Would you force them into the same school as Europeans go to?—No.

2904. Would you make the schools for them of a literary or principally of an industrial character?—In small places in the country I would try to go further than at present. In towns I would never mix the children. As a matter of fact, European children often go to native schools in the country, but it is not desirable.

2905. If you do have compulsion, what sort of schools would you provide for the natives, literary or industrial schools?—I should not make them industrial schools. I do not approve of these big boys and girls going to schools in towns; they ought to go out to work.

2906. If you do force black boys into these schools would you make the schools more of an industrial character than they are now. There is a complaint that coloured boys are not trained for their future vocation in life, that they learn in school what they do not want afterwards, in fact rather learn idleness?—In towns, I would make all girls learn sewing, and so on, but I should not recommend anything industrial for boys. You cannot teach them to work with a spade in town.

2907. Why not. Suppose they worked for two hours a day in the garden?—It is not desirable. The parents in most cases desire the help of their children. I would not have a lot of idle boys and girls.

2908. Could not two hours a day be utilised in teaching the native children some industrial sort of work?—I do not think so. The girls can learn sewing, but there is a difficulty with the boys. They get into an idle sort of way, and it is more play; they do not work. I have seen it in Kafirland. There they are trained in industrial institutions to work, but they work in a most slovenly way.

2909. The complaint is that they learn how to read and write, and even a little Latin sometimes, and when they go out among farmers, they are not useful as servants; would it not be a good thing, in view of that complaint, that they should have some sort of industrial training?—You cannot carry it out practically without such an expense as is not warranted. I have seen a good deal of it. I have been in charge of an industrial institution myself. Boys who learn carpentering or shoemaking you can make work hard, but in the case of boys who have to dig a hard piece of ground for two hours a day, you must be with them all the time, or they will only play.

2910. Two hours a day would not be much time lost to the superintendent, would it?—It might answer at a large place like Lovedale, but if you attempt to carry it out throughout the country, you will find, I believe, that it would not answer; certainly not in town.

2911. *Dr. Berry.*] Where you propose making education compulsory in towns, do not you see any plan of making that education partly industrial and partly literary. The complaint is that the native boy who is sent to school in a town and gets literary attainments, becomes too big for his boots as the saying is; would it not be possible to give him some idea of the dignity of labour by teaching him to work?—They do not learn the dignity of labour; I see no remedy. I have had natives who have been taught a trade thoroughly. When I was in Natal, for instance, one boy was trained in bootmaking, and he has since worked in Natal as a bootmaker, and he brought me over £30 to take care of. They will work in that way, but if you attempt to teach them spade work it is most unsatisfactory. A great deal depends upon the climate and the weather. If you can lead water over the land something might be done, but if not it is no good.

2912. *President.*] If you compel these coloured boys to go to school, what school would Government have to send them into—which denomination?—I am not prepared to say what is the best course.

2913. What is your opinion about night schools; have you anything to suggest?—We have one in connection with the natives at the location.

2914. How many are there in it?—It varies very much. I should be afraid to say.

2915. *Dr. Berry.*] Who teaches?—The same master who teaches in the day school.

2916. Does he get anything extra?—I think so.

2917. *President.*] Does it answer well?—I believe it does good. Our native minister can speak better about it than I can.

2918. *Dean Holmes.*] I believe your lordship has been eight years in Grahamstown ?—Yes.

2919. Have you had much to do with education ?—Yes, a great deal, both here and elsewhere in South Africa, before I came here. I have had both to start as well as superintend education, but I should prefer speaking as to broad principles rather than details.

2920. *President.*] Is your lordship acquainted with the present undenominational public school system in this Colony ?—Yes.

2921. Do you think the poorer class of children are sufficiently provided for ?— In this place I think there is sufficient provision. I think the Government should use all the appliances they have and make the most of them, and the result would then be more satisfactory than by any addition on new principles in the present order of things. There are, I think, four or five general principles that the Government should proceed upon. First of all, the inspection of schools should be more efficient and constant. I do not mean more efficient as regards the inspectors themselves, who are thoroughly satisfactory. If we get Government aid, we ought to submit to any degree of Government inspection. Secondly, and this I consider a very important point, there should be more regard paid to the qualifications of teachers. I do not say that a certificate should be required in every case, because there are not sufficient teachers to meet the demand, but that the teachers should be more carefully approved as regards their qualifications than can be the case at present. Inefficient teachers are worse almost than none at all. In the third place, the Government should require proper accommodation and appliances for school purposes. The school buildings are in some cases very inadequate and inefficient. In the fourth place, a thoroughly effective conscience clause should be insisted upon. This, I think, would meet the difficulty. With regard to the waifs and strays, whom you must compel to go to school, there are Roman Catholic, Anglican, and Wesleyan schools, as well as private schools. There are schools enough, and the Government should satisfy themselves that these schools are well conducted. You might have a Visiting Board consisting say of the Mayor, the Magistrate and two or three others, who should have the right to visit schools. If children are found not going to any school, and growing up to be a curse rather than a blessing to society, they should be compelled to go to some school. If the religious difficulty is raised, it could be met by the children learning some secular subject during the time devoted to religious instruction. It seems to me that by this means economy to the Government would be secured, and more enthusiasm would be called forth in the promotion of education. Then again, I think the present grants are insufficient. When a school gets beyond 50 or 100 children, £75 a year is not enough to provide for a proper teaching staff, and so a school may become inefficient. With regard to the proposal on the part of the Government to establish fourth class undenominational public schools, I should suggest that they must be careful, inasmuch as there is a fallacy lurking in the word "undenominational." No school is really and absolutely undenominational. We have had in our schools Jews and Roman Catholics, though they are professedly Anglican. The visiting body I suggested, consisting of the Mayor, the Magistrate, two Government representatives, and two local men, should have the power to visit a school at any hour of the day. In our schools you find that the mixing of boys and girls leads to a little trouble sometimes. There is not proper and adequate inspection insisted upon with regard to water closets and so on, and I take it that the public is as much interested in the moral character of the children who are growing up, as in their literary knowledge, for you may train up very clever children, who may become adepts in committing fraud and other crimes in after life. I should like to see Government grants made proportionate, as is the case in the north of Ireland, where every school that has fifteen children receives aid. The Government conditions must be complied with, and the Inspectors satisfied that there is proper teaching and proper accommodation, as well as an effective conscience clause. As I said just now, you cannot have a thoroughly undenominational school. I do not know of one anywhere.

2922. Supposing all the conditions you have referred to were complied with, the fact still remains that the Government has now by law no power to bring into existence any school to meet a demand, except through the medium of a voluntary body. Do you think, in view of that, it would be a good thing to have a Board which should have the power to initiate new schools and improve existing schools, having full regard to all vested rights, and also recommend further aid where they thought it was deserved. At present there are no schools where you can run these waifs and strays into. You cannot force them into a first class undenominational public school ; it is too expensive, so that other schools must be brought into existence, and there is now no body to do that except voluntary bodies ?—Is it not best to try encouragement first before you attempt

D

*The Right
Rev. the Bishop
of Grahamstown.*
———
Sept. 3rd, 1891.

compulsion. In the case of children not attending any school, perhaps the parents are negligent. There are in Graham's Town the Shaw Hall School, our own Good Shepherd School, and the Roman Catholic Schools. These schools might have a little more encouragement from Government, and I do not see why it should not help any proper school that does good work for the country. It remains to be proved, I think, that there is not sufficient accommodation here in Graham's Town for the children of the poorer classes. I think there is. It certainly seems a very anomalous thing that a public school where parents can afford to pay good fees and send their children, should get something like £700 or £800 a year, while another school where the education of the poorer classes is provided for, gets only £75 a year. With better encouragement of a practical kind there would be more efficiency.

2923. Would not your complaint best be met by creating a Board, which would be able to approach the Government and point out what the local wants and anomalies are, and rectify any difficulty?—I cannot say. Local Boards would mean local taxation, and there is a great trouble in even getting the streets and reservoirs properly attended to. There would be a cry for economy and cutting down of expenditure, and I do not think you would improve the system very much by creating local Boards with the power of local taxation. I should prefer a Visiting Board, before which complaints could be brought. Suppose, for instance, a school violated the conscience clause or sanitary conditions, proper representations could be made and the matter rectified, and the school must suffer so far as the grant is concerned. Local Boards are always for economy, and you would not find a liberal system of education promoted. The great difficulty is to get proper sanitary conditions in any town, not only for children, but also for resident adults. It would be very hard to stir up such Boards to enthusiasm. Enthusiasm for the poor comes from religion, and you must use that power.

2924. *Dean Holmes.*] You were saying that the teachers were inefficient, would you be in favour of having a training college?—I think training colleges should be encouraged, but it is a little premature to require a very high certificate from teachers in this country at present. You cannot do it in regard to mission schools proper; there is not a sufficient supply yet. The teachers should be approved by the Inspectors. Their work should not be merely confined to passing the children in certain standards, but the discipline of the school should be enquired into. We are hoping to start a normal school in Graham's Town. It is a great want at present.

2925. You are in favour of having a boarding training college for teachers, where they could come for a certain time from different parts of the Colony?—Yes.

2926. You said you would like all voluntary schools to be aided; would you apply that to schools where there were only three or four children—private adventure schools?—I would apply the rule that prevails in the north of Ireland and give a grant for fifteen children, provided the necessary conditions were complied with.

2927. Would you on principle aid private adventure schools?—Yes. I think some parents feel that their children are better attended to where the number is small.

2928. That principle would have to be applied all round. Suppose there is a flourishing private school already making a very handsome profit, would you allow that to have its grant the same as others?—I do not see any reason against it if you want to encourage education in the country; but I was dealing simply with education for the poorer children, where no profit would be likely to be made. I do not see why we should not encourage every school that is doing work. The country wants its citizens educated. Of course you must take care that the education fulfils certain conditions. When a school fulfils the conditions of efficiency and thoroughness, and is safeguarded as to religious wants, then I feel persuaded it would be more economical for the country, and better results would be obtained than by starting fresh schools.

2929. *Rev. Cortze.*] Would not what you suggest lead to the breaking up of the system, and support private schools?—I do not see that it would if you require all the conditions to be fulfilled. There must be a room of adequate size, and a certain plant is necessary. It is a grave matter to start even a small school, and requires a good deal of outlay. A poor lady sometimes has half-a-dozen or a dozen children in a stuffy little room, but no Inspector could pass such a school as qualified to receive a grant. It would be much easier for a religious body to have a good school with a large room and an efficient staff, than for private persons to meet proper requirements. You find that most of these little schools are started by impecunious ladies without very much qualification for teaching. It should be a condition that the teachers are efficient, if grants are assigned.

2930. *President.*] But will not these schools be multiplied if you give the aid you suggest? Why should they not be multiplied if they fulfil the conditions.—I do not think you would find that fresh schools would be started in opposition to well ordered schools. My great principle in education is free trade all round under certain conditions.

The Right Rev. the Bishop of Grahamstown.

Sept. 3rd, 1891.

2931. Then the poorest go to the wall, do they not?—I do not think so. The principle has been accepted with regard to farm schools.

2932. Unless voluntary or religious bodies come forward to do the work of the State?—Stringent conditions must be complied with, and it is not an easy matter; but religion will supply the motive power.

2933. *Dr. Berry.*] The legislature has decided that it will give aid only to undenominational schools. That is the established system, and it seems as if it were not to be undone. Can you suggest any way by which on that basis the school system can be advanced and developed?—The present business of the State is to see that good education, apart from religious subjects, is given within certain hours.

2934. *President.*] Have you formed any opinion with regard to the bi-lingual difficulty, the teaching of Dutch and English?—One language should be the vehicle of instruction in a school. I do not see why it should not be Dutch as much as English. Let there be free trade. If Dutch is required, let the vehicle of instruction be in Dutch and the examination in Dutch. The thing will settle itself in time by the demand. It is a matter of demand and supply. If there is a Dutch population in some out of the way place, I do not see why they should not have all the teaching in Dutch; but as I say the demand will ultimately settle that question.

2935. Suppose that parents prefer a boy being taught English, and they also wish Dutch taught, and there is an examination afterwards in that language in the Elementary examination; do you think it wise to have such an examination?—In an Elementary school a child requires the whole time to be devoted to primary subjects. In the upper schools Dutch should be put on an equality, or perhaps rather more than an equality with French or Latin. In primary schools there is not time for children to learn thoroughly more than the subjects before them, and I think you must have one vehicle for teaching—let it be Dutch, English, or Kafir. I would rather have a school taught in Dutch and the examination papers in Dutch than have an additional subject put as a strain upon the children. It would bear hardly upon English children. I think that Dutch should be rewarded, as it is required for official purposes and so on.

2936. Do you think there ought to be an optional paper in the Elementary examination?—Children should be allowed the option of being examined in Dutch or English. Questions might be set in Dutch and the candidates allowed to reply in Dutch, if it is their language; two sets of papers in fact.

2937. English being the vehicle of instruction in most of the Elementary schools, do you think it advisable, in view of Dutch being used by so many, that there should also be an examination paper in Dutch in the Elementary examination?—Not in the Elementary, but in the Higher examinations I think so.

2938. *Rev. Coetzee.*] But Dutch is excluded in the Elementary examination now?—If Dutch is the home language of a child, and it is easier for it to answer in Dutch, do not let it be at a disadvantage. At the same time, a child's time should not be wasted unnecessarily. In primary education it is all it can do to master the three r's, and if you get English children to learn the grammar of Dutch you handicap them in their Elementary education.

2939. *President.*] With regard to the natives, do you think there should be more industrial training?—There ought to be industrial schools. But if you send a Kafir child to any school, it gets taught habits of discipline and order to some extent, and wants are created which will have to be supplied by labour. There ought to be industrial schools where trades could be learnt. But a Kafir child who has been to an ordinary school will want to dress better; it will not be satisfied with just a kaross or blanket. Tastes and wants will be formed and created; these must be supplied; and the native will find he has to work. Natives as a rule only require very Elementary teaching—just reading, writing and arithmetic—and such teaching should be encouraged for the good of the country. Industrial schools, likely to be of much practical service, can only be promoted in comparatively few centres. Opportunity should also be furnished for natives who wish to qualify themselves as teachers and who give proof of their earnestness by self-help, to proceed in higher education. Those who will profit by doing so at present are comparatively few.

Graham's Town, Friday, 4th September, 1891.

PRESENT :

Sir J. D. BARRY (President),

Dean Holmes,
Mr. Rowan,
Rev. Moorrees,

Rev. Coetzee,
Dr. Berry,
Mr. Theron.

Mr. J. Slater examined.

2940. *President.*] I believe you are editor of the *Journal* newspaper in Graham's Town ?—Yes.

2941. And you are a member of the Undenominational Public School Committee here ?—Yes.

2942. Have you also had some experience in educational matters ?—Yes, ever since I came to South Africa, both as a teacher myself and as being interested in schools.

2943. Can you offer any suggestions upon the question of the irregularity of attendance of children in town schools ?—On the question of irregularity of attendance of children, I am requested to give the opinion of the committee of the public school, and it is my own opinion. We think that the only way to deal with the matter effectually is to insist upon all children attending school ; compulsory education in fact.

2944. How would you work it ?—I would interfere with the present system as little as possible. Where you have a Public School Committee, I would deal with it if it were possible. They have covered the ground for years and done good service, and they are doing good service, I think. The example of England shows that such bodies have acquired an interest which ought not to be ignored.

2945. How would you work the compulsory system through them ?—Of course it would be necessary to find out in the towns all the children not attending school, private or otherwise. The parents must be informed that they must send their children to school, and if more accommodation is required than already exists, then I think the Government should in the first place call upon the committee of the public school to find it. If they say they have their hands full and do not want to do it, then the Government might establish a Board School.

2946. *Mr. Rowan.*] Under the present system the Government has not the right of doing so. You would have to alter the system, and I understand you are not in favour of altering the system ?—I would alter it as little as possible. I have the example of the English system before me. In cases where the voluntary system suffices, I would not introduce a Board School ; in cases where it does not suffice, the Government should step in.

2947. *President.*] You say that where there is a deficiency, the undenominational school at present in existence should undertake the task, and if they will not, then establish another school ?—I think so.

2948. Is not that rather a departure from the English principle ?—I think Dean Holmes will bear me out that that is the plan adopted in England, that if they find a voluntary school on the ground doing the work, they do not put a Board school there.

2949. Yours is not a voluntary school, is it ?—Ours is entirely a voluntary school.

2950. You get a large grant from Government, and inasmuch as you get that benefit, ought not the duty to be imposed upon you of finding these schools ?—I would give them the option. I do not think the public school in this town would hesitate to do so, but I cannot speak about other places. If it was found that there were 200 or 300 children in the streets, not going to school anywhere, I think the Government might say to the Public School Committee, you must either provide for these children or we shall.

2951. You are in favour of establishing a Board or some public body to fill up the gaps, are you not ?—Yes, where there are gaps.

2952. *Dr. Berry.*] Is that confined to towns ?—I should adopt the principle of compulsory education everywhere, both for whites and blacks, but like a great deal more of our legislation in this Colony, I would make it permissive; the Governor could decide whether it should be applied to any particular district.

2953. *President.*] You think that ultimately compulsory education must come and ought to come, but you would proceed by degrees ?—Let it come as soon as you can, but we must move cautiously in this country. That is why I would not advocate going beyond towns in the first place. Wherever you have a school that children can conveniently attend, education should be made compulsory, and I say that on the principle that the State cannot afford to have any of its children in utter ignorance.

2954. *Mr. Rowan.*] Is the attendance irregular in the schools with which you have been connected ?—We have not any great complaint that I know of in this town.

Mr
J. Slater.

Sept. 4th, 1891.

2955. What is the percentage of children in attendance compared with the number on the books ?—At the Shaw Hall mission school there are 250 names on the books, and the attendance this morning was 200.

2956. *Dean Holmes.*] Do you see any objection to the appointment of a truancy officer to take to school the children found in the streets, and an attendance officer to visit the parents in the place and enquire whether such children are receiving instruction ?—I do not see how compulsory education is to be enforced without some such officer.

2957. Would the people object to it as inquisitorial ?—I do not think they would object in towns. I cannot speak so well about the country. The situation of the country is such that it must be dealt with very carefully. I think people in towns would feel that it is perfectly right the children should be educated.

2958. *President.*] Can you apply the compulsory system in towns without touching the blacks as well ?—You cannot do so in towns, I mean on the locations. I have had some conversation with gentlemen who are concerned in the education of the natives, and there is a minority of Christians round, and these have to bear the whole brunt; the school has to take in the heathen children for nothing, because if they do not make up a certain number their grant gets stopped when the Inspector comes round. The end of that is, that the Christian people have to pay the whole, and the heathens get their children educated for nothing. I think where there is a headman in a village, and a school is established, it is only fair that we should insist that all the children should go to school and share with the rest.

2959. And those who can pay be made to pay ?—Yes. The natives can all pay a very little.

2960. Then you think the compulsory system can be applied to locations ?—I should begin cautiously to apply it.

2960A. Would you have literary schools only for natives, or would you have the training to a great extent industrial ?—The literary education should be of the simplest character. I think it is a mistake to have anybody in the country who cannot read, write, and cypher, and have some little knowledge of history, geography, and so on, which is necessary to make any human being fit for his work, but we are all of opinion that it is highly desirable the natives should have some kind of industrial training besides, and especially spade husbandry. What we want is that the natives should be good agriculturists. If you go much further and teach them carpentering and so on, then you come into collision with the tradesmen of the country, and it becomes very unpopular. Everybody would like to see the native boys taught to dig and plough and so on, and the native girls taught to sew, wash, get up linen, and such things. These subjects should be joined to their other education, as we hope they may thereby get their living.

2961. Would the establishment of such compulsory schools for natives interfere with labour in the country, or would it have a tendency in many cases to induce the parents of children who do not like industrial work to leave the towns and go into the country ?—In every school where native children attend throughout the country, I would insist upon it that they had some industrial training along with their other teaching, whether in town or country. I would not propose to go to any great expense, but they should be taught to work and not be allowed to idle their time away.

2962. Do you see any difficulty in starting an inexpensive industrial school in Graham's Town, at the location for instance ?—It might be done in connection with the school. The teacher might have a piece of land and employ the boys on it.

2963. Do you think your mission school would fall into such a system if it were one of the conditions upon which the grant is perpetuated, or increased possibly ?—Yes. I am sure the native minister is strongly of opinion that industrial training should form part of the teaching of the natives.

2964. Have you any knowledge of the industrial training schools in England ?—It is a long time since I was in England. Industrial schools would be an expensive matter, but in every school where natives should be taught how to use simple implements. Without making carpenters of them, I think they might be taught how to use the plane, hammer and saw, which would be very useful for them, but if you train them for regular trades, then you encounter the opposition of the townspeople, who would say, we have to apprentice our children to learn, while you teach these people for nothing. That will not do.

2965. Would you debar the blacks from going to any other literary schools, if they pay for their teaching ?—If they satisfy the Government that they are being properly taught, I should say nothing at all.

2966. Whether they were public or private schools ?—Yes.

Mr.
J. Slater.

Sept. 4th, 1891.

2967. With regard to their admission to public schools, do you see any barrier or real objection to it. Suppose a coloured boy presents himself at an undenominational public school and offers to pay, can you debar him?—The difficulty of colour is inseparable.

2968. How would you got over that?—In the first place, the natives would not want to come; that is one great comfort.

2969. Suppose they do begin to obtrude, or wish to obtrude, what barrier, if any, would you make?—It is within measurable distance. It will come some day, and there will be great trouble when it does come. The white people will not associate with them.

2970. Would it not be a good thing to have two sets of literary schools. At your own public school for boys I believe you have started two preparatory departments, one for ordinary pupils, and one in which the door is open, so to speak, for boys with whom the others do not wish to associate?—That is so.

2971. Does that work well?—Yes; it works in this way, that the two classes cannot very well associate.

2972. How do you keep them separate, by fees?—Yes. They do not mix in any way, but even the fact of their being on the same ground in the drostdy is found to be an objection by some families who are better off; they do not like it.

2973. What have you done in consequence?—I think we shall have to move one school away somewhere else.

2974. Then practically the same difficulty with regard to social distinctions arises among whites?—It is not so bad. If the boys I refer to were clean and better behaved, they would not be so objectionable, but when you talk of mixing whites and blacks it is impossible. I have seen them associate at Lovedale, but it would not be endured throughout the country I am sure. I do not think the natives themselves wish it either.

2975. Dr. Berry.] With regard to locations, do you mean the term to apply solely to town locations, or locations in districts?—Wherever natives are; any place where there is a school. I was alluding to Peddie. It was a missionary there who told me that he could not get the heathen natives to pay; they came for nothing in great numbers.

2976. Would you make industrial training a compulsory part of education as well as the literary part?—I would. I am anxious that the natives should be taught spade husbandry.

2977. Would you be in favour of supplementing such a system by any provision whereby a reasonable number of such natives in locations might have an opportunity of going to some higher industrial institution, as a reward for extra diligence or proficiency?—Those of the natives who are a little better off, will insist upon being better educated. Whether it is our business to undertake it, I do not know.

2978. President.] Would you be in favour of giving bursaries to those who are advanced, and help them to get on to a higher grade, if they at the same time wish it?—It would only be fair, but I should keep it limited. You want a certain number of natives as teachers, ministers, and interpreters, and a limited number you might provide for in the way of bursaries; but as a rule, I notice that the natives are anxious to get book-learning. They are not so anxious to get industrial teaching.

2979. To some extent does not that apply to white children; ought not industrial teaching to be more imported into our white schools than it is?—The time that boys have for education in the Colony is very limited, and it is a fact that we almost give them what is called "a lick and a promise." They are not taught as thoroughly as they should be in schools.

2980. Dr. Berry.] Have you any trade class in connection with your undenominational public school?—We have a carpentry class.

2981. Is that well attended and taken advantage of?—It is satisfactory.

2982. Is it for European boys?—Yes; that is all.

2983. What class of boys usually attends that?—All classes.

2984. Town boys or country boys?—We have not so many country boys there at present.

2985. What teacher comes there to give instruction?—We pay a carpenter, and the system works satisfactorily. We are also endeavouring to arrange for classes for elementary agriculture, a knowledge of soils and so on, of a simple character.

2986. Do they pay a fee in the carpentry class?—I think 2s. 6d. a quarter, or something of the sort is paid for materials.

2987. Rev. Moorrees.] When is the instruction given?—I think twice a week, in the afternoon, after the school work is over.

2988. Dean Holmes.] It is not included in the regular school time, is it?—No.

2989. President.] Do you take in boys from elsewhere for this class?—Not to my knowledge.

2990. *Dr. Berry.*] Do the boys complete the articles?—They would know how to make a bench or a chair, and if one of these boys becomes a farmer, he can repair anything in his own house in a tolerably satisfactory way.

2991. You do not turn out articles for sale do you?—No, we do not make a trade of it.

2992. *President.*] Do you find it too expensive?—It is not at all expensive.

2993. *Dr. Berry.*] Has anything to be taken out of the school funds for the support of this industrial teaching?—I think the Government gives us a small grant, about £10 a year, I am not sure.

2994. *President.*] Do I understand you to say that you would like the public school to remain under the present system of guarantors as long as they like, and as long as they perform their duty to the satisfaction of the Government, and then, if there is a gap created outside of them, or by their giving up their work, the Board is to step in; is that so?—Yes.

2995. *Rev. Coetzee.*] With regard to native schools, did I understand you to say that you would be in favour of industrial training in every native school, or at certain centres?—In every native school teachers should be required to be able to give a little instruction in elementary agriculture and a simple knowledge of the use of tools and so on. I would hardly call it carpentering for fear of making tradesmen jealous.

2996. Who is to find the tools?—The Government must be liberal.

2997. And the materials?—It is easy to find a little wood.

2998. Have you any idea what it would cost to have such a branch established in every school?—I would not make a branch of it; it should be part of the regular work.

2999. Would every teacher be capable of giving that instruction?—I should require him to be capable.

3000. You would make it part of the curriculum of the school?—Yes. I think that every native should be expected to know how to use his hands. The great cry of the country is that the natives will not work, so let us teach them that.

3001. Are the teachers who take charge at present capable of imparting such instruction?—You cannot deal with the existing race quite so well, but you might require it in future, the same as you require anything else.

3002. *Mr. Theron.*] I take it that you mean this, that these native schools in locations are mostly conducted by native teachers?—Yes.

3003. And in their training they should be required to get some knowledge of these things?—At least of agricultural names.

3004. And for the future you think teachers should know that it is required of them to be able to conduct such instruction?—That is my desire.

3005. It would be no extra expense?—No.

3006. *Dean Holmes.*] Is it not your experience that whenever an additional subject is imposed, existing teachers make themselves immediately conversant with it, so as to be able to carry on their school more efficiently?—If it is a case of book learning they will, but when it is a question of using spades and ploughs it is different. You must get that into them earlier.

3007. *President.*] If you start the system within a reasonable time, inasmuch as there would be more coloured boys taken into these schools under any compulsory system, a slight additional grant would enable the schools to have competent teachers to deal with industrial matters, would it not?—Yes, if needful.

3008. Do you think that managers and teachers would fall in with such a system?—Gradually. They are fully convinced of the necessity for it.

3009. *Dr. Berry.*] Are you among those who think that the time has arrived when natives should be compelled to pay a little more for their education than they have been paying hitherto, natives in locations for instance?—Yes, they ought to be made to pay under the present system; some pay rather more than they should, and some rather less. The missionary who has the Christians under his thumb can make them pay, but the heathens will not pay. The headman ought to be made to collect from them, it should not be the missionary's work. The Government ought to instruct the headman of a location to collect from every family a small fee.

3010. *President.*] Would you have a hut tax?—What the missionaries now do is to have certain families who will pay a shilling a month each family. If pressure was brought to bear on the headman there would be but little complaint, but at present they say they were not engaged for this work, and they will not do it.

3011. Is your opinion generally shared in?—I think I am pretty safe in saying that what I have stated is the general opinion, but I speak from a more intimate knowledge with the Wesleyan body.

3012. What additional facilities do you think could be given to meet the wants of children of railway employés?—With reference to that subject I may say that I have

Mr.
J. Slater.

Sept. 4th, 1891.

received a communication from the teacher of the railway school at Alicedale. He says :—

At present the children of railway servants may travel free by rail to and from school, daily.

The chief defects of this arrangement appear to me :—

1. Some children cannot avail themselves of this privilege on account of their great distance from the nearest school, or—in the case of branch lines—from the absence of convenient trains.

2. The Railway Time Table cannot be arranged so that children from different directions may all arrive and depart at the same time ; consequently, even when the trains are punctual, children arrive and depart in batches, an irregularity which interferes very much with the efficiency of school work. For example, Alicedale school hours are 9 a.m. to 12·30 p.m. and 1·30 to 3 p.m.

Alicedale children attend	..	.. 9—12·30	1·30—3
Port Elizabeth line ,,	..	.. 9—12·30	1·45 leave for train.
Graham's Town ,, ,,	..	.. 9—12·30	2·10 ,, ,, ,,
Cradock ,, ,,	..	arrive 9·25 (This train is generally cancelled;next 11·30 Train before 6·30 a.m.)	2·45 ,, ,, ,,

Every change in Railway Time Table affects the times of arrival and departure.

3. Children travelling long distances daily in the guard's van are too much fatigued by the rough journey to study to much advantage while in school.

Allow me to call your attention to the following extract from the last report on the Alicedale Public School by Mr. J. H. Brady, M.A., deputy inspector of schools :—

" Nearly, if not quite, all the pupils are the children of railway employés. The majority of them live at Alicedale, but 17 come in every day by rail from the stations and platelayers' cottages along the line. Even if the trains are punctual, some of these arrive an hour late, but, as a matter of fact they are sometimes much later. This irregularity, of course, is injurious to work, but the great distances which some of the children travel are of much greater moment. Last year 4 children travelled 58 miles, and 3 children 44 miles every day.

What is urgently needed here is a Government boarding-house for railway children, so as to allow them to come on Monday morning and leave on Friday afternoon. Alicedale is excellently situated for such an establishment, being at the junction of three lines. There is a building in the camp belonging to the Railway Department which with slight alterations would be very well adapted for this purpose, and a grant of £10 or £12 for each boarder equally divided between the Railway and Education Departments would suffice."

A number of boarding-houses at intervals along the lines and in connection with public undenominational schools would, I am sure, meet the case of railway children, if placed under good management.

3012A. What steps in your opinion should be taken to give Boards of Management perpetual succession in their office ?—In Grahamstown, I may say, we wish to have our school incorporated as a high school ; we have had it before our minds for some years. Sir Sydney Shippard went so far as to prepare a Bill of Incorporation for us, but there was some objection, and it was not carried out. In the larger places, the school should work towards being an undenominational high school or college, so that it might eventually be affiliated to the university of the country.

3013. Would not that tend to shut out the educational interests in the districts, and lead to your becoming a close corporation ?—A certain portion of the members might be official members, for instance, the Mayor and the Civil Commissioner. They should always be upon the public school committee ex officio.

3014. If your idea was carried out, you would not be quite a public school, you would be shutting the door as it were ?—I remember Mr. Merriman taking me up very sharply about that. He said, you are not a public school, but still we do the work.

3015. But other schools say we do the work too. St. Aidan's College, for instance, would say give us an Act of Incorporation, we will do the same work ?—St. Aidan's does not stand upon the same ground that we do. We are strictly undenominational.

3016. They say they will satisfy all the conditions you do, and there is the difficulty. If you are to be a public school, you must take in the highest and the lowest. Practically you are not undenominational, you are allowed to have the religious teaching that the managers provide ?—We do not provide any religious teaching, we are strictly undenominational. Our head master is an Anglican, and he conducts devotions morning and evening according to his own wishes. We are there and see what goes on, and we do not object.

3017. The other schools say they are the same, that they have no undenominational teaching, and yet they get nothing, while you have a large grant. They do exactly the same work as you do. If you had an Act of Incorporation, it would really enable you to shut your doors to any who did not satisfy your conditions, and you would no longer be a national school?—There is no element of exclusiveness in connection with the public school.

3018. Would it not be a good thing if a School Board were to be started, and take the place of the guarantors of the public school?—I am not of that opinion. The plan works very well at present. You have got men interested in education who work for the love of it, and if you had an elected body like the Town Council, they might wish to keep down expenses as much as possible, and they might not be men interested in education.

3019. Suppose you make it obligatory upon them to find schools to the satisfaction of the Education Department, and if they did not, then give the Education Department power to step in and find them at the expense of the ratepayers; would not that meet the difficulty?—Why wish to overturn a system which works well already?

3020. There are those who say it might be improved. The guarantors are a fluctuating body and you want to make them permanent by making them a close body. That is the difficulty?—There is a difficulty, and I am not quite prepared to say how it should be dealt with. I maintain that you ought to show the utmost consideration for the public school system and for the guarantors, because they have done good work for so many years. I think no one pretends to say that our public schools are other than undenominational.

3021. Rev. Moorrees.] Do not you think it is a very great disadvantage at present that there is nobody who could hold public school property. Would you be in favour of some plan to create the present school committees corporate bodies, or would you prefer a new kind of board altogether?—I want to see them incorporated, so that they can hold property and be continuous. Vacancies might be filled up in any way you like.

3022. Mr. Rowan.] How are you to make that provision, because this body of guarantors only exists for three years. At the end of three years they may be nowhere. Such difficulties have arisen in the Western Province. A body of guarantors, men who take an interest in education, start a school and erect buildings. After three or six years the children of these men are educated, or these guarantors themselves have removed from the district, and the building belongs to nobody?—I suppose the law can deal with that, and make it a corporation as long as it lasts, and then, should they cease to do any business, it might be provided that the property should belong either to the Government or to the parties who found the money.

3023. But how would you provide for the transfer of the buildings?—I think that is a legal detail.

3024. President.] Is it not better that at the end of three years the guarantors should go out, and a Board be elected by the ratepayers. Would not that create greater interest in education throughout the district, and satisfy local wants better than by making this close body which may in some cases be very good, but being a close body might exclude those wishing to be admitted and who have a right to be admitted?—The best results in the country have been obtained by these close bodies.

3025. Rev. Coetzee.] What do you think of the establishment of an over Board for the district, leaving existing schools to have their own managers and internal arrangements, such over Board providing schools where they are required, holding property in trust, and taking to a certain extent the place of the guarantors?—I am afraid you would not get an intelligent Board. You would probably get a class of men more interested in keeping the rates down than in advancing education.

3026. President.] But if you make it their duty to do it, the Government supervising them and keeping them up to the mark, such Board would have power to deal with local bodies. They would approach such a body as yours, and if you are doing work to the satisfaction of the Government, they would say go on and we will leave you alone, but if not, then they would report it to the central authority. Would not such a proposal embrace your present arrangements. Why need it destroy or supersede them?—It looks to me like having another set of masters besides the department over the committee.

3027. Dr. Berry.] Unless you have a general School Board in a district, who is to administer or manage these schools?—They are managed now very well.

3028. But if you call into existence schools that do not exist, you would have to levy rates to keep them going. Who is to manage all those things and hold the school property, unless you have some sort of Board in the division charged with the

Mr.
J. Slater.

Sept. 4th, 1891.

maintenance and administration ?—I do not see why the Government if it finds the money for the buildings should not hold them. I am terribly afraid you would not get intelligent men on these Boards. Even in England the School Boards have furnished subject matter for criticism.

3029. May not that criticism be applied to all local institutions, still they do some good ?—The present plan would work well if the inspection was a little more frequent. You do not want any more than that.

3030. But it does not cover the whole ground, it is not complete, is it ?—If you speak of natives, everything is tentative, and must be very cautiously altered ; if you speak of Europeans, I have said what I would recommend doing in every town.

3031. Is not the necessity which you see for caution every reason why a local Board should deal with the matter best ?—What good could an over Board do for us here. We have given no cause for complaint as long as we have been working.

3032. *President.*] Do not you think an elected body such as is proposed would be an advantage ?—I think that you would be creating machinery that is really unnecessary.

3033. Your opinion is that it is better to form the present committees into a corporate body ?—I am distinctly of that opinion.

3034. Have you formed any opinion with regard to the teaching of English and Dutch ?—Speaking for the schools I am interested in, there is every facility given for instruction in the English language, and Dutch is studied as a separate branch ; in the public school considerable attention is given to it. It is not desired except by those who wish to pass examinations for some reason or other.

3035. You give them an opportunity by having a master ?—We have a master.

3036. Does that answer all requirements ?—Yes.

3037. Do you think there ought to be any alteration in the Elementary examination with regard to language ?—I think it is not fair to insist upon English children learning Dutch for the examinations. They do not want it, and if you make it an extra subject it adds to the difficulty, especially where children are at school only for a short time. I am of course only speaking of this place. I see that in some parts of the country there are communities that speak nothing but a variety of Dutch. I would not insist upon those people taking their instruction in English if the parents object. I should not think it right to force them. You must not compel on either side.

3038. *Rev. Coetzee.*] What would you suggest in order to give some encouragement to Dutch ?—I do not want to encourage it.

3039. *Dean Holmes.*] Seeing that this is a bi-lingual country, do you think it would be fair to have in the Elementary examination a paper set either in Dutch or English ?—That would be a fair arrangement. Those who had been taught through the medium of Dutch might have a paper set entirely in Dutch and *vice versâ.* I would give the candidates their choice.

3040. *Rev. Coetzee.*] Are you acquainted with the wants and requirements of the Dutch population ?—I have been studying the matter ever since I came here, or rather trying to do so.

3041. Can you express any definite opinion as to their requirements ?—I came across Dutch a good deal in the Free State. The Volksraad was every now and then at us to teach Dutch. I was co-rector of the Grey College. The parents themselves did not care much about Dutch, nor the children, and I believe that to be the case in nearly all the places where the two languages have come together. The necessity for English is so great, and the parents think that children will pick up enough Dutch. I try to allow everybody the same freedom that I claim for myself. In places where nothing but Dutch is spoken, if parents wish nothing but that language taught, I cannot say anything against it.

3042. Suppose they want their children to be taught English and Dutch ?—Let them have it ; but I would not make it a part of the Elementary examination. It is not elementary work in my opinion to learn two languages ; and if they are going to be taught Dutch, they should be taught proper Dutch, not the language that is commonly spoken in this country.

3043. Do you know the difference between the language spoken by the majority of people and proper Dutch ?—Yes, I do to some extent. There is rather less inflection in what you would call good Cape Dutch than in the Dutch of Holland.

3044. Do you know that there is not much difference between the language spoken by some people and proper Dutch ?—That may be so in the peninsula perhaps, but as a rule, I have never come across farmers who speak much else than the taal. They may understand the other, but they do not talk it. I think if you insist upon children learning the Dutch of Holland, it will be a trouble to them, and prove of comparatively little use, as it is not a language that is likely to be spoken by a large number of people.

3045. *Rev. Moorrees.*] Do not you think that the programme of the examinations rules to a great extent the instruction given in our schools ?—Yes, disastrously.

3046. If the Dutch language is excluded from the Elementary examination, would not that tend to discourage the study of the language ?—Yes, it would; and that seems to me a thing we should aim at most vigorously. I was born and brought up in Wales, and I saw there the effect of two languages on the population. The population was kept in perpetual isolation and jealousy because they spoke in another language; and as long as that is the case in this country, as long as people are confined to another language, they will be kept in a state of jealousy and suspicion, and prevented from uniting. It seems to me that we could not curse our country with a worse thing than trying to perpetuate two languages.

3047. Would it not be better for both classes of the community to learn each other's language than for one to try and stamp out the language of the other ?—I do not require that. I distinctly said that in a case where a community chooses to have education in Dutch, I would not interfere.

3048. But you wish us to aim at discouraging the Dutch ?—That is only my thought; my wishing does not affect it. I give that advice to my fellow colonists, but if a man wants to perpetuate Dutch, or there is a school where only Dutch teaching is wanted, very well.

3049. You are aware that Belgium is a bi-lingual country ?—Yes.

3050. And it is one of the most intelligent countries in Europe, is it not ?—Yes.

3051. In that country it does not do much harm to have two languages apparently ?—It does here. It separates us, and we do not mix as we ought.

3052. *President.*] If it is thought desirable to have a Dutch paper at the Elementary examination, in what form would it be least objectionable ?—It seems to me that you might have a separate paper set to test proficiency in Dutch, and give rewards, and publish a separate list. That would be fairer than mixing it up with the general examination, and making children who do not want to take the Dutch paper stand lower than if they had taken it. It is really a question of compulsion.

3053. It has been suggested that a Dutch boy educated in Dutch, is to a great extent handicapped, and inasmuch as he is so handicapped, you should create a sort of rude equality by having a paper in Dutch which should to some extent handicap the English boy. Is not there some principle of fairness in that ?—It is not fair to handicap anybody, and I do not see why you should put difficulties in the way of an English boy. At the same time, I would give every facility to those who wished to have Dutch.

3054. Would it not be wise to have in the Elementary examination papers in several alternative subjects, and give the candidate an opportunity of displaying his knowledge in any one or more ?—I should have thought the object of the Elementary examination was for the University to express its opinion as to what elementary teaching ought to be, and examine in a few elementary subjects.

3055. If there were three papers in the Elementary examination, would not the mass of boys take up Dutch, and if they did, would it not be a good thing for the country, and lead to the people mixing more and getting hold of each others ideas more readily. A boy who passed in Latin would get his marks accordingly, and French the same ?—Latin and French are not elementary subjects. Dutch is an elementary thing with boys who have been talking it all their life, and I would give them equal facilities and set an extra paper for proficiency in Dutch or proficiency in English for boys brought up in Dutch, setting them in an equal position as regards marks, and to the Dutch paper, separate bursaries or honours might be attached.

3056. Do not you think it is wise to hold out some inducement to the English boy to take the Dutch, and in order not to handicap him, give him the option of another subject ?—I do not consider that elementary work.

3057. *Dr. Berry.*] You say that you would have no objection to a separate paper in the Dutch being set for the Elementary examination, giving rewards for those who attain a certain amount of proficiency in the examination, would you also insist that any pupil who was to be rewarded for that proficiency should also attain a certain standard of proficiency in other subjects ?—Yes; I think that is quite necessary, but I would not insist in the Elementary examination upon two languages. I am contending for freedom; that no child should be forced to learn a language which his parents do not wish him to learn; but practically it would come to what you say, that even in English, as well as reading, writing and arithmetic, the boys would be so educated that they would be able to take a pass in all those subjects.

3058. *President.*] What contribution would you expect from local bodies in support of schools ?—None. The municipalities are already heavily burdened, and their income is small. They find it difficult to carry out the necessary improvements in the towns, and to impose more burdens upon them would be very unpopular. Direct taxation does not find favour either in town or country, they would rather see Government find the money. It comes to the same thing in the end.

3059. And do you think that all education should be controlled from the centre, without any local control?—Yes; I do not see any advantage in the suggested change.

3060. *Rev. Coetzee.*] Would you be in favour of raising the grants to two-thirds of all the expenses connected with schools?—I may say that in our own school we are not illiberally treated by the Government. We just come out. We got half, and whether we have a right to ask more than that I do not know. Government gives us nearly £600 a year, and that is good deal to give.

3061. Is there ever a call made upon your guarantors to make up the deficiency?—Never.

3062. *Rev. Moorrees.*] Would you have any objection to make local bodies pay whatever deficiency there might be in the accounts of the school?—It is not that I would object, I am afraid they would object.

3063. *President.*] Is it fair that they should be called upon to do so, do you think?—I have spoken with the ex-Mayor on the subject, and he said he thought that if a small portion was demanded, there would not be any objection.

3064. *Dean Holmes.*] If there was a deficiency, would you be in favour of the Government paying half and the local authorities half?—Some such arrangement as that might answer. My objection arose from the fear that a small rate would soon grow into a large one.

3065. That fear does not exist in the minds of all municipal bodies, because certain municipal councils are already guarantors. Would you object to its being made a permissive arrangement for municipal bodies to take the management?—I do not see the slightest objection to that.

3066. I mean make it permissive for towns to rate themselves?—No; I do not object to that. I do not mean to say that they should go beyond existing schools.

3067. *Dr. Berry.*] Where public undenominational schools exist, and they want to get rid of their obligation, would it not be a good thing to have a local Board ready to take them in, if they require to annihilate themselves and to have perpetual succession?—Yes. As long as existing interests work well, that is all right; if they do not work well, Government might step in.

3068. Do you know anything about the wants of children belonging to the agricultural population?—I do not know anything about that.

3069. Can you suggest any means for securing the fuller use being made of the opportunities afforded for education?—I think the grants which Government makes to European mission schools are not sufficiently generous. In the case of the Shaw Hall mission school which I visited this morning, there are 250 children on the books, and Government gives £75 a year towards the teachers. They also give towards three pupil teachers, but the whole grant only comes to about £100 a year. Considering what the Government gives to other schools of a more advanced character, this is a very poverty-stricken provision. I think in the case of mission schools in towns, Government might be more liberal than they are. The result in our case, and it must be the same with other schools in town, is that we are sorely cramped. We cannot provide adequate books, maps, and so on, and we cannot employ the teachers we should like. The dealings of the Government are not so generous as they should be with regard to these schools.

3070. Could there in your opinion be one general system of contribution on the part of the Government to the poorer whites in these mission schools?—I would rather leave it to the Education Department which has managed things on the whole hitherto so well.

3071. Suppose you were in the department and had to deal with the subject, what would you do?—I cannot say.

3072. *Mr. Theron.*] With reference to your mission school, is it managed by a committee of managers or a Board?—There is a committee of managers.

3073. And still it is a mission school?—Yes. It is called a mission school.

3074. Are you required by the regulations to have a board of managers for mission schools?—It is called a mission school, but really it is a fourth-class school.

3075. In that case, would it not be better to change the name and make it a fourth-class school under the existing managers of the public undenominational school?—I do not know that the name would signify very much. I should be sorry to disturb the management of that and similar schools, as they are under the care of the churches, and are very well conducted.

3076. You mean to say that they are more or less sectarian?—Not sectarian. They are carried on by a sectarian denomination; but they are undenominational.

3077. *Mr. Rowan.*] Is the Shaw Hall School carried on by the Wesleyan body?—Yes.

Mr.
J. Slater.

Sept. 4th, 1891.

3078. It is under a board of management, but still it is a mission school belonging to the Wesleyan body?—It is a misnomer to call it a mission school. They are all white children there; but the parents cannot afford to pay very much.

3079. *President.*] The Church appoints the committee of management, and makes up any deficiency, does it not?—Yes; they often have to do it.

3080. *Mr. Theron.*] Instead of that committee, appointed by the Church, would you object to the school being placed under the supervision of the same committee which manages the other schools; would that make any alteration?—Not in this particular case.

3081. *Rev. Moorrees.*] Sir Langham Dale proposed that Cape Town should be divided into districts for the purpose of these mission schools, the inhabitants of any district electing the managers for such mission school; would you be in favour of some such plan as that?—We should be very sorry to interfere with the working of these mission schools. As far as we have seen, they work well.

3082. You prefer the management as it is at present, and larger grants?—Yes.

3083. *President.*] Do you think that is better than fourth-class public undenominational schools?—Yes.

3084. *Dean Holmes.*] You would like the mission schools to be continued exactly as they are now under the present managers, and yet obtain the grant suggested for the fourth-class schools?—Yes.

3085. *President.*] And make an industrial department compulsory?—Yes.

3086. *Rev. Coetzee.*] How many mission schools are there in Graham's Town attended by whites?—I think three.

3087. Are there any mission schools attended by coloured people?—Yes.

3088. How many?—I have not any knowledge of them.

3089. *Dr. Berry.*] Have you any objection to the existence of more than one first-class school in a division?—There might be circumstances under which another first-class school might be required, if there are two towns in a division. Where there is only one town in a division it is not advisable.

3090. Why not?—There is not sufficient element to support it.

3091. *President.*] Where you have in one town, like Graham's Town, three first-class schools all working and doing well, are not you contradicted by facts?—The support of the schools here is largely from the outside.

3092. Suppose all the schools were willing to submit to inspection, would it not be a good thing?—I do not see it. I think the system of quiet instruction is far better than these examinations, which simply disturb the steady teaching of the school. I am afraid that is so in every school.

3093. You think we are over-examined?—Yes. I think so. One of the difficulties with regard to ladies' boarding schools is the great expense for boarding, which is found almost too much for country families to pay. They complain that it amounts to £80 or £90 a year. I think Government might help private schools that are doing good work, by giving a capitation grant, some payment by results, or some grant for boarders.

3094. *Dean Holmes.*] Would it be a good principle that private adventure schools should be aided. Suppose such a school is carried on for individual profit, any grant made would only be increasing that profit, would it not?—I do not contemplate that.

3095. There are about fifteen schools in Graham's Town carried on for individual profit, are there not?—I was not thinking of schools of that kind. I was thinking of quasi public schools.

3096. *Rev. Coetzee.*] There is sometimes a difficulty found in providing suitable boarding buildings; what would you suggest with regard buildings for schools aided by Government?—The Government ought to help I think. I should not say it was wrong if a small rate were levied, but if we introduce the principle, it would soon mount up to a heavy sum.

3097. You have been some time in the Free State; the buildings there are erected at the expense of the Government mostly, I believe?—Yes.

3098. Could not the same principle be applied here?—I should prefer it. I think the Government ought to find the money; it is the best way.

3099. *President.*] If that is done, the property ought to be vested in a public body. What body would you vest it in?—I think in the case of any incorporation, the Mayor of the town and the Civil Commissioner should certainly be members of the council, indeed in the case of every public school I should like to make them *ex officio* members, as you thereby ensure a certain amount of publicity and Government interference.

3100. If something like an elected body is created, you would like the Mayor and the Civil Commissioner to form part?—Yes.

3101. Could you suggest any others who should be added?—I do not think of any others.

Mr.
J. Slater.
—
Sept. 4th, 1891.

3102. You said just now that you thought the ratepayers would not be competent to elect. The ratepayers elect members of Parliament who have to legislate for the country, and although not competent themselves to go to Parliament, they generally know who are the best men to represent them. Do not you think the ratepayers, if the duty were imposed on them, would elect the most competent men to have charge of educational matters ?—They might ; I cannot tell. I do not think they have done so in England particularly. It has been a question of politics and various other things.

3103. *Rev. Coetzee.*] Suppose the Government finds the buildings, who will decide whether it is necessary to erect a school building in a certain place or not ?—I suppose the Government will have certain rules to go upon by which they will decide whether another school is required in that place. I think in England they go by the population, but I am not prepared to say.

3104. Have you anything to say on the subject of industrial schools ?—My committee thought it was a very good thing to be tried, but it has not been a very great success.

3105. Are there any night schools in existence here ?—I do not know of any.

3106. Have you formed any opinion as to their desirability ?—Theoretically they are desirable, no doubt, but practically we have tried them here without much success.

3107. Have you tried a night school in connection with your public school here ? —Yes.

3108. Why did it fail ?—I do not think boys want to be at school after dark.

3109. And it is not judicious for girls you think ?—No.

Sister Cecile examined.

Sister Cecile.
—
Sept. 4th, 1891.

3110. *President.*] I believe you are Mother Superior of St. Peter's Home, Graham's Town ?—Yes.

3111. How long have you been in the Colony ?—Eight years.

3112. How long has the Home been established ?—Eight years next October.

3113. What expenditure has been incurred in establishing it ?—We have incurred £4,500 odd in the purchase of property and buildings, and there is another outlay of £4,000 ; £8,500 altogether.

3114. Have you an industrial department ?—Yes. There are 45 boarders, who go in purely for industrial work ; they are the lowest class whites. Mr. Brady inspects the school, as we want to work on the English rules of certified schools.

3115. Do these children receive a free education ?—It is practically free.

3116. Both board and education ?—Yes ; practically.

3117. Do not you get any aid from Government in connection with that school ? —No aid beyond the secular education.

3118. What do you call your mission school ?—" The Good Shepherd."

3119. How many children are there in that ?—There were 100 last Monday morning.

3120. Boys, or girls ?—Boys under seven, girls, and infants.

3121. No boys over seven ?—No ; we found that it was undesirable to keep them there after that age.

3122. What aid do you get from Government for this purpose ?—£75 a year.

3123. Do all the children who go to the Good Shepherd receive industrial education ?—Not all ; only our own boarders.

3124. Why not ?—We have not the money to do it. £75 barely covers current expenses.

3125. Do you find this industrial department is a good one ?—We have only seven children out ; five are thoroughly satisfactory, and two not very.

3126. What is the nature of the industrial work ?—Cooking, baking, housework, laundry work, and needlework. We are about starting knitting machines, but that is rather an expensive business. We got them out from England. The great difficulty is the strong prejudice against white children being taught industry.

3127. Do you find that that prejudice is being perpetuated ?—It is considered beneath a white woman's dignity to scrub.

3128. Do you make them do industrial work ?—Yes.

3129. You think it is absolutely necessary ?—Yes ; a certain amount of manual work. They have plenty of outdoor exercise. We have had a good many children who have been in prison.

3130. Does it contaminate the other children, being brought into contact with them ?—We have tried to isolate them as much as possible, if the district surgeon considers it desirable when they come.

3131. Still you carry on the work as one school, do you not ?—Yes.

3132. The object is to train the poorer class of European girls for domestic service ?—Yes.

3133. And you think it has been a success ?—Yes, on the whole.

3134. What literary education do you give them ?—We try to take them up to the sixth standard if possible. They all work up to the third standard. This is what Mr. Brady says in his report, " 36 of the pupils are inmates of the St. Peter's Home, an institution in which girls of European race after being rescued from destitution or crime, are brought up, with the object of being fitted to be domestic servants. They are given a sound elementary education, and a good training in housework, including cooking, baking, housemaid's work, and laundry work. The object of the institution is from every point of view most beneficent and praiseworthy."

3135. You say that the children from there go to the Good Shepherd school ?—Yes.

3136. Where they get literary education ; the industrial training they get in St. Peter's Home ?—Yes.

3137. With regard to mission schools, do you think the Good Shepherd school you have just mentioned would be better if it had an industrial department ?—Yes, but it would mean an additional grant. All the children who pass out of the two schools ought to be able to help themselves as much as possible with ordinary industrial work.

3138. It would not interfere with their education, but train them better in fact for future life ?—I should think so.

3139. Do you think this mission school would be better for having an industrial department, where the children would be obliged to undergo some industrial training in connection with their education ?—If it could be managed, it would undoubtedly.

3140. How could you do it most inexpensively ?—I have not thought of that sufficiently. I know nothing about boys. Some plan might be devised, I dare say.

3141. Could you provide for their industrial training in St. Peter's Home ?—It would be at some considerable cost I am afraid. It could be done.

3142. Can you conceive any means by which it could be done away from the Home ?—That would be more expensive still. A certain percentage of the work the children were engaged upon would be spoilt. It depends upon how much they spoil.

3143. You think it is desirable that there should be an industrial department in connection with every mission school ?—Yes. The idea that labour is unbefitting for white people ought to be eradicated.

3144. You try to do so as far as you can ?—Yes, we do with our own children.

3145. Have you any other children elsewhere ?—A mission school at Port Elizabeth, mostly coloured children. There were 173 at Mr. Brady's last inspection. He says in his report :—" The teaching throughout is brisk, the discipline and behaviour of the pupils good, and the work, as a rule, as good as can be expected. The class rooms are brightened with pictures, and simple object lessons form part of the course, but only in the upper classes."

3146. You make object lessons part of the teaching ?—Yes, we have object lessons in all our schools.

3147. Are the children forced to learn any particular creed ?—We have had a conscience clause : some have used it, and some not. It was in this department that Mr. Brady asked us to take railway children with a view to their learning some industrial work. That is partly why we are enlarging our buildings.

3148. Are you prepared to take the girls of railway employés ?—Yes ; girls only, if it can be under Government, but we should not like to begin it without.

3149. What would you be willing to take them for ?—Not less than £12 a year. We could take them for that if we were sure of getting it, and if we had forty children.

3150. You would feed and teach them for that ?—Yes ; but we should expect to get a grant for school materials.

3151. Would that be an additional £2 a year ?—Not so much as that ; but it would mean a considerable difference if we got materials at a reduced rate.

3152. Have you any knowledge of the children of railway employés ?—We have had three children of railway employés and they have been exceedingly nice English country people.

3153. Have they been satisfied ?—Yes. There is one pupil teacher at Port Elizabeth, doing very well.

3154. Did you teach her ?—Yes ; we had her in our mission school here.

3155. Are you training pupil teachers ?—Yes.

3156. Yours is a sort of normal school for girls ?—We have three ex-pupils holding mission schools, and seven are under training now.

3157. And you say that you would like to come under Government inspection ?—Yes. We should be exceedingly glad if an Industrial School Act, such as obtains in England, could be passed.

Sister Cecile.

Sept. 11b, 1891.

3158. Are you familiar with the working of those industrial schools?—Yes; we work our own schools on the same lines as the English rules.

3159. Do you think we ought to embody the English Act in some form?—I think it would work well.

3160. Have you had any sort of unpleasantness with regard to religious differences in consequence of what you have done, and the way you have carried on the school?—No. We have had several parents say they would rather their children did not have distinctly Church of England teaching, and they have not been in.

3161. Have you satisfied the parents by what you have done?—Yes. In St. Peter's school we have had several cases. That is a higher grade school. We have had none in the poorer schools.

3162. Then you have another school?—Yes; a school that corresponds to an English higher grade school. The pupils are prepared for the Teachers' Examination.

3163. How would that compare with the boys' school?—I imagine that it is on the same level as the boys' first-class public undenominational school.

3164. How many children are there in it?—There were 80 in school this morning. Our chief difficulty is that we cannot get a qualified Dutch teacher. We have tried for years to teach Dutch, and we should very much like to get a good teacher, as well as some authorised series of Dutch books. Many parents wish their girls to learn Dutch, and we have given them either that language or elementary Latin; if we could all combine to pay some Dutch teacher who would give instruction in all the Government aided schools, it would be a great help.

3165. *Rev. Coetzee.*] Do the pupils prefer taking Dutch?—Yes; we have tried to encourage them to do so, and we have taught them as far as we can, but it is a very difficult matter when there is really no qualified teacher.

3166. *President.*] Do you find that they take kindly to Dutch?—Yes, and they would do so much more if it was thoroughly taught.

3167. Does that school get any aid from Government?—No.

3168. Are there not similar schools in Graham's Town, such as the Wesleyan High School?—We are below the standard of the Wesleyan High School.

3169. What are the fees?—25s. a quarter. We have arranged the school in standards up to the sixth standard, and then we have an extra class for those going in for the Teachers' Examination.

3170. Then the children in that school are a little older than those in the mission school, and of rather a higher class?—Some come on from the mission school. Some of our children have passed on to the Wesleyan High School and some to the Diocesan Girls' School.

3171. Do you think the graded system is a proper one?—Yes; it makes method more easy.

3172. You said that you would like to be under Government inspection; do you think it would be a good thing to have a public local body in the nature of a School Board?—I am not qualified to say, but I think we should be the better for a little more unexpected examination. The moral condition of the schools would be better. We all go on the system of cramming for the annual examination, more or less.

3173. Are there any coloured children in your school?—There are some who are slightly coloured.

3174. Have you any rule with regard to admission?—No, not unless we know them to be extremely undesirable children who would contaminate the others; then we refuse them. One family has been round all the schools here, I think.

3175. Is the matter ever put to the children whether they would like a pupil admitted?—Yes, we have occasionally done that in the higher grade school; but there has never been any ill-feeling. At the beginning of this present quarter a child with some colour came to be admitted. The girls expressed a strong opinion that there would be no ill-feeling, and she came in and has done well. She is a bright, intelligent child.

3176. Could you suggest any means of dealing with this question of colour?—I think it is a matter of discipline.

3177. With regard to natives, do you think such children ought to have industrial training?—The trouble here is that white people set themselves against manual labour so very much. They complain about the coloured people being idle, but if they worked more themselves, the coloured people would work more.

3178. In the Good Shepherd school you would have an industrial department?—Yes, if possible.

3179. Would you have an industrial department for all native children?—I do not know enough about the natives to be able to say. I have never worked with them, but I imagine that they need it quite as much as if not more than Europeans. With regard to what I stated just now as to the terms on which the girls of railway employés

Sister Cecile
Sept. 4th, 1891.

would bo taken at St. Peter's Home, I think I might say that board, lodging and tuition would be given for 25s. a quarter, to be paid by the parents in advance, the Government contributing a corresponding amount for each child, provided also that a free railway pass is granted to the principal of the school. Clothing, of course, would have to be provided by the parents.

Rev. Canon Mullins examined.

Rev.
Canon Mullins.

Sept. 4th, 1891.

3180. *President.*] I believe you are at the head of the Kafir institution here?—Yes.

3181. Does it work well?—Very well indeed. We have apprentices who work us such all day long, and all the boys in the institution work for two hours every afternoon at some industrial work or other.

3182. Is that a condition of their admission?—Yes.

3183. Do they have spade industry, and such like?—Yes. There are large gardens under cultivation, and they do spade work.

3184. In your opinion, is it a good thing for natives to have such industrial work?—Yes; the very best thing. It is work that I superintend myself always every afternoon. I hardly ever miss it.

3185. Would it be a good thing if that sort of industrial training for blacks was extended if possible to mission schools?—Yes, certainly.

3186. I presume it would have to be conducted in an inexpensive manner to be at all a success, would it not?—Yes. I can see a great many difficulties in the way.

3187. Suppose mission schools got a small grant from Government on condition that they imported this kind of work, how would you set about carrying it on?—The only thing one can imagine you would be able to carry out would be garden work, and of course that immediately involves the expense of land. It is no use to have industrial work for an hour or two hours a day, or whatever the time is, unless it is really made work. It is no good to send half a dozen boys together to work on a piece of ground. They require supervision, and they must be made to labour according to their age, capacity, and bodily strength. Some boys come who are able to do book work, but they are not able to do hard manual labour, and I set them accordingly to what they can do.

3188. Then the industrial work would depend very much on the character of the place, and the opportunities afforded?—Yes. At the location here there are large native schools, and it would be very easy to buy some property and have it fenced in and made use of. One great drawback is that the boys are often unable to see the result of their labour. It frequently happens that good honest work is put into the ground, and for want of fencing, animals get in and destroy the crops, which is very disheartening.

3189. Could not the erection of fencing form a part of their work?—No. That is just the sort of work they cannot do properly. They would put up a fence, and the cattle would knock it down the next day. It must be done by a competent hand.

3190. I believe you have had an agricultural school here?—Yes.

3191. It has been suggested that if you had an agricultural school for boys, you might use them as managers in some sort of way in connection with an industrial department, working the coloured boys; could that be done?—It would never answer. Everybody who has had anything to do with natives knows that they must have their orders from the "boss." It does not do to have messages sent.

3192. If an industrial school were established here, would it be likely to cause the black children, who do not like such work, to go away to other parts?—They are entirely dependent upon their parents. As long as their parents live in the location they would be with them.

3193. Would the parents like such training?—I do not think they would object to see their children properly taught. I have never had parents object to their boys being put to manual labour; it is quite an understood thing.

3194. *Dr. Berry.*] Where do these boys in your institution come from?—From Natal, the Transvaal, and Bechuanaland.

3195. How are they paid for?—They pay £8 a year, and there is a Government capitation grant. We supply the rest.

3196. Do the boys all pay something?—Yes. Some have been paid for by European friends; they are orphans—but there are only two or three.

3197. How long has your school been at work?—Since 1860.

3198. Have you any record of the after history of the boys who have left school?—Yes.

3199. Can you tell us how far their industrial training has been of any use to them?—It is difficult to follow them, as they drift away, and you lose sight of them. I was, however, able to trace the majority of the boys. Of course, there were a good

F

Rev.
Canon Mullins.

Sept. 4th, 1891.
many failures; but a large number were still earning their livelihood honestly. The majority of the lads are trained as teachers, and they go out and begin life at that. The payment we are able to give them as schoolmasters in small native schools is very low, so they often take service at a higher wage.

3200. Have you anything to show how far their industrial training has been of use to them in after life?—I know three carpenters in Queen's Town, but the difficulty is that European tradesmen are averse to working with them. I know a builder here who hired a good native half-caste, and the second day the man went into the shop to his work, he found all his planes glued fast to the bench. The white men did it, as they said they would not work with him. The best way is to let them work by themselves. I have a man in the location, and he has plenty to do; he is always provided with work of one kind or another.

3201. *President.*] Do they go about among the farmers and work?—I do not know. They may. It is very hard to keep up a correspondence with a number of boys; they drift away.

3202. Some become teachers and missionaries, do they not?—Yes; there was one man who called to see me yesterday, whom I had not seen for ten years.

3202A. *Dr. Berry.*] Are any of the boys educated to become practical gardeners?—Yes; every boy in the institution who is able has two hours work a day. I tell everyone I hope whenever they leave the institution they will be able to say they can dig, but they are ashamed to beg. Every boy is taught really to work.

3203. Have employers of labour made application to you for the services of these boys?—Yes; but naturally having had rather a better education than they get in the mission schools, they looked for something above manual work. They can do it, and they have always got that to fall back upon. I have nine going in for the Teachers' Examination this month. We educate them up to the fifth standard; we are required by the Government to do that. I have often had people apply to me for boys who have not been able to pass their examination, and they have always been satisfactory, good industrious fellows. Only this morning I had a gentleman asking if I could not recommend a boy. He said he had a boy from me for five years before, and he was excellent.

3204. Some boys might be fit for literary training and others for industrial training?—Yes, it is only a mere handful who are able to pass the examinations. They have to do it all in English; they think in Kafir or Sesuto and then translate it into English in all their work, and they are handicapped in that way.

3205. *Rev. Coetzee.*] What capitation grant do you get from Government?—£12 for boarders and £15 for apprentices.

Rev. Father Simeon examined.

Rev.
Father Simeon.

Sept. 4th, 1891.
3206. *President.*] You reside in Graham's Town, and your clerical duties take you a good deal along the line of railway, I believe?—Yes.

3207. Do you come a good deal in contact with railway employés?—Yes. For the last three years I have been going over the whole distance between De Aar and Alicedale.

3208. Visiting each house?—Yes. Not each house in the camps, but the houses of the gangers and sub-gangers.

3209. Have they a large number of children?—They vary very much. There are some families with seven or eight children, while others have none.

3210. Are they anxious about the education of their children?—Yes, one and all. They talk about it each time I visit them.

3211. How has that want been supplied hitherto?—Those living in cottages within reach of any station schools have made use of the trains as far as they could. There have been attempts in two or three centres to start station schools in accordance with the scheme of last year.

3212. Have they been successful?—No, I should say not. I know one that has been successful, but that is because there are a good many farm children who live near and support it, but in other cases they have not been a success.

3213. Is that for want of numbers?—Yes, and also for want of funds. The funds to make up the subsidy required by the Education Department are not sufficient. There is a school at Tafelberg. The Railway Department carried out its promise and put up a building. It has been up for eight months.

3214. How were the children to get there?—By train.

3215. Do you think that is a wise thing?—No. I do not see how the thing is to work unless much larger grants are made.

3216. Is not travelling daily along the line objectionable for these children?—Yes, the parents object very much to it, even where they can send their children.

Rev.
Father Simeon.

Sept. 4th, 1891.

3217. What is the best means to adopt, do you think ?—I think the best thing to do is to have a good central boarding school or schools.

3218. How many children would you collect ?—My experience actually extends between De Aar and Alicedale, but if you take the Graaff-Reinet line, I should imagine, you could collect from 80 to 100 children of both sexes, say 50 of each. I think I am well within the mark. I can give you the figures. Between De Aar and Alicedale there are 44 boys between the ages of 7 to 14 inclusive, and within the same district there are 36 girls, that is entirely exclusive of the children within reach of any of the existing schools, which are at De Aar, Naauwpoort, Mortimer, Cookhouse, and Alicedale. It is also exclusive of Cradock, where there ought to be a school, and there is not.

3219. Why do not the 44 boys use these schools ?—Because there is no boarding arrangement, and the trains do not suit.

3220. Can you give the number of children between Alicedale and Port Elizabeth or between Port Elizabeth and Graaff-Reinet ?—No. I have not ascertained that.

3221. What would be the best way of providing for these children ?—I have come distinctly to the conclusion that it would be best if possible to have a central school at Graham's Town for girls. I understand that at St. Peter's Home they are willing to take them. We made an attempt about eighteen months or two years ago. I had a long talk with the Mother Superior, but some difficulty arose.

3222. Did it arise on the part of the Education Department ?—No. It fell through : the thing could not be done on a large scale, and sufficient confidence was not inspired.

3223. I see that Mr. Howell, the traffic manager, reckons £24 a year for board and tuition, but the Mother Superior at Graham's Town says she could do it for £12 ? —So I understand. That is what they told me at the time, that they could just barely do it for that ; that is to say they would not actually be losers. Of course there would have to be a sufficient number.

3224. Do you see how they could be better or more cheaply provided for than at St. Peter's Home ?—No ; I do not think so.

3225. Would it be an advantage to girls to go there ?—Yes, I think so distinctly. My opinion is that it is a good thing to take them away from the associations and surroundings along the line of railway.

3226. From what you know of the parents themselves, would such a school be acceptable to them for their daughters ?—Yes, I think it would distinctly.

3227. Do you think it better to keep the boys separate from the girls ?—Yes ; I think so.

3225. What provision would you make for the boys ?—I think a good boarding establishment in Graham's Town would be the best thing. Of course the boys would cost a good deal more than the girls, because you have not the voluntary association in their case, who would be willing to give the education practically for nothing. For the boys you must have a thoroughly good master, and I should suggest that the best thing would be, as there is nothing of the kind in existence, for the Government to make a definite grant, say £500 a year, on the understanding that there were 50 boys in the establishment, and £300 a year, on the understanding that there was a minimum of say 25. My reason for suggesting that is this : you cannot help seeing that the starting of anything of the kind is the really crucial time of difficulty ; when once you have got the school going, the difficulty is not so great. The chief thing is to get the children. Railway people are very slow indeed to have their confidence gained, and it would take a period of about two years for the thing to grow and develop itself. In this case the parents would have to pay £10 to £12 for each boy

3226. Would it require £20 a year for a boy ?—Yes; taking everything all round.

3227. It has been suggested that there are buildings at Alicedale which might be utilised for the purpose; do you know anything about them ?—I know the buildings— they belong to the Railway Department ; but I do not think they would do for a school ; they are wooden buildings, but I do not think they are large enough for the purpose at all, and moreover I consider that Alicedale itself is a very undesirable place. It is exceedingly hot in the summer—one of the hottest places I know of in the whole of the Eastern districts. The Bushman's River runs round the camp, and there are pools of stagnant water. I should be very much afraid of epidemics breaking out among the children. I think Alicedale is not suitable.

3228. You think the parents would prefer Graham's Town to Alicedale ?—I have no doubt they would.

3229. What do you think ought to be the proportion of the grant from Government for boys and girls ?—From the conversation I have had with the Mother Superior of St. Peter's Home, I think a grant of £6 each would suffice for the girls, the parents

Rev.
Father Simeon.

Sept. 4th, 1891.

finding a similar amount. I have made careful enquiries during the last fortnight from every parent and from the inspectors on the railway, and they all of them have told me the same thing; that they considered if they got a good education for their children, as well as boarding, and they had to pay say £1 a month for one child and 15s. a month for the others, it would be a very liberal arrangement. I was very careful how I put the matter to them so as to elicit what they really felt.

3230. What would you propose in the case of boys?—In the case of boys, the wisest thing would not be to ask for a capitation grant for the reasons I have explained, but to get a grant for the school, and then when the thing was thoroughly established, a capitation grant might be obtained.

3231. But suppose the Government spent £300 or £500 in starting the school, and no boys came?—I do not anticipate that. If assistance were given to a boys' school in the way of capitation fees, the difficulty would be to find a master who would undertake all the risk. It is better to put it on a good basis at the beginning.

3232. Do you know of any volunteers in this place who would undertake such a work?—My impression is very strong that there would be volunteers if the Government made such a grant as I have suggested.

3233. *Dean Holmes.*] We have had it stated in evidence that the railway employés were not prepared to pay more than 1s. 6d. a week, do you think such is the case?— All I can say is that all those who have spoken to me on the subject, after carefully going into it, have said they could pay £1 a month. 5s. a day is the lowest wage a ganger gets, and some get 8s. 6d. a day. Some spoke of 25s. and 30s. a month.

3234. Could not you make provision for those who wished to avail themselves of some other opportunity for education, such as farm schools?—To a certain extent. Here and there there is a farm perhaps near the station or centre. There is such a school working at Sherborne, and the Middelton school is more a farm than a station school. Where you can find a farm near enough for the purpose it would work.

3235. Would it facilitate the starting of farm schools if the Government gave a capitation grant on a liberal scale for the children of gangers attending?—At certain points it might, but it would not meet all the needs.

3236. *President.*] You think it is better for educational purposes to have it more concentrated?—Yes.

3237. And the men would prefer it themselves?—Yes.

3238. *Dr. Berry.*] Would there be any objection to starting a school, say at Cradock?—No; I think not. My feeling is that if Graham's Town was not considered suitable, the next best place would probably be Cradock, but one objection to Cradock is the very fact of its being a large and increasing railway centre, and I think it is better to remove children from these surroundings, and impart a fresh discipline which would make an impression on their lives. On the other hand, it is fair to say this, that if the school were at Cradock, you could work in as day scholars the children living in the camp, as there are locomotive, maintenance, and traffic employés. No doubt that would decrease the cost of the establishment by some £70 or £80 a year.

3239. *Dean Holmes.*] Might it not be better to have a boarding establishment at Graham's Town, and ordinary schools at Cradock, Alicedale, and De Aar?—Yes; that is my opinion.

3240. *Dr. Berry.*] Up to what standard would you propose to bring these boys and girls; what class of school would you set up?—I would not advocate more intellectually than simple reading, writing, and arithmetic, but I would have technical teaching, garden work, and various trades.

3241. Would you propose to work that in with the school?—Yes: it seems to me that that is really what is most wanted and would help most in after life.

3242. Up to what age would you maintain the children at school?—Fourteen would probably be found to be the limit. Parents look to the children going to work after that and bringing in something.

3243. And at what age should they begin?—Seven is the youngest age at which they would let them go away from home.

3244. Would you propose to make it compulsory on all railway children to attend some school?—If Government saw their way to making it so, I think it would be desirable, but one cannot help seeing that directly you touch on compulsory education for one class in the colony, Government would be dealing with a very difficult question. Theoretically it is desirable no doubt.

3245. Suppose it were made compulsory for localities, could not the people along the line be made localities for this purpose?—Yes; that might be so. The only point to be considered is whether any of the parents would object so strongly as to give up their situation, and thus the Government might lose valuable servants through it.

3246. If it was known beforehand that it was compulsory, the men would not join the service unless they were prepared to accept the condition?—That is true.

Rev.
Father Simeon.

Sept. 4th, 1891.

On the other hand, I suppose that any ganger or second man can leave at any time by giving the usual notice, whatever may be his pledges as long as he remains in the service.

3247. It strikes one that unless there were some means of compelling railway children to attend school under such a system, it might be a risky matter to set it up?—Possibly the Railway Department or the Government might see their way to stopping so much from each man's pay for educational purposes in the same way as stoppages are made for rent and sick fund.

3248. *Mr. Theron.*] Has there been any intention to start a railway school at Cradock station?—There was such intention. About two years ago, the men, through a ganger who is residing there, sent me a petition with about 30 signatures, stating that there were some 53 children who would be sent to school if one were started, and I was asked to see what could be done. I accordingly secured the promise of the services of a lady, but for some reason or other, possibly because this ganger was not thought the right person to take the initiative, the thing came to nothing, and nothing has been done since. I have spoken to the station-master, Mr. Hyslop, who is anxious about it, several times, and he has told me the same thing, that the difficulty was to get a sufficient number of persons to become guarantors and start an undenominational school.

3249. Do these children you refer to receive any instruction at present?—A certain number of them go to school in Cradock. There are three schools there, but a great many receive no instruction at all because the charges are too high, and also because the parents do not like to send their children across the bridge; they consider there is danger from the traffic.

3250. Did you make any application to the Education Department for a grant for the proposed school at Cradock, or was it not far enough advanced for that?—There was no need to make actual application. The school was to be worked under the circular issued by the Railway Department and the Education Department together in May, 1890. It was under that circular that the effort was to be made, and if the school was started, we could have got the premises from the Railway Department, and a grant of books and money from the Education Department.

3251. But I understand there is a number of these railway children at Cradock, at present not in school?—Yes; I understand a considerable number.

3252. *Dr. Berry.*] I suppose your proposals have reference entirely to the children of European parents, have they not?—Yes.

3253. Is there any necessity to make provision for native children along the line?—Yes; I think so certainly, but I know very little about the natives, not understanding the language, so I have been obliged to pass them over in my work. Every ganger has several men under him; these reside along the line, and I notice a good many children about.

3254. *Mr. Theron.*] I suppose these native labourers you speak of shift about; they are not engaged under any contract, are they?—Still there is a large and increasing number who devote themselves to this kind of work altogether.

3255. Would you approve of both white and black children being collected in one school?—No. They would have to be dealt with separately altogether.

3256. Are there any other centres similarly situated to Cradock, where there are children who do not receive instruction at present, and ought to receive it?—There are no large centres on the Midland Line that I know of. There is a large opening for work of every kind among the natives along the line.

3257. *President.*] Would Alicedale or Cradock be good places for them?—Yes; if you could secure that the children would be paid for regularly.

3258. *Mr. Theron.*] Under present arrangements, you think there is not sufficient provision to meet the requirements of railway people along the line, as far as education is concerned?—That is so, undoubtedly.

3259. *President.*] Are those parents who accept your ministration along the line generally Church of England people?—Out of the 44 boys I have referred to, there are 23 Church of England, 2 Wesleyans, 2 Dutch Reformed Church, 1 Roman Catholic, 2 Lutheran, and 4 Scotch Presbyterian, and what the remainder are I have not noted down. I am not certain about them.

3260. *Dr. Berry.*] Referring to the 44 boys, would you consider this number a fair average, or exceptionally small or large?—I consider that of that number 29 would almost certainly be sent to school; the rest are doubtful.

3261. As far as the average number of children in families is concerned, is that fairly representative from year to year?—I think so. I have not noted down those children below seven years old. There is a large number of little children below that age.

Rev.
Father Simeon.

Sept. 4th, 1891.

3262. *Mr. Theron.*] Are these children all stationed at cottages along the line?—Yes; taking the whole distance between Aliecdale and De Aar and Colesberg: the cottages are placed every five or six miles along the line. There is a great difficulty with regard to the trains. Trains which run suitably for the school at Mortimer, for instance, would not suit for the school at Tafelberg or Naauwpoort. As a case in point, I might state that two years ago the school at Naauwpoort was very flourishing; there were some 45 or 50 children, because the trains in both directions happened to fit in, but the last working time-table issued has completely upset all that, and I am told that the number of children has fallen to 21 or 22. There used to be children from Hanover Road and the cottages between.

3263. *President.*] But even if the trains ran to suit, I take it you think it would be better for the children to be at boarding-school?—I think so, undoubtedly, and I believe the parents feel it. Of course, the schools that exist are better than nothing; but many parents speak of them as very unsatisfactory, and not what they could wish for their children.

Mr. F. M. de Vries van Hijst examined.

Mr.
F. M. de Vries
van Hijst.

Sept. 4th, 1891.

3264. *President.*] I believe you are Dutch Master at St. Andrew's College, Graham's Town?—Yes; and I also teach French and German.

3265. Are you a Hollander by birth?—Yes.

3266. Have you had experience in teaching before you came here?—Yes; for about 9 years in England.

3267. Is there a large number of boys at St. Andrew's College under your teaching in the Dutch language?—Altogether about 65 or 66. About 7 or 8 learn French, and a couple German. I do not teach them all myself, the classes are too large. I teach altogether about 83 out of 129 boys.

3268. Do they take Dutch voluntarily?—Yes.

3269. Is there a growing desire to learn Dutch?—The majority of the boys who come take up Dutch in preference.

3270. Do you teach what is called High Dutch?—Only High Dutch.

3271. How do you think this bi-lingual question ought to be treated?—At the college Dutch is taught like any ordinary modern language would be in an English school, through the medium of English, till the pupils get very advanced. Very few of our boys are Dutch. The classes are all conducted on the English school system: English text-books are used, and translations made from English into Dutch and from Dutch into English.

3272. Do you consider that the best way of teaching?—Yes, I think so.

3273. Is the result satisfactory?—Yes; as far as examination goes it is. It may not be so satisfactory for the sons of Dutch parents perhaps: they might like rather to have Dutch teaching altogether, but it is impracticable at our place.

3274. Would it be wise to have Dutch teaching everywhere in the Colony as far as you know?—I know very little about the Colony. I have not been west of the Midland railway. I have not been in the Dutch districts.

3275. With regard to the Elementary Examination, it is proposed that Dutch should be added as an optional subject and the marks counted: do you think that would be wise?—I would I think be very unfair. It may be all right for the Dutch part of the Colony, but it would be extremely unfair for the English part. It would give some the advantage of five papers, while others only had four.

3276. How would you recommend the matter should be treated if there is a desire to have Dutch encouraged?—I would suggest that there should be a double set of examinations, one of which should be in Dutch, the Dutch paper taking the place of the English paper, keeping the present subjects as they are, and giving as an optional fifth subject Dutch, French, German, Latin or science. Give every candidate a chance to take up the fifth paper.

3277. Would you limit the candidates to the subjects they took up?—It would hardly be fair to limit them in some schools. I think a large range of subjects should be given.

3278. What range would you give?—I would give the choice of Dutch, French, German, Latin, and Elementary Science.

3279. As there are so many of your boys who go in for Dutch, if they had the option, would not they choose that?—The majority of them would not choose Dutch, and I should not be prepared to advise them to take it.

3280. Why not?—It is difficult for English-speaking boys to get a proper hold of Dutch. It is a difficult language. If I had to prepare a boy for examination, I would sooner send him in for French than for Dutch, as it is much easier to work up the French language.

Mr.
F. M. de Vries
van Heijst.

Sept. 4th, 1891.

3281. Would science or Latin be chosen?—Latin in our place, because it leads to the School Higher and Matriculation. The boys go in for the Elementary examination because they cannot go in for the School Higher without passing it; that is really the only reason.

3282. So that they are already handicapped?—Yes.

3283. And you would handicap them further if you imported another subject, would you not?—Certainly.

3284. *Rev. Coetzee.*] Are there many Dutch boys attending your school?—There are a few boys from the Free State, and three or four from the Cradock district.

3285. How many take Dutch?—About 80.

3286. The great majority are English boys are they not?—Yes.

3287. Is there any need for teaching Dutch in a place like Graham's Town?—In some of the examinations it is compulsory, and then there is a desire for it, seeing that it is a language which is very much made use of in the country. The desire is to learn Dutch rather than French or German.

3288. You said that Dutch is a difficult language to master, but candidates for the Civil Service Examination seem to master it very easily, do they not?—I do not think very easily. I have had three years' experience of teaching it, this is my fourth year, and I have found that they do not take to it so easily.

3289. Have the candidates made any complaints about it as far as you know?—Not to my knowledge. I know from the amount of work it takes me to teach the Civil Service class.

3290. From your experience you infer that there is a growing desire to know the Dutch language?—Yes, I should say so. I can only speak as to Graham's Town. I have hardly been out of this place.

3291. *Dr. Berry.*] Is it not fair to suppose that a number of the boys being educated in your school are looking forward to entering the Civil Service?—Only a small number.

3292. What is the stimulus they have for learning Dutch?—In the natural school course they are expected to take up a modern language, and in this country Dutch is more useful than French or German. For Matriculation they must take a modern language, and they naturally find that Dutch is a much more sensible subject to take up here.

3293. Do not you think that the plan you propose for getting over the difficulty would rather destroy the elementary character of what is called the Elementary Examination? I myself from what I know, should prefer that the Elementary Examination was left as it is.

3294. Suppose it is found necessary to do something to meet this bi-lingual difficulty, what would you say to having a separate paper in Dutch altogether, and letting the marks count on a separate list?—It would give an advantage to those who passed. Suppose anyone wished to employ a lad, he would rather take someone who was proficient in five subjects as against four.

3295. Suppose you had a separate list altogether and endorsed on the certificate that such a candidate had passed in Dutch, the list being published by itself? I do not think that would be fair to those who are not in a position to take up Dutch. Others may have a knowledge of Latin, French, or German that they are not examined in, and therefore the examination is not a fair test of the acquirements of the boy.

3296. *Rev. Moorrees.*] I understood you to say that giving an alternative subject with Dutch in the Elementary Examination would discourage the study of Dutch in Graham's Town: is that so?—If Dutch is added to the Elementary Examination the way to meet it would be to give the choice of another subject as well.

3297. You are probably aware that in Holland and almost all continental countries children begin the study of foreign language at a very early age?—Yes.

3298. So that it is not always considered as destructive of the elementary character of education to begin a foreign language at an early age?—No; but such Examinations as the Elementary in this country and the university local examinations in England are not known in Holland, or they were not when I left there.

3299. Does it clash with the elementary character of education?—No, not in the least. I myself began to learn French when I was ten years of age.

3300. Why do you think it would destroy the elementary character of our Elementary Examination if Dutch was introduced?—English children find any modern language very difficult to master, so as to be able to be examined in it.

3301. It was said that if Dutch were given in a separate paper it would not be a fair test for the other candidates who cannot take Dutch, but who know other subjects, but is not that the case now with a Dutch child. He knows Dutch, but has no chance of displaying his knowledge in the Elementary Examination?—If Dutch children go to school on English lines it is not so unfair. It may be to a certain extent, but when

Mr.
F. M. de Vries
van Hijst.
——
Sept. 4th, 1891.

speaking to a Dutch schoolmaster from up country, he told me that he found it easier to teach young Dutch children English, than to teach them in Dutch.

3302. As a teacher, do you think that it is a scientific plan to teach a child through the medium of a foreign language ?—I think not.

3303. The child is placed at a disadvantage, is it not ?—Yes, certainly.

3304. *Mr. Theron.*] Am I to take it that you do not mind about placing a child at a disadvantage so long as you benefit the English boy ?—I am speaking from a business point of view.

3305. You compel a boy to know Dutch when he wants to pass the Civil Service examination, but you compel a Dutch child to start in a foreign language and handicap him from the beginning ?—That can be met by another suggestion. Let there be two complete examinations each of about equal difficulty, with two separate lists.

3306. *Rev. Moorrees.*] Would that be practicable do you think in the present circumstances of the Colony ?—I think so.

3307. Would you get teachers qualified to teach all the subjects in Dutch ?—It would be the business of the Education Department to get them. At the same time, I do not believe you would get many candidates to take up the Dutch Examination, not even Dutch boys.

3308. But suppose you cannot get teachers competent to teach them ? -If you cannot, then you cannot examine the candidates.

3309. *Mr. Theron.*] In the commercial world, a knowledge of Dutch is desirable, is it not ?—Yes, but it is not required. You can do all your business, and travel from one end of the world to the other without knowing a word of Dutch.

3310. You said I believe, that you know very little about the Dutch districts of the Colony ?—Yes.

3311. In the Elementary Examination you would allow an English boy to have four subjects in his own mother tongue, and then if he chooses Dutch say as an optional fifth subject, you would give him extra marks for that ?—Yes, of course.

3312. And if you compel a Dutch child to pass in the four required subjects in English, and he does a Dutch paper too, would you give him also extra marks for that ? —Certainly.

3313. *Rev Coetzee.*] Why do you consider it desirable to know Dutch ?—Because there is a great deal of Dutch spoken in this country. I myself believe that it will not be so for ever.

3314. Are any of your pupils studying German or French ?—In the whole school about 25 learn French. I have about 10 pupils.

3315. *President.*] Do any of the pupils learn German ?—None at present. Occasionally there are one or two who learn it.

3316. And Latin ?—The whole school learns Latin, except a few in the upper division.

3317. *Dr. Berry.*] I understand your recommendation to amount to this, you would add several subjects to the Elementary examination, any one of which would be compulsory on the candidate ?—Any one of which he might take optionally.

3318. Those who elect to take a fifth subject would stand at a very considerable advantage over those who only take four ?—Yes.

3319. Would not that destroy the elementary character of the examination, considering the circumstances of this country. This examination is supposed to be for the encouragement of merely elementary attainments, and does it not cease to be so the moment you add a linguistic subject like Latin, French, or German ?—The whole examination ceases to be an examination of an elementary nature by making it compulsory for those who wish to go higher.

3320. Would it not be better to abolish the elementary examination altogether ; that is to say, not make it incumbent on a boy who goes in for the higher examination to pass the elementary ?—Yes.

3321. *Rev. Moorrees.*] Do you think that a language of the country ought to be put on the same level as a foreign language, as regards marks ?—I can only speak from my own point of view. For the boys who come to the college, Dutch is a foreign language, with very few exceptions.

3322. In a general way, should a child score the same number of marks for a foreign language as he should for his own mother tongue, the language of the country. Is Dutch one of the languages of the country, in your opinion ?—It depends upon the kind of Dutch. The Dutch you find in modern Dutch books, or Elffers' Grammar, I believe, is not the language of the country.

3323. Is the difference between the Dutch spoken here and the High Dutch greater than the difference between some of the dialects spoken in Holland and High Dutch there ?—No ; very much the same.

3324. You would not say because in a province of Holland they speak a dialect, that Dutch was not the language of the country, would you?—No.

Mr. F. M. de Vries van Hijst.

Mr. W. C. Meredith examined.

Sept. 4th, 1891. Mr. W. C. Meredith.

3325. *President.*] I believe you are principal of the undenominational school here?—Yes.

Sept. 4th, 1891.

3326. And you are a graduate of the London University?—Yes.

3327. How long have you been head of the school?—I have been for two years at Graham's Town. Before then I was three years in Cape Town, and before then I was five years teaching in England.

3328. What is the percentage of attendance in your school?—About ninety-five per cent. on the average.

3329. And in the branch school?—I cannot say. In the preparatory school it is quite as good as in the upper school.

3330. How do you think the irregularity of attendance in towns can best be dealt with?—I should say by an attendance Act, much in the same manner as in England.

3331. Would that operate on coloured children as well in towns?—I think so.

3332. Do you think the effect would be good?—I think so decidedly.

3333. What schools would you force children into who are not receiving any instruction at all, those who cannot pay?—They should be put into the lowest State aided school there is in the town.

3334. Which is that?—There are State aided mission schools here.

3335. Could they be run into your school?—Some of them might go into the branch school, I daresay.

3336. At present you are not bound to take more than a certain number, are you?—We can take any number we can find room for. We could find room in the branch school for from 80 to 100 children altogether; about thirty in addition to our present number.

3337. You are not bound to take them, are you?—No.

3338. Would you take them for nothing?—I suppose some provision for that would be made in the Act.

3339. You think that Government should make some pecuniary provision?—Yes. We are only bound to take one free scholar for every twenty or thirty who pay.

3340. How would you propose to give Boards of Management perpetual succession?—In the case of our school the property was acquired by the school committee at public auction in the way of direct purchase, but with regard to the manner in which, or the means by which payment was made, I am quite ignorant, the event having taken place long before the period of my connection with the school, and no opportunity having been given me for enquiring into the state of the finances at any time anterior to my appointment.

3341. How would you give perpetual succession in such a case?—There should be some means of incorporating the School Board or Committee of Management.

3342. If you did that, would not it become a sort of close body, giving it this property which has been acquired, and shutting out a mass of children from the use of the school?—I do not see that incorporation would necessarily imply that it would be a close body.

3343. *Dean Holmes.*] Would it not destroy its character as a public school?—I think not. I see no reason why it should.

3344. *Dr. Berry.*] Are you in favour of keeping the public undenominational school here under the control of a public representative body?—Yes.

3345. You would not be in favour of any Act of Incorporation which would destroy the character of the public control now in force?—Certainly not.

3346. *President.*] What body would you suggest should have control of the property?—I think Divisional Councils should be responsible generally throughout the division for the schools. There might be either a sub-committee of the Divisional Council or there might be a body chosen at a separate election.

3347. *Dean Holmes.*] Practically you would propose to introduce the board school system?—Yes, in a modified form.

3348. *President.*] Why do you suggest the Divisional Council in preference to the Municipality?—Such schools as ours are only situated at the seat of a Civil Commissioner, and thus they belong in a certain manner to the division as well as to the municipality.

3349. You want to give them a larger range?—Yes.

3350. Are you in favour of a Board elected by the ratepayers, in whom the property should be vested?—Yes.

3351. *Dr. Berry.*] Suppose a compulsory Education Act is introduced, and additional school accommodation was required in Grahamstown, would you be in favour of placing the management of those schools and the control of any further grants, in

Mr.
W. C. Meredith.

Sept. 4th, 1891.

the hands of a representative body, or in the hands of voluntary bodies such as the church authorities?—I think they should be in the hands of a public representative body. I think there are schools at present established, such as mission schools, which may be made use of, but while they should be left under their present management, the managers should be responsible to this public representative body, which would be responsible to the Government for the state of all the schools.

3352. *Rev. Coetzee.*] And the managers should be responsible to the Board?—Yes.

3353. *Dr. Berry.*] Take the case of the Shaw Hall mission school in this town, attended by over 200 white children; do not you think it a misnomer to call that a mission school?—I do.

3354. Do not you think it would be better if such a school came under the control of a publicly elected representative body?—I should like to see it so, but I do not think the managers of such schools would give up their present control.

3355. If the necessity arises for developing our educational system, under whom is the management to come—public representative bodies or close corporations?—Ultimately under public representative bodies, but I should not be in favour of any violent change at once.

3356. You would be in favour of introducing a system which would pave the way to what you consider a better arrangement ultimately?—Yes, I do not think that fourth-class schools should be introduced where there is sufficient accommodation in the way of mission schools already. It would be unfair to the vested rights of the mission schools I consider.

3357. Many of these mission schools are no longer such; would it not be better in large towns at once to incorporate them in the public undenominational school system?—If the managers of the schools and those who hold the property consent.

3358. Has no one else a voice in the matter?—The managers only have a right to the disposal of their school buildings.

3359. It is the educational arrangements I am speaking of, and the grants?—The public have a voice to a certain extent certainly, but I think the rights of the congregations to whom these schools belong and which they have acquired, should be respected.

3360. If the schools are taken advantage of very largely by children who do not belong to the denomination which rules them, how does your argument stand affected?—If mission schools wish to obtain any State aid, they should be responsible to a central Board for the state of their schools, but the management of the finances, the engagement of the teachers, and minor questions might be left in their own hands.

3361. Would not that Board conflict with the operations of the public representative Board?—It would be the same Board. The managers of the mission schools should be responsible to the Central School Board to which all the other schools are responsible.

3362. Then they would practically come in under the public representative system?—Yes, they would if they obtained any State aid at all.

3363. *Rev. Moorrees.*] Many of the religious bodies have made large sacrifices to establish these mission schools, and on that account it would be unfair, would it not, to take away at once the management out of their hands?—I think so.

3364. As regards the question of perpetuating the present school committees, do not you think that their fluctuating character makes the position of the teachers very insecure?—I am hardly qualified to say. I have not experienced anything of the kind myself, though I can easily conceive such a case.

3365. After three years the body ceases to exist, and then the contract between it and the teacher is at an end, is it not?—There is one fact which tends to maintain the continuity, and that is that the new committee is chosen from the former list of guarantors, not from the general public meeting. The first list is compiled at a general public meeting, but afterwards, the Committee of Management is chosen at a meeting of guarantors, so that the guarantors are very likely to remain the same body they were three years before.

3366. *Dean Holmes.*] The new managers are under no liability to keep on the old teachers, are they?—No, not at all.

3367. *Dr. Berry.*] As a matter of fact, the Board of Managers, when their time is about to expire, often give notice to the teachers that their services are no longer required, do they not?—I was not aware of that.

3368. *President.*] How would you provide for the tenure of public school property; in whom would you vest it?—I had thought of a scheme which is, to some extent, identical with the recommendation of the Commission which sat in 1879:—First, that the Divisional Council should be responsible for all the schools in its division. There might be a sub-committee of the Divisional Council, if desirable, and then in towns and villages there should be a special Board elected by the ratepayers or householders, responsible to the Divisional Council. They might manage their own finances, and report their state periodically to the Divisional Council, which should be also directly responsible for all such schools in the division as are not held by the smaller Boards. Then I think that funds should be provided by a local rate on the Municipalities for each school within the Municipality, and an equal amount should be contributed by Government, and whatever deficit there is, should be made up by the Divisional Council. I do not think there would be a large deficit.

3369. *Mr. Theron.*] For the finances required in the district would you levy a rate?—If they do not come under any Municipality they should be under the Divisional Council.

3370. You would not tax a Municipality for schools outside that Municipality, would you?—No.

3371. That you would leave to the Divisional Council?—Yes.

3372. *Rev. Coetzee.*] With regard to the constitution of Divisional Councils, are you acquainted with it?—Yes; I do not know whether in all cases it is fit to provide an Educational Board, but I think that might be held in check by the Government Inspector. Divisional Councils would be responsible to the Government Inspector for the state of the schools in the division. If he finds that the school is not satisfactory, he has to tell the Divisional Council what he wishes done, and if it is still found to be unsatisfactory, the Government should bring pressure to bear on the Divisional Council.

3373. *Dean Holmes.*] Would it not be better to elect men conversant with educational matters. The members of the Divisional Council might know only about matters connected with roads?—I do not know how you could have such an election. It is probable they might elect the same men.

3374. *Dr. Berry.*] What you contend for in the main is the elective constitution of the School Board, is it not?—Yes.

3375. *President.*] And that this Board should be responsible to the Government for all the schools in the district, imposing on it the duty of filling up all gaps either by starting new schools itself, or recommending other bodies who will satisfy the Government?—Yes.

3376. And then the Government contributing a certain fixed sum all round as aid?—Yes.

3377. Should that aid be in proportion to the average number of children in attendance, or would you have any other method?—I should like to see a regular ratio of the income of the Municipality devoted to schools, that is to say, make education free, and let a fourth or a fifth of the total income be devoted to schools, to be met by an equal amount from the Government. If education were free, there would be but little objection to an additional tax by the Municipality.

3378. What do you think the Government ought to contribute to schools; what would be the cost of each child?—I think the Government should contribute about the same as it does now: about £3 16s. is the average total cost, and the Government gives rather less than half of that

3379. Suppose the Government said to the School Board that it was prepared to give that amount, the Board providing the school, and any deficiency come out of the rates; would that be a fair means of dealing with the matter?—No. In a large town there would be many children whose education would cost more than £3 16s. per annum, while in villages where the people are comparatively poor, there would be many children whose education would cost very much less than £3 16s. per annum.

3380. On what principle would Government give the aid?—I think a fourth or a fifth of the total municipal revenue should be devoted to schools, and then this should be met with an equal amount from the Government.

3381. Suppose the schools pay, then there would be no need to devote anything, would there?—I think you would find there would be a deficiency.

3382. *Rev. Coetzee.*] Are you aware that the income of some municipalities does not exceed £300 a year. I know many cases, and that would only give you £75?—There would be a very small school to provide for perhaps.

3383. *Dean Holmes.*] Do you know any country where one-fourth or one-fifth of the municipal income is devoted to school purposes?—Yes, France. The deficit is made up by the Government, which amounts to nearly one-half of the total cost.

3384. *Rev. Moorrees.*] Education is free in France, is it not?—Yes.

3385. *President.*] Would you advocate free education in this country?—Yes, certainly.

3386. *Dr. Berry.*] You are, I understand, in favour of free education by means of local rates?—Yes, by local rates and the Government making up the deficiency.

3387. *Dean Holmes.*] Is it really requisite, considering the condition of many people in this country?—Yes; it is an aim towards which we should work.

Mr.
W. C. Meredith.

Sept. 4th, 1891.

3388. *President.*] Is it not the primary duty of parents who can pay to contribute towards the education of their children?—They would contribute through the taxes and the local rates.

3389. *Dean Holmes.*] Would you apply free education to every condition of life in the colony?—Up to a certain standard. I do not mean higher education. I think, however, the fees for higher education might be very much lowered.

3390. Would you abolish all voluntary effort?—Voluntary effort could not be abolished. If anyone chooses to keep a private school, they would be responsible for it entirely. If the Inspectors did their duty and the Government properly saw that their commands were carried out, there would be very little chance for an inefficient public school.

3391. Would you like to assimilate our system to what it is on the continent, where, for the most part, everything is entirely under the Government?—I think I should.

3392. *President.*] How would you manage about the natives, would you have free education for them?—I am not qualified to speak on that question. I do not know whether they would submit to it. From what I have heard, I fancy they would not. I believe to a certain extent that compulsion would be better for them. The following, I may say, are the main outlines of a scheme I would propose for the educational administration of the colony. I would recommend:—

1. THE PROVISO that present vested interests should not be interfered with except by choice of the persons or societies in whom they are vested.

2. That the Divisional Councils, the chairmen of which represent the Government, be responsible to Government for the efficient provision for education in their divisions, with the exception of certain State provision to be mentioned afterwards.

3. That in each division there be at least *one* high school, to be placed at the seat of the Civil Commissioner, and others if deemed necessary; such high schools to be endowed at first by the State with large and suitable grants of land, and also with annual pecuniary grants, calculated on the basis of the population of the division, but with as little fluctuation as possible.

4. That the high schools thus established be on a perfectly undenominational basis, admitting religious, but not doctrinal, instruction, with the usual "conscience-clause."

5. That the high schools shall be under the financial control and general regulation of the Divisional Council or a Committee of Education thereof, the C.C. to be the chairman.

6. That in every municipality or village community there be established educational boards, to consist of, say, five members, two elected at a public meeting of ratepayers, two nominated by the Divisional Council, and one, the chairman, nominated by the C.C.

7. That such educational boards be responsible for the creation, maintenance and financial control, within their districts, of either or each of the following two classes of schools, as they may deem necessary:—

(a) Middle Schools,
(b) Primary Schools,

on a perfectly undenominational basis, of course making the best use possible of such schools as are already established.

8. That if it shall appear that there are already in existence, in such towns or villages, schools under denominational management which may be deemed, from every point of view, efficient to carry on the work of these lower-class schools, the educational boards abovementioned shall be empowered to assist such agencies rather than establish fresh schools under section 7.

9. That the high schools, middle schools, and primary schools, be of distinct grade in the superior limit of the education to be given in them, but that this shall not hinder every such school beginning its educational work at as low a standard as its managing council may deem advisable. This is supported by reasons, 1st of economy, 2nd of continuity in teaching.

10. That present Boards of Managers of first class public schools of the higher division shall have the option of becoming incorporated and forming institutions distinct from the present scheme, though they shall not be prevented thereby from supplying the place of the high schools of the divisions.

11. That such present Boards of Managers, as wish, shall have the option of entering and forming part of this scheme.

12. That since the main principle of "Free Education" is merely commutation of taxation, the endeavour should be made throughout every division to make all school education perfectly free in the manner contemplated in the following sections, the preference in such work to be given to the undenominational schools, but extended as soon as possible to every class of school.

13. That the support of schools under " Educational Boards " be partially met by the revenue of the municipality or village community ; an amount in fixed proportion to such revenue, say ¼ or ⅕, being regularly devoted to education and being adminis- tered by the Educational Board.

14. That the amount contributed towards education, as in section 13, be supplemented by an equal amount from the State, to be distributed through the Superintendent-General of Education.

15. That the high schools of the divisions, in addition to the State grant already (section 3) contemplated, derive support in the first instance from the municipalities in which they are situated, and secondly—in such a manner as to make up deficiencies—from the Divisional Councils.

16. That in case schools are needed in the division in places beyond the range of the " Educational Boards " of municipalities or village committees, the Divisional Council shall be directly responsible for the establishment and control of such schools, such schools, however, not to be of a grade at all higher than the primary schools.

17. That all accounts of the revenue and expenditure of " Educational Boards," from whatever source the revenue be derived, be audited annually by auditors appointed by the Divisional Council ; and that a sum not exceeding a certain fixed proportion of the Divisional Council's rates be then devoted from those rates to the meeting of deficiencies in the various school accounts.

18. That the completed statements, showing the amount derived from the Divisional Council by each school, be then forwarded to the Department of Public Education.

19. That all school property in the division should be, as contemplated above, the property, for school purposes, of the Divisional Council, account to be rendered annually to the Education Department of the manner in which it has been appropriated.

20. That all schools receiving aid as above be subject to regular inspection by the officers of the Education Department, and in educational matters be *solely and entirely* subject to the Educational Department ; and that the Government shall hold the Divisional Council responsible for carrying out in the division the wishes of the inspector.

3393. Do you think it would be wise to have more industrial education in our schools ?—I doubt whether in the present state of the colony it can be managed. I should be very glad to see it.

3394. Do you think that technical education can be improved ?—I do not think you have the material for it at present.

3395. Do you mean there is no money ?—There would be a difficulty in getting the necessary appliances for an extensive scheme of technical education.

3396. I believe you have an industrial department in your school ?—Yes. There is a small carpentry class.

3397. Is it held after the ordinary school hours ?—Yes.

3398. Are special fees charged for that ?—No. There are no fees at all.

3399. Do the boys take to it kindly ?—Yes, and the parents like it. The class is generally quite full. It is optional with the boys to learn, and sometimes a parent requests that if there is a vacancy, his boy may be sent to fill it.

3400. Is the time for this taken out of play hours ?—Yes.

3400A. Is there any Government grant made towards that class ?—Yes. £50 a year.

3401. *Dr. Berry.*] Does that go to the teacher of carpentry ?—His salary is £48 a year, and we have to find tools and materials.

3402. What does your school get altogether from Government ?—£700 a year.

3403. *President.*] Is that for every department ?—It includes the branch school, preparatory school, and the carpentry class.

3404. *Dean Holmes.*] Are you in favour of introducing the so-called fourth class public undenominational schools ?—If you keep up the present system of school committees, I should be in favour of introducing them, but under the proposed system, the municipality would be responsible for the efficiency of all its schools, and it would devote as much money to them as it could spare. I think the fourth class public undenominational school system would be very good.

3405. *President.*] I understand that you would elect a Board responsible to Government for all schools and allow existing schools to go on if they satisfy the Government and the local Board. When they do not give satisfaction, and where there are gaps, you would let the local Board bring into existence other schools, Government in every case contributing its aid according to the system you have suggested, but what that aid is to be, must be determined by the circumstances of each school ?—Yes.

Mr.
W. C. Meredith.:

Sept. 4th, 1891

3406. What additional facilities do you think can be provided to meet the wants of the children of the agricultural population?—I am not qualified to speak as to that.

3407. With regard to the further facilities for giving instruction in both the English and Dutch languages, and how far that object can be attained through the medium of the elementary and other examinations. Have you made any provision for Dutch in your school?—We have a special teacher for it. We had a special teacher for French, but at present we have not.

3408. How many of your boys take Dutch lessons?—About 50 out of 120.

3409. Is it optional?—Above a certain standard in the school every boy is compelled to take either French or Dutch, and they generally choose Dutch because they fancy it is likely to be more useful to them in after life. I think we have at present about five or six boys learning French and 50 Dutch.

3410. Do those 50 boys learn Dutch with a view to the higher examinations, or because they prefer it?—In the first place because they prefer it to French as a rule. I have had instances of boys when working for examination, dropping Dutch and taking French. They must take one modern language.

3411. *Dean Holmes.*] How many hours a week do you devote to instruction in Dutch?—Ten hours. It would be less if we had not a civil service class.

3412. *President.*] Why are the boys compelled to take one modern language? —It is part of our school curriculum.

3413. *Dean Holmes.*] You say they take Dutch because it is likely to be useful to them later on; in what way?—I do not know that it is very useful except for the civil service examination. Colloquial Dutch is not taught; none of the boys know it.

3414. *Mr. Theron.*] Do you know any school where colloquial Dutch is taught?— I do not.

3415. *President.*] How would you meet the language difficulty in the Elementary examination. Is it necessary to add a Dutch paper?—No, I think not. It would destroy the elementary character of the examination, unless pupils who have been aught in Dutch, and know it, choose to take a Dutch paper instead of an English paper.

3416. You mean examine them throughout in Dutch?—That would be the fairest way, to give every paper in Dutch, to hold two Elementary examinations, one in Dutch and one in English, and have the lists separate.

3417. Do you think it would be wise to have a fifth paper in Dutch, giving the candidates an opportunity of answering it, and adding the marks to the aggregate?— It would not be fair. There are many English boys who have not taken Dutch at all, whereas most Dutch boys speak English.

3418. Have you several Dutch speaking boys in your school?—I do not think we have one at present. Generally about one per cent.

3419. *Rev. Coetzee.*] Who is the Dutch teacher?—Mr. Rowan, son of the Inspector.

3420. *President.*] Would you suggest that there should be an alternative fifth paper in the Elementary examination?—Then it would in my opinion be no longer an Elementary examination. If there is a Dutch paper added there should be an alternative modern language or science paper.

3421. *Dean Holmes.*] Would you have Latin?—Yes.

3422. *President.*] Do all the boys learn Latin?—Yes.

3423. In the Elementary examination their knowledge of Latin is not tested, is it? —No.

3424. *Rev. Moorrees.*] Do you know that on the continent a second language is not considered to destroy the elementary character of the education; boys begin very young to learn a second language, do they not?—Yes. I am aware of that, but the character of the teaching is very different here to what it is on the continent, and the character of the examinations also.

3425. *Dr. Berry.*] What is your opinion with regard to the Elementary examination; would you like to see it abolished?—I should regret its abolition, because I think it has done a great deal of good, and its tendency is to raise elementary education, but I think it is becoming rather more than elementary. Some parts of the papers are rather beyond the scope of boys of thirteen.

3426. *Dean Holmes.*] Would you be in favour of exempting boys who go in for the higher examinations from having first to pass the elementary?—Yes. It interferes with the ordinary curriculum of education. We send in a good many boys for the Elementary examination, some pass and some fail. The boys who fail, if they want to go in for the School Higher examination, are thus put back another year.

Mr.
W. C. Meredith.

Sept. 4th, 1891.

3427. *Rev. Moorrees.*] English and Dutch being the two languages of the country, would you give both those languages a higher average of marks than foreign languages? —Yes, provided the examination papers were exactly alike in character.

3428. In examinations where English and another language are compulsory, and a second language is optional, would you be in favour of giving to Dutch, as being one of the languages of the country, a greater average of marks than you would to German or French?—The second language taken should be neither English nor Dutch. English and Dutch should be alternative for the first language to be taken, but neither English nor Dutch should be the second language. If a second language is to be taken, one of the others, French, German, or Latin should be chosen.

3429. *Dean Holmes.*] Would you have the same examiners for both?—I do not know whether you could do that. I should prefer to have the same examiners.

3430. *President.*] Do you know anything about night schools?—I believe there is a night school in Graham's Town, and I think there are several efficient ones in Cape Town. I have worked in a night school in Cape Town. The subjects were principally elementary, but I have also had a civil service class at night and taught higher mathematics and classics.

3431. *Rev. Moorrees.*] Is it a system that ought to be developed in your opinion? —I think so. The difficulty is to find the pupils. I should have thought in Graham's Town we should have found a fair number of pupils, but I do not anticipate much success. Those who really need the education will not come for it.

3432. Can you assign any reason for that?—I suppose the character of the country and the fine evenings have something to do with it.

3433. *Mr. Theron.*] Have the fees got anything to do with it?—I cannot say.

3434. *Dean Holmes.*] Are you aware that in Graham's Town we have a grammar school, not aided in any way by the State, and that that grammar school is now having a night school?—Yes.

3435. So that the system is being tried?—Yes. We intend to start a night school ourselves.

Graham's Town, Saturday, 5th September, 1891.

PRESENT :

Sir Jacob Dirk Barry, Knight (President),

Mr. Theron,
Dr. W. B. Berry,
Rev. A. Moorrees,

Rev. Cootzee,
Dean Holmes.

Rev. Charles Taberer examined.

Rev.
Charles Taberer.

Sept. 5th, 1891.

3436. *President.*] What are you?—Resident Missionary or Principal of St. Matthew's Mission School at Keiskama Hoek. It is a missionary and industrial institution.

3437. Do you receive aid from Government?—Yes.

3438. For the industrial department?—Yes; but it is more for the boarding department. A small proportion of the grant-in-aid is given to trade teachers, but the principal part is for the board of the native boys in the institution. A grant is given of so much per head for a certain number of apprentices resident in the institution, and an allowance is made for two trade teachers.

3439. Is this teaching carried on in the institution under your supervision?—Yes.

3440. What trades do you carry on?—Wagon-making, blacksmiths and tinsmiths' work, carpentering and gardening.

3441. Do day boys come to the school as well?—Yes; they attend the day school.

3442. What work do they do?—The boys attending the day school from the outside kraals do no industrial work, they go home immediately after school. The boarders do two hours industrial work a day, but the apprentices work at their trades all day long.

3443. The boarders who are scholars and not apprentices, do two hours manual work a day?—Yes; every day.

3444. Do you find that a good thing?—An excellent thing.

3445. Do you think industrial departments ought to be encouraged?—Most certainly.

3446. Do the scholars come with the view of learning a trade?—No; they come for education, but two hours manual work is compulsory.

3447. Is that technical or rough work?—Just rough work about the place, gardening and so on

Rev.
Charles Taberer,

Sept. 5th, 1891.

3448. What do they pay ?—£6 a year themselves.

3449. Do you see any means of getting more of the native parents to go in for the education of their children ?—I think the education that is now available for them need not be improved upon at present, but what I should like to do myself would be to increase the facilities for giving industrial education.

3450. How would you propose to do that ?—It is a very difficult matter.

3451. Could you not give industrial education to the day scholars ?—No; not very well, because they are scattered about the mission district. There is no location on the mission itself. They live from one to four miles away, and it would be impossible after school hours to keep them at industrial work unless they are also fed, and a midday meal would involve expense.

3452. Need the midday meal be anything but mealies ?—Mealies, Kafir corn, or beans.

3453. Could not that be provided inexpensively for those who attend ?—The expense depends very much upon the season of the year. The last two or three years it has not been expensive, but there is the further expense of providing tools, and of deciding what work they are to do, as there is no market for sale of produce within 28 miles of the mission.

3454. Could not some portion of the time devoted to literary work be given to industrial work, so that the children could come to school for the same number of hours ?—I am afraid the number of hours devoted to literary work could not well be diminished, because of the irregularity of attendance. ¦If they only received two hours' instruction a day they would learn very little in the course of the time they attend school—that is, the majority of the scholars; it would practically amount to almost nothing.

3455. At any rate they would have some industrial work ?—Yes; that would do some good, but I question whether they would come for that, knowing that it is taken away from the usual school hours. If it were made a general thing all over the colony, they would fall into it gradually perhaps.

3456. How would you cure the irregularity of attendance ?—I suppose by establishing compulsory education directly, or in some way indirectly.

3457. How would you establish it directly ?—To do so in the country districts would to my mind be practically impossible. It could only be done by police supervision or by an attendance officer, and the levying of an education tax. There are two ways of doing it, either by imposing a tax of so much per hut in the native locations or so much per householder. I am rather inclined to say the better plan is so much per householder. A householder may have several huts. Without a valuation of property such as we have in towns, I do not see how we can impose a tax in proportion to the amount of property. There might be something similar to the late house duty.

3458. How would you propose to levy a householder's tax ?—So much per householder, to be collected in the usual way by the Government officials. There is no doubt at all that natives should be made to pay more than they now do for what they receive in education. At present they pay practically nothing, except in boarding institutions, where they are compelled to do so. In outstation schools the fees are very seldom insisted upon and very seldom paid. If there was some tax, it would be equivalent to a compulsory fee.

3459. If they had to pay this tax, you think the children would come to school ?—Yes; because a native will always try to get an equivalent for his money.

3460. Do they like education ?—They are being trained to it now gradually. They see the value of it, but still there are a number of them who do not, and it would be a means of bringing them, if not from a missionary, from a practical, point of view to understand the value of it.

3461. You say that you would prefer a householder's tax to a hut tax ?—By a householder's tax I mean a tax in proportion to a man's wealth, and that is not tested by the number of huts. I could point out cases where a native with a single hut is much better off than another with three or four huts.

3462. Do you think the property of householders can easily be ascertained, so as to tax them in proportion to their property ?—Not easily. There would be far more difficulty in that than in a simple householder's tax, without ascertaining the value of a man's property. Every head of a family should be taxed.

3463. How much should he pay ?—From 10s. to 12s. 6d. a year, I think.

3464. Could every head of a family pay that for education ?—Yes, I think so. I do not mean to say that it would not be better probably to tax in proportion to property, but I can see difficulties in the way. You must have the property assessed all over the country, and it would cost an immense amount of money before you got at any result.

3465. You think that every Native householder would be able to pay from 10s. to 12s. 6d. a year for the purpose of education, and it would be a good thing ?—Yes. Rev. *Charles Taberer.*

3466. *Dr. Berry.*] Would you levy this rate whether a householder has children or not ?—Yes. Sept. 5th, 1891.

3467. *President.*] Is this suggestion familiar to the native mind in the Transkei ? —I believe that in certain parts of the Transkei something like a tax for educational purposes is going on now, but it is voluntary, carried out through the influence of the magistrates.

3468. You think the natives appreciate it, and it would be a good thing to make it law ?—They do not all appreciate it. I should judge that the tax would only be paid by those who really wished to educate their children, unless it was really made law.

3469. Do you think it would be a good thing for the natives if it is paid ?—Yes.

3470. And it would advance education of the best sort, which you say ought not to be merely literary but also industrial ? —Yes.

3471. Could anything in the way of levying a tax be carried out at St. Matthew's ? —I think it could be done in the whole of the Keiskama Hoek district or the King William's Town district. There is no location at St. Matthew's. My work extends over a large district.

3472. If you got the money from such a tax, how would you carry out this industrial education among the natives in certain centres?—I ought to say that this tax is not the best thing to my mind that I should like to see in connection with schools, but it appears to me to be the only way out of the difficulty. I should like very much better to see the people appreciate education and pay school fees voluntarily, but as they will not do so, they must be compelled, and the only way to compel them is through the Government. The Government must step in, and in some way force them to do what they will not do willingly. Hence this tax seems the only way out of the difficulty.

3473. Would it tend to instil habits of industry into the native mind ?—Yes, if we could increase the facilities for industrial education.

3474. What sort of industry would you recommend ?—A little of everything; spade and garden industry should be taught more than anything else, probably because the natives at present are really the labourers.

3475. Do you think something of the kind could be worked through the mission schools ?—I think it would involve a good deal of expense.

3476. Would you recommend something of the kind being tried in towns where there are locations, through the agency of mission schools that are willing to do the work ?—I think so. I should advise its being done in all places where practicable.

3477. Would a simple industrial school be very costly if it were worked through a mission school ?—They must have land, and I am afraid you would not get missionary superintendents to undertake it to any extent, if it involved them in financial liabilities.

3478. You do it yourself, do you not ?—I have done it, and I am prepared to go on with it.

3479. And you have done it with great success it seems ?—I do not know that others would attempt it, and any success I may have had may be partly owing to local favourable circumstances.

3480. Would it not be a good thing to look out for men, like yourself, willing to do the work ?—Certainly.

3481. Would it not be more beneficial for the natives to have industrial training ? —Yes; but you must have land, and also a market for your produce when you have got it, otherwise, whatever you grow will be wasted. There must be a regular organisation if the thing is to be in any way useful or successful.

3482. *Mr. Theron.*] Would you make the tax you referred to general over all the native territories ?—Yes; as far as practicable.

3483. How would you collect the tax ?—I would make it general. It can only be collected in the same way as the late hut tax was collected, through the Government officials. At Keiskama Hoek it was always taken to the clerk-in-charge at the office, and receipts were given them. We have no inspector of locations in the Keiskama Hoek district.

3484. There are inspectors of locations in the Transkei, are there not ?—Yes, there are in parts of the country, but I am not certain about this.

3485. Would you apply the amount thus collected exclusively to the native territories for their education, or would you distribute it towards education in other parts of the Colony ?—My idea is that it should go into a general fund, and let it be for distribution through the Education Office, according to the reports of the inspectors, and the desirability of increasing the number of schools in certain places.

[G. 3—'92.] H

3486. You would not impose the tax on the European population, would you?—No; I might say that if I were to impose a fee to-morrow for the native children, they would go to another school, where they would be taken for nothing. In the same way, if other schools impose a fee and I do not, then my schools are filled.

3487. Why are not you in favour of a hut-tax?—A hut-tax would lose its distinctive character with the natives very soon; they would forget that it was for the purpose of education, and it is well to keep that before their minds.

3488. You think it should be collected exclusively for educational purposes?—Yes; it should not lose its force as an educational tax.

3489. *President.*] Could not the chief man in the kraal himself aid in collecting the tax?—As far as my district goes, they are incapable of doing anything, and a better and more intellectual set of men should be appointed as headmen.

3490. *Dr. Berry.*] Would not the best plan be to have a school district, with a School Board in King William's Town to collect this money and administer it?—It would involve secularizing all our schools.

3491. Why should not they be secularized?—I think that every denomination wishes to keep its own children under their own supervision, and provide religious instruction for them. We naturally all like to do this, and should be very averse to throwing the whole educational work of the district into the hands of a Board, because that would mean distinctly secularizing education, on the principle of the Board schools in England. I do not say there are not many things in favour of it. The clause in the Educational Act providing for religious instruction in undenominational public schools is to a great extent a dead letter.

3492. Need it necessarily do that. Could not a local School Board for the district of King William's Town collect the tax and administer it?—It seems to me that the secularization of the schools is necessarily involved in the question.

3493. Why should it be more involved in such a system than if the money were paid over and distributed by a Government officer?—I am afraid that it is involved in both systems.

3494. Would it not better meet the requirements of the case if the whole thing was done locally?—The power of the Board would have to be limited to a great extent, or secularization must follow.

3495. *Dean Holmes.*] Would you object to such a Board. Suppose each school retained its own existing management, you would then have two controlling powers, would you not?—That would be a complication of the machinery. Denominational interests would be certain to creep into a Board of this nature, and it would be a question whether, in all cases justice would be done—whether the places that most deserved a grant would get it, and whether undeserving places would not get more than they ought. There is, moreover, an equivalent to such a Board already in existence in the Educational Department.

3496. Suppose the grant were allocated by the Government Inspectors?—I should much prefer that, whatever denomination they belonged to.

3497. *Dr. Berry.*] You could even have a school district not coterminous with the whole division. The division might be parcelled out into various small districts, and each district have its own independent management?—That, to my mind, would be better, but not satisfactory, as the schools of various denominations in this district overlap each other.

3498. If you have the general Government giving a subsidy to schools, that involves a certain amount of supervision on the part of the Government, and if you have the local Government also giving a subsidy, that necessarily involves a certain amount of supervision; you must in some way or another, on your own recommendation, provide both for general or State supervision and for local supervision. What suggestion have you for the institution and maintenance of local control in cases where you think local taxation is advisable for school purposes?—I do not see any better way than the present way of administering the education funds in any native district, provided the natives can be made in some way to contribute more towards their education. I cannot bring myself to approve of these Boards as affecting the natives.

3499. *Rev. Moorrees.*] Is the grant you get from the Government proportionate to the part contributed by you?—The grant given by the Government is much larger than the native contribution.

3500. If you take the total you receive from the Government and the total you get from other sources, whatever they may be, would those two amounts be equally proportionate, more or less, or is the Government grant much more?—It depends upon whether we reckon the salary of the missionary, which comes from another source altogether. They would be about equal if all other sources of revenue are included.

3501. So that your church has not to make any special sacrifice to keep things going?—No, but special sacrifices have to be made to start work, putting up buildings, etc.

Rev.
Charles Taberer.
— —
Sept. 5th, 1891.

3502. *Dr. Berry.*] It is a matter of complaint from other centres that there is nobody to control the setting up of schools in native districts; that what may be called school areas overlap, and the work is overdone, districts are over-schooled, and there is really no control as to the number of schools that may be set up in any particular division. Is that the case ?—This overlapping exists in some districts, and it appears to be the outcome of a liberal recognition of denominational education in native schools by the Education Department.

3503. Has that difficulty arisen under the present system of management ?—Yes, but I think it is very probable that when applications for grants have been made, the question of distance from existing schools has not been stated.

3504. Does not that seem to point to the necessity of a local over Board in the district, so as to prevent the waste of public money and local taxation ?—I think the difficulty would be met by this tax. The tax would involve free education.

3505. How would the difficulty be obviated simply by the imposition of a school tax ?—The scholars would all swarm to the school where there was the best teacher. As they can get into each school for nothing, they would naturally go to the best, and the others would go to the wall.

3506. Then it would resolve itself into a question of the best or worst teachers ?—Yes.

3507. Would the natives be adequate judges of that ?—Yes, immediately.

3508. On what basis would they judge ?—They generally know what is best for their money. Scholars would soon find out which is the best teacher.

3509. If the other schools were still getting the grant, how would they lapse ?—The children would go to the best teacher, and Government should step in and say, one good school is sufficient and the others must go—that is in places where schools distinctly overlap each other.

3510. But Government has practically the control at the present time and it does not say so does it ?—It ought to say so. It is understood that within a certain number of miles a second school should not receive aid, at least I have hitherto understood so.

3511. The danger of overlapping which now exists would be met by the principle that natives when they come to pay their school tax, would choose the best school, and the other schools would fall to the ground ?—Yes.

3512. *President.*] You think the tax should be distributed in proportion to the number attending the school ?—Yes.

3513. Are you still of opinion that a local over Board will not assist in this difficulty at all ?—It would assist, but it involves the danger of secularization, which I do not like.

3514. *Dean Holmes.*] How many of the boys in your institution are under industrial training ?—There are 25 regular apprentices in residence and 14 boarders. The former work all day and receive instruction in the night school; the latter do two hours industrial work daily.

3515. Have you a girls' establishment ?—Yes.

3516. How many boarders have you among the girls ?—24 in residence. They do washing, ironing, sewing, scrubbing, and such like domestic duties. Some of them are apprentices. The scholars work two hours daily and the apprentices work almost all day long.

3517. Do the girls pay the same fees as the boys ?—They are a little lower.

3518. Have you many applications from native children for admission ?—Yes; many more than I can accommodate.

3519. Is there a great desire on the part of natives for an industrial training ?—Yes; I have sent away during the last six months at least fifty applicants for admission to the boys' industrial departments, and in the girls' department, I have sent away about twelve applicants. In July, on the opening of the schools, I had not sufficient room, there were so many applications to come as apprentices to learn sewing, cutting out, ironing, etc.

3520. Have you an industrial teacher for the girls ?—Yes; there is a lady matron in charge. She has the supervision, and that is her chief duty.

3521. Is there a grant from the Government for that purpose ?—There is a small amount given to her as sewing mistress, £10 a year, but that does not of course cover the salary of the lady matron, provide rooms, or anything else. The balance of her salary comes from other local sources.

3522. *Dr. Berry.*] Such a system as you have at your institution is perfectly inapplicable to the whole division of King William's Town, is it not ?—Yes, unless men and means can be found to apply it.

3523. Is there any suggestion you can make for generally giving industrial training of a lower class to the poorer body of natives throughout the division; suppose it is found to be necessary to add some kind of industrial training, how would

Rev.
Charles Taberer.

Sept. 5th, 1891.

you propose that it should be initiated?—That is a broad question, and one great difficulty is the race feeling that may exist in the Colony about so much money being expended upon the natives, and tradesmen objecting about the facilities given to the natives to learn trades. They say that the bread is taken out of the mouths of European mechanics by what is being done. To my mind nothing that would be generally successful can be done without the direct supervision and control of the Government, and the total expense of any industrial institution must come from the Government. Whether it is a small or large one, it must have supervision and control, and there must be a managing man who must receive his salary from the work he is doing. You must have buildings and appliances even for farming, and to establish small industrial centres inefficiently conducted about the King William's Town district would be worse than none at all. I am fully convinced that no efficient work can be done at a small centre with only the native teacher in charge, and at the larger centres the missionary bodies have not sufficient funds to come forward to put up buildings and provide all the necessary appliances. This must be done by the Government, and the whole thing must be under Government supervision and control. If such institutions were established by Government, the nearest missionary could visit the institution in his religious capacity and give religious instruction to the boys and girls resident at the place. It should be a Government scheme altogether. The tax would only cover the simple education in the schools.

3524. Have you observed that lately very serious complaints have been made about the whole method of educating the natives in the Colony?—Yes.

3525. What do you take to be the nature of those complaints?—They arise partly from a feeling that exists that the natives ought not to be anything better than servants; that education is not good for them, and that the raw Kafir is much better than an educated Kafir. Many of the colonists also disapprove of the expenditure of so much money on industrial education, fearing their competition with European mechanics.

3526. What reply have you to those complaints?—I may say that I issued a pamphlet four or five years ago on the whole subject. In the first place, as to educating the natives at all, my opinion is that the complaint is without foundation entirely. They have as much right to education as we have. They pay their proportion to the revenue through taxation, and the more educated they are the more they will contribute to the revenue, in that a desire is thus created for imported goods upon which duty is paid. Looking at it from a missionary point of view, of course we come out here to make them better, but they cannot be made better without intellectual training in conjunction with Christian teaching. I am very strong on the point of this intellectual training, for although it indirectly benefits the individual native, it is a far greater benefit to the whole community. Industrial training is not appreciated generally because it involves a little suffering perhaps and some complaints from English mechanics, although they really only imagine they have a grievance. Some years ago, a native boy would not have found a place in a shop in King William's Town, but now native carpenters go over the Colony and are readily employed, because they work for less wages. Then comes in the cry of mechanics and others, but the answer to that is, that no great good can be done in this way without adversely affecting a few. The history of civilization and the invention of machinery, etc., prove this.

3527. Your idea is that these natives in the mass must receive a certain amount of intellectual training as well as industrial training?—The one is impossible without the other, except, perhaps, actual spade industry. A native can never become a carpenter unless he has a certain amount of intellectual training. Without this he would be puzzled to know what the one-eighth or one-sixteenth of an inch means.

3528. At the same time you say it is impossible to give that amount of intellectual and industrial training on the large scale you try to carry it out at St. Matthew's?—Yes; impossible in that funds are not available.

3529. In the district of King William's Town, I suppose there are 12,000 or 15,000 children of schoolable age. How are we to take the mass of these children and give them a certain amount of intellectual and a certain amount of industrial training?—It is impossible, as I have said without the aid of Government or munificent charitable benefactions. You can only take a certain portion without the establishment of very large industrial institutions all over the place at a vast expense, and then the question arises as to what you are to do with the things when they are made in these institutions.

3530. What is the best thing to be done in your opinion in return for this school tax which you propose to put upon the native householders?—The tax would be an indirect compulsory act. I do not mean it to refer to industrial education, as it would not cover the necessary cost. I should look upon this tax not as class legislation, but as a compulsory school fee, equivalent to the fees paid by Europeans in town schools, and the sums guaranteed by Europeans in support of such schools.

3531. What is the best return in the way of education you propose to make for this tax?—If the tax would cover the expense of both intellectual and industrial training, it should include both. I do not believe in any education for natives which does not include industrial training.

Rev. *Charles Tatever.*
Sept. 5th, 1891.

3532. Would you leave the direction of the quality and amount of the education to be determined by the central Government or the Education Department?—Yes.

3533. Your idea is that it should comprise as far as possible intellectual and industrial education going side by side?—Yes.

3534. You have no suggestion beyond this, that the education of the mass of these natives should be left in the hands of the Government?—No local body would, I believe, and no missionary can possibly carry out these things at their own cost; it can only be done through the medium of charitable contributions for the purpose, and these are most difficult to get. They can only as a rule be obtained in driblets, and an institution can only be raised after many years of perseverance. The colony must come to see that it is a good thing for the community at large, and that it must be done at the public expense. If the colony cannot refund itself through this tax, it should consider itself refunded by the good done to the community at large, although a few individuals may suffer by the advancement of civilization among these people.

3535. Your point is that the administration of this fund, and the determination of the quality and extent of the education for the natives is better left in the hands of the central Government than in the hands of any local Board in the district?—Yes.

3536. *Rev. Moorrees.*] Do you think it is practicable to have some kind of industrial class attached to every native mission school, or to most of them?—That would be impossible except at centres, because at other places, at out stations for instance, only native teachers are in charge, and in four cases out of five, native teachers would neither be disposed nor competent to give any sort of industrial training, not even spade industry, that would be satisfactory to any Government Inspector. I should like it to be done, and it is very advisable, but the difficulty is how to do it.

3537. *President.*] In face of the difficulties, would you sooner leave it undone?—I would sooner leave it undone, unless it were done well. I would leave the tax to be used for literary education as it at present exists, and let industrial training be imported when it can be, and the sooner the better.

3538. Would not you help those missionary bodies that are prepared to introduce industrial education in connection with their work. Should not they be helped if they are prepared to undertake it?—Yes.

3539. Who would you leave to judge as to whether they are to be helped; would it not be a wise thing to have a local Board to report to Government upon what they propose and advise the central Government as to whether they should aid or not?—No, our present inspectors are quite competent to do that.

3540. *Dr. Berry.*] You say that you would leave the literary education as it at present exists?—I would do so because we cannot help it. I would rather not do so. I say that it is impossible at our *out stations* to tack on industrial training that would be satisfactory.

3541. On what ground do you defend a literary education for these people?—Because it is better than none; they must be educated.

3542. Why is it better than none. A great many people say that such is not the case, do they not?—They must learn to read their Bible and read the newspapers; absolute literary ignorance has never been considered good for any nation.

3543. Why should they have literary education?—Why should they not be educated?

3544. *President.*] Is it not better for these natives to know how to herd sheep or dig than read the newspaper?—Our forefathers were not left without literary education, and why should the Kafir nation be singled out in the matter from the rest of the world.

3545. *Dr. Berry.*] There must be some philosophical reason for teaching these natives. In their savage condition they are practically without literary ideas, and if we are to put literary thoughts into their brains, we must have some philosophical basis for our recommendation?—The basis is, that it is necessary and useful to these people that they should be advanced. Public policy—good Government and civilised advancement demand it.

3546. It may be useful, but are you adopting the best method of giving them a useful thing. This literary education is a method, it is not a thing; and why should we adopt that method in preference to any other? It has been adopted all over the world. It is a natural consequence of human life, and why the natives of this country should be left in darkness as to their literary education I cannot understand.

3547. *Rev. Moorrees.*] Those natives who have learned a trade, do they stick to it?—Generally they do.

3548. *Dr. Berry.*] Can you trace the record of any of your apprentices?—Yes; with a little trouble I could trace a number of them, as I did some years ago when the Education Department requested me to do so.

3549. Is there no means of calling out these people's efforts?—No special means that I am acquainted with. I have never been able to get them to give liberally towards industrial buildings of any kind, but for church and school building purposes I have often received very fair donations from them.

3550. *President.*] If you were in the position of the Government and had to get all these taxes, and the duty was imposed upon you of finding industrial as well as literary education, how would you set about it?—As far as literary education is concerned, I do not see that I could improve upon the present way of managing native schools by the Education Department. As to industrial schools I have never supposed that this tax would cover the expense of erecting special industrial institutions. If I were the Government and had fully decided that such institutions were necessary and desirable for the development of the country (as personally I have decided), I should freely support the institutions that are now doing good work; and, as there is no probability that many others will be raised by missionary bodies or charitable enterprise, I should choose some suitable localities in large native centres, keeping in view the necessity for providing a market for goods made, etc., and I should erect at the public cost such desirable institution, expecting a return for the outlay financially in exactly the same way as railways or telegraphs are expected to produce revenue, and a most valuable indirect return would be secured in the advancement of civilization in the country by means of such institutions and the general good to the public at large. Generally—as the Government—I should endeavour as far as possible to always keep before me the necessity for associating literary with industrial education, and in any such establishments erected solely at Government cost it would be necessary, as no special missionary body would have any control, to arrange for the religious and moral training of the resident apprentices and workers.

3551. Who is to have charge of the literary work?—The appointment of such teacher should rest with the Government.

Rev. Gana Kakaza examined.

3552. *President.*] I believe you are native minister at the Wesleyan mission station in Graham's Town?—Yes.

3553. Have you anything to say upon the subject of industrial schools for natives?—My idea is that our children should not only have a literary education but also have industrial training. It would be good for them.

3554. Do you think that could be carried out inexpensively here?—I think it should be done by Government. At places where there are very many people and there is a sufficient number of boys who attend school, I think some trades should be taught.

3555. Would not you let all the boys who come to school do some work with their hands as well as their minds?—Yes.

3556. Would it not be a good thing to teach them spade industry, gardening, and so on?—Yes.

3557. Do you think that could be done in town?—I think so.

3558. Would the natives be willing to pay a hut tax for their schooling?—I think so; those who send their children to school.

3559. Would it be wise to make all the householders in the location pay say 10s. a hut, and have a good school established, with no fees?—Those who send their children to school should pay, but I do not think it is right to make all pay compulsorily.

3560. You cannot have a good school unless it is a pretty large one, and you want a number of children to attend. If it is good for these children to go to school, should not their parents be compelled to send them as they do in England?—There are some people who do not yet understand the advantage of education, and I do not think it would be just to make those pay who have no children.

3561. *Mr. Theron.*] Do all those who send their children pay regularly?—Not all.

3562. Is it fair that some should pay and others not?—No.

3563. I suppose you like good education for your people, do you not?—Yes.

3564. Do you object to pay for it?—No; but I do not see why those who have no children should be made to pay.

3565. But if the Government levied a tax all over the Colony, they would have to pay, would they not?—Yes, if it was the law.

3566. And suppose the Government makes a law in this case?—I would not consider it just to those who have no children.

3567. *President.*] What are you ?—Resident Roman Catholic priest at Graham's Town.

3568. Have you been a long while in the Colony ?—Since 1873.

3569. I believe you have had a good deal to do with education ?—Yes; I take considerable interest in it.

3570. Have you yourself been on a public school committee ?—Yes; at Queen's Town for three years.

3571. You know the working of public undenominational schools ?— Yes.

3572. How many Roman Catholic schools are there in Graham's Town ?—There are two different establishments, the Convent and St. Aidan's College. The convent is more for the lower education of boys, and St. Aidan's, the higher. The convent school is for girls and also boys up to the fifth standard, when that class of boys generally leave school and go to work. If there is any very intelligent boy in the school, he gets a free place in the college when he passes the inspector's examination, that is to say, if his parents wish him to continue his education.

3573. Are these schools aided by Government ?—Only the Convent mission school.

3574. In the Convent is there a school which is not a mission school ?—There is a Convent higher school for girls with 56 boarders.

3575. That is not aided ?—No.

3576. How many children have you in the mission school ?—There are 211 on the roll at present, all whites, and 113 in the Convent higher school, and 60 at St. Aidan's.

3577. What aid do you get ?—£75 a year.

3578. Do you educate blacks at all ?—We have no mission school for blacks here, except a tentative one, where there are 20 or 30 children. It is not aided.

3579. Has much progress been made in education in your opinion ?—Since I came to the country in 1873, great progress has been made as far as education is concerned. The schools have increased from 430 to 1,500 ; the grants in aid from £27,000 to over £100,000, and the number of scholars enrolled from 30,000 to 80,000. The standard of education has also been raised considerably on account of the University examinations and school standards. The number of passes shows a great increase. This has been largely owing to the principle of the Education Department, under Sir L. Dale, to aid voluntary efforts ; indeed, I look upon the system as purely voluntary, both on the part of committees of public schools and the religious bodies who try to fulfil the elastic conditions on which aid is given. In this way much progress has been made up to the present time, but after doing all this, there still remains a great deal to be done as far as the Government is concerned, because comparing the census and the Education Department returns, half the white children in the country, about 30,000, are still unaided and untouched by Government aid or inspection, and are likely to remain so unless voluntary agencies are still further recognised as Dr. Dale proposes.

3580. How many of those who are unaided by Government are in school ?—We cannot tell. Sir Langham Dale says there are 10,000 at private schools ; but I think there would be more. He wrote before the census.

3581. By what process do you arrive at that ?—From my knowledge of the country and the towns. Except in out of the way rural districts, children are more or less at some school or another.

3582. How many are educated in voluntary schools unaided by Government ?—That I cannot say. We have no record of those schools. Of the 30,000 white children that are aided, there are 10,000 in "mission schools" simply classed as natives, or receiving the same aid as if they were natives, so that considering the small amount of grant given to native schools and the very fixed lines with regard to those schools, there are only 20,000 children who receive the full advantage of the large Government grant of £100,000. The 20,000 receive the major part of the grant, leaving out the 10,000 whites that are classed as natives in mission schools, and leaving out the 30,000 not touched by the Government aid at all. Hence it is a matter of consideration how far educational aid can be extended, so as to bring the other 30,000 within touch of Government assistance and inspection. That would, I think, materially improve education in town and country.

3583. You say that 30,000 children broadly are not aided by Government ?—Yes.

3584. And a large proportion of those educated by private voluntary efforts are unaided?—Yes.

3585. And the remainder are totally uneducated ?—Yes, those on scattered farms, and a certain number of the truant or very poor class in large towns.

3586. Can you state roughly what is the number of white children untouched by education?—I am unable to do so till the census is finished.

3587. Have you any scheme to propose whereby they could be brought into touch with the Government?—The schools that are in existence in the country and doing educational work should, after inspection, be in some way or another brought under the Government. Those children who are not touched either by voluntary or Government schools in the country would have gradually to be gathered together into school by means of some district Board or school attendance committee, the same as in England, whose business it should be to attend to the local supply of schools, both in town and country, especially in the country. The Education Department at present has no initiative power with regard to the establishment of schools in any place. The Inspectors go round the country, and only stay at a school for a few hours, examining as quickly as they can, and going off by the next post. They have not the time, as their number is so few, to enter very much into the question of the supply of schools in a district, and even if they know there is a want, they have not time to stay and talk the matter over, and go about among the field-cornetcies to see what number of children are without education, and discuss the best means of establishing schools where possible, by stimulating local efforts and offering Government aid under certain conditions

3588. You mean that they have neither the power in law nor the knowledge of local circumstances?—Yes; and they have not the time on account of their small number.

3589. How would you remedy that?—There might be some kind of local Board for the district. It might take the form possibly of what they call "school attendance committees" in England, which provide for three-fourths of England outside of London and have no rating powers, whose principal business is to see that the school supply of a locality or district, is adequate; and if it is not adequate, they report to the Government about it. Of course those on such a Board in the Colony if they are at all anxious for education, would try and show the parents where to establish schools or how to get the children to school. There are a great many people in the rural districts or country who do not seem to know how to get a school together. There is very little machinery to put them in the way of it, outside the zeal of the Churches; especially of the Dutch Reformed Church.

3590. Do you speak from your own experience?—Yes.

3591. And you think a local Board would be one means of spreading this knowledge?—Yes; when I say local, it should cover a good area, say a district, and work through parents and the local managers of each school.

3592. Would you say an electoral or a magisterial district?—The fiscal district in some places and in others a larger area.

3593. Corresponding with what the Divisional Council would cover?—Yes; such Board would be like an attendance committee in England, or in large towns something like the Council of education in Liverpool. This Council generally gets the heads and managers of the various schools in the town to unite in some common action with regard to things which it is possible for them to do together, but which they could not do separately.

3594. Can you illustrate that in some way?—This Council would see to the attendance. They ought to know the number of school children in the district and the number of those attending school or otherwise, through the field-cornets and magistrates, clergy and other people, who would be in touch with the different localities and would be able to tell how many children were not at school, and whether it was possible in any way to get a number of these to unite to make up any kind of school, telling them that if they did, the Government would be urged to assist in some measure, so as to stimulate local effort. In this way, every little community where there were children near enough to go to school, would be urged to have a school of its own. This body could help to organise existing schools, and ask the Government to send a suitable inspector to give assistance. If there are building grants required, which is a serious difficulty in this country, they might urge members of Parliament or the Education Department to attend to such matters. They might possibly get those personally interested to offer a portion of the cost, and the Divisional Council or ward where the school was, might be got to contribute, or they might in some way negotiate a loan from the Government for building schools, on the same principle as the Irrigation Act, where repayment is spread over a length of time. At present, the ward or church body cannot make themselves heard unless a member of Parliament happens to be interested in some particular locality, and then perhaps they may get some favour shown them. The wants in regard to school buildings are not considered as a whole, it just depends upon the chance of having some influence with a particular member of Parliament or member of the Ministry in office.

Rev.
Father Fitz Henry.
——
Sept. 5th, 1891.

3595. *Dr. Berry.*] Would you make such a Board a corporate body charged with the holding of school property in the division over which they have administration?—It might come to that, but at present perhaps seven-eighths of the school property is in the hands of private bodies who will not part with it.

3596. Would you give them power to hold such property as they came into possession of?—That would be another question. If schools are built with Government money, then they should be vested in the Government as is the case in Ireland. There, buildings erected by the Education Department are vested in the department, and those buildings which are not built for the Education Department are vested in the body which provided them.

3597. *President.*] Suppose a school Board were elected, would you vest in such Board the buildings that were erected out of Government money as well as those furnished in other ways?—It would be a simpler plan to vest the property in the Education Department in connection with the Civil Commissioner for the time being.

3598. You would vest it in the name of the Civil Commissioner under the control of the Board?—Yes; it would be under the immediate control of the local Board or school managers.

3599. How would you have the Board in your sense appointed?—There should be some kind of nomination. I would give the Divisional Council a voice in the matter, and also the Municipality, and the other nominations might possibly be by the Government to secure full representation of all educational interests.

3600. Would not you move in the direction of making these Boards elective when people are more interested in education?—They would be nominated by representative bodies, and so far they would be elective.

3601. Would not the electors know more about the particular qualifications of a man suitable to be on the Board than a body like the Divisional Council, whose function is more the making of roads?—I should not care to have the ratepayers the electors, if you can get a Board in a simpler manner. I do not think we have come to the time for that, or the need of it.

3602. Suppose this Board finds an educational want to exist, ought they to have the power to supply that want with the aid of the Government, given on a certain principle. If it is to be merely an advising body they are comparatively not of much use, are they?—An advising body would be useful under the present circumstances of this country, because there is a great deal of voluntary effort in the direction of education everywhere, only needing direction. Practically speaking, all the education we have is from the voluntary efforts of the people, and interest in schools is increasing.

3603. Should not this body have power to initiate and start schools where they are actually wanted?—I do not think that could be done, unless such body had the power of raising money by a school tax levied in each division.

3604. Do not you think they might have the power of raising money for the purpose—not necessarily spending it?—People are averse to being rated for their neighbours' schools. I have made enquiries all over the country, and I am sure there would be an outcry. People do not like to be forced. A great deal more might be done voluntarily than by forcing direct taxation upon people; they are opposed to the principle.

3605. If you had this advising body to advise starting schools at the expense of the general Government, would not it happen that such body having no responsibility and not having to put their hands in their pockets, might advise a great many expensive things which might be very awkward for the general Government and prevent their acting; whereas if the ratepayers had to pay the deficiency which occurred after the Government had aided, the Board would be more circumspect in their advice?—The Education Department always has a check, and as now, would only supplement local voluntary effort under definite conditions.

3606. Suppose the Government acts on their advice and there is a deficiency, who is to pay it?—The local managers.

3607. You would have more guarantors brought into existence than at present?—Yes; people interested in the school, whether church bodies or a number of farmers in the ward. These would be responsible: every new school, new guarantors, either parents or church bodies or both combined.

3608. Is not the guarantee system an evil. Is it fair in your opinion to call upon guarantors constantly to pay deficiencies?—It is not the fact that guarantors, as far as public schools are concerned, have ever paid very much. People who are not legally guarantors have paid a great deal more in providing education for the 10,000 white children in mission schools, for instance, for the last 30 years. Guarantors are generally interested parents of the richer classes. Churches have to provide for the poor.

[G. 3—'92.] I

Rev.
Father Fitz Henry.

Sept. 5th, 1891.

3609. *Dr. Berry.*] Who asks them to do it?—Their conscience and sense of duty. The voluntary principle is general in this country. Dr. Ross in his report on Cape schools expresses his surprise at the amount of voluntary effort in the Colony that has established so many schools. The guarantors of a public school are a voluntary body, and they guarantee for a public school, but they do not undertake to teach anybody except those who can pay a certain fee. As soon as a number of guarantors have formed a certain committee, generally for the promotion of education among the better class, the sons of merchants, lawyers, clergymen, in town or village, they stop short, and do not provide for the poorer white children. That is the reason why so many white children of the poorer class have been forced into the coloured mission schools, and there they have remained for 20 or 30 years, while the local guarantors for the higher class schools have profited by money granted that was equally intended for the poorer lot.

3610. *President.*] Unless you impose on the Board the duty of starting schools, what guarantee have you that it will be done. Is it not a good thing to put upon them the absolute obligation of finding schools adequate and filling up the gaps either at the expense of the body which they represent, namely the ratepayers, or such voluntary body as they can point out as being capable of doing the work to the satisfaction of the Government?—I do not object to anybody finding schools. The only difficulty I see is in practice, the opposition of people in a very sparsely populated country to provide the money by local rates for any schools that are not within their own reach: we cannot put a school at each farmer's door.

3611. But if a Board is created with the duty imposed upon it of finding schools, and they represent the ratepayers, they would like to spend as little as possible and not involve the ratepayers; so they might approach these volunteers and get them to guarantee schools to the satisfaction of the Government if they get the aid; but in addition to that, if they cannot find the guarantors, ought there not to be a duty imposed upon some public body of finding schools adequate for the wants of the district. That seems to be the defect of the present system?—The practical difficulty is in regard to the rating powers and the feeling the country has against it, unless every family is supplied with a suitable school near enough to it, and we are far away from that at present. They object to paying for other people for many years till a school comes into their neighbourhood. If you give aid or make up a deficit for one school, then in order to get the ratepayers to acquiesce, you must make up the deficit in every school. If a district Board were to establish a school in some corner perhaps 30 or 40 miles away, and send a teacher there, it would not be in a position to directly manage and control it. Local parent-managers should pay the deficit. If extremely poor, Sir Langham Dale provides itinerant teachers.

3612. But is it not proper that people living at that distance should get a school?—My contention is that if farmers at a distance were approached and shown how they could get a school of their own, they would pay for it in a great measure, along with the Government grant as at present, without a call on the rates. Free schools are far away yet.

3613. Suppose they happen to be very poor, ought there not to be power vested in the Board to start a school which may possibly involve some little call upon the ratepayers. Is not the principle fair and sound?—If the ratepayers of a locality were willing, and no opposition was raised, it would be a good thing. I fear opposition and mal-appropriation.

3614. You said that the guarantors have hardly ever been called upon to pay; does not that show that if the Board does its duty and gets the help which you propose the Government should give, the ratepayers will virtually hardly ever be called upon to pay anything, while they will have the control, as they ought to have, of their own public schools?—I do not know what it might be in practice, but it is the principle of a general school tax that I do not think would be pleasing to the people, except in exceptional places and restricted areas.

3615. If they once begin to understand it, do not you think they will appreciate it and work into it?—It may come to be appreciated in some districts where there is a full supply of schools. Of course a Board might approach Divisional Councils and get a voluntary grant from them, if made legal. No school tax would pass through the Cape Parliament.

3616. How would you provide for the attendance of children at school?—There are certain places where the power of compulsion is needful, especially in large towns for truants and negligent parents.

3617. If in large towns the power of compulsion is needed, do not you think there ought to be vested in the Board to a certain extent the absolute duty of finding schools if the present accommodation is inadequate, into which children should be forced?—In large towns the accommodation is adequate, if not more than sufficient. It would be matter of detail for the Education Department. In Cape Town, Sir Langham Dale says there are sufficient school places, and it is the same I think in Port Elizabeth and Graham's Town, King William's Town and East London.

Rev.
Father Fitz Henry.

Sept. 5th, 1891.

3618. Might not this want be created at any moment and be supplied by some machinery brought into existence by law?—The school attendance committee might if they found there were not sufficient places for the children, call upon the managers of existing schools to enlarge them.

3619. *Dean Holmes.*] At whose cost?—If the existing schools were for the very poor, then the Government ought to aid by loans or grants as is done for richer children now.

3620. *Dr. Berry.*] Who would make up the rest of the contribution?—The local managers of the schools.

3621. *Dean Holmes.*] Suppose they say they will not, what power would you have to supply the deficiencies?—I think they would do it as they have done it. As far as building grants are concerned, the Government ought to lend the money if not give it. There are sufficient schools and free places for the very poorest children in Graham's Town at the present time. I should like to have a School Board, but not Board schools. It would mean more system, more zeal, and less expense to local rates.

3622. *Rev. Moorrees.*] If a School Board is established, and that School Board is obliged to find schools all through the district wherever they are needed, would not they have to erect schools in localities where schools cannot possibly pay?—If the onus was thrown on them and the means provided by the ratepayers, then of course they should do so.

3623. If they had to establish say three or four schools of that kind throughout the district, would not the deficit afterwards put a very heavy burden on the ratepayers?—Decidedly; I can imagine a case where there is in the distant part of a district a necessity for a building. That building might be a moveable building, as the children might not always be there in sufficient number; or it might be an immoveable building; and to find that building, I think the Government might give a certain amount from the Divisional Council rates, and a certain amount would come very likely from voluntary contributions on the part of friends. When the building is once there, if the people were absolutely so poor that they were unable to pay any fees, which I hardly think would be altogether the case, they could be given a schoolmaster by the Government, an itinerant schoolmaster at £5 or £6 a month, according to present regulations. There would always, I take it, be a certain amount of local income when once the school was built.

3624. If we had these Boards, and they were obliged to find out of the pockets of the ratepayers provision for such cases, would not the amount to be so paid be enormous? —I do not think the ratepayers would agree to any law involving large expenditure.

3625. *President.*] Would you under certain circumstances have one-third of the expenditure on buildings fall upon the rates?—I think that would be a good thing if no one got the lion's share. Several schools require repairs or additions to make them suitable.

3626. The moment you agree to that, does not it show that the ratepayers ought to have a voice in the whole matter of expenditure?—It is one thing to assist to establish a school, and another thing to be prepared to pay the deficit from year to year, which would very often be unlimited if local managers were not responsible and could come on the rates for the deficit.

3627. Do not you think it would be a good thing and tend to interest the local ratepayers, who are in many instances parents of children, in the general system of education for the district?—If all the districts were populous and commencing to build schools everywhere, and everything was new, then it might be recommended, but at the present time you have, through the voluntary efforts of public school committees in every town and village, and religious bodies in larger centres, a large system of schools of various and suitable kinds started all through the country, and you must deal with those first; and unless you take these fully into account, you immediately have opposing elements in any body that has the power of rating for schools, necessarily ignoring all the others. Farm schools, boarding schools, native schools, and many efficient private schools could not receive aid from local rates; their supporters would object to be rated for other schools. It is unfair and impracticable, outside of small one-school communities.

Graham's Town, Monday, 7th September, 1891.

PRESENT:

Sir J. D. BARRY (President),

Mr. Rowan,
Mr. Theron,
Dean Holmes,

Rev. Moorrees,
Rev. Cootzee,
Dr. Berry.

Rev. Father Fitz Henry further examined.

Rev.
Father Fitz Henry.
Sept. 7th, 1891.

3628. *President.*] How many children do you think are not receiving education? —The exact number we cannot tell till the census returns are published. Sir Langham Dale says there are 10,000 educated in private schools and 8,000 not accounted for. There may be more than 8,000 possibly not accounted for, but not necessarily without any instruction.

3629. How are the other 12,000 to be accounted for, because they exist?—They exist, but we cannot say whether they are under instruction or not. I believe a good number are under some kind of instruction.

3630. What is your estimate of the number of white children not under instruction at all?—It is difficult to form an estimate.

3631. If there are 20,000 totally uneducated, how would you reach them?—I do not think there are 20,000 without instruction. A great many might be receiving a very poor education, because there is no aid and no inspection, and where that is wanting, except in the case of a few rich people's schools, the teaching must be weak. It is weak even where there is aid for want of better teachers.

3632. Do you think it is actually the case that those who receive instruction are poorly educated?—The greater number is poorly educated, as not five per cent. pass Standard V at inspection.

3633. How are they educated, in your opinion?—In private adventure schools that are always changing, or by private tutors or teachers uninspected. In the richer private schools, results tested by the University are good.

3634. How would you remedy that?—By extending as far as possible the facilities that are at present offered by some new regulations.

3635. In what way would you extend them?—There are two ways. First, by increasing the efficiency of the present white mission schools, so as to secure the teaching of the children who go there, and then by having some organizing inspector or some other means to multiply the farm schools and schools of that kind in the country; also by adding to the number of district boarding schools where it is possible in towns as well as country, in order to reach specially the rural population, and the better training of pupil teachers.

3636. How would you extend the farm schools without giving them Government aid?—I would give them Government aid as at present, and keep up a supply of good teachers for them.

3637. How would you alter the present system of Government aid so as to reach them?—I should not alter it at all. It is not fully taken advantage of as yet.

3638. Then the present system is enough for the purpose?—Yes, as far as the means are concerned, but it requires to be a little more known among the people.

3639. Do you think the white mission schools should be a little more aided?—Much more. The mission schools are not giving at present in my opinion a sufficiently good education to the class of children attending them, for want of funds to secure a better class of teachers.

3640. Do you think there would be an improvement if they were more aided?—Yes.

3641. You are speaking as to white children?—Yes.

3642. Would you introduce industrial education as an adjunct, in the form of object lessons and technical education?—As far as practicable it would be most advisable: manual not so much as technical.

3643. Do you think the present mission schools could be developed into something which could have such a department added and worked into the system, considering the teachers and the material they have?—Perhaps immediately it could not easily be done, because you want the teachers and a little more organization among them.

3644. How would you provide for those mission schools which are mostly denominational, and therefore not touched by any present system of Government aid?—The Government does aid these schools, and also helps to provide teachers.

3645. But it does not indicate who shall be teachers. Is not that a defect in the mission schools?—The Government has power to veto a teacher as in undenominational public schools. The Government in about four or five different training schools are now training elementary teachers under church management.

Rev.
Father Fitz Henry.

Sept. 7th, 1891.

3646. For mission schools?—Some will be for mission schools. Pupil teachers are now actually being trained by church bodies specially for their own schools and farm schools. Still there is a want in quantity and quality.

3647. Would it be a good thing if the Government insisted upon mission schools having efficient teachers and examining them?—The Government at present always asks for the certificates or credentials of every teacher, and they would be more strict than they are if they thought they could get a supply; but knowing that they cannot, they take the best they can get. The Education Department is doing its best to get this supply, and Sir Langham Dale in his last report says he feels the want of efficient teachers.

3648. Do you think these mission schools will consent, and ought to consent, to have teachers who are certificated by the Government, if they can be procured?—A number of mission schools have certificated teachers.

3649. Ought they universally to have certificated teachers?—As soon as possible all of them ought, and would very soon, if salaries were higher.

3650. Would they be willing to receive them?—They are doing their best to have them, and they would have more and better teachers if they had more to pay them with; £25 a-year grant per teacher in a white mission school is hard on the poor.

3651. You say there is a third class of private adventure schools where children receive some sort of education?—Yes; a large number of these schools in towns are started for a short time; many are infant schools.

3652. What would you do with them?—We could not close them, but I should make all Government schools and existing schools of a permanent character that were necessary and suitable, as good as possible by further aid, and then in time the others will give way, as happened in England and elsewhere.

3653. Would you have these private adventure schools inspected?—If they wish to be private, you have no right to inspect them. In Germany, however, as a rule they do not allow private adventure schools, but denominational schools are aided. A restricted Government system produces private schools.

3654. *Dean Holmes.*] Are you aware that in England private adventure schools have to be certified as efficient, otherwise a child's attendance is not reckoned?—The school attendance committee must be in some way satisfied. There is no rigid inspection. There are so many schools in England that are above the elementary class which are not touched at all by the Government boards of compulsion. I am in favour of general inspection.

3655. *President.*] You think the Government ought only to aid these improved mission schools?—A certain number of working mission schools that are necessary and suitable to each place, taking into account vested interests, efficiency, and population.

3656. It has been suggested by one witness that Government should aid all private effort that is up to the mark; do you agree with that?—I should not like to agree to a proposition of that kind. It would lead to a multiplication of schools not having a permanent character, and would produce no good result in the long run. There should be some special reason for aiding such schools, as when the undenominational public school falls into the hands of a clique.

3657. You think it should be a condition of aid to voluntary schools that they be placed under Government control?—They should be under Government control in some shape or another, either under the Education Department, or in connection with a public school or some local body that might be created hereafter as an over Board.

3658. Denominations are volunteers; do you think all their schools ought to be under Government control?—If they be aided, then they should be inspected. If they are not aided, you have no right to interfere; practically you could not do it unless you offer aid.

3659. Do you think any system of compulsion ought to be applied in town to secure attendance?—Except in the case of truant children who have got beyond the control of their parents or guardians, or where the father is away, and they run about the streets.

3660. Suppose the parents do not wish to send their children to school, ought not they to be forced to do so?—If it is due to negligence on the part of parents, some power of compulsion would be useful. The administration of that power, however, as has been the case in England and other places, should be carried out very gently.

3661. Can compulsion be used in the case of children going to denominational schools?—Yes; it makes no difference. The school attendance officer in any town must take into account all the schools in that town, whether public or private. He should be a Government officer—not appointed locally.

3662. Do you consider the system of fees a good one?—I think so. It is the custom of the country, and besides, if we abolish fees, then the taxes would have to bear the burden. The late Mr. Samuels, the inspector, in his report said that it would

Rev.
Father Fitz Henry.

Sept. 7th, 1891.

cost the Cape one million of money to do what New Zealand has done without fees. There is not much expense in collecting fees; generally the masters do it.

3663. Is it not employment which masters would sooner not have and had better not have?—It may be a necessary evil, but if you cannot get the fees in any other way what are you to do?

3664. Would the absence of fees increase the attendance in this country, or not? —Very little, if at all, in mission schools, because the fees are so low now. In the class of schools where the poor children go, they are as low as threepence a week and there are free places.

3665. What fee should the Government insist upon in the case of aided schools? —It depends upon the grade of the school, upon the locality, and upon the parents.

3666. Do you think there ought to be a maximum fixed in the case of mission schools for whites, or should it be left to the Department?—The fees must be regulated by each locality and almost by each school.

3667. Would you say that Government aid should not be given to any school where the fee exceeded a certain amount per week; for instance, that no school should get aid where the fee is more than ninepence?—I do not think the English idea of "ninepence" applies to this country. A mission school is an elementary school only.

3668. Do you think the condition of aid in a mission school ought to be that the highest fee was limited to say ninepence a week?—I do not agree with the principle, but practically the fee very seldom goes above ninepence a week. They are very glad to get ninepence in most cases.

3669. How would you reach children who are in no school at all?—It depends upon where they are. I think the supply of schools in all towns, if not in all villages, is sufficient. Compulsion should be used to a certain extent, and in addition to this, the influence of the teachers should be exerted, and the grant might be given more or less according to the attendance. The managers of the schools might become truant officers, and urge parents to send their children to school. The defect in large town schools for the poorer classes is not so much in the children not going to schools, but the irregularity of attendance. They come three days in the week and stay away two, and the teacher has to teach the same lessons very often, two or three times over, consequently, at the end of the year, though there has been a great deal of work, there is very little result to show for it.

3670. Would it not be a good thing if our schools in towns were fewer in number and the attendance larger, and the attendance officer also prompt in his duties?—I do not think that practically we could have many less schools than there are in the larger towns. There might be a few less possibly when a separation is made between the whites and blacks in a number of the mixed mission schools.

3671. If there were fewer schools in Graham's Town for the lower class whites, would not they be more efficient?—In Graham's Town there are three large church mission schools. These are attended by about 200 children in each school, or a little more. The buildings belong to three different churches, and the children have been gathered together by the various denominations, and are influenced to attend. They are well looked after, and the churches are interested in these schools. If the Government or the Education Department proposed to amalgamate them in one school it would have in the first place to build a school for the 600, which would cost a large amount of money. It would cost in this country about a shilling a cubic foot for 140 feet for every child; some £4,000. The money would have to be found for the building, and then the different churches would say they did not want their children to leave the schools where they were. Two or three days ago there was a meeting of the representatives of these mission schools in Graham's Town with regard to the proposal about the fourth class schools, and the question of amalgamation or re-construction upon other lines than those at present existing was discussed. All the managers said that they did not wish to give over the management of their schools; they wished to keep the children in the same buildings, and if there was a School Board in Graham's Town for that class of children, large or small, they would still keep as many children as they possibly could. A certain number would go to that school, and then you would have four schools instead of three, and greater cost and less results. A few of the poorer children would possibly be well taught at the Government expense, or that of the rates, as long as the school continued, and the rest of the children would be without any assistance whatever.

3672. Would not this fourth class school within a measurable time draw all the other children into it if it is the best school?—I think it would lead, as was the case in England in 1870, to a sort of cut-throat action if the Government forced purely undenominational schools upon the people against the wish of the churches. English board schools have not absorbed the church schools, and Chamberlain says, never will; some local church would absorb very soon such schools, and the others would keep up private schools.

Rev.
Father Fitz Henry.

Sept. 7th, 1891.

3673. Has not that cut-throat policy, as you call it, been beneficial in England, and productive of immense public good since 1870 ?—By accident, perhaps.

3674. Why by accident ?—As soon as the School Board in England finished its work of school supply which was necessary, then the School Board lenders were not satisfied with that, but they commenced immediately to cut into all the work that had been done for fifty years before, and they are still not satisfied.

3675. But has not that insatiable desire to cut in resulted in the public good ?—If the educational wants of the country are supplied sufficiently and satisfactorily, then one school interfering with the other is no longer educationally good. Rivalry is good up to a certain point in education just as in trade, but beyond that, somebody has got to suffer. Some rivalries are healthy ; some destructive.

3676. Do you consider the system of rivalry raised by the board schools in England is prejudicial to public interests ?—If persisted in.

3677. When must it stop, and where ?—It is very hard to say when it must stop ; it will not stop as long as the ideas of it's promoters remain as they are, and those ideas are not wholly educational. If it were not for political motives, the School Board supporters in England would not do half as much as they have done. If there was no Church of England influence ruling three parts of the education of the country, you would not have so much School Board zeal, and if there were no Conservatives, you would not have such a Liberal cry for free education. Much of the cry is outside educational motives altogether in England.

3678. But does not the fact of so many children in this Colony not being reached by any education, show the necessity for creating fourth class schools of some sort for the poorer children ?—If the Government entered into a simple arrangement with the present managers of mission schools, they could call these schools what they liked, so long as the present managers had fair influence in the management of the schools ; then you would have the use of their buildings and you would have their support. Children unreached are not in large towns where you propose these fourth class schools.

3679. Would not the effect then be to force into these mission schools possibly the children of parents who have no wish to use these mission schools or denominational schools ?—Practically there are very few children in any town who are not in one or other of the mission schools.

3680. But under a system of compulsion, would not the parents of Jewish children, for instance, prefer to have a school which was not denominational at all ?—These mission schools in practice are just as undenominational as any school you can have. Many Jews prefer schools under Roman Catholic management. Their conscience clause is stricter.

3681. If they are undenominational, why not have one big undenominational school into which they can all go ?—I say they are undenominational as far as any interference with the religion of the children is concerned. They are not undenominational in their management, inasmuch as they belong to a church body, but I can quite conceive of a public undenominational school being just as much in the hands of a church body as any of these mission schools that are now clearly in the hands of a church body. In this country you can hardly use the word "undenominational" in connection with the management of any school. The denominational forces are so strong in this country, that except those forces neutralize each other in any particular instance, some one or other denomination has the dominating influence in the schools, and just as much and sometimes more so than in the mission schools to which you object. In no case can you bundle all a town's children into a big school.

3682. Suppose that Government allied itself with one of the schools, making that one totally undenominational in it's teaching, would not the effect ultimately be to draw all into that undenominational school ?—That might occur in the course of two or three generations, but I doubt it, and in the mean time education suffers. Moreover, it would not be right for the Government to ally itself with any denomination for a purpose of that kind to the exclusion of others, equally deserving.

3683. For the purpose of making it totally undenominational in it's teaching, I say ?—To all intents and purposes the teaching at present is non-sectarian, that is, there is as much use of the conscience clause made in these mission schools, as far as I know them, of all denominations, as there is in the public schools, for you have children of all denominations going to the mission schools, and you never hear very much outcry about any undue religious influence, while the majority receive positive religious instruction as in so many undenominational public schools.

3684. Then I understand you to say that whether through prejudice, sentiment or whatever it is, there are forces in existence which will prevent the Government starting beneficially fourth class public undenominational schools ?—Yes, I think there are only about twelve large towns with over 2,000 population, where the question of fourth

Rev.
Father Fitz Henry.

Sept. 7th, 1891.

class schools *versus* mission schools really presents a difficulty. Outside of those there is generally only one undenominational school in all the other places in the Colony for whites.

3685. In Cape Town is there not a necessity for creating another school to reach the lowest class of whites. Sir Langham Dale says so, does he not ?—Cape Town is different from other towns, and has to be dealt with specially. Ragged schools are needed.

3686. As we grow in numbers, will not the same difficulty arise elsewhere. We grow slowly. Would you start a fourth class undenominational school in Cape Town ? —The difficulty is, who is to manage such a school ? I do not know Cape Town, and therefore I cannot speak accurately as to it. There is a number of white mission schools in Cape Town, and I should make some arrangement whereby these mission schools might be called public elementary schools, or fourth class schools if you will, under church and parental management and guarantee.

3687. How would you force them to receive all the poorer children brought by the attendance officer ?—He has no right to bring a child to any particular school ; a child or parent must choose the school.

3688. Suppose the child holds its tongue and says, I will not go to school ?—Then the parent can speak.

3689. Suppose the child has no parent ?—If there be no parent or guardian, I presume the magistrate would step in and apprentice it.

3690. Where would you take such a child to, to the Roman Catholic, Church of England, or Dutch Reformed Church school ?—As those schools have a conscience clause as in the case of public undenominational schools, you can take the child where you like, or to the nearest school.

3691. Would it be fair for the attendance officer to take all such children to one school ?—The parent or guardian should name the school.

3692. And where there is no parent or guardian the officer should exercise his own discretion ?—Yes ; the schools are all equally undenominational under a conscience clause.

3693. And would you force these schools to take them without payment ?—If the Government provides a sufficient amount of aid to carry on the school, say for 100 children, it makes very little difference whether they take 20 additional children free or not. There is a point beyond which they cannot take them because they cannot do the work for the money.

3694. Then if the Government pays according to the number, you think these denominational schools or mission schools would take the children upon receiving an additional grant in proportion to the number ?—I think so. Government cannot force a school to supply education, unless it gives that school the means, especially the poorer class of schools.

3695. It is stated that in the undenominational school here they have two branches, one the upper and the other the lower, and the managers have been forced into that arrangement by the lower social position of some of the white children. How would you deal with that in these mission schools ?—The children in the mission schools are generally of the same social class ; there may be one a little above or one a little below, but one or two does not much matter, they are nearly all of the same social class, and there is no difficulty ; the course is the same.

3696. But do not you think the difficulty may arise elsewhere ?—No ; the public school here commences a course of instruction which does not end at the three r's . Those boys who have to be put into the branch school, finish their course of instruction at the three r's ; it is purely an elementary school ; the other boys in the higher school aim at matriculation, the school higher, or the civil service examination, as final.

3697. Would you limit these mission schools to teaching the three r's ?—Yes ; they should be purely elementary schools, covering the standards.

3698. What school would you provide for those who wish to go beyond that ?— The children attending the mission schools, as a rule, or with very few exceptions, go to work as soon as they reach the fifth standard. As a matter of fact very few of them reach the fifth standard.

3699. Do the children of the middle or trade classes go to the mission schools ?— Artisans send their children. Few of the "middle class," if there is such a class.

3700. Do not they aspire higher than that in many cases ?—Not unless they are well to do.

3701. What school would you have for them ?—As a matter of fact, in towns they go to a higher grade school.

3702. Such as St. Aidan's College ?—Yes ; or to the public school or grammar school.

3703. Have you anything to suggest with regard to St. Aidan's; is there any- thing unfair in the Government action towards such a school, taking into considera- tion that we are dealing with Elementary education?—St. Aidan's school is a higher grade school or college; it does not merely aim at teaching the three r's and merely elementary work; it collects from all parts of the country the sons of the better class of the farmers and professional men, and merchants, and gives them a higher educa- tion, similar to that imparted in the higher grade first class schools, or in what we might call University Colleges. We have passed during the last seven or eight years a good proportion in the matriculation and civil service examinations, and some higher. It ought to receive aid; Sir Langham Dale intended to bring it under the Higher Education Act, with St. Andrew's and the undenominational public school.

Rev. Father Fitz Henry.

Sept. 7th, 1891.

3704. As an elementary school, you do not think it is entitled to or requires aid? —It is not an elementary school. It would have to be classed as something different, as a University College or a District Boarding School.

3705. There is elementary teaching, but that does not require aid does it?—Of course we have a preparatory department where the pupils are trained for something higher, but it is done in a different manner from that adopted in a simple elementary school; Latin is taken at an early stage, also Dutch and French.

3706. Is the character of the teaching similar to that at St. Andrew's College?— Yes, as far as it goes to the survey and B.A.

3707. But you receive no aid at all?—No.

3708. Do you think you should?—St. Aidan's College and schools of that kind for the higher class of children have arisen from the necessities of the country, as they afford boarding facilities, and having met the wants of education in this way, they might with advantage be inspected if they wished to be aided by the Government, and also aided under some of the heads into which the Education Department divides undenominational schools, district boarding schools, and colleges under the Higher Education Act.

3709. What principle of aid would you apply to non-aided elementary depart- ments?—In Graham's Town we have St. Aidan's College, St. Andrew's College, the Wesleyan High School, the Diocesan Girls' School, the Convent School, and a Diocesan Grammar School. These schools are providing for a large number of children outside Graham's Town elementary and higher education. I believe there are some 300 children boarding at these schools, or boarding in the town and going to school in Graham's Town, and they come from all parts of the country. They are the children of taxpayers, and they centralize at Graham's Town. Because we receive no aid or inspection from the Government, the parents cannot tell, except so far as by the result of the University examinations, how the schools are conducted at all. The parents are scattered over the country in various parts, and have not facilities for educating their children locally, so they send them at great expense to some central place where they can get a decent education; hence I think that schools which are really doing a good work for the country should be aided and inspected.

3710. To what extent would you aid them?—I would not lay down any particular amount of money, but I would grade the schools by inspection, so that they should be equal to the first, second or third class public school as the case might be, boys and girls, and aid accordingly. In the case of St. Aidan's, it would be more like a university college, something like the Gill College at Somerset East, which collects a large number of students at a suitable centre for boarding and supervision.

3711. You think that each school should be aided according to its grade?—Yes.

3712. Similar to the aid given to public undenominational schools, according to their grade?—Yes. That would meet the justice of the case, and I do not think it would interfere with the first class school, because each institution has its *raison d'être*, although in the same town.

3713. You think that as long as they are not aided they would have some grievance as tax-payers?—Yes; and education is injured to a certain extent.

3714. Would not the effect of giving this aid be to multiply these schools and possibly bring into existence a Salvation Army school for instance?—Schools of the class referred to require a large sum of money to start them, and they are not multiplied often. At Port Elizabeth there is the Convent school, which since its establishment has cost in sites, buildings and other expenses £27,000, also a costly ladies' collegiate school. St. Aidan's College in Graham's Town has cost £17,000. I do not know how much the Wesleyan High School has cost, but I should say between £7,000 and £10,000. I do not think these schools would be multiplied; they are schools for the whole of the Eastern Province, not simply for Graham's Town or even Albany. They take children from all parts of South Africa. At St. Aidan's there are boys from Cape Town, Kimberley, Johannesburg and the Free State, as at Rondebosch and Stellenbosch.

Rev.
Father Fitz Henry.

Sept. 7th, 1891.

3715. Where is the limit you would make ?—This class of schools would come under Sir Langham Dale's idea of district boarding schools. In his reports from time to time he expected that the district boarding schools would multiply, but they have not done so, because there is always a difficulty with regard to the money for large buildings, especially in the country, and therefore the children concentrate in the towns where buildings and the appliances for education are more easily obtained. They come to central places for discipline and " finishing."

3716. If I understand you rightly, you think the principle of district boarding schools ought to be applied to schools in towns ?—Yes; in towns as well as in the country, irrespective of boarding departments attached to undenominational public schools.

3717. Would not the effect of that be to strip the undenominational public schools of pupils ?—As a matter of fact that has not been so to any extent.

3718. If they are better aided they would perhaps be more efficient, and in that way prejudice the undenominational public schools would they not ?—They would not be necessarily better aided.

3719. But if they are aided in addition to their present means, might it not be the case ?—In practice they do not. The Paarl, Stellenbosch, Graham's Town are examples.

3720. But will they ?—The class of children coming to these schools of different grades come because they cannot get, nor would they get if they stayed, the same kind of education nearer home, except in very few instances. Parents send children to boarding schools for training as well as for mere knowledge.

3721. You said you thought it was most desirable to have an industrial department in connection with every mission school. White children as well as black require some sort of industrial education, do they not ?—Yes.

3722. If that be so, could you have efficient industrial departments in connection with every mission school, and would there not require to be concentration to have an efficient industrial department in connection with any elementary school ?—That would depend upon the kind of industry needed or practicable.

3723. What kind of industry do you think is needed for white children attending mission schools in Graham's Town ?—All they have been able to do in many places in England in that way under similar circumstances, has been a certain amount of needle work for girls and instruction in the use of tools for boys. In country schools in Ireland there is a garden attached, and the boys do a certain amount of cultivation; but you can do but little industrial work, where you have children only staying at school till they are 12 or 13. It must be very elementary and very limited, that is in the mission schools I speak of. In the case of needle work for girls there would not of course be much difficulty, and where there is a large number of boys, you might have a class for teaching the use of tools. In England in a number of places, the voluntary schools associate for the purpose of giving lessons in special industrial branches such as cookery and elementary science, just as the larger board schools do; and there is no reason why in Port Elizabeth, Graham's Town, King William's Town, and such places, if the teachers were available, certain days might not be appointed for holding these classes at central places.

3724. The pupils coming from the various schools to a certain centre for industrial education ?—Yes; if you had an over Board that would be able to bring all the schools and all the managers in touch with one another on an equal footing.

3725. Are you in favour of an over Board for that purpose ?—Yes. In connection with the supposed clashing of boarding schools in towns with the established first class school, I might remark that I do not think it would happen. As an example of that, in connection with the Convent in King William's Town, there are 100 boarders, the children of poor farmers and German immigrants, and some railway children I believe. They pay a very small amount of money and these children receive only an elementary education in the three r's. Some remain till they have passed the fourth or fifth standard, and these children while they are at school, as far as the means and circumstances at present allow, do receive a certain amount of industrial teaching. They have to do a good deal of work in the kitchen, dormitory, and garden, also washing and ironing, and they learn habits of industry in that way. The school was established specially for such class of children in that part of the country, and it has proved a great help in every way, without any interference with the young ladies' boarding department of the public undenominational girls' school in that town.

3726. What do they pay ?—Up to £2 a month. Sometimes their friends pay the fees, and people give subscriptions in aid. Part of the cost comes out of the higher boarding school, and the sale of garden produce also helps to support the institution.

3727. What is the higher school ?—There is a higher girls' boarding school of eighty for another class of children, who pay fairly well. There are among these latter about 20 girls (some of them of poor but respectable parents), who are kept there to be trained as teachers. Neither of these two boarding departments can, according to the regulations, at present receive any aid from Government, because there is a first class school with a boarding department for girls in the town. In that department there are 26 young ladies only.

3728. And they will not take assistance elsewhere than from you ?—Most could not pay the undenominational public school fees. The undenominational public school boarding department gets special aid from Government, as well as teachers' salaries and building grants.

3729. Why do not they go there ; is it on account of religious feeling ?—In the first place, these are children of poor farmers and railway employés, and they have not the money to go to a young ladies' school. There is of course some feeling about religion. In the case of the public undenominational school at King William's Town, the property is vested by a special deed in trustees belonging only to the English, Wesleyan, and Presbyterian churches, and the guarantors, according to the trust deed, must be members of those churches, and thus the Lutherans, Dutch Reformed, and Roman Catholics are excluded from any management in that public school, so that even if we wished to guarantee or take our share in the management, and send our scholars, we are excluded. We have therefore to deal with facts as we find them, whether you have denominational or undenominational over the door ; useful and necessary schools should not be excluded for the sake of a meaningless name, whatever the management.

3730. You said that it would be a good thing to have an over Board to urge united industrial education ; how would it work to cause such union ?—There is need for union between the managers and the teachers of the various kinds of schools that are established in the large towns. Each school grows up on its own lines, under its own management, and with its own object in view of higher or lower educational work, connected or not with any church, and this has continued for the last 20 years. We are therefore at the present time in face of a certain number of facts that we possibly, if we had to begin again, might have changed, but we must take things now as they are. I think a great deal of good might be done if there was some Board to bring managers and teachers into touch with one another.

3731. So as to have, among other things, one school for industrial purposes ?— Yes, and scientific teaching, drawing, and special subjects under special masters.

3732. Might it not ultimately be for literary purposes also ?—Not necessarily. It might be for pupil teachers training.

3733. Possibly it might lead to a combination for all purposes except religious ?— It would lead to better educational results, anyhow, but you cannot have all the children of one town without social distinctions of colour, creed, or grades of education in one school. You must separate blacks and whites, and boys and girls, into different grades. You must make the best of what material you have, and where it is possible to bring about any combination, to do so ; a village or a farm centre may be content with one school ; large towns must have many.

3734. Do you think a Board would have a good effect altogether ?—A Board more or less like the school attendance committees in England, which cover a very large area, and are very successful in their work might, with certain modifications, be suited to our circumstances here, not so much for towns as for town and district ; possibly it might develope into something better ; but you would have to begin very tentatively if you wished to get your ideas carried out by the country and by Parliament, once you speak of levying a local school rate on a fiscal or electoral division.

3735. Suppose you recognise all existing institutions, and you have this over Board elected by the ratepayers, with the duty imposed upon it of filling up the gaps and satisfying the central Government that there are sufficient schools for all the children in the district, the Government contributing largely towards education, do not you think such a Board would supply a want which at present exists ?—I am afraid the temper of the country would be against such a Board with rating powers, no matter how useful it might be. It may come.

3736. Do not you think it ought to come ?—If there is a special necessity for it and a general desire for it, and if such Board would take into consideration the many efficient institutions existing, and religious feelings as in Canada and Scotland, there would not theoretically be an objection to it. I may say that Cardinal Manning, through Mr. Arthur O'Connor, M.P., in England, at a great meeting held lately in London, countenanced a scheme for uniting the rival educational elements in England by having a representative School Board with power over every school in the district, giving to local managers in existence, or who may come into existence, the power of managing their schools internally, and then this body would have the power of distributing more impartially than is the case now any sums of money coming into its hands from rates or grants in aid.

K 2

Rev.
Father Fitz Henry.

Sept. 7th, 1891.

3737. Then they would have control over the rates?—They would have rating powers; but the rates would no longer be for the exclusive benefit of board schools.

3738. Did he not contemplate that the Government should also contribute something?—Of course; it was proposed in order to avoid the injustice of having one set of schools supported out of the pockets of other people who have to support their own schools as well. That state of things does not obtain here.

3739. You think that is a good scheme?—Theoretically.

3740. Why not practically?—Because in this Colony we have all voluntary schools, and also you have to take into consideration the kind of people that we have here and their ideas. You require a liberal educational spirit which will lead people not to mind taxing themselves or their neighbours for a good they don't share.

3741. Would not the effect of a scheme like Cardinal Manning's be to get good educational men elected on the Board?—Yes; in England.

3742. If the Government has the power to force that Board to do its duty, do not you think there would also be an inducement for the electors to put upon it the best men from an educational point of view?—Yes; but the difficulty is to get a rating Board made the law of the Colony.

3743. Suppose the ratepayers see that the guarantors in our public schools virtually never put their hands in their pockets, what practical objection is there to their nominees occupying the prominent position of being on the Board and advising the Government?—The fear on the part of the public would arise from this fact, that now the guarantors scarcely ever pay anything because of their responsibility, and so they make the fees come out, but if they were an irresponsible body, the deficit in the schools would be x or y.

3744. Is not that a good reason why you should make them responsible, and also make the rates responsible, because then the Board would represent the ratepayers, and they would take care that the expense was not great? If they represented the ratepayers, you would have a Board something like the Divisional Council, and they would not represent education. If I had the power of taxing you without any responsibility on my part, I might have an educational article that you would not like to pay for.

3745. Would not there be every inducement to elect good men?—I am afraid not. Suppose the Commission did propose such a thing to the country as local managers and an over Board, theoretically I would have no objection, but it should in any case be proposed permissively to the different districts. There are some districts or centres that might easily accept it, especially where there is only one school or a full school supply. In all the large places, however, there are so many interests involved, that people would be afraid either that too much money would have to be paid or that the money would not be equally distributed, especially with the experience of the past. The public school committees were supposed to have the function of these School Boards, but they exercised their power in keeping the money grant for a certain clique in every town. In Port Elizabeth, the Grey Institute has been established since the year 1856, with a large amount of money from the Government and also from lands, but they only cover 440 children in a population of 2,000 white school-going children in the town up to the present time.

3746. Suppose there was an obligation imposed in that case, which there is not now, of finding adequate schools for all the poor children in the place, to the satisfaction of the Government, they would then be forced to cover the whole and be less exclusive, would they not?—They would possibly reply that they did as much as they could for better education with the money they got. If they had had rating powers they would have covered more ground. But now the ground is covered by voluntary bodies and the needs of 1865 are met.

3747. Would not they have done their work better also?—They would, but now the school supply I think in Port Elizabeth is full. The schools are as it were crystallised. If the Grey Institute put a school in a part of the town where there were 400 children, they might not get ten into it.

3748. I suppose you have a fair knowledge of this district, have you not?—A fair knowledge.

3749. What additional facilities do you think can be provided to meet the wants of the children of the agricultural population in this country?—Taking the Albany district and its census population, we have 100 more children at school than one-sixth of the white population, and taking the supposed number of children throughout the Colony not accounted for, if we divide them over the 70 fiscal districts, they only amount to about 100 to 200 in each district. They may be more in one district than another. The facilities for children in the country are, thanks to Sir Langham Dale, so far as the Government is concerned, very fair: the thing is to try and make these advantages more known, and bring the people into touch with them, either through organizing Inspectors or an over Board. Clergymen and others could use their influence. The defect is not so much the want of school buildings. There are often groups of families in the country in isolated parts who need to have a circuit teacher or a farm school governess or tutor at homesteads. Clergymen might give more time among their own people, and try and get suitable teachers for them.

Rev. *Father Fitz Henry.* Sept. 7th, 1891.

3750. They should act as attendance officers in a way?—Yes, and helpers in many ways.

3751. People in the country districts would be able to reach a local Board better than the one central authority or the Inspector who only came occasionally, would they not?—Yes. Any local Board could make itself acquainted through the field-cornets and other means with any deficiency. If they could not put a school at each man's door, they could try and induce the people to send their children to farm schools. There are at the present time considerable facilities not taken advantage of.

3752. You think an over Board would be useful in utilizing more the present facilities afforded by the Government?—Yes. An over Board or school attendance committee might do that, even though it had not any rating powers. The school Boards in England were established to supply schools that were wanted in dense and poor populations, and to make up the deficit; the school attendance committees were appointed in the year 1876, under Lord Sandon's Act, to compel children to go to schools that were already provided for them, as they were in a great part of England by various agencies and denominations.

3753. *Mr. Rowan.*] How are the attendance committees paid?—I do not know that they are paid at all; they are voluntary and elected by the Board of Guardians. I believe they are unpaid, and they appoint local people to aid them. In this country, neither in the towns, villages, nor where there are groups of farms, is there much need for building schools; the deficiency in this country is more in regard to the isolated farmers' children. In Cape Town Sir Langham Dale says there are places enough for 7,000 children; in Port Elizabeth and Graham's Town there are also places enough, so I do not think that new buildings are absolutely required. Some schools need additions. The deficit in England is owing a great deal to the fact that the children in the elementary class of school are poor children, not able to pay the fees for a good education, but here in this country, outside the poorer mission schools, they are as a rule able to pay, and you are not likely to have a deficiency if the school is well managed. In the poorer class of mission schools where there might be a deficiency, that might be reached by a more liberal grant on the part of the Government. As to small village schools or where there are groups of farms, they generally fix upon a certain sum that they can pay every year, and they make it up without ever thinking of coming upon the rest of the ratepayers for it, so in this country it is only in the case where guarantors might stop paying, and there was a danger of the school collapsing, that an attendance committee might keep it going and say there must be a school, charging the local municipality or the Village Board, perhaps, with the cost, until some agreement was come to; but that would not be for very long probably. In the distribution of any money raised by the rates for deficiencies, there would be a difficulty, because the schools in this country are not homogeneous as they are in England. In England you have in the county a large number of elementary schools all of the same kind, but here you have a grammar school, a higher class public school, a village school, and private schools, boarding schools, &c., and the difficulty would be to which of all these schools would you pay a deficit. Graham's Town might object to pay a deficit in Bathurst, or *vice versâ.* The school attendance committee cannot build or carry on schools in England, but in this country, if there was need of a school, they might urge the people locally interested and the Government, and possibly the Divisional Council, to get a school built. The school attendance committee can also compel attendance in the local schools that are provided. The truant officials would be under the direction of this committee, though appointed by Government, and they would have to ascertain the number of schools in town and country, through the magistrates, field-cornets, police, or ministers of religion. If the school supply, whether farm school or otherwise, was deficient, or even if they found the teaching was weak, they could call in the services of an organizing inspector, schoolmaster, or clergyman to assist. That is one of the things very much needed in this country, somebody to teach the teachers how to teach. Most elementary teachers are untrained, and very often do not do their work to much purpose. It would be a good thing sometimes if they could have somebody even to classify their schools for them. You sometimes see in the Inspector's report " classification not good," and this injures the school work. Then such a Board might help in securing or suggesting competent teachers, and also assist further the creation of farm schools by urging the use of the farm school grants. They would also recommend

Rev.
Father Fitz Henry.

Sept. 7th, 1891.

schools of different grades already existing in large towns as Government schools under one name or another, and be able to advise whether the supply for a town was sufficient or not. In that way they would prevent the too great multiplication of schools, and yet retain existing efficient schools. Now, everybody tries to get a school where and when he can, and by any influence that he can; there is no one to supervise the whole of the schools in any one town or district, and bring those schools into touch with one another. It could also approach municipalities or divisional councils in case there was need for additional school buildings, and greater accommodation for existing schools. It could also negotiate loans from the Government for building purposes, like loans for irrigation, &c. This would be a way of improving a great number of our schools that are, according to the Inspectors' reports, in great need of improvement, even in towns. In Port Elizabeth, there is the nucleus of such a committee in the Teachers' Union. They have a depôt, and get different kinds of books from various publishers, so that all teachers can go there and select. They could also make an agreement between one school and another to use more or less the same kind of books in the same grades as far as possible. If they were under one Board, the classes in the different schools in a large town might be better graded, so that if children went from one school to another, which they are very much in the habit of doing, the difficulty would be in a measure met. They could also regulate the holidays. They might have in a town one higher class school, that would be really a high class school, where those who wished to continue their education for a time might go to, and there might be municipal bursaries and other favours connected with these schools. Some point of union is wanting between the various jarring elements at present, and I think in this way, each school would be got to do a certain amount of graded elementary work. Then they might as they do in Liverpool and several places in England, secure one teacher each for drawing, music, calisthenics, science, the teaching of agricultural chemistry, and so on, in cases where each school could not have a separate master for these special subjects. One teacher might be able to do all the science teaching in a town perhaps with the same set of apparatus. In some parts of England they go about with a set of apparatus to various schools, visiting them at certain hours each week. Men employed partly by the Government and partly paid by the fees of the students could do a certain amount of work of that kind. There are a great many pupil teachers in all the large towns, and what is a great want I think in this country, is good elementary teachers, both for town and country places. The pupil teachers at present are not well trained; they do a certain amount of teaching, but they have not method mistresses over them sufficient to give them a training at all equal to what pupil teachers in England receive. There might be a method master or mistress in central places who could give lectures to the pupil teachers, and possibly to the teachers themselves. As an instance, to my knowledge, Mr. Brady advised that a method mistress should be employed for the assistant teachers and pupil teachers in a certain school, and he said that after this instruction for about six months, he saw the greatest difference in the manner of the teachers and in the way they did their work when he came to the same school again. He said he was only sorry he could not remain for a time himself, so as to show them how to do their work just a little better. The exact training of pupil teachers, day scholars or boarders, is a thing that is much needed in this country. An attendance committee of the kind indicated would also inform the Education Department as to local needs and also bring pressure to bear on members of Parliament to urge the claims of a district in the Legislature. At present, unless you have a member of Parliament with the ear of a Minister, you can get nothing, although you see all your neighbours getting windfalls ; but if you had a representative committee of this kind, things would be different. Another thing is, they could get the rates removed from all the schools in towns. At the present time, according to a calculation I have here, some five or six schools in Graham's Town have to pay £183 in one year for municipal rates; and divisional rates for last five years as, for instance, the Public School, £51 ; St. Aidan's, £90 ; St. Andrew's, £23; Wesleyan High School, £58; Diocesan Girls' School. £44 ; and the Convent School, £44.

3754. *Dean Holmes.*] But there are other schools paying rates besides those, are there not ?—St. Aidan's, the Public School, Diocesan Girls' School, the Wesleyan High School, the Convent School. Shaw Hall, Good Shepherd, the Home, St. Bartholomew's, Diocesan Grammar School, and the three Kafir schools paid altogether £183 to the municipality last year. They tell me the Divisional Council took off one-third of the valuation as a favour, but they might put it on any year, according as they are in want. I should also add that the Divisional Councils in the Colony are £50,000 in debt, and the Municipalities are nearly £900,000 in debt. Graham's Town is some £30,000 in debt. That is one practical difficulty I see against any scheme for rating, while these bodies are nearly a million pounds in debt. I think they might, however, relieve the schools from the payment of rates, and also give bursaries to deserving scholars. They might also assist by giving sites for play-grounds, as it would not cost them much. I do not think Parliament would give Municipalities and Divisional Councils power to rate for educational purposes, looking at their present necessities, however good the thing may be theoretically. You might perhaps have it permissive, and give rating powers to those who wished it, where the schools are few, and they would not be likely to enter into competition with one another. At Uitenhage, for instance, the management of one school is under the Divisional Council; I do not know whether or not there is any murmuring about it. It paid a small sum of £37 lately towards a branch for poorer boys.

Rev.
Father Fits Henry.

Sept. 7th, 1891.

3755. *President.*] If all the schools are doing well and paying, and you give them something more from the Government, where is the fear?—Some schools are paying ones. The Uitenhage girls' school pays so well that the local church body or Kerkeraad, according to the Inspector's report, can put £300 from the school into the church treasury every year. If there is a deficit in three years time, and you put it on the rates, the people who pay the rates would turn round and say, where is the money you saved?

3756. If the schools are paying now, the rates would not be touched, would they?—As long as the responsibility of meeting the deficit is thrown upon the people interested in each school, there will never be a very large one, but if it is thrown upon others they will not care much about collecting the fees or curtailing expenditure.

3757. Would it not be well that this ideal Board should be placed under the control of a central department to see that they did their duty?—Yes. In England, if the school attendance committee is in default, the Education Department has the power of sending down someone to do their work for two years or till they are willing to take it up again. That is a power I would give here as well.

3758. Suppose such a Board is created what would you do with regard to the property of undenominational public schools?—At present, three-fourths of the property belongs to the Dutch Reformed Church, and is lent to aid in the education of the country, and it is not likely that they will part with that property.

3759. How is the property lent?—They allow the local public school committee, whether it is in connection with the church or not, to use the school-room for a small rent.

3760. Does not the Government also contribute?—In some cases the Government has given building grants, on condition that the property is used for school purposes for twenty years.

3761. At the end of twenty years, any improvements revert to the original owners of the property, do they not. If it is a church property, it goes to the church?—Yes.

3762. Do you think that ought to be so. Would it not be a good thing to make it a condition of aid in future that it should always be public school property?—The school committees might be willing, but if the church body to whom the property belongs was not willing, what can you do, unless you give a loan only where property is not public.

3763. *Dr. Berry.*] Suppose they were willing to part with it to a Board?—The Board might buy it for school purposes and vest it in trustees.

3764. Then you would give the Board power to hold property?—I would prefer to give the Government power to hold all public school property.

3765. Why not vest the power in a Board?—We have no Boards now, only local committees using church property, Government property, or property in trust as at King William's Town.

3766. *President.*] The proposed Board would be a corporate body, would it not?—The local Boards at present are voluntary bodies, and you cannot incorporate a voluntary body. The simplest way would be, if there is a school building erected with public money, to have it vested in the Government, represented either by the Education Department or the Magistrate, or both together, as they do in Ireland.

3767. Why not in a Board?—If a School Board for the whole district with the right of succession is created, you might make it a corporate body. A school attendance committee in England is not the holder of property, but the local managers or church bodies. I would have no special objection if such a Board is called into existence, to it's becoming the holder of property. The Hon. Mr. Justice Smith in the Commission of 1879 thought it unnecessary, as trustees could always be appointed.

3768. Would you make the Civil Commissioner a member of that Board?—Not necessarily.

3769. Would you put the Civil Commissioner for the time being on the over Board?—I think so, as Government pays so much.

3770. Would you make him the chairman?—Not necessarily. They could elect their own chairman.

Rev.
Father Fitz Henry.

Sept. 7th, 1891.

3771. Who else would you put on the Board?—It should be partly elective and partly nominated.

3772. How many members would you put on the Board altogether?—In England it is regulated by the population of the district. The minimum is five and the maximum fifteen.

3773. *Dean Holmes.*] How many should be elected, and how many nominated?—I would suggest that three should be elected and two nominated, and in that proportion.

3774. Nominated by whom?—By the central Government.

3775. *President.*] Would you have the other members elected by the voters for the Divisional Council or members of Parliament?—I would not be in favour of going to the electorate as a body at present, but if so, I would say that voters for the members of Parliament should elect, with a "cumulative" provision, as in England.

3776. The majority elected by the ratepayers and two nominated, with the Civil Commissioner in addition; is that what you suggest?—Yes; in case such a Board is proposed at all.

3777. Have you anything to say about the facilities for the education of the children of railway employés?—I think you should concentrate the teaching where you can, as at Alicedale and Burghersdorp now, and where you cannot, deal with individual cases in the best way possible in connection with neighbouring farm schools, for instance.

3778. Do you think the existing machinery for the education of these children adequate or otherwise?—It is rather inadequate, on account of the poverty of the people and their comparative isolation.

3779. *Dr. Berry.*] You think there is need for further assistance in the matter?—Yes, in establishing schools at more centres.

3780. *Dean Holmes.*] You speak of the poverty of the railway employés; are they not a comparatively well-paid class?—I mean they would not be able to send their children as boarders, away from home, unless assisted very much.

3781. *Dr. Berry.*] Are you acquainted with the facilities offered?—Yes.

3782. Do you think they are adequate?—I think there is every desire on the part of the Government to help them as far as possible, but the difficulty arises from the circumstances of the case. Unless you undertake to board all the very isolated railway children in some central place, you cannot cover the whole want. You might do a great deal by removing men with families to certain centres near school accommodation for a time, but I believe they say that the exigencies of the service will not always admit of that.

3783. *President.*] You would suggest that the bachelors should be placed in isolated places and the married men removed nearer to school centres?—Yes, as far as possible, and it could be done more than it is if the sub-inspectors wished.

3784. *Dr. Berry.*] Would it not be a good thing to take these children if possible away from local influences on the railway and place them at some boarding school at a distance?—It is simply a question of expense.

3785. *President.*] Do you think they would be better at a boarding school than isolated along the line?—If they could get a short time at a cheap boarding school, the discipline and example would be of great benefit to these children, if it was only for a year. I know that is the case with certain railway children at the convent lower boarding school at King William's Town, but of course we cannot expect the country to do everything for these people.

3786. What would be the cost of boarding a child here in Graham's Town?—I have formed no opinion. I suppose the cost would vary with circumstances and the hire of buildings.

3787. *Dr. Berry.*] It has been suggested that the influence of the railway on these children is not desirable, and that in their own interests it would be better that they should be taken away?—They are much in the position of isolated farm children. The influence of a place like Alicedale might be prejudicial, but I do not know that the evil, except in special localities, is so great that you are called upon to deal with it directly.

3788. *Dean Holmes.*] Are you aware that Sir Langham Dale says that further facilities are not required?—He means facilities apart from taking away the children and boarding them, I suppose. The railway people might be urged to form groups of schools and unite with the farmers. It is a matter of organization; you must either do that, or put the children at a boarding school at the expense of the Department. I do not know what else you can do. In some cases families remain at one place a long time without any means of instruction at all. Sir Langham Dale's offers are adequate. It is for maintenance engineers and clergymen to take them up.

3789. *Dr Berry.*] Are you in favour of extending to the children of railway employés the capitation grant of £3 given to children in farm schools?—Yes.

!Rev.
Father Filt Henry.

Sept. 7th, 1891.

3790. Would you extend the facilities also to the children of the trading class in the country—say Kafirland traders. Might not they also come under the benefit of these capitation grants?—The children of traders, railway employés, and farmers should be equally assisted. Their circumstances are the same.

3791. *President.*] Have you thought of the subject of night schools?—I think that night schools would be useful. They are needed very much.

3792. Do you limit yourself to Graham's Town, or do you speak generally?—In all towns they would be useful.

3793. *Dean Holmes.*] Both for boys and girls?—Girls generally receive a better education than boys in this country, with few exceptions.

3794. *President.*] What would you do for boys in the way of night schools?— Boys leaving school at a comparatively early age, as they often do here, might be encouraged to continue their studies in night schools. It would often prevent their getting used to the freedom of the streets and beyond the control of their parents.

3795. Are there any night schools in existence here in Graham's Town?—Yes; but very small and irregular.

3796. What are they in connection with?—There are some private night schools. At present in the Convent school they have a continuation school for boys who have to go to work at an early age. Some boys we cannot get to come.

3797. How would you create these schools?—Large public or white mission schools having a certain influence over their scholars might have a continuation school for boys who have to leave with a very poor education, as the greater number do.

3798. The same school buildings would be used for the purpose, I suppose?— Yes, if no others are found available.

3799. How would you find teachers?—There are possibly young teachers, zealous and earnest, who would be willing for a certain remuneration, either from fees or a capitation grant from the Government, to teach in these night schools a certain number of evenings in the week.

3800. What fee do you think should be charged?—I cannot fix any particular fee.

3801. *Dean Holmes.*] What would you say to ten shillings a month from the boys themselves?—It would depend upon the class of boys. Some of them, perhaps, earn a little money for their parents, and could not pay so much. The boys who are better off probably remain at the ordinary day school, and do not want a night school. Perhaps they might pay half-a-crown a month.

3802. What contribution do you think the Government should give?—It would depend upon the number in the school.

3803. Should the Government give as much as the boys give?—It would be best determined by some local committee or by an over Board for instance. It would depend upon what they get teachers to do the work for. Some might do it voluntarily perhaps, while others would want to be well paid.

3804. *President.*] Ought there not to be some sort of system throughout the country?—It depends upon the class of school and scholars in each locality. The elementary subjects should be first attended to.

3805. Would you have more than one class of night-school?—They would be all of an elementary class; not necessarily the same subjects taught. Some boys would need to rehearse what they had gone over before; others might possibly be induced to learn a little more.

3806. *Dean Holmes.*] Would you approve of a capitation grant from the Government, provided a certain number of attendances was made?—The school should begin with a certain number fixed by the Department, and then a capitation grant on that number and above it would be the easiest way.

3807. Provided a certain number of attendances were made?—Yes. That should be the rule, and the number should be checked.

3808. Something like the English plan?—Yes.

3809. Are you aware that in England, evening schools can be called into existence without there being a school attendance committee or school board, merely by voluntary agency, applying to the Government, and if the school is kept open 45 times, then it is inspected and a grant is made?—Yes. The same thing could be done here, and they could be inspected as farm schools are by local headmasters of undenominational public schools.

3810. *Dr. Berry.*] Could not you graft some kind of technical education on to these night schools, such as drawing for instance?—Drawing is one of the subjects taught in England, and would be most useful.

3811. *President.*] Have you considered the matter of technical education?—No, not in this country. Technical education is determined by local wants. It is little use teaching the use of machines to South African boys, because there are no machines or

Rev.
Father Fitz Henry.

Sept. 7th, 1891.

manufactures to speak of. You may teach agriculture where it is an agricultural country, and the use of tools in an elementary way to boys who are likely to have to live by their labour. That is about all you can do in this country. There is a certain point to which we can go in preparatory work in technical education and no further. The Kindergarten begins it: manual training in drawing to scale, use of tools on wood and iron, sewing for girls till the time for leaving school comes; we can do no more.

3812. Would you connect an agricultural school and a technical school in one. Take Graham's Town, for instance, would it be wise and practicable to start such a school?—In a large number of schools in this country the elements of agricultural science could and ought to be taught. An agricultural school proper for young men would include much technical work in connection with farming.

3813. Even in mission schools?—Yes; to boys over the fourth standard, who would be able to read a book fairly well, and who were likely to take to farm life afterwards.

3814. It has been said that the mission schools were intended for the blacks; in your mission schools the children are wholly white, are they not?—Yes; and it has been always so.

3815. How would you provide education for the blacks?—I have no opinion in detail beyond this, that the teaching of the coloured classes ought only to reach a low standard, say the third standard, but unfortunately very few even reach that. If you have a good teacher, he can do a great deal in these schools if the children remain any length of time.

3816. Would you have anything else besides literary teaching?—They might be taught a little gardening where there is ground about the school, as is the case in Ireland in many of the national schools.

3817. You think they should do a certain amount of work daily as part of the school instruction?—Yes; I should insist on manual work of some kind daily.

3818. Does the plan you refer to succeed in Ireland?—Yes; the boys like it. Many teachers are trained to give it, or go to model schools for a "vacation course."

3819. What time would you devote to such industrial teaching?—About an hour a day would suffice. The great thing is to initiate the boys into habits of labour at an early age, and in connection with land.

3820. Would you apply compulsion in towns?—I think so, where there are sufficient schools for natives.

3821. Where would you draw the line between blacks and whites in Graham's town?—There would be no difficulty in Graham's Town. In Cape Town there might, but they can manage that among themselves.

3822. How would you manage it?—One or two coloured children in a white school would not be noticed very much perhaps, but there is just a point where you destroy a school by the introduction of coloured children.

3823. What power would you give the truant officer in regard to colour, if he has to collect these boys from the streets?—He should use his discretion.

3824. Take coloured boys to a coloured school, and white boys to a school for whites?—Yes; he must use his eyes, and study the feeling of the place. He ought to know.

3825. Have you considered the language question at all?—I have not been much in the Dutch districts.

3826. In Ireland the bi-lingual difficulty has existed, has it not?—Yes, to some extent. From an educational point of view, if you in any way force the partial study of two languages, or if in the case of Dutch in the Elementary examination, you destroy its elementary character and deprive a large number of candidates from going in for that examination, you injure education; but, from another point of view, if you have to deal with a people and their language, a certain amount of latitude must be allowed, as in the case of the Welsh. The Welsh language is much more difficult even than Dutch to learn, and the school authorities have allowed the people to use the Welsh language in the parish schools, principally in the lower standards, where the teacher avails himself of the spoken language to teach English, and *vice versâ*, with the two translations. Instead of grammar, they have in some of the schools used the translation from one language to another, which is one method of teaching grammar, but the Welsh people have a desire to preserve, in some degree, their own language. At the same time, they do not allow it to interfere with their keen desire to acquire English, the result of which is that the knowledge of Welsh to a certain extent is spreading, but the knowledge of English is spreading more in places where, perhaps, English was never spoken before, according as the bi-lingual schools spread.

3827. That is the result of using Welsh to some extent in explaining the English teaching?—Yes; it helps in the elementary lower standards in teaching; that is, in

places where there is no English spoken at all. According as there is a wider know- Rev.
Father Fitz Henry.
ledge of English, there is then less necessity for the use of Welsh. Sir Langham Dale
encourages the study of Dutch wherever it is possible to teach it. Sept. 7th, 1891.

3828. Would you have a Dutch paper introduced into the Elementary examination as an optional subject, adding the marks to the sum total?—If you add Dutch as an optional subject, you would have then to give those not taking Dutch the choice of some other subject to make the examination fair.

3829. What other subject?—There might be a number of subjects or languages, as the case might be. One school might teach French, another German, another elementary science, or a primer of agriculture, or domestic economy.

3830. If Dutch were imported as a fifth subject, what would be wise to add as an alternative subject?—French or German, or Kafir in the case of Kafir candidates; some elementary science, or Latin, which would not be so very difficult for those preparing for the School Higher examination.

3831. Do all your boys at St. Aidan's learn Latin in the upper school?—They all learn Latin, with the exception of a few who are very young, and a few who leave it off, and go into the Civil Service class.

3832. *Dean Holmes.*] Would not you destroy the character of the Elementary examination if you added a fifth language paper?—From an educational point of view it would raise the standard of the Elementary examination too high for a considerable number, to whom it is now a final examination, but you might divide it into two parts, one division taking the present four subjects alone, and the other five. Have two classes and an extra list, as in the teachers' examination. That is one suggestion.

3833. *President.*] Seeing that so many boys learn Dutch, and so many who go in for the School Higher examination learn Latin, and a good many learn elementary science, would it be weighting the boys too much, do you think, to give an extra paper?—I do not think, in the case of schools like ours, they would mind whether there were four or five subjects. A number of the small staffed schools, with perhaps only one teacher, might experience a difficulty in getting instruction for the extra subject to balance Dutch, which cannot be taught in a large number of Eastern schools.

3834. Have you a teacher for Dutch in your school?—Yes; at St. Aidan's. A good many boys like to go up for the Civil Service examination, or they prefer Dutch for business purposes.

3835. Have you many Dutch boys at your school?—Scarcely any.

3836. *Dean Holmes.*] Are you in favour of relieving candidates for the School Higher examination from the necessity of passing the Elementary examination?—It might be optional. There are many candidates who would do better to go on to the higher examination without a serious break by the way.

3837. Do you think the Elementary examination very frequently interferes with the teaching of the school?—Yes, especially in the higher schools. The Elementary examination might be the finishing examination for a number of scholars. In the latter case, we don't complain.

3838. *President.*] How would it do, not to make the Elementary examination a necessary step to the higher, but import into it Dutch as a fifth subject?—That might answer in some cases, where facilities for teaching Dutch exist; not in other places.

3839. *Rev. Moorrees.*] As a matter of fact, you know that a good many Dutch boys now have taken Dutch while preparing for the Elementary examination, so that in reality the Elementary examination for them has lost its elementary character?—For all those boys who take an extra subject it has.

3840. So that the elementary character of the examination exists only for the English boys, not for the Dutch boys does it?—There are many Dutch boys who do not study grammatical Dutch.

3841. Speaking generally?—For those it has lost its elementary character; to a Dutch-speaking boy not so much.

3842. If we add Dutch to the Elementary examination, and give the option between French and German, or another subject, do you think it fair to assign the same number of marks to French and German as to Dutch?—It would be more difficult for an English boy to learn French or German, especially from an English teacher, than it would be for a Dutch-speaking boy to learn high Dutch from a Dutch teacher. If marks were given for actual work done, the boy who has to learn a strange language from a strange teacher, if he answers the paper equally well, has really done more work than the Dutch boy who has a general acquaintance with the subject, and is among Dutch surroundings, and with a Dutch master. If you wanted to promote Dutch, then of course you might give more marks in order to induce children to take Dutch rather than French or German, but if it was a case of marks for actual mental work, it would be different. In practice, Dutch is taken in preference wherever it can be taught.

L 2

Rev.
Father Fitz Henry.

Sept. 7th, 1891.

3843. The disadvantage for an English boy studying French or German would not be half so great, would it, as the disadvantage for a boy who has to do all his subjects in a foreign language?—That would depend very much upon the bringing up of the Dutch boy. A Dutch boy who studies on to the point of the Elementary examination knows English, if not from his home associations, from his school companions, nearly as well as a good many of the other boys; grammar is learned best by using two languages.

3844. But still, from an educational point of view, you are aware that the boy who has to acquire not only the knowledge, but the medium through which that knowledge is given him, is at a disadvantage over against the boy who knows the medium?—That is true. If a Dutch boy has not a sufficient knowledge of English, or has not acquired it within a certain time, he is labouring under a difficulty for a time.

3845. *Rev. Coetzee.*] What would you say to putting a Dutch boy on the same footing as an English boy with regard to the examination?—I do not know any way of doing it except by having an optional class with five subjects and a class with only four subjects. A number of small schools might be hurt in this way. Children would not have the opportunity of going in for the Elementary certificate, which they covet and prize, and education would be injured on account of the small staff of some schools not being able to teach the optional subject. In the larger schools it does not matter.

3846. *President.*] Would you suggest that in the Elementary examination a fifth optional paper be added and the result endorsed upon the candidates' certificate?—That might answer the purpose.

3847. *Mr. Theron.*] Do you know the relative number of Dutch and English children attending the schools of different classes?—I have not seen it stated anywhere.

3848. To which nationality would the largest number belong, do you think?—I think to the Dutch nationality but not necessarily to the exclusive Dutch speakers. Dutch candidates for the Elementary examination are bi-linguists from an early stage.

3849. So that virtually you would place the largest number of children at a disadvantage for the sake of the minority?—I do not see that there is a disadvantage. It is as difficult for an English boy to learn French or German as for a Dutch boy to get himself up in Dutch. They are as equal as we can make them. There is nothing to show that many Dutch boys are debarred from the examination through their want of understanding the English medium of instruction.

3850. Looking at the number of candidates going up for the Elementary examination, and the number going up for the Higher examination, we see that the former is the real test for the largest number, do we not?—I do not know that I ever counted the number of English and Dutch names respectively upon the elementary list, but I think a very fair proportion, if not the larger proportion of the names are Dutch, which would show that Dutch boys are able to do very fair work in comparison with English boys. It would be an interesting thing to go over the names of an examination paper of any one year.

3851. Suppose that was a final examination for all children, then you would compel the majority to take up a foreign language from the starting point to the end?—I am afraid we have not reached that being the final examination, when out of 22,000 children inspected of the mission schools, only 74 reached the fifth standard a short time ago, and out of 60,000 white children only 610 passed the Elementary.

3852. *President.*] What do you infer from that?—It indicates a very low standard. I might say, comparing late examinations, that more Kafir children in the Transkei schools passed in the fifth standard for the numbers, than in the white and mixed mission schools of the Cape Colony.

3853. *Dr. Berry.*] Is not the highest percentage on the average attained actually by the farm schools?—I think so. I have the statistics. The farmers' schools, taught by private tutors and governesses give the best results for the numbers.

3854. *President.*] According to the present system are the farm schools inspected?—Yes, every one.

3855. Do you think they are adequately inspected. Would not a Board inspector be more satisfactory and get more frequently at these schools than the present system?—Practically he might be the same man who now examines the schools.

3856. Are you aware that the inspection of the farm schools is not done by a Government inspector, but by the heads of public undenominational schools told off to do the work?—Yes.

3857. Are you aware that it has been stated that when the inspectors do inspect these farm schools, their inspection does not verify that of the heads of schools?—Yes; that may occur in cases where the teacher of the farm school is not very able, and where the local school teacher who inspects is disposed to be more or less lenient either towards the farmer or towards the teacher.

3858. What would you suggest should be done in that case?—I do not think that there is reason to make any change in the matter, because in these cases you must not expect as good teaching from a private teacher who is perhaps uncertificated, with farm children whose minds are not so well developed, as you would in the case of a school of the same grade in town. A certain amount of allowance must be made for circumstances. I might say also that some teachers on farm schools are better than many town teachers, and the results are better. In some cases I know of, the examination was just as strict, or more so, than that of the inspectors in ordinary schools, and I know also cases where a single teacher on a farm school passed fairly well the pupils on the farm, in the standards, and some of them even Dutch children, in the Elementary examination without ever leaving the farm, and in a comparatively short time and an early age, so that it very much depends upon the teacher that you get, and the talents of the pupils.

Rev.
Father Fitz Henry.
Sept. 7th, 1891.

3859. *Rev. Moorrees.*] Would it not be in the interest of the inspecting teacher to keep the number of passes down if he possibly can?—No; it is nothing to him.

3860. Does it not show badly for his school, if the proportion of passes is greater in the farm schools than in his own, and is not the temptation rather towards stringency than leniency?—There might be a case of rivalry between a very successful farm school and a local town school not far distant.

3861. *Dr. Berry.*] Would not that rather be an argument for having assistant inspectors. Is it not desirable to have uniformity of inspection in the interests of the pupils, teachers, and all concerned?—It might be the best plan, but the schoolmasters know exactly the standards, and how much it is that makes the standard. The present mode of inspection works well enough.

3862. Would it not be better, generally speaking, to increase the number of inspectors?—Generally it would. They do not reach sufficiently the schools they ought to inspect at present, let alone the farm schools.

3863. *Mr. Theron.*] You said that only a small percentage of these pupils comparatively come up to the standard of the Elementary examination; is that so?—If they go beyond the fourth or fifth standard, and the parents wish them to remain further at school, they are generally sent to a town boarding school. I speak of farmers.

3864. Suppose that is the case, do you hold that the medium of instruction for these children who have such a short time at school, should be in a foreign language or their own; which would benefit them the most?—In the case of children who remain but a short time at school and who do not know any language but their own, educationally it is better to teach them anyhow to read first in that language that they know. The position is very much the same in dealing with Kafirs, or Welsh and Gaelic speaking children.

3865. Then you would make the medium of instruction the mother tongue of the child?—If you give the child a year or two's instruction, it is better for the child to learn how to read in the language that is familiar to it, and it is easier for that child then to pass on to a new language later on that may become neccessary for it afterwards, than to try to teach it words that it cannot at all understand. Of course you have in a bi-lingual country all grades of knowledge of the other language; some who know a little, some who know more and some nothing. You have to judge of each case according to circumstances and teach accordingly.

3866. You would not compel an English child to take the Dutch language, or be instructed through the medium of Dutch, suppose he has only a short time for instruction would you?—I would give him instruction in his own language as absolutely neccessary in his after life.

3867. And you would do the same to the Dutch child?—Yes.

3868. Suppose the medium of instruction is in the Dutch language, would you consider an English child handicapped in that way?—The English child would be handicapped in two ways educationally. He would not learn how to read as well in his own language, and then he would be learning a language that would not be of so much use to him as English would. In the case of a Dutch child in similar cicumstances, although he would be handicapped as far as learning his own language was concerned, it would be counterbalanced by the use which he could afterwards make of English commercially in a country like this, speaking his own, but knowing how to read and write English as well.

3869. Then you mean to say that Parliament was wrong when it compelled candidates for the civil service to pass an examination in Dutch?—Civil servants have to earn their bread by their knowledge of Dutch very often as a *sine qua non:* It is a personal choice.

3870. Why should the Government demand it from the civil servants in an English Colony?—They pay the civil servants to attend to the wants, from a Government point of view, of a large portion of Dutch speaking people, and consequently, as in the

Rev.
Father Fitz Henry.

Sept. 7th, 1891.

Indian Civil Service, Englishmen are obliged to learn the languages of that country, so Dutch is required in a large Dutch speaking colony.

3871. Then you hold the idea that you must first commit an injustice that afterwards you may correct it ?—It does not follow, the cases are quite different. In the one case, the Civil Service, you pay a man for a certain kind of work which he cannot do unless he knows Dutch ; in the other case, the ordinary scholar, he is his own master, and chooses which language will serve him best, or both according to his opportunities.

. 3872. To what class do our civil servants mostly belong, Dutch or English ?—There used to be a large number of English, but the number of Dutch is increasing I have heard.

3873. Would they be equal do you think ?—I cannot tell.

3874. Do you think the Government of an English colony is not acting fairly towards the civil servants to compel them to pass an examination in Dutch ?—They do not act unfairly to the English; they do not compel them. If they choose to enter the Civil Service to attend to the wants of the Dutch people, then it is their duty to learn the language, as well as being a personal gain.

3875. But under any circumstances, whether they have to attend to the wants of the Dutch or English population, they must pass an examination in Dutch before they can enter the civil service, must they not ?—Yes ; because Dutch is so generally useful in the Civil Service, and they may be removed at any time, perhaps from a place where English only is spoken to a place where Dutch is spoken.

3876. You like to do justice to the Dutch population in that case ?—Certainly, and without any injustice to others.

3877. But not in school examinations ?—I do not say I would do injustice in school examinations. The cases are not parallel.

3878. Have people taken more to learning Dutch lately ?—Yes, very much so, wherever practicable.

3879. And are you going to throw stumbling-blocks in the way ?—For the class of pupils as a rule who go in for the Elementary honours and Matriculation examinations the advantages are equal as far as I see. The Dutch boys soon become fairly acquainted with English, and generally desire to have as good a knowledge of English, if not a greater knowledge, than of high Dutch. Dutch would be the stumbling-block to the English really.

3880. Would you consider it fair on the part of the Dutch population if they should stamp out the English language altogether ?—That was done in the case of Alsace and Lorraine since the time of the German invasion, by means of German schools and schoolmasters, and by the iron rule of Bismarck. No French language was allowed there, and the newspapers even were ordered to be printed in German, the consequence of which is that in one generation German has come to be generally spoken. Such methods, fair or not, are out of the question here.

3881. *Rev. Meorrees.*] Do you know the feeling of the inhabitants of Alsace and Lorraine against the German Government ?—Of course it is not amicable.

3882. Do you see any chance of stamping out the Dutch language in this country ? —In the first place, I do not want to see it stamped out. I should like to know Dutch myself well as far as that is concerned. The only thing is, you may afford every facility for learning Dutch, and in some degree favour its teaching, without injuring education or doing injustice to other people. That is the only point where I draw the line. I respect the sentiments of a people even in the matter of a language which may not perhaps be beneficial to them; if they like it, let them have it.

3883. Why should it not be beneficial : are you acquainted with Dutch literature at all ?—No. I know there is a Dutch literature, but compared with other European literatures it has not the same likelihood of spreading or being known, whatever its intrinsic merit. The translated works of Hendrik Conscience are in all our Catholic libraries.

3884. Do you think if you exclude Dutch from the Elementary examination you discourage the teaching of the language ?—I think that giving a place to Dutch in the Elementary examination would give an impetus to the teaching in many places where it is not well studied now.

3885. *Mr. Theron.*] From your observation, do not you think that these two languages will, perhaps for generations to come, have to go hand in hand in this country ?—It is likely.

3886. And if so, is it not better for one to help on the other instead of discouraging it ?—I do not want to discourage it ; the only difficulty with me is that in asking me to learn the language, something is imposed upon me that I do not want or is out of my reach, just in the same way as if I wanted you to learn something that was very pleasing to me which you did not like, and of which you did not see the value.

Rev.
Father Fitz Henry.

Sept. 7th, 1891.

3887. Seeing that the Dutch population, which is the largest European population in the colony, do all they can to encourage in their children a desire for English, do not you think it would be well for the English to do the same to the Dutch?—A great many of the English boys in the higher schools do learn a great deal more Dutch than ever they learned before, and it is only up to a certain point in the educational life of a child where you can do very much with a second language not locally spoken. Among the great number of English speaking people in this country, the difficulty is not how to learn a little more Dutch, but to learn even the rudiments of English. Where a Dutch child knows only its own language, I would say make the most of that language, and the same with regard to an English child, because our standards of education, whether Dutch or English, are so very low that you do not get very far into either of them: aiming at both we master neither.

3888. In the cause of education itself, would it it not be a duty on the part of the English to encourage Dutch so as to raise the standard?—It is encouraged so far as the Education Department is concerned. Encouraging Dutch where it is not heard or can't be taught, raises no standard.

3889. Up to a certain point you would allow us a certain privilege, but when we come to the real point of union, namely, the Elementary examination, where we say, give us an optional test for our children and your children, there you object?—I do not object to two optional tests. I object to an optional test which favours you only. If it is one optional test, and that Dutch, it is out of my reach, and it is not optional to me, though it is to you.

3890. French and German are not recognised official languages in this country, whereas in Parliament and the law courts, Dutch and English are used are they not?— If there were the same means for teaching Dutch to an English child in the Eastern Districts as in the Western Districts, the difficulty would not arise, but in a great number of the schools in the Eastern Districts, there are no means for teaching Dutch. We are not all M.L.A.'s, and we try to avoid the law courts.

3891. *Rev. Moorrees.*] If the means were available, what would you do?—It is very likely that optionally we would learn Dutch. At St. Aidan's, where they learned French or German, as soon as a Dutch teacher came, they took Dutch and I do not know that very many learn either of the other languages now, so it is satisfactory where you have the means, but in a large number of schools there is really no means of learning Dutch, while many teachers are able to teach French, German, or science, or the elements of agriculture.

3892. *Mr. Theron.*] You take a Dutch child from home, and compel it to learn four subjects in a foreign language, and you place it on an equal footing with another child who has had its instruction in its own tongue; does it not seem hard?—Children are different from grown-up people in learning a language. If you take Dutch children away from home to where English is spoken, they acquire just as much knowledge of it very soon as children brought up in it, without losing their mother tongue: besides, it is begging the question to suppose that all Dutch candidates have no acquaintance with English from an early age.

3893. Will just picking it up be of any benefit to them in an examination?— They do pick it up and make a very good figure in the examinations, as against the English. I see a great many Dutch names at the top of the list always.

3894. Take the case of two children, English and Dutch, and train them in the four subjects required, and suppose the English child takes a liking to Dutch, and takes the Dutch paper, would you reward that child?—Yes, if the University examination was arranged like the University examinations in Ireland, where fourteen subjects are written at the top of the Result List, and as you run along you find the number of marks a boy has got in each. He can take fourteen subjects, or he can take only two, or he can take honours in any particular subject. Everyone can take as much as he likes; but constituted as the Elementary examination is, of course, many boys might know things for which they do not get much credit, such as music or drawing, or Latin, which do not come within the scope of the examination. I would recommend the Irish mode of marking and then add Dutch to the examination: Few could object, as Celtic in Ireland with bursaries.

3895. *Rev. Moorrees.*] In the matriculation, Greek is optional, and there is no alternative subject. If a boy takes Greek, the marks are added to the total. If he does not, he loses the marks. There are many schools where there is no occasion to learn Greek, and yet the pupils desire to go up for matriculation. That is not considered unjust, is it?—With regard to Greek, the University may in its profound knowledge have some recondite educational reason for imposing Greek, but if they do impose it, everybody starts fair. It is a tongue foreign to all. It is necessary only to those who go higher. It is only when students are very young that the medium is difficult to one and not difficult to the other, speaking of Dutch and English scholars.

Rev.
Father Fitz Henry.
Sept. 7th, 1891.

3896. During the time that the one is acquiring the medium, the other can go on increasing his knowledge, so I should say the one has a start before the other ?—The results we have do not show that in the case of Dutch and English children going in for the examinations, the Dutch are behind. If you can show that there is a great number of boys who are prevented from passing the Elementary examination because they cannot well do so in English, and because their Dutch is not recognised, and that therefore they are handicapped and their education lowered, then you would have a good case.

3897. I cannot show that the Dutch boy does not pass well, but is it not very likely, if you take the average, you will find that Dutch boys pass their examinations at a later age than the English boys ?—That may be so, but perhaps they have commenced their education later also, or stay longer at school.

3898. If two boys start at the same age and in the same school, and one has to acquire the medium and the other has not, will not one have to take a longer time than the other ?—It is difficult to give an answer to a general question of that kind, considering differences in brain power.

3899. Take it that all things are equal ?—The one may lose the time, but then he has *two* languages to make up for it.

3900. *Dr. Berry.*] Would the fairest way to get over this difficulty be to set a paper for the Elementary examination in both Dutch and English, and let the results be tabulated accordingly ?—I do not think that would satisfy the people who want to promote Dutch in English schools.

3901. Would it be fair ?—Yes; theoretically it would, but it would not settle the question.

3902. If that is impracticable, does it not seem that the only other way is to give the option of a separate paper in Dutch, and let the marks be counted on a separate list ?—Yes; that or the Irish method of marking.

3903. What do you say to the proposal to make the Elementary examination either wholly in English or wholly in Dutch, at the option of the candidate ?—I say it would be impracticable, even from a Dutch point of view.

3904. Why ?—First, there are no schools up to that grade which are wholly taught in Dutch, with books and masters fitted for that work; they could not do it, and if they did do it, they cut children off from learning English, and that would be an injury to children in a commercial country like this. The parents would object; hence the dissatisfaction with the Grey College in Bloemfontein.

3905. Then that seems to prove that the bulk of the examination must be conducted in English ? —Yes, whether the candidates are Dutch or English.

3906. Then it seems fair in the same way that children who get an education in Dutch, or whose mother tongue is Dutch, should have an opportunity in the same way of proving that they have the knowledge?—Yes; and of course meeting the desire of their parents and their countrymen to foster their native language. I attach some importance to that, apart from the value it may be to them in their after life, and on that account I should educationally give way a little, in order to meet that desire, which is quite legitimate, provided no positive injustice were done to others.

3907. We are told that if you introduce languages into the Elementary examination, you overload it altogether; looking at the bulk of the children in this country, is that your opinion ?—Yes; three-fourths in 1889 did not go higher than the Elementary: 610 Elementary, 160 Higher.

3908. Then we are shut up to the one alternative of having an optional Dutch paper, and adding the marks on a separate list ?—Yes; as the simplest plan.

3909. *President.*] Would it not be better to have a fifth paper in the Elementary examination, with alternative subjects, science being one ?—If you gave special separate marks for Dutch, it would not injure the elementary character of the examination so much, but I do not think the advocates of Dutch would be satisfied with that, because it would not tend so much to encourage the study of Dutch as making it quasi-compulsory.

3910. *Dr. Berry.*] Would you be in favour of giving bursaries to boys at the top of the list ?—Yes; it would be more encouragement still than the other way, and candidates would have a chance of getting special rewards, but I do not know whether it would satisfy those who want Dutch fostered.

3911. Can you give us any information about the aiding of private adventure schools in the north of Ireland. We are told that they are aided by the Government if there are 15 children in attendance and fulfil certain conditions ?—I never heard of any such schools as "private" schools. They may be Presbyterian minority "national" schools in a Roman Catholic parish.

3912. *Rev. Coetzee.*] I understood you to say that you would like to have district boarding schools established in town as well as district. Would that necessitate their being arranged in several grades like other schools, first, second and third, or would they all be the same standard?—I should be very glad if the Commission saw its way to recommend the recognition of graded boarding schools for the farming population in towns as well as in the country districts, on account of the greater facilities for finding suitable buildings and suitable teachers, and also the proximity to the church and nachtmaal meetings. Such schools would be under the inspection of the Government, and it might be so arranged that country people could combine and put a district boarding school in any town where there were easily acquired buildings. It would help education considerably, and these schools might be graded according to their curriculum and the social standing of the pupils. This has been done already in some cases, although not exactly in accordance with the letter of the regulations, but Sir Langham Dale has four or five times in his reports urged the advisability of doing it as a matter of simple justice to the people who have already got such schools together; and he has already I think, under one name or another, through what he calls the elastic power given to him in the administration of affairs, and the division of the Parliamentary aid, granted assistance to such schools in and around Cape Town, some as district boarding schools and some as training schools for teachers. Some time ago he mentioned that he wished to give a grant to the Rhenish Institute at Stellenbosch, although there is another first-class girls' school in the place, on account of the buildings and the management, and the fact that the Rhenish mission people centred a number of their children in that place. The existence of the other school, which practically they could not avail themselves of, did not much matter.

Rev. Father Fitz Henry.

Sept. 7th, 1891.

3913. Was it started?—Yes, I believe so. The Estimates passed through the Parliament for a grant in aid.

3914. *President.*] Is not the effect of that, that there are two first-class undenominational schools in one place?—Yes. Both teach religion, only one is called religious. It comes to the same thing; the mode of appointing managers is the only difference.

3915. In order to effect that, was a public meeting of householders convened?—I do not think so. Managers' names appointed by the Department and a conscience clause only.

3916. Do you think that Sir Langham Dale, under this elastic power which he has, could start St. Aidan's school for instance, in Graham's Town, as another first-class public undenominational school aided by Government?—He could do so, perhaps, if approached on the subject. Three large unaided schools in Graham's Town are in the same position. He has done so in the case of the Paarl Schools. There they have four first-class schools; the Upper Paarl Boys' school, Upper Paarl Girls' school, gymnasium, and the Girls' first-class public undenominational school in the Lower Paarl, as well as the Wellington Boys', and the Huguenot Seminary and Blauwvalley. Each of those gets from £200 to £500 grant, and also about £600 total for having boarding departments, about £200 for method teachers to help and train pupil teachers, and £2,000 on Estimates of 1891, for building grants, so that in the Paarl division alone, they get yearly something like £4,000. All these schools so near one another are really rendered necessary by circumstances. One is a training institution for girls, another is a higher grammar school for boys, called the gymnasium; they must have 200 or 300 boarders altogether, and these schools represent not the district but perhaps the half of South Africa. Hence other centres should be treated similarly.

3917. Do boys come there from beyond the Colony?—I daresay they do. The fact of one public school, whether for boys or girls, being in a place, should not necessarily be a reason why boarding schools should be aided there. There should be an amount of consideration and latitude given to further the interests of education. As an example of that, in Port Elizabeth at present there is not any first class girls' school, but there is a large number of scholars in private schools. The Convent in Port Elizabeth, though I do not suppose they would place themselves under the present Government regulations, has spent on its educational establishment up to the present time £27,000, and they only receive £75 a year from the Government, and the Ladies' collegiate nothing. Regulations made in the year 1865 have never been altered to any extent since, to meet such cases in larger towns, and here especially. Regulations are needed to meet the ever growing necessities of different places.

3918. What would you suggest?—I think that in the case of existing boarding schools, either for boys or girls, that have special reasons for their existence, and where they could not be considered as directly interfering with the local Government aided schools to any appreciable extent, the Education Department should have the power of aiding and inspecting them, according to their several grades, and of exacting certain guarantees from approved managers; some managers being parents of the pupils.

M

Rev.
Father Fitz Henry.
——
Sept 7th, 1891.

3819. *Rev. Coetzee.*] Do you think it is advisable to have uniform books for schools of the same grade throughout the colony?—I do not think it would be advisable or even practicable. The schools are under so many different managers that you cannot compel it, although a school board, with all the schools in any one district under its charge might do so. I should like also to recommend the granting of building loans for school purposes. Whatever decision with regard to school boards the Commission may come to, I should be strongly of opinion that such school board or school attendance committee, one or the other, should be optional, and as far as rating is concerned, it should come on later and be permissive, or left to the municipalities or divisional councils. A new rating body will not be passed in a Cape Parliament for years to come. I think the Commission should not lose sight of all that the Roman Catholics have done for education. I have obtained from Bishop Ricards a list of the amounts of money spent in different towns in the Eastern Province in his vicariate for sites and school buildings, and especially for the introduction of teachers, both for the natives and for the white children up to the present time. In the course of some 40 years it amounts to no less a sum than over £100,000, and I say that any regulations which would tend to exclude or ignore those who have spent such a sum upon education would certainly be unjust and unfair, and prejudicial to the cause of education in general. In pleading for consideration for our efforts, I of course, include similar and greater efforts of other Church bodies in the same direction. I am glad that Sir Langham Dale has so long steered clear of the "religious difficulty"—the source of so much injustice and ill-feeling in England, by giving freedom of religious instruction in all Colonial Public Schools, according to the wishes of the majority of a Management Committee. Once that principle is conceded, the poorer children in the white mission schools cannot be denied the same privileges under say—some combined management of their parents and church bodies. We must not secularize the schools of the poor. Sir Langham Dale warns us against imported educational fads in the matter of school management. He distributes grants in aid under 12 different heads at present, so elastic has his administration necessarily become. I believe that increased Government aid for the poor, the training of elementary teachers, voluntary zeal, and a system of responsible local management under the Municipality, an over Board, or the Department, with due consideration for the linguistic and religious sympathies of the people, will give us a just and efficient national system of education. The following is an account of the expenditure on school sites, buildings, teachers' residences, cost of introduction of teachers from Europe for European schools and Native missions in the Eastern Province by the Rev. Bishop Ricards since 1850, exclusive of yearly maintenance:—*Graham's Town*—Already expended, £5,000; Convent, £4,700; St. Aidan's College, £17,900; *Port Elizabeth*—Marist Brothers' Schools, £5,370; Convent, £27,750; *Uitenhage*—Convent, £2,000; Marist Schools, £3,000; Trappists' Mission (Native), £5,800; *King William's Town and East London*—Convents, £23,700; St. Joseph's Boys, King William's Town, £1,300; Izeli Industrial Farm School, £2,000; *Kei Lands* (Native Mission), £2,200; *Graaff-Reinet* Mission School, £410; *Bedford* Mission School, £350; *Port Alfred* Mission School, £450; Passages and outfit of Jesuit missionaries for Native Missions, £4,000; Total, £105,930.

Rev. Father Berghegge examined.

Rev.
Father Berghegge.
——
Sept. 7th, 1891.

3920. *Rev. Moorrees.*] I believe you are Dutch teacher at St. Aidan's College, Graham's Town?—Yes.

3921. How long have you been there?—About 4½ years.

3922. Do you find there is an increasing desire for instruction in Dutch?—Yes; the number of pupils taking Dutch has greatly increased. There are 50 who learn Dutch.

3923. Do you think the study of Dutch should be encouraged in this country?—I think so.

3924. Are you at all acquainted with Belgium?—Not much.

3925. Do you know that there every facility is given for instruction in two languages, Dutch and French?—Yes. I know there is a great struggle going on, and in all provinces they have equality for both languages.

3926. *Mr. Theron.*] Will you explain the kind of equality?—You can take what language you like, but all officials have to know both languages.

3927. *Dean Holmes.*] Are not they divided by a distinct line?—They are very distinct.

3928. *Rev. Moorrees.*] Except in the towns?—Yes.

3929. Do you think that the exclusion of Dutch from the Elementary examination discourages the study of the language?—Yes. You might give an additional paper in

Dutch and let it count for marks, or you might put both languages on the same footing, so that a boy could take either the Dutch or English paper.

Rev.
Father Berghegge.

Sept. 7th, 1891.

3930. If Dutch were added as an optional subject in the Elementary examination, and the marks counted, do you think that would be unfair towards the English child ? —No. I do not see that it is unfair. The boy who does more should get more.

3931. Dutch being one of the languages of the country, if the option is given between Dutch and another language, do not you think the language of the country ought to have a greater percentage of marks in the examination ?—If you want to promote French or German, you must do the same, but that is not asked.

3932. But ought not Dutch to receive more marks than other languages which are foreign to the country ?—Yes ; if you want to promote it you must make it worth while.

3933. *Mr. Theron.*] Those boys taking Dutch in your school now, are they all preparing for the Civil Service examination ?—Some for the matriculation also.

3934. Are any of them below the standard required for the Elementary examination ?—No. Those who go in for the Elementary examination next year are beginning to learn Dutch.

3935. Are those Dutch or English children ?—Perhaps there are one or two Dutch ; the rest are all English.

3936. Why do they learn Dutch for the Matriculation examination ; it is only optional, and is not required, is it ?—The parents desire it.

3937. Do you think they feel that it is a necessity for them to know the Dutch language in a colony like this ?—I think so.

3938. From your experience, if you had to instruct a child from the commencement, so as for it to make the greatest progress in the shortest time, in what language would he derive most benefit ?—From his mother tongue.

3939. So that whenever you give a child from the commencement instruction in any other language than his own, you handicap him ?—In some way, yes. It makes it more difficult.

3940. *President.*] What do you think is the best way to arrange the Elementary examination so as to get over this bi-lingual difficulty ?—I think the fairest way would be to have a fifth paper, with several alternative subjects, and give the candidates the option of choosing whichever they wish.

3941. From your experience, if you add a Dutch paper, as it has been suggested, in which form do you think it would be fairest and best all round, looking at the desire that exists to encourage Dutch ?—If you have a fifth paper, such as French, German, or science, I do not see what it has to do with the question, which is, what is the best means for giving instruction in both the English and Dutch languages.

3942. If there was an optional paper in Dutch, the marks for which counted in addition, would that be fair to the boys in your school ?—I do not see how the others who do not take the Dutch paper would suffer.

3943. But suppose a boy does not know Dutch at all ?—It is his own fault ; he should have learned it.

3944. But suppose he has not learned it ?—All I can say is, one boy has more brains than another.

3945. *Dean Holmes.*] Would you add, say twenty subjects in the same way, and let a boy get extra marks for each subject ?—Yes.

3946. *President.*] Would it not be unfair to a Kafir boy who goes up for the examination ; he has to learn Dutch, English and Kafir, has he not ?—I do not think it is unfair. You have to take Dutch in the Civil Service examination, and I have heard something about suspending that examination, because there are so many going in for it, but I would say rather make it more difficult. You might say that boys should first pass the Matriculation before they go in for the Civil Service examination, and then they would be better up in Dutch than they are now. The great difficulty is they will not learn the grammar. As long as they know how to translate, that is enough for the Civil Service examination. There is not sufficient inducement for them to take it up well. They should first pass the Matriculation examination and then go in for the Civil Service examination ; they would by this means get a better foundation in both languages, English as well as Dutch, and the Government would get a better class of men.

3947. If what you proposed were carried out, would it not shut out more English boys from the examination ?—English boys are not so stupid—all my boys here are English. Of course it would make the examination more difficult.

3948. *Rev. Coetzee.*] If the examination were made more difficult, you do not think it would shut your boys out ?—No.

Rev.
Father Daignault.

Sept. 7th, 1891.

3949. *President.*] What are you ?—I am principal of St. Aidan's College here.

3950. Have you heard the evidence given by Father Fitz Henry ?—Not all.

3951. Can you suggest any way to secure fuller use being made of the opportunities afforded for education ?—I think that in the present state of the colony where such a large number of our boys and girls are educated in mission schools and higher grade schools belonging to church bodies, if our system of education is really to be made national and universal, Government aid ought to be extended as far as possible to such schools, provided they be willing to submit to Government inspection. Government aid in my opinion should not be confined to undenominational schools. As one of the reasons for this opinion, I would point to what has been done already by religious bodies. If one were to overlook the educational work done by the Dutch Reformed Church, the Church of England, the Roman Catholics and the Wesleyans, as church bodies, there would be comparatively little to show. I think therefore, the Government should give substantial help to such voluntary agencies, considering especially the great sacrifices they have made so far for the good of education. At St. Aidan's we have so far spent over £20,000 ; some £17,000 in buildings, besides large sums of money in bringing out teachers from Europe. Much also has been spent in buying land to provide playgrounds for the students, &c., &c. What I say of the Roman Catholics applies also, I am sure, to other church bodies. The convents in this and the other Vicariates have gone to very great expense to promote education. The results of the public examinations show that we compare favourably with other schools which receive Government help ; for example, I may mention that this year a girl, from Rosary Convent, carried off the silver medal offered for competition by the Port Elizabeth Municipality. At Kimberley, it is a girl from the Convent who won the gold medal under the same conditions. I need not speak of the excellent work done by the Dominican nuns of King William's Town ; it is known to all. Here in Graham's Town, out of nine candidates sent up by the Convent for the Elementary examination, only one failed. At St. Aidan's, owing to the comparatively small number of students, we cannot boast of having passed a large number of boys, but the percentage has been very fair. This year we sent up five boys for Matriculation, and passed four ; we sent up six for Honours and passed five. It will thus be seen that the work done in these schools, even when judged by Government standard, is good, and therefore calls for encouragement. I would further say, that the present undenominational schools do not and cannot afford sufficient accommodation for our boys and girls, nor could the Government alone provide for all the educational wants of the colony, and therefore it is unfair to keep only undenominational schools and deny every help to the denominational ones, when the former cannot do the work the latter are doing so well, and which otherwise would remain undone. It may be of interest to know that since 1870 the English School Boards have spent £22,508,322 sterling to provide 1,784,995 places in school, whilst voluntary schools, during the same period, have provided 1,745,519 places, *i.e.*, nearly the same number as School Boards, without costing the ratepayer one penny. It is also interesting to know that the Paris School Board has spent during the last 10 years more than £26,000,000 sterling in providing school accommodation for children formerly educated in Catholic schools. I quote these figures to show that if the Government wanted to do the work that is being done by religious bodies in the colony, they would have to go to fabulous expense, and that it is wiser to make use of and develop the facilities afforded by religious bodies.

3952. You think you ought to have help if the others have ?—Yes.

3953. Would not the effect of that be to make the Government expenditure enormously larger, without promoting the interests of education, because they would only then be paying for work which is already being done without being paid for ?—I can hardly think the Government would be so ungenerous. Moreover, besides doing an act of simple justice, it is evident that Government help would render our efforts much more efficient.

3954. You think you ought to be paid for the work you have done or will do ?—I say we ought to be helped.

3955. How do you want to be helped ?—In the same way as the public undenominational schools are helped. There is also the fact that Sir Langham Dale, whose impartiality, talents and desire to promote education everybody recognizes, has stated that schools like the Convent and St. Aidan's are deserving of Government help.

3956. Was that in the last report ?—In the report for 1889. No one better than the Superintendent General of Education is able to judge of what is fair in this matter. He thinks that schools of this kind ought to be helped. Some one might say that such appropriation of Government money is against the law. But as, has already been stated by Father Fitz Henry, schools which do not actually come within the strict letter of the law have been helped by Sir Langham Dale, for instance, at the Paarl and also at Burghersdorp, and I think the Good Hope Seminary, in Cape Town. I see therefore no reason why similar help should not be extended to other schools in the same circumstances. Rev. Father Insignanlt. Sept. 7th, 1891.

3957. In what way would you extend the help; what would be a fair contribution per head in your opinion ?—The Government should extend proportionally the same help which is given to the public undenominational schools of the Colony.

3958. Would not the cost be very enormous if you give those bodies carrying on good work as much as the public undenominational schools get ?—The number of such schools judged by Sir Langham Dale as worthy of receiving Government aid is not very large. Furthermore, Sir Langham Dale, in his evidence before a former Commission, said there was a very large amount of money voted annually by Government for education, which he had really no means of expending. My opinion is, and it is shared in by many others, that there is really no undenominational school in the colony; it is a misnomer. There may be a few cases where a school approaches something like undenominationalism in its character, but taking the Colony as a whole, the public schools are mostly in the hands of the local predominating religious body. Here in Graham's Town the children of Anglican parents go to St. Andrew's or some other such school; Catholics send their children either to the Convent, St. Aidan's, or the Catholic mission school; other religious bodies have also their own schools, and there remain not many children who make use of the public undenominational school. Last year, if I remember rightly, there were 155 students on the rolls of the public school here; but what is that compared with the scholastic population of Graham's Town, and yet for these 155 scholars the public school received nearly £800 pounds. In many a small village where nearly all the people are Dutch, the form of election of managers is gone through, but as far as religion is concerned, it is a mere *pro forma* election, and the school is in reality a Dutch Reformed school. The more so, because since the passing of the Hofmeyr clause, the managers are allowed to have religious instruction given, and even the catechism taught in the school. It is therefore next to impossible to see what real difference can exist between such a school and an ordinary Convent school.

3959. *Rev. Moorrees.*] How would you alter that ?—I do not find fault with what is done; but if Government money can be given in this way to some religious bodies, it can be given also to others.

3960. *President.*] It has been proposed that there should be a Board established. If it were, would it not be a good opportunity for you to ventilate your present grievances ?—I think a certain kind of Board might be a very good thing, but I want to ventilate my grievances to the present Commission. Besides, I will make a point of bringing them before the Board, should it ever come into existence. Indeed, I did not mean to ventilate grievances, but to expose a means of " securing fuller use being made of opportunities for education."

3961. How would you reach those who are outside all school aid altogether. Suppose a school Board was brought into existence to fill up gaps and hear grievances such as yours and put them before the Government, do you think it would be a good thing ?—A Board which would see to all the needs of a district for which it was elected would be an improvement on the present system. Such Board however ought by no means to have the power of levying rates or taxes, and should be independent of any particular school.

3962. Would you have it elected ?—Partly elected and partly nominated by the Education Department.

3973. Have you taken an interest in night schools, or have you anything to suggest in regard to them ?—They would supply a real want in towns.

3964. Do you agree with Father Fitz Henry ?—Yes, I agree with what he said on this subject. I think that something ought to be done for children who are constantly seen in the streets, the waifs and strays.

3965. Would you run them into school through a truant officer ?—Yes if necessary.

3966. What schools are you familiar with yourself in Europe ?—I come from Montreal in Canada.

3967. Can you recommend any suggestion from there ?—I think the Canadian system of working schools would give very good results in this colony. We have there some of the difficulties we meet with here. But in Canada they have tried to meet the requirements of even very small minorities in small villages.

3968. The schools are helped all round ?—Yes; the chief lines of the system are these : There are two Boards, one for the Catholics who are the great majority in Lower Canada, and the other for the Protestants. The money is provided proportionately to the numbers of these two great bodies in the country, and the members of each Board have power to give money as requirements demand.

Rev.
Father Daignault.

Sept. 7th, 1891.

3969. Would you have two Boards here ?—I think it is not necessary. I brought forward the example of Canada because there is a principle of fairness about it which we would do well to imitate.

3970. How is the language difficulty dealt with in Canada ?—There is perfect liberty for anyone to learn what language he likes.

3971. In the same school have you two systems of education, one in French and the other in English, or have you separate schools ?—In the French schools French is the medium of imparting knowledge, and in the English schools it is English. In the French schools English is taught, as a secondary subject, and in the English schools French is taught in the same manner. There is no Government University. There are several Universities, and each one gives its own degrees and has its own examinations.

3972. Are not the examinations given by the Government ?—No ; there is complete liberty.

3973. Do you think it would be wise to have two sets of schools here, Dutch schools and English schools ?—I cannot speak with authority on that subject, but if you wish to go on the principle of fairness, and if it be possible, I would say have the Dutch boy taught in Dutch and the English boy taught in English, if their parents so wish. That is how it is done in Canada.

3974. *Dr. Berry.*] In this vicariate are not you charged with some superintendence of native education ?—Yes.

3975. Can you tell us something about your system of education ?—We give very elementary education to our natives, but we teach them also to cultivate gardens, agriculture, and something about trades, such as masonry and carpentry. That is all that we have been able to do so far.

3976. How many have you at your school at Keilands ?—We have bought a property, and about 200 natives have come gradually to settle on it. The children go to our school, and they are trained there.

3977. At what age do you take them in ?—Practically there is no limit of age.

3978. Is there any limit to the time you keep them. How do you get rid of them ?—When they can earn some money for themselves, or work for their parents.

3979. Do you turn them off, or do they go of their own accord ?—It is not very long ago since we began our mission, and we have not experienced yet this difficulty.

3980. Have you any views with regard to native education generally ?—The children ought to receive a fair elementary education and be trained to habits of work, especially agriculture and trades, so as to enable them to build houses for themselves. It is a disgrace that natives who have been so long in our midst should not have learned to build European houses, and not know how to make doors, windows, wheelbarrows, and carts for themselves. I think that so far from the white artizan suffering from it, it would be a real benefit to him if the native would take to European habits. I think the example set in the United States is very condemnatory of what takes place here in the colony, and people coming from America are surprised to see how low down in the scale of civilization the blacks are here, although they have been so long in contact with the whites.

3981. Do you begin with a literary education for the native children ?—I would not call the education we give them literary at all.

3982. How would you begin with the youngest ?—When very young, they are taken out by one of our brothers to do some light work in the garden ; the bigger boys till the ground, cut down trees, trench, and do other similar work.

3983. Do you teach them to read at the same time ?—If they are able to learn, we teach them to read and write, and also the rudiments of arithmetic.

3984. Why do you do that ?—Because we believe in raising these people from their state of complete ignorance to a higher state.

3985. Why is that teaching necessary so to raise them ?—Because without this kind of learning they would be unfit for the ordinary duties of life.

3986. Many people say it is a wrong way to raise these natives by teaching them to read and write ; why do you do it ?—They have a mind, and it ought to be developed by education. I think, however, that it would be a mistake to educate them above their station, or to neglect the teaching of manual work.

3987. Have you had any experience in the teaching of the North American Indians under the Canadian Government ; how do you begin there ?—We begin there exactly as we do here. We teach them elementary education, and also how to work.

3988. Do the two go hand in hand ?—Yes ; at our school at Dunbrody they have to do a certain amount of work each day.

3989. You think that both must go together, the literary and the industrial ?—Yes ; it would not be good for the natives, in their present state, to be brought up at once to learn Latin and Greek, etc. I think it is a mistake, except in a few exceptional cases.

89

Rev. Canon Espin examined.

3990. *President.*] I believe you are principal of St. Andrew's College, in Graham's Town?—Yes.

3991. Have you anything to suggest with regard to the questions submitted to the Commission?—Most of them lie outside my experience, as I have been connected rather with higher education in the country, and as far as I understand, the questions relate mainly to public schools and providing facilities for the education of the lower classes of the population.

3992. Do you think it is expedient to establish school boards?—If you mean elected school boards I should say not. My mind is rather against it. I should rather have officers appointed by the central authority at Cape Town. I think that would work much better than elected school boards.

3993. What officers would you appoint?—I should have thought the inspectors might with advantage be considerably increased in number, and the inspections be more frequent. If you wish to introduce compulsory education in towns, I should have thought it might be done through a local authority, either the Divisional Council or the Municipality.

3994. Would not that be a board?—I should not advocate an elected board in the towns.

3995. Have you any particular grievance?—No; but I quite agree with what the last witness said, that it is fair and right that good educational work should be helped all round.

3996. You do not put that forward as a grievance, do you?—Of course we should be very glad to receive Government aid.

3997. Do you not receive it for your lower branch?—No.

3998. Have you a Dutch master?—Yes.

3999. Has he lately been introduced?—Since 1888.

4000. Have you Dutch boys in the school?—Yes; several. A large number of the boys learn Dutch.

4001. What is your opinion with regard to instruction in the Dutch language?—I think that facilities should be provided for those who wish to learn the Dutch language.

4002. Are they sufficiently provided in your school?—I think so.

4003. Is there a growing desire to learn Dutch?—Yes, the number of Dutch pupils is increasing, and has been for the last two or three years.

4004. To what do you attribute that?—Partly to the Civil Service examination, which makes Dutch a compulsory subject. That has had a great effect.

4005. Do your boys go in for the Civil Service examination?—Yes, a great many. They learn Dutch on that account, and then again the extension of railway has brought us more boys from up-country.

4006. Have you boys from the Free State and Transvaal?—Yes.

4007. I suppose you send up boys for the Elementary examination; do you think it desirable that there should be a Dutch paper added to that examination?—No. I think it is a good thing to keep that examination as it is. It is a good test of a plain English education. It is not intended I should say for such schools as St. Andrew's, and they only send up boys for it, because they cannot compete for the Higher examination, unless they first pass the Elementary. If the Higher examination could be entered upon without first passing the Lower, we should not go in for the Elementary examination at all.

4008. Then in fact the Elementary examination does not bring out all that you teach in your school?—No; the third form, which prepares for the Elementary examination, takes up Euclid, Algebra, Latin, and Greek, in addition to other subjects.

4009. Do you think the Elementary examination interferes with the ordinary curriculum of school work?—To some extent it does.

4010. You would in fact sooner be without it, would you not?—If you were allowed to enter for the Higher examination without passing the Lower, it would be a help.

4011. Do you teach French and German?—We teach French; two or three pupils take German, and a large number Dutch.

4012. If the Elementary examination is continued as it is, do you think it desirable to add Dutch as a paper, in view of the increasing desire to learn the language?—I do not think it is desirable. I see no objection to letting those who like take Dutch as a sort of extra subject, and put some distinguishing mark after their names to show that they have passed in it. The Elementary examination is really intended as the test of a fair English education, and directly you introduce languages, it is a new feature and alters the character of the examination.

Rev.
Conon Espin.
Sept. 7th, 1891.

4013. If Dutch is introduced, how would you do it ?—What is needed is one examination which should include fairly the whole of the school course.

4014. Would it do to have several alternative papers, and let candidates choose ? —That would help us perhaps.

4015. In view of the desire which is apparently evinced even at your College to take up Dutch, do not you think it would be wise to give some sort of stimulus and a good stimulus to the language ?—I do not think anything more than what we have is necessary as far as we are concerned. The boys show themselves quite anxious to learn Dutch already, and they do not require any further stimulus.

4016. Is it an advantage or otherwise to have two languages ?—I think that bi-lingualism is a misfortune to a country.

4017. Why ?—It tends to inaccuracy. We do not make one another understand. Although the precise words of the two languages may agree, the idioms are often different, and a boy gets misunderstood a good deal I think. It tends to inaccuracy, and to some extent makes truthfulness more difficult.

4018. *Rev. Coetzee.*] Would you be prepared to give up the English language ? —One language is better. Without expressing any opinion as to the relative merits of the two languages, bi-lingualism is a distinct misfortune.

4019. *President.*] In Germany there are two languages even in the higher education ; in fact, in the higher education a second language is always required, and so far from proving an obstruction, it is considered to increase accuracy of thought ?—The acquirement of another language is a distinct thing from a second spoken language being in common use.

4020. Do you consider Latin an advantage ?—It is an immense advantage to learn Latin, it tends to accuracy of thought.

4021. *Rev. Moorrees.*] Do you think that Dutch boys are at a great disadvantage in having two languages ?—I think they are at a disadvantage certainly.

4022. *President.*] In order to remedy that disadvantage would it not be well to have an optional Dutch paper which would count in the Elementary examination ?—I should have no objection to allowing Dutch boys to be examined and have a separate paper, but I should not be in favour of counting it in the aggregate marks. It seems to me that in an English colony, the English language must have a certain advantage. The Germans in this country, as well as the natives, are under the same disadvantage in regard to the Elementary examination.

4023. *Rev. Coetzee.*] In what sense do you call this an English colony. It is a dependency of England, but if you take the Dutch speaking population they are in the majority, are they not ?—I merely state the fact.

4024. *Dr. Berry.*] Would you be in favour of awarding bursaries to those passing well up in Dutch ?—Yes, certainly.

Graham's Town, Tuesday, 8th September, 1891.

PRESENT :

Sir J. D. BARRY (President),

Mr. Rowan,
Dean Holmes,
Rev. Moorrees.

Rev. Coetzee.
Mr. Theron,
Dr. Berry.

Mr. F. Howe Ely examined.

Mr.
F. Howe Ely.
Sept. 8th, 1891.

4025. *Mr. Rowan.*] You are deputy inspector of schools I believe ?—Yes.

4026. How long have you been in the service ?—Since January, 1875.

4027. What divisions does your present work comprise ?—Queenstown, Cathcart, Stutterheim, Komgha, East London and King William's Town ; broadly between the Keiskama and the Kei.

4028. Have you all the different classes of schools connected with the Educational Department in your district ?—Yes, I think so.

4029. Have you any idea of the number of children in your district of a school-able age not in any actual attendance at school ?—I have a very large native population in my district, but the census returns are not yet completed, so I am unable to say.

4030. Cannot you give a rough estimate of the number of children in your district not receiving any instruction ?—No ; it was made out three years ago.

4031. Do you think there is irregularity of attendance ?—There is irregularity of attendance, but the parents of many of the children in town schools are so poor that they are obliged to employ the children in domestic work. A year or two ago especially the depression in trade was very great, and people were great sufferers. I am speaking of the white population.

Mr.
F. Howe Ely.
——
Sept. 8th, 1891.

4032. Are there portions of your district where the attendance among the coloured children is irregular?—There is constant irregularity among the coloured people. The attendance varies very much according to the season of the year. The children are taken out of school to assist in various agricultural operations, and in wet weather it is very difficult to get anything like attendance with the natives.

4033. Are you in favour of compulsory measures being taken?—I think you might have modified compulsion in towns. It would press hardly upon a good many people.

4034. *Rev. Moorrees.*] In what way should any modified form of compulsion be carried out in towns?—The only way I can see is to have a truant officer constantly going about picking up the waifs and strays.

4035. And with regard to the coloured people?—In towns you might apply the same rule to coloured people, and take the children into different schools.

4036. *Mr. Rowan.*] Could the same system be applied also to large mission stations and locations?—Yes; mission stations. I do not see how you can apply it in such a district as Khama's country for instance. I do not think that Khama himself could compel the people. As it is, he is the chief of the district, and the attendance is still irregular.

4037. If he received aid on condition that he saw children went to school, and while at school they received some industrial training, would not there be a motive which is not in existence now?—At stations like Annshaw, where a missionary is actually resident, such a scheme would be possible; but besides the station schools, there is a very large number of schools in Khama's country away from direct missionary influence, and I do not think you could force children to go to school there, because a large proportion of the population is heathen, and they would just as soon not have any education at all as have schools in their midst. If we had a purely Christian population, a scheme of compulsory education might be feasible, but with these people I do not think it can be carried out.

4038. *Dr. Berry.*] If you were to levy a tax for education which would fall on these people too, would not that gradually bring them into the system?—Possibly it would.

4039. You would be in favour of gradually introducing compulsion even into such localities as Khama's location?—Yes. The natives themselves, those who send their children to school, are in favour of compulsion, because it would relieve them of a certain amount of fee paying, but that is merely an imaginary thing. The Christian natives would like compulsion, so as to force the heathen to send their children to school and so contribute to the school.

4040. So they would be aiding you in a way at any rate with their sympathy, and Khama himself would aid in that direction?—I do not know that Khama has such influence as all that.

4041. You speak of Khama because he is the headman in your district?—Yes.

4042. *Mr. Theron.*] Do you think there would be any objection on the part of these natives if such a tax were imposed upon them?—I think there would be great objection on the part of the natives, but it is a thing that should be done.

4043. Then you agree with the Rev. Mr. Taberer that that would be the only means to make these people take to education; that they would make better use of education if they had to pay?—Yes.

4044. *Rev. Coetzee.*] How would you regulate the tax for education; should it be so much per family?—There are two or three ideas on the subject. Mr. Dick, the Special Magistrate of King William's Town, is in favour of a half-crown tax for every man, but I think that that would be an almost impossible tax to collect, whereas a hut tax of half-a-crown could be collected by the ordinary revenue officer of the district. I do not think there would be any difficulty in collecting that tax or any tax that might be fixed.

4045. Would not a poor man have more to pay than a man who was better off if a hut tax were imposed. Sometimes a native may have three huts, but still he is a poor man all the same. Would not you be in favour of a tax assessed on the property of a man?—I think a hut tax of half-a-crown is best.

4046. You would not tax every householder?—No.

4047. *Mr. Theron.*] Are you in favour of a tax being levied for school purposes?—Yes, certainly.

4048. And that you would use for the benefit of the natives for whom it was collected only?—Yes.

4049. How would you collect it, what officers would you employ?—The ordinary revenue officers.

4050. *Dr. Berry.*] Would you have no special machinery?—No.

[G. 3—'92.]

N

Mr.
F. Howe Ely.
—
Sept. 8th, 1891.

4051. You do not propose that this tax on the hut holders should do away with the grant for educational purposes from the public revenue, do you ?—No. I would use the tax just as you would use the rate on Europeans in case it were determined to establish board schools. The Government grant, the rate, and the fees should all go together.

4052. Would you in any way apportion the Government grant in accordance with the amount raised locally. Is there any principle you would recommend to the Commission for adoption in that respect ?—I should feel inclined to give them a very large proportion from the general revenue, because at present the Government grant is given to these schools without any guarantee on the part of the natives that they shall pay anything. It is understood as a rule that they shall contribute £10 a year towards the salary of the teacher, but as a fact, they contribute a very small portion indeed of the £10, and the teacher has to take what he can get.

4053. Mr. Rowan.] Would you apportion the Government grant then according to what the natives paid or according to the attendance at school ?—I think I should apportion it in accordance with what they paid, rather than according to the attendance, because it is very difficult to get at the actual attendance in a native school. The returns in the native schools, I am afraid, are not as strictly correct (I do not mean to say that they are wilfully falsified) as they would be in European schools, because in European schools the register is marked at a certain time, and although the instructions are that the register in the native schools shall be marked immediately after the religious service, I am afraid that the native teacher too often marks it at the close of the school, when the children have dropped in and been there some time during the day. They may have been there so far, but it is not according to the European idea of attendance.

4054. Mr. Theron.] You hold that this tax would take the place of the guarantee system existing among the Europeans to a certain extent ?—Yes.

4055. Dr. Berry.] How would you administer this local fund in the case of native schools ?—I should have Boards of Management, or School Boards, of which the missionaries should be ex officio members.

4056. And the money would be sent back to these Boards ?—Yes.

4057. And these Boards would then have a jurisdiction coterminous with any particular area ?—There would have to be an over Board, and then different localities must be managed by sub-Boards, I should say.

4058. President.] And the over Board having power to delegate its powers to any sub-committee in a town or locality ?—Yes. I think you would have to work in some such way, and it would be necessary to enlist the sympathy of the mission-aries by having them on the Board.

4059. Dr. Berry.] How would you have this over Board appointed, should it be a nominee or an elected Board ?—I think among the natives, it should be a nominee Board.

4060. Mr. Rowan.] When speaking of Boards, do you refer to Boards simply for mission schools, or Boards for all classes of schools ?—I thought we were talking specially as to native education.

4061. President.] Do not you think it better to have one Board for a whole district for whites and blacks, and let this Board delegate its functions with regard to the natives to committees in any locality where they are, and with regard to schools for whites, deal with them in such a way as they may deem best, making it incumbent upon them to satisfy the central Government that they are providing schools both for blacks and whites throughout the whole district ?—I do not think there would be anything impracticable in that.

4062. Rev. Coetzee.] Are there many native schools in your district ?—Yes.

4063. Are they spread over a large area or close to each other ?—They certainly extend over a very large area, but many of them are very close to one another.

4064. What is the average distance that the majority of the schools are apart ?—Some of them are quite six miles apart; others again are very close together; a great deal too close.

4065. Are they all denominational schools under the supervison of missionaries ?—Yes.

4066. Do you think it is advisable to adopt another system, so as to secularize the education given to the natives ?—I do not think by changing the system that we should secularize it more than we have done with the European population.

4067. Is it advisable to secularize the education and have purely undenomina-tional schools ?—Yes, I think so.

4068. With regard to teachers, are they native or European ?—The great majority are native.

4069. Are they all competent ?—The smaller schools get such a little aid that you can hardly expect very efficient teachers.

Mr.
F. *House* Ely.

Sept. 8th, 1891.

4070. What is done by the Education Department when their incompetence is shewn to exist ?—If a teacher is reported as quite incompetent, he is generally dismissed.

4071. Have any of the schools in your district been closed on that account ?— Occasionally ; more so previously than of late.

4072. *Dr. Berry.*] Over what time would you suggest that the education of an ordinary native child should extend, or up to what standard ?—Personally I should be inclined to limit it in the case of out-station schools to the third standard.

4073. *Mr. Rowan.*] Would you be in favour of giving a labour certificate, suppose a child reached the third standard say, upon its leaving school, similar to what they have in England, stating that the child has passed that particular standard and may now be employed ; and also lay it down, that no employer is to take any child into his service unless it shall have a certificate, making the certificate as low as you can ?— The labour difficulty is the great trouble in this country, and I am afraid by doing that, we should hamper it even more than it is at present.

4074. *Mr. Theron.*] With regard to taxing the natives, has it been brought to the notice of these people that there is such an idea ?—I have for years been telling them that the time must come when the Government and Parliament will not be satisfied with promises, and that they will have to contribute towards their own education, in fact the people themselves are getting very desirous for education, so much so, that according to the *Christian Express* newspaper published at Lovedale, which may be looked 'upon as the native organ, the £ for £ principle could be largely extended with advantage to the natives. I am not of that opinion myself, but that is the opinion of the *Christian Express.*

4075. So that by imposing such a tax, there would not be any fear of the natives looking upon it as an infringement of the rights and privileges enjoyed by them for so many years through their having to pay for their education ?—I do not see how they could ; it certainly would not be for want of warning on my part that the time would come when they would have to pay

4076. It has been placed before them ?—Yes ; I have placed it very clearly before them.

4077. And as far as the better class of natives is concerned, they are all willing to submit, and they think it necessary ?—If it were general, they would fall in with it.

4078. *Dr. Berry.*] Would you be in favour of the pass system for an ordinary native child from the lower to the higher schools. For instance, a large training or industrial institution, supported by the Government, seems to draw its pupils, according to the present arrangement, on no recognised principle at all. Ought not there to be some system whereby an ordinary native child could be promoted or advanced to one of these higher institutions on the usual terms ?—They have the power to go there if they like. I think that is an evil which will remedy itself, because at Lovedale, according to the last returns, they have about 654 pupils. It comes to a question of accommodation, and they cannot admit more there.

4879. Are there free pupils there among the number ?—There would be in what is called the station school. They pay, I think, a small fee. From the station school they go into what is called the institution, if they advance at all.

4080. How are they admitted from the station school into the institution ?—They are kept in the station school till they pass the third standard, and then they go on.

4081. Would you be in favour of extending or maintaining that system ?—I think it would be a good thing if standard three were made the standard of admission into these higher institutions, places like Lovedale and Heald Town, which are purely training institutions.

4082. *President.*] Do you think these missionaries would be able to supervise an industrial department in connection with their ordinary mission schools as has been suggested ?—In connection with the station schools, I think that is practicable, but it is utterly impracticable at the out-stations.

4083. What would you do in that case ?—I do not think you can do anything.

4084. *Dean Holmes.*] The truant officer, as we understand, is only to pick up the children in the streets ; would you approve of an attendance officer to visit the parents as is done in England ?—Yes.

4085. Suppose this officer found a number of children not attending any school, into what school should he have the power to send them ?—It would largely depend on the class of child.

4086. *President.*] Can you work that well under the present system without a Board ?—It would be difficult to work it well. I know of a case where an Indian woman sent her child to the public undenominational school and it was objected to. I do not know what the result was, but legal proceedings were threatened. If it had been persisted in, the managers thought it would have resulted in the closing of the school.

Mr.
F. Howe Ely.

Sept. 8th, 1891.

4087. Under the present law, could the managers refuse such a child?—I do not think they could upon the fees being tendered.

4088. What do you think ought to be the power of the managers in such a case?—Where the managers are responsible, as they are under the present Act, for the maintenance of the school and the payment of the teacher's salary, they should be allowed to refuse any child whose admission would prove mischievous to the school, without saying more.

4089. *Dean Holmes.*] Would it be the duty of the Government to provide schools for waifs and strays who could not be taken into the ordinary schools?—You can hardly legislate for individuals. In the particular case I mentioned just now, there was no mission school, and that was a hardship for the parents.

4090. *President.*] Ought not the power to exclude to be given, provided there is another school in existence to which the child can go?—If the presence of the child is likely to prove detrimental to the school.

4091. *Dr. Berry.*] When children are excluded and there is no other school where they can be sent, should the Government allow the parents a capitation grant for their education privately?—If the family is large enough, but it could hardly be done for one or two children.

4092. On the general question, would you be in favour of extending the system of capitation grants to such children as a means of remedying any supposed injustice to a child who could not be admitted to a public school where there is no other school in the place?—If there is a sufficient number of children excluded from the public school for whom no other provision is made, I do not see any objection.

4093. *Rev. Moorrees.*] Would you be in favour of a capitation grant?—I would put them, in that case, on the same footing as the farm schools.

4094. Would you do that in the case of one or two children?—Certainly not. Only where there was a sufficient number. You want five in the case of a farm school.

4095. Would you be in favour of giving such a grant in a village?—Yes, if there is no other provision for the education of these children.

4096. Would you not extend that system to coloured children on farms, and give them a capitation grant too, if they are excluded from any school?—The difficulty with coloured children on farm schools would be to find a teacher.

4097. But if they found a teacher?—I do not see how you could very well object. Under the present system of grants to farm schools, a farmer gets a tutor or a governess, and he has to pay him or her a salary and provide board and lodging, and in aid of that he gets a certain capitation grant as well as a certain payment by results, according to the examination.

4098. *President.*] Suppose a farmer has twenty servants who have children, may he consider them as entitled to a capitation grant?—A farm labourer would not be able to get a competent teacher for whom he could provide board and lodging and pay the salary; the capitation grant alone would not cover the teacher's salary, and you would not get a competent man.

4099. Do you think the system of capitation grants ought to go right through on the farms if they can manage to find teachers?—Yes. If a farmer treats his servants as members of his family, then you have a separate regulation. If the number of children on a farm, or two or three farms grouped together, comes to ten, then the school ceases to be a farm school and draws a higher grant as a public school of the third class on farms..

4100. Even if they are black children?—Yes, it does not matter.

4101. Are there any schools in existence like that?—Not that I know of.

4102. *Rev. Coetzee.*] Suppose coloured children are able to do manual labour on a farm and the farmer has made an agreement to the effect that those children shall be engaged in doing the work of a farm, and at the same time the head of a family gets a teacher, how would you regulate the schooling for the coloured children and work such a school?—That is rather a legal question.

4103. *President.*] Could you suggest some means by which servants on farms could receive some sort of education, without interfering with their work?—As a matter of fact, the farmers prefer not having natives who are at all desirous of education. An educated native avoids the farmers as a rule.

4104. Suppose there was an inclination to have such educated natives on farms, how would you meet that; by night schools?—You could only meet it by night schools, because the kind of labour they have here is chiefly day labour.

4105. In that case would you give an additional grant to a farmer, if the teacher is willing to undertake the work of a night-school?—Yes.

4106. *Rev. Coetzee.*] Could not the natives engage another teacher on the farm for a night-school, without the consent of the farmer?—Not unless they are prepared to provide for the board, maintenance and salary of the teacher.

Mr.
F. Howce Bly.
Sept. 8th, 1891

4107. *Mr. Theron.*] What do you mean when you say that educated natives avoid the farmers ?—I think they feel that they can get higher wages elsewhere.

4108. *President.*] Is there any other reason. Is it because they have better opportunities for the education of their children elsewhere ?—It is chiefly because they get better wages in towns and on the railway.

4109. *Mr. Theron.*] Are you convinced that that is so, that they get higher wages in towns than on the farms ?—I could not be sure of it, but I think it is the case.

4110. Have you ever heard of anything to that effect from the natives themselves, or is it your private opinion ?—It is my private opinion.

4111. *President.*] Do you think if industrial education is more general among the natives in the native schools, they would be more inclined to take regular service than they are now, and that habits of industry would be promoted among them ?— The great advantage of the industrial institutions is that it teaches the natives to use their hands, and being under strict discipline, they are trained in habits of industry and method. As a matter of fact, the native is averse to labour, and he cannot stand either mental or bodily strain for long. You will find in your own experience, that native servants after a time want to go home and rest. The work that is done at the institutions is useful as a beginning, but it will take a very long time before you actually instil habits of industry into the native mind.

4112. *Mr. Rowan.*] With regard to the establishment of School Boards, would you have one such Board over each fiscal division ?—If you adopt the principle of over Boards.

4113. That is to say, you would have an over Board over the Boards of each separate district ?—Yes.

4114. How are the separate schools to be managed ?—By sub-committees.

4115. Would you bring all classes of schools, both denominational and undenominational, under this Board ?—I think it would be an advisable thing to work the denominational schools into the general system of the colony.

4116. *Dean Holmes.*] Leaving them under their existing managers ?—If the managers would fall in with the Government requirements. There is no doubt there has been an immense amount of voluntary effort, and in any scheme that might be devised, that effort should be recognized.

4117. If there is any deficiency in mission schools, do you think it should also be made up out of the rates ?—The awkward part of it is. we have mission schools and mission schools. If you refer to mission schools in town, I should certainly have the deficiency made up out of the rates, but in the case of natives. a tax has been already suggested.

4118. *Rev. Coetzee.*] Suppose an over Board were established over a fiscal division containing several schools of different grades, how would you distribute the money raised by levying a tax. Suppose there is in one school a deficiency of £5, in another £20, and in another £40, on what principle would you distribute the money between those schools ?—I think you would have to divide it *pro rata*.

4119. And tax the whole fiscal division for making up the deficit in each of those schools. Would you tax the whole district for that £5, say ?—If you had one general fund I would.

4120. Suppose you had a school attended mostly by the children of the aristocracy, and there happened to be a deficit of £10, say, is it not probable that the lower classes will object to paying towards the schooling of the better class by making up such deficit ?—It is not very likely to happen, and I do not think the rates should be applied to anything beyond elementary education.

4121. *Dean Holmes.*] Would you apply a similar rule to that which exists in England, where the fees are not beyond a certain sum ?—Yes.

4122. *Rev. Coetzee.*] Suppose it is found impracticable to have an over Board, what else could you suggest instead of the present guarantee system ?—I am not prepared to make any other suggestion.

4123. You think that the only way to obtain perpetual succession would be this arrangement of over Boards ?—I think so. The Superintendent-General of Education, in his report for 1890, says :—"There is no provision for the continuous management of the schools, and the appointment of a new committee and the renewal of arrangements for aid every three years place the teachers in some difficulty and uncertainty. It is desirable to alter this and to provide for the security of the school property. School committees should be incorporated by law, and have perpetual succession, with power to hold property, moveable and immoveable, and to sell, transfer, lease, or otherwise dispose of such property, and provided that it shall not be lawful to dispose of any immoveable property without the consent of the Governor."

4124. *President.*] Can you suggest any scheme ?—I am afraid I cannot.

Mr.
F. Howe Ely.

Sept. 8th, 1891.

4125. Have you considered Sir Langham Dale's proposition as to fourth class public undenominational schools?—Yes, I gather that he wishes to turn the present mission schools into public schools, on the same principle as the undenominational schools of the colony.

4126. Dean Holmes.] Only mission schools where whites are attending?—Yes.

4127. President.] And withdraw these schools from the denominations?—Not necessarily, though the effect might be such.

4128. Dr. Berry.] If additional accommodation is to be provided for white children in towns, would you prefer having the public undenominational school system developed, so as to meet that want, or would you increase the mission school system as at present exists: in towns I am speaking of?—I should feel inclined to develope the public undenominational school system. •

4129. Would your recommendation in favour of a School Board for the district include these fourth class public undenominational schools?—Yes, I think so, with the same condition I mentioned before, that present interests should be conserved, and provided they are willing to come under the Government system.

4130. With reference to districts largely occupied by natives, do you think there ought to be two Boards, one for the administration of education among Europeans and one for the administration of education among natives: or would you have simply one Board for both?—I think the idea of an over Board for the whole district, both European and native, with sub-committees, is the most expedient.

4131. Would you give to that Board power to regulate the number of schools in a district that are to draw public money?—I think so, and for this reason, that owing to denominational zeal, the schools are in many places overcrowded. I have referred to that in my last report to the Government. You cannot find teachers for these mission schools, and you are obliged to take just what you can get.

4132. How would you start when the Board is called into existence; would you say that the Board should issue a notice to the effect that all managers of schools who wish their institutions carried on under the administration of the School Board of the district should notify accordingly, and let it decide what is to be done with every individual school?—Yes. My reason for suggesting that missionaries should be members of the local committees is that they may see the natives are fairly handled, and that they get a fair proportion of the grant and of the rates.

4133. Would you say that if a missionary or a denomination wishes to set up a school for which the local School Board says there is no need, it should do so at its own risk?—I think the advantage of a School Board is that it will prevent the needless multiplication of schools.

4134. Where they are multiplied out of the jurisdiction of the Board, you would say, let it be done at the expense and risk of the denomination?—You cannot stop it. I may say that I have found three schools within a certain area, two of which are supported by Government as mission schools, where one would be sufficient, but for denominational differences.

4135. President.] How would you act in such a case?—If we had this Board, it should determine which school should receive aid or where any other school might be created, always preserving existing rights.

4136. Where they receive aid, would you disturb things?—Yes, certainly.

4137. Rev. Moorrees.] If a church or missionary society, getting the Government grant goes to the expense of erecting a school, would it not be unjust for the Government to take the grant away afterwards?—I think if the schools are too close, and one school would supply the wants of the locality, there is no injustice done by removing one.

4138. Would there not be very great danger of injustice being done by these Boards if they had to select from a certain number of schools, which were going to receive Government aid and which not; would not the denomination which is strongest on the Board carry on its school perhaps at the expense of the other, which deserved the aid better?—I think that could be guarded against. The missionaries would be there to represent the interests of the several religious denominations, and it would have to be a question of give and take.

4139. Dr. Berry.] Would you have an appeal to the Education Department in case of any school being threatened with abolition?—An appeal would always be from the Board to the Government, I take it, and local interests might be safeguarded in that way. I think that in the case of mission schools, there should be a distance of at least six miles between any two schools.

4140. Would you be in favour of having any Board of Control for Native Education for the whole of the frontier districts, so as to direct it into proper channels, in the same way as the University exists to direct the education of Europeans into proper channels, or would you say that such control and administration should rest

97

entirely with the Superintendent-General or the Minister of Education for the time being ?—I would be in favour of its being under the control of the Superintendent-General of Education.

Mr.
F. Howe Ely.

Sept. 8th, 1891.

4141. Under whose control should the question of Native education and Native labour as affected by education be placed ?—I would not divorce European and Native education.

4142. You would let things remain just as they are as far as general control is concerned ?—Yes.

4143. *President.*] You have already stated your views in writing with regard to the question of English and Dutch ; have you anything further to add ?—No.

4144. *Rev. Coetzee.*] The Dutch people complain that they have a grievance, inasmuch as Dutch is not recognized in the Elementary examination ; how would you meet their wishes and remove that grievance ?—You would be giving the Dutch boys or whoever took up the extra subject, an additional means of obtaining marks.

4145. The Dutch say they are in the majority and their language is officially acknowledged, but in the Elementary examination they are excluded, and no facilities are given for showing that boys have acquired proficiency in the language ?—To that I would reply that by the time a boy is capable of going up for the Elementary examination, he has attained such a mastery of the English language that it is no disadvantage to him at all.

4146. Suppose an English and a Dutch boy start at the same time, which of the two would be first capable of passing the examination, the Dutch boy or the English boy ?—The only way out of the difficulty that I see is either to put the two languages upon an exactly equal footing and set the same papers in both, letting the Dutch boys take their examination in Dutch and the English boys in English, or else adopt the resolution which was passed at the Teachers' Conference at Kimberley, namely to have a Dutch paper for those wishing to take it up, and let the marks be endorsed on the certificate.

4147. What do you think of having an alternate subject ?—I feel very strongly that as soon as you begin adding to the syllabus, you will change the character of the examination.

4148. What do you think of doing away with the Elementary examination altogether, and when the Inspector comes round to do his work, let him give a certificate to each candidate passing the fifth Standard ?—I do not think that pupils would look upon that as the same thing.

4149. *Dean Holmes.*] That would not affect schools not under Government inspection either, would it ?—No.

4150. *President.*] How would it do to relieve boys wishing to go up for the School Higher examination from the obligation of passing the Elementary examination altogether. The Rev. Canon Espin seemed to think that his boys would prefer it ?—I think most teachers would prefer it.

4151. Do you think it would be in the interests of education ?—Yes, I think so. Teachers complain that there are too many examinations, and they do not dovetail into one another, that a subject required for one examination is frequently of no use to a candidate preparing for the next in the ascending scale. I stated that in my report, and Sir Langham Dale in his last report says on this subject, "the great evil of our time is the multiplicity of subjects introduced into the ordinary course of schools : pupils learn a little of everything and nothing thoroughly."

4152. Do you think if boys wishing to go up for the School Higher examination were relieved from the obligation of passing the Elementary, a fifth paper might be set in the Elementary examination, either Dutch or some alternative subject ?—Even in that case you would have a certain number who would go up for the Elementary examination as their final examination.

4153. If it is their final examination and they want to stop there, would it be unfair or unwise to make them take Dutch, or rather hold out a strong inducement for them to do so, seeing that they will probably stop in the country and ought to know the language, or do you think even in that case it would be wise to have an alternative subject ?—I think it would be wise to have an alternative subject, if you are determined to have a fifth paper.

4154. But you are not in favour of a fifth paper under any circumstances ?—No.

4155. *Rev. Coetzee.*] What would you suggest in order to encourage and promote the study of the Dutch language ?—You might give bursaries or prizes for it as a special subject.

4156. *Dr. Berry.*] You would not give a bursary for Dutch alone, would you ; you would insist upon a candidate shewing his proficiency in other subjects as well in the Elementary examination ?—One-third of the aggregate marks is the pass in the Elementary examination, and I should separate the Dutch from the rest of the examina-

Mr.
F. Howe Ely.

Sept. 8th, 1891.

tion in this way, that if a boy passed the examination and attained a certain proficiency in Dutch, which of course I should leave the examiners to determine, then he should receive a bursary, but I would not allow a boy who did not take Dutch to suffer. It should be a special subject, carrying a special prize, but it should not interfere with the rest of his work or the rest of anybody else's work. In my opinion, a boy who passes the four elementary subjects should be eligible for a bursary for Dutch.

4157. *Rev. Moorrees.*] I understood you to say that you are not in favour of adding another subject to the Elementary examination?—I think its elementary character would be changed by the addition of an extra subject, and if we allowed the pupils of public schools to go in for the Higher examination without passing the Elementary, there would be no need to make any change.

4158. On the continent, children begin at a very early age to study two languages, and that is not considered destructive of the elementary character of their instruction, is it?—We have in the Eastern Districts comparatively very few Dutch speaking people; I speak of my own district at all events, and the fact is, that to a great majority of children Dutch is entirely a foreign language, while English is not, so that you start with a facility already.

4159. Do not you think that in the Midland Districts and a great part of the Western Districts, Dutch children are as totally ignorant of English practically as English children here are of Dutch?—I am not prepared to give any answer to that question. My own knowledge of the Karoo districts is confined to towns where I should certainly say the knowledge of English is much greater than the knowledge here is of Dutch on the part of English children.

4160. Do not you think there is cause for complaint when in a bi-lingual country one of the languages is totally excluded from the first examination?—There is, of course, a sentimental grievance to begin with. There is the sentiment of the majority to be considered, but as to compelling boys to learn English, if there is any compulsion, I look upon that as a very decided advantage to a Dutch boy, because you are teaching him what is practically the almost universal language of commerce. English is a language with which you can travel through the greater part of Europe. Everybody who knows anything of Dutch will admit that it has a very rich and powerful literature, but the amount of Dutch which an English boy will acquire will be so small, that he will be unable to make any use of it as far as reading even an ordinary Dutch book goes, and the consequence will be, that as soon as he has passed his examination, he will return to the minimum of subjects that will help him through. There is a great difference between the two languages.

4161. But we do not ask the same for Dutch that we are ready to give to English. We make no complaint that English is the language of the examination, we only ask for one paper to be added?—If you had a special paper for Dutch, I think it would meet the difficulty.

4162. Would it not be a discouragement for a Dutch boy to take up Dutch, if he has to do so without any additional advantage to himself?—He does not take it without any additional advantage; he is eligible for a bursary for that special subject, and thereby you encourage the language.

4163. *Mr. Theron*] Can you give us any idea of your own, as to the best way of meeting the difficulty?—The really best way would be to encourage among children a love of reading Dutch, but the practical difficulty about the thing is, that out here we have not got proper Dutch school books to work with.

4164. Do you say that because you are not acquainted with our Dutch literature?—Children get a certain amount of proficiency, that is all; of course, there is a Dutch speaking population, and there is preaching in Dutch, so that it is necessary for those who wish to attend the ministrations of the Dutch Reformed Church, that they should understand the language.

4165. Do you think the Government made a mistake when they insisted upon Dutch being compulsory in the Civil Service examination?—No.

4166. Do you think candidates for the Civil Service should pass their examination in Dutch properly, or in a slipshod manner?—If a candidate consulted his own interests, he would do his best.

4167. Would you help him to do so?—Yes.

4168. And the best way is to begin young, is it not?—Yes, if you can.

4169. But you want to stop a boy at the Elementary examination?—I do not want to stop him.

4170. You compel a Dutch boy to pass four subjects, in English, and then when we say, give a paper in Dutch, you do not like to place him on an equal footing with an English boy?—He would get the advantage of the special paper, which has been suggested.

Mr.
F. Howe Ely.

Sept. 8th, 1891.

4171. By insisting upon Dutch in the Civil Service examination, do you or do you not acknowledge that it is one of the official languages of the country?—It is one of the official lnuguages.

4172. If so, should it not be placed on an equal footing with the other official language?—If you can work it in. I speak only of districts in which my special work lies, and there I do find that there is a difficulty in making English boys take up Dutch for the Elementary examination; but more than that, I find that Dutch parents themselves request that their boys may not be taught Dutch. I had a case the other day at Glen Grey, where a question arose about changing a farm school into a circuit school, and the gentleman whose farm it was, asked me whether the Educational Department would have any objection. I remarked that one of the conditions was, that the teacher should be able to give instruction both in Dutch and English, and that the teacher whom they were then employing, and they wished to keep on, could not speak Dutch. The answer was, we do not want our children to learn Dutch; we want them to learn English. That was a Dutch family. In Tarkastad, the teacher told me that he had a larger number of children attending at the end of last year than more recently; the parents had withdrawn them from the Dutch class, in order that they might give attention to other subjects.

4173. *Rev. Moorrees.*] Might not one of the reasons for that be that Dutch is not recognized in the Elementary examination?—It might be; but I noticed in the last Elementary examination, out of 132 candidates who passed in Class I, 61 were Dutch names; in the Matriculation, out of 41 who passed, there were 25 Dutch names.

4174. What does that prove?—That Dutch is cultivated and taught in the schools for the benefit of those who wish to go on for the examinations.

4175. Do you think it right that Dutch, which is one of the languages of the country, should be put as regards marks on a level with a foreign language. I mean in in the School Higher and Matriculation?—I should think that high Dutch to an ordinary colonial boy was almost a foreign language.

4176. Dutch being the language of the country to such a large extent, is it right that it should be put on a level with foreign languages such as French and German in the examinations?—I should be inclined to think that if it came to a matter of marks, the scholar who took up the more difficult language should have the higher marks.

4177. Is that the principle followed in the examinations; do you give more marks to the French than to the English paper?—No.

4178. Why would you do so with regard to Dutch. If you acknowledge Dutch to be one of the languages of the country, should it not have a higher proportion of marks than French or German?—I would put it exactly on an equality with English.

4179. *Dean Holmes.*] Do you mean you would give an equal number of marks?—I would have the same paper in Dutch and in English; two sets of papers.

4180. *Mr. Rowan.*] What contributions should be expected from local bodies such as Divisional Councils and Municipalities?—I have answered that question in my written reply to the circular issued by the Commission.

4181. What more do you think can be done to meet the wants of the agricultural population?—That is a question I am not prepared to answer. The great difficulty is the distance.

4182. *Mr. Theron.*] Have you any farm schools under your inspection?—No; they are inspected by the local teachers.

4183. *Rev. Coetzee.*] Do circuit schools answer?—I think they ought to. I have no practical experience.

4184. Are there any circuit schools in your district?—One or two; they are quite new.

4185. *Rev. Moorrees.*] Have you anything to say as regards the wants of the agricultural population?—We cannot do more than is being done already. As far as the Government is concerned, the grants are very liberal, and they seem anxious to do all they can, but the difficulty about distance seems insurmountable.

4186. At present, the Government does not like to give the capitation grant for district boarding schools to schools in town; do not you think if a boarding school in town is really doing the work of a district boarding school, it ought to get the capitation grant for poor children—the £6 grant?—Yes.

4187. Have you thought of any plan for reaching the isolated farm children?—That is a very difficult question.

4188. *Dr. Berry.*] Would not local Boards be more likely to grapple successfully with that question?—You have to deal in this case with individuals, there is the difficulty.

4189. *Dean Holmes.*] Have you anything to suggest about night schools; have you any in your district?—Not that I know of. I think they are desirable, though I

Mr.
F. Howe Ely.

Sept. 8th, 1891.

am very much afraid that the experience will be what it has been in Natal, that they will answer for a time only. There the attendance was good at first, but it fell off.

4190. Are there night schools in Natal?—There are Government aided night schools. They were begun in February last. The attendance was satisfactory at first, but it has been gradually getting less.

4191. *President.*] Why do you think the attendance is likely to fall off?—Like many other things in the colony. There is a night school here carried on by Mr. Parkhurst.

4192. Do you know what the system is in Natal?—No.

4193. How would you work night schools here?—On the plan of continuation schools, through whichever body takes up the work.

Rev. G. W. Cross examined.

Rev.
G. W. Cross.

Sept. 8th, 1891.

4194. *President.*] I believe you are Baptist minister in Graham's Town?—Yes.

4195. Have you any acquaintance with educational matters?—Yes. I have been a teacher.

4196. I believe you have also been appointed by the Government to inspect the farm schools in Albany?—Yes.

4197. Have you visited them?—Yes.

4198. Are the facilities afforded for meeting the wants of the children of the agricultural population sufficient or not?—I think the facilities are very good, but there is certainly not so much use made of them in Albany as there ought to be.

4199. Why not?—I can hardly understand why. Possibly the facilities are not known generally by the farmers who most need them. It is about five years ago since Sir Langham Dale asked me first to go out to the farm schools in Albany. At that time there were two, now there are seven I think, and I believe that covers all Albany. I have not inspected one in Lower Albany, as the time has not yet come round, but all these schools, I think, have been started through my being able to make known the advantages to the farmers and the opportunities that they have. It seems rather difficult to get this knowledge spread among the farmers. The very people who most need the help do not take newspapers, so that even if the Government intimated through that medium this plan of helping the farmers, I do not see how it would reach them. If some circular could be left at every farm, by means of the police or in some other way, it might help the matter a little. I think we are more behindhand in Albany than other districts. In Bedford, very many farmers avail themselves of the Government grant.

4200. Is not that to some extent because the farmers are poorer here?—It is just the very poor farmers who need the help.

4201. *Rev. Moorrees.*] The farmer has to contribute something, has he not?—The farmer makes an agreement with a tutor or governess as the case may be for the salary.

4202. Do not you find that there are many farmers too poor to pay the portion of the salary that falls on them?—I have been to farms where the salary is £24 a year, which is very little; and a good part of that is supplied by the Government; I do not think there are many farmers unable to pay a few pounds, but still, they could not get a good tutor for that.

4203. *Mr. Theron.*] Is not there a difficulty sometimes about a suitable place for holding the school in, or a dwelling for the teacher?—Yes, I have seen very unsuitable rooms used for the purpose; I have, however, always found the Educational Department very welling to help. I do not know that any farmer has made application for help in building a school room, but whenever any farmer has made application for furnishing a school room, he has always received help.

4204. The arrangement is, that the aid can only be got from the Government after a school has been twelve months in existence, and a teacher perhaps requires his pay quarterly or half yearly. Does not that interfere?—I never heard that the aid is obtained from the Government before the end of the year.

4205. In any of these schools that you inspected, are there any indigent children, or children of bywoners, as we call them?—Yes.

4206. Do they make use of these schools?—I have inspected this year one circuit school in a very poor district, and it seemed to me that the children of bywoners did make use of it.

4207. Was the capitation grant for indigent boarders received there?—I do not think there were any boarders. It is rather a densely populated part, Fouteinskloof, in Albany.

4208. Are they white children there?—Yes, all whites.

Rev.
G. W. Cross.
Sept. 8th, 1891.

4209. *Rev. Moorrees.*] Have you thought of any plan to meet the case of isolated farms?—The farm school grant as it is called, meets such cases, but it wants to be more generally known.

4210. In our district, unless a farmer has a certain number of children, five at least, or gets a neighbour to help make up the number, he cannot employ a teacher and cannot get the grant. Is not that so?—It seems to me that the circuit school grant would come in there.

4211. *President.*] Would you suggest in the case of isolated farms, that the farmers should get some privilege, if they send their children into town?—There is at present a provision for that—a £6 capitation grant in aid of boarding.

4212. Might that be altered in any way for those who can prove that they are in indigent circumstances?—In many places the charge is £45 a year for boarding alone, and £6 would not aid a farmer very much. In Graaff-Reinet I understand, board and education can be obtained for £30 to £36 a year, and a grant of £12 say would be a considerable help to a farmer.

4213. *Rev. Coetzee.*] You would be in favour of doubling the capitation grant and making it £12 a year in the case of indigent farmers?—I think the case of indigent farmers is very well met by the grants to farm schools. I am quite sure there are farmers who would be willing to take children for £12 a year, and half of that would be paid by the Government.

4214. *Rev. Moorrees.*] Do you think that the capitation grant should be extended to farm schools for indigent boarders?—Yes.

4215. *Dean Holmes.*] Have you found any great difficulty in obtaining teachers for farm schools?—Some difficulty. I think perhaps the supply is increasing now; but you sometimes find teachers who are utterly unqualified men, and who can do hardly anything.

4216. We have it in evidence that there are teachers as much as seventy-five years of age. Do you think more inducement should be held out with a view of securing a better class of teachers?—I am not so sure. I find that the best teachers in those farm schools as a rule are those who just make it a stepping-stone to something better. They get a few years experience at a farm school, and then go to a public school.

4217. So that a young teacher might begin at a farm school, gain experience, and then go on to a higher class of school in town?—If he has a teacher's certificate I should say yes. In nine cases out of ten a farmer would do a wise thing to engage such a young teacher, although holding a teacher's certificate does not always signify a qualification to teach. I have known men without a certificate who were better than teachers who had one, some, for instance, who have been educated in Europe in public schools, and are thoroughly qualified, but simply because they have not the Cape certificate, they are not eligible for the higher grant.

4218. *Mr. Theron.*] Have you come across cases where the parents have employed an elder girl or boy who have been educated at a public school to teach the other children?—Yes. One of the best schools I inspected was taught by the daughter of the house. She had a certificate.

4219. You do not think that is objectionable, do you?—No. I only know of one instance, and that was certainly a good school.

4220. Have you ever come across farm school teachers who have complained about the grant having been received by the farmer and never paid over to them?—No; I never came across such a case.

4221. I know it has happened that farmers have drawn the grant, and never paid it over to the teacher; is not that a drawback?—The grant is not due to the teacher; it is due to the farmer, and if a farmer asks my advice about it, I always tell him to make a definite agreement with the teacher about salary.

4222. If there was an over Board in existence for the whole district, elected by the ratepayers, would it not tend to greater interest being taken in education?—Yes, I think so.

4223. Do you think it is advisable to have some such Board?—The question is, whether it is practicable; it is certainly advisable where it is practicable.

4224. Do you think it is practicable?—I can conceive some places where it is not. In many towns, for instance, it would interfere too much with the existing interests.

4225. Supposing such Board confines itself to filling up gaps, leaving existing interests as they are, would that answer?—Yes, if it provides for existing interests.

4226. *Dean Holmes.*] You mean provided it left existing schools under their present management?—Yes. What I mean is this: suppose we take a case like Somerset East or Port Elizabeth, where there are large educational establishments, with considerable endowments; it might be that you would elect an over Board in such a neighbourhood that would work against some of those schools.

o 2

4227. But no over Board could establish a school without the sanction of the Educational Department, and the Department would take care that there was nothing of that sort, would it not?—Quite so. It wants guarding. If you can guard existing interests, such a thing would be very desirable.

4228. *President.*] What do you think is the great defect in the present system, if any?—I think one principal thing is the want of perpetual succession.

4229. What steps should be taken to give Boards of Management perpetual succession; how would you provide for'that?—I could not give an opinion to touch the general question, because I have not had an opportunity of studying it in other places than this. In villages and in towns where there is not competition through existing interests, I should say that a School Board would be the very best means of meeting the wants of the neighbourhood, giving perpetual succession, and providing for the tenure of public school property.

4230. Would you vest that property in the Board?—Yes.

4231. I believe you are yourself a guarantor of the public school here; have you transfer of your school property?—Yes.

4232. In whose name is it?—I do not know in whose name it is transferred; most likely in the name of the chairman for the time being.

4233. At the end of three years, the committee of management becomes defunct, and another may be called into existence, may it not?—Yes; the old Board keeps on till the new one is elected

4234. Suppose they fail to elect a new Board at the end of three years?—Such a thing could not happen. As soon as the time has expired, the Government demands other names.

4235. How do you get the other names?—There are volunteers.

4236. Is there a public meeting called?—Every year there should be a meeting called, but I am afraid that some years that has been omitted.

4237. Have you ever called a meeting within the last five years?—Yes, within the last three. The meeting is convened by public notice.

4238. Who comes to the meeting?—Those people who are interested generally.

4239. Any besides the guarantors?—Yes, often.

4240. Where do you meet?—In the Town Hall generally.

4241. How many attend?—I cannot say.

4242. As a rule, the same guarantors come in again, do they not?—I have been altogether nine years a guarantor of the public school. There are not many guarantors now that were on when I was first elected, possibly only about one. From the very fact that a man is a member of the public school committee, he is also a guarantor. In the case of this particular school, we have often discussed the matter how to provide for the tenure of the property and ensure perpetual succession. We have thought that we ought to be incorporated by a short Act of Parliament.

4243. Why should you be incorporated more than any other Boards that exist elsewhere?—If there are other Boards existing under the same conditions, I would apply it to them as well.

4244. If this over Board comes into existence, could you not invite them to become holders of the property and have it vested in them?—But the over Board is not in existence.

4245. Suppose there is such a Board?—That would alter the circumstances.

4246. Can you conceive of any interest they would have outside yours?—No, not if it were a thoroughly representative Board.

4247. Do you think an elected body is the best?—Yes.

4248. If it is the duty of the Board to fill up gaps, there might be perhaps some poorer centres requiring help, which would involve the Board in some expenditure outside the aid which Government gives, might there not?—At present the Government gives aid on what is called the £ for £ principle. We have a public school here, and if we found that we did not meet the public demands, we could extend, and as we extended we could get help from the Government.

4249. How do you mean extend?—Take a case like the Grey Institute with its two branches, one at North-end and one at South-end. In those branch institutions, they provide education for the poorer classes, and they are assisted by the Government on the £ for £ principle.

4250. *Mr. Theron.*] By whom do you think the over Board should be elected?—I should say by the people most interested certainly.

4251. Would you take the Parliamentary voters' list for the purpose, or the Divisional Council list?—I can hardly say. It would greatly depend upon where the money is to come from. I should be inclined to make the franchise for the Board as wide as possible.

Rev.
G. W. Cross.

Sept. 8th, 1891.

4252. Why not then adopt the Parliamentary franchise?—I think you are safer by making the franchise pretty wide, and you would be more likely to ensure the education of the whole community perhaps by adopting the Parliamentary franchise.

4253. *Dean Holmes.*] I presume the Education Department would always control such a Board, as it does in England, and step in where it saw a want is not supplied in any district?—Yes.

4254. So that that would remove your objection that the wealthy might say they will not provide for the poorer classes, or the latter say they do not care; the Department would step in and compel certain action to be taken?—All I care about is that the needs of a neighbourhood shall be provided for, and when it hinges upon the question of franchise, I am inclined to think that the wider you make it the better.

4255. *President.*] You think the Government should contribute half, and then if after the fees have been added there is a deficiency, the Board should be responsible out of the rates for making up that deficiency?—Yes; I am inclined to think so.

4256. Do you think the effect of that would be to bring upon the Board men regarded by the public as best fitted to deal with educational matters as a rule?—I hope so. I cannot say: There are so many motives and interests come into play in a popular election that you cannot tell very well what may take place. I still think that in some cases an Act of Incorporation would be advisable.

4257. *Dr. Berry.*] Would you give to this Board the power to fix the fees in public schools?—Yes; we have that power at present. I should say that it is to a large extent under the control of the Education Department. If we have had any difficulty, we have always been advised through the Inspector.

4258. Do you think it would be fair for the Department to give as large a grant in aid of the schools under the control of a School Board, as what that School Board raised by means of fees or from other sources. On what principle would you regulate the relation of the fees to the Government grant in amount?—I should be inclined to have it on the £ for £ principle, that is to say, supposing we could guarantee to raise either by fees or by subscriptions £100, not less than £100 should be given by the Department.

4259. *President.*] Suppose there are no fees at all, or very few, as in the case of poorer schools, what is the principle upon which the Government should pay. In England they have a fixed amount; 17s. 6d. is the maximum, and 10s. has lately been added under the Free Education Act, making 27s. 6d. altogether. That is what they consider secures free education?—In this country we have next to no direct taxation, and when we do have it, it is regarded as very obnoxious, as in the case of the late house duty. If you make a direct tax for education, you will have an enormous amount of local opposition to contend against.

4260. *Dr. Berry.*] You mean if you make it a charge on the local rates?—Yes, or a special charge.

4261. Then you would endeavour to raise as much of the school revenue by fees as possible?—Yes.

4262. And claim from the central Government a grant equal to what you raised by fees?—Not less than that.

4263. *President.*] Ought not the contribution from the Government to be fixed; is it not better to have it on the principle of numbers, and pay so much for each class of school as per the average number of scholars in attendance?—At present there is no danger of a richer school getting as much as it pleases, or of a very poor school getting less than it ought to get. Take the case of the public school; suppose it were in our power to double the fees all round, so that we could double our income, we should only get a certain amount for every master, that is all, and we should only get a master to every 30 or 40 boys, as the case may be, and the same with a poor school. Suppose there is a school that pays the teacher £160 a year, then it can get half of that from the Government.

4264. One of the evils complained of with regard to the present system is this: You have a school with 200 or 300 boys, and you cannot get from the Government more than a certain sum for the teachers, and the result is, that while that school is doing what is really Government work, it gets paid a very small sum, while on the other hand, a higher class school with very few pupils gets a large amount in proportion to the number of those pupils. That has been stated as a grievance?—The schools that get a small amount elect to get the small amount, that is to say, they will not bring themselves under the conditions of the Public Undenominational School Act in order to get the grant.

4265. If they did, children would not go there, for you find that children go to the mission schools because they are cheap. Your fees prevent a great many going to your school, do they not?—I think the public school system can produce an education as cheap as mission schools.

Rev.
G. W. Cross.

Sept. 8th, 1891.

4266. But they do not, do they ?—In many instances I think they do.

4267. In the mission schools the fees are twopence, threepence, and sixpence a week ?—I think in King William's Town the fees are quite as low as that in connection with the Dale College. It is not a mission school, but a branch school of the Dale College, and I could give the Commission an instance of a third class public undenominational school that provides absolutely free education, and does well. That is at Kareiga Valley.

4268. How does it manage that ?—The residents in the neighbourhood guarantee the schoolmaster's salary and make it up by subscriptions, and all the children come without paying fees.

4269. Then the guarantors are out of pocket ?—Yes, but their children are getting educated. There are some very poor people in the neighbourhood, but their children have as good a chance as the others. That is a case in which the present undenominational system meets the requirements.

4270. Mr. Theron.] You have had a pretty wide experience of the present system; with the exception of the defect as to want of continuity of managers, have you found any other fault in the system ?—I have not had so much experience as you give me credit for. I cannot call to mind any instance of the abuse of privileges or any case where the needs failed to be met, except that I have not seen so much provision made for the education of the natives as there might be.

4271. Dean Holmes.] Have you known any cases of hardship to teachers under the present guarantee system ?—No. I have sometimes thought that the system is made for teachers. The guarantors cannot get the money that has been promised them until the teacher has signed an affidavit that he has been paid all that is due.

4272. The Board of Managers goes out at the end of three years, and their contract with that teacher comes to an end, and there is no compulsion for the new Board to take on that teacher again, is there ?—I have never known that.

4273. It might be a hardship, might it not ?—Yes.

4274. You can imagine that in a village, where party feeling runs high sometimes, coercion might be resorted to, in order to get rid of a teacher rather unfairly, might it not ?—I suppose it might, but I have never met with a case.

4275. Dr. Berry.] Is it your opinion that the general standard of education as seen in our schools is very low or very high ?—It is neither.

4276. Does it satisfy you ?—Not yet, but it is improving.

4277. What statistics have you got to show that it is improving ?—I can see that it is improving here in Graham's Town. I have had 14 years experience here, and for 9 years I have had a seat on the School Board. I would take the public school or almost any of our large schools, and I notice that the children are being sent earlier to school. When I first knew this school here, the preparatory class was filled with boys over twelve years of age, and many up to sixteen or seventeen, whereas now the preparatory class is filled with children from six to eleven years of age—possibly twelve, but the average age is about 8½ years.

4278. If you take the figures of the Education Department I find that during the last ten years not quite six per cent. of the total scholars attending school reach the fourth standard of attainment; would you not reason from that that the general education of the country was rather poor and weak ?—Yes, I should.

4279. Would not that lead you to suppose that there must be a defect in the present system somewhere ?—I am inclined to think that it is attributable to the fact of the sparseness of the population and the immense distances that most people live from schools, so that the children are neglected at an early age; they do not get sent to school to learn the first standard or the second standard work, till they ought to be in the fourth standard work, and then they have two years possibly at school.

4280. Is not that only another way of saying there is a defect ?—Yes; I can imagine a more perfect system.

4281. Does it not seem to indicate that a remedy is needed somewhere and must be applied ?—I think so.

4282. Do you see any promise of a remedy in this School Board system and its possible development in particular localities and the facilities it would offer for reaching sparsely peopled districts, as well as in the general increase of interest that it would create among the community ?—Yes; generally speaking, if it is practicable in any neighbourhood to have the whole community responsible for the education of all children it would be a good thing and increase the interest taken in education, and lead to a great deal more effort being put forth.

4283. Mr. Theron.] Are you positive of that ?—No, I cannot be positive; but I should judge that that would be the tendency. It is reasonable to suppose it.

4284. Dr. Berry.] It is a good thing in these as in other matters, is it not, to try and include as many people as you can in furthering the object you have in view, -Yes.

4285. *Mr. Theron.*] If the Board were elected by the Parliamentary voters, do you think by that means you would get the best men, men really interested in education?—On the whole, yes. With our present institutions it seems to me to be the only way. I could imagine the whole thing being worked from the other end, from the Education Department, but I do not think that is possible in a country that has a Parliamentary franchise so wide as ours. Rev.
G. W. Cross.
Sept. 8th, 1891

4286. Do you know the difference in the qualification of those who vote for members of Parliament and those who vote for members of the Divisional Council?—Yes. One is a £25 and the other a £75 qualification.

4287. You say you think you would get the best men elected by this means, but cannot you conceive of some election cry being raised, such as extravagance on the part of the Board, and the necessity for retrenchment, through means of which the cause of education might suffer?—I would prefer to trust the people generally than any particular class, especially the class that has property, as they will have to pay most of the rates. In all these things, I do not find that local influence works more say in a Parliamentary election than it does in a Divisional Council election; indeed, I think that local influence is greater in a Divisional Council election.

4288. Take the case of a small village, where you have the largest number of electors in the country and the smallest number in the village, would you in that case adopt the same franchise?—It would very largely depend upon the provision you propose to make for education. If you are going to provide only for the villages, then it seems to me unfair to put the control of their school under people outside, but if you are going to take the whole district, and say that there shall be sufficient school accommodation for every child in the district, then I think that the whole district should be represented at the Board.

4289. But still you have the smallest number of voters in the town and the largest in the country, and you leave the largest number to rule the smaller number, because they can put in whom they like. Would not the town schools suffer on that account?—I do not think so. It seems to me that the great trouble has been this. Up to now you had a certain advantage in the towns that the farmers did not get in the way of education, and I am afraid there would not be a disposition on the part of villages to bear their share of the additional expense for providing for education in the rural neighbourhoods.

4290. From your argument am I to take it that the country would be able to put all their members in in opposition to the town?—I should think not. It is not likely that you would have all the country uniting against the village.

4291. Still they may be in the majority, would not that?—If you govern by majorities, the minorities must submit. The hardship has been not in villages but rural districts. The villages and towns have had unfair advantage; that is now being redressed by the farm school grants, and in some cases it has made a great difference. Formerly a farmer was put to a very large expense in order to get his children educated at all, whereas the villagers or townspeople could get education for very little indeed. All the Government aid came into the towns and villages at one time.

4292. Would the establishment of a School Board rectify that?—It might do so.

4293. *Rev. Moorrees.*] Are you in favour of the establishment of a Board or not?—Taking it as a general principle, yes. It is a thing that ought to interest the whole community, and if you give the whole community work to do, you will interest them. I do not think there is any better way than that.

4294. *Mr. Theron.*] Do you know that in the constitution of our Divisional Councils, the country sometimes has to suffer for the benefit of the town?—I have not noticed it. I have lived out here five years, and seen Divisional Council elections.

4295. Would you give this School Board rating powers?—If it is necessary I should. I take it that the most important thing is, to get education diffused as widely as possible, but if you are going to bring the greed and selfishness of the people into play against that, it would be rather a bad thing. At present, a great deal of money is provided from the public funds, and all of us have to contribute, but we do not pay it directly and we do not seem to feel it, but if there is a penny or a two penny rate or something of that kind added on to the Divisional Council tax, I am afraid there will be a great outcry. The question is just this, am I in favour of direct or indirect taxation for this purpose? In this country I think for the present, indirect taxation is most likely to be effective.

4296. Then the School Boards need not have rating powers?—At present the guarantors have to be responsible for a certain amount, and I would have the proposed Boards similarly responsible.

4297. Would you take the power out of the hands of the Education Department with regard to the distribution of the money?—No. In the case of the grant for

Rev.
G. W. Cross.

Sept. 8th, 1891.

farm schools, for instance, it is not given until the Government official has reported, and then there is a result grant as well. If four children have passed in the fourth standard they get £1 extra each.

4298. *Rev. Moorrees.*] Are you aware that in the smaller villages there is almost every year a deficiency in the accounts ?—I am not aware of it.

4299. As a matter of fact, the guarantors have sometimes to pay very largely out of their own pockets, have they not ?—In the case of a school I am connected with, a third class school, everything comes out of the guarantors' pockets, except the Government aid.

4300. *President.*] They have in fact established a system of free education among themselves ?—Yes.

4301. *Rev. Moorrees.*] Would you give to the proposed School Board the power of recommending certain voluntary schools for Government aid, private schools started by some private body ?—I do not think private schools should receive Government aid. Only representative bodies under public control should receive Government aid. If the schools are to be supported out of the rates or taxes, then the ratepayers or the taxpayers should be the managers, as the case may be.

4302. *Rev. Coetzee.*] Do you know of any case where a school has been closed or the teacher dismissed because a fresh guarantee list could not be got up ?—No, it has not come under my personal knowledge. I have known a school to lapse because they could not get a suitable teacher.

4303. Your knowledge is mostly confined to this place and district, is it not ?— Yes, and King William's Town.

4304. *Rev. Moorrees.*] According to your opinion, are the defects of the present system so great that a change is urgently required ?—You will, I think, meet the case better by development than by revolution.

4305. Would the Board School system be a development or a revolution in your opinion ?—I certainly should like to testify that I think the time has come for compulsory attendance in villages and towns.

4306. *Dr. Berry.*] Would you apply that compulsory system to whites and blacks ?—Yes, in villages and towns. I would not go so far as to express an opinion as to its applicability to locations.

4307. Have you anything to say on the question of language ?—I have given some little thought to the matter, and I think it would be a misfortune to change the character of the Elementary examination by adding another subject. If it is necessary to provide for Dutch as well as English, I do not see any objection to having the papers printed in the two languages. The only radical alteration that it would necessitate would be an alteration in the literary paper ; you might have to take a Dutch author instead of an English author. I think it would be a misfortune to make the examination to consist of five subjects rather than four.

4308. *Dean Holmes.*] You think it would destroy the elementary character of the examination ?—Yes. It seems so to me, and I have had a great deal of experience one way and another, that the Elementary examination as it is, commends itself universally to teachers, public as well as private, and it is increasing in popularity every year, and not only so, but it is more reliable as a standard than any other examination conducted by the Cape University.

4309. You would be in favour of abolishing the Elementary examination altogether as a stepping-stone to the Higher examinations, letting candidates if they like, go straight to the higher ?—I should be inclined to do that. At the same time, I can see the danger of conducting an examination in the higher subjects without having any guarantee of the foundations or ground work. The papers at present in the School Higher examination do very little to enquire into what you might call the ground work of knowledge, but if there can be some guarantee that that has been attended to, then students might go straight on as you suggest. I should say, for instance, that a fifth standard public school certificate, or some other test, might do instead of the Elementary examination.

4310. *President.*] Suppose there are not these two sets of papers you suggest, and it is advisable to have Dutch introduced into the Elementary examination, what do you think would be the best way of doing it without any injustice ?—The Elementary examination seems to me to be very important, because it means the beginning of a career and not the finish. If you substitute for it a public school certificate, as has been advocated in some cases, then the scholar may feel that he has come to the end of his course, whereas if he takes a University examination, he feels he has only begun his course. I think it is very desirable that the beginning should be such that a boy of thirteen of ordinary abilities should be able to take it.

4311. *Rev. Coetzee.*] Is it right because it is the beginning of a boy's career that the Dutch language should be excluded from the Elementary examination ?—I do not propose to exclude it. I say have two sets of papers.

4312. *Dr. Berry.*] The impracticability of that is that boys whose mother tongue is Dutch in this colony could not as a rule tackle a geography paper in Dutch, or a history paper in Dutch, or an arithmetic paper in Dutch?—I think the difficulty could be got over.

G. W. Cross.
Sept. 8th, 1891

4313. *Rev. Moorrees.*] Would you do anything to promote the study of Dutch in that way?—If it is a question of promoting the study of Dutch, and not affording facilities for giving instruction in the language, I do not see any better way than giving bursaries. You find no difficulty in getting boys here in Graham's Town to study Dutch, boys who mean to go in for the Civil Service, because there is a prize at the end of it.

4314. Is it not but fair in a bi-lingual country that a boy should have a right to expect that his own language should be recognized in the first examination?—I am only afraid you will alter the character of the examination if you have five subjects and two languages. You will find that at least a year will be put on to the average age before a child undertakes it.

4315. Then according to your idea a Dutch boy must be severely handicapped, because he has to learn the Dutch language in addition?—I would let the same paper be printed in both languages, or if it is not desirable to have the paper all the way through in Dutch, just have the literary paper in both languages.

4316. You say that if you add another language paper, you will alter the elementary character of the examination. Take the Dutch boys of the country; they have in addition to all the other subjects to study the Dutch language also, so that they are severely handicapped, are they not, if the adding of one language to the examination is such a severe matter?—My proposal meets that case exactly, because the paper can be taken either in Dutch or English as the boy chooses. I suppose that you are correct in saying that the Dutch boy is severely handicapped. It seems to me quite clear that the three papers, mathematical, geographical, and historical, must be just about the same in any language; the only paper that could give any difficulty would be the grammar or literary paper, so I say let that be in the two languages.

4317. In continental countries it is not supposed to alter the elementary character of study to take up a second language at a very early age, is it?—I do not know whether you have noticed that as a rule Englishmen are slow linguists, possibly Frenchmen are too, but Germans are not, and Dutchmen are not; so that you might find a German child very quick with a couple of languages, but not able to compete with an English child in some other studies.

4318. Then because the English boy is slow in acquiring languages, the Dutch boy must suffer?—The Dutch boy is quick in acquiring languages, and the Dutch boy gets all the advantage when he comes to the Higher examinations.

4319. We are talking of the Elementary examination?—I would propose to take off the handicap which you seem to think exists by an alternative paper.

4320. Going to the Higher examinations, do you think it is fair that one of the languages of the country should be bracketed with German and French, which are foreign languages, and receive an equal number of marks with those languages?—I should say certainly if the same time is given to the papers.

4321. You would not make any difference between the different papers?—In matriculation, one modern language besides English is necessary, and therefore, one modern language I should say would have about the same number of marks as is given to any other three hours paper. They are all three hours papers.

4322. Do not you think it right for a native of this country to study the Dutch language if possible?—It strikes me that there is the question of patriotism involved, which I can thoroughly understand. I remember, for instance, our own people going out from Holland to America, simply because they were afraid of getting absorbed, and losing their language and customs. Naturally that is a question that presents itself in one light to you and in another to me.

4323. You would not do anything to induce children of English parentage to take up the Dutch language, short of compelling them?—I would not do that, not put it over French or German. If I were a Dutchman, I certainly should.

4324. *Dr. Berry.*] The country does offer an inducement, by giving a reward in the Civil Service for those who take Dutch; is not that so?—Yes.

4325. *Mr. Theron.*] Have you ever seen girls pass the Civil Service examination?—Not yet.

4326. *Rev. Moorrees.*] Is making Dutch compulsory in the Civil Service examination a reward, or is it not rather an obligation, because it is needed in the business of the country?—To students it is a reward.

4327. Am I to understand that you hold that Dutch has been made a compulsory subject for the Civil Service examination as a reward for those knowing Dutch, or is

Rev.
G. W. Cross.

Sep'. 8th, 1891.

it made compulsory because the necessities of the country require it?—I should say that it was made compulsory by the examiners, because the country requires it; but I say further, that it does act as a reward to the students in our schools and colleges. If the question asked is this, how to promote the study of the Dutch language, I say it is solved by the Civil Service examination.

4328. But only a small proportion comparatively, go in for the Civil Service examination?—Then there is the plan of giving bursaries.

4329. *President.*] Are you in favour of giving bursaries?—Yes. I may say that practically Dutch would do me very little good here in Graham's Town.

4330. Have you anything to say on the subject of night schools. Have you ever had one?—No; but I take great interest in the matter, and I should very much like to see something done; we are thinking it over.

4331. Would you give those who have gone through a course of education an opportunity of continuing their studies or taking up other subjects?—If we made education compulsory in towns and villages, then night schools can only be extension.

4332. Do you think that night schools could be established on farms?—I do not know. With regard to children on farms, you find it very frequently happens that they have to work pretty late in the evening.

4333. Have you anything to say on the subject of technical education?—No.

4334. Are you in favour of it, and do you think that it has been hitherto neglected?—There is a great demand for technical schools. At St. Andrew's College here, provision is made for boys to learn carpentering if necessary, and I know it is done at the public school.

Mr. A. C. McDonald examined.

Mr.
A. C. McDonald.

Sept. 8th, 1891.

4335. *President.*] What are you?—Government agricultural assistant in Graham's Town.

4336. What are your views regarding the present system of guarantors. Should it be done away with, and the rates be liable for any deficiency in the school, the School Boards, if established, having the duty not merely of finding schools for whites, but also for natives?—In my opinion, the system in vogue of only a few persons guaranteeing any deficiency in school funds is not a very practicable one, and I think the time has now arrived when all owners and occupiers in each district and town should be liable to taxation, assessed upon the respective value of their holdings; such taxation to be borne in equal half shares by the proprietors and occupiers respectively. A Board of Directors should be established in each district (to be tri-annually elected by the ratepayers), who should be authorized to impose the necessary taxation and be entrusted with the formation, management and control of schools in their respective districts, for whites, and in case of need for the natives; but with this condition, that their actions as such Board shall be subject to the approval and confirmation of the Education Department of the colony.

4337. In your opinion should compulsory education be applied?—Compulsory education is, I think, a necessity in the case of whites, and all between the age of 9 and 15 years, or the former until they have arrived at a certain standard of proficiency in education which some may attain to before the latter age, should, if living within a radius of ten miles of an established school, be compelled to attend for such a period as may be fixed by the Board and confirmed by the Education Department, during each year, either until they have arrived at the age of 15, or such sooner time as in the case of their having attained the standard of proficiency laid down; or, unless good and sufficient reason can be given by the parents or guardians of any child to the contrary. The fees payable for such tuition and instruction should be within the discretion of the Board. In the case, however, of children living without the radius of such school, it should also be made compulsory, but for shorter periods and with a reduction in the fees so as to meet the question of increased expenditure which would necessarily be incurred in such cases by their having to board and lodge elsewhere than with their parents. With natives it should also be made compulsory in the case of those living in all established locations, but their education should partake more of an industrial nature. With regard to those living outside locations or on farms, it might be left optional. My reasons for drawing class distinction are: That in the case of the former the children are allowed to grow up to lead a lazy and indolent life, and in consequence, when they enter service, they are found to be untaught and undisciplined workmen, whilst those brought up on farms are more or less trained and taught to work in the tending of sheep and cattle and in husbandry from their early youth, and in the majority of cases they will be found to be more or less efficient upon entering regular service.

4338. *Dean Holmes.*] Would not you apply compulsory education in towns to chil- Mr.
A. C. McDonald. dren under nine years of age?—Boys under nine could not very well come long distances. You might in towns, compel them to come at a younger age. In Graham's Town they Sept. 8th, 1891. come to school at six or seven.

4339. One of the difficulties is, that they are so short a time at school, as they are wanted for work at an early age, and if they do not go to school until they are nine, they are not likely to get much instruction?—In the country you cannot expect a boy to come nine or ten miles to school, until he is at least nine years of age. Very many children are uneducated, because they cannot come to the schools.

4340. Then the age of nine would apply to the country, but not to towns?—Yes.

4341. *Rev. Coetzee.*] Are you in favour of compulsory education for all classes, including the blacks living in locations?—Yes.

4342. How would you supply them with school accommodation if education was made compulsory?—Districts would be rated and compelled to provide school buildings.

4343. At whose expense?—The ratepayers.

4344. *President.*] Do not you think if compulsory education is applied to locations, and not in the country, heads of families would in many cases leave the location rather than be compelled to send their children to school?—I have no doubt that such would be the case in many instances, but then they would of necessity have to go on to some farm where their children would be subject to much the same sorts of training as they would receive at an industrial school. Besides, I consider if such a step were taken by them, it would not only prove of material benefit to themselves, but to the colony at large, in so far as, that instead of leading a lazy and useless life in the location, they would with their families then enter into service on farms, which would be the means of supplying the insufficiency of labour, so keenly experienced by many of our farmers at the present time.

4345. Can such industrial schools be universal and cheap?—Yes, in the following manner:—Let them be established on farms in close proximity to locations, and if possible where parts of the land are, or could be, put under irrigation. Tobacco, fruit, and garden produce generally could be extensively grown, which would afford sufficient employment for, and instruction to a large number of boys, whilst at the same time a fair amount of literary education might be imparted to them; and further, should any show a disposition for masonry, carpentry, &c., instruction in these could at little cost be supplied. On these lines and under proper discipline, our natives may be developed into more serviceable workmen, and better suited for their future calling, whilst the returns and profits derivable from their labours, upon the school being thoroughly established, would go far towards defraying the expenses thereof.

4346. Can you suggest any means of introducing a system by which whites and natives could be educated together on some farm, which would be of benefit to both in the pursuance of agriculture to which so many of our youths devote their lives, and at the same time they would be suited for their respective future positions of employer and labourer?—In my annual report to Government for 1891, I had occasion to refer to the subject of agricultural education, and in doing so made the following remarks:—"That Government take over a farm in some central part of the colony where the arable land should be put under irrigation. The holding to be large enough to support a stud of improved cattle, sheep, and horses, and a fair number of colonial cattle for experimental purposes, the surplus of which could be disposed of at an annual sale to be held each year for that purpose. Only persons who have completed their general education should be admitted, and should be obliged to reside at the farm, unless under exceptional cases where the students lived within reasonable distance of the school. The course of lectures and operations to last for about six months each year, during which period the head veterinary surgeon, an agricultural chemist and botanist could be taken into requisition, and short courses of lectures given by the tobacco and other experts on subjects of interest to the farmers, the general agricultural classes to be taken by the principal. By means of a combination of school and farm with a proper staff of experts, such a course of special instruction could be provided as would be most useful to the agriculturist, that is to say, by classroom and outdoor instruction, the general principles of agriculture and the various sciences connected therewith could be taught, as well as their sound application to the cultivation of the soil, the rearing of stock, and their treatment in health and disease, and the processes and products of the dairy, together with the working and general business of a well-managed farm. An agricultural institution based on such lines, would, I think, be popular with young farmers, many of whom could devote part of their time each year to acquiring a knowledge of the various subjects and branches connected with their calling, and even the older farmers might be induced to occasionally visit the farm and thereby gain some useful

Mr.
A. C. *McDonald.*

Sept. 8th, 1891.

information. Experiments for testing the suitability of imported seeds for the colony, such for example as the rust-resisting power of different varieties of cereals, could be conducted on a sufficiently large scale to make the results somewhat reliable." Now, if a school was once established on the above lines, then from it could be taken such students as were found qualified to impart the necessary knowledge of agriculture, who together with a master trained in the imparting of literary education would be able to conduct a school for the whites and natives together, giving the former more of the literary and scientific education, and the latter less of the literary and the entire manual labour. By such a course their respective positions could be maintained.

4347. Should both English and Dutch be taught at the established Board Schools? —This is a matter which I think should be left to the discretion of directors, who being elected by the ratepayers of the district, ought to be the best judges. In some parts of the colony, English is almost solely spoken—in other parts Dutch—what we want is education for the masses, be it in English or Dutch or both. Only let each district be treated separately, and the circumstances taken fully into consideration and the directors be allowed to act accordingly.

4348. What are your views with regard to the working of denominational schools? —With denominational schools already in existence or likely to be established hereafter, and in cases where tutors are kept, I would recommend no interference whatever, beyond insisting on an annual or half-yearly inspection by such persons as may from time to time be appointed by the Educational Department for the purpose of ascertaining whether a sufficient education is being imparted to the pupils. At the same time, I should recommend that these schools receive some Government aid.

Port Elizabeth, Wednesday, September 9th, 1891.

PRESENT:

Sir J. D. BARRY (President),

Mr. Theron,	Rev. Coetzee,
Dr. Berry,	Rev. Moorrees.
Dean Holmes,	

Mr. Edward Noaks examined.

Mr.
Edward Noaks.

Sept. 9th, 1891.

4349. *President.*] I believe you are a graduate of the University of Cambridge ? —Yes.

4350. And you are Rector of the Grey Institute at Port Elizabeth ?—Yes.

4351. Had you before been devoting time to education ?—Yes, in England.

4352. Do you know the English system of education ?—Yes.

4353. With reference to the question of irregularity of attendance in town schools, does such irregularity exist as far as you know ?—I should say that the attendance in Port Elizabeth, which is the only town that I am acquainted with, is good, and compares favourably with the attendance in England.

4354. What percentage of those on the roll attend daily ?—At the branch schools of the Grey Institute, about 85 per cent. and at the Hill school up to 95 per cent. on the average.

4355. Do the poorer classes attend at the branches of the Grey Institute ?—Yes.

4356. What is the cause of this regular attendance ?—I attribute it to the system. We are very particular about attendance.

4357. In what way ?—If a child is absent from school, he is expected on returning to school to bring a written excuse from his parents, stating the reason, and if the reason is not considered satisfactory, some pressure is brought to bear on the child, and also on the parent.

4358. What pressure is brought to bear on the parents ?—I would myself write and enquire, and express an opinion on the subject.

4359. What are the fees payable by the parents for children attending such schools as you have mentioned ?—At the branch schools, which are not for the very poor, they vary from 5s. a month in the upper standards down to 3s. a month for infants; and at the Hill school, they vary from twelve guineas a year in the upper forms down to five guineas a year in the lower forms, the fees being divided into four quarters.

4360. Do the bulk of the children pay fees ?—They all pay, and pay regularly.

4361. You have no free scholars ?—There are certain foundation scholarships, for which money has been funded so as to pay for them, and we have at the branch schools some half-dozen pupils altogether, the children of poor parents and widows, who are admitted free by the Board.

4362. On whose application ?—The matter is brought before the Board generally by a clergyman who is interested in the case, and the Board considers it on its own merits, and it has the power to remit the fees.

4363. Both the schools you mention are for the whites; rather a high class of school are they not?—There are very few coloured children at all; not more than two or three altogether, I think.

4364. Have you any knowledge of schools for the poorer classes?—I am acquainted to some extent with what is going on at White's Road mission school, but not an accurate acquaintance. That is in connection with Trinity Church.

4365. Have you any knowledge of St. Paul's Mission School?—I have examined that school and can speak very highly of the work carried on there.

4366. Do you know about the attendance there?—Not definitely. I believe it is very good.

4367. What are their fees?—They are about the same at St. Paul's as they are at our branch schools in the higher standards. They are lower in the lower standards.

4368. What are they in the lower standard?—I could not say definitely.

4369. Do you think there is any necessity to do anything to secure the regular attendance of children actually on the roll, more than is now being done; do you think a compulsory system would be wise?—According to the last census returns, the number of children in Port Elizabeth not attending any school at all must be fairly considerable.

4370. What do you take it to be?—I could not say definitely.

4371. Do you think those children require to be induced to go to some school?—Yes. I know some cases of my own personal knowledge where white children who ought to go to school are not attending.

4372. Are those the children of poor people who cannot pay?—Yes.

4373. Do you know any cases of children of parents who can pay but will not?—No.

4374. With regard to those who cannot pay, how do you think they ought to be brought into school?—To meet their case, if one free school were established in a town, the parents of poor children might send them there, and I think, in that case, children who are loafing about the streets might be compelled to attend these free schools.

4375. You would apply compulsion to them?—Yes.

4376. You would compel the parents to make their children come?—Yes.

4377. Through attendance and truant officers?—I think that the present police would be sufficient.

4378. As attendance and truant officers?—As truant officers.

4379. Who ought to be the attendance officers; do you think the masters would be sufficient?—I think if the children were in attendance, the teaching influence would be sufficient to make them attend satisfactorily.

4380. Suppose they are not in attendance, in order to find out where these children are, would not you have some officer to visit the houses of the parents?—Not at present.

4381. You think an attendance officer is not absolutely required, but only a truancy officer to take up the children found about the streets?—I think the influence of the clergy and others interested in the welfare of the poor would be sufficient.

4382. Would you apply this to blacks as well as whites?—I think that for the black children there ought certainly to be separate schools.

4383. Would you apply compulsion to both classes?—Yes.

4384. If there are separate schools, should they both be free?—Yes.

4385. Do you think the nature of the education in both schools should be identical or in some respects different, in consideration of the future calling of the whites and the future calling of the blacks?—In the case of coloured children I should certainly like to see the education different to what is given. I think it should be more of a mechanical description, and girls should be trained definitely for domestic service, and learn needlework and so on; but of course so far as reading, writing, and arithmetic goes, I think the education would have to be the same or pretty nearly the same in each case.

4386. And the same with the boys?—Yes

4387. And what would you add in the way of industrial education for them?—In the town schools I hardly see what could be done, but in the country they could be taught gardening and so on.

4388. I see that in Natal, all, both boys and girls are taught to sew, and are made to keep their clothes in good repair. The boys cultivate the garden and field crops, and the girls in town are taught house work. Does it not suggest itself to your mind as being the right thing?—Yes. For very young children there might be the Kindergarten system, or some development of it, for both sexes.

4389. In the case of European children, would you also apply some industrial education of a little higher character in the way of mechanical instruction?—It would be useful, but I do not think myself that very much can be done in school. The giving of an elementary education takes up almost the entire time.

Mr.
Edward Noaks.
——
Sept. 9th, 1891.

4390. Do you think the present system of mission school teaching fails in respect of not training children industrially?—Our mission schools here are not properly speaking mission schools; they are schools just like the third class schools.

4391. These mission schools in towns as well as mission schools up country would seem to fail in not adding an industrial department. Would that be better for the natives themselves in your opinion?—I think so decidedly.

4392. You said you would apply compulsion to natives, can you suggest any means by which you could make parents more interested in their children going to such schools? What do you think would be the best means?—I cannot think of any other means than general influences such as the influence of clergymen and those who have to deal with them.

4393. If you levied an education tax on the natives, do you think they are likely to be taught by degrees to appreciate the value of education?—No, I think it might have a contrary effect. I think that an education tax would be resented to some extent and would not be welcome.

4394. If they knew that the money was to be spent on the education of their children, would not they come to appreciate it by degrees?—I very much doubt it.

4395. What would you suggest?—Compulsion, together with general humanizing influences.

4396. Do you think the truant officers should operate both on blacks and whites so as to get the children into school?—Yes.

4397. *Rev. Coetzee.*] If you have compulsory education, you will have to provide the necessary school accommodation, will you not?—Yes.

4398. How would you suggest finding school buildings, both for blacks and whites?—In the case of school buildings, I think the municipalities and the Government might very well be expected to contribute on the £ for £ principle for all that were considered necessary.

4399. And you would levy a tax for that purpose?—Yes.

4400. For both classes?—Yes; whites and blacks, so far as I can see. It is not to be expected that parents should contribute towards school buildings. So far as my experience goes, that has never been done successfully. Buildings, if wanted, have to be erected through some extraneous means; they cannot be paid for out of school fees. You require that the Municipalities or the Government should start the buildings to begin with, and I would suggest the £ for £ principle.

4401. If compulsory education is applied here, would you have sufficient school accommodation for the children?—The present school buildings are, I think, pretty crowded at present, and if many more children were compelled to attend, additional buildings would certainly have to be erected. The attendance at many of the schools, especially the mission schools, is very crowded now already, and I should not wish to see waifs and strays from the streets imported into the existing schools as free scholars; it would have a bad influence upon them. If free schools were established for the waifs and strays, some parents who are poor would gladly avail themselves of them to send their children, in preference to those schools where they are now paying. If a building is established for free education, it would be utilized.

4402. With regard to the natives living about here, have they properties that can be taxed?—There are huts in the location, but I am not familiar with the matter. The mission schools I am acquainted with have white and coloured children.

4403. *Mr. Theron.*] Would you be in favour of keeping the two races distinct?—Yes.

4404. *Dr. Berry.*] If any further development of the public-aided school system is required in the Colony, what lines would you advise we should proceed upon; would you be in favour of developing the public undenominational schools, or the mission schools?—I am in favour of the lines suggested by Sir Langham Dale on the whole. I think that in every village where there is only one school, that school ought to be an undenominational school; but in towns like Port Elizabeth, where there is a sufficient number of parents belonging to a particular denomination, if they want to have a school of their own and a staff of their own, I can see no reason why they should not have their wish gratified—making use of denominational agencies to work these poorer schools. Various safeguards would be required in that case, and I think there ought to be a public audit of accounts.

4405. If you encourage denominational education in the larger towns, would not the infection spread to the smaller towns also?—The Education Department would have to step in and say whether in a town there was room for a school in connection with a particular denomination. If there was not a sufficient number of pupils for a particular school or number of schools in existence, there would be no cause for starting a new denominational school.

Mr.
Edward Noaks.

Sept. 9th, 1891.

4406. Would not there be a constant desire to make a case, and would it not be very difficult for the Education Department to resist the outcry of the denominational bodies in the smaller towns. Would it not lead to endless disquietude and disruption of the whole educational interests?—I do not apprehend that there would be such an outcry. I think it would chiefly apply to the class of schools that Sir Langham Dale is contemplating, the fourth class public undenominational schools, which we have already in existence. In Port Elizabeth we have in connection with St. Peter's Church an excellent mission school. The Marist Brothers also have an excellent school connected with the Roman Catholic Church, and the only question is, whether, if Sir Langham Dale's proposals are carried out, these schools would not be better found than they are at present. At present the maximum grant is £75 a year, and they can get no grant for buildings, hence the schools are crowded, and the staff is not so good as it might be. The effect of Sir Langham Dale's proposals is to give a large grant to existing so-called mission schools, and this would help them to be more efficient. At St. Paul's school lately they have raised funds to erect a corrugated iron building for boys   That is all they could manage, as they are not sufficiently wealthy.

4407. *President.*] How many children are there?—Upwards of 250 altogether, girls and boys. It is not satisfactory that children should be taught in a corrugated iron building—the heat in summer is insufferable.

4408. *Dr. Berry.*] You said that it should be incumbent on Municipal and similar bodies to assist in the erection of school buildings, that is to say, that public money would have to be spent. Does not the expenditure of public money on school buildings imply that there should be public control. How can you dissociate the two ideas of public expenditure and public control?—In this case there is public control; enough I think to ensure efficiency. What more public control is wanted I cannot see. We have inspectors who inspect these mission schools and guarantee their efficiency, or otherwise; and if you have a body of gentlemen of a particular denomination interested in a school and anxious to undertake its management, and the parents also wish the school to be under a particular influence, I cannot see why they should not have their wish.

4409. Suppose in your town and in other towns there is no accommodation in the mission schools for those driven to school under any compulsory system, under whose control are the new schools to be set up?—That is a difficult question. It ought to be undenominational, I consider, unless a strong case is made out that there is a field for a denominational section. Unless the denominations are sufficiently strong to have a school of their own, then I think there ought to be a public undenominational school, where all children are upon the same plane.

4410. *President.*] Do you consider it was present to the mind of Sir Langham Dale in suggesting the fourth class public undenominational schools, that he should have an opportunity of further aiding these existing mission schools under that system?—That was my impression.

4411. Is it not rather a misnomer to call such schools undenominational? Why not call them fourth class public schools?—I think that would be preferable.

4412. Do you think the term "undenominational" might be struck out in regard to all schools?—Yes, I think so.

4413. *Dean Holmes.*] You said you would make the police truant officers. Would not that be rather treating children as if they were criminals and create a prejudice against the system. Would it not be better to have a proper attendance officer, a municipal officer for instance?—It was the question of expense that led me to think the present staff of police would be the best agency.

4414. Might it not have the effect I refer to on the minds of rather sensitive people?—I should not expect the parents of these unfortunate gutter children to be a very sensitive class.

4415. It might happen that some children did not belong to that class, and the police in the exercise of their duty, might think it necessary to take up these children?—I think the police would have to be under somewhat stringent regulations. It would not be within their province to take up any child found in the streets between school hours, there would have to be some further collateral circumstances in order to give ground for the conviction that a child was not attending school. These waifs and strays must be knocking about in the streets and known as gutter children.

4416. Habitual loiterers?—Yes.

4417. *Dr. Berry.*] If the expense of the truant officer was met by a Government allowance, would your objection disappear?—No. I think there would be so little work in a town like Port Elizabeth for a truant officer that it would not pay to create such an official.

4418. Do you speak locally?—It would apply to all the larger towns also.

Mr.
Edward Noaks.

Sept. 9th. 1891.

4419. *Rev. Moorrees.*] Would you apply the principle of Government aid to denominational schools of a higher grade?—I am in favour of it as a question of principle. In England we see the denominational system side by side with the undenominational system, both producing good results, and one obvious advantage is, that supporters of a particular denomination contribute funds towards the schools, and in that way the State is spared the expense; but I should be very sorry to see any clashing of the two systems. I prefer myself the undenominational system, but on that account I am not opposed to the existence of the other.

4420. Would there not be a danger of their clashing, if Government supports an opposition school?—It would require a very firm voice in the Education office to be able to say such and such a school is wanted or is not wanted.

4421. Are you in favour of giving Government aid right through?—I ought to explain that I am not in favour of very large schools. In America there was at one time a feeling that there was a great advantage in having schools with 1,000 pupils, with several parallel classes. If that were the case, then I think one would be compelled to draw a line and say, only undenominational schools can be admitted.

4422. You do not think that large schools are so beneficial?—In any school where there is a sufficient number of pupils to form a class in each grade and standard, the school is large enough.

4423. *President.*] What do you consider a sufficiently large size?—On the average, 30 pupils to a standard, and there are five standards. That would make the school 150 to 200 pupils. I consider that large enough.

4424. *Rev. Moorrees.*] That would not apply to the preparatory department, would it?—I would have an infant department; that would be an additional 30 pupils.

4425. *Dr. Berry.*] Is it your opinion that where the number of pupils at a public undenominational school in town did not exceed 150, five classes of 30 each, grants in aid should not not be given to any denominational school?—Certainly not.

4426. *President.*] In Graham's Town you have three denominational schools working side by side, have you not?—And they are crippling each other.

4427. Would you make an exceptional case with regard to a school like St. Aidan's at Graham's Town?—Certainly.

4428. *Rev. Moorrees.*] Have not the Roman Catholics the same liberty to enter the public undenominational schools as others?—Yes; but as a matter of religious conviction they say they will not send their children to schools where they may not be taught religion right through the school hours. They are not content with having liberty to teach religion for one hour a day, but they must be able at any moment—in a history or geography lesson, for instance—to refer to religion, and as they hold that conviction, I think it is right that they should be allowed to have schools of their own if there are children enough to fill those schools.

4429. *President.*] Provided they place themselves under inspection?—Yes.

4430. *Rev. Moorrees.*] Would not the Government be thereby helping to train children in the Roman Catholic religion. It would be paying in order to enable them to have Roman Catholic instruction right through, would it not?—Roman Catholic taxpayers have a perfect right to have their children trained as Roman Catholics if they are in sufficient numbers to be able to have a school without undue expense to the community.

4431. *President.*] You would not contribute to a school if there was merely religious education—you would require a certain standard to be arrived at in secular instruction, would you not?—Certainly; I would not make religious instruction the sole thing.

4432. You would insist upon their attaining a certain standard in secular subjects?—Yes.

4433. And you would make that a condition of payment?—Yes.

4434. *Rev. Moorrees.*] Is not the advantage given to Roman Catholic children of secular instruction in the public undenominational school?—I understand that they take this view: that they do not want to have secular instruction divorced from religion. Rather than that, they would prefer not sending their children to a public undenominational school. They consider that there ought to be the option of introducing religion at any time, if necessary, during school hours.

4435. If they carry that out, then the Government, in giving them money, would virtually be assisting to train the pupils in the Roman Catholic faith, would it not?—The Roman Catholics claim to have State aid in consideration of the secular instruction which they impart; but they also claim the right to be able to impart religious instruction simultaneously with the secular instruction, and if that is not possible for them, then they will not send their children to undenominational schools.

4436. Would you extend that same aid, for instance, to the Dutch Reformed Church?—Yes.

4437. Would not that virtually break up the whole system?—My impression is that at present the public undenominational schools are influenced to a great extent by the Dutch Reformed Church, and their religion is introduced into those schools in the colony.

4438. Have you any proof of that statement?—From conversation with teachers, and I have met a good many, that is the impression formed on my mind—that religion is introduced into the public schools; indeed, that there are very few schools in the colony in which religion is not introduced.

4439. In making such a statement, it would be just as well to name instances so as to enable the Commission to test its accuracy?—I do not wish to say that they are doing what is not allowed by the Education Department. The Department provides for one hour's religious instruction a day. I do not say the Dutch Reformed Church teach religion right through the school hours.

4440. *Rev. Coetzee.*] Do I understand you to say that the Roman Catholics would not be averse to coming under the public school system, provided that control and management is allowed them to a certain extent?—I have spoken with representatives of the Roman Catholic body on the subject, and my impression is that they would gladly come under the system if they had the control and management.

4441. *President.*] Subject to inspection?—Yes.

4442. *Dr. Berry.*] And provided they were allowed to appoint their own teachers?—Yes.

4443. *President.*] Would it not be well that the Government should have a right to insist upon teachers being up to the mark also?—Certainly.

4444. Do you think they would consent to satisfy the Government, or whatever the controlling body may be, that their masters are up to the mark, by having them certified, or coming up to some standard?—That I cannot say. It would be very reasonable, and ought to be so.

4445. *Rev. Coetzee.*] Does the Education Department take into consideration, when it approves or disapproves of the qualification of a teacher, the denomination to which he belongs?—At present not at all. No questions are asked, at least I have never heard of it.

4446. As the religious bodies in this country take a great interest in the advancement of education, would it be advisable or beneficial to the cause of education generally to do away with all voluntary agencies and secularise education altogether?—No, I think it would be a mistake at present. I am in favour myself of undenominational education. That is what I should like to see all over the country, but as we have these denominational bodies with their particular wishes, I think they have a fair claim.

4447. *President.*] You would work through them, provided they do their work efficiently?—Yes.

4448. But always leading in the direction of undenominational education?—Yes. That is the best chance of getting undenominational education eventually.

4449. Are you acquainted with the guarantee system?—Yes.

4450. You are aware that at present the guarantors have to make up any deficiency. It is one of the objects of our enquiry whether contributions should not be expected from local bodies towards making up any deficiency. Can you suggest any means of supplying the place of the guarantors by any public body?—There is a plan which I think might be adopted, namely, having modified School Boards; not exactly like those in England, but adapted to our circumstances, and they should be compelled to make up any deficiency in the school revenue; the Government contributing as at present to the salaries of the teachers. Any deficiency would be a claim on the Municipality or the Divisional Council, upon a precept to the Education Department to that effect.

4451. Would it be wise in your opinion to make such a Board control a large area, including the whole district say, so as to undertake the work of filling up gaps where educational facilities are wanted throughout each fiscal district, and so making all the inhabitants of that area interested?—I think it would be very desirable to have such a body, but there would also be room for smaller bodies.

4452. Suppose you had an Upper Board, through which the smaller bodies could work, would that answer?—Yes, very well.

4453. Do you speak from experience to some extent?—Yes.

4454. You are in favour of an over Board to fill up all the gaps where schools are now wanting?—Yes.

4455. If necessary, the Government contributing together with the rates to meet any deficiency throughout the district?—Yes.

4456. Would that best secure what you call free schools?—Yes.

Mr.
Edward Noaks.

Sept. 9th, 1 91.

4457. What contribution ought the Government to give under such circumstances, so as to prevent the ratepayers looking upon it as a direct tax on them. At present, most of the schools are worked without any loss. Should there be one distinct amount per number of children in attendance or on the roll ?—I think the present arrangement is an excellent one, the Education Department representing the Government what is wanted, and then certain grants in aid are given for the teachers' salaries in proportion to the number of children on the roll. In that case the Education Department has the control.

4458. That is to say they do not get the grant unless the conditions are complied with ?—Yes.

4459. Do you think that might be made universal throughout the Colony ?—Yes. I can see no objection to it.

4460. Then virtually this Upper Board would take the place of the guarantors, would it not ?—Yes.

4461. Should this Upper Board have the power to work through denominational schools, and allow those interested in denominational schools to come in and take the grant from Government upon its recommendation, so as to relieve the tax-payers where the Upper Board considers it desirable ?—Yes, I think that would answer, the control always being left in the hands of the Education Department.

4462. And also in the hands of the Upper Board to see that they fulfil the conditions ?—Yes.

4463. The Central Government still looking to the Upper Board for the performance of the conditions ?—Yes.

4464. Through the denomination, if necessary ?—Yes.

4465. Would the effect of that be eventually to cause these denominational schools by degrees to see the wisdom of coming in under what you consider the public school system ?—I don't think in itself it would have much direct influence upon the proportion of the two schools, but it would prevent the establishment of denominational schools in the future which were not really required by the demands of the neighbourhood.

4466. Do you think there are too many denominational schools in certain parts ? —I think there is a strong tendency that way.

4467. Do you think this would check it ?—Yes.

4468. Do you think it would also have the effect of interesting people more in education and making volunteers work side by side effectively with undenominational bodies through the medium of the Board, removing some of the asperities which are supposed to exist now ?—My experience is that asperities do not exist to any very appreciable extent.

4469. But if any did exist, would not the effect be to modify them, if denominational bodies found that through the medium of these Boards they found they could get some aid from Government ?—I think it would cause more satisfaction on the part of the denominational bodies with our present system.

4470. Do you think it would tend to promote elementary education generally ? —Yes.

4471. Have you anything better than that to suggest, either your own idea or what you have heard ?—I think that is a system which would work.

4472. Would you have the Upper Board elected by the ratepayers throughout the district wholly or in part, or would you have the members nominated by elected bodies ?—The plan that suggested itself to me was that the Municipality or the Divisional Council should choose from their own number say half of the members of the Board, the electors in the district choosing the other half—choosing them for their educational qualifications, while those elected by the Municipality or the Divisional Council would be appointed for their business qualities generally and their knowledge of the actual requirements of the community. I think that would answer.

4473. What should be the maximum number of members on the Board ?—I think 15 or 20.

4474. Would not that be too large ?—It is difficult to get a quorum sometimes.

4475. If you had a few, would not they consider it their duty and privilege to be present and make it a regular business ?—If there was a Board of 15, and they appointed a permanent committee, that committee would probably do all the real business.

4476. You would have a large Board, even up to the number of 15 if necessary, with power to delegate their functions to a sub-committee ?—Yes.

4477. What do you think should be the minimum number ?—I think about five.

4478. Would not three be able to keep the thing going in a small town ?—I think five is better.

4479. Would you pay the members ?—No.

117

4480. You think that non-payment ought to be an absolute condition ?—Yes.

4481. With a view to secure those really devoted to the cause of education ?—Yes.

4482. How would you provide with regard to country members attending. Should they also attend without payment, or would you give them anything at all ?—I did not contemplate giving them anything at all.

4483. Have you considered whether those elected by the country would probably be gentlemen who had been engaged in farming pursuits and had retired, and would thus be able to give their time to the matter ?—I think that would very likely be so.

4484. Do you make non-payment of members an important point because you want to work the thing cheaply ?—Partly that ; I think it would be better not to make any payment.

4485. The effect of this system would be if there is a deficiency, and the Board itself starts its own school, that deficiency would come upon the ratepayers, would it not ?—Yes.

4486. Where there is a deficiency, but the Board does not start its own school but works through a denomination, that denominational or volunteer body would have to pay the deficiency itself, would it not ?—With regard to denominational schools, if they came in under the system, I would let them also have the deficiency supplied through the ratepayers.

4487. Would not the effect of that be to have a number of denominational bodies working ineffectively ; would not you make it a condition that they should be themselves guarantors after receiving the aid from Government ?—The deficiency would be very small.

4488. But would it not prevent a deficiency if the denominational body received aid from Government on condition that they were responsible for any deficiency. Ought not that to be a *sine qua non* ?—I do not want to see any distinction made either as regards building grants or the supply of any deficiency, but at the same time, the Education Department would have a difficulty to prevent this conflict, but merely requiring the denominational schools to supply any deficiency would not have any great effect.

4489. If a denominational school knows that it receives Government aid, and then undertakes to start a school, do not you think it is fair, if there is a deficiency in the working, that they should be responsible ?—That introduces a difference certainly.

4490. In the case of other schools it would fall on the rates ; do you think the ratepayers ought to object to pay that deficiency ?—None whatever.

4491. Is that principle acted upon elsewhere ?—That is a small matter compared with free education throughout the country, and that seems to be the principle which is forcing its way elsewhere. The amount which the tax-payers would be called upon to pay in this case to meet the deficiency would, I am convinced, be very small.

4492. Would it be still smaller in consequence of the rate-payers themselves having the management of the money ?—Yes.

4493. You say that the alternative to that is free education, in which the State finds means of educating all. Do you think we could work free education in this Colony ?—No ; not at present.

4494. Why not ?—There is not any demand for it. The colony would require educating up to it, and then it would at once cut off as it were voluntary agencies, and the country would be so much the loser. It would be considerably more expensive than this other scheme.

4495. All the voluntary agencies would cease, and the burden be thrown on the State, would it not ?—Yes, and also the school fees, which many parents have no objection whatever to pay.

4496. Is it not the duty of parents to pay the school fees for their children when they can ?—In most cases parents prefer to do so, and by paying fees of a higher or lower grade they have the choice of schools of a higher or a more elementary character, and there is an advantage in that.

4497. It is the primary obligation of parents to pay the fees if they can, is it not ? —I think so.

4498. What do you conceive to be the principle why the State should supply a large portion and the local body should also contribute, and have the immediate management ; upon what is that based ?—The contribution of the State seems to be based upon inspection by the State, the grant depending to some extent upon efficiency as evidenced by inspection : and then the local body has a smaller rate to collect, and that causes less friction. The incidence of taxation which is raised by the State is spread over a larger area and is more equable.

4499. Upon what principle of fairness do you call upon local rate-payers to pay anything ?—On this principle : the local area has a certain voice in regard to education. One area would want a very high class school and another not so high a class school,

Mr.
Edward Noaks.

Sept. 9th, 1891.

o 2

Mr.
Edward Noaks.

Sept. 9th, 1891.

and they ought to pay in proportion to the education which they actually require; that is a reason for making the local area contribute a certain proportion.

4500. It is to the interests of the local community that all children within that area should be educated in the way they wish them to be educated is it not?—Yes; and it excites a certain amount of interest in the education of a small section of the community if they are themselves required to contribute.

4501. Does that fit into the principle of local self-government best?—Yes.

4502. In England, the State now contributes 27s. 6d. per head, and by that means it is supposed that free education is secured to all children. Suppose the Government here contributed a definite sum for children on the roll or in attendance, do you see any objection to that, leaving the money in the hands of the local Board to work with?—In England, the State contributing this 10s. a year, in lieu of school fees, enables the different local bodies to organise to a certain extent. In some schools the 10s. a year is to be used toward reducing the school fees by a certain amount; in other cases, they are going to abolish the fees altogether, and in others again, they are going to abolish the fees only in the case of higher class schools, so that they are enabled to adapt themselves to their own requirements.

4503. Do you think in this country the State could fix a definite sum, as is done in England, to be paid towards all children on the roll throughout the Colony?—I do not think that would be a good principle to introduce.

4504. Why not?—Take the case of Port Elizabeth, there are different classes of schools where parents pay definite amounts. If you take the first class public school, the Grey Institute, there the grant from Government is a good deal larger than it is to one of the inferior class schools, and that is necessary to keep up the higher grant. That is a far better arrangement than making certain payments per head.

4505. Would not the superior wealth of the upper classes and their ambition, enable them to get a higher class school provided out of their own private means, even though they only get smaller aid from Government?—I think the more wealthy parents in this Colony at any rate are very few and far between, those who require no assistance as it were. I think the fees at the Grey Institute, which is a well endowed institution, are as much as parents can conveniently pay, because the cost of living is expensive in this Colony. The Grey Institute has an endowment of £1,000 from grants of lands contributed by the municipality at its foundation, and also by Sir George Grey, who allocated certain lands. It receives about £1,100 from Government in aid, and there is rather more than £1,100 received in fees roughly speaking. That is apportioned between the three schools, the Hill school and the two branch schools.

4506. How many pupils are there in the Hill school?—160. There are 250 in the North End school, and about 150 in the South End School—about 500 in all.

4507. And your income is about £3,200 a year?—Yes.

4508. What is your expenditure?—At present, the revenue is slightly less than the expenditure. It varies a little from year to year.

4509. At the Hill School, where you say there are 160 boys, what is the expenditure?—About £1,000 a year, or more, is spent on teachers.

4510. Is there a good deal spent on maintenance and boarding?—No; there is no boarding department.

4511. Is the balance of £2,200 spent on the other two schools?—Till recently we have had an interest account of £400 payable on a debt, but it has been reduced gradually, and now we have a debt of about £2,000, on which we pay interest.

4512. Did you pay off the debt annually?—We were paying off £450 a year. More than £1,000 a year is spent on salaries.

4513. How many children do you think there are in this town requiring education?—I cannot say.

4514. What is the population according to the last census?—About 25,000.

4515. How many of those are white?—I cannot say.

4516. Over 2,000 whites ought to be under education here if we take the white population at 13,000, yet in the Grey Institute we find there are only about 500 being educated, and that is the Public Undenominational School here. How is it the Grey Institute does not reach all those children?—There are various mission schools for white children.

4517. How is it, with all its aid, and with all its machinery and its efficiency, the Grey Institute has not reached the children who are now in the mission schools?—The buildings are one great drawback which every school has to contend with. We have as many children as our buildings can hold, except at the Hill school, where there is one class-room we could utilise, but at both the branch schools the buildings are full.

4518. Then the effect of removing denominational agencies from all participation in education would be to necessitate a large expenditure on buildings, would it not?—Unless the present buildings which are used by the denominations were handed over

Mr.
Edward Noak.

Sept. 9th, 1891.

or secured in some way. I think that accounts principally for the fact that our system has not extended itself further. There have been from time to time suggestions made that existing denominational schools should come in under our system.

4519. If the denominational schools are bought or the buildings secured by the public undenominational school authorities, would you get into these schools the bulk of the 2,000 children just referred to, who are not at school now?—I think under the present system our numbers will not increase very greatly, because certain school fees have to be charged to meet the expenses. In the higher classes twelve guineas a year is the charge, and parents cannot pay more than that. The number who can pay it is limited.

4520. Why do not you reduce your fees so as to invite these 2,000 children to come to school?—Our buildings are fully occupied now, without launching out into more expenses. With reduced fees even we could not get these children to come, and then we feel that the present existing agencies do overtake the work, mission schools for instance.

4521. You do not think it fair to try and break them down?—Not in that way. We should be glad if they would come in under our system, but they do not wish to do so.

4522. *Rev. Coetzee.*] Have you any school properties in this place?—We have three buildings.

4523. In whom are they vested?—According to our Act of constitution, they are vested in the managers for the time being.

4524. Have you an election of managers every three years?—Every year. Our board consists of 20 members, and the Municipal Council elect seven. Then the parents have the power of electing eight members from their own number, subject to a certain pecuniary qualification. They must have contributed £5 in school fees during the twelve months preceding. In this body, which holds office for a year, the school funds are vested for the time being.

4525. *Mr. Theron.*] Is not your institution incorporated under a special Act?—It is under a special Act.

4526. *Rev. Coetzee.*] With reference to the suggested Over Board; are you acquainted with the large rural districts in the Colony?—No.

4527. Suppose they were divided into six different wards, and each ward was provided with a school, and there is a deficiency of say £5 or £10 in one of the schools in a ward, would you tax the whole district in order to make up the deficiency in that particular school?—I think so. I should suggest that; but I should not suggest if there was a surplus in one school taking the surplus of one school and applying it to a deficiency in the other. If there was a small surplus, it should be applied to the purposes of the school itself, decorating the walls, or something of the sort. If there was a deficiency in a particular school, it should not be borne by that particular school or ward, but by the district, spread over it as widely as possible.

4528. Would the proposed Board have to find school accommodation for the natives in that district too?—I have not thought of that.

4529. *Mr. Theron.*] The whole of your argument simply applies to European children does it not?—My knowledge of the country districts is extremely limited, and I do not feel competent to express an opinion upon the question as to whether a ward or a larger division should raise the necessary funds.

4530. *Rev. Moorrees.*] Would you apply the system to natives and whites equally?—I have been contemplating Europeans all through far more than the natives.

4531. *Rev. Coetzee.*] With regard to the 10,000 white children throughout the Colony supposed to be in mission schools, have you formed any idea as to what it would cost to erect buildings so as to supply these 10,000 with the necessary school accommodation?—It would depend very much on the kind of building erected. At South End, the Rev. Mr. Smith, who has charge of St. Peter's Mission School, erected a building that will accommodate 80 children at a cost of less than £200, but then he knew how to do it. The walls are made of concrete, and the building is very nicely ventilated. It is a schoolroom worth seeing.

4532. In erecting school buildings, what space is required for each child?—In the Board schools in England, 10 square feet for each child is considered to be the proper amount of space, but in voluntary schools that is not insisted on; 8 square feet is the minimum.

4533. In this hot country how much space should be allowed?—I cannot say exactly. Something more than in England; 12 feet perhaps.

4534. Are your school buildings exempt from municipal rates?—I believe so, except the water rate.

4535. And other school buildings?—I do not know.

Mr.
Edward Noaks.

Sept. 9th, 1891.

4536. *Dr. Berry.*] Would you be in favour of giving this Board any control over or any power to direct the quality of the education in the area which it is supposed to superintend?—I think it would have power to make representations to the Education Department, but the Education Department should be the arbiter as to the character of the school required in the district.

4537. Would you give to the local Boards such as you would like to see called into existence the power of saying, within certain limits, or any limits, what amount and what quality of education should be given in any particular district?—I think the local Boards should certainly have the power of choosing whether there should be a first, second, or third class school. I think in the circumstances of the Colony any additional efforts like that should be supported by voluntary aid. In some of the larger School Boards at home I believe they do take over technical instruction, but it is only very few schools where they find it possible to do that. I do not think it would be advisable to give every School Board in this Colony the option of doing it, and lavishing money on an expensive undertaking, which after all might be found to end in failure.

4538. Would it not be well that local bodies should have a distinct say in that matter. If they choose to take the risk, and find the means, is there any reason why they should not have power to direct it?—If permission were given to them to decide in the matter, but the permission ought to be subject to revision by the Education Department.

4539. With its sanction, you would give local bodies power to regulate to a certain extent the quality and amount of the education within their area?—Yes.

4540. The number of white children attending the schools here is put down by the Education Department at 1,100. You say the number of children educated at the Grey Institute is 500. It would therefore appear that about 1,600 European children are being educated here under public inspection. Can you give us any idea of the quality of the education supplied to children in schools not under inspection?—I know very few. There are three or four well known Institutions in Port Elizabeth doing thoroughly good work. The Diocesan Grammar School is not inspected, the Girls' Collegiate School is not inspected, Miss Peacock's school for girls is not inspected, and the Rev. Mr. Pritchard's school for boys is not inspected. Certainly a fair proportion of the remaining children are in well known hands.

4541. Quite half the European children in this town are being educated in mission schools, are they not?—Yes.

4542. Is the education supplied there of the quality that a European child in a town of this character ought to have?—In the schools I am familiar with the style of education is very nearly, and in some respects it is quite the same as we give in our branch schools, and the children really attain a very high order of excellence. St. Paul's Mission Schools, especially the Girls' Department, do very good work indeed. The children are brought up to the fifth standard. They are only mission schools in name, and the amount of grant they receive is only £75 a year.

4543. How many children would these schools cover?—At St. Paul's schools there are 291 children, and at White's Road Mission—also a very good school—there must be almost as many.

4544. It is stated by the Education Department that in the mission schools at Port Elizabeth 1,118 white children are getting their education; you say that about 500 are in the three mission schools with which you are well acquainted; where are the other 600 children being educated?—There is a large number of mission schools in Port Elizabeth; there must be very nearly twenty altogether. At the Marist Brothers School the children are nearly all white; there are about 200 there I should say at a guess. These schools are all well looked after, and at St. Paul's school they attain a really high standard.

4545. Do you believe that in the interests of the European population of Port Elizabeth, where so many children are being educated at these mission schools, anything is necessary to be done to raise the general standard of education among them?—I think the standard of education is satisfactory in these higher mission schools; the others I have no knowledge of.

4546. *Dean Holmes.*] Can you tell the Commission how many school places there are in Port Elizabeth?—I do not know.

4547. *Rev. Coetzee.*] Suppose this Over Board decides upon establishing a school in a certain locality, and the Education Department objects and refuses to pay the grant, how would you meet that case?—The school would not be established under Government aid.

4548. Would the Board then make up the deficiency by taxation?—According to the plan I had thought of, the Education Department should issue a precept for taxation. In every case taxation should only be resorted to with the sanction of the Education Department.

4549. *President.*] So as to have a check upon extravagance ?—Yes.

4550. Suppose the Board does not bring into existence a school that the Education Department thinks ought to be brought into existence, what machinery would you then bring into play to create such a school; would you allow the Education Department to establish a school after notice to the Board and at the expense of the Board, the Central Government contributing its quota and working the school till the Board takes it over and works it ?—Not at present. For the successful working of the school the consent of the district would have to be required.

4551. Suppose the district determined not to have education, and the Board thinks it ought, should there be power vested in the Central Government to say, it is a want, and you must supply it ?—I would not apply compulsion, except in the case of the most elementary education.

4552. To create a ragged school, for instance ?—Yes, if it was not in existence.

4553. You would allow the Government to start such a school, and contribute its quota, the Board working it, and if there is any deficiency make the ratepayers pay it, but in that case you think the deficiency would be necessarily very small ?—Yes.

4554. *Rev. Moorrees.*] Would not that destroy the representative character of the Board ?—Only in the case of the most elementary class of school, or the free school we were contemplating, where there is no education being given. If that is demanded, I would compel the ratepayers in such a case, and the Government should contribute its quota.

4555. *Mr. Theron.*] Can you call to mind any case where the real necessity for the establishment of a school in a certain ward has been reported to the Education Department by the Inspector, and the Department has not made provision in one way or another ?—I do not know of any such case.

4556. *President.*] Have you thought of the subject of giving Boards of Management as at present existing under the public undenominational system perpetual succession. Suppose we do not bring into existence this Board, how would you give perpetual succession ?—That is not a question that I have considered. The evils of the guarantee system most public school teachers are acquainted with I think.

4557. What are they ?—At present, a school collapses at the end of three years; virtually the Board ceases to exist, and the engagement with the teacher ends. The school may be closed, or pressure may be brought to bear upon the teacher to bring about his dismissal. How far that is done I am not in a position to say, but there is a strong feeling among public school teachers that there is no real security for their tenure of office under the present system.

4558. Do you consider that an evil ?—I think it is a very great evil.

4559. Is it not one means of getting rid of a teacher who is not very efficient, but with regard to whom you cannot point to any decided inefficiency ?—I think in such a case a teacher ought to be dismissed on his own demerits, and not that the whole system should be rendered insecure.

4560. But might it not very often happen that a teacher who was not very efficient would continue, with the object of earning his pension ?—A system which does not give a secure tenure of office is simply a direct encouragement to inefficient persons to join, and it excludes efficient teachers.

4561 Would not an efficient teacher be secure and sure of employment, especially looking at the want of efficient teachers which is said to exist ?—I have known cases of undoubtedly efficient teachers who have been dismissed through some friction that has arisen.

4562. Can you point to any such case ?—I would rather not mention names; but I have known cases where it has happened.

4563. Should not a Board have the power to dismiss teachers who are not efficient as they think, without being able to point to any actual demerit ?—I look at the matter from a teacher's point of view, but in case of a dismissal I think the consent of the Education Department should not be required in the first place, but if the teacher appeals against his dismissal, and thinks he has been dismissed on what he considers wrong or insufficient grounds, then the Education Department should step in and be able to exercise a veto if necessary; not in the first instance, but only in case of an appeal.

4564. Does not the character of a school depend upon some quality in the teacher which you cannot directly point to as indicating either efficiency or inefficiency ?—I have known of cases where a school has thriven and been efficient, but owing to some friction, which always tends to become greater and greater, a good teacher has been dismissed, whereas if there were more security in the tenure of the office, the occasions for this kind of dismissal would be removed. If it were felt that a teacher had a greater hold on his position, there would not be the same tendency on the part of members of the Board to do things in an irritating way so as to cause friction.

Mr.
Edward Noaks.

Sept. 9th, 1891.

4565. Then you would give the Board power to dismiss a teacher, allowing him an opportunity of shewing to the Education Department that his dismissal had been wrong, but always presuming in favour of the Board's decision?—Yes. The Education Department should be the judge. I do not think in such a case that a teacher would very often find it to his advantage to stay on even if the Board continued him in his position.

4566. *Rev. Moorrees.*] You mean that in this country for a good man so many opportunities are open, where the post is secure, that he would not care to take the insecure position of a teacher?—From a teacher's point of view, the great drawback to the profession at present is, that they have not any adequate tenure of office. At the end of three years the engagement ceases. A man naturally wishes, when he settles in a district, to be able to look ahead to some extent. I have known cases where the teacher has come into collision with a member of the Board of Managers perhaps, and although an efficient man, on account of some extraneous cause, he has had to leave, and every teacher knows that there is this insecurity.

4567. *President.*] If you perpetuate the succession, the same thing would happen, would it not, unless you control the Board, and say they cannot dismiss a man?—The managers must, of course, have the power of dismissal.

4568. *Dean Holmes.*] Would you allow an appeal to the Department in every case?—Yes.

4569. *President.*] Has the guarantee system any other evils, in your opinion. Do you think it fair to throw on a few a burden that ought to be distributed among the many?—That is an evil, decidedly.

4570. Have you known of any cases where deficiencies in the school funds have arisen?—I have heard of such cases.

4571. Does it not come hard upon the guarantors?—Yes.

4572. And you think the ratepayers ought to be called upon in such cases, where the school is efficient?—Yes.

4573. How would you propose to give perpetual succession to this Board of Management other than by an Over Board?—Upon the plan of allowing the municipality of a district to appoint, say seven members. That involves perpetual succession in itself, because from year to year there would be new members appointed; there would be a new election at all events on the part of the municipality, and I think that would give the required element of stability to the Board.

4574. Would you transfer to the Boards the duty of guarantors in all public undenominational schools?—Yes.

4575. Do not you think it would be fairer if those School Committees or Boards of Management which are working efficiently had the option of remaining outside till such time as they wished to be absorbed by the new Board, or would you absorb them at the end of the three years?—I would leave the option with the whole district if they are satisfied with the guarantors, and they wish to continue some time longer.

4576. Do you know how public school property is vested at present?—I only know about the Grey Institute.

4577. You have got an Act of Incorporation, have you not?—Yes, the property is vested for the time being in the managers. There must be the signature of three managers before the expenditure of any money.

4578. And your real property is vested in them?—Yes.

4579. How would you vest the property of first class public undenominational schools elsewhere?—In the case of our Board, if any member of the Town Council dies or goes away, a successor is at once elected. There is a notification to that effect.

4580. Suppose there is an advertisement, and nobody comes?—The Civil Commissioner and the Mayor are *ex officio* members.

4581. *Dr. Berry.*] Do I understand that you are agreeable to certain School Boards for districts being called into existence. and that you see no objection to giving them power to hold public school property?—I see no objection.

4582. *Mr. Theron.*] Would you have any objection to vesting the property in the Education Department?—Yes. I think it would be safer to vest it in the local Boards. I consider that the Education Department is more concerned in the administration of large questions.

4583. *Rev. Coetzee.*] Suppose the Civil Commissioner was joined with the Education Department?—Being in favour of local self-government as far as possible, I would still prefer that the local Board should have the school property vested in it.

4584. *President.*] How do you think it is possible to secure fuller use being made of the opportunities afforded for education. Have you any trade classes?—No.

4585. Are you in favour of night schools?—Quite recently we have started a Dutch class in the evening, for the upper school, but it is not largely attended. There

Mr.
Edward Noaks.

Sept. 9th, 1891.

does not seem to be much demand for it. Other attempts have been made in past times to start night schools, but without very great success.

4586. Ought they still to be attempted, do you think?—I do not think they will do much good.

4587. *Dr. Berry.*] Was the attempt made for the benefit of the pupils of the Grey Institute, or generally?—Generally, for the whole town.

4588. *President.*] Have there been night schools for other studies besides Dutch?—We are prepared to start a Civil Service Class in the evening as soon as there is any demand; but as yet there is none.

4589. You think, altogether, at present there is no demand for night schools, and you do not advise embarking upon them?—In connection with the Railway, I believe something might be done. The Railway is having an Institute started now, and probably some of the employés would go to night schools.

4590. With regard to the question of language, have you a Dutch master at your school?—Yes; we have one this term, and we have commenced instruction in Dutch.

4591. Are there many anxious to learn it?—Yes; in the upper classes. The boys, I think, prefer to learn Dutch to French, as being more immediately useful.

4592. Do they take to Dutch more than they did formerly?—I only know of one case of a parent who does not wish his son taught Dutch.

4593. Do you think the study of Dutch ought to be encouraged?—Not encouraged in so far as it would interfere with English. I have no hostility whatever to the Dutch language; but it would be a great pity to foster the study of Dutch, if the study of English is not to be encouraged even more at the same time. I see no danger to the study of Dutch being encouraged among Dutch or English children; the best way to bring about the ultimate triumph of English is to encourage both languages, I think. From a sentimental point of view, it would be a great pity to discourage the study of Dutch, because I believe in the long run that would have a contrary effect, and cause it to be perpetuated longer than it would otherwise be.

4594. You think if it is encouraged, the result will be to show that English will prevail?—Yes, in the long run.

4595. Therefore, taking that point of view, you are favourable to encouraging Dutch?—I would hardly use the word "encourage." I have no wish to see it discouraged.

4596. Do not you think, in view of the fact that the majority of the white population of the country is Dutch, something ought to be done to promote the use of good Dutch?—Certainly, I think among the Dutch-speaking population the study of classical Dutch would be an advantage.

4597. How would you best secure that without interfering with the true educational interests of scholars?—I do not see what more can be done than is done now. The Education Department at present enables any school to take either Dutch alone or English alone, whichever is considered best by the School Managers, and every facility is given for the teaching of Dutch. I should be sorry to see Dutch introduced into the examinations from political objects.

4598. You mean you would be sorry to see political objects cause its introduction?—Yes. The subject was discussed in detail at the last Teachers' Conference held at Kimberley, and the decision arrived at was one that recommends itself to most teachers in the Colony, that in the Elementary examination those who wish to take up Dutch should be allowed to do so, but as an extra optional subject, and that Dutch should not be included among the strictly elementary subjects of that examination.

4599. That would force all children to learn it?—Yes.

4600. Would it, in your opinion, be a disadvantage if all children were forced to learn Dutch?—There would be this disadvantage; it would cause ill feeling. I wish to see English boys learning Dutch, it tends to unite and amalgamate the two nationalities, but if you make it compulsory, it would have just the opposite effect. The more English know of Dutch and Dutch of English, picking it up voluntarily in the ordinary way, the more it will conduce to the spread of good feeling in the colony; but if you make it compulsory for English boys to learn Dutch or Dutch boys to learn English, it would have a very bad result.

4601. You think that if Dutch were made a fifth subject in the Elementary examination it would be virtually compelling English boys to take it if they wanted to get a place?—Yes.

4602. If it did not cause that ill feeling you speak of, would there be any harm from an educational point of view?—There is just as much mental training by learning Dutch as French, if you take the two languages up to the point we teach them at school. You do not teach all the subtleties and niceties of a language, but as a training in grammar and translation, Dutch offers the same sort of facilities as French; the only drawback is the want of good text books in the Dutch language.

Mr.
Edward Noaks.

Sept. 9th, 1891.

4603. Then it would not, from an educational point of view, do any possible harm if Dutch was a second language?—I should like to see a second language throughout the colony instead of French.

4604. Why should not we have it?—If it was introduced into the examinations it would produce irritation.

4605. If it becomes a second language instead of French, and from an educational point of view there is no harm, if you have the books, would not it become advisable, within a measurable time, to have an examination in Dutch and prepare in that language?—The papers should always be strictly optional. It should be optional to students for instance, to take Latin, French, or Dutch for instance.

4606. *Rev. Moorrees.*] Are you in favour of that?—Yes, in the Elementary examination.

4607. *President.*] If that is done, will not Dutch be taken up at the Elementary examination, and thus the study of the language would be promoted?—Probably. I should like to make not only Latin, French and Dutch alternate subjects, but also science. If it lay between French and Dutch, a great majority would take Dutch certainly, but there would be ill feeling.

4608. But for that ill feeling, is not there a very strong motive for inducing children to learn Dutch, so as to facilitate inter-communication with one another?—It is very desirable, no doubt, but any attempt at compulsion would be bad.

4609. What other means would you suggest to encourage Dutch; would you give bursaries to those taking a high position in Dutch in the Elementary examination?—If bursaries were introduced at all, they ought to be for Dutch and English conjointly, so that it could not be said that one language was being fostered or favoured in preference to the other. It is just as desirable that the Dutch-speaking people should learn English as that the English-speaking people should learn Dutch.

4610. Suppose you give bursaries to those taking the highest places in the Elementary examination in Dutch, it would virtually not be fostering Dutch any more than English, would it?—If bursaries are given for Dutch as an alternative subject, bursaries ought also to be given for other alternative subjects at the same time.

4611. *Dean Holmes.*] Would you add a fifth paper in every case to the Elementary examination?—No. The decision arrived at by the Teachers' Conference was that the examination should be left alone so far as the elementary subjects are concerned, but that it should be optional with candidates to take Dutch or Latin or French or science separately, and separate class lists would be brought out in the order of merit. Bursaries might be attached to these if you liked.

4612. The Elementary examination would be complete in itself as it stands at present, with some optional subject which could be endorsed on the certificate?—Yes.

4613. *President.*] Why should not you have an examination in Dutch alone if they like it, and have the candidates' names published according to the place they take in Dutch, and have an endorsement on the certificate to that effect. What harm is there in that?—It might be endorsed on the certificate, but the system of including marks for Dutch and various optional subjects in the Elementary examination is objectionable.

4614. Would it not be fair, seeing that a Dutch boy is taught in English, and has to acquire it through an English medium, that some little inducement ought to be held out in the way of bursaries to those who attain a high place in the Dutch paper?—I think then there ought to be bursaries for those who pass well in the English paper. I would like to see the two languages put on the same footing as far as possible. At the present time, the medium of education is English, even for Dutch-speaking children, and that cannot be avoided on account of the text books. It would be impossible to bring out text books in Dutch as a commercial success, and as they learn Dutch through the medium of English, it is inevitable that they should be examined in English. I believe now if the option were given to Dutch-speaking boys of writing their papers in Dutch, not one in a hundred would accept the alternative; they would all write their papers in English. That would be the result, as they are more familiar in expressing their thoughts on special educational topics in the English language.

4615. *Dr. Berry.*] Do I understand you to say that no candidate should be eligible for a bursary who does not obtain a pass in the ordinary elementary subjects of the examination, or would you say he must be in the honours list before he can obtain a bursary?—I think so. The municipality, for instance, gives a silver medal for the highest in the Elementary examination, but it is never given unless the candidate gets into the honours division. I should not give a bursary unless honours had been obtained.

4616. *Rev. Moorrees.*] You say you would not discourage the study of the Dutch language, but is it not a discouragement of any subject if it is not included in the examinations?—My feeling about the Elementary examination as a teacher is that the present subjects for boys of 13 or 14, are enough for examination purposes. Every teacher desires to have a good number of subjects which are not going to be examined upon. It is almost essential in educating boys that they should not be only working at subjects they are specially preparing for purposes of examination.

Mr.
Edward Noaks.
Sept. 9th, 1891.

4617. As a matter of fact, the instruction of boys extends beyond the limits of the Elementary examination?—Yes. They are learing languages and science simultaneously; but it is not desirable at so young an age that they should be examined either in a foreign language or in a science subject. It is better that the examination should remain as an Elementary examination on elementary subjects.

4618. Would there be any harm in setting a very simple paper in Dutch?—My conviction as a teacher is, that at the age of 13 or 14, a foreign language or a science subject cannot form the subject of examination with much advantage, and they ought to be taken up with a view to examination.

4619. Are you aware that Professor MacWilliam differs from that view?—Yes.

4620. What is your objection to his plan?—I have had several discussions with him on the subject. I think if his plan were carried out, it would spoil the character of the Elementary examination.

4621. Would it not be better to have that slight disadvantage, if it is such, and by that means conciliate a great part of the population, in fact the majority of the European population, who feel that they have a grievance through their language not being recognised in the Elementary examination?—If what the Teachers' Conference proposed was adopted, they would be able to be examined in Dutch if they wished.

4622. Would you not thereby impose on the Dutch child what you would not impose on the English child, namely, make him prepare five subjects while the other child has only to prepare four?—Some teachers would take up the four elementary subjects and one other, but my own feeling is against that. I prefer to take up only four at the same time; my boys would be doing other work, learning either a foreign language or science, but I should not wish them to be examined in that, or even in Latin, at so early an age. But still, teachers would have the option, and that should be sufficient for the advocates of Dutch.

4623. Do you consider that a concession made to the Dutch boy?—I should not care to employ the word "concession," but it seems to me to be a reasonable course to pursue with regard to the examination. It enables those who wish to be examined in Dutch to take it up, and, so far, it is certainly an encouragement. At the same time, it is a very great pity to encourage any subject by means of an examination. A subject should appeal to students on its own merits.

Mr. R. H. Hammersley-Heenan examined.

4624. *President.*] I believe you are District Railway Engineer at Port Elizabeth? —Yes.

Mr.
*R. H.
Hammersley-Heenan.*
Sept. 9th, 1891.

4625. And you have been so for some time?—Yes.

4626. Are you intimate with the wants of the employés along the line; do you visit them from time to time?—Yes; I have examined into the matter very carefully between here and Graaff-Reinet, and right away up the main line to Alicedale, and also to Grahamstown.

4627. What do you think their wants are?—The Government have assisted us in every way in their power, and so has the General Manager, to get schools established at different points. The Traffic Department, with the permission of the Government, has also arranged for the children to be conveyed by all trains, both passenger and goods, from the various cottages to the schools, and these schools, although faulty, are an inestimable benefit to the people who live along the line, as they would otherwise have no possible means of educating their children.

4628. How many schools have you along the line between here and Cradock?— I am not in charge of the Cradock line. There is a school at Alicedale and one on the Graaff-Reinet line; there is one at Glenconnor and, until recently, there was one at Klipplaat; also one at Addo.

4629. Why was the school at Klipplaat abandoned?—For want of support.

4630. How many children are there in the schools between here and Cradock?— You may take it that there is about a child and a half for every mile of line.

4631. Are those children all at school?—Not all.

4632. How many miles is it from here to Graham's Town?—106, and 186 to Graaff-Reinet. I cannot say how many children are at school altogether. There are, I think, 37 at Alicedale, 14 at Glenconnor, according to the last return, and at Addo about the same number as at Glenconnor. As to Middleton and Cookhouse I cannot speak with certainty, as they are not on my district, but I should think about 46.

R 2

Mr.
R. H.
Hammersley-
Heanon.

Sept. 9th, 1891.

4633. That would make 111 children at school out of 438, according to your calculation?—There are also children being educated at Uitenhage, Port Elizabeth, Graham's Town and Graaff-Reinet. I may say that I have endeavoured as far as possible, to bring the men with large families near to school centres.

4634. How many children should you say are out of school?—About 25 per cent.

4635. That would be about 109 children?—Yes.

4636. How do you think the wants ought to be met of those who cannot attend the existing schools?—The trains do not run to suit the children, and the distances are very great in some cases. It would be a good thing if some cheap boarding school could be established at certain centres.

4637. The mother superior at Graham's Town has offered to take the girls of railway employés, board and educate them for about £12 a year; with books, stationery, and so on, it would come to about £14 a year. Do you think that plan would answer?—Yes, but I doubt whether the men with their present pay could afford that.

4638. Have you tried to ascertain from them how much they could afford?—It varies very much.

4639. The Rev. Father Simeon suggested that where there is one child, £1 a month could be afforded, and 15s. a month for the second; call it 12s. 6d. on the average. Suppose the Government were to contribute half, could the men manage the rest, do you think?—Yes; they might, but it is doubtful, and there is also the religious difficulty to be faced.

4640. It seems that about £20 a year would be required to board and educate a boy at certain centres, and it was suggested that £500 should be spent in starting a school for them, the men contributing. Would that work?—If a ganger has three children he might possibly be able to contribute 30s. a month, that is ten shillings for each child, but the sub-gangers would only be able to contribute about half of that. For about every nine miles of line there are three white men, one of whom receives 8s. 6d. a day, but the other two get only 6s. a day, consequently it is easy to see that the latter two could not contribute in the same ratio as the first.

4641. Dr. Berry.] Is that exclusive of Sundays?—Yes; unless they get an order from the Engineer to work on Sundays, they are not paid.

4642. President.] What do you think the men could fairly contribute for the education of their children?—Irrespective of the number of children, I should say the men under me would be able to contribute possibly on the average £1 a month each.

4643. How many children would be the average in a family?—They average about three.

4644. That would be 6s. 8d. for each child per month?—Yes.

4645. Are there not some families who could contribute more, where there is only one child for instance?—No. There are not many men who have only one child. For my own part, I am rather in favour of getting more of the farm schools, because if you take the earning portion of the community away, you render it more difficult for farmers to establish schools. In some places I have arranged with the farmers that they should send their children to the railway school, and they give a guarantee sometimes, so that the schools have half railway people and half farmers' children. I do not think it would be just to encourage those earning public money to send their children away, while the farmers, many of them poor, are trying to establish schools. It is much better to concentrate and establish a better school.

4646. Where would you establish farm schools along the Graaff-Reinet line?—I would have one at Klipplaat. There is one already at Glenconnor, a farm and railway school: and I would establish one at Aberdeen Road. I think for the present, that would meet the requirements.

4647. How many railway employés' children do you think would concentrate at each centre?—About 7 or 8.

4648. And how many would you expect from the farms?—About the same number.

4649. Then they would fulfil the conditions of a farm school?—Yes, getting £30 a year. The Government up to the present time has never refused our application for a house and other little things, such as tables, &c.

4650. Could the children be boarded at the farm schools, or would they be carried daily to and from school?—The trains are at their disposal if they run to suit. As to boarding, they would have to make their own private arrangements with the stationmasters. On the Graaff-Reinet line the trains are not very suitable. A girl might act as nurse to the stationmaster's wife perhaps, and in that way the expense would be reduced, but you cannot have any fixed arrangement.

4651. With regard to girls, it has been stated that it would be better to concentrate them in certain centres, as they would get a better education, and be under better influences than when isolated on the railway. Do you think there is something in that?—I do, after they are a certain age.

Mr.
R. H.
Hammersley-
Heenan.

Sept. 9th, 1891.

4652. Therefore, where practicable, you would concentrate the girls in a town, the Government contributing £6 a year ?—Yes.

4653. And with regard to boys who can find the means of getting to town ?—There would be some difficulty about the boys. I do not think that anything at all should be contributed for them, and indeed I could not recommend that the boys be sent away. I would let them go to farm schools, and pay the regular tariff, which is low.

4654. Then you think there is sufficient provision for the boys already ?—Yes, if you multiply the number of schools and increase the grants, which are at present too low. £30 a year is not sufficient for a school like this one at Addo, which is doing very good work. It permits of but a miserable pittance for the unfortunate teacher.

4655. Upon what principle would you increase the grant; according to attendance ?—Yes. I would increase the Government grant in direct proportion to the number of children attending the school.

4656. What would you make the grant ?—Where there were over fifteen children I would make the minimum grant £50 a year.

4657. And for less than fifteen £30 a year ?—Yes.

4658. Dr. Berry.] The Government now give £3 a year for each child, but the limit is £30. No school can draw more than £30 a year. Would it not meet the case if that limit was withdrawn or raised ?—That would meet it. At the present moment, a farm school is started with 10 or 12 children with a grant of £30 a year. I would make the capitation grant £3, with a limit of say £50 a year.

4659. Mr. Theron.] Are you acquainted with the regulations relating to railway schools ?—Yes.

4660. I believe the Education Department contributes £30 per annum for a daily attendance of at least ten scholars, and the Railway Department contributes also. Is that so ?—Yes.

4661. So that the actual amount is £60 ?—No ; the Education Department contributes £30, and the Railway Department gives an equivalent in the way of accommodation and school furniture.

4662. Dr. Berry.] The Government limit is £30 a year, is it not ?—Yes.

4663. President.] You suggest that it should be £50 a year instead of £30 ?—Yes

4664. Mr. Theron.] Can you give us any information about technical instruction ?—I do not think there is anything more sadly wanted or required in this country at the present moment than a technical school.

4665. President.] What sort of a technical school would you advocate ?—A school somewhat similar to such institutions in Ireland, that send lecturers at different periods in the year to lecture on science. They take the necessary apparatus with them, and teach natural philosophy, chemistry, magnetism, electricity, the properties of steam, and so on.

4666. When you say that the schools send forward men, do you mean that you would create teachers ?—No. I may say that I am most familiar with Ireland, and in Dublin they have got a Government school of arts and sciences, which sends out to different towns once a year, I think, a qualified man to lecture for a term of three or five weeks, as the case may be, on some branch of science. At the end of that time, examinations are held, and those who have qualified themselves up to a certain mark, get a certificate, which serves good all their life to admit them into higher schools, when they go out into the world.

4667. Does this lecturer go to individual schools ?—No ; he takes the Town Hall perhaps, and brings his apparatus and appliances there at the cost of the State.

4668. Rev. Moorrees.] Is he a teacher in an Art school ?—Yes, and a qualified university man, so far as I remember.

4669. President.] Is he trained in an Art school before he is sent out as a lecturer ?—He may be. The position, which is a good one, is obtained by competition.

4670. Where would you have the centres ?—That is rather a difficult question to settle. I have been thinking a good deal about it, and I would suggest one in Cape Town, one in Kimberley, and one in Graham's Town or King William's Town. Graham's Town perhaps is the best place of the two, as you have an admirable museum there.

4671. Would you have only one lecturer in each place ?—In Cape Town you would want two, and in the other places one.

4672. What would he do ?—If he had ten or twelve towns to visit, I would only keep him a month at a time in one place, unless it was a place of importance. Then he might remain for two months.

4673. Would he lecture in the daytime or at night ?—At night. In Ireland these lectures are invariably conducted at night from seven till half-past ten. During the day he has to prepare all his apparatus and get everything ready for the lectures, which are mostly experimental.

Mr.
R. H.
Hammersley-
Heenan.

Sept. 9th, 1891.

4674. What is the fee?—There is I believe no fee at all, or a very small one. The lectures are absolutely free I think.

4675. How many lectures would they give in a week?—On some subjects they lecture for five weeks, and lecture five times a week on such subjects as magnetism, electricity, philosophy, and chemistry. It all depends on the subject.

4676. Who would you expect to attend these lectures?—Young men wishing to improve themselves who are employed in shops and stores, and who under present circumstances will never be able to rise beyond their present position, for want of this technical knowledge. It is most lamentable to think what a number of things we import from England, which might be made in this country, if there was the necessary training. We have had several young fellows in our works, but as a rule, they display very great ignorance in regard to mechanical appliances, &c.

4677. Do you think that five weeks' lectures at certain centres would supply that knowledge sufficiently?—I do. A month's lectures at each place once a year would give young fellows, if they were inclined to learn, an enormous advantage, and enable them to read technical books with profit.

4678. What stimulus would you give to young men to take to it in the first instance?—I would not allow any boys into our workshops unless they had a certificate, if there were such schools.

4679. Do you admit them now without any certificate?—Yes, we do.

4680. At what age are they admitted into your workshops?—At 14 or 15.

4681. What is the qualification for admission?—There is practically none.

4682. Do they get a salary?—Yes; they get $2\frac{1}{2}$d. or $3\frac{1}{2}$d. an hour for the first, second, and third years, I think.

4683. How many hours are they at work?—Eight hours.

4684. They get from 2s. to 2s. 6d. a day?—Yes, somewhere about that. Mr. Thornton, the locomotive superintendent, could give you very detailed information on the subject of technical education. He has struggled to get over the difficulty himself by getting up classes for his boys.

4685. What do you think would be the expense of bringing one of these central institutions into existence?—I am not able to say.

4686. What would be required besides the lecturer; I mean in the way of appliances?—You would want a lecture room. The apparatus would cost from £300 to £500, I should say, and the lecturer would carry that about everywhere.

4687. What do you think you could get such a lecturer for?—£300 a year perhaps.

4688. Are there any qualified men in the colony?—None who would be likely to take the appointment, but they could be got from Europe.

4689. Could you connect that with an agricultural school in any way?—I do not know what the agricultural schools are doing. They surely teach chemistry.

4690. We have had an agricultural school at Graham's Town which has come to an end because no boys for whom it was intended came. The reason was that their parents thought they were better occupied at school, and as soon as they left school they went home?—I think you would find the same with a technical school such as I propose, unless you made it a *sine quâ non* that no boy should be employed unless he had a certificate. Let them feel the necessity of knowledge.

4691. Do you think a good number would attend under those conditions?—We must employ many dozens of white boys on our railways and public works. It is a well known thing that an Africander colonist will never get beyond a certain point, the sole reason being that boys, although many of them are higher in intelligence and brightness than the ordinary English boy, have not had the same chances and opportunities for acquiring knowledge and expanding their minds.

4692. Getting into the Government workshops might be an inducement for a certain class of boys. What inducement would you hold out for boys who wanted to become farmers or go into business?—You could not say to a boy, "You shall not be a farmer unless you have a certificate," but you could refuse him admission to the Government workshops and Government service generally unless that condition was complied with.

4693. Is the system in Ireland connected with any school?—The Commissioners of National Education in Ireland have control of it, I believe.

4694. *Mr. Theron.*] In a place like this, is it not desirable that the senior boys of the public school should attend such lectures as you speak of?—Yes. It would do them an immense amount of good. I mean it for every boy who likes to attend.

4695. *Dean Holmes.*] Would you have a practical class attached, like the School of Practical Engineering at the Crystal Palace?—Yes; I would teach them, for instance, how to connect up a battery, the rudiments of chemistry, magnetism, electricity, and so on.

4696. You would leave teaching them casting and so on till a later stage?—Yes; I would leave that as a special branch to be learned in the shops. I would treat technical education as a part of everybody's education.

4697. The theory first and then the practice?—Yes, and I would not allow them into the workshops unless they had a certificate.

4698. *President.*] Could anything of that kind be connected with the South African College, do you think?—Certainly.

4699. And the higher schools in Graham's Town?—Yes, and Kimberley; also the Grey Institute in Port Elizabeth.

4700. *Dr. Berry.*] Would it not be valuable for young men who intended to become telegraph clerks, for instance, to attend such lectures?—Yes, of great value.

4701. Are they being reared in the colony?—The Government a very short time ago had to introduce a large number of telegraphists, which ought not to be the case, because we have plenty of boys who, if they were properly educated, would be well suited for the work.

4702. Do you think any special school would be advisable in addition to general lectures?—I think it would work in this way: If you had a lecturer coming here once a year, Mr. Noaks and the other heads of educational establishments in Port Elizabeth would take good care that they had trained their boys up to a point at which they were fit to receive the instruction, and if certificates were granted, the probability is that they would try and do credit to their respective schools by securing these certificates. Mr. Noaks, I believe, already teaches the elements of physics and chemistry also, but he is powerless to go beyond a certain point, as he has not the apparatus nor the time at his disposal.

4703. *President.*] Would you give bursaries in connection with the lectures?— Inasmuch as the Government would have to provide the lecturer and the apparatus, it would be better I think not to burden them with anything else. Of course private effort might do something in that way.

4704. *Mr. Theron.*] You think granting a certificate would be sufficient?—It ought to be, and I think the recipients would be very proud of it.

4705. *President.*] Have you thought at all of the subject of night schools?—I think these technical lectures should be delivered at night.

4706. I mean continuation schools for young men who have to go out to work at a pretty early age?—The Traffic Manager and myself talked of doing something in that way, but we found very great difficulties in the way. Boys and young men seem to like freedom in the evenings, and they do not care to go to school.

4707. What sort of night school do you think is likely to be permanent?—I think boys should be fairly educated before they are put to work, and then they will need little beyond the instruction they can give themselves if they have anything in them.

4708. But if they are educated, and still have a desire to go to a night school?— I do not think they would have any difficulty in getting persons to help them if they are desirous of learning. At Uitenhage there are some of our workmen who I am told are always willing to teach them, but it is a difficulty to keep up a night school.

4709. Then you would not advise the Government to establish any scheme of the kind?—No. If there is any necessity for it, it will come from the people themselves.

Port Elizabeth, Thursday, September 10th, 1891.

PRESENT:

Sir J. D. BARRY (President),

Rev. Morrees,	Dr. Berry,
Rev. Coetzee,	Mr. Theron,
Dean Holmes,	Mr. Rowan.

Rev. Dr. Wirgman examined.

4710. *President.*] I believe you are Rector of St. Mary's Church, Port Elizabeth? —Yes.

4711. Have you taken great interest in school work?—Yes.

4712. Formerly, I believe, you were vice-principal of St. Andrew's College?—Yes.

4713. What further facilities do you think can be afforded for giving instruction in both the English and Dutch languages, and how far can that object be attained through the medium of the elementary and other examinations?—I look upon the language question from the point of view of a citizen and an educationalist. To begin with, this country, as far as I can see, must be bi-lingual, and you can no more attempt to dispense with the Dutch language in South Africa than you could attempt, with any reasonable hope of success, to dispense with French in the province of Quebec. I think

Rev.
Dr. Wirgman.

Sept. 10th, 1891.

both languages ought to have equal rights, as they have in Parliament and in the law courts. I am inclined to think that the suggestions put forward by Professor Mac-William, of the Gill College, Somerset East, with regard to adding a Dutch paper to the Elementary examination worth consideration, but I am not of opinion that any other foreign language should be regarded as an alternative for Dutch, which is one of the languages of the country. I think that to make our children of English descent learn the Dutch language and prepare in Dutch for the Elementary examination would be a very useful thing. It may be said that this would give a great advantage to Dutch-speaking boys, but on the other hand, it must be remembered that when English is the medium of instruction, Dutch-speaking boys are to a certain extent handicapped, and a little make-weight by having a paper in Dutch in the Elementary examination would just about pretty fairly balance the disadvantages they would have through English being the medium of instruction. I am also of opinion that to maintain the equal rights of the two languages, if a Dutch-speaking boy wishes to answer his questions in any of the examinations conducted under the authority of the Government in Dutch, he should be allowed to do so.

4714. Do you mean answer the questions in all the papers ?—If he likes—all that are practical. It is a thing to be aimed at.

4715. *Mr. Rowan.*] Would you be disposed to give additional marks for the Dutch paper ?—Certainly.

4716. To be added to the other marks ?—Yes.

4717. *President.*] And you would give no alternative ?—No. I do not think it is advisable to adopt altogether the principle that the Transvaal Government has adopted, and have Dutch the medium of instruction. One of the most eminent ministers of the Dutch Reformed Church told me some little time ago that he regretted English had not been made the medium of his own education, as a boy, as he considered it an advantage. I should not be disposed, therefore, to recommend making Dutch the medium of instruction, but with regard to everything else, there should be an absolute equality between the two languages of the country.

4718. If a boy wants to be examined in Dutch, how would you work it ? Would you have all the papers published in Dutch and English ?—I should leave that as a practical question to be solved by the University authorities.

4719. In what way ?—I do not think it is for me to point out the way.

4720. You would have to provide an examiner, would you not, if there was one Dutch boy wanted to be examined ?—I consider that it would be dealt with without much trouble. I am not at all sure that very many would take advantage of it, but I do not see any more practical difficulty than there is in printing the public documents in two languages.

4721. You would have two sets of papers, one in Dutch and the other in English ? —Yes, if it were necessary.

4722. And if any boy wanted it ?—Yes.

4723. Then if one boy wanted it, you would have to start the arrangement at once, would you not ?—Yes.

4724. That would be the result of what you suggest, namely, two sets of papers, would it not?—Yes. I think that whatever practical inconvenience is found, such a course would be counterbalanced by the feeling throughout the country that the two languages were placed in educational matters on the same equal footing that they are in Parliament and the law courts. I only lay down general principles that I think ought to guide the country in dealing with the question of language. I do not pretend to go into details.

4725. *Rev. Coetzee.*] Your idea is not to advocate having two sets of papers in Dutch and English, but to give an opportunity, if candidates prefer it, of having the examination in both languages ?—Exactly. That is my feeling.

4726. *President.*] You have spoken from a citizen point of view; will you speak now as an educationalist ?—I should not like to speak from that point of view, as I am not directly connected with any educational institution.

4727. *Dr. Berry.*] I understand that you have two ways of getting over the difficulty ?—I do not go into details, but only lay down general principles. I say there should be absolute equality between the two languages.

4728. How do you secure that equality in the way you propose ?—I consider that the extra marks a Dutch boy would get for his Dutch paper would about make up for the disadvantage he would be under compared with the English boy.

4729. Would you compel every English boy to learn Dutch ?—Certainly. I should like to see every Dutch boy learn English and every English boy learn Dutch.

4730. Is not that compelling the direction which a young man's education should take ?—Not in this country.

4731. If you compel a boy to learn Dutch, is it not directing his course of educa- Rev.
Dr. Wergman.
tion compulsorily?—I look upon the matter from a citizen's point of view, not as an
educationalist at all. In this country we have two languages. They are equal in Sept. 10th, 1891.
Parliament and in the law courts, and they must be equal in educational matters.

4732. Is it not better for a young man to be brought up to regard himself as a
citizen of the world rather than as a citizen of a remote part of it?—I do not think we
can afford to disturb the ideas of South African patriotism by substituting cosmopoli-
tanism for it; it is a great danger to the country.

4733. Is not patriotism of that sort a very selfish sort of thing?—No. I do not
think so. The patriotism that ought to be put into the minds of a young man here is
that he is a South African first, and an Englishman afterwards.

4734. How does that kind of patriotism affect the Kafirs?—I should submit that
that question is hardly within the scope of the Commission's enquiry.

4735. You said you were favourable to Professor MacWilliam's recommendation,
and he places Sesuto and Kafir alongside Dutch, does he not?—I only endorse his
recommendation so far as it touches the idea of an alternative Dutch paper.

4736. You would not encourage boys to study any other language here but
English and Dutch?—No. The study of Kafir may be a necessity for certain purposes
in the Civil Service and so forth in the Transkei.

4737. So is Dutch, is it not?—We have got to consider this country with a view
to Europeans in the country and with a view to the two European languages in the
country, and we are not going to consider other people as being a factor of equal
importance in national, political, or social life.

4738. The Europeans have to govern the Kafirs, and it is necessary from that
point of view that Europeans should know something of their language and ideas, is it
not?—There need not be a public examination; those who want it may learn it themselves.

4739. Could not the same be said with regard to Dutch?—I do not think so.

4740. Do you agree with Professor MacWilliam's recommendation that a weak
paper in English may be compensated for by an equally weak paper in Dutch?—I
should be disposed to agree with him.

4741. Would not the practical outcome of that be that two weak papers would
take the place of one good one?—There you are getting into educational details, and
I do not feel myself competent to give an answer that would be worth having on
that point.

4742. Then we may fairly take it that your views are not in the interests of
education, but in the interests of politics?—Exactly; upon this subject.

4743. *Mr. Theron.*] I believe you have been travelling a good deal through the
country, have you not?—Yes.

4744. Do you know the requirements of the country?—I do.

4745. Should you like to educate the Dutch population just as well as the English
population?—Exactly.

4746. So that it would not be well, even from an educational point of view, to
leave the Dutch people uneducated?—Certainly not.

4747. Particularly in their own mother tongue?—Yes; that is my view.

4748. Is it felt to be a necessity, even in the Government service, that civil
servants should pass an examination in Dutch?—Certainly.

4749. Why is that insisted upon?—It is one of the languages of the country, and
cannot be done without; it is indispensable.

4750. Do you hold then that the Dutch language is officially acknowledged?—Yes.

4751. And as such it ought to be encouraged?—Certainly.

4752. *President.*] You said you thought there ought to be no public examination
in Kafir; that there is no necessity for it?—I do not think so.

4753. How is it that in India where we govern a large native population there
are examinations in native languages for civil service candidates?—I should say that
the parallel between the natives of India and the native races of South Africa is a
parallel that scarcely applies. The natives of India can only be governed through the
medium of their own languages. Although a knowledge of Kafir is necessary for
certain Transkeian officials, we teach the natives in our schools English, and English is
becoming more and more known among them; and the native population in this
country does not present at all a parallel with regard to the linguistic difficulty to the
natives of India; they are not equal to them either socially or intellectually.

4754. The principle of examination in India is because the officials come into
contact with the natives constantly in everyday life, and it is required in the administration of the country, is it not?—I do not think it is advisable in this country.

4755. *Rev. Moorrees.*] Do not you think before that question is entered into, the
natives ought to have equal rights in Parliament conceded to them?—Yes.

Rev.
Dr. Wirgman.

Sept. 10th, 1891.

4756. *President.*] Do you know anything about the facilities for the education of the children of railway employés?—I know something about the work that is being done on the railway, and I should like, from an outside point of view, to state that I think on this system, from Port Elizabeth to Graham's Town and from Alicedale to Cradock, the most convenient centre for railway children to be educated at is Graham's Town, and I have been told that the mother superior of S. Peter's Home is ready to enter into arrangements with the Government to take the girls of railway employés and board and educate them for about £12 a year. From what I know, through going backwards and forwards on the line, I think that is very well worthy the attention of the Government.

4757. What would you propose for boys? —With regard to the education of boys, I think school facilities might be given at De Aar. At Alicedale and De Aar there might be establishments where boys could be boarded cheaply.

4758. *Mr. Rowan.*] How are these boarding departments to be supported?—The Government ought to give special facilities I think under the circumstances.

4759. *Dr. Berry.*] Why should the Government give special facilities for, the railway employés and not the police?—The railway employés are isolated about the country in the cottages along the line, and they are placed there by Government at a special disadvantage, hence the Government ought to treat them differently to other civil servants.

4760. Do you know anything about the distribution of the police throughout the country?—The police are shifted about more than railway employés, and therefore have better chances of getting their children educated than maintenance men who remain in one cottage perhaps for four or five years.

4761. You propose to erect boarding establishments and educate the railway employés' children at the Government expense?—I do not say entirely at the Government expense, but I think the Government ought to treat the children of railway employés with more consideration than other civil servants, because of their isolation. I only wish to give a general view.

4762. Would you object to applying the same principle also to the children of policemen in isolated situations?—If they could be got under the same scheme.

4763. Would not there be some outcry in the country if the Government were to offer facilities for such persons and not offer the same facilities to other people in poor circumstances in isolated positions?—I do not think so. I think the country generally is inclined to treat the railway employés with consideration.

4764. *President.*] Do you know what is being done for farm children?—Yes.

4765. Could not railway children be worked into those farm schools?—I do not think so.

4766. With regard to boys, what contribution ought the Government to give?— I have not gone into any figures, and should not like to say.

4767. The Rev. Father Simeon suggested that the Government should start some central boarding establishment for them. Do you approve of that?—It is worth thinking of, but I should not like to pin myself definitely to such a proposal.

4768. What contribution do you think the Government ought to give?—I should not like to say.

4769. From your communication with railway men, what do you think they can afford to pay?—I cannot say. I would sooner leave that to Mr. Heenan. I do not know their circumstances sufficiently.

4770. Mr. Heenan thinks that these children of railway employés can be worked into farm schools, and you differ from him?—Yes, I differ from him there.

4771. Do you know anything about mission schools?—I should like to state that a Bill has been introduced into the New Zealand Legislature providing for a general system of aiding all denominational schools as a substitute for the present system of State aided undenominational education. The broad principles of the measure are, that in every district where the denominational schools are doing their work properly, under Government inspection, the Government shall not come in with a State aided undenominational school to interfere with them. The Government State aided undenominational schools in New Zealand would only come in where denominations have failed to do their work. That has been introduced into the New Zealand Parliament as a measure of economy.

4772. Has that measure passed?—Not yet.

4773. Have they undenomination l schools in existence in New Zealand?—Yes; and they are found to be very costly, more costly than the country can afford. One of the newspapers, the *Southern Cross*, commenting on the measure says, "If this Bill is carried, people will rejoice, not only as regards their pockets, but as regards the faith of their forefathers, and children will have religious education." I should like to say that I have had to inspect mission schools in my rural deanery, and I have inspected a them from time to time as diocesan inspector in religious knowledge, and I wish to testify to the efficiency of all the mission schools in this district. They are doing really sound educational work, but the defect in regard to the mission schools is the mixing of the two races. I should like to see the Government aid the different denominations in providing schools which would enable us to keep the two races distinct. I do not mean by that that the Kafir race is not kept distinct; they are kept distinct. The Kafir mission school here in connection with St. Stephen's is in a high state of efficiency. I have paid it surprise visits and inspected it as well.

Rev.
Dr. Wigman.

Sept. 10th, 1891.

4774. *Mr. Rowan.*] Are you in favour of fourth class public undenominational schools ?—No. I want Government to give denominations larger grants, so as to enable them to take a school like the White's Road mission school and cut it in two, so as to divide the races. That is the great difficulty. I do not think it is good for European children to be mixed up with natives. I could not conscientiously support the idea of fourth class public undenominational schools, but my theory is, that the State should superintend the present grants for mission schools to such an extent that we might be able to separate the races.

4775. How would you superintend them ; according to attendance and efficiency ? —Yes, and according to the result of inspection. It would be very easy, if we had an additional grant, the same grant that it is proposed to give these fourth class public undenominational schools, to separate the European children from the native children, and teach them separately and efficiently. At present, the inadequate Government support prevents it.

4776. *Dr. Berry.*] According to your plan, why should not we put the Grey Institute under your rural deanery, as well as any other schools ?—I do not want that.

4777. Why do you want the others ?—The Grey Institute is an endowed school.

4778. But you want the Government to endow the other schools, do you not ?—I do not say endow them, but give a larger grant.

4779. A larger grant would be endowment, would it not ?—You cannot say that a larger Government grant on the principle of payment by results, that can be taken away at any time, is an endowment. The Grey Institute has £800 a year coming from quitrents. That I call an endowment.

4780. A large Government grant is practically an endowment to a school, is it not ?—I do not think so. It is not called so in any other country in the world.

4781. They are called Government aided schools officially. The Grey Institute is an aided school, and you want a school to be set up in connection with your church, which shall have larger aid from Government, and still be under the direction and administration of your church. Why cannot that principle go all round, and the Grey Institute, which is also aided by Government, be put under your control ?—You cannot interfere with existing facts.

4782. But you propose to interfere with existing facts ?—No ; I want new facts brought to light. If Government gives me the money, you will see I will make a fact with it. I would cut that mission school in two, and see that the white children are not mixed up with the others. Another £50 a year would do it.

4783. If your principle is introduced, it practically cuts at the existence of all Government aided schools, does it not ?—You would really make the Government aided system a house divided against itself, one part being conducted by the churches and another conducted by a small body like the Grey Institute ?—That is what it is now.

4784. Is not that an evil ?—No ; competition is the soul of business, even in educational matters, and if things get too much into one hand it is bad.

4785. Then it is to keep up this competition and rivalry that you advocate the system you speak of ?—Not necessarily. I have other reasons for advocating it. One of them is this, that I consider it is the duty of members of the English church to provide in the day schools for efficient religious instruction as well as secular instruction. Every denomination must agree that the Education Department here has been most friendly to the different religious bodies, but in Australia and New Zealand the public undenominational school system has done the greatest possible harm. The most ridiculous questions are sometimes put to children.

4786. Then generally you would say that if any development of the system of education is required in this colony, it should be on denominational or mission school lines in preference to public undenominational schools ?—Yes ; I should prefer the lines of the New Zealand Bill I have referred to. Such a change would not have been proposed there after so many years unless the public had found the present system was not only costly but inconvenient in other ways.

4787. *Mr. Theron.*] Do you want to alter the present system of mission schools, or simply increase the Government aid so as to enable them to separate the two races ? —I should desire to see such an increase of Government aid given to the existing mission schools for the poorer classes as would enable us to educate the white children separately from the coloured children.

Mr.
George Cassé.

Sept. 10th, 1891.

Mr. George Cassé examined.

4788. *President.*] What are you ?—I am assistant teacher at the Grey Institute.

4789. Where else have you been a teacher ?—I was headmaster at the Cradock public school till quite recently.

4790. Have you been anywhere else ?—I was in Graham's Town for six months temporarily and also at the Grey Institute previously.

4791. Can you say anything about the wants of the agricultural population ?— I should like to propose something which I have already proposed to Sir Langham Dale. A farmer has his children at a farm school, and when they reach a certain age, he wants perhaps to send them to a public school. If he does so, he reduces the number below the minimum required in a farm school. What I proposed was, and Sir Langham Dale agreed with me, that those children who are transferred to a public school from a farm school should be still allowed to count in the farm schools so far as the grant is concerned. I know cases where farm schools have been broken up for the want of some such provision.

4792. Would not the effect of that be that the Government would contribute twice over to the farm school and also to the town school ?—I do not propose that the particular children transferred to a public school should get the farm school grant, but that the remaining children should get it. I have myself gone to a farm school and found boys of eighteen being taught by a young lady not much older. I said that such boys ought to be sent to a public school, but the farmer replied that he could not afford it, as if he did so he would lose all the grant for the remaining children and he would have to dismiss the teacher.

4793. How many were there ?—Six. Two of them should have gone decidedly to a public school, and the farmer would have sent them but for what I say. He would have lost the grant for the remaining four children, and they would have received no education.

4794. *Mr. Theron.*] The grants to the public schools where those boys could attend are not made on the principle of numbers, so that it would not interfere, would it ?— No. I know as a fact that a good many of the poorer children in agricultural districts get no education at all.

4795. Is that in Cradock ?—Not merely in Cradock ; there are some there, but all through the Eastern Province. It is a very serious matter. I think the field-cornets of each district should be instructed to report the number of children who are not at school at all. That could easily be done. It should be the business of the people in the nearest town to try and arrange something for them. The minister of the district generally does that sort of thing, but he would have the information before him more definitely if he got it in a formal way from the field-cornets.

4796. *President.*] Do you think it would be wise to bring into existence some local power such as a School Board elected by the ratepayers to create schools to meet these emergencies ?—Yes. The Government should also contribute. The field-cornets could report to the Board and they could establish schools where necessary. Many of the bywoners' children are not receiving any education at all, while Kafir children in towns are taught.

4797. Suppose there is a deficiency after the Government has made its contribution and the fees have been collected, who ought to pay it ?—The local rates ought to be applied to the purpose. In some schools that is so already. In Cradock, for instance, our school was under the Town Council, and the local rates were responsible for any deficiency.

4798. Did that work well and to the satisfaction of the ratepayers ?—Decidedly.

4799. Have they ever had to pay ?—Not a farthing. The fact of their being responsible creates confidence at once in the school.

4800. So that the school is frequented and sought after ?—Yes, and teachers will go to a school of that kind where they would not care to go to others.

4801. *Rev. Moorrees.*] The great difficulty with regard to the isolated farming population is to get suitable accommodation for boarders and teachers, is it not ?—Yes.

4802. Have you thought of any plan to meet that difficulty ?—Itinerant and circuit teachers meet it to some extent, but of course if we had a Board they could work in this direction and superintend the whole thing. I know that in some farm schools the farmer does not care to have these very poor children associating with his own. I think there ought to be some mode of compelling them, but that is impossible I am afraid.

4803. To start a circuit school you must have at least two centres. Very often you can find one suitable place, but not a second. Would you be in favour of calling a circuit school by another name, and giving a grant to one place, if it does the work required ?—Yes, certainly. Some children are engaged in agricultural labour necessarily for some part of the year, and during the remainder of the year they get instruction from a circuit teacher who goes round, so that they get partially educated in that way.

4804. As far as you know there never was any deficiency at Cradock?—No, although money was borrowed by the school from the municipal council and interest had to be paid out of the school revenue, until the debt was wiped off by a grant from Government.

4805. *President.*] What steps should be taken in your opinion to give Boards of Management perpetual succession, and provide for the tenure of public school property?—I do not see why you cannot make municipalities or divisional councils responsible as far as the buildings are concerned. That would ensure perpetual succession, as the property could be vested in those bodies.

4806. *Mr. Rowan.*] Would you keep the present guarantor system intact?—If it does remain intact, then the school buildings should be vested in the divisional council or municipality.

4807. *President.*] Would you also shift the responsibility from the present guarantors, say to a Board elected by the ratepayers?—Yes. I should much prefer that certainly, but the present bodies have already too much to do in many cases, and I do not think they would be suitable. Any Board should be elected specially for educational purposes.

4808. Do you think the burden thrown on the ratepayers would be great?—I do not think so. If these local Boards were made responsible for the buildings alone, the Government could treat with them, and the management of the school could be left to local committees. That would secure perpetual succession, I think. When the school at Cradock was taken over by the municipal council, all difficulty ceased.

4809. *Dr. Berry.*] Do you know anything about the education of children in towns?—Yes.

4810. Suppose it is deemed advisable to recommend that in all schools aided by Government a separation should be made between the European and the coloured children, would you advise that such separation or segregation should be carried out by the development of what is generally known as the public undenominational school system, or by the development of the mission school system?—I think the public undenominational school system is preferable.

4811. Have you made yourself acquainted with Sir Langham Dale's recommendation as to fourth class public undenominational schools?—Yes.

4812. Are you in favour of the principle he lays down?—I think it is highly advisable that the children should be separated by some means or other.

4813. *President.*] The method you have not thought of?—No. I cannot give an opinion as to the method—not a decided opinion at any rate.

4814. Have you anything else to suggest?—A great deal of dissatisfaction exists among teachers in consequence of the frequent dismissals without rhyme or reason. I should like to suggest that an appeal to the Superintendent-General of Education should be allowed in the case of the dismissal of any teacher. That was, I may say, generally approved of by all the teachers at the recent conference held at Kimberley.

Mr. A. S. Marshall Hall examined.

4815. *President.*] I believe you are headmaster of the Diocesan Grammar School here?—Yes.

4816. How long have you been so?—For nearly two years.

4817. Are you a graduate of the Oxford University?—Yes.

4818. Have you been engaged in educational pursuits elsewhere in the colony?—Yes. At Umtata, in the St. John's diocese, I was headmaster of the Diocesan Grammar School. That school was formed by being separated from the mission school.

4819. Have you been engaged in Switzerland also?—Yes. I was Government inspector of schools in certain departments. I was engaged by the Cantonal authorities.

4820. What Canton?—Vaud.

4821. Were you there long?—For four years.

4822. Can you speak with regard to the establishment of public undenominational schools in towns where there already exists an efficient denominational school?—My experience is that it is a very great hardship that undenominational schools can be and are occasionally established at the expense of an efficient denominational school.

4823. How would you remedy that?—It is rather a difficult question. The case in which I had personal experience was one in which I consider the regulations laid down by the Education Department were infringed, that is to say the meeting was not duly called nor were the resolutions passed by it adhered to. That was at Umtata. The result was so to handicap what was then the Diocesan Grammar School, that it

Mr.
A. S. Marshall
Hall.

Sept. 10th, 1891.

practically divided the allegiance of the town; we had to decrease the staff, and generally it interfered with the efficiency of the school.

4824. Is it still in existence?—Yes. The public school has so far been a failure that they are now going to amalgamate the two.

4825. Under what system?—I do not know. It is not yet decided. It was a Church of England school, that had for ten years carried on all the education in the place, and then owing to its being called a Church of England school, and not a mission school, which it had been originally, it became the Diocesan Grammar School, and owing to that development, a certain amount of ill-feeling arose, and a public undenominational school came into existence.

4826. What would you suggest?—The only thing I can suggest is that the controlling machinery should not be quite so cumbrous. It is allowed to slide a little at some places where there is apparently no means of checking the statements made by outsiders or interested people.

4827. Do you think it would be a good thing to create local Boards?—Yes. That would be a way out of the difficulty.

4828. Would you have representations made to the Board who would be the best judge as to whether a second school should come into existence?—Yes. It should be under the control of the Education Department, as a final court of appeal.

4829. Does the grammar school you speak of get any aid from Government?—None whatever. It did originally. Before it was organised as a grammar school it was a mission school. We separated the coloured children from the whites, and put the former into the mission school and created the grammar school for the whites. The result was, that competition came in. That was an instance of the separation of the two races not being a success from an educational point of view.

4830. Mr. Theron.] When that separation took place between the two races, was it after they had been some time together in one school?—Yes. They had been together for some time; I forget how long. It was for some years they had been drawing aid from Government as a joint school, the only school in existence in the town in fact.

4831. Suppose the two races had been separated from the beginning, would any grievance then have arisen?—No. It would have been difficult to do so, because under what class would you bring the school for whites.

4832. Suppose you had mission schools for both?—If that could have been done, it would have met the difficulty.

4833. So that if the Government grant was increased so as to enable you to conduct two schools on race lines in such a place, no difficulty would arise?—Exactly.

4834. From your experience at Umtata, do you think it desirable that the two races should be mixed in one school?—Umtata is not exactly like most other colonial towns; the distinction between colour there is very marked indeed; you have not the number of gradations you have elsewhere. Most decidedly it is desirable that the two races should be kept separate.

4835. Do you think that should apply here in Port Elizabeth?—Yes; at White's Road mission school for instance.

4836. You think it is worth while making some sacrifice to separate the two races from the beginning?—Decidedly.

4837. President.] Would you have a colour distinction?—The gradations are so very fine that it is difficult to draw a marked line between the two.

4838. What would you make the line of distinction if you had to lay down a school regulation in print?—I think you might say children with some European parentage, even if there was a little colour. That seems the only practicable way.

4839. Dr. Berry.] Would you give managers power to exclude, without assigning a cause in any case?—Certainly.

4840. President.] Would you have an appeal against the managers?—I think it is desirable always to have an appeal in cases where the control is so purely local as it would be.

4841. To whom would the appeal lie?—To the Board that might be created, or if there is no district Board, then to the Education Department.

4842. Rev. Coetzee.] How would you create these Boards?—In the case of municipal areas, I should have the Board, elected by the municipal ratepayers, and in case of country districts by the divisional council ratepayers outside the municipalities.

4843. President.] What do you think of a Board elected by the ratepayers of the whole district to control all the schools within that district, including the town schools?—I think it is desirable that in certain towns the town interests should have control of the districts within their township.

4844. Rev. Coetzee.] Would you be in favour of laying down a system of education for this country in which there would be left scope to religious denominations to take an interest in education?—Quite so. Of course it would even in that case be subject

Mr.
A. S. Marshall
Hall.

Sept. 10th, 1891.

to public control. Speaking as to existing schools, where any one religious denomination was not in such a large majority as to make it practically very little hardship to others to have to send their children to school, I should place that religious denomination in such a position that it could carry on its school in such a way that it would take the place of the public undenominational school, always laying it down as a *sine qua non*, that any denominational school which plays the part of a public school should have a conscience clause with reference to religious education, and be subject to inspection at all times.

4845. *President.*] With reference to the question of language, is there more than one language taught in the schools in Switzerland?—There are three,—German, French, and Italian.

4846. What is the mother tongue of the bulk of the boys?—In the Canton of Vaud it is French, but that is the language of the majority. The language of two-thirds is German, and the remaining one-third French and Italian.

4847. In the Canton of Vaud where you were, did the majority speak French?—French was the official language.

4848. How do they deal with the question of language there?—Three languages were taught in the schools, but the medium of instruction was French.

4849. How do they use the other two languages in teaching?—The other two are optional. Switzerland is a peculiar country in some respects. The different cantons keep very much to themselves, and it is not easy for a Swiss citizen to change his canton. He has to go through a rather elaborate system of getting permission from the communal or district authorities and then the cantonal authorities before he can change his domicile from one part to another. Both the chief languages, French and German, are pretty well known throughout colloquially, and as a rule they do not trouble themselves to learn more than the language of their own canton grammatically. In the higher grade schools all three languages form part of the regular school curriculum. These are optional, but they are all taught grammatically.

4850. In the primary schools you say they generally limit themselves to learning one language grammatically?—Yes.

4851. And in the canton where you were it was French?—Yes.

4852. Was that the medium of instruction throughout the school?—Yes.

4853. Did the boys all understand that language?—Perfectly.

4854. *Mr. Rowan.*] Is that the only language spoken in that canton?—In the northern part they speak a very mixed patois, Gothic in its roots, and German more or less in form. It is a peculiar language and has arisen in a somewhat similar manner to Cape Dutch. As a rule, the mountaineers speak it; it is a dialect and forms no part of the school education.

4855. *President.*] That would be a German dialect, would it not?—Yes.

4856. And yet in the canton the medium of instruction is French, is it not?—Yes.

4857. Is there any system of examination there?—Yes, in all schools.

4858. In the primary schools?—Yes.

4859. In the primary schools was there an examination in any other but the French language?—No, only in French.

4860. Does that primary examination correspond to our Elementary examination here, or is it higher?—It is a lower standard.

4861. What examination there corresponded to our Elementary examination?—There are three ranks of schools in Switzerland—primary, secondary, and what we would call a finishing school or gymnasium. The examination for the second grade schools almost corresponds to our Elementary examination here.

4862. Is there an examination in any other language but French in the secondary schools?—Yes; in French, and Italian if required.

4863. Is German also optional?—Yes.

4864. Is there a system of marks?—Marks are given.

4865. Are the marks published?—No; it is not competitive, it is merely a pass examination.

4866. They have to pass in French, and they may take up the two other languages?—Yes, and in that case they have to pass in those two languages. Failing in the optional subject has the same result as failing in one of the compulsory subjects. Suppose a boy had been taking up German when he was in a French school, he would have to obtain the requisite number of marks in German in order to pass into the higher grade school.

4867. Must you pass in two languages before you get into the higher school?—No, only one; whichever language you choose to take you have to pass in. French is compulsory.

4868. Are not they obliged to take up all three languages?—No, only French.

Mr.
A. S. Marshall
Hall.
—
Sept. 10th, 1891.

4869. *Rev. Moorrees.*] Do they make some distinction between the use of languages of the country and foreign languages ?—A very important distinction. Failing in a language like English, which is not a language of the country, would have no effect on the pass examination for the higher grade schools.

4870. *Mr. Theron.*] Failing in one of the languages of the country would affect the pass, would it not ?—Yes.

4871. *Dean Holmes.*] A candidate is not compelled to take more than one of the languages of the country, is he ?—No.

4872. *Rev. Moorrees.*] Is it considered destructive of the elementary character of instruction for a boy to take up a second language for the examination ?—No, not as regards the three languages of the country.

4873. *President.*] What are the other subjects in which they are examined in order to pass ?—The history of their own country, and the usual subjects such as we have here—reading, writing, arithmetic, and dictation.

4874. Then the other subjects are similar to our four subjects ?—It is not so high as the Elementary examination ; it is nearer our fourth standard.

4875. And the fifth subject would be language, which they might take up if they like, and if they fail in it it would cause them to fail in the examination altogether ?—The principle in Switzerland is this : There is a fifth language paper, with say 100 marks attached. A boy who takes up French alone would get the maximum of 100 marks ; a boy who takes up French and German would get the maximum of 50 each. If he takes up two and fails in one, he would not pass in language.

4876. What was the result of that ?—I could not say ; it was evenly divided. A great number of children would take up both languages, and in the southern part (the Lake of Geneva side) they nearly always took up one ; it depended upon the district they resided in.

4877. *Dean Holmes.*] Were there any instances of their taking up three languages? —No, not in the Elementary examination, that I remember.

4878. *Rev. Moorrees.*] From your experience in Switzerland, do you consider that it would destroy the character of the Elementary examination here if another subject were added ?—It depends to a very great extent on the way it is done. It could be done without destroying the elementary character of the examination.

4879. *President.*] How could it be done ?—English is the medium of instruction in all schools, and I should have thought myself that in cases where the medium of instruction was Dutch, the whole examination might be conducted in Dutch as far as can be, with subjects such as geography, history, and so on ; and composition, which has to be written, might be in Dutch in the case of Dutch children ; but I think if any attempt were made to substitute Dutch in places where English was the general language spoken in the school by children, then it would seriously interfere with the elementary character of the examination ; that is, as far as my experience goes in the Eastern Province.

4880. Why should it do so here and not in Switzerland ?—Here the two races are widely separated. Throughout the Eastern Province, as a rule, there are very few children who can read or write Dutch proper, although they may know something of "kitchen" Dutch, as it is called, whereas in Switzerland, throughout the country, those who take German take it because their own family or their connections are German, and they hear it spoken as often as French, and read it as often as French. Here there is such a very distinct line between the two languages, so far as my experience in the Eastern Province goes, and it would not act in the same way at all.

4881. Can you devise some means by which those who speak Dutch and use English as the medium of instruction should have some benefit from the knowledge they have acquired, without handicapping unduly the English boy who knows nothing about it ?—I should allow them to reply to all the papers in Dutch that it was possible to do. It has occurred to me that extra marks might be given to any Dutch boy who chooses to answer his paper in English, and any English boy who answers in Dutch in the same way. I have thought that that might work.

4882. *Rev. Coetzee.*] What would you say to having the subjects arranged in columns, and have a language column like they have in Switzerland ?—It works very well there ; whether it would here I cannot say, but I think it might be made to work.

Rev.
Father Strobino.
—
Sept. 10th, 1891.

Rev. Father Strobino examined.

4883. *President.*] I believe you are at the head of the Roman Catholic schools in Port Elizabeth ?—Yes ; the convent and mission schools, and the Marist Brothers' school.

4884. Do those schools get any contribution from Government ?—The high school gets no contribution ; only the mission schools.

Rev.
Father Niobino.

Sept. 19th, 1891.

4885. Are there boys and girls there ?—Yes. We have about 500 children, and we get altogether from the Government £270 a year. We have the St. Augustine's school, the school at the North End and the South End and at the convent.

4886. Is the attendance of the children regular ?—It is very good ; we cannot complain.

4887. What is the percentage of attendance to the number on the roll ?—We have 505 children on the roll, and the percentage of attendance is 375. We cannot complain about the attendance ; as a rule it is very good.

4888. Would you suggest any means of increasing the regularity of attendance. How do you induce it ?—At present we give attendance marks in the schools and also medals. At the end of the month, the manager goes into the school, either myself or my substitute, and reads out the marks of the children, and then rewards of some kind are given. So that the children have an inducement.

4889. Is there any other inducement ?—We speak to the parents very often from the pulpit, and so on.

4890. Do you remit the fees in consequence of regularity of attendance ?—Not unless the parents are poor.

4891. Would you be at all in favour of compulsion, with attendance and truant officers to look after the children not at school ?—As far as my experience goes since I came to this country, I think the parents are themselves anxious to send their children to school if they have the opportunity. It is only perhaps in country places where there is much difficulty, but the Government has arranged to give grants for farm schools, and I fancy that supplies the need without compulsion. I am only speaking of our own denomination.

4892. With regard to children who do not go to school at all, do you know anything about them ?—There are a few cases of children who do not go to school in Port Elizabeth even among our own people, but they are mainly the children of poor parents who require the services of the children.

4893. How would you deal with them ?—I think they ought to be in school. Government should take the matter in hand, and see that the parents give education to their children.

4894. If they cannot, do not you think the State ought to step in ?—Yes.

4895. And have attendance and truant officers ?—Yes, certainly.

4896. Would there be room in the existing schools for these children ?—For the children of our people there would be ; we have made ample provision.

4897. Would your people like some officer of that kind to help you to bring the children to school ?—I can hardly say whether they would all like it. I do not know that they would have any objection as a body.

4898. If such children are brought to your school, would you be prepared to receive them upon the present system of aid ?—We would have to make provision for them. We would not allow them to mix up with the other children.

4899. If you took them, what do you think would be fair to you ?—The Government ought to make us some allowance.

4900. Something like what Government does now in connection with mission schools, in proportion to the number attending and the efficiency of the school after inspection by the Government Inspector ?—Yes.

4901. Have you seen Sir Langham Dale's suggestion about fourth class public undenominational schools ?—Yes.

4902. What do you think of that recommendation ?—I understand it to b that the present mission schools, in so far as the whites are concerned, are to be changed into fourth class public undenominational schools, and that the present mission schools are to be retained only for the coloured children, and then, that the present mission schools containing white children are to be aided of course a little more than they are at present, if they are made undenominational, with a Board of Managers. That is what I understand.

4903. Do you think that could work into your system ?—It would work into our system only with this proviso, that a Board of Managers be chosen from among the members of that denomination to which the present buildings and lands on which school buildings are erected belong. I do not think that a denomination would be willing to hand over to a Board constituted of people belonging to several denominations their lands and school buildings.

4904. Suppose your buildings are used by your own denomination receiving this aid, and your denomination has the management, subject to supervision and inspection at all times of some officer like the Government Inspector, would that suit ?—Yes ; but I should like to explain that we would object to have a Board of Managers telling us, for example, what staff of teachers we are to employ in our schools, or removing teachers from one place to another without our consent; and to provide against that,

[G. 3—'02.]

Rev.
Father Strobino.
——
Sept. 10th, 1891.

we would insist that the Board of Managers belong to the denomination to which the school belongs; and whatever changes are to be made in the staff of teachers and the routine of the school, and so on, should be subject to the control of the Government or the Education Department; but not to the whims and fancies of people who perhaps have not the same feelings and ideas that we have at present.

4905. Would you object to your being required to satisfy the Government or the controlling body that your teachers were competent; that is to say, that they were certificated teachers, and had passed examinations to qualify them?—Yes, certainly.

4906. What do you think you ought to get for such additional teaching, if you took in these children picked up in the street?—So much per head. We would be satisfied with Sir Langham Dale's proposal as far as aid goes, if the thing could be carried out in that way, provided we had the management, always of course under the superintendence and direction of the Education Department.

4907. In order to start this school you would have to collect the householders in your neighbourhood to see whether they approved of your having this undenominational school. Would that be fair?—There might be too much interference; we might be in a minority in some places.

4908. If there was a general Board for the district, with the power of dealing with these questions, are you not more likely to be dealt with fairly by them?—I do not think as a body we would like that; we would prefer to deal direct with the Government.

4909. What part of Europe do you come from?—From Italy.

4910. Is there any difficulty about language there?—No; I come from Piedmont, and French is spoken in most parts there. They teach in Italian and give a pass in French.

4911. Do they get passes for passing in French?—Merely a certificate, in which it is stated that the boy or girl has passed in French.

4912. Is that endorsed upon the other certificate?—No. It is a distinct certificate entirely.

4913. Is it valued there?—In most districts it is.

4914. Is French generally spoken among the lower classes?—No; it is rather a *patois* of German and French.

4915. Have you anything to say on the subject of language in regard to the Elementary examination here?—I would not make Dutch compulsory in the Elementary examination, but I would give rewards in the shape of bursaries. That would be an encouragement to pupils to learn Dutch, and it would not diminish the chances of a pass in the case of those not knowing Dutch.

4916. How would it do to have a fifth paper in the Elementary examination with three alternative subjects, and give a boy the opportunity of taking which he liked, the marks counting?—I do not think that would be fair in the Elementary examination, because it is as a rule pretty hard now, without adding an extra subject, such as language or science.

4917. Do you teach elementary science?—Yes.

4918. *Dr. Berry.*] Is it the case that boys in your school are encouraged to prefer going in for the fifth standard rather than the Elementary examination?—They are not encouraged, but the boys themselves prefer to satisfy the Inspector that they have reached the fifth standard to going in for the Elementary examination.

4919. Have you any objection to boys going in for the Elementary examination?—No. I encourage it.

4920. *Rev. Moorrees.*] Does that apply to the poorer schools only?—Yes.

4921. *President.*] Do you teach Dutch in your school?—Not here; in our other schools we do.

4922. *Rev. Coetzee.*] Is your experience confined to this place?—I was at East London for six years.

4923. Have you been in the up-country districts at all?—No; I have not been in a Dutch district.

4924. Then you cannot express any opinion as to the wants and requirements of the Dutch country people?—No.

4925. *President.*] Have you anything like industrial education in your school?—We are starting it for white children in connection with the orphanage.

4926. What sort of education do you propose to give boys?—Teach them trades. The thing is still in embryo; but our intention would be to indenture certain boys to good tradesmen in the town in the daytime, and they would come back to the establishment in the evening. In a few years time we hope to be able to increase that and establish industrial schools in the country.

4927. Would you encourage night schools?—Yes. When the boys I speak of leave their work in the daytime, they will come home and have an hour in the night school.

Rev.
Father Stichino,

Sept. 10th, 1891.

4928. Literary instruction you mean?—Yes; elementary literary work.

4929. Have you any night schools in operation?—Every winter we establish a school at the North and South End.

4930. How many pupils are there in each?—About twenty in each school on the average. As the weather becomes fine, the numbers fall off.

4931. Do you consider that night schools are useful?—Very useful; and we find that for the three winter months they are appreciated. We provide the teachers and a room.

4932. What fees do you charge?—A shilling a week.

4933. Do you think if the Government gave aid it would be productive of benefit?—Yes; but a night school all the year round would not answer. It would only answer in winter.

4934. In what direction do you think the Government can aid best?—It might make a grant towards night schools for three months in the year in proportion to the numbers attending, and subject to inspection.

4935. What grant do you think the Government should give?—I think if we got £5 per school for three months in the year it would be a help.

4936. You say you would only want it for a quarter of the year?—It is not practicable to carry on the work longer than that, here, at all events.

4937. How many boys would you expect to be in attendance here?—About twenty; not more.

4938. Do you know anything about technical education, here or elsewhere?—No.

Rev. S. Brooke examined.

Rev.
S. Brooke.

Sept. 10th, 1891.

4939. *President.*] I believe you are Rector of St. Paul's, Port Elizabeth?—Yes.

4940. Have you a large mission school?—Yes. I have four mission schools under my charge. St. Paul's girls' school, with 200 children; St. Paul's boys' school, with 61; St. John's mission school, with 137; and St. Stephen's boys' and girls' school, with about 60.

4941. What is the total of all?—About 450.

4942. What is the average attendance?—About 80 per cent.

4943. Do you consider the attendance pretty regular?—It is very regular indeed, especially in the girls' school. In the Kafir mission school, that is St. Stephen's, it is not so regular. There is a smaller number there now.

4944. Do you think you could or should be aided at all in securing better attendance?—The great thing is for the parents themselves to be anxious. In the case of Kafirs, the native teacher says it is a great difficulty to get them to attend regularly; any little excuse will keep them away.

4945. Is it the fault of the parents or the children themselves?—It is the fault of the parents.

4946. Do you think the principle of compulsion, with attendance and truant officers, would assist?—There would be a difficulty in the case of the Kafirs; the locations are so spread about; but, possibly, it might be beneficial. At the St. Paul's school our numbers are large and the standard is high. According to Mr. Brady's last inspection, we reached the highest class of any. There were eleven in the fifth standard, and his report is exceedingly favourable to us. I do not think it is right that St. Paul's school, where there are European children, should be placed on the same level as a mission school like St. John's or St. Stephen's.

4947. Are they principally white children at St. Paul's school?—Yes, all whites.

4948. You think you ought to have a higher grant?—Yes; and be ranked in a different class.

4949. You would like to receive a grant according to numbers and according to results?—Yes.

4950. What do you think would be fair for you to receive by way of aid from Government, according to the number on the register at St. Paul's?—We ought to have some aid towards assistant teachers, which we do not get. We get pupil teachers. In the Grey Institute branch school at the North End, a quarter of a mile from us, a similar school to ours, they have a fewer number of scholars and a lower standard.

4951. What aid do they get?—£163, and the number of pupils is 246. Not only are we unable to get aid towards assistant teachers, but we cannot get aid towards buildings. I have spent about £1,250 on buildings, but we cannot get any assistance.

4952. How could a grant for buildings be given to you when it is to improve your own property. To-morrow you may withdraw altogether from the Government if you like?—I really consider that our school is as much a public school as any other, and as good.

T 2

Rev.
S. Brooke.
—
Sept. 10th, 1891.

4953. Do you think your church body would be prepared to give over the title to the buildings to a Board or the Government for school purposes?—For school purposes I am sure they would. We could not make away with it as church property, but it could be so arranged that it might be always kept for school purposes.

4954. Suppose your body discontinued the work by some accident or other, the Government money would have been spent upon it, and the title would be in your body, which would be a loss to the country, would it not?—The church is a public institution, and it would not be likely to cease educating the children belonging to it, and other children who came. There is another thing which I think places us at a disadvantage as regards teachers. The teacher has been 23 years mistress of the school, and all those years she has had a very favourable report. She has a good service allowance of £12, and would consequently be entitled to a very small pension, while teachers in other schools, who get a larger good service allowance, would receive a larger pension.

4955. Have you seen Sir Langham Dale's proposition for fourth class schools?—Yes.

4956. If that principle were applied to your school, would it satisfy you?—It would. I think that in all equity, and considering the work we are doing compared with other schools, we are entitled to it.

4957. Is it your intention to make your school one of those fourth class schools?—Yes, it is. Sir Langham Dale has been very favourably disposed towards our school, because of the good work we have done for so many years. It was the first school of the kind in Port Elizabeth.

4958. Do you understand that before you could have that benefit, the householders in the neighbourhood must approve of it?—Yes, and I am sure they would. The churchwardens also would do anything the Government wish, so that the school might be continued.

4959. Suppose the householders in the neighbourhood voted against it?—They appreciate the school too much for that.

4960. Would you be favourable to the establishment of a board elected by the district to superintend the distribution of the grant?—Yes.

4961. Do you think anything like an industrial department might be attached to your school?—I hardly think there is any necessity for it in Port Elizabeth. It would require large funds also to carry it on.

4962. *Dean Holmes.*] Have you had any experience of night schools here?—Several times I have given my school-room to persons wanting to open night schools on their own account, but they have been a failure.

4963. Why?—The young fellows do not seem anxious to improve themselves. A few of the parents may wish their children to attend, but they do not seem to take to it.

Rev. Cuthbert E. Mayo examined.

Rev.
Cuthbert E. Mayo.
—
Sept. 10th, 1891.

4964. *President.*] What are you?—Precentor at St. Mary's, Port Elizabeth.

4965. Do you know anything about night schools?—Yes. I have one, called St. Mary's night school.

4966. How many attend?—Thirty-five.

4967. What is the age of those attending?—From nine up to twenty-six.

4968. Do they attend the day schools at all?—No; they are boys out at work, and they belong to all denominations.

4969. What do they pay?—2s. 6d. a month; and they learn reading, writing, and arithmetic.

4970. Do they attend throughout the year?—They began on the 16th of June, and I intend to carry on the school till the end of October. It ought to be for six months, and we might begin a month or a month and a half earlier.

4971. Would you advise the continuance of the school in summer?—I think not. I doubt if it would answer then.

4972. Have those who attend been at school any time?—Some of them have. I should say the majority.

4973. Some have not been to school at all, I suppose?—You can hardly call it being at school.

4974. How many classes are there?—Three.

4975. How many teachers have you?—Three.

4976. Are they teachers from any mission school here?—No, they are young fellows in business; it is quite voluntary on their part. Besides the ordinary education, I teach book-keeping and shorthand, for which they pay more. Shorthand is ten shillings a month and book-keeping five shillings a month.

4977. Do the pupils attending those classes come also only part of the year?—Yes.

Rev
Cuthbert E. Mayo.

4978. Do you think the Government ought to aid you?—I think it would distinctly strengthen the school.

Sept. 10th, 1891.

4979. Upon what principle ought aid to be given?—I think in a case like that, a grant of £40 would not be too much.

4980. One witness told us that he thought a grant of £5 would be enough for his school carried on for three months in the year; why would yours require so much more?—Perhaps he can get his teachers to work for nothing.

4981. But you said that your's worked for nothing?—They do now, but it might not go on for ever. Voluntary effort is all very well, but you cannot always get it. I happen to be blessed with suitable teachers at the present moment. Then again, many might volunteer who could not teach.

4982. Do you think that the principle of aid should be in proportion to the number of persons taught?—Yes.

4983. You now charge you say 2s. 6d. a month; suppose the Government gave 2s. 6d. a month per head; would that be satisfactory?—That might do.

4984. Is there not any fear of these night schools interfering with the day schools?—I do not think so.

4985. Ought not boys of nine years of age to be in a day school?—They ought to be, but circumstances may compel them to go out to work for their parents.

4986. Are you in favour of compulsory education?—I think it would be a good thing. I would say that every child should be compelled to attend school unless it could show that it had passed the third standard.

4987. You think those who have passed that standard, whatever their age, should be exempt from the operation of the Act?—Yes.

4988. Have you thought of the subject of industrial schools?—Yes. I think that industrial classes might be formed in night schools to aid young mechanics, who although out at work, want more theoretical experience than they possess.

4989. Do you think you could start such a school here?—I think I could in connection with our present night school.

4990. What aid per head would you require?—I have not considered that. It would all depend upon the instructors.

4991. You think it could all be worked into one thing, excluding from it the younger children?—I think so.

4992. Do you think it would be a good thing if the Government appointed someone to attend and give lectures for a month or so at a time?—Yes, I see no reason why that should not be done.

4993. Would you invite such a lecturer to come if you could get him?—Yes.

4994. Could not you work this night school undenominationally, not in connection with any particular school, and ought it not to be so worked?—I think so, decidedly.

4995. Do you think there ought to be only one such school in a town?—Yes.

4996. How would you select the teachers for it?—That could only be done by those who are known to members of the local committee of the school.

4997. Should the committee determine which denomination it preferred to work the school?—If it grew and developed it would be necessary to have some sort of Board.

4998. Elected by the ratepayers?—I should say so, and work subject to the approval of the Government.

4999. Do you think that any Government grant to a night school should not be given till there is a certain number of pupils in actual attendance?—Yes.

5000. What number would you say?—I should say twenty for this town. You might have sliding scale.

Mr. W. R. Clarry examined.

5001. *President.*] I believe you are a teacher?—I am Elementary teacher at White's Road mission school, where there are 224 children, boys and girls, of the very poorest class, mixed races and religions as well.

Mr.
W. R. Clarry
—
Sept. 10th, 1891.

5002. Do these children pay fees?—Yes, one shilling and two shillings a month.

5003. Is the school in connection with any particular church?—Yes, the English Church.

5004. Do you get any grant from the Government?—£75 a year.

5005. How many teachers have you?—I have an assistant teacher in the infant school. There are two departments; the juvenile department and the infant department. I have a female teacher and a monitress for the juvenile department, and to supply the place of a teacher in the infant school I have to take pupils from my first class to do the work.

Mr.
W. R. Clarry.

Sept. 10th, 1891.

5006. What is your own salary ?—£175 per annum.

5007. What does the female assistant receive ?—£3 5s. a month.

5008. And the monitress ?—£18 a year.

5009. Have you trained them yourself ?—The one who is at present paid was a former pupil in the school.

5010. Is it in your opinion desirable that the mixture of races should continue ?—Speaking for my own school, we have got along very pleasantly with the mixed races, but I should not like to see it applied to the whole colony in mission schools, especially where there is not a male teacher in charge.

5011. Why ?—As Sir Langham Dale justly says in his report, the undue familiarity of a coloured boy with a European girl may not take place in school time, but it may develope in the course of a few years and be prejudicial.

5012. How would you distinguish between the races ?—That is a very knotty point.

5013. Suppose you had to divide them, what principle would you go upon ?—Unless the parents were European, or the mother and father had some European blood in them, it seems to me that the only way would be to put children into the coloured department.

5014. How would it do to have the managers of the school to decide the question ?—That might do, subject to an appeal to the Board.

5015. Do you consider that your school ought to receive further aid ?—Certainly.

5016. How much would you say ?—The number of children we have at present is 224, and out of that number I have 64 Europeans, which is a school of itself. The Government only give us £75 a year, and I think that we ought to have at least double that; in fact, were it not for private and voluntary subscriptions, we could never keep up the school.

5017. Do you get anything for buildings ?—We get nothing. We contemplate building, as the Town Council has given us a piece of ground.

5018. Are you collecting funds for it ?—Yes, voluntary subscriptions.

5019. Do you expect the Government to contribute ?—We have asked them, but they will not give us anything, as it is a denominational school.

5020. Do you admit any children ?—Yes.

5021. Have you any special religious teaching ?—We teach reading the Bible, the Lord's prayer, and the ten commandments.

5022. You think it would be fair for the Government to contribute to a building which is church property ?—Although nominally it is an English church school, we educate all colours and creeds, and the school building which is contemplated would be for the benefit of the public; therefore it would really come under Sir Langham Dale's new scheme of fourth class public undenominational schools.

5023. Would you be prepared to hand over the property ?—I should think so, for school purposes.

5024. Outside your church ?—That I cannot say.

5025. Dean Holmes.] What is your percentage of attendance ?—As a rule I should say it is about 70 per cent.; it has been over 80 per cent.

5026. To what do you attribute irregularity of attendance ?—To carelessness on the part of the parents a good deal.

5027. Do you think the fees have anything to do with it ?—The fees are very low; there are none lower in the town; a shilling and two shillings a month.

5028. Would it help you if an attendance officer was appointed to go round and look up the children ?—It would help greatly.

5029. President.] You think these children require to be looked up ?—Yes. I have often to send out myself to look them up.

5030. Dr. Berry.] What do you mean by irregularity of attendance; a child staying away half a day or a whole day ?—Staying away more than a day at a time. As a rule, if a child is absent more than a day, I find out where it is. Very often the child is away through the negligence of the parents.

5031. Dean Holmes.] Does it not frequently occur that if a child does not come to school the first two days of the week it stays away the rest of the week ?—I make the children pay monthly. They would do what you say if they had the opportunity.

5032. Do they pay in advance ?—No; but if I can possibly get the money in advance I take it.

5033. President.] If your school was free do you think you would have a larger attendance and it would be more appreciated ?—I do not think so.

5034. Neither by blacks nor whites ?—No. I have been 17 years now in this work; ever since I left school almost.

5035. Were you trained here ?—Yes.

5036. In which school ?—In the present mission school where I am now teaching.

5037. *Dr. Berry.*] Are you eligible for the good service allowance ?—Yes. I was eligible for it after five years' service. I have received it regularly every year, and after 17 years good service, I only get £12 a year. An ordinary elementary teacher in a public school gets £15 a year after five years' service.

Mr.
W. R. Clary.
Sept. 10th, 1891.

5038. Why do not you join that department ?—Somebody must teach these children, and I like to stick to my present work.

5039. Is there anything taught in your school that could not be taught in a school which would be the same as one of Sir Langham Dale's fourth-class public undenominational schools ?—We teach exactly the same ; reading, writing, and arithmetic.

5040. Do you teach more ?—The only thing I do not teach which is in the scheme of the fourth-class public undenominational schools is drawing. I teach vocal music and the outlines of geometry.

5041. *President.*] Why do European boys come to your school instead of going to the other schools?—They cannot afford to pay the higher fee in the Public Undenominational School.

5042. And the coloured boys ?—They will not receive them in the public school.

5043. You do teach religion in some form I believe ?—Yes ; mostly the Creed, the Lord's Prayer, and the Ten Commandments.

5044. Do any of the parents object ?—Not in the least.

5045. Suppose they did object ?—Then I should give them some other work during the time of religious instruction. There are only two in the whole school who would be likely to object, and they are Jews.

5046. Have you any Malays in the school ?—Yes, a large number.

5047. And they do not object ?—No.

The Hon. W. H. Pearson, M.L.A.

5048. *President.*] I believe you reside in Port Elizabeth ?—Yes.

The Hon.
H. W. Pearson,
M.L.A.
Sept. 10th, 1891.

5049. You are a Member of the House of Assembly, and you have also been Mayor of Port Elizabeth for many years ?—Yes.

5050. Have you been on any Boards of School Management ?—I have been on the Committee of White's Road School.

5051. You are acquainted with the present system of guarantors ?—Yes.

5052. Do you consider that a defective system ?—The present system is practically a persuasive one. You get up boards of management by persuading people, and you assist them with money voted by Parliament. There is no compulsory force in the system.

5053. Do you think that something more is required ?—It depends upon whether the country is willing. There are two elements—the persuasive element and the compulsory element. If you pass an Act of Parliament in this country making Education compulsory, you enter upon a new system, and may probably destroy a great deal of the voluntary effort now displayed.

5054. Does the present system reach all the poorer class of children ?—No ; certainly not.

5055. Do you think they ought to be reached in some way from a national point of view ?—Certainly. I think the State ought to see that everybody is educated up to a certain point. Elementary education ought to be provided for all, without any distinction of creed, class, or colour.

5056. Do you think the present system accomplishes that ?—No.

5057. How would you reach the poorest class most economically, retaining as far as possible the lines of the present system ?—It would be very difficult under the present system. At one time, when I was in office, I had a long talk with Sir Langham Dale about the matter of the fourth-class schools, which were to be a superior kind of mission school. We also talked about adopting some sort of inspection with a view to getting children into school, by sending an attendance officer round. The first proposition was that municipalities should pay for that ; but that seemed a point we could not carry at all. Then it was suggested that the Education Department should pay for it, but the question arose whether, although it might be applied to a few towns, it could be applied to the country, as the expense would be so great. The end of it was that the thing dropped. I found here, when I was Mayor, that notwithstanding the existence of very many schools, a large number of the poorer classes were not educated : not always people who could not afford to have their children educated, but people who did not care about it. Take some of the labouring people for instance, they get high wages ; but owing to drink or disorderly conduct of some kind or other, they do not care about educating their children. They get, perhaps, from 8s. to 10s. a day, yet they say they cannot afford to educate their children, and consequently they do not go to school.

The Hon.
H. W. Pearson,
M.L.A.
———
Sept. 10th, 1891.

5058. Although in reality they can afford it?—Yes. It is the same with regard to the hospital. Directly one of these men meets with an accident, he goes into the hospital; but he does not pay anything, because improvidence has left him helpless, and his wife and children have to be kept by charity. Then, again, you have another class of people here, and I suppose elsewhere, the pure natives, for whom there are no efficient schools. There are also the half-castes, some of whom are very poor and deserving of consideration. They have come to me many times and complained. They say that under the old Herschel system the schools were practically free, and all were treated alike; but now they cannot get that kind of training for their children. If they have any colour and they send them to a public school now, they are not happy, as such a distinction is made. All these things are constantly cropping up, and they present a great difficulty indeed. I hardly know how they are to be dealt with satisfactorily. The pure natives can get some kind of education in locations and elsewhere, but the difficulty is to deal with the mixed race in towns.

5059. And the pure whites too?—If the pure whites do not get education, I am afraid it is because they do not choose.

5060. For them the mission schools are open, are they not?—Yes, the better class of whites are not satisfied with the mission schools, and they use the other schools when they can.

5061. Do you think it is desirable to separate the pure whites and the half-castes if you can?—I think it will become a necessity. The only thing is, more expenditure, either more charitable help or Government aid. It is a mere matter of building schools and maintaining teachers. Take the case of the Malays in Cape Town, and Port Elizabeth also; they want a school of their own. Some of them attend the White's Road mission school here, and they are satisfied so far, but then those who can afford it say they want a better education.

5062. You say that the State ought to find schools?—The first duty of the State is to compel its population to be educated in the elementary branches of knowledge at all events; it is a necessary of life.

5063. How do you think the State can best reach those children who are not now in school?—That is a difficulty that has always seemed very great, unless you adopt the compulsory system.

5064. Do you think it wise to try it?—I doubt if the country will pass it.

5065. Not for the towns?—Many are in favour of it, and some I know are against it. I do not know how the balance would be.

5066. Do you think it might be tried here?—Yes; here and in Cape Town, and a few other centres perhaps.

5067. If you try it, you must find schools where the children can be educated without payment if they have no means. How would you do that, and who do you think ought to contribute?—That will be a bone of contention. I do not believe the country generally, even in towns, would go in for the School Board system of England or America. I do not think you would get the people to agree to a rate; the prejudice would be too great.

5068. In principle is there anything opposed to it?—No. It is sound in principle.

5069. What proportion do you think the Government ought to contribute out of the general revenue, and what proportion ought to fall on the rates?—I do not think you can draw any definite line. You have the example of other countries; some contribute all and some nothing. In America, it falls entirely on the rates and lands, but here you have no lands that would be available.

5070. What do you think ought to be done here?—I think the Government should step in in this country. Of course more money would be wanted to do the thing efficiently. I do not think it necessary to establish new Boards; Municipal Councils or Divisional Councils might be charged with the duty, and if you had a general Act of Parliament, those bodies should be bound to see that everyone in their respective districts, municipal or divisional, was educated up to a certain point, the State paying a certain proportion of the funds. In England, for instance, it is different with the police to what it is here, and a somewhat similar plan might be applied to education. Every county is called upon to find sufficient police, and whatever the expenditure may be, the Government pays a certain proportion, I think one-fourth, whatever it may be, but they must have sufficient police; and I think in this country, as general feeling goes, the only way to proceed with compulsory education would be to insist upon Municipalities or Divisional Councils seeing that everybody of all classes and colours in their area received education up to a certain point to be approved by the Inspector, the Government paying a certain proportion of the expense.

5071. How should the deficiency be made up?—By the rates.

5072. *Mr. Rowan.*] Should not the Government pay half the deficiency ?—I think not. I think the Government should pay a certain proportion, say one-fourth or one-third, or one-half, to be fixed by Act of Parliament, of whatever the proper expenses are as approved by the Education Department.

The Hon.
H. W. Pearce,
M.L.A.
Sept. 10th, 1891.

5073. Suppose the fees are not sufficient, together with that aid, to work the school ?—Then the rest must come out of the money at the disposal of the Municipality or Divisional Council.

5074. If that be so, would it not be better to elect a special body to do the work, rather than impose it on the Divisional Council or Municipality ?—It would have its advantages, but you must look at the additional expense.

5075. Is not the Divisional Council elected for purposes connected with road-making ?—If you imposed the duty upon them of providing education, I think it would tend to improve the status of these bodies, and properly qualified men would, no doubt, be elected. There is one danger that I foresee, and that is, that directly you do away with the persuasive element you have now and make it compulsory, you to a certain extent possibly abate voluntary effort.

5076. Have you followed the development of education in England ?—I cannot say that I have paid sufficient attention to it, but I know the mission schools here want better buildings and better accommodation than they have got.

5077. Suppose the present mission school system is continued as it is, would you propose to contribute anything towards their buildings if they undertook the further work of educating the poorer classes ?—I do not think you can get any competent education without good buildings. When I was connected with the Grey Institute, I held that we ought to get the best buildings possible for the school ; it is part of the elementary education.

5078. You think that a larger amount ought to be contributed for buildings ?—Yes ; very much larger.

5079. Suppose you contribute to the mission schools, which are nearly always in the hands of denominations, how would you deal with the properties upon which this money is spent ?—What the Government contributes will have to be Government property.

5080. You would make it a condition, would you not, that where money is spent, the property should be devoted to school purposes ?—Where Government grants money, it should have for ever a certain amount of control over the property. I believe in the Government system of education, the Government giving educational aid all over the Colony, religious education and the sects and parties coming afterwards. You cannot very well mix them up together under an Act of Parliament. An Act of Parliament is the Act of the people for the people, and everbody is entitled to its benefits, rich and poor, in the land alike.

5081. You know as a fact, that notwithstanding that principle, the mission schools are denominational bodies and do good work ?—Yes. They do very much good.

5082. Would you do anything to destroy them ?—No.

5083. Would you do anything to perpetuate them ?—The only way to perpetuate them is to give them money more freely.

5084. Would you be in favour of doing that ?—Yes.

5085. What additional aid would you give. £75 a year is now the maximum ?—It would vary in different localities. I should be inclined to apply the £ for £ principle.

5086. Would you give them aid as second and third class public undenominational schools, if they proved themselves after inspection to be doing good work ?—I do not think you can do that. The Government might maintain its own schools more as primary schools.

5087. *Mr Rowan.*] Would you not take the attendance and the efficiency into account in granting aid ?—Yes ; I do not think the Government should do anything here in Port Elizabeth that would interfere with the Grey Institute as a school. Properly speaking, the Government school here is really the Grey Institute, and in Graham's Town certain schools have been established, and these are the schools in which the Government should take most interest, and in regard to which more money could be best supplied.

5088. Who are the best judges as to when interference would be justified, the Central Government or local authorities ?—The Education Department as it is now. I would leave it to them, you cannot leave it to any body locally.

5089. Why not ?—Local prejudice would immediately come in and render the thing liable to be upset by the conflict of opinion.

5090. *Rev. Coetzee.*] In what way would you find the buildings for district boarding schools in the country ?—Under the present system, boarding schools in the

u

country are brought under the persuasive system. If you pass an Act of Parliament that every rustic is to be educated up to a certain point, it will require a very large vote to carry it out. The idea of the Government for years past has been to assist these people; it is a matter of coaxing. Sir Langham Dale comes to Parliament and gets as much as he can for his department; one year more than another, and he applies that money in the best way he can. If you make a hard and fast rule that every child in the country must be educated, you will want enormously larger votes or rates, one of the two. Suppose you agree to give the Grey Institute power to teach all the people in the municipality, and provide sufficient buildings, they would want a very large amount of money for buildings, a far larger amount than the mission schools are satisfied with, but these mission schools should have proper buildings and proper appliances; they must not be makeshifts, which they are at present. I think if there was a Board, the tendency would be greatly to increase the rates, as has been the case in England.

5091. Suppose you had a Board, would that Board have to deal with the native schools within its area?—Clearly. I do not consider there is any exception. A native has his rights just as much as any other man, and he should get them. If I were on any Board, I would never recognize any difference in any class of the people, no matter what their colour, class, or creed. The Grey Institute only wants money, and then one of the first things would be to establish a good native school, and then a school for the mixed coloured classes, not pure natives.

5092. *President.*] How is it that in the Grey Institute you have no half-caste children?—We never had money enough.

5093. But if a boy is sent there, he is not received, is he?—He cannot be without damaging the school. There are the mission schools. The Grey Institute never had the means of carrying out the provisions of its charter, nor has the South African College.

5094. You spoke of a coloured man who complained to you that his son could not get in did you not?—He would not be happy if he was there.

5095. Would you take him in?—I cannot say; but I know if he was there he would not be happy.

5096. Practically such a child is excluded; is not that so?—Yes; by the force of circumstances.

5097. So that Sir George Grey's object has not been attained?—Practically not. We have never had the money to carry it out.

5098. At the Grey Institute, I believe, about 500 only are educated out of something like 2,100?—Yes, something of the kind. We educate up to the limit of our means.

5099. Do you know anything of the proposal that has been made in New Zealand for the Government to give aid at the rate of £2 a head all round to all schools that educate children up to a certain standard?—I do not know anything about that.

5100. Would anything of that sort answer here do you think?—No; you would bring down some schools and bring up others, and you would get an inferior education for the whole community to what you have now.

5101. And some of the lower class schools would get more than they are entitled to, would they not?—Yes.

5102. Our social grades necessitate different classes of schools, do they not?—Yes; uniformity is impossible.

5103. Do you think industrial education might be more associated with literary education?—In some cases it might be, but it depends upon what it is to be.

5104. Do you think industrial education is desirable?—Certainly.

5105. Is it desirable for Europeans?—Not to the extent of doing away with apprenticeship.

5106. Apprenticeship is the form in which you would consider industrial education most desirable?—Yes.

5107. With regard to industrial education for natives, do you think it should be universal, so as to train them for their future calling?—The question is, what is their future calling? In the country you can train them for agricultural pursuits, but not in the town here.

5108. In the country schools do you think it would be desirable?—Everywhere, if you can afford it. In England there is a good deal of talk about technical education in connection with arts and sciences, but there is not any demand for the same class of people here. You would be putting people perhaps beyond the means of getting a living.

5109. The mass of the natives in this country devote themselves to manual labour, do they not?—To pastoral and agricultural pursuits in the country, and to manual labour in the town.

5110. Should their training be more or less in that direction?—If you can train them so as to prepare them for the farmers, it would be a good thing.

5111. Do you think it would be a good thing to associate some industrial training with the literary teaching in the mission schools in the country?—I do not know much about the country; in towns I do not think it would answer.

5112. Mr. Slater seemed to think it would answer in a place like Graham's Town?—I do not know how far it would answer here. You might put the natives to such trades as tinsmiths or blacksmiths, but then you have the difficulty of their coming into competition with European artisans, although of course they are not equal to them. You cannot train them for the callings they are most employed in in town, such as porters in wool warehouses, and so on.

5113. If a coloured boy is handy with the spade and a girl with her needle, do not you think that is an advantage?—Yes. It ought to be the part of every girl's education to learn needlework. That is part of the elementary education. I do not mean embroidery and the like.

5114. And you think coloured boys should be taught how to use the spade?—In a town like this you have no opportunity of teaching them that. It would do for the country. You must always look to the future of children, and direct their education with a view to their getting their living afterwards.

5115. Assuming Boards of Management to remain as they are now, how would you give perpetual succession to school property?—If you had an Act of Parliament whereby the Government or the Divisional Councils could become holders of the property, you would have perpetual succession.

5116. Which would you prefer, to vest it in the Government or Divisional Councils?—If you give Divisional Councils the management and the power of rating, then you should vest the property in them. If property is given as a donation, it should be the Government. For the present, I should advise the donating system; let the Government do it. The country is not in a position to have taxation through Divisional Councils for educational purposes.

5117. What further facilities do you think can be afforded for giving instruction in both the English and Dutch languages, and in how far can that object be attained through the medium of the Elementary and other examinations?—The difficulty is this, that proper Dutch is nearly as much a matter of educational study to the ordinary Dutch children of the country as English, or Latin, or anything else. I have often felt myself that it is really a hardship for little Dutch children, who have never heard anything but Dutch, to have to learn English; still there are advantages in it, and it is a question what we are to do in this country. I do not agree with having two systems, English and Dutch; I think we must try and work together, because we have to live together, and in the future more and more it would be an advantage for every Dutch person to know English and every English person to know Dutch. In the meantime, I do not think you can make any definite line. The great difficulty hitherto has been to get Dutch teachers of any competency. We have one now in the Grey Institute, and I believe in Graham's Town also they teach Dutch. When you come to the examination question, you must talk to the University about that. I would not like to give an opinion. It would not do to put an English boy at an absolute disadvantage. You must not make Dutch compulsory for him, and degrade him because he does not know it. There would be a sort of revolt against that. All these things want careful management, and any change from the present donative system under the Education Department to the compulsory system must be tentative. I doubt if you would be able to carry an Act of Parliament that is absolute all through.

5118. Adopting that tentative method with regard to language, what would you suggest as the best means of leading on to a wider knowledge of the Dutch language without irritating anybody?—Special prizes might be given for Dutch in the examinations, the same as for French or other languages, but I do not think you can refuse anybody because he has not learned Dutch.

5119. There are four subjects now in the Elementary examination, and it has been proposed to add a fifth paper in Dutch and let the marks count; do you think that would answer?—Other things being equal, I have no objection, but do not put the boy who does not bring up a Dutch paper under any disability. Until lately, an Englishman's son had no means of learning Dutch; there was no Dutch teacher in the place. You cannot send such boys up for examination and debar them from passing because they do not know Dutch.

5120. They would take a lower place, but they would not be debarred would they?—I object to their taking a lower place. Let there be an alternative subject if you like, and give marks in that subject. There might be three or four languages, and a candidate could choose which he pleased.

5121. And you would give him marks?—Yes.

The Hon. H. W. Pearson, M.L.A.

Sept. 10th, 1891.

u 2

The Hon.
H. W. Pearson,
M.L.A.
——
Sept. 10th, 1891.

5122. Would you give bursaries to those taking a high place?—Yes, any reward you like and which the University can afford.

5123. Do you think that ultimately Dutch ought to form a subject in the Elementary examination?—I do not see how you can use the word "ultimately"; it depends altogether upon the tone of the population. If five-sixths of the people are Dutch twenty-five years hence, Dutch will have more predominance in the University than English, but if there are five-sixths English, it would be quite the other way. The growth of the population will decide that question. If you have great success in the north, and a million English people come to Johannesburg, it might alter the balance of things. You can only speak for the day, and only legislate for the day, in this country.

5124. *Rev. Moorrees.*] A Dutch boy has to receive all his instruction through the medium of English, so that practically he is put at a disadvantage, is he not?—I think if you make Dutch compulsory, candidates would not go up for the examination. It would not answer. If I had any control, not one should go up in any case, for my opinion is, that public examinations cripple the educational power of a school. They interfere with the ordinary school curriculum, which should be arranged to suit the capacity of the scholars.

5125. *Dean Holmes.*] You would invite some sort of local examination of the school instead?—Yes. I consider that you do not make the most of your pupils when they are set to work to pass a certain examination controlled by the Cape University.

5126. *Mr. Rowan.*] Has not the introduction of Dutch into the Civil Service examination done a great deal to promote the teaching of the language?—I would not like to say.

5127. *President.*] Would you like to start night schools here?—I do not know whether they would answer, they might perhaps, if Government would give something in aid. You must get teachers in the first place, and most of them have enough work to do in the daytime.

5128. *Dean Holmes.*] Could it be done if there were voluntary teachers?—Yes; Government might establish a night school here with independent teachers, but I do not believe in getting teachers who are otherwise employed as such. If a man has to work at night, his work in the day must suffer.

5129. *Dr. Berry.*] Is there a class here that would be benefited by night schools? —The sons of mechanics and others might be.

5130. Do you think it would be well to make an effort in this direction?—I think so, decidedly.

5131. Would it be for those who have already left school?—Yes. The sons of artisans and others. I would be glad to see a night school or two.

5132. On what principle would you give Government aid to such night schools; on the capitation grant principle?—I think I would grant aid according to results to a certain extent, or on the £ for £ principle. In many cases such a school might be self-supporting.

5133. *Dean Holmes.*] If you had aid from the Government, you would require inspection would you not?—Yes.

5134. It seems that a night school cannot be continued more than a few months in the year; would it not be difficult to get inspection during the time it met?—Yes; there is that difficulty; but all these things are tentative.

5135. *President.*] Have you formed any opinion about technical education?—I would have it wherever it was possible.

5136. In what form would you give it a start here?—You must have an Arts professor; the ordinary teacher here cannot do it. We used to have two professors at the Grey Institute; and I think it was a great mistake of the Government to take them away. They thought it was expenditure for nothing. I have always wanted them to get them back. I think the Government should pay about one-third of the salary of such a professor, the school something, and the pupils something. He should have a right to take as many pupils as he can. I should like to see a professor attached to the Grey Institute, teaching not only the pupils there, but to be a professor for the town, so that he could fit young fellows to go into the engineering workshops, and so on. He should teach them something beyond mere drawing; a little bit of whatever is required. Chemical training to a certain extent is wanted. I think a Science and Arts professor for Cape Town and here might be obtained, and paid partly by the Government, partly by the school, and partly by the pupils.

5137. It has been suggested that at a few large centres there should be lecturers, and that they should go about with their apparatus to different places, delivering lectures for a month or so, and at the end of the time the pupils should be examined, receiving a certificate if they pass, and making it a condition that all those wanting to get admission into the Government workshops should possess such a certificate. Do you think that would work?—It might work as a tentative thing; but a month's teaching would not be sufficient. The bulk of the boys would forget all about it.

5138. They would prosecute their work in the railway shops would they not?—The workshops cannot take many.

5139. *Mr. Theron.*] Would not such a project be a stimulus for our colonial youths?—Yes; but I do not like a smattering of anything; I like thorough education. It is better for a boy to know how to read and write well, than to have an indifferent knowledge of several things.

5140. *President.*] Would you suggest that these lecturers should attend at different schools?—It might answer here, and in some places, but not in all.

5141. *Dr. Berry.*] Suppose you get such a professor or lecturer as you suggest, the Government guaranteeing one-half of the salary, would it not be a good thing if the municipality had power to guarantee the other half?—Yes; a very good thing.

5142. And make it a permanent institution in a town like this?—Yes; but of course you cannot force it on municipalities; that is the difficulty. I do not think there would be any trouble here in carrying out the general principle of having the Government contribute so much, the school so much, and the pupils the balance.

The Hon.
H. W. Pearson,
M.L.A.

Sept. 10th, 1891.

Mr. John McIlwraith examined.

5143. *President.*] I believe you are Mayor of Port Elizabeth?—Yes.

5144. Have you ever had anything to do with Boards of management of schools?—I have been a member of the Grey Institute.

5145. You know the principle of school committees and guarantors?—Yes.

5146. In whom would you vest the property belonging to these school committees?—I think in a Board.

5147. But the Board goes out every three years, and it may not be perpetuated?—I do not see why municipalities or divisional councils should not step in and take the place of the guarantors.

5148. And you would vest the school property in them?—Yes.

5149. Ought that to be acceptable, do you think?—I think so. If that was the case, it would make the citizens of a town take much greater interest as to who they put upon these Boards.

5150. And it would promote interest in education?—Yes, I think so.

5151. Do you think it would create any friction which does not already exist, or would it have the contrary effect of allaying any friction that might exist?—That is a very difficult question to answer. The religious education given in denominational schools comes in.

5152. Would you preserve the existing rights created in school bodies, and keep the mission schools going on?—Yes. Unless the whole system of education was to be remodelled.

5153. Would you give the Board an opportunity, where a mission school ceases or wishes to transfer its work to the Board, to step in and undertake the duties?—If the Board thought that school a necessity, I should consider it part of that Board's duty to see that the school did not fail.

5154. Would you give the Board an opportunity of recommending to the Government to give aid to such schools if they do their work well?—Yes. I think so.

5155. You would have the Board responsible for education?—Yes; and for the maintenance of the school so long as it was a necessity.

5156. *Dr. Berry.*] Would you be in favour of compulsory education of the children in a town like Port Elizabeth?—I do not consider that Port Elizabeth has quite got the length of compulsory education, but I should like to see education put within the reach of everybody, and if they do not embrace the opportunity, it is really their own fault.

5157. Is not this a matter in which the State may fairly demand from its citizens that they should see it carried out?—Yes; but I do not think we have quite reached the state of compulsory education yet.

5158. Not even in towns?—I doubt it.

5159. *Mr. Rowan.*] You are more for persuasion than compulsion, I take it?—Yes. This is too young a country for compulsory education.

5160. *Dr. Berry.*] Does the same thing apply with regard to regularity of attendance. Would you not apply any compulsion to, or exact any fine from parents for inattention to this matter?—I do not think so yet.

5161. Whose duty, in your opinion, ought it to be to provide educational facilities for all the children of a town like this?—I consider the Government ought to take a leading part in it.

Mr.
John McIlwraith.

Sept. 10th, 1891.

Mr.
John McIlwraith.
Sept. 10th, 1891.

5162. Do you think they ought to take the sole part?—No. I do not think we have reached that point in our history when the Government should do that, but I consider that the Government ought to assist in education in every possible way, and make good sound education so cheap and so easily within the reach of everyone, that there would be really no excuse for all not being educated. That might be done by giving liberal grants for the purpose of education in every town throughout the country.

5163. Would you be in favour of a body like the municipality of Port Elizabeth being responsible for any deficiency that might arise in the management of the schools?—I do not see any objection, if that was the law. I consider the municipality is quite a sufficiently capable body to undertake the responsibility.

5164. Would you go so far as to say that municipalities might very advantageously have power to assist in a system of higher education than what is carried on in the primary or elementary schools; for instance, for the development of a system of lectureships and professorships in arts and sciences?—That is a very complex question. We have an art master in the town who teaches mechanical drawing and painting.

5165. Who pays him?—He gets so much from each of the schools.

5166. Does Government assist to pay him?—No, I do not think so.

5167. Take the case of lads who are no longer at school, and are learning some mechanical trade, should anything be done for the purpose of promoting technical education. There is a general outcry in the colony that such lads are very inefficiently trained, and in fact have really no teaching at all in their particular trade, and there is no way of getting it at the present time?—Industries in this colony are in their infancy, and the proportion of lads who learn trades is very small indeed. There is no doubt if there were evening classes, that would enable them to gain a good theoretical knowledge of their trade, and prove a great assistance, but up to the present we have found in Port Elizabeth, that evening classes are not a success.

5168. Have they been carried on on lines that would be likely to secure success?—Yes. In many cases boys leave school at about fourteen, just at the very time when they are beginning to derive the full benefit from the efforts of their teachers, and in their case continuation schools held in the evening ought to prove very useful. I believe the one cause why these schools are not so successful is, that the struggle for existence is not so great as it is at home, and lads are not called upon to put forth the same effort.

5169. That is with reference to what we call literary training?—Yes.

5170. With reference to technical instruction, such as carpentry, engineering, cabinet making, telegraphy, and any of those subjects, do not you think we might do something in the way of training boys in that direction?—If it can be done, it is a first rate idea, but the great difficulty is, our population is so small and scattered.

5171. In Port Elizabeth, you have a large population, have you not?—Yes; something of the kind might be attempted.

5172. Do you think the community would assist in any way?—If the Government paid half the teacher's salary, I think the town would make an effort to provide the rest.

5173. Do you think they would provide a suitable building or give a room in the Town-hall say, where a lecturer could have his class?—Yes; that difficulty might be very easily overcome.

5174. Do you think there is a need here for something of the kind?—I fancy we are hardly ripe for it yet. We have an art master here, and any mechanic who wishes to acquire knowledge of mechanical drawing, can attend Mr. Leslie's classes in the evening. Any lad wanting to go into the workshops say, can, if he chooses, perfect himself in many important matters that appertain to his trade.

5175. You say they do not take advantage of this?—Not as they ought to do.

5176. What is the fee?—The fee for mechanics is very low, I believe.

5177. Are there not perhaps branches of study that might be more enticing and more engaging than drawing, such subjects for instance as chemistry, optics, mechanics, and physical science generally?—Yes, but as a rule, the lads in Port Elizabeth go into stores or become carpenters or builders or something of that kind.

5178. As carpenters and builders, would not they be all the better for a little technical training?—Yes.

5179. It is found in England that those who go in for these classes are much better fitted for their trade than those who do not. They get a higher wage also and generally succeed better in life. Is not that so?—Yes; schools that impart a sound technical knowledge take the lead.

5180. You are not against anything of the kind?—No; I should assist it if it was not too great a burden on the community. Of course the difficulty would be to work it into all the different schools and make it available for them.

Mr.
John McIlwraith.

Sept. 10th, 1891.

5181. Could not students attend these lectures in the evening?—Yes. Of course it is only recently that the giving of technical instruction in schools has come to the front. If we had more manufacturers in this country, it would become a very important matter.

5182. Is not this the very way to start them?—It would be very well worth trying in Cape Town, Port Elizabeth, and perhaps two or three other towns.

5183. What is done for the native population in the location in the way of education?—They have their own mission schools.

5184. Are they in a position to pay a small rate towards defraying the cost of those schools?—Perfectly.

5185. Would you be in favour of giving the municipality or some other body authority to levy such a rate upon these people for educational purposes?—Yes; I do not see any objection to that.

5186. Do you think it would promote education among the natives by making them take a greater interest in it?—I think the education of the natives up to a certain point should always be made compulsory.

5187. And you would carry that principle out so far as to levy a small rate to defray the cost?—Yes; and I would make the children attend school up to a certain age. I consider that if you get a certain amount of education into a native, you create in him civilized aspirations and wants which he must supply.

5188. *Mr. Theron.*] How would you levy that rate on the natives?—In the same way as other rates are levied, such as a water rate, for instance.

5189. Would you do it by way of a hut tax?—It might be done in the way of a capitation tax upon the adult males, on the household, or the hut; but sometimes two or three families stay in one hut.

5190. Would you apply this tax solely to the natives or would you mix it up with an educational tax generally?—I do not think we should have separate legislation or a separate tax for the natives. If there is going to be a general rate levied by the municipality, or if money is raised by the Government, a certain portion should be put aside for the support of the native schools, because they must be kept by themselves; they cannot be mixed up with other children.

5191. Suppose you apply that principle to the Transkeian Territories, where there is a mass of natives, and tax them for education, you would not put that money into the general treasury, but keep it separate for their own education, would you not?—In cases like that yes.

5192. Would not the same principle be applicable to towns also?—You could make it so.

5193. Would not you create ill feeling in the native mind when he does not see a *quid pro quo* for the money which he pays for the education of his children?—We should have to see that they did get a *quid pro quo*, and indeed give them a little more perhaps than they paid in.

5194. It would be a separate tax on these natives would it not?—Separate as far as the amount goes.

5195. In that case would it not be difficult to keep it separate from the European population for their wants?—It is simply a matter of account.

5196. If they were taxed, would they take more interest in education, do you think?—I think so; where they see that they get the value.

5197. *Dr. Berry.*] Has such a proposal ever been contemplated in this municipality?—We have never meddled with education. We have just given a few prizes to encourage school work.

5198. *Dean Holmes.*] Have not you given grants of land for school purposes?—Sometimes we have given to various schools a piece of land that they have applied for.

5199. I believe you have given a piece of land to the White's Road mission school?—Yes; they had a piece before and they sold it for the theatre site, and they have got the proceeds of that. There is another piece which we had to apply to the Government for, and now we have got it, we have handed it over to them for the purposes of a mission school. We have given grants of land which are of no value to us, irrespective of any denomination; we have done it pretty well to all.

5200. *Dr. Berry.*] What would you consider a fair tax per hut or per householder in the location for school purposes. Do you charge municipal rates there?—I think there is a hut tax. The location is self-supporting; the municipality makes nothing out of it. We simply make it pay its way, and give the natives the full benefit.

5201. What amount does each hut contribute?—I think it is 10s. or 12s. a year.

5202. Would that be an excessive tax for them to pay for school purposes?—A native can pay more than a shilling a month; he is better able to pay for education in a place like this than hundreds of white families are.

Mr.
John McIlwraith.

Sept. 10th, 1891.

5203. You would not object to a shilling a month on each hut, would you?—No.

5204. That would bring in £400 or £500 a year?—Yes, about that.

5205. Are you in favour of giving the natives more industrial education?—The difficulty is that you cannot get a white carpenter to work alongside a black one. I think their destiny for the present is to till the ground.

5206. *Rev. Coetzee.*] What suggestions can you make for improving the education of the rural population?—I consider the farm school system is a very good one, and it ought to be fostered in every possible way.

5207. Can you suggest any additional facilities outside farm schools and circuit schools?—No. I have thought over the farm school system a good deal, and I think, considering the very scattered nature of our population, that system is nearly as perfect as possible. I consider that the Government have spent money very wisely and well in promoting it.

5208. What plan can you suggest in order to induce the farmers to make more use of the existing facilities?—It is very hard to bring pressure to bear on the farmers. Many of the children have long distances to travel to school. That is a question which I think the farmers are better able to deal with than townsmen.

Port Elizabeth, Friday, September 11, 1891.

PRESENT:

Sir J. D. BARRY (President),

Mr. Rowan,　　　　　　　　　　Dean Holmes,
Rev. Moorrees,　　　　　　　　 Dr. Berry.
Mr. Theron,

Rev. Dr. Hewitt examined.

Rev.
Dr. Hewitt.

Sept. 11th, 1891

5209. *President.*] I believe you are incumbent of Holy Trinity Church at Port Elizabeth?—Yes.

5210. And *ex officio* chairman of the White's Road mission school?—Yes.

5211. Have you also been connected more or less with education for a long time past?—Yes. I was second master at the Cathedral Grammar School in Cape Town some years ago, and I have also been on school committees at Riversdale and Bredasdorp.

5212. Are you familiar with the Dutch language?—Yes.

5213. Have you had the management of mission schools?—Yes.

5214. Has the attendance of children in these mission schools been regular as a rule?—No; it has not been what it ought to be. The schools do not attract all the coloured children they ought to attract. Speaking of my experience of the mission schools at Worcester, I may state that if you drive through the location there you will find a number of children who ought to be at Mr. Esselen's school, but are not.

5215. What is the reason?—I think in many cases it is poverty; want of clothes very often; and in some cases it is owing to carelessness on the part of the parents.

5216. With regard to those children on the roll, is there any irregularity of attendance from your experience?—Certainly.

5217. How would you remedy it?—I am hardly prepared to say. It is very difficult to persuade parents to send their children regularly.

5218. Do you think it would be wise to adopt any system of compulsion in towns?—Yes, I do.

5219. Would you have attendance and truant officers appointed?—Yes.

5220. Who would you employ as such officers?—I think the police would perhaps inspire most awe in the minds of the coloured people. Special police might be told off for the work.

5221. Do you think there would be school room sufficient to receive all the children brought in?—At Worcester, a place I am well acquainted with, I think Mr. Esselen's school would want enlarging, or else another school might be established in the middle of the location, which would meet the requirements perhaps.

5222. If a school were established in the middle of the location, would you draw into it all the coloured children apart from the white?—No; certainly not.

5223. Would you keep them mixed up?—Yes. There are some white people living in the location, and if they choose to send their children, I would let them.

5224. Would you, as a rule, have separate schools for whites and blacks?—Not mission schools.

5225. What is the advantage of having the two races mixed together?—There are a great many poor people who cannot afford to pay the fees at the public undenominational schools, and if they were excluded from the mission schools, they would be forced into them.

Rev.
Dr. Hewitt.
Sept. 11th, 1891.

5226. Is that the only reason?—Yes; I think so.

5227. If you did provide other schools for the poorer white children, do you think it would be wise and remove any objection?—I do not think very much would be gained by it. In my opinion it is not necessary to separate the poor white and the poor coloured children.

5228. *Mr. Rowan.*] At Riversdale, did you have the whites separate from the blacks?—Only in the case of girls. It was not an absolute rule that if a child was coloured it was to be excluded from Mrs. Beerling's school there.

5229. *Mr. Theron.*] If provision were made for the poor whites in one way or the other, would it not be desirable to have this separation of the two races?—Yes. If there were mission schools for the white children, it would be an advantage then, in some respects, I have no doubt.

5230. *President.*] Would there be any disadvantage?—I cannot say there would be.

5231. Do you think it is expedient if possible to have the whites educated in one school and the blacks in another?—Yes. It is not inexpedient; it might have disadvantages.

5232. Where a school is mixed for boys and girls, do you think it is still more prudent to have a division?—In the case of mixed boys and girls it would be better to separate them.

5233. If you had them separate, upon what principle would you be able to lay down a rule for the purpose without creating friction?—That is where the difficulty would arise.

5234. Can you give us a definition of "white" and "coloured"?—I should be opposed to leaving the managers to decide it, and from my own experience it would be a most difficult thing to do. I have known families belonging to the farming population who were certainly several shades darker in colour than many of the coloured people, and yet these people would be received I suppose into a white school, while children of a much lighter colour would be excluded.

5235. *Rev. Moorrees.*] What is your objection to leave this point in the hands of the committee to decide?—It would lead to endless difficulties, and the committee, I think, would involve themselves in disputes in a matter of that kind which would bring about trouble, and probably break up the school.

5236. Would not they be the best judges as to what would damage the school or not?—They might do it in the interest of the school, and unconsciously and unintentionally damage it. I should certainly be very much opposed to leaving it to the schoolmaster.

5237. *President.*] How would it do to leave it to the children to vote?—That would not do.

5238. *Mr. Theron.*] Have you been manager of a public undenominational school?—Yes.

5239. Were there ever any coloured children present?—At Worcester one was, but I was not a manager there.

5240. Was that child admitted?—Yes, upon the order of the Superintendent-General of Education, to whom the father appealed. The father said it was a Government school, and he insisted upon his child being received, and if I am rightly informed, the child was received upon the order of the Superintendent-General of Education.

5241. Was there any difficulty experienced among the children or parents?—There was a feeling against it. In the first place it was an illegitimate child.

5242. Would you continue that system of obliging managers to take in coloured children when they presented themselves, because it is a public school?—I suppose a public school is intended for the public; and coloured people in that case are part of the public.

5243. Under the present system, the public take an interest in the school and guarantee its establishment, and provide for any deficiency. A parent who has never subscribed a penny towards it may come and present his child, and all those who have guaranteed the school must suffer. Is not that so?—That parent is a taxpayer and contributes indirectly to the Government grant.

5244. But is it desirable in the interests of the school itself that such a state of things should be continued?—Personally I should prefer not having such children; but in the case I mentioned it was an illegitimate child.

5245. *Dr. Berry.*] Do you see any necessity for making any recommendation under that head?—I do not. It is a case which practically settles itself.

5246. You think the troublesome cases that have occurred are so exceptional as not to be worth taking notice of in the general system?—Yes, that is so.

5247. *Mr. Theron.*] Is it not better to make some provision than allow it to occur, and perhaps be the ruin of the school?—The schools have been going on very well for

Rev.
Dr. Hewitt.

Sept. 11th, 1891.

a long time without being ruined by anything of the kind, and I do not see why any more trouble should arise in the future than in the past. We know, as a matter of fact, that the coloured people do prefer to have their own schools and would not obtrude themselves unnecessarily. It is the same with regard to mission work. They prefer having their own mission chapel to worshipping in the same building with Europeans; they come to look upon it as their own property, and I do not think they are likely to force themselves offensively upon the European population.

5248. *President.*] Where individuals do insist upon it, you would give them the right, provided there is no other disqualification than that of colour?—Yes; if they pay the fees, conform to the rules, and observe the sanitary arrangements of the school, it would be simply a matter of justice.

5249. In order to provide schools for any increased attendance, what would you suggest?—In the first place I should leave it to the present agencies, such as mission schools. No doubt they would do all they could, and if the Education Department found that there was still a large number of children unprovided for, then would be the time to step in and make further provision, but as long as existing arrangements are working satisfactorily, I should not interfere with them.

5250. Would you contribute anything additional to these mission schools, in order to induce them to receive these children, who might be paupers and unable to pay?—The Government reserves to itself the right of admitting a certain number of free scholars, and if that number were exceeded, I do not see much difficulty in the Government making an ordinary grant to provide extra accommodation.

5251. What additional grant ought they to make?—I was thinking more of an additional school than of an additional grant.

5252. Suppose it is an additional school, would you have it an undenominational school?—If any religious body came forward and was willing to start a mission school, certainly. I suppose in the case I mentioned just now, if Mr. Esselen saw a chance of establishing another mission school with a totally different grant in another part of the town, he would do so. He is a man with a great deal of energy.

5253. Suppose there were two or three applicants to start such a school and get an additional grant, how would you solve that question?—That I can hardly say. I do not think it would be likely to arise. Perhaps the fairest way would be to allow those who have worked in the mission school at the place the preference.

5254. In whom would you vest the decision?—In the Superintendent-General of Education in every case.

5255. Have you seen Sir Langham Dale's scheme of fourth class public undenominational schools?—Yes.

5256. Would that meet the want?—No; not as long as mission schools can be started.

5257. You think that mission schools are better than fourth class public undenominational schools?—Yes, in my opinion.

5258. Might not Sir Langham Dale's suggestion be applied to a mission school; and if there is no mission school, it might be applied to what is called an undenominational school. Is there any reason why that aid should not be applied to a mission school?—If a religious body is willing to find a certain proportion of the expenses of the school, in all fairness that religious body should be allowed to carry on its work.

5259. You would be in favour of allowing the Superintendent-General of Education to give aid to a mission school that works with a conscience clause?—Yes.

5260. *Rev. Moorrees.*] Would you apply that principle right through and give aid to higher denominational schools also?—If there was an opening for them.

5261. You would leave the Superintendent-General of Education to judge?—He has been the judge in time past, and I think he has always given satisfaction in his decision where schools were wanted. I know that in Cape Town he has suggested where with advantage a school might be started, and adopted the scheme of anyone willing to come forward and work a school.

5262. *President.*] Are you in favour of having several first class public undenominational schools in a town?—I do not think there would be several. I do not see any objection to it if they are at opposite ends of the town. In connection with the Grey Institute there are three different establishments.

5263. *Dr. Berry.*] Suppose there was a Minister of Education, would you be in favour of placing the right of disallowance in regard to a second undenominational school in a town in that officer?—No. I think you would be bringing it within the range of politics.

5264. Who would have the right of disallowance then?—I suppose there would be an Under Minister; but I should be opposed to leaving the question as to a second undenominational school to political parties.

5265. *Mr. Theron.*] Is not the Colonial Secretary the responsible head now ?— But he never interferes.

Rev. Dr. Hewitt.

Sept. 11th, 1891.

5266. *Dr. Berry.*] In the absence of the Superintendent-General of Education, and if a Minister of Education comes into existence, in whose hands would be placed the right of disallowance ?—In the permanent head of the department.

5267. Would you prefer that right of disallowance being so placed to its being placed in a Board locally established to superintend educational matters ?—I think I should.

5268. *President.*] Has it occurred to you that possibly a district Board might be brought into existence which could fill up the gaps where educational facilities were required, with the approval of the Superintendent General of Education, who also should have the the power of instructing such Board to supply the want ?—My only experience of Boards is at the time the Worcester public school was guaranteed by the municipality, and that did not work well. It seemed as if the school under that management was really left very much to itself. The headmaster in most cases did not feel himself called upon to use very great influence to fill up the number of pupils, and there was always a large deficiency, which had to be paid by the municipalty. That was my experience. It became quite a burden, and at last it was abolished. Now they have a school on the ordinary system of guarantors.

5269. Suppose a Board had been elected only for educational purposes by the ratepayers, do you think the same thing would have happened. Would not it have brought a class of men on to the Board willing to devote their attention to educational matters who would be quite unwilling to undertake municipal affairs ?—I cannot say, I hardly think it would. In these cases you have the same electors, and they would practically put in the same men as they put in for the municipality ; and they are not always the best persons fitted for it. I may mention that I had a personal grievance with regard to the Worcester municipality. On several occasions I was nominated by members of the municipality as a member of the School Board, but I was always vetoed. I was never on the public school committee at Worcester, although I was at Riversdale and Bredasdorp, and I think I may say I have done a good deal towards education in both those places. As soon as the guarantee system was adopted, they came to me and asked me to become a guarantor, but I declined.

5270. Then they went on working without you ?—Yes.

5271. *Mr. Rowan.*] Do you approve of the guarantee system ?—Yes, I do.

5272. *President.*] Have you found it everywhere working well ?—At the end of three years there is a lapse. A number of people go away perhaps, and very often debts are left, and there is no permanent succession, so that it is difficult to know who is responsible.

5273. What would you suggest to meet that difficulty ?—I am hardly prepared to propound any scheme, but there should be some system whereby perpetual succession could be secured. In connection with White's Road school, as it is a close corporation, we fill up our own vacancies as they occur.

5274. *Mr. Rowan.*] Have you ever been called upon to make up any deficiency ? Yes ; I have out of my own pocket.

5275. Do not you consider that a hardship ?—It may be a hardship, but in the cause of education I submitted to it.

5276. But is it fair that the burden of education should rest upon a few public spirited individuals, and not upon the general body of ratepayers ?—Of course those most interested in establishing and keeping a good school going will come forward and guarantee, and the parents of children who want a good school would consent to become guarantors.

5277. *President.*] Are not the wants of the poorest classes likely to be neglected where you have no local body whose duty it is to find schools for them, and who can be approached by those wanting schools ?—That has not been my experience so far. Not only are there mission schools which supply the wants of the poorer classes, but there are also private schools in many cases for children who cannot afford to pay the public school fees.

5278. Do not you think it is a defect in the system that there is no one charged with the absolute duty of bringing into existence schools to supply the wants of those who are in no school now, and who cannot pay ?—No ; I can hardly say I do, because religious bodies undertake that duty. If the clergyman of any place found that any members of his own congregation were without education, he would exert himself to obtain it for them.

5279. With regard to denominational bodies, ought not there to be a duty imposed upon them of receiving without payment all the children who offer themselves or who are brought to them by the attendance officer ?—Under the conscience clause

Rev.
Dr. Hewitt.
Sept. 11th, 1891.

they would not have the right to refuse. Practically there is no want now of any additional school space that I am aware of.

5280. And until the want arises, you would not have the present machinery added to at all ?—I think not. My experience of Boards is that it is very difficult to get the members together ; what is everybody's business is nobody's business, very often. At Worcester, where we had most intelligent men on the Library Committee, there was the greatest difficulty in getting a meeting once a month. Matters might be left in the hands of the head of the district. The Civil Commissioner very often is the best man to leave them to.

5281. *Dr. Berry.*] You said that you would be in favour of having compulsory education in towns ?—Yes.

5282. Has it occurred to your mind whether there ought to be any limit in regard to the population of towns where you would apply compulsory education. What would be the minimum ?—The town I was thinking of was Worcester, which has a population of about 4,000. There is a large number of children there not going to school.

5283. Would you say wherever there was a Village Management Board or Town Council it should be applied ?—You might put it in that way.

5284. Would you apply it to what are called mission stations or mission villages in the colony ?—Yes, certainly. At Genadendal they have great difficulty in getting the children to attend. At Elim it is better. That is held on a different tenure. It is the private property of the Moravian Missionary Society, and if the people misbehave themselves they are turned off.

5285. Would you apply it to all races, sexes, and colours in towns ?—Yes.

5286. In Port Elizabeth, according to the census returns, there ought to be something like 2,500 native children in school, but as a matter of fact there are only about 1,100 in school. Upon whom should the obligation rest of providing schools for the others ?—I suppose it must rest with voluntary bodies.

5287. *Mr. Theron.*] Is this a moving native population here ?—No, permanent I should say.

5288. *Dr. Berry.*] Do you think it is right that the State should content itself with waiting upon the voluntary efforts of individuals ?—If compulsory education is carried out, the State would ascertain what provision there is, and then if they found that it was inadequate, they would make further provision.

5289. Upon whom would they call to make the provision ?—They would probably say to us at White's Road, are you prepared to enlarge your schools so as to admit a certain number more ; if we say no, they would go somewhere else, and if nobody can, they would have to start a public school.

5290. *President.*] At present there is no machinery for starting such a school, is there ?—The Civil Commissioner could call a meeting.

5291. Suppose that is done, and the poorest classes want a school, but they cannot guarantee, what then ?—The poor might not be able to guarantee, but why should not other guarantors come forward as in the case of existing schools.

5292. *Rev. Moorrees.*] Even if there existed a local Board, then in the case of such very poor children almost all the money would have to be forthcoming either from the Government or the local rates. If the Government in the case of such poor children were to offer to the local school committee, in cases where the denominations do not come forward, a liberal grant in aid, do you think there would be any objection on the part of the local committee to establish schools ?—I do not see that there could be.

5293. *Dr. Berry.*] In Port Elizabeth we find that in the mission schools there are about 1,100 European children being educated, and as a matter of fact we find in looking at the statistics year after year, that not quite six per cent. of the population reach what is called the fourth standard. Do you think that such education is really adequate to the wants of the European section of the population at the present time ? —I do not believe in over educating these people.

5294. Does not the present state of things tend to a low state of education in the colony ? —Not so far as the lower orders are concerned. Those who are fitted to occupy better positions will attain a better education.

5295. Children in other countries who have not means of their own for education, get it at somebody else's cost, or at the cost of the State, and they get a much better education than children here get ; the consequence is, that our children are handicapped, and are displaced in situations of usefulness by those who come from abroad. Is not that the case ?—The State must raise the standard.

5296. Are you agreeable to a general raising of the standard and the means of education for European children in this colony ?—If it is practicable. I suppose the Education Department has fixed a standard which is attainable. It is no use fixing a standard which nobody attains to.

159

5297. The Education Department does not fix the standard, does it?—There is a certain number of scholarships and a certain number of free scholars. As a matter of fact, I have been interesting myself quite recently in getting children presented to scholarships in the Grey Institute, a class which would otherwise be attending mission schools. Then again, the education given by the Marist Brothers is admirable education for the class of children who avail themselves of it.

5298. *Rev. Moorrees.*] Are you aware of the fact that in a good many mission schools the teachers are able to work up the pupils to a higher standard?—Yes.

5299. *President.*] What step should be taken to give the Boards of Management perpetual succession, and provide for the tenure of public school property?—Our own school works very well; it is a close corporation.

5300. Where the Government contributes to any school building, should that be considered public school property?—I think so.

5301. If that be so, then the Government cannot give grants to mission schools? —They do not, as a matter of fact.

5302. You do not suggest that in future anything should be given to mission school buildings from the public funds?—No, I should say not.

5303. Would not the effect of that be to make the buildings inferior and unfit in many cases for school purposes?—No; because of course we should try to attract children to our schools, and to that end we should make them as good as possible, so as to compete with the public schools. The Government would insist upon having a certain amount of accommodation afforded, and that accommodation must be at the expense of the denomination that supplies it.

5304. Do you see that denominations have an opportunity of starting good buildings without aid from Government?—Yes.

5305. *Rev. Moorrees.*] If provision were made that at the end of three years half the managers should retire and the other half remain, you would have a perpetual Board as long as the school lasted, and there might be another provision that in the event of the school failing, the property should revert to the Education Department; would that answer?—I think that would meet the case, if a certain number retired by rotation.

5306. *Dr. Berry.*] In that case the guarantors would be left with the debt. Would not the effect of that be to check any real improvement in our schools, because guarantors would not be likely to come forward when they saw what was before them? —The Education Department is the body to see that there is improvement.

5307. But the risk lies with the local guarantors, does it not, and that being so, is there not a serious danger of all efforts to improve the tone and quality of education being repressed?—I do not think so. Those people who live in towns will study their own interests, and provide as good an education as they can for their children.

5308. Will you point out any case to me where when the guarantors were called upon to pay up, the inhabitants of the locality have come forward and taken the burden upon themselves?—Behind the actual guarantors there is always a list of sub-guarantors.

5309. Can you point to any instance where when guarantors were called upon to pay up, the community have stepped forward and taken the burden upon themselves? —No, I cannot.

5310. *Rev. Moorrees.*] Do you know of any case where bazaars have been held for the purpose of making up a deficiency?—Yes, frequently.

5311. And are there cases also where not only the guarantors but the public have contributed?—Yes.

5312. *Mr. Theron.*] You said just now that the buildings would revert to the Government and the guarantors be left with the debt, would that apply to buildings in which no Government money had been invested; where they were the sole property of the community?—If it was private property, it would be unfair for the Government to appropriate it. At Worcester, the property belonged to the Dutch Reformed Church.

5313. It would only apply in cases where Government aid has been given for buildings?—Yes.

5314. In that instance, the Government should either sell the buildings or do what they liked with them, refund the amount they had contributed, and return the rest to the managers?—It would not revert to the Government, but to the Education Department.

5315. *Dr. Berry.*] Suppose a body of guarantors start a school and desire to put up a property worth say £2,000. They raise half the cost, £1,000 on mortgage, on which they have to pay £60 a year, and the cost of repairs may come to £50 or £75 a year. The school is therefore charged with a sum of perhaps £120 a year, which could be called money devoted purely to educational purposes upon whom

Dr. Hewitt.

Sept. 11th, 1891.

should devolve the payment of that annual charge ? Under present circumstances, it is taken out of the fees, which seems a very great hardship on those boys who are getting their education.

5316. Do you think any remedy ought to be applied to meet such cases ?—The remedy ought to be applied by having the money before you begin to build.

5317. Where is the money to come from ?—If you have not the money, do not build.

5318. Then how is the school to go on ?—The only way is to hire a building.

5319. But the rent must be paid, must it not ?—The rent would not amount to much, and you would not be saddled with a large debt. I am opposed to building unless you have the money to build with, and where managers cannot build, they should hire.

5320. *Rev. Moorrees.*] As Government gives half of the funds wherewith to buy property, would you be in favour in future of it's giving half of the rent in cases where school property is hired ?—Yes, that would be fair.

5321. *President.*] And in all cases where Government does contribute money to buy property, at the end of twenty years, it should be public school property ?—Yes, where Government contributes anything towards building, and the money is spent on that building, it ought always to become public school property.

5322. *Dr. Berry.*] Would you be in favour of giving half of the rent to mission schools held in premises which are rented ?—No, only those schools that are on the same footing as those where the Government has given money to build.

5323. Would it not as a matter of fairness, lead to the Government considering the question of making a grant for building or repairs to every public school in the colony ?—For enlarging buildings, but not for repairs, provided the enlargement is in the opinion of the Government required.

5324. *President.*] What additional facilities can be provided to meet the wants of the children of the agricultural population ?—There are generally centres at which the agricultural population is somewhat thicker than at others. If farm schools could be established there it would be a good thing.

5325. Ought anything more to be provided than is provided under the present regulations ?—I think the regulations are sufficient if they were carried out on a larger scale. There are more centres perhaps where farm schools could be established, if the farming population knew more about the facilities. In the Karoo it is very difficult to establish farm schools where the farms are very far apart.

5326. What would you do in a case of that kind ?—I am not prepared to say. In the case of railway children, where they are taken to the Buffels River School on Monday morning, and brought back on Friday, some difficulty is experienced : they manage to get some sort of lodging ; but what to do in the case of farms which are miles and miles apart, I am not prepared to say ; it is a very difficult question.

5327. I believe you are well acquainted with the Dutch language ; you read and write it do you not ?—Yes.

5328. Have you mixed much with the Dutch ?—Yes.

5329. Are you acquainted with the present facilities for giving instruction in the Dutch and English languages ?—Yes.

5330. Would you add to them ?—I do not think there is any great necessity to add to them.

5331. You know that managers have the power to instruct in Dutch if they like ?—Yes.

5332. Do you think that is enough ?—Yes.

5333. Are the existing text books sufficient ?—I cannot say that I am familiar with what the existing text books are. I have had nothing to do with teaching Dutch of late. I have no doubt they are the best of their kind.

5334. Have you come across any grievances in connection with instruction in Dutch ?—I have never heard of any.

5335. Do you think the desire for learning Dutch can be promoted through the medium of the Elementary or other examinations in the colony ?—It is provided in the School Higher examination. There Dutch is an alternative subject, and that is sufficient I think. If there was a demand for Dutch in the Elementary examination, it has struck me that instead of English history, Dutch and Cape history might be an alternative subject.

5336. Then the time of the Dutch boys would be saved in that way, would it not ?- Yes.

5337. You think that Cape history should form part of the Dutch paper ?—Yes.

5338. Can you work history and Dutch into one paper ?—Yes ; I think so. I should be very sorry to make history disappear from the Elementary examination altogether. There ought to be some history, and therefore I think they ought to begin with the history of their own land. Dutch and Capo history might fairly be combined, and put as an alternative subject, instead of taking up English history.

Rev.
Dr. Hewitt.

Sept. 11th, 1891.

5339. You would not increase the number of papers?—No.

5340. It has been suggested that a fifth paper should be added, and that those who go in for Dutch should have the benefit of increased marks; would that answer in your opinion?—That would be unfair to those who did not take it.

5341. Could you suggest any other means for promoting the acquirement of Dutch through the examinations?—No.

5342. Would it be a good thing to have two sets of papers, one in Dutch and one in English, and two forms of instruction; would that be wise from an educational or from a national point of view?—I do not think it would.

5343. Do you think the Dutch wish it?—I cannot say I do to any great extent, and I am pretty familiar with the mind of my Dutch fellow colonists. Speaking as to Worcester and Riversdale, I am not aware that any grievance is felt.

5344. Rev. Moorrees.] You do not think that they would wish to have a separate examination in Dutch?—I should not think so.

5345. Mr. Rowan.] What do you say to an easy Dutch paper similar to the English paper as a fifth subject?—Then you must give a fifth subject to the others, or you handicap those who do not take up Dutch.

5346. Do not you think that a boy who has to take five subjects would be more handicapped than a boy who has to take four?—Not if he gets an additional number of marks. I should be opposed to setting a separate Dutch paper unless it were compulsory.

5347. President.] What would you think of having a Dutch, Latin, French, German and Elementary science paper, putting them all as alternative fifth subjects, giving the candidates an opportunity of choosing, and then adding the marks to the total?—That would be too much for the Elementary examination.

5348. Rev. Moorrees.] Would not the danger of your plan be this, that the English boy would be discouraged from taking Dutch in the Elementary examination, and have to take it as an alternative with English history?—If they prefer English history, it shows that they do not care to take up Dutch, and they are not bound to do so.

5349. Very likely they might have taken up Dutch if they could have had English history also?—I do not think that English boys are so keen upon acquiring languages that they would take up Dutch unless they were obliged.

5350. Ought we not to encourage them as far as possible?—I do not think so.

5351. In a bi-lingual country, ought not both languages to be encouraged?—It is an advantage no doubt, but most boys in this country know quite enough Dutch for all practical purposes.

5352. Dr. Berry.] Have you any acquaintance with Professor MacWilliam's scheme on this subject?—I have read it.

5353. What is your opinion about it?—It is very much on the same lines as mine, namely, that Dutch should be an optional subject in the Elementary examination.

5354. Would it give a decided advantage to pupils attending some schools and not to others?—It is a question of supply and demand. The Grey Institute has obtained a teacher for Dutch.

5355. What chance would children in mission schools have, if Dutch, French, German, and elementary science were alternative subjects? —Such a programme would be too difficult for them, therefore I would not include those subjects in the Elementary examination.

5356. Have you any suggestion to make for altering the method on which the Elementary examination is conducted?—No.

5357. Do you think any evils are connected with the present system of examination?—Not that I know of. I am generally appointed commissioner to conduct these examinations, so that I know about the matter.

5358. Would you be in favour of publishing the rank simply of the honours list, leaving all the candidates below that to pass?—It does not make much difference.

5359. Is not the present plan objectionable for boys going in for the School Higher examination, that they should be compelled to pass the Elementary examination?—No. It is a very good preparation for more difficult examinations. It makes them familiar with the form of the examination.

5360. President.] Do you know anything about technical schools?—I think that industries might be taught very much more largely throughout all the schools, white and black.

5361. What should be the nature of the industrial teaching for blacks?—The industry of the district should be taught; for instance, at Worcester I would teach wagon making, carpentering, and so on.

Rev.
Dr. Hewitt.

Sept. 11th, 1891.

5362. Would you make it a condition of additional Government aid being given to mission schools, that they should have some industrial department in connection with them ?—It is a condition at present that where there is an industrial department, additional aid is given. I should be disposed to encourage it as far as possible, but I would not make it compulsory at present. Take the case of a town like Port Elizabeth, I do not see how industrial training could be enforced here, but it might be in villages and smaller towns.

5363. You would encourage it where it could be done ?—Yes.

5364. Is it not desirable that native education should be industrial to a great extent ?—Yes.

5365. More so than it has been ?—Certainly.

5366. Would it be expensive to import such industrial teaching ?—Yes ; I have no doubt it would be.

5367. Would you have spade industry taught ?—Yes, wherever it was practicable.

5368. And the girls taught needlework ?—Yes. There is a danger of drifting away from industrial pursuits and taking to easier occupations, or no occupations.

5369. Do you think the natives have been rather over educated from a literary point of view ?—I do not think they have been over educated exactly, but the teaching them that which would be of more use in after life has been neglected.

5370. You would have industrial added to literary teaching ?—Quite so.

5371. And in towns you would compel them to come to these schools ?—Yes. I quite agree with what Mr. Postma has said on that subject, that industry is decaying even among the Dutch farming population. I can remember that many years ago nearly every farmer had his blacksmith's shop, and could furnish whatever was wanted. Old Mr. Theunissen, of Somerset West, was a most accomplished wagonmaker.

Rev. D. J. Pienaar examined.

Rev.
D. J. Pienaar.

Sept. 11th, 1891

5372. President.] What are you ?—Minister of the Dutch Reformed Church at Uitenhage.

5373. I believe you were previously minister at Aliwal North ?—Yes.

5374. Are you acquainted with the educational wants of the agricultural population ?—Yes.

5375. Is the irregularity of attendance of children in town schools such as in your opinion to require some additional means to improve it ?—Yes.

5376. What would you suggest ?—I think the proposal of Sir Langham Dale ought to be tried, namely to have as an experiment attendance and truant officers in towns.

5377. Might that system be applied to Uitenhage ?—I think so.

5378. Both to whites and blacks?—I cannot speak as to blacks. I think there should be some officer under the supervision of the magistrate to look after the children not attending any school.

5379. Do you think the parents generally would like it ?—I do not know whether they would like it, but it would be a good thing.

5380. Are there many white children in Uitenhage not in any school at all ?—There are a good many not in school. There are small schools in the town, but I do not think their work is very satisfactory. They may not do much harm, but it would be much better if the children attending these cheap private schools were at a public school. They do not learn enough, and they are not under proper supervision or inspection.

5381. Would you interfere with them ?—You cannot force these people to shut their schools.

5382. Have you a first class public undenominational school in Uitenhage ?—Yes.

5383. Ought the fees to be made cheaper do you think?—We have made an attempt in that direction. It was not levelled chiefly at the private schools, but in the interests of the children of poorer parents in the town we started a branch of the Boys' Public School, and that branch school is mixed. We went to the Divisional Council for a grant, and applied also to the Town Council for a grant, and both those bodies assisted us. Half of the teachers' salary we get from Government. We call that a branch school, because there are other mission schools in the town supported by the Government.

5384. Do you apply the grants from the Divisional Council and the Municipality wholly to this branch school ?—Yes.

5385. Does that result in a surplus or a deficiency at the end of the year ?—There has not been a deficiency yet as far as I know. The school is in a very flourishing condition.

5386. Are the fees very low ?—Yes ; threepence and fourpence a week, and a good many children attend gratis.

Rev.
D. J. Pienaar.

Sept. 11th, 1891.

5387. Upon what principle do you admit children gratis ?—There are parents who have three or four children in the school, and we do not make them pay for all perhaps.

5388. Do you exclude any children ?—If a parent earns so much a day, beyond a certain limit, we do not admit his children, but encourage him to send them to the public schools.

5389. Do many of the railway employes use your school ?—Yes.

5390. Are there English children there ?—Yes.

5391. Is there an English mission school as well at Uitenhage ?—I think so. For coloured children there is more than one mission school.

5392. Do you think that the school wants are sufficiently supplied at Uitenhage ? —Yes, in the town.

5393. You want the attendance to be more regular, and more children brought in ?—Yes.

5394. You think there is school room enough ?—Yes. There is the Boys' Public School and a branch school in connection with it for the children of poor parents, and besides that, there is the Riebeek College, and also a public school for girls.

5395. Would you admit coloured children into the branch school ?—No. There are mission schools which supply the wants of the coloured children.

5396. Do you think it is well to have blacks and whites in separate schools or not ?—The coloured children should be in separate schools.

5397. How would you draw the line between blacks and whites ?—That is a very difficult thing, because the parents soon complain. There was one case in the Riebeek College that I remember. A little girl was admitted, and all at once the parents commenced to be dissatisfied; they did not complain formally or officially, but reports were spread about in the town, and people threatened to take away their children. We spoke to the Lady Principal, and she managed the thing quietly.

5398. How ?—I suppose she spoke to the parents.

5399. Was the child kept at school ?—No, she was taken away.

5400. Was there any other school for the child to go to ?—Not any school of the same class as the Riebeek College.

5401. Then the child suffered in consequence ?—Yes, but had she not been taken away, the whole school would have suffered.

5402. What do you think ought to be done in such a case ?—It is a very exceptional case.

5403. In a place like Cape Town it might often arise, might it not. The Malays for instance are ambitious, and many of them are wealthy ?—I would establish a different school.

5404. *Rev. Morrees.*] They would be able to pay for the school, I suppose ?—Yes.

5405. *Mr. Theron.*] When you speak of irregularity of attendance, do you allude to those children whose names appear on the roll and who do not attend regularly, or children who are not at school at all ?—Those who are on the roll attend as a rule very fairly, although the attendance could be better perhaps. Sometimes there are a good many poor people who do not take enough interest in the education of their children and let them run wild. Those children should be looked after by a truant or attendance officer.

5406. Would that be the proper way of gaining those parents over to take an interest in education ?—It would amount to a kind of compulsory education; you would have to force them, but you force them in their own interests, and in towns especially, such as Uitenhage, it would be a very good thing to have compulsory education.

5407. Suppose you did force the children into school, can you force the parents to pay for them ?—The Government ought to provide for them.

5408. But suppose the parents can provide for them themselves ?—I do not know how to act in such a case. If the parents are really very poor, a certificate might be given as to their poverty, and the children could be admitted free, but in cases where they can pay, I do not know exactly how to act.

5409. What is the percentage of children on the roll in attendance ?—I can speak as to the Riebeek College with more certainty, although I am on both Boards. In one case I am chairman and secretary of the school. I think perhaps 80 per cent. are in attendance

5410. Are you satisfied with 80 per cent. ?—100 per cent. would certainly be better.

5411. If there was a truancy officer, would you give him the right to enter the houses of the parents and speak to them or would you compel them to send their children to school ?—Perhaps it would be a good thing to appoint two kinds of officers, one to attend on the parents and speak to them and use moral suasion, and

Rev.
D. J. Tienaar.

Sept. 11th, 1891.

another to work with the class of children who are running wild in the streets, the waifs and strays.

5412. Have you provision for those waifs and strays in your school at Uitenhage?—We have a school.

5413. Would provision have to be made for them?—Yes. I would have a separate school.

5414. *Dean Holmes.*] Who would you call upon to provide school accommodation for these waifs and strays?—We have a cheap school at Uitenhage, supported by the Divisional Council, the Municipality, and the Government, and we hire a building. We would take white children in there. That school has been started to meet the wants of the poorer people, but all do not make use of it, and we cannot force them.

5415. Suppose these children are absolutely paupers, who is to pay for their education, the Government or the Municipality?—I think the Government ought to pay the whole cost of the education.

5416. At what rate per head?—I would say threepence a head per week.

5417. Could you afford to educate 100 children at threepence a week each?—We do that now.

5418. You get your grant from the Government, do you not?—I would have a separate cheap school for them.

5419. Is there any building which you could hire for the purpose?—At present not. We contemplate building on the premises where the Public School now stands. We have a large piece of ground. That is my proposal, although some members of the committee are not exactly in favour of it. They are afraid lest the class of very poor children taken in there might injure the other school, but I do not think it. It is a large piece of ground.

5420. Is your proposal to build the school by voluntary contributions?—Yes, but we want aid from Government too.

5421. *President.*] In what proportion?—We have already written to the Government and applied for assistance and received a reply. Sir Langham Dale promised to put something on the estimates, but I do not know whether he has done so. On the Board of Managers for the school for poor children, we have members of the Divisional Council and Municipality and two outsiders, Dr. Vanes and myself. At Aliwal North, we worked a mixed school, and some months before I left, we put that school under the Town Council, who appointed three of their own number and two or three outsiders, and I was one. Shortly after I came to Uitenhage, the Civil Commissioner who took great interest in educational matters, asked me whether we should not put the school under the Divisional Council, and I said, yes. I had a little experience of a public body, and I thought we ought to go to the Divisional Council, because the school was needed, there being so many children. The Divisional Council took over the school, and appointed a committee, consisting of three of their own number and two outsiders. That committee repudiated the former debt of £1,012, and the Government made us a present of £1,000, wrote it off, and we paid the £12. Dr. Vanes and myself accepted office as outside members on certain conditions. The first condition was, that the managing Board, consisting of three members of the Divisional Council, should have a free hand and not be hampered too much; only in financial matters there is a kind of veto. The first Tuesday in the month we have our meeting, and the next day the Divisional Council meets. That school is now in a flourishing condition. We have appointed a first class teacher, and about two years ago we commenced with 38 boys; now we have over 168.

5422. *Dean Holmes.*] Who pays the deficiency, is it the divisional Council?—The school is well endowed. They have large pieces of ground, and these are let to people on certain conditions.

5423. Is anything provided out of the rates?—Yes.

5424. *Dr. Berry.*] Before the £1,000 debt was paid off, who paid the interest on that sum?—Shortly after we took office, the debt was cancelled.

5425. Do you know how the interest was paid?—I believe the old Board paid it, but I cannot say for certain. I believe that they could hardly do it.

5426. *Dean Holmes.*] Did Government write off the interest year after year?—I know we only paid the £12.

5427. *Mr. Theron.*] Are there any other schools in Uitenhage similarly situated, under the Divisional Council?—No.

5428. Are the mission schools under the Divisional Council?—No. They belong to different denominations.

5429. *Mr. Rowan.*] Have you a boarding department in connection with the boys' school?—There are some boarders.

5430. *Dean Holmes.*] What is charged in the boarding department?—£36 a year for girls and £40 a year for boys.

5431. Does that include tuition?—No. It is merely for boarding.

Rev.
D. J. Pienaar.
Sept. 11th, 1891.

5432. *Dr. Berry.*] Who are the managers of the Riebeck College?—The Board consists of members appointed half by the Dutch Reformed Church and half elected by the public.

5433. Who are the guarantors?—That is a difficult question to answer. Some think that the Kerkeraad of the Dutch Reformed Church are the guarantors.

5434. Who are the guarantors of the Riebeck College?—I consider there are none; but there is a difference of opinion about that.

5435. Have you sent in any answer to the circular issued by the Commission dated March 3rd last?—Yes. We sent it at the very first meeting we held.

5436. *Dean Holmes.*] What is the franchise under which the three members are elected by the public?—All the householders in the town.

5437. Is it the Parliamentary franchise?—The householders and ratepayers in the town.

5438. *Mr. Rowan.*] Have you had anything to do with a school supported entirely on the guarantee system?—Yes.

5439. Where was that?—At Aliwal North, before the Municipality took over the school.

5440. What do you think about the guarantee system?—I have one great objection to it, and it is this, that at the end of the three years, it is very difficult to get people with public spirit enough to come forward and sign the sub-guarantee list. On one occasion, we called a meeting for two successive weeks, and only three or four persons mustered, and it was very hard to get the guarantee list filled up to the amount required by Government.

5441. How many guarantors' names did you secure?—I cannot say exactly, but we should have secured a good many more names had it not been for the fact that a good deal of feeling was created in the town, and there were parties against each other. It was not a normal condition of affairs. As a rule, we have very hard work in getting about twenty names.

5442. Have you ever been called upon to make up any deficiency?—Fortunately I have not.

5443. You may be liable for the whole deficiency at Uitenhage, may you not?—We take pretty good care not to work the school at a loss.

5444. *Dr. Berry.*] Where the householders elect the whole of the managers, should not the Municipal Council find the amount of any deficit that arises in the funds, and where the Dutch Reformed Church as a body and the householders as a body elect the managers, would it not be fair that the deficit should be made up by the Church body and the municipal body?—It would not be unfair, I think. The school exists there for the public.

5445. Then, in your opinion, local public bodies should be responsible for deficits in public schools?—Yes It comes to that. I do not see why two or three people interested in education should do all the work.

5446. Personally are you in favour of local public bodies being responsible?—Yes.

5447. Would you be in favour of their being responsible for the whole deficit, or should the Government pay any portion after it has already contributed its quota?—I think so.

5448. *Mr. Theron.*] Would you extend that principle that the public should pay to other schools also; would you extend it to mission schools?—I have not had any experience with mission schools. I have not given the matter a thought.

5449. Would you make your school an exception, or would you apply it to denominational schools in your town?—Denominational schools I regard more or less as private schools, and I am not at all for denominational schools.

5450. You tax the ratepayers for your school, to pay for the deficit, do you not?—That is a public school, and everybody can make use of it.

5451. Why are you averse to supporting denominational schools?—The State should not be called upon to teach creeds or doctrines of any sort. I think that doctrines ought to be taught in Sunday schools and in the churches, but not in public institutions.

5452. Have you any proof that such things are taught in denominational schools?—There is a school at Uitenhage, and I think it is inspected by the Deputy Inspector, but I would not say for certain, and in that school I know that Church doctrines are taught.

5453. How do you know that?—I can read the advertisement, which is as follows. "Commercial Boarding School, Uitenhage. (Directed and taught by the Marist Brothers, under the distinguished patronage of His Lordship the Most Rev. Dr. Ricards.) This school, lately enlarged, possesses a magnificent dormitory, well ventilated and fitted up with every modern convenience. Baths, class and study rooms

Rev.
D. J. Pienaar.
Sept. 11th, 1891.

spacious and airy. The object of this Institution is to impart to the pupils a good, sound education, based on Catholic principles: to train them to virtue; to implant in their minds useful and necessary knowledge which will enable them to qualify themselves for a mercantile career. The Brothers, ever anxious for the formation of the moral character of their pupils, never leave them to themselves nor commit them to the care of employés. The Brothers accompany them in their walks, are present at their meals, superintend their recreations and direct their games and amusements. By this constant watchfulness, disorderly conduct is checked, punishment obviated, and self-respect maintained. Every opportunity is afforded for the discharge of all religious duties, and no pains are spared to prepare the children for first Holy Communion. Pupils may enter at any time of the year. Pension, which is £40, is payable quarterly in advance, and charged from date of admission. For particulars apply to Brother Noctaire, as above." As I have said already, I cannot say for certain that that school is inspected, but at all events I am decidedly against the State paying for teaching the doctrine of any Church.

5454. Does that advertisement appear in the Uitenhage paper?—That is taken from the " Record and Beaconsfield Advertiser."

5455. *President.*] Does that school receive Government aid?—I believe so. There is a Roman Catholic School at Uitenhage which gets £45 a year from the Government, £627 10s. from other sources, and £60 school fees.

5456. You do teach some religion in the public undenominational school, do you not?—Yes; but according to the regulations, we do not make that the chief object as the Marist Brothers do. Their chief object is to prepare children for Holy Communion and their Church.

5457. If their chief object is that, but at the same time they train the children in secular subjects up to the mark required by Government, do you think the country can complain that it does not get its money's worth for teaching 103 children in that school?—It is not fair to other denominations who do not use the school. They want to get these children to their own Church.

5458. *Mr. Theron.*] You do not object that such a body should out of the general revenue receive £45 a year, but you object to taxing individuals through Divisional Councils or Municipalities to make up the deficiencies?—Yes.

5459. *Dr. Berry.*] Generally, you dislike education on denominational lines, do you not?—I am for secular schools, undenominational altogether. Doctrines, creeds, and catechism, should be taught by the Minister.

5460. *Dean Holmes.*] Would you banish all religious instruction from these schools?—The public schools worked on the present system answer well, and a child is not forced to attend religious instruction, but the chief object of the Marist Brothers schools is to train the children on the denominational principle.

5461. *Dr. Berry.*] Is the Commercial Boarding School a mission school?—I only know that a Roman Catholic school at Uitenhage gets a grant.

5462. *President.*] What additional facilities can be provided to meet the wants of the children of the agricultural population?—The Government is very liberal, I think, but some plan or other should be adopted to supply the farmers with better teachers than they have. As a rule, the teachers generally employed on farm schools are incompetent, and not really the class of persons who ought to teach children.

5463. How would you remedy that?—I can hardly say. It is a difficulty which we have to contend with in the country districts. There is a Normal College at Cape Town for training teachers, but a good many go to the Free State and Transvaal, where they get higher salaries.

5464. *Mr. Theron.*] Do you think the pupil-teacher system ought to be encouraged?—We have tried that in Uitenhage. Very often people come and ask me to supply them with a teacher, but they make certain stipulations; among other things, perhaps, they say they want one able to teach Dutch, and that is difficult to obtain. I know a case where one of our most promising young ladies in Uitenhage passed several examinations, but she does not know Dutch. She could have had several situations in the country, but not knowing the Dutch language, she was debarred.

5465. To supply that want, would it be well for our pupil teachers to have the requisite training?—That would be one way of obviating the difficulty. Another way would be to try and induce the farmers to send their children to towns to school, but then again the boarding difficulty comes in. We should have more assistance from the Government to establish cheap boarding houses in towns. People can pay the school fee, but the boarding expenses come very heavy.

5466. *Rev. Moorrees.*] Would it be a good thing to encourage the farmers to send their children into town if possible, rather than have them at farm schools?—I prefer sending them to town; they learn better manners in town and become more polished, and their minds are expanded.

Rev.
D. J. Pienaar.

Sept. 11th, 1891.

5467. Do not you think where a boarding school in a town is doing the work of a district boarding school, the capitation grants allotted to district boarding schools should be allowed for such schools also?—Yes. That would certainly be a great assistance. Then the boarding fees could be made so much lower.

5468. Are there many poor farmers in your district?—Yes, very many.

5469. Do you think the system of circuit schools meets their case fully?—I do not know much about circuit schools from experience. We applied for one, and got the reply that there were no funds.

5470. Is there any opening for circuit schools?—Yes.

5471. If you could get the grant, could you in that way provide for the wants of these poor farmers?—To a certain extent we could.

5472. Have you thought of any other means that could be devised to bring education nearer to the door of isolated farmers in your district, or say districts like Victoria West?—The poorer farmers generally live in a kind of cluster; the farms are near each other as a rule, and farm or circuit schools are wanted. The better class farmers can send their children to school in towns.

5473. Do not you find that very often there is a difficulty in getting a school-building or a house for the teacher?—That is a great drawback.

5474. How would you provide for such cases?—As a rule, we generally have to content ourselves with just a small room. In the district of Uitenhage, for instance, there are two or three of these schools, conducted in buildings which are not at all suited for the purpose, but we cannot run into debt for building.

5475. If the Government gave a small grant towards the erection of a small building, could you find the rest?—It might be done in that way. We have already applied for money, before the last Session of Parliament, but we got a reply to the effect that there were no funds.

5476. You are alluding to schools on farms?—Yes.

5477. Would the building be on private or public property?—If it was erected on a farm it would be private property.

5478. Whose property would the building become?—That is just the difficulty.

5479. Mr. Theron.] There are many farm schools in the Uitenhage division, are there not?—Yes.

5480. Do not they supply the wants of the division?—Some of them are outside my parish, and others are very small schools. I do not know much of them. The schools at Wolvekop and Koraansdrift are pretty fair schools; they are third-class Government schools.

5481. Dr. Berry.] If you had a School Board in your division, with power to hold property, would that assist you at all in the way of getting such buildings as would be necessary for the whole district?—Yes. The great drawback of the present system is that the school committee is a fluctuating body and cannot hold property. If we could have a School Board, it would obviate the difficulty.

5482. Would the establishment of a School Board with power to hold property facilitate the establishment of schools for the poorer people among the agricultural population?—Yes, I think so.

5483. In what way?—Such a Board would have more power than the present school committees. I take it that they would have the right to levy a rate directly or indirectly through the Divisional Council, and generally they would have more power to act.

5484. Would you give such Board the right to expropriate land for school purposes if it could not procure it from the owners on proper conditions?—I do not think it would be unfair.

5485. Mr. Theron.] Suppose a farmer objects to give a grant of land and objects to have a school on his farm, would you in that case give land to build a school on?—I can hardly say what would be the result of his objecting. If the farm is in a central position, with other farms near, it would simply enhance the value of the man's own property to have a school there.

5486. But a farmer might not care to have the nuisance of a number of children running about his farm, might he?—There are difficulties of course, but I should be in favour of creating a Board so as to have a perpetual body. The great objection I have to the present system is that the school committees to do not continue in office and cannot hold property.

5487. From your experience, what sort of a Board would you prefer; an irresponsible Board?—It could be arranged for the Board to be under the supervision of the Superintendent-General of Education.

5488. Would a Board constituted like the one you have at Uitenhage, consisting of three members of the Divisional Council and two outside members, be likely to work

Rev.
D. J. Pienaar.

Sept. 11th, 1891.

successfully?—Yes; but there is always the danger of the Divisional Council vetoing our resolutions if there is a difference of opinion; then the system might not work well.

5489. Whatever Board you create, do not you think there must be some check on expenditure?—I think so.

5490. Do not you think the members of the Divisional Council, which has to levy the rates, should have a place on the Board?—Yes, if you can find in the Divisional Council men competent and willing to take an interest in education. Very often these men are elected simply with a view to their knowledge of roads and such things, but they may know very little about education, and not care much about it.

5491. Would you create a Board with the power to levy rates, in case of a deficiency?—Yes. I think there must be such a Board, but if they levied rates directly, I fear it would be unpopular. It should be done through the Divisional Council.

5492. Have you never heard of Boards being done away with in consequence of their having too much spending power without any check upon them?—I have not had any such experience.

5493. In any case, if the Board does not levy a rate directly but indirectly, do not you think the body levying such rate should have some representation on the Board?—Yes; if it is practicable; if there are men capable of sitting on an Educational Board, then I think it is an advisable thing. We are working on that very principle in Uitenhage.

5494. And up to the present it has worked well, has it not?—Yes; but I do not know what might happen in the future.

5495. *Dr. Berry.*] You would not object to the Divisional Council having power to nominate certain members of the School Board, would you?—I would not object to that.

5496. *President.*] Have you formed any opinion with regard to the question of language?—There is a great demand in the colony for more Dutch being taught. Up to now, the Dutch language has been treated very stepmotherly in the schools, at least in the schools I have had to do with. In the school at Aliwal North, when I came on the committee, Dutch was made an extra subject, and pupils had to pay for it, like Latin and other higher subjects. I was really the only Afrikander on the Board; the other members were English and Scotch. In Uitenhage also, according to my experience, Dutch has not been treated as it ought to be. I attribute this not to the teachers or the managers, but to the fact that in the examinations, Dutch is in the background as it were, and is treated as a foreign language altogether. The teachers are compelled to devote all their attention to other subjects, and they put Dutch aside as much as possible. My opinion is that if in some of the University examinations Dutch could receive better attention, the teaching of Dutch would be encouraged. The examinations are looked upon as a kind of advertisement for the schools, and they all try to pass as many candidates as possible.

5497. Suppose there was a separate paper for Dutch and a bursary awarded to those candidates who distinguished themselves, would that be satisfactory?—That would be something, but I am afraid there would still be a grievance.—There is not enough encouragement given to the language.

5498. Would you like all the papers to be in Dutch and all in English, and then let the boys choose?—I am afraid that would not work well either; I think you should give an extra paper in Dutch and assign extra marks for it, and add them to the total.

5499. Would that be fair do you think to those who do not know Dutch?—I do not see that it would be unjust to the others. It is to their own interest to know Dutch in this colony.

5500. Would it be fair to a boy who had been educated for the last three or four years in English?—It cuts both ways. The whole of the examination is conducted in the English language, and that is a foreign tongue to Dutch children, who are consequently handicapped. I can speak from personal experience, for even to this day English is not quite natural to me. I am not free in English, and I know a great many Dutch persons who are exactly in the same way. It takes a long time for Dutch children to prepare for the examinations when the sole medium is English. I consider that Dutch children are much more handicapped than English children. Then if a candidate takes fewer subjects, he can prepare himself so much better in those than another who takes all the subjects.

5501. At St. Andrew's College, Graham's Town, they say there are no fewer than three subjects the pupils take up which they are not examined in; it is part of the school course and part of a liberal education?—To learn Dutch is also part of a liberal education.

5502. Would it be fair to introduce it at once, when you know as a fact that so many boys do not learn Dutch. Should not there be some notice?—The subjects for examination are generally announced a full year beforehand. They are out already for 1892. I maintain that up to now, Dutch has been in the background.

Rev.
D. J. Piennat
Sept. 11th, 1891.

5503. Do you want to force every boy to learn Dutch if he does not want to?— Boys are forced to learn Greek in the Matriculation, where the marks for Greek count. At the time of the Synod, a sub-committee was appointed to report on this question of Dutch, and that report was printed. Before I saw it, one of our ministers spoke to me, and put the matter in such a way as to lead one to think we were going to force every one to learn Dutch in the colony, and take the Dutch paper in the examination, not as an optional subject, but as compulsory. He did not say that, but it was the impression I got, and I said I would not vote for it, that it would be unfair to English children. When I came to the Synod I saw that such a thing was not proposed.

5504. What alternative did you propose?—I simply said I was not going to vote for it.

5505. If there were two or three alternative subjects, such as French, German, or Elementary Science, and the candidate could choose from these, would not that be fair?—I think that Dutch should not be on a par with French or German; those are foreign languages, while Dutch is the language of a large proportion of the white population of South Africa. French is hardly of any use in this colony.

5506. Dutch it seems is not taught properly now, so that most boys would have to start fresh, would they not?—Dutch is not taught properly simply because the children who learn it are placed at a disadvantage in the examination.

5507. Dr. Berry.] If you take the frontier districts, Dutch is hardly needed, and it is not much spoken, so that if your suggestion were carried out, it would simply throw the bulk of the prizes and rank in the Elementary examination into the hands of boys in those districts where Dutch is spoken in the Western Province, would it not?—I cannot see that. My opinion is that there is a very small area in the Cape Colony where only English is spoken. In an English town like Port Elizabeth there is much more Dutch spoken than some people imagine.

5508. Is it taught in the schools here?—Now it is. At the Grey Institute they have a teacher. They once wanted me to come over from Uitenhage and teach Dutch.

5509. Is there any other Dutch teacher here?—I cannot say. There was a strong feeling before the session of Parliament to have Dutch taught in the Grey Institute.

5510. President.] Do not you think it would be fair to have alternative subjects and let the boy choose?—My opinion is that it would be a great advantage for English children to know Dutch.

5511. Why force the advantage, if parents do not want it for their children?—I do not think that it is forcing it. It would be forcing it if we said Dutch is a subject in which you must pass, but as long as you leave it to the candidate and hold it out as a kind of stimulus, it is encouraging, but it is not forcing. We are all along forcing Dutch children to learn English.

5512. Mr. Theron.] You are aware, are you not, that candidates for the Civil Service must pass an examination in Dutch?—Yes.

5513. Have you ever heard any complaint about that?—No.

5514. Is it not compulsory there?—Yes.

5515. Are there not many young men who pass the examination and never get a situation, or at all events have to wait a long time before they do?—I cannot speak with certainty as to that, but I should imagine it is so.

5516. Dr. Berry.] But the number of candidates for the Civil Service is very small compared with the thousands of boys and girls who go up for the Elementary examination, is it not?—That is true; but the Dutch paper there would be simply an elementary paper.

5517. Would not your proposal practically compel every boy and girl to learn Dutch, and every teacher to make Dutch an essential part of the school course?—Yes, quite so.

5518. And discourage other branches of learning?—Against compelling English children to learn Dutch, I would put the fact that we have been all along compelling Dutch children to learn English, and there is no complaint about that, because we say that it is in his own interest for a Dutch child to learn English.

Mr. A. McQuaig examined.

5519. President.] I believe you are a teacher at the North End branch of the Grey Institute?—Yes.

Mr.
A. McQuaig.
Sept. 11th. 1891

5520. How many children have you in your school?—There are 217 on the books.

5521. What is the percentage of attendance to the number on the roll?—About 84 per cent.

Mr.
A. McQuaig.

Sept. 11th, 1891.

5522. Do you think the attendance can be increased?—Yes, by adopting compulsory education.

5523. Could you get more children into your school if that was in force?—Yes; but we should want more accommodation.

5524. Do you know anything about night schools?—I do not think there is any call for night schools here at present.

5525. Are you acquainted with the present guarantee system?—Yes, I may say that I was for 7½ years assistant in the Bedford public school, and during that period our numbers varied from about 60 to a little over 40; they went back. It was a first class school. Some of the guarantors did not care to sign a fresh list, as they thought they would have to put ther hands into their pockets to pay the teacher, and the consequence was, that the school was in danger of falling through at any time. Another thing I should like to mention is the abuses that can be carried on under the guarantee system. A teacher for instance can be dismissed without any reason.

5526. Did they dismiss you?—I was once under notice for no reason connected with the school, but I believe one or two of the committee thought they had a grievance against me, but pressure was brought to bear from outside, and they had to retain my services.

5527. What recommendation have you to make as to that?—I think that as all appointments are made with the approval of the Education Department, so all dismissals of teachers should be approved of by the department. A school may be brought down through no fault of the teacher, who may lose his good service allowance by the parents withholding their children.

5528. Why did the school at Bedford go down?—It was partly through the establishment of farm schools, which absorbed many of the children. It was through no fault of the teachers.

Dr.
A. Vanes.

Sept. 11th, 1891.

Dr. A. Vanes examined.

5529. *President.*] What are you?—A medical practitioner at Uitenhage.

5530. Have you been long in the colony?—I have been twelve years in Uitenhage.

5531. Are you a member of any school committee?—Yes. There is the first class school for boys, another for girls, the Riebeek college, the Memorial school, and the night classes connected with the Railway Institute.

5532. Is the attendance good?—In Uitenhage the attendance is good. We have had at times a little difficulty, but we insist upon the head master bringing up a report, and if there is anything in the way of irregularity of attendance, some one enquires into the matter. We find that system works very well.

5533. Are there children receiving no education who ought to be got into school? —Two years ago we made an inspection at Uitenhage, and as the result of that, we decided to establish an elementary school, with fees of two pence a week. That school had to be subsidized by a special grant from the Town Council. They gave £37 and the Divisional Council gave £37. The Government also contributed, and we opened the school, which has been a most unqualified success. There are about 100 boys in attendance, and most of those 100 boys never attended any school before. Some had been at private schools in the town, and the inspector told me that many of them who had been in these private schools for two or three years, could not pass the first standard; their education had been more or less wasted. This cheap school has met the difficulty, and at the present time there is hardly a white child in Uitenhage who does not receive education.

5534. Could compulsory education be applied to whites or blacks with advantage? —It could in regard to the whites, but I cannot speak as to the others.

5535. What additional facilities can be provided to meet the wants of children of persons employed on the lines of railway?—I discussed that question with our master, Mr. Savage, and as the outcome, after some correspondence, a school at Glen Connor has been established to provide for the education of the children of platelayers. The Rev. Mr. Pienaar and myself travelled up the line on one occasion, and we questioned the employés as we went along, and found that a number of the children could neither read nor write. The train picks up the children and delivers them at the school about 10 o'clock in the morning, and they return to their homes by train in the afternoon. That system works fairly well. I was at the school a little time ago, and I could see a very decided progress. The Graaff-Reinet line is the line that is worst patronised in regard to traffic, and there the train difficulty is the greatest; but if the plan can work there, it can work on the other lines where the traffic is greater and the children are more easily picked up.

5536. Where else would you create centres?—It might be arranged for children to be picked up at crossing places on the line.

Dr.
A. Vanes.

Sept. 11th, 1891.

5537. Can the farmers' children avail themselves of these schools?—They would be somewhat in advance of farm schools, a slight improvement on them; they would rank more as fourth class schools.

5538. Is it not advisable to do everything to invite farmers in the neighbourhood to send their children to these schools?—Farmers' children attend the school at Glen Connor. The fee is sixpence a week, and the Government grants £30 a year. We take the fees and pay the teacher, and the school works very well.

5539. Do you think any further facilities ought to be offered?—The schools are a very fair success up to the present, and as the result of a little further experience, we might be able to suggest some improvement, but it is difficult to propose any drastic changes.

5540. Where the children cannot avail themselves of this, ought not there to be some means of concentrating in some town those children who cannot attend?—I have often thought that over, but I hardly know what to suggest. I am railway medical officer at Uitenhage, and know these people very well indeed, and I think the provision that has been made in our own district is ample, as far as Kleinpoort.

5541. How far is that away?—Sixty-four miles from Uitenhage.

5542. With regard to the girls, is it not advisable to concentrate them in towns?—Undoubtedly there are advantages in that. I do not mean to say that the present system is perfect, but it is fairly so, and to a certain extent meets a good deal of the difficulty.

5543. What additional facilities can be provided to meet the wants of the children of the agricultural population?—I think the farm schools are very good, but at the same time they do not fulfil all the educational requirements. I think it would be very much better if we could take the farmers' children and concentrate them in the suburbs of a town not smaller than Uitenhage, where in addition to literary education, they could be taught practical agriculture. There should be some land surrounding the school, which the pupils might cultivate, and the produce would help to support the school. I would devote the mornings to instruction in reading, writing, and arithmetic, and in the afternoon teach technical work. It would be an advantage if periodically some of the pupils could be sent to see the produce sales in Port Elizabeth, as it would give them an insight into the prices, and so on, and would prove a very practical kind of education in mercantile requirements, as they would not then be the dupes of Boer-*ecrneukers* as they often are at the present time. It would also tend to lessen the friction that exists between town and country, and they would in time be able to embark in new industries. I know a farmer in the Long Kloof, Humansdorp, who grows peaches in large quantities, and he cannot do anything with them. Now if these boys were acquainted with tinsmiths' work, they could make cans and preserve the fruit. Again, in the same district, the farmers do not use very much in the way of agricultural implements, for the simple reason that they do not know how, but if there was more technical education, such implements would be appreciated; the farmers would grow their produce cheaper, and make greater profits. I think such a school as I have suggested would be self-supporting. The children would have to be cheaply boarded, and they would grow most of the produce. You might introduce the making of certain agricultural implements which are now imported, and the sale of these would also help to support the school. If this were done, the young fellows would be able to return to their farms thoroughly fit to go in for practical work. If you look at some of the gates that are made now, they are very miserable things, and the same with fencing. I think therefore if the children of farmers could be educated on some such lines as those I have indicated, it would be a great advantage.

5544. *Mr. Rowan.*] Are you acquainted with the agricultural colleges in America?—No.

5545. *President.*] Have you anything to suggest about Native education?—I do not know very much about it. I should imagine their training is not altogether satisfactory, but I am not an authority. I know that if I want a groom, I have to teach him what he has to do.

5546. Would you apply industrial training to Natives?—There is a certain amount of industrial work which Natives could with advantage do, such as rough carpentering work. I know a good many in Uitenhage who are able to do that.

5547. Is there any other work you would teach them?—Rough industrial work generally.

5548. *Mr. Theron.*] Have you considered at all the higher branches of technical education for the whites?—Yes. I think we might do very much in the way of training our children in that direction. They talk about protection of colonial industries, but I do not see that it would answer under present circumstances. If you went in for it to-morrow, you would have to import mechanics to do the work, and

Dr.
A. Tanes.

Sept. 11th, 1891.

they would want tempting wages to come out here, so that the goods would be produced at a high cost. If on the other hand, we trained our children to industrial pursuits much could be done without the aid of protection. Uitenhage is very favourably situated as regards facilities for technical education. We have here large railway workshops, where there are competent mechanics and excellent teachers. I know one little boy in the tinsmith's department only fourteen years of age; he has been there only two months, and can work well enough to make cans for fruit. We have tried to start technical work in connection with our boys' school, teaching them tinsmiths and and blacksmiths' work, and I think they will take kindly to it. After a few lessons they seem to enjoy it, and some look upon it almost as a recreation. I am myself very fond of amateur mechanics, and have a small workshop. You want a technical school to be placed if possible in some industrial centre such as Uitenhage, where teachers can be trained, mechanics specially selected from the large number of men employed in the Government workshops.

5549. *Rev. Moorrees.*] Would you be in favour of having a few such schools in certain centres in the colony ?—Yes. It would be a great advantage. I asked our acting head master whether it would not be possible for him to spare time twice a week so as to allow the boys to go in for a little technical education, but he said no, the educational standards were such that they did not admit of it, and he rigidly boycotted it.

5550. *Mr. Theron.*] What would you suggest as the best plan by way of a stimulus to such mechanical work ?—I have a little machinery myself, sufficient to equip a workshop, and if the idea had been entertained, I should have suggested getting a few model engine castings and so on, and teaching the boys to use their fingers as well as their minds. I would give them a practical idea of what a steam engine was, and if a boy was to learn to make a model, it would be an intelligent amusement for him. I should have been glad to give my workshop free, and the boys could go there twice a week say ; but I do not see why each school should not have its own workshop. The cost of equipping it would not be great. The machinery would not cost more than £100, and with that you could do a great deal of intelligent model making. You could make a half horse power steam engine for instance. I trained one boy myself, and he turned out to be a most valuable mechanic. He used to make his own patterns, and he made also a model locomotive which is in the museum. That was all done in my workshop. The total cost of the necessary machinery would not be more than £100, and it would train boys to use their fingers. We train their mind now, and very often they have not the power to carry out the ideas which their minds originate.

5551. What means would you suggest to excite in these boys some desire to come to such workshops?—Such a school as I was suggesting would be a sort of stimulus if it were carried out. In addition to that, certain prizes might be offered for the best model engine made by boys under a certain age.

5552. *Dr. Berry.*] What do you think of founding lectureships in arts and sciences in large towns ?—I doubt if they would be an unqualified success. Our mechanics have never attended lectures, and they are too theoretical. Practical training is more wanted.

5553. Certainly; but in very few towns do we find gentlemen who take such a practical interest in the matter as yourself, and who are so ready to assist ?—There are such people if they were only looked for. I saw lately a mealie sheller made by a Dutch farmer : a rough and ready apparatus, but it worked well, and he certainly deserved the greatest possible credit for it. It was a patched up affair, and there was a good deal of originality about it, but he did the whole of the mechanical work, and he had moreover not had any technical experience. If the Government encouraged the thing, you would soon find people would take it up.

5554. We want some means by which you can make it attractive do we not ?—That is not difficult. Nothing is more attractive than mechanical work to a boy, but it must not be too theoretical. He likes to see how things are done.

5555. *President.*] How would it do to have a lecturer in the town-hall here for six weeks or two months, and then have an examination ; if a boy is proficient, give him a certificate which would enable him to go to the railway workshops at Uitenhage or Salt River ; would that answer ?—I do not know whether it would. In Birmingham, which is my native town, lectures are given on technical subjects such as chemistry, but they are very thinly attended, even with a large population.

5556. If there was a certificate to be gained which would be of use afterwards, would not that prove an inducement ?—I doubt it.

5557. *Dr. Berry.*] Are you in favour of attaching lecturers to the workshops at Uitenhage and compelling apprentices to attend them ?—There would be a very great advantage in that, and to a certain extent we have tried it in the night schools con-

Dr.
A. Vanes.
Sept. 11th, 1891.

nected with the Railway Institute. We have a drawing class, which is taught by a blacksmith, and it is a great success; but very much depends on the teacher. The apprentices are taught drawing and other elementary subjects.

5558. Are you acquainted with trade classes attached to public schools ?—Not practically. I can imagine what they are.

5559. *Rev. Moorrees.*] Could such an institution as . ou suggested just now for the benefit of farmers' sons be started at Uitenhage ?—I think it is about the most suitable town in the colony. It possesses certain unique advantages and is within twenty miles of Port Elizabeth. Boys could go there and see something of the produce sales, which is a very important thing, and then we have the large railway workshops in the immediate vicinity, which is also a great consideration. Then again, a tract of land can be got, which could be irrigated and cultivated. In this way a certain gap which seems now to exist between the farming community and the town might be filled up, and good would be done all round.

5560. Do you think the Uitenhage people would make an effort on their side to get such an institution started, with Government support ?—They have been very anxious to do all they can to start schools, and I think they would do anything reasonable in their power.

5561. *President.*] Have you anything to suggest on the subject of night schools ? —We have had to inaugurate night schools in connection with our Railway Institute. Some little time ago, we examined the boys attending the classes. When they came, many of them could scarcely read or write, but they are now quite proficient in elementary work We started this night school, and we were told by the Railway Department that if it was a success they would give us a grant, but we have managed to keep the thing going without the slightest assistance from the Government, and it has undoubtedly done a great deal of good.

5562. *Dr. Berry.*] Who teaches there ?—Mr. Miller, the teacher at the Memorial school in Uitenhage, the cheap school.

5563. *President.*] The boys work as well, I suppose ?—Yes. They work in the daytime.

5564. How old are they ?—Various ages, from 13 to 19.

5565. *Dr. Berry.*] Has there been no objection to the teacher giving assistance in the night school ?—That has never been thought of. I do not think they would raise any objection.

5566. Have you got any grant now ?—No.

5567. How long has this night school been in operation ?—It has been working for 12 or 18 months. We cannot get a grant, although we have applied several times. We use the Railway Institute. There is a certain debt on it, and the Institute Committee pays the rent. It is built on Government ground and technically it belongs to the Government, but to all intents and purposes it is the property of the Institute Committee.

5568. Do you admit boys who do not belong to the railway ?—We have not done so hitherto, but I do not think there would be any objection ; I can see none.

5569. Do you think such night schools could be started at other places ?—I see no reason why they should not. Very much depends on the teacher, as the discipline of a night school is quite different to the discipline of a day school. There is a certain amount of voluntary effort made in night schools.

5570. Is anything done for girls in the night schools ?—Not hitherto.

5571. Do you think girls could with advantage get instruction there ?—I think so, but not to the same extent as boys. Girls can go to school in the day time.

5572. *Dean Holmes.*] Do you think it advisable to have night schools for girls ?— I have not thought much about that.

5573. *President.*] Have you ever thought of having early morning schools for girls. I believe such schools are held in some parts of Europe ?—They might be useful.

5574. *Dr. Berry.*] What do you think would be a fair grant from the Government ?—£30 a year.

5575. How many pupils attend ?—About twenty in each class, and there are two classes.

5576. *Rev. Moorrees.*] What are the school hours ? –We commence at seven and go on till half past nine, four evenings a week : two for drawing and two for elementary subjects, reading, writing, and arithmetic. The boys appreciate the school, and there seems to be an increasing desire on their part to attend.

5577. *President.*] We have heard that in summer the attendance at these night schools drops off ; is that so ?—I think the classes are continued in summer, but I know they have been very much handicapped by the pressure of railway work on the Bloemfontein line extension. The boys were not able to attend in consequence of having to work overtime.

Dr.
A. Vanes.

Sept. 11th, 1891.

5578. *Mr. Theron.*] Has your night schools been inspected?—We got no grant, but the Government can inspect the school at any time they like if they will only give us a grant.

5579. *Dean Holmes.*] Have you had any independent examination?—We cannot get it.

5580. Cannot you get some schoolmaster to come and examine the school?—The boys are taught by a schoolmaster at present, but we should prefer the Inspector examining the school.

5581. *Mr. Rowan.*] Have you ever been a guarantor?—I am a guarantor now in two schools, but we have a sub-guarantee in one case from the Divisional Council, and in the other from the Dutch Reformed Church.

5582. Have you ever been called upon to make good any deficiency?—We have taken good care to manage the school properly. I am not altogether in favour of the Divisional Council taking the guarantee of the school. Persons elected to the Divisional Council are all very well for supervising roads and bridges, but it does not follow that they are versed in educational matters, and they are not in many instances. Our divisional councillors do their best in the matter of education, but it does not follow that all Divisional Councils would. They are chosen for a specific purpose. The rate-payers ought to have an opportunity of going at their convenience and voting for those men who are best adapted for looking after educational interests. At present, any half-dozen people can go to the magistrate's office, and in five minutes select their cronies and put them on the Board, and that is done not in the interests of education, but from party spite. There ought to be due and proper notice of the meeting.

5583. Would you have a Board of Management elected for the division, with power to supervise all the schools?—Yes.

5584. Including mission schools?—Yes.

5585. But you would respect existing rights, would you not?—Yes.

5586. Would you impose on the Board the duty of bringing into existence new schools that might be necessary for keeping the education of the district up to the mark throughout?—Yes.

5587. Suppose there is a deficiency in the school revenue?—I think the Board ought to have power to levy a small rate, perhaps through the divisional council, to meet any deficiency. It seems very unfair that a few men should have to bear all the brunt. I have no children myself, and can derive no prospective advantage in any way.

5588. Do you think some such plan would work?—I think it would.

5589. Would it tend to soften any asperities that now exist?—I think a thoroughly representative Board would work very well. It must be selected, not from the town but from the district, and there would have to be regular meetings.

5590. Would you be in favour of paying the members?—I would only allow them travelling expenses, the same as in the divisional council.

5591. *Rev. Moorrees.*] Would you have a representative for each field-cornetcy? I would say that the Board should be thoroughly representative.

5592. *Mr. Rowan.*] Would you be in favour of a nominee Board?—No.

5593. *Dr. Berry.*] Would you be in favour of having the schools in the district managed by a local committee under this Board?—I do not see any harm in that. With regard to the Glencounor School, the Government insisted that there should be three managers, and they were to be selected from the Railway Department. We had the greatest difficulty in getting them. It is not always you can get a sub-committee.

5594. Where a sub-committee could be found, would you be in favour of having it?—There would be no objection to it. A Central Board would have this advantage, we would know what teachers to send to the various farm schools. If one failed, we would have a spare or relieving teacher under our control, so as to supply any possible deficiencies or vacancies. We often have to do it in connection with our Uitenhage Schools.

5595. Under such a system, would you be in favour of all the school fees in the district being payable to the Central Board and allocated to the various schools?—There would be some difficulty in that, as there would have to be some means of collecting the fees.

5596. Would the Government grant be paid in one lump sum to the Board?—Yes; that would be an advantage.

5597. And by it allocated to the different schools?—Yes.

5598. Subject always to an appeal to the Education Department?—Yes.

5599. Are there many natives in your district?—Yes.

5600. Would you be in favour of levying a tax on them to support their own schools?—I do not think they would pay very much in the way of rates, but I do not know sufficient of native schools to say.

5601. Would you be in favour of taxing the European population of a division, in order to give schools to the natives?—I quite think the natives should be taught to work, and then if they were useful to the Europeans, the Europeans might pay as you say, but as long as the natives are taught the rubbish they frequently are in some of the schools, I would say not.

Dr.
A. Vann.

Sept. 11th, 1691

5602. *Dean Holmes.*] What is it you object to in their training?—I have seen myself a good many instances of educated natives, who are of very little service. I know from experience, if I employ a Kafir groom, no matter what wages I pay, I invariably get a man, who has never been taught anything of the work I want from him. He knows nothing of grooming, nothing about the proper feed for a horse, nothing about putting a horse shoe on, or attending to the horse generally, and nothing about mending harness. He is absolutely ignorant of all these things, but no doubt he has been taught at school Latin and Greek, which are of questionable use even to many white people. As long as the natives are educated thus, I do not think the Europeans should be called upon to pay anything for them.

5603. Would it not be an infinitesimal proportion of the natives who are taught Latin and Greek, and that perhaps for a special purpose?—I do not know. I know that on one occasion my groom was what would be called an educated native. He was very willing, but very stupid at any practical work.

5604. You would prefer industrial to literary training for natives?—Their training should be suited to their future requirements. They have to live by their hands and not by their brains, and they ought to be taught to use their hands intelligently.

5605. Would you educate them up to the third standard?—I think as long as a native can calculate what his wages are, it is sufficient.

5606. Have you considered the question of language at all?—Yes. I know the question of English and Dutch is a very vexed one, and there exists a good deal of prejudice in the matter. When once that is set aside, there will be very little difficulty. Dutch no doubt is very useful and ought to be taught, and we must admit that the bulk of the population speak it. Any person who can speak two languages is in a better position than a person who can only speak one. The only thing is that Dutch should be taught thoroughly; there is a very indifferent knowledge of the language, and when it is taught in school, it should be followed up afterwards, so as to be acquired perfectly, just as you would acquire a thorough acquaintance with German or French. I speak Dutch myself very indifferently; but even what little I know is of very great use to me. It enables me to put myself in communication with people. Even during the last twenty-four hours I have had to see a sick person, and I could not have understood what was the matter with him (without an interpreter) unless I knew something of Dutch. In that way, Dutch is very useful to me, far more use than other languages, such as French or German would be; another advantage in fostering the Dutch language is, that it would tend to diminish that want of unity among the two European nations which at present exists in South Africa. If they knew more of one another, they would find out that they had very much more in common than they think they have at present. If each spoke and understood the other's language, the difficulty would be very greatly met.

5607. *Rev. Moorrees.*] Should the study of Dutch be encouraged in the examinations?—What I should like to see would be the encouragement of Dutch voluntarily, persons coming to realize its advantages. I think it should be made compulsory at the Elementary examination.

5608. *Dean Holmes.*] Would that be fair to a large portion of the population?—Perfectly fair; they are living in the colony. If they like to handicap themselves it is their own fault.

5609. Would not the effect of that be to induce parents to send up their children for the examinations of other countries, and set up another standard?—I do not think so. I know there is a little prejudice in Uitenhage. An hotel-keeper, for instance, told me he was not going to have his child taught Dutch, but he admitted afterwards that he was wrong, and his child is being taught the language now.

5610. Do you foster the teaching of Dutch in the public school?—We do what we can, but that school has had a great deal of difficulty to contend with. Three years ago it was in a chaotic state, and it had to be slowly built up. We have not been able to do all we should like, but if I continue to be one of the managers, I shall be glad to do all I can to encourage the teaching of Dutch.

5611. *Rev. Moorrees.*] I suppose you are aware that the course of instruction at school is to a certain extent guided by the programme of the examinations?—Yes, unfortunately.

5612. So that if a subject is left out in the programme, it discourages taking up that subject, does it not?—It does. We have to teach the Government standards, and the Government standards are fixed, and we do not know altogether the requirements of the colony.

Dr.
A. Vance.

Sept. 11th, 1891.

5613. *President.*] What would you do if you were arranging the subject?—Parliament ought to take some interest in the matter and fix the standards. There ought to be a Parliamentary Committee.

5614. How would you arrange the Elementary examination?—A good knowledge of reading, writing, and arithmetic should be made compulsory; also a certain knowledge of colonial history and geography, and the European languages spoken in South Africa—Dutch and English. Chemistry should be included also, and elementary science.

5615. *Mr. Rowan.*] If you introduced a Dutch paper into the Elementary examination, would it not tend to destroy its elementary character?—It ought not to. No subject could be more advantageously learned than Dutch.

5616. *President.*] Do you think it wise to have an elementary science paper?—Yes. I also think the teaching of chemistry is, as a rule, begun too late.

5617. How would it do to have a fifth paper in the Elementary examination, and give candidates the option of choosing either Dutch or chemistry?—I think that Dutch ought to be something more than an optional subject. What you suggest would not be sufficient.

5618. You think it ought to be compulsory?—Yes, in the interests of South Africa.

5619. *Rev. Moorrees.*] Do we educate our children for Europe or for the colony?—A child ought to conform to colonial requirements; we educate to that end, and undoubtedly one important thing is a knowledge of Dutch.

5620. Do you speak Dutch?—Indifferently. I speak it, but I cannot write it. I may say that I feel the want of Dutch every day.

5621. *Mr. Theron.*] Do some boys of Dutch parentage consider that they have finished their education when they have passed the subjects at present prescribed in the Elementary examination?—Many do not go beyond that, but I should not think they were sufficiently educated. Many other subjects could be taught.

5622. Must they not of necessity study Dutch as well as English?—I think so.

Mr. J. M. Thornton examined.

Mr.
J. M. Thornton.

Sept. 11th, 1891.

5623. I believe you are Locomotive Superintendent in connection with the Cape Government Railways, and reside at Uitenhage?—Yes.

5624. Can you give us any information on the subject of technical education?—I am of opinion that the night schools at Uitenhage in connection with the Railway Institute should receive greater support from the Government. Mechanics with a knowledge of the rudiments of such subjects as physics, applied mechanics, geometry, and chemistry might be imported from England, who could be employed at their trade in the workshops during the day, and in the evening conduct classes at which the subjects referred to would be taught to the young men and boys engaged in the workshops.

5625. Are there competent men in the colony?—Very few; but as I have already stated, mechanics with the necessary technical knowledge might be imported.

5626. And they could teach in the evening, you think?—Yes.

5627. And the Government could utilize these men in the workshops during the day?—Yes, as mechanics.

5628. Mr. Heenan thought it would be advisable to have lecturers at different centres, who should go about the country with their apparatus. Do you think that would answer?—I do not think that the proposed scheme is of a practicable nature. Boys enter the workshops about the age of fourteen and remain until they are twenty-one years of age, and it is during that period they should be taught in the evenings the theoretical part of their work.

5629. Could you make it a condition that if the boys gained a certain amount of knowledge at those lectures, certificates should be given them which would pass them into the Government workshops?—You might make admission to the workshops conditional on attending the evening classes.

5630. What other inducement would you offer?—You might offer prizes.

5631. At how many centres do you think technical schools could be started with any moderate hope of success?—At Uitenhage, Cape Town, East London, and perhaps at Kimberley and Graham's Town. You could not hope for much success at places where there are no workshops.

5632. And would you connect them with the evening schools?—I think so.

5633. Would you make it attractive to boys at schools to attend them also?—I think that every inducement should be held out to attend such schools either by offering them prizes or by promising them employment in the workshops, should they obtain satisfactory certificates.

5634. Would you connect them in any way with a system of agricultural teaching?—Yes; the practical part might be learnt in the workshops, such as to be able to repair a plough or a force pump, and the theoretical part might be learnt at the evening classes.

Mr.
J. M. Thornton.
—
Sept. 11th, 1891.

5635. Would such a school be expensive to start?—No; I do not think it would be expensive.

5636. Could you give the Commission a general outline of what you suggest should be done in the way of technical education?—The training of the boys in the Uitenhage workshops has engaged my attention for the last few years, and I have given every encouragement to any movement which has had for its object their physical development, their intellectual advancement, or the improvement of their moral condition. My action in this matter has been influenced, not so much by philanthropic motives, as from the advantages which will accrue to the Department, by filling the workshops with men of a high moral character, who will have been specially trained both practically and theoretically for the work they will have to perform, which consequently would be executed more efficiently and economically, and thus dispense with the unsatisfactory and expensive alternative of procuring skilled mechanics from Europe, many of whom, owing to the faulty system of selection, are incompetent, unsteady, and unsuitable. Evening elementary classes for reading, writing, arithmetic, and mechanical drawing, have been in existence for the last two years in connection with the Railway Institute, Uitenhage, but only thirty out of ninety boys attend, owing to want of funds to provide teachers, insufficient accommodation, and the absence of the necessary authority to enforce attendance. This state of affairs could be easily rectified, by giving the Locomotive Superintendent power to engage competent persons as teachers, and employ them during the day in the workshops as draughtsmen, clerks, timekeepers, and mechanics, and as teachers during the evening to conduct the classes; it would also be necessary to endow the Superintendent with authority to enforce attendance, and to have the requisite models and diagrams made. The actual cost to educate these ninety boys, on this system, I estimate would be not more than £200 per annum. The sons of farmers would be employed in the workshops between the ages of 15 and 18 years, and during the day time, they could be found work in the fitting, millwright, carpenter's and blacksmith's shop, and in the evenings they could attend the classes of instruction. The wages for such boys according to the present scale would be:—1st year, 8s. per week; 2nd year, 10s. per week; 3rd year, 12s. per week. As these wages would be insufficient to maintain these lads in board and lodging, and presuming they were sons of poor farmers, it would be necessary to provide a boarding house, superintended by one of the teachers, whose wife could look after the catering. I estimate that such an establishment would cost the Government on an average 5s. per week per boy. Three years of such training would qualify a boy to superintend, operate, and maintain any mechanical contrivance used in connection with farming pursuits, such as steam engines, thrashing machines, steam and hand pumps, ploughs, &c. I might state, I do not anticipate there would be much difficulty in obtaining the proper stamp of men as teachers, provided I was permitted to employ them in the manner suggested.

Mr. John Buckley examined.

5637. *President.*] What are you?—Inspector of Police at Port Elizabeth.

Mr.
John Buckley.
Sept. 11th, 1891

5638. Have you been here long?—Yes, twelve years.
5639. Is it part of your duty to look after the natives?—Yes.
5640. How many locations are there here?—Four.
5641. Do you inspect them from time to time?—Yes.
5642. Are there many children there, who do not go to any sort of school?—A great many.
5643. They do nothing?—Yes.
5644. Could they not be sent to some school with advantage?—I think so.
5645. What sort of education do you think would be best for them; should they be taught some industrial work?—I think so.
5646. Working with a spade and rough carpentering?—Yes.
5647. How many of them are there in the location?—About 700 or 800, if not more.
5648. Would you have a school in the location?—Yes.
5649. Is there a place there where you could start a garden for them to work in, or something of that kind?—Yes; it might be done in the Valley.
5650. What other industry can you suggest for these natives?—They might learn brickmaking and basketmaking.

Mr.
John Buckley.
Sept. 11th, 1891.

5651. Would it be a good thing if this formed a part of their education ?—I think so ?

5652. *Dr. Berry.*] Is the native population of Port Elizabeth pretty stationary in the town ?—Yes.

5653. Will the children who are now growing up in Port Elizabeth eventually take service in the town ?—Yes.

5654. Those natives who are now labourers, have they been brought up in the town to any extent ?—A great many of them.

·5655. Has the bulk of them come from a distance, or have they been brought up in town ?—They have come from a distance I should say.

5656. Is that going on now, or has it stopped ?—It is hard to say.

5657. Do these people support their own churches in the location ?—I do not know.

5658. Is there a Kafir schoolmaster in the location ?—Yes.

5659. Who pays him ? I cannot say.

5660. Do the children pay anything ?—I do not know. The superintendent collects the hut rents ; they pay 10s. a hut to the municipality.

Port Elizabeth, Saturday, September 12th, 1891.

PRESENT :

Sir J. D. BARRY (President),

Rev. Moorrees.
Mr. Rowan,
Dean Holmes,

Mr. Theron,
Dr. Berry.

Rev. J. Pritchard examined.

Rev.
J. Pritchard.
Sept. 12th, 1891.

5661. *President.*] What are you ?—I am congregational minister of the Kafir native church here.

5662. Do you get any aid from Government ?—Yes. £60 a year.

5663. How many children have you at school ?—60

5664. Do they pay any fees ?—Yes, from sixpence to a shilling per week.

5665. Are there any who pay nothing ?—Yes, a number. I should say 25 out of the 60 ; but then we have an allowance made by the London Missionary Society which covers that.

5666. What sort of buildings have you ?—We have a very nice schoolroom. It is vested in the Congregational Union of South Africa.

5667. Who built it ?—The London Missionary Society.

5668. What has it cost you ?—I cannot say ; it was built many years ago.

5669. Is the attendance at the school regular ?—Yes, very.

5670. What is the percentage attendance of those on the roll ?—At the last inspection it was 45 out of 60.

5671. Do they come specially for the inspection ?—No.

5672. Do you think other means than those existing should be resorted to to secure attendance ?—Yes. I have been here nine years, and I know something about the natives. I think instead of having so many of the present existing native schools, there should be but one school for them. At present we have for the Kafir speaking population three schools, one Episcopalian, one Wesleyan, and our own. Among the Europeans there is the idea of denominationalism, but such a thing does not really exist among the Kafir speaking population. There may be a congregational church, or a Wesleyan, or an Episcopalian ; the natives will go to either. In the three schools there are six teachers, and I suppose there are not more than 250 children all told. If we had one principal school, into which all the Kafir children could go, and one chief teacher with three or four subordinates, it would answer every purpose and save a large expense.

5673. How would you find a building large enough for such a school ?—The Government would have to make a grant towards erecting a building, and doubtless the town would contribute liberally towards an object of that kind.

5674. Would not the other buildings do ?—They are not large enough.

5675. Would they be wasted ?—No, they could be used for Sunday schools.

5676. Were not they brought into existence for the purpose of a day school ?—No. The present building I have was originally a Sunday school and intended for such. It has only been within the last ten or eleven years that we have had a day school for blacks in connection with our church at all.

5677. Then your work is among the blacks ?—Purely.

5678. What would become of your school ?—The children would go to one central school.

Rev.
J. Pritchard.

Sept. 12th, 1891.

5679. And you would confine yourself to church work ?—I do not teach. The congregation would have to contribute towards the maintenance of the teacher, and there should be a Board consisting of the representatives of the various churches.

5680. What is to become of the three schools and the three sets of teachers ?—Places could be found for them. There is a scarcity of teachers in the country. I only speak as to Port Elizabeth; I do not know whether the idea of one central school could be carried out in other places.

5681. If such a school is established, should there be an industrial department in connection with it ?—Certainly.

5682. What would be the nature of the work ?—Blacksmiths' work, carpentering, and so on.

5683. And spade work also ?—The difficulty would be as to the ground. I think there should be needlework for the girls.

5684. Do you think such an industrial department would be expensive ; can you point to any place where such a thing is worked inexpensively either in this country or elsewhere ?—I cannot.

5685. Would you apply compulsion to natives in the town ?—Certainly.

5686. How many hours a day would you devote to industrial pursuits ?—I would have five hours altogether at school : two should be devoted to industrial pursuits and three to literary training.

5687. Would you begin with industrial training ?—No, with literary training.

5688. How would you constitute the Board if your idea was carried out ?—I would have representatives from the various churches.

5689. Would it not be better to have representatives elected by the ratepayers ?—They could have that if they chose.

5690. Why do you say representatives from the various churches ?—The churches would naturely take an interest in working the school where their children were, and it would be more likely to be successful I think than otherwise.

5691. Dr. Berry.] Would that be a fourth class public undenominational school ? —Yes.

5692. And you would bring that into existence for natives as well as for Europeans ?—Yes. I may say that the Inspector, Mr. Brady, and myself have had a long discussion on the subject, and he is quite of my opinion in regard to the matter. He has to devote three days to inspect three small schools in Port Elizabeth, whereas it could be done in one day when he is here in town.

5693. President.] With whom else have you discussed the matter ?—With the Wesleyan minister.

5694. With the Church of England minister ?—No.

5695. With the Romanists ?—No. They have not any adherents among these natives.

5696. Mr. Rowan.] Would you create a separate school or take one of the existing three schools ?—Neither of the three schools is large enough.

5697. Would you have a school at the location ?—It must of necessity be there.

5698. Are any schools there now ?—They are all there.

5699. Dr. Berry.] What percentage of Kafir children go to school ?—It is difficult to say.

5700. It is estimated that there are about 600 children of schoolable age in the location altogether ; would that be about the number ?—Yes.

5701. President.] Would there be about 300 at school ?—Yes.

5702. Dr. Berry.] Have these natives been a long time in town, or do they come and go ?—Some of them have been a long time here.

5703. Is there a large body of children growing up, likely to be permanent residents ?—Yes.

5704. It is with a view to providing education for these that you suggest this scheme ?—Quite so.

5705. President.] Would you have coloured masters ?—Yes.

5706. Are they procurable ?—Yes.

5707. What do you pay them ?—I pay my present teacher £80 a year.

5708. Dean Holmes.] What sort of training would these children have ?—Up to the third standard.

5709. President.] Would you be able to conduct an industrial department ?—I think so. The girls learn sewing at present.

5710. Are any of the teachers brought up at Lovedale ?—All our principal teachers come from Lovedale. Our present teachers are not competent to teach industrial work.

Mr.
D. Lumsden.
—
Sept. 12th, 1891.

Mr. D. Lumsden examined.

5711. *President.*] I believe you are a merchant at Port Elizabeth ?—Yes.

5712. Are you a member of any School Board ?—I am on the Board of the Grey Institute.

5713. I believe you have taken a great interest in municipal matters from time to time ?—Yes.

5714. Are you a member of the municipality ?—Yes.

5715. Do you consider the present system of guarantors a good one ?—If a school is to be a permanent institution, I fear you would never get such a thing as voluntary guarantors. Unless there is some power to levy a rate, I do not see how you can make the schools permanent.

5716. Do you approve of the system of rating ?—Yes. I think a School Board ought to be appointed, with rating powers.

5717. You think that system must come and ought to come ?—I think so.

5718. Have you any knowledge of the working of schools in Scotland ?—Yes.

5719. Does the Board principle work well there ?—The system has been very much altered the last two or three years, it is quite different from what it used to be. First of all, there was no Government assistance, then the Government assisted to a certain extent, and now it has become free education. It has developed very rapidly.

5720. Was the old system of parish schools a good one in Scotland ?—Very good.

Mr. James Brister examined.

Mr.
James Brister
—
Sept. 12th, 1891.

5721. *President.*] I believe you are a merchant at Port Elizabeth ?—I have been. I have now retired from business.

5722. Have you been a long time resident here ?—Yes, many years.

5723. I believe you have large interests in Port Elizabeth ?—Yes.

5724. Have you been Mayor ?—Yes, two or three times.

5725. I suppose you understand the present school system and also take some interest in general school work ?—Yes.

5726. Are you a member of the Grey Institute ?—Yes; *ex officio.*

5727. It is found that there are here roughly about 600 white children not traceable to any schools and about 600 blacks also; have you formed any opinion as to what ought to be done to get these children into school ?—I think it is very necessary that every child should be educated, and if the State spends money for that purpose it does wisely.

5728. Do you think the necessary machinery ought to be brought into existence to attain this object ?—I quite think so. Every child should have an opportunity of getting education.

5729. What scheme should be adopted do you think ?—I think it should be worked partly through the Divisional Council, as being a representative body and having an organisation already formed. There might be three members chosen to assist the Divisional Council, and these together should form a committee to supervise the education of the district.

5730. *Mr. Rowan.*] Who would you have to elect the three members?—The ratepayers.

5731. *President.*] Would you have the Civil Commissioner on the Board or any other permanent member ?—It depends to a great extent upon the character of the official. If he was a man who took a great deal of interest in education and had the time, it might be a good thing. Our magistrate here has not the time, although he is a capital man. He is really unable to attend to the Divisional Council work, his time is so taken up. He did attend the meetings at first, but he found it almost impossible.

5732. Do you think the Board should elect its own chairman ?— I think under all the circumstances it would be best.

5733. Would you vest in such Board the public school property of the district ?—Yes, I think so.

5734. And the deficiency, after the Government has contributed its quota and the fees have been exhausted, should be paid out of the rates you think ?—Yes, out of the divisional rates.

5735. Would you give the Board the power of rating, or would you give them authority to instruct the Divisional Council to collect the rate, so as to simplify matters ?—I would adopt the latter course; we do not want two collectors. If possible, we ought to save expense in the machinery, and there is already an organization at hand. The Divisional Council has got its offices and so on, and the same place of meeting would answer, only on different days.

5736. Do I understand that the reason why you suggest three members should be joined with the Divisional Council is that you would then get men who might be unwilling to do duty on the Divisional Council, but would be willing to work in educational interests?—Yes; you get a different class of men.

5737. Do you think such a plan would increase the interest of parents and the community generally in the education of the district?—I think so.

5738. *Rev. Moorrees.*] Would such a Board be for the whole district?—For the whole of the Divisional Council district.

5739. Would you put all the schools under the management of this one body?— Yes; and if there is any deficiency, such body would have to find the money. If you have taxation, you must have representation.

5740. Would not the same end be attained if the Divisional Council were represented in every school committee in a district?—Then you would have two bodies and two expenses. There would have to be separate offices and a separate secretary. The secretary of the Divisional Council I think has not very much to do in most divisions. In rural districts as a rule, the men who compose the Divisional Councils are not men probably who take much interest in education, therefore you must have an educational element so to speak incorporated with the Divisional Council so as to get the interest you require. If not, I am afraid in some districts it will be a dead letter.

5741. Would not your object be gained if instead of having one body as you propose, we just had the school committees as they are at present, one portion elected by the ratepayers and one portion appointed by the Divisional Council, but let every school committee treat directly with the Divisional Council instead of having a body between them and the general body of the whole district?—Then I think the Divisional Council would say they had no responsibility, and it is a powerful body to some extent and it is to them you have to look for the means to carry on this warfare.

5742. You have wards in the Divisional Council; suppose a school is started in one of these wards, could there not be a school committee to manage the internal affairs, consisting say of two members elected by the Divisional Council voters, and the member of the Divisional Council for the division having an *ex officio* seat on the committee to guard the interests of the council as far as spending money is concerned, because you are aware doubtless that great complications sometimes arise in these outlying districts?—There is this difficulty; the member for the Divisional Council might have no interest in that ward, and only the two committee men might attend, and they could do nothing; they might probably be divided in their opinion. You must remember that the Divisional Council is not a paid body.

5743. Would not some body be required in the ward to look after internal arrangements, the school attendance, and so on?—They might form a sub-committee.

5744. Do you know as a matter of fact that a good many School Committees now in the country districts consist of three members only?—But those three members probably are interested in the object they have in view, and will attend. My experience of divisional councillors is that they are somewhat lax in their attendance; indeed I should be disqualified myself if I do not attend the next meeting, though it is no fault of my own, as I have been away in Cape Town and elsewhere. Had I been in Port Elizabeth I should have attended as punctually as any man.

5745. *President.*] Would you empower this Board to delegate its functions to volunteers or to sub-committees in various parts, so as to carry out educational objects? —If you could get two or three persons interested, who would devote their time to assisting the general body, I should have no objection.

5746. If the Board finds that there are volunteers in certain centres willing to do the work and carry on the school without any expense to the ratepayers, would you delegate to them certain functions and recommend that they receive a grant, and so attain the principal object which is the education of the people?—Yes; but they would be under the control of the central Board.

5747. The Board itself would have to find schools to the satisfaction of the Superintendent-General of Education?—Quite so.

5748. With regard to the natives, what is the best form of native education. Do not you think it ought to be more industrial than literary in its character, so as to fit them for their future avocation?—Most decidedly.

5749. If you were a member of the Board, what sort of industrial training would you suggest should be part of the education in a native school?—Wagon building, carpentering, brickmaking, and so on. We are always short of labour of that kind.

5750. Is that the case throughout the colony more or less?—I think so.

5751. Would you have spade industry also?—You might have a garden or a small model farm. I think it is a great mistake to give these people only a literary education.

5752. Do you think the same principle ought to apply to the schools for the poorer whites; would you teach the children of artisans the same industries?—We must not attempt too much.

Mr.
James Brister.

Sept. 12th, 1891.

z 2

Mr.
James Brister.

Sept. 12th, 1891

5753. If you had to formulate a rule, what line of demarcation would you make between black and white, so as to guide the managers of the schools?—That is a very difficult question. It would have to depend a great deal upon the good common sense of the schoolmaster.

5754. Would you leave it to the authorities?—I think so. I would leave it to each authority to exclude or otherwise. If there was a hard and fast rule laid down, they would not be so anxious to carry it out, but if you give them the responsibility and they want to make the school a success, they will endeavour to get over these difficulties.

5755. Suppose the parent of a coloured boy has means and is ambitious for him to get on, but the managers of a school think his presence would be detrimental, what sort of redress would you give in such a case?—I think these people might have their own collegiate institution to meet such cases. They can provide for themselves I think, and it might be a question whether the Government would assist. If they succeed in getting together a certain sum of money, I think the Government might perhaps contribute, as it is a laudable object.

5756. Would you rather wait till the occasion arises before binding the hands of the Government in any way?—Quite so.

Rev.
George Smith.

Sept. 12th, 1891.

Rev. George Smith examined.

5757. *President.*] You are Rector of St. Peter's, Port Elizabeth, I believe?—Yes.

5758. Is it a Church of England mission?—Yes.

5759. Is your school for boys or girls?—It is a mixed school.

5760. What aid do you get from the Government?—We have two schools. We get £75 a year for one and £30 a year for the other.

5761. Are they both mixed schools?—Yes.

5762. In different parts of the town?—Yes.

5763. How many children are there in the school for which you receive £75 a year?—184, and in the other 112.

5764. Are there any other Church of England mission schools here?—Yes. There is the White's Road mission school. I think they have about 200 children : at St. Paul's mission school there are about the same, and at St. John's about 150.

5765. Between 800 and 900 boys and girls altogether?—Yes.

5766. What fees do you charge at St. Peter's?—Our fees are very uncertain. They are supposed to be 3d. and 6d. a week, but there is a very large number unable to pay anything.

5767. Do you take them for nothing?—Yes.

5768. You never refuse any child?—Never.

5769. Is there a deficiency in the funds of the school in consequence?—Yes ; I have to make it up out of my own pocket.

5770. What is your salary?—I have always made it a rule to take my own salary out of the school, and with that salary I receive and my own money I make up the deficiency. I teach in the school, and I am obliged to do so, because otherwise we should not have a sufficient number of teachers.

5771. How many teachers are there in the school besides yourself?—There are myself and three others in the £75 grant school.

5772. And in the other?—Two teachers.

5773. Then yourself and five teachers are covered by the two grants of £75 and £30?—Yes.

5774. What buildings have you?—They have been built out of our own money. The £75 school has been built by ourselves altogether; for the other, a building is now being put up by one of our church people, who will give it to us at his death.

5775. Then they will both be church property?—Yes.

5776. What did it cost to put up your building?—Our actual expenses in connection with the £75 school have been £445.

5777. What is the size of the building?—There is one room 45 x 20 ; another 45 x 21, another 35 x 16, and another 25 x 18.

5778. Is that all in one school?—Yes.

5779. What space do you give to each child?—About 15 feet per child.

5780. *Dean Holmes.*] Is yours a very fluctuating school?—Yes. Sometimes we have a great many withdrawn, but this year very few indeed have been withdrawn, It fluctuates from year to year.

5781. *President.*] Is yours a satisfactory school building for the number of children actually in attendance?—There is plenty of room. Mr. Brady, so far as our buildings are concerned, is very much pleased with them.

5782. Do you think for about £500 a building could be put up to meet the wants of the poorer class of children?—It depends upon who builds it.

5783. If built by yourself?—Yes.

5784. Can you give us any suggestion to guide us with regard to other school buildings elsewhere of a similar character and constructed in the same way. Ought the amount to exceed £500 if care is taken?—I daresay it would exceed it by nearly 100 per cent.

5785. Why do you say that?—I will explain to you how I build my schools. I have eight Kafirs and one white man, and I superintend the work and explain to them exactly how to go on, and keep them straight. They are not built of brick or stone, but of concrete.

5786. Do you get concrete here?—We dig it out. If we have a piece of ground to build a school on, I dig the rock out and build a wall with it. You can get concrete almost anywhere in South Africa. I may explain that many years ago we had an old temporary building lent us, the roof was falling in, and myself and my school boys put up a school. We excavated the rock and built the walls. It took two years.

5787. Were the boys attending school?—Yes, in the afternoon.

5788. Were they day scholars?—Yes. They did the work voluntarily.

5789. Do you think the training was good for them from an educational point of view?—Yes; it was just the education they wanted.

5790. Would you encourage some system by which all the children in attendance could get more or less some such industrial training in addition to their literary teaching?—Yes.

5791. What sort of industries would you suggest; would you teach them how to construct their own schools?—Without wishing to be egotistical, I may say that that would ordinarily speaking be impossible in South Africa. You would require too much knowledge and too much influence over the boys.

5792. What other simple industries would you suggest so as to create habits of industry in the children?—I think it would be an excellent plan if the Government could take boys and apprentice them to various trades.

5793. But while they are at school, what sort of industries would you teach them?—It would be very expensive. Where there are Government workshops, boys might go there in the afternoon, and it would be a very good thing if carpenters' work could be taught in the schools. Girls I think should be taught dressmaking.

5794. Would brickmaking answer?—No; it would not do here.

5795. Would gardening work answer?—Yes, in certain cases; and tree planting. All the trees we have around St. Peter's have been put in by the boys entirely.

5796. What part of the day would you devote to industrial training?—I would begin with religious teaching, then literary instruction, and then finish off with industrial training, say for two hours. It is necessary to have the industrial training afterwards, because it makes the boys' hands shake so.

5797. Would you have a higher class of industrial training for the better class of boys?—We have not any of the better class; they are all poor.

5798. Do you think, altogether, that the character of the native children would be improved by a regular system of industrial training?—Yes; certainly.

5799. Practically, in your school the system is being carried out, is it not?—It has been so far as opportunity offered.

5800. Are the children better for it?—Infinitely. For instance, I give a prize to the boy who builds a summer house or takes care of the plants, and that sort of thing.

5801. Have you a summer-house?—I have my own, but I give the boys plants, provided they build their own summer-houses, and I encourage them in that way.

5802. You follow them out of school into their social life?—Yes.

5803. Do you think that is the best means of divorcing natives from any bad habits?—I cannot speak of natives; we have none. They are poor white and poor off-coloured children of various shades.

5804. Is it expedient to have separate schools for blacks and whites in your opinion?—I would suggest that the following course be adopted, namely, to have two schools, one for whites and the other for blacks, leaving the upper school authority the power of excluding children who may be in his opinion unfit to mix with the others and prejudicial to the interests of the school, without assigning any reason. Then the other school should be left for the residuum. In the school for which I receive the grant of £30 a year, I have Malays. I work the above system in my two schools. The school with the 184 boys is the upper school and the other is the lower class school. I built a school specially for Malays, because their moral character and their social habits are so horribly disgusting and loathsome. It is impossible for them to mix with my other children. They asked me for a Malay school, and I built them one. Then they said they did not want to be by themselves, but among the white children; but I said that was impossible.

Rev.
George Smith.

Sept. 12th, 1891.

5805. That is the school where the 112 children are now ? —Yes; mixed boys and girls, principally Malays.

5806. Are there any Kafir children there ?—No. Any child that I consider would be prejudicial to the one school I send to the other. I may say that I have a most intimate acquaintance with nearly every child at the South-End. I know their habits, their antecedents, and their homes.

5807. Virtually you are an unpaid attendance officer without compulsory powers ? —Yes, I am. I very often go out in the street and find children not going to school. I send them in, and if possible get some fees out of them, but if not, then I make it up out of my own pocket if necessary.

5808. Would you suggest that there should be some further machinery than moral suasion. Should there be some power of compulsion through the aid of a truant officer ?—I think if I could lower my fees universally there would be no need for it ; the children would come voluntarily.

5809. If you lowered the fees so as to virtually make it a free school, could the system of compulsion be applied successfully, even to those who will not come ?—I think so.

5810. Very often those who will not come are the ones you ought to bring there, are they not ?—Yes. They ought to be brought in.

5811. Sometimes the parents want the services of the children, do they not ?— Yes, it would be a very excellent thing if children were forbidden to work under a certain age.

5812. What age would you fix ?—Twelve or thirteen if possible. They are very often taken away from school just when they are beginning to learn. A large number of boys and girls, nine or ten years old, go out to work.

5813. Where would you begin your school age ?—I would not care to begin with children under five. It is a great mistake to send them younger than that.

5814. From five to twelve you would compel all children to attend, would you not ?—Yes. If needful, the age might be extended to fourteen. I would suggest that a boy should not be permitted to go out to work under fourteen, unless he has passed the third standard.

5815. If he has passed the third standard at twelve, he might go out to work ?— Yes.

5816. *Mr. Rowan.*] Are you in favour of a labour certificate, that is to say, give a child a certificate that he has passed the third standard ?—Yes, but not before twelve years of age.

5817. *President.*] Would you make that universal throughout the colony ?—There would be a difficulty in enforcing it in many portions, but I would certainly do so in towns.

5818. Would you limit it to towns ?—I think it would be advisable to begin with the larger towns and extend it.

5819. *Dean Holmes.*] Have you considered Sir Langham Dale's proposition of fourth class public undenominational schools ?—I may say that the Rector of the Grey Institute, Mr. Noaks and myself, have had a good deal of conversation about that. I went to him and said I was perfectly ready to come under that system, provided I had some guarantee that our present independence could be maintained. Nearly all the mission schools belonging to the Church of England in South Africa are the property of the See, and therefore it would be impossible for any undenominational Board to occupy them except at the pleasure of our own tenure; they would not be able to have complete control of the buildings, and moreover, we should need some guarantee that our present religious instruction would not be interfered with, because if we could not give religious instruction, it is no use ; we might shut the schools at once. We talked it over, but Mr. Noaks could not see any way out of the difficulty.

5820. Has the conscience clause been put in force in your school ?—I have had one or two instances, not more, where parents have asked to have their children excused. We have had all denominations. I go to the parents and tell them that we have catechism and religious instruction in the Bible for an hour every day, and I ask them if they have any objection to their children receiving that instruction. I talk the matter over and endeavour to persuade them, if possible, but if the parent has any objection there is an end to the matter. We take the child and give it other work to do in another room while the religious instruction is going on. The plan pursued in some schools, as I have heard, of placing, say, Roman Catholic children on one side of the school and the other children on the other side while religious instruction is going on is not fair. I give a boy or girl some other work to do in another room while the others receive religious instruction. I think they should be entirely separate.

5821. It has been suggested that there should be a School Board for a district or town ; would you have any objection as far as you are personally concerned to bring your school under such a Board?—It depends entirely upon the composition of the Board and its power. The position, I take it, is this, we are willing to spend certain money on our schools and to submit to any test or any inspection that the Government may choose to put upon us, but we do not want to be interfered with in our religious instruction in any way.

5822. Would you like to come under some system by which, if there was a deficiency in your school revenue, it could be made good?—No. I would rather deal with the Government direct.

5823. *President.*] Suppose a Board is brought into existence more or less representative of the people, and the Government allows all existing institutions to receive the aid which they now do as long as they fulfil the conditions upon which the aid is given, but it imposes upon the Board the duty of filling up all the gaps, either by aiding existing institutions or starting others where they are of opinion that the existing institutions are not altogether the best form of meeting the deficiency, giving the Board also the power to do any future work through volunteers as at present, the Government in that case contributing upon a more liberal scale than they do now, do you think such a system would be acceptable to you, your property in land and buildings remaining as now but you being subject to inspection and examination?—I would prefer remaining as I am.

5824. Suppose the Board had the power to help you without disturbing your organization?—It might be an advantage from a financial point of view.

5825. *Rev. Moorrees.*] Which would you prefer, getting greater aid from the Superintendent-General of Education or from such a Board?—From the Superintendent-General of Education.

5826. *President.*] Are not the local wants of the people better ascertained by such a Board than by the Superintendent-General of Education?—I think when the Inspector comes round from time to time he is quite capable of judging.

5827. Suppose he does not come at all; he is not always here to be approached by the people in regard to their needs, is he?—He is here every year.

5828. Do you think that is enough?—He generally spends a month in Port Elizabeth.

5829. *Rev. Moorrees.*] You think that such an inspector would be a more impartial judge than a local body which might perhaps be divided by party feeling?—Yes; and I should be very much afraid of party feeling arising.

5830. *President.*] In what way could it prejudice you if your existence is not dependent upon the Board?—There is nothing to prevent the Board in course of time advocating most strongly entirely undenominational education.

5831. But they cannot destroy you if you go upon your present lines, can they? —We have a very large school at South-end, and the Grey Institute also spends a large sum on a school there, but they do not offer to use us in any way at all. They simply wanted to extend the Grey Institute there and get a good many children, and so do we.

5832. What is your idea about the Board School system?—Knowing Port Elizabeth intimately as I do, I have no hesitation in saying that I would far rather deal with the Department of Education direct, and I should prefer the scheme of fourth class public undenominational schools, dealing direct with Cape Town, to the formation of a Board for Port Elizabeth. I have been brought into close contact with the business men and town councillors of this town, and I do not consider that any control exercised by them would be more beneficial to the cause of education than that at present exercised from Cape Town through the Deputy Inspector.

5833. *Dean Holmes.*] Have you given any consideration to the subject of night schools?—I have had a great deal to do with and I have spent a great deal of money on them, but I find they are very difficult indeed to work.

5834. What are the practical difficulties?—I find a room, lights, and everything, but there does not seem to be any ambition among the boys. When once they go to work they seem to drop everything.

5835. *Dr. Berry.*] Do you speak with reference to Port Elizabeth?—Yes. I cannot get any ambition into the boys.

5836. *President.*] What stimulus have you tried to induce them to attend?—I have had meetings, and got a piano, and chess, draughts and so on, and done everything I could to get them to attend. I have had as many as 45 boys in the night school. It lasted four or five months, and then dropped off. Then I started it again after that, and 30 or 40 boys came, but it again dropped off.

5837. *Dean Holmes.*] How would it be to have it only for three months in the year?—I have done that, but there is great difficulty in keeping it up even for three months in winter. It will start well, that is all. Then there is another thing. I have a schoolmistress who is a professed dressmaker, and I should be quite willing to set

Rev. George Smith.

Sept. 12th, 1891.

Rev.
George Smith.

Sept. 12th, 1891.

apart certain hours in the week to teach girls dressmaking, which is very needful I think : mine is nearly the only school in Port Elizabeth where girls are compelled to learn plain sewing, not fancy work. You will sometimes go into a school and find a girl doing crochet work or crewel work, while her dress is in rags.

5838. *President.*] That sort of work you do not encourage ?—No. As regards standards of attainments, a great many boys pass the fourth standard and then go to work. I would like to suggest by the way that practice should be put before vulgar fractions. I make a great point of that.

5839. Why ?—If a boy goes into an office, he can apply his knowledge of practice at once. A boy has perhaps a large invoice to work out, and he does it by multiplication. When asked whether he does not know practice, he very often has to say no, although he has passed the fourth standard. I rarely pass a boy in the fourth standard, because I make them all learn practice, and practice comes in the fifth standard. It is very easy to teach.

5840. Do you think Government could hold out any inducement to encourage night schools, which you cannot do for want of means ?—I do not see what they can do. I have thought it over many times. What I would suggest is this, that Government might increase the grant to mission schools, and we could then lower our fees, and thereby increase our efficiency.

5841. And render night schools unnecessary ?—Practically so.

5842. What would you recommend ought to be the system upon which the Government should proceed ?—They might do what is done at home, give so much per head on the average attendance.

5843. What ought Government to give, do you think ?—Our school grant amounts to £75 a year, and our fees I think amounted to £261 15s. 7d. last year, for 426 children.

5844. Would £1 a head do ?—Yes ; then we could lower our fees to a penny for infants, threepence up to the second standard, and sixpence above that. We could do very well then.

5845. Could that be applied throughout the colony ?—Yes.

5846. Would you apply it to blacks as well as whites ?—I do not know anything about actual mission work. I am not in a position to say.

5847. Suppose you got £1 a head from Government, you would not want any aid for buildings, would you ?—No.

Cookhouse, Monday, September 14th, 1891.

PRESENT:

Sir J. D. BARRY (President),

Dr. Berry, | Dean Holmes.

Mr. H. Veary examined.

Mr.
H. Veary.

Sept. 14th, 1891.

5848. *President.*] You are stationmaster at Cookhouse ?—Yes.

5849. Is there a school here ?—Yes. I am chairman.

5850. Is it a Government school ?—Yes ; we got a grant of £30 a year under the circular issued by the Railway Department in May, 1890.

5851. How many children are there ?—The average number is 31, mixed boys and girls.

5852. How many teachers have you ?—Only one.

5853. Do any coloured children attend ?—No.

5854. What are the fees ?—Two shillings a month per child.

5855. Does the school give satisfaction ?—Yes ; every satisfaction.

5856. How far is the school supposed to reach each side of the line ?—Twenty miles each way. Children are brought to school daily by train.

5857. Do any farmers' children avail themselves of the school ?—None at present.

5858. Are they likely to do so ?—I do not think so.

5859. Do any village children come ?—Some of the children about the station do.

5860. Is there anything further you can suggest that might be done in the way of education ?—I do not think anything more can be done; we are getting on very nicely.

5861. How long has the school been in existence ?—About four years.

5862. Has it always given satisfaction from the first and worked well, or has it lately improved ?—It has improved lately since the present teacher has come.

5863. *Dean Holmes.*] Is the teacher certificated ?—I cannot say whether she is or not. She has good testimonials.

5864. *President.*] What do the parents get in the way of wages as a rule ?—I believe a ganger gets from 7s. to 10s. a day.

Mr.
H. Veary.

Sept. 14th, 1891.

5865. Are they all gangers' children at the school ?—Gangers and second men. The second men get 5s. 6d. a day.

5866. Among the gangers are there any who have daughters who would be better for being sent away from home to a boarding school for a time ?—I could not say.

5867. *Dr. Berry.*] Do you think the railway children are exposed to any bad influences about here at all ?—None whatever.

5868. What ages are the children mostly in the school ?—They range from four to ten or eleven.

5869. *Dean Holmes.*] Does the railway department provide the schoolroom ?—Yes.

5870. And a house for the teacher ?—Yes.

5871. *President.*] Is there any industrial training given ?—No ; it is just ordinary third class school teaching.

5872. *Dr. Berry.*] Do your trains suit very well for bringing the children to school and taking them back ?—Very well.

5873. Is that why the school is such a success ?—No doubt.

5874. Is there any difficulty in getting the children up and down the line ?—None whatever. They are granted free passes once a month.

5875. Do they travel without any protector ?—Yes ; the guard of the train keeps au eye on them.

5876. *Dean Holmes.*] And you look after them when they arrive ?—Yes.

5877. *Dr. Berry.*] Do you think anything can be done by set up a boarding school here for the children ?—I daresay something could be done.

5878. *President.*] Would anybody here undertake it ?—I cannot say. The old hotel building might be used for the purpose perhaps, but I think the Government have that in view for some other purpose.

5879. Do the children come by goods train ?—Yes.

5880. How far is Cradock from here ?—Fifty-five miles.

5881. Is the school at Alicedale working well ?—Yes, I believe so.

5882. Have they a good teacher ?—Yes.

Richard T. Pearce examined.

Richard T. Pearce.

Sept. 14th, 1891.

5883. *Dr. Berry.*] What are you ?—A ganger.

5884. How long have you been here ?—Over two years.

5885. Have you any children ?—Yes ; three go the station school here.

5886. Are you satisfied with it ?—Yes, quite so. There is another ganger here who has children going to school.

5887. Are the fees too high ?—They are plenty high enough for the wages we are getting.

5888. How much do you pay ?—Sixpence for each child. It is not so much the fees, but food and clothing have to be provided, which is as much as a poor man can do.

5889. *Dean Holmes.*] Do you know any of the men about here who would like to send their children to boarding school where they could get a good education away from home, suppose the Government made a liberal grant to meet the case ?—My children are all small, and I would sooner see them all round the table.

5890. *Dr. Berry.*] Is that the general feeling, do you think, to keep the children at home ?—The children are all small here. I do not suppose the oldest child going to school is more than fourteen.

5891. Then £1 5s. or £1 10s. a year is as much as you can afford to pay for the education of a child ?—Yes.

5892. Would £6 a year be out of your reach if it included the boarding of such child ?—I think so. It would mean that you would have to get a lot of clothes for the children if they were sent to boarding school. I would like to give them a good education, but I think they are rather too young to be sent away from their mother.

5893. How do the children manage who come here to school from up the line ?—They bring some food with them.

5894. Do you think there is any need for starting a boarding school at Cookhouse for the children ?—No.

5895. They just stay in the school while they are here and go home in the evening ?—Yes, they get their breakfast at home, bring their dinner with them, and get home in the evening for their tea.

5896. *Dean Holmes.*] Do the trains suit ?—Yes.

5897. *Dr. Berry.*] Is there no danger about these children travelling alone ?—No.

5898. Do you think there are any bad influences for young children about here ? I do not think so.

5899. Are there any native children about ?—Yes ; along the line.

AA

Richard T. Pearce.

Sept. 14th, 1891.

5900. Is anything being done for their education?—I do not know. There is a large location in the neighbourhood.

5901. Do the men who work along the line live in the location?—No; they live by the cottages. Kafirs come from their country for two or three months and go back again when they have saved a little money.

5902. Have you been at any other place in the railway service?—Yes; at Naauwpoort and Commadagga.

5903. Are there facilities there for schooling as good as they are here?—There is no school at Commadagga Station. There was a Dutch school about a mile and a half from the station when I was there. There is a school at Middleton.

5904. Is there a school at Naauwpoort?—Yes; a good school.

5905. Do any of the gangers' children go to farm schools?—I do not think so.

Somerset East, Monday, September 14th, 1891.

PRESENT:

Sir J. D. BARRY (President),

Dean Holmes, | Dr. Berry.

Professor Robert MacWilliam examined.

Professor Robert Mac-William.

Sept. 14th, 1891.

5906. *President.*] I believe you are principal of the Gill College here?—Yes.

5907. How long have you been so?—Nearly eleven years.

5908. Where were you engaged before that?—I was English lecturer in the Church of Scotland training college at Aberdeen.

5909. Do you know the Scotch system of education thoroughly?—Yes. I was connected with it from fourteen years of age as pupil teacher and head master, and Training College lecturer.

5910. Have you anything to say on the subject of irregularity of attendance?—I do not think I have anything to add to the reply I have sent in to the printed circular. As it is, the attendance is not so irregular that it could be very well improved.

5911. *Dean Holmes.*] What is the percentage of attendance to the number on the roll?—It is very large as a rule at the Gill College, from 90 to 95 per cent. I should say.

5912. *President.*] Do you know the compulsory system that exists in Scotland?—Yes.

5913. And in England?—Yes.

5914. Are you in favour of School Boards?—Yes.

5915. If a School Board comes into existence, would you give such Board the power to request the Government to bring the compulsory system into operation in such areas as it indicated?—I do not think that would be possible or advisable, inasmuch as it would tend to keep the rural population outside that area for fear of compulsion.

5916. Would it not be well to apply the system in towns, and then if it works, extend it to the country?—How would you draw the line between white and black?

5917. Is not there a practical line drawn now; do not the black children generally attend one class of mission school and the whites another?—In the Eastern Province they do, but so far as I understand, in the Western Province, it is much more difficult to draw the line than it is here.

5918. Would you exclude the blacks altogether from the privilege of being educated?—Not at all.

5919. Then why not include them under such a system of education in towns?—I should certainly be in favour of making provision for their education.

5920. If there is provision both for whites and blacks, would you give the Board power to request the application of the compulsory system in certain areas?—I do not think I should recommend such a strong measure as that to begin with. If the Board gets the authority, it brings compulsion to bear on the parents. I am looking at it from a parent's point of view.

5921. What harm would it be to the parents?—It would tend to keep the parents outside the area. They would stay in the country and not in the town. A man will often do willingly what he will refuse to do under compulsion, especially the farmers. Farmers will often come into town with their families in order to have their children educated.

5922. But the compulsory clause would not touch them, would it?—If the law were compulsory, they would not come into town.

5923. From your knowledge, has compulsion had that effect elsewhere?—It has had a very bad effect in Scotland.

5924. In what way?—With regard to the public estimate of education. Formerly even poor parents made every possible effort to educate their children, and they looked upon it as a duty; now that it is a matter of compulsion, they kick against it, and take their children away as soon as they have complied with the conditions. I could see that before I left.

5925. What have they to do in order to comply with the conditions?—A child must be educated up to I think the fourth standard. After the age of thirteen, practically, parents withdraw their children from school in Scotland. I do not say they all do, but specially that class which compulsion is intended to effect.

5926. Before the compulsory clause came into effect, did these people send their children to school?—In almost every case, in the country districts.

5927. You mean to say that in Scotland, compulsion has had the effect of getting fewer children to school than before, in proportion to the population?—In the country districts at any rate they stay a shorter time.

5928. Compulsion is found to work well in England, is it not?—Because in the rural districts of England, the state of education was very much behind what it was in the corresponding districts of Scotland.

5929. Then where education is backward, it is a good thing to have compulsion?—Yes. The poorer working classes in the large towns especially were very imperfectly educated; the old parochial system had completely broken down.

5930. Then do I understand you to say that in towns, where the attendance is irregular of children who ought to be on the roll, it would be a good thing to have some system of compulsion?—I do not say absolute compulsion, but there should be some means of bringing pressure to bear.

5931. Would you be in favour of an attendance officer whose duty it should be to visit the houses of parents whose children did not attend school?—It depends very largely upon the kind of officer appointed. If he were a sensible man it might have a very good effect.

5932. Do you think it would be wise to have a truancy officer for children found about the streets during school hours, he taking them to some school to be provided?—At present that is impossible.

5933. Why?—You cannot compel a child to go to school where possibly no Government school exists.

5934. But suppose schools are brought into existence for the purpose of receiving these waifs and strays and giving them an elementary education, either voluntary or Government schools?—It would certainly be very much to the interest of the children; but at present I could not recommend an absolute compulsory clause. I think a Permissive Compulsory Act might answer.

5935. Can you suggest any improvement on the present system of managers. You say in your reply that it would be better to have the whole Board properly elected, but that such a plan would require some effective check to prevent extravagance. If a School Board consisting of five members was constituted, two elected by the ratepayers, two nominated by the Divisional Council, and one appointed by the Government, would such a Board be more likely to check extravagance than one elected directly by the ratepayers?—No, I do not think so. To some extent the nomination of members by the Divisional Council might answer, but the question arises, is it advisable to have such members. A School Board exists for educational purposes, and we know that members of Divisional Councils are in many cases about the last possible persons one could wish to see in charge of education.

5936. What check upon extravagance would you suggest?—All expenditure should require the sanction of the Education Department before it is embarked upon. I mean expenditure on school buildings and so on. Very often in the case of a public Board, if they can trust to getting money on the £ for £ principle, they will make a special effort to raise their quota so as to get the benefit of the other, and in that way they might go beyond what the central Government cared to spend.

5937. What you wish is, that no expenditure undertaken unless with the sanction of the central Government?—Yes; practically it comes to that. The only thing is, if they persist in carrying out anything the central Government refuses to give a corresponding grant for, it must be done entirely at local expense.

5938. How would you protect the interests of teachers?—I believe the educational system will never be satisfactory until the consent of the Superintendent-General of Education, or whatever Government official represents that officer, is required for all dismissals as well as for all appointments of teachers. I would rather perhaps put it this way: in order to avoid friction, in the case of all head teachers in schools, the consent of the Superintendent-General of Education or any other Government official representing him should be required for dismissal as well as for appointment, and in the case of assistant teachers, the consent of the head teacher in the school should be required in the same way.

Professor
Robert Mac-
William,
—
Sept. 14th, 1891.

5939. *Dr Berry.*]. You mean to say that the Board should have no power to elect an assistant teacher without the consent of the head master?—I think it very inadvisable.

5940. *President.*] Nor the power to dismiss?—No.

5941. Would it not be better to give the power to dismiss provisionally, subject to an appeal to the central Government, whose refusal to endorse it should be final?—No; it is much better the other way. The School Board, if they know they have to give reasons, will hesitate about what they do. If there is real ground of incompetence, the teacher can be dismissed all the same. The mischief done to education by the arbitrary power of School Boards is much greater than what would be done the other way.

5942. Are you against the present system of guarantors?—Yes, entirely.

5943. What do you consider are its evils?—It throws the whole burden upon a small number of people, and very often on those who are least able to bear it. The guarantors are generally the most intelligent people, but not the wealthiest.

5944. Do denominational influences creep in at the same time?—They would creep in in any case, whether the Board was elected or otherwise. Then again, another evil is, that the schools are not continuous.

5945. Do you think a School Board elected in the way you suggest, would make the whole district interested in education?—I think so, and it would have a good effect. At present, at the end of three years, the school committee ceases to exist, and there is a general complaint that it is difficult to get young men to become teachers, the reason being that there is no continuity of office. If they become unpopular from any cause, no matter whether it is connected with educational work or otherwise, they do not need to be dismissed; the school lapses, and they are thrown on the world, possibly some of them married men with a family.

5946. Would you vest all undenominational school property in this Board?—Yes.

5947. Would you have any Government element on the Board at all, a Government nominee?—No. I think the Government would be sufficiently represented by the control I have suggested of the Superintendent-General of Education. I have generally found that with a Board consisting partly of elected members and partly of nominees, there seems to be a natural antipathy between the two, which leads to bad results.

5948. You would neither have a Government nor a Divisional Council nominee on the Board, but make it wholly elective?—Yes.

5949. *Dean Holmes.*] What would you make the franchise?—The usual Parliamentary or Divisional Council franchise.

5950. One is lower than the other?—I should prefer the higher.

5951. *President.*] And you would have a Board for the whole electoral district?—Yes. If you had a wholly elected Board, it might perhaps be necessary to have local representation to make sure that the country districts had an opportunity of bringing their wants before the central Board. It might be necessary almost to have the Board elected with some reference to field-cornetcies.

5952. Would you be in favour of a cumulative vote, so as to have minorities represented?—No. I should be in favour of the electorate being divided into wards. Each field-cornetcy should elect one representative for the Board, but it would be a matter of arrangement as to how this could best be done. I think the cumulative vote misrepresents the electorate as a rule. The only cumulative vote I would have would be this—If there were six or seven members to be elected, I would not compel a voter to give all his seven votes, he may give only one vote if he likes.

5953. Would you have the wards divided in proportion to population?—I would suggest the field-cornetcies as the most convenient arrangement at present. As far as possible the population should be represented.

5954. *Dr. Berry.*] Would you give the Board any control over the course of study in the school?—I do not think it is possible with any Government system; you have the curriculum laid down from head-quarters. So far as the optional subjects are concerned, outside the Government minimum, of course the Board would necessarily have the control. Practically they would have the whole power outside the Government requirements, and they could make whatever arrangements they liked. If it was a question involving the expenditure of money, it would depend upon whether the Government agreed with them or not.

5955. *President.*] If such a Board were brought into existence, what power would you give it over the education in a district. Would you bring all the undenominational schools under such Board?—Necessarily.

5956. And also the mission schools for whites and black?—That I do not know. I think it is very greatly to be desired that mission schools should all come under the power of the general School Board also, but I am not at all sure that it would be possible to bring that about at any rate for some time.

Professor
Robert Mac-
William.

Sept. 14th, 1891.

5957. *Dean Holmes.*] Would you allow them to come under, provided they retained their own managers?—I do not see any serious objection to it. There are, I know, difficulties which might arise.

5958. You know that nearly all the schools in the colony are denominational as a matter of fact; the managers have virtually the power to order what religion shall be taught in school?—As a matter of fact they do not often excercise that power.

5959. Suppose for instance, the preponderance of managers in any school were members of the Dutch Reformed Church, they could have that form of religion taught in the school, could they not?—Yes, certainly.

5960. And the same with Wesleyans?—Yes.

5961. Therefore in a sense they are denominational, are they not?—Yes; outside the conscience clause.

5962. *President.*] If these Boards are elected, do you see any objection to make use of these denominational agencies where they exist?—The question is, what would happen in the case of rating.

5963. Would you apply the rates to their assistance?—I do not see any reason against it, if the popularly elected Board consents, but before allowing any grant to be given to denominational schools, one purely undenominational school should be an absolute necessity in each division under the new system.

5964. *Dean Holmes.*] Would you not prefer to substitute the word secular for undenominational?—Not at all, but I should prefer leaving out the word undenominational and simply call them " public schools," which would more accurately describe the fact.

5965. *Dr. Berry.*] Do you mean to say that you would give grants from the local rates in aid of voluntary schools?—Yes. It would come to that if the Board agrees to take over a denominational school. It should lie between the local Board and the local managers of the denominatioual school as to whether they could make such arrangements as both could agree to.

5966. You would allow the local rates to be used for that purpose, without local control?—There would be local control if such an arrangement were carried out. The present managers of the denominational schools would practically be a sub-committee of the elected Board.

5967. Would you have the same arrangement as to the appointment and dismissal of teachers in the denominational schools under the local Board as the other?—I look upon the ideal system as doing away altogether with denominational schools.

5968. *Dean Holmes.*] You would accept the existing state of affairs and try to work it into something better, until something more perfect is attained?—Yes. In order to avoid the undenominational schools being swamped altogether, I would insist upon each School Board having at least one such school.

5969. *President.*] With regard to the blacks, how would you deal with them under this system?—I think the white School Board should at present have charge of all the education of the blacks. You cannot have a separate School Board for the blacks.

5970. What sort of education would you impart to the blacks?—I should like to see industrial education much more largely developed.

5971. Would you leave the blacks under the agency of the mission schools?—At present I do not see that anything else can be done.

5972. But you would as far as possible have an industrial department in every native school?—As far as possible I would; but I doubt whether it would be possible at present.

5973. Why?—The population is far too much scattered, and the cost of maintaining anything like an efficient industrial department would be pretty large.

5974. In towns, where you have native schools, would you not apply the system, and could not spade labour and gardening be taught?—Yes, garden labour is a good thing, but the great difficulty in regard to this matter is the splitting up caused by the different sects. In the location here you have three mission schools. I think one industrial department ought to do for the three; but I question whether it would be allowed to.

5975. Could one industrial department be brought into existence to serve all three through a Board without friction. Is there any reason why there should be friction at all?—If they could agree to abolish two of the schools, it would be much more effective.

5976. *Dean Holmes.*] You mean to say there are three weak schools which might be made one good one?—Yes.

5977. *Dr. Berry.*] Would you leave the local Board to deal with that question of shutting up the two schools and strengthening the other?—The local Board would not have the power to shut up any mission school, but the right to accept it as a school receiving a Government grant.

192

Professor
Robert Mac-
Williams.
———
Sept. 14th, 1891.

5978. *President.*] You would not have a breach of contract with existing schools, but allow them to go on, and if the Board chooses to recommend any of the schools, you would give them a slight benefit?—Yes, certainly. The only question is, how long that engagement necessarily lasts before such a contract is binding on future elected Boards. That, I am afraid, might in some cases lead to friction.

5979. *Dr. Berry.*] Do you know much about the location here?—Not a great deal.

5980. Are the natives who live there able to pay a school tax to help support their own schools?—I think they pay a considerable sum as it is in support of the mission schools. They are all mission schools in connection with the churches, and I have reason to believe that they subscribe very handsomely.

5981. The complaint is often made that it is the willing ones who are made to contribute, and that a lot of people cannot be got to contribute in any way, or pay the fees for their children. Would it be possible, as far as you know of the location, to impose a small tax on each householder or each hut to keep the thing going?—I think it should be done.

5982. *President.*] And then making it a free school virtually for the natives?—I would tax them as well as make the fees. I would have the fees low, and have a general tax for any deficiency.

5983. *Dr. Berry.*] Would you let the Municipal Council collect the tax and hand it over to the Board?—In every case the School Board would collect the tax through either the municipality or the Divisional Council. The Board would not have power to levy the tax itself. It would be a matter of arrangement whether you confined the school rate to the Divisional Council, or whether you divided it *pro rata* between the Divisional Council and the Municipality.

5984. What contributions do you think should be expected from local bodies, such as Divisional Councils and Municipalities, in support of schools and for the erection of buildings. Suppose a Board recommends to the Government a voluntary body such as a mission school, and the Government contributes, what should such contribution be?—In every case half the expenditure should be paid by the central Government up to a certain amount.

5985. Would it not be better to fix a certain sum?—I do not think so, because the population is so unequally distributed. The cost of maintaining a good teacher for a school of thirty or forty children is just as much, or nearly as much, as for a school of 100 children.

5986. *President.*] Would you limit the sum to a certain sum per head?—I would deal equally all round.

5987. You would find out what the expenditure was, and contribute half, subject to the condition that all expenditure is submitted to the central Government?—Yes.

5988. And you would make the rates liable for any deficiency?—Yes. That involves that the elected School Board of the division has first the power of saying whether it will accept these voluntary schools or not.

5989. *Dean Holmes.*] Seeing the dislike there is to direct taxation in this country, how would it be for the deficiency to be made good by a moiety being paid by the Government and a moiety by the taxpayers, letting the Government grant stand as it is. Would that make it more palatable?—I do not think so. It is not the amount of the tax. I have known men who would utterly refuse to pay 5s. who would give voluntarily £5, simply because they could do it of their own free will. It is the principle of the thing, not the amount.

5990. *President.*] What would be the amount of the contribution to school buildings if volunteers were accepted or recommended by the local board?—If the thing were to start afresh, I think the £ for £ principle would work all round.

5991. Where a volunteer body has its own property, would you expect it to give up that property absolutely for school purposes?—I think it would be wise if they did.

5992. Suppose they refused?—If they retained the ownership of the buildings, I do not see that they can expect the grant. The grant they could get then would only be for the annual expenditure for carrying on the work.

5993. If you elect a Board for school purposes, how would you enable them to collect the rates for the amount of any deficiency. Should they levy a rate themselves, or send a precept to the Divisional Council?—To the Divisional Council or the Municipality, as the case may be. It is desirable not to multiply rating powers. If possible, the rate should be all got through the Divisional Council.

5994. *Dr. Berry.*] In the case of any large towns, would you separate the Municipal area from the Divisional Council area for school purposes?—I am afraid that in some cases it would be necessary.

5995. In such cases would you give the Municipality rating power?—Yes; if it was considered necessary to separate the Municipality.

Professor
Robert Mac-
William

Sept. 14th, 1891

5996. *President.*] To whom would you give the power to separate it?—In some cases it might be advisable to have a Board for the town and a Board for the country, but the more they are brought together, the better for the country, not only educationally, but otherwise.

5997. Do you think such a Board would be more likely to meet the wants of children in agricultural districts than the present system?—I think so.

5998. Local wants would become better known to the Board, would they not?—Yes, necessarily so.

5999. So there would be two agencies at work, the Board and the central Government. Would you give the central Government the power, if the Board neglects its duty, of finding sufficient accommodation, to step in and find it at the expense of the Board?—Certainly, that is necessarily involved.

6000. *Dean Holmes.*] Do you mean to the extent of compelling them to build at the cost of the rates?—Yes, a minimum of one school to begin with.

6001. *President.*] Is not one defect in the present system the lack of power to fill up any gap where it exists; there is no such duty imposed on any one, is there?—That is a great defect in the present system. There is no duty imposed on any body to start a school or keep it going. That is the chief want.

6002. With regard to the wants of the agricultural population, do you think the present farm school system is altogether adequate?—It is a very great improvement on anything we have had before.

6003. Do you think the farmers fully understand what the facilities within their reach are, and how they can get their wants supplied?—I think they are getting to understand it. I think doubling the grant for uncertificated teachers has been a most mischievous thing. The objection I have to the present system of grants to teachers in country schools is, that while formerly £1 was given to uncertificated teachers and £2 to certificated teachers, now £2 is given to uncertificated teachers and only £3 to certificated teachers. The difference between the two is made less than it was before.

6004. You think it ought to be the other way on?—Yes; and the uncertificated teachers should not be encouraged in any way.

6005. Are they not encouraged because of the want of a sufficient number of certificated teachers?—I think there is a very considerable number at present, but they are not so well utilized as they might be. I think it is advisable to have a better and more extended system of training teachers; one normal school is not sufficient.

6006. Would you have a normal school in other centres besides Cape Town?—There should be at least one other in the Eastern Province, and they should be under Government and not under one of the churches.

6007. In Cape Town is the normal school under a church?—Yes, practically so.

6008. Where would you start such a school in the Eastern Province?—At Graham's Town, perhaps. I think the system that Sir Langham Dale suggested last year might be utilized, namely, the addition to three or four of the largest and most important schools of a class for training teachers, with additional teachers paid by Government. Sir Langham Dale offered to make some arrangement in connection with the Gill College last year.

6009. Are you aware as a matter of fact, that teachers are trained, but they go off to the Transvaal and the Free State?—Yes.

6010. How would you stop that?—By offering better salaries in the colony and improving the position of teachers. You will always get teachers to work for less if you have anything like fixity of tenure.

6011. *Dean Holmes.*] You would not give absolute fixity of tenure, would you?—No; but reasonable fixity.

6012. *Dr. Berry.*] Would you be in favour of delegating the functions of the Board in any way to local committees?—In the abstract not, but under the existing circumstances of the country, I do not see anything else that can be done. It might be the most satisfactory way out of the difficulty, provided it is made compulsory for them to have one school directly under themselves, one purely public school.

6013. Suppose a school was set up in a field-cornetcy, would you have a sub-committee in that field-cornetcy?—I do not see any reason why, if it is found convenient, a School Board should not have the power to nominate a local committee to keep up the buildings and so on, but they would have no status from a Government point of view.

6014. *President.*] Do you know anything of the circuit school system?—Very little.

6015. Do you think anything further should be done to meet the wants of the agricultural population?—The present facilities should have more time to develope. I think nothing more should be done at present.

Professor
Robert Mac-
William.

Sept. 14th, 1891.

6016. *Dr. Berry.*] Are you in favour of the local Board having its own inspector? – No.

6017. Are you in favour of increasing the present number of Government inspectors? —I think it would be advisable, as the schools are increasing in number.

6018. Do you like the system of the headmaster of a public school going out to inspect farm schools?—I think it is advisable. I inspect all the farm schools in this division.

6019. *Dean Holmes.*] What is your objection to the Board having its own inspector to visit the schools much more frequently than the Government Inspector can visit them?—It means a new head master with no responsibility, and knowing nothing whatever of the circumstances of the school. If there is to be any combined inspection, it should be done by the head master of the principal school. You utilize his experience.

6020. What is your objection to the system of having Board inspectors?—Inspection is a necessary evil, but it is an evil, and therefore the less of it the better.

6021. Would you like to adopt the German system of having a number of sub-inspectors to go and pay surprise visits to the schools, men who have been themselves teachers?—I do not believe it works well where it is tried.

6022. Have you had any experience of the German system?—Not practically. I have been through some of the German schools.

6023. Do you know the system?—Partially. I have once or twice been subject to surprise visits. The inspector thought it his duty just to walk into the school without knocking at the door. It was a surprise, but generally speaking, when teachers are subject to that sort of thing, they organize a code of signals, and they are all on the look out in the district beforehand.

6024. Can you suggest any way whereby fuller use can be made of the opportunities afforded for education?—You have got an expensive system of education in the colony, largely supported by Government, and young people are induced to go forward to higher education, but when they pass the University examinations it is no value to them, from the point of view of making a living afterwards.

6025. What would you do?—I think that for all admissions to the Civil Service, at least the Matriculation examination should be made compulsory.

6026. You think that no one who has not matriculated should enter the Civil Service?—I think so, and I look forward to the time when every magistrate should be an LL.B. At present a young man who has a friend in the service can manage to scrape through, but I would insist upon the University standard for those entering the Civil Service.

6027. Are there any night schools here?—No. I should like to see them organized, but practically we have had no time to do it with our pressure of work.

6028. It has been said that night schools when they are started, go on fairly for about three months in the year, during winter, but the moment that summer comes on, the attendance drops off, is that so?—I think they should be dropped. I do not think it is possible to carry them on all through the year.

6029. Would you have them for children who have not been taught, or more as continuation schools?—It would depend largely upon the circumstances of the district.

6030. What would be the case here?—Here it would benefit those who have been partially taught.

6031. Would you teach scientific subjects?—That would be very desirable, and I should like to see the University local examinations extended, so that there should be something to test the knowledge acquired,—something like the Science and Arts department system in England.

6032. *President.*] Where would the examining body be?—It should be in connection with the University.

6033. *Dean Holmes*] Should any grant be given by the Government do you think?—I think so.

6034. On any defined principle?—I do not know of any principle except a capitation grant or a pass grant.

6035. You think the school should be open so many nights and so many attendances made, and the inspector must be satisfied, and then the capitation grant might be issued by Government?—I do not see any other way.

6036. *Dr. Berry.*] How would you propose to pay the science lecturers?—A great many persons at home do it for the love of the thing. In the Science and Arts department in England, the payment depends upon the number of passes, but that is not entirely satisfactory. Here I suppose you would have to utilize the existing staff of the public schools in the case of teachers who have time and knowledge enough to undertake the work.

Profe-sor
Robert Mac-
William.

Sept. 14th, 1891.

6037. Would you be in favour of giving a grant for the necessary apparatus ?—I think it would be necessary.

6038. You would not limit these lectures to boys getting ordinary teaching would you ?—No They would be specially for those outside that.

6039. *President.*] Have you an agricultural school here ?—Yes.

6040. Has it answered well ?—I think so. I believe the success here has been due to the literary and agricultural instruction being in the same building, and to the harmony existing between the two. They are not under the same management, but we always try to suit each other, so as to interfere as little as possible with the classes, and that boys may attend the agricultural classes in addition to their ordinary work.

6041. Do the two things fit in ?—To some extent it interferes, but we endeavour to minimise it as far as possible.

6042. At what age can boys, without injury to themselves, take up in addition to their literary education, the agricultural instruction ?—I should not like to say definitely. At present we are experimenting. They are not encouraged to take it up before they are sixteen, but at present some of the boys are below that age.

6043. Have you any acquaintance with technical schools ?—No.

6044. *President.*] Have you given any attention to the question of instruction in English and Dutch in schools ?—Yes.

6045. Can you offer us any suggestions with regard to that ; do you think the present system sufficient ?—At present I believe that nearly as much as possible is done in every school that I am acquainted with where Dutch is required. Provision is made for teaching it, but I am afraid that it is not always very well taught, because it is of very little value in the examinations.

6046. Is that the reason why you think it is not well taught ?—Generally it is left to the junior teachers. I attribute it partially to the difficulty of getting competent men to teach the language.

6047. How would you supply competent teachers ?—If it is considered necessary to bestow greater attention upon the teaching of Dutch, no doubt teachers could be supplied from those trained in the Colony, in the Normal College.

6048. Do you think there is a supply of teachers readily at hand to meet this want ?—I think so ; and I believe that the teachers now engaged could do much better work, if it paid, so to speak, from an examination point of view.

6049. Are the parents anxious, do you think, about Dutch being taught in the schools ?—I do not think they are anxious for a very great deal of it.

6050. Would you be in favour of altering the system as to making English the medium of instruction ?—In the public schools, no. I think in the farm schools it is very advisable that teachers should know colloquial Dutch, in order to make plain what they do in English. Then again, there is a great want of proper text-books. The only books they can get are really in English.

6051. *Dean Holmes.*] Do you mean the *taal*, or proper Dutch ?—It practically answers to such English as would be spoken by country people in England or Scotland, the dialect of the place, which does not differ so very much from Dutch proper.

6052. *President.*] What is your opinion as to the introduction of Dutch into the Elementary Examination ?—I believe that Dutch could be added to the Elementary Examination with profit. My suggestion with regard to the Elementary Examination is, that the present four subjects should remain compulsory ; let it be possible to pass with those four subjects, and much more carefully limit the history and geography that are prescribed ; sometimes the papers set in those subjects are altogether beyond what should be expected : too difficult, in fact. For instance, in the geography paper of last year, one question was, give a list of the provinces of Holland. If a question of that sort is asked, you might in the same way ask the divisions of all other countries in Europe, and that is perfectly useless for a Cape child. The amount of time involved in preparing him to pass such an examination is out of all question beyond the value of it.

6053. *Dr. Berry.*] Was that question you refer to indicated at all ?—No. It came under general geography. I do not think the question, give a list of the English counties, would be a proper one. The same thing applies to a great extent with regard to history. I sympathize very much with the examiners, for they must be driven to despair almost sometimes in varying their questions. As the examination stands at present, the amount of history and geography may be made so heavy that these two subjects alone are more than a child can manage in a reasonable time.

6054. You mean that a certain amount of indiscretion is applied to the examination papers in those subjects ?—Yes. Then I think that one additional or optional subject should be allowed, and I would have as a fifth paper the following five languages, Dutch, French, German, Kafir, and Sesuto, any one of which might be taken up, and the marks count and be added to the total number of marks in the Elementary Examination. Those who preferred to take Elementary Science

Professor
Robert Mac-
William.

Sept. 14th, 1891.

instead of a modern language could do so as a fifth subject. I would also add Latin. In my opinion, science of a simple kind is an elementary subject, and more advisable than a second language, that is, from an educational point of view. This subject is one of the most important I imagine that teachers have at present to consider. Even if it is admitted that the question is one of politics and sentiment rather than of education pure and simple, that only makes it the more urgently pressing, and the more important from the administrative point of view, for nothing, hardly even the practical value of the education given, has so much influence on the work of the public schools of a country as those same factors of politics and sentiment. The wish of what I may call the Dutch party is that Dutch, as the mother tongue of so large a section of the population, should have some weight given to it in the Elementary School Examination. The reply of the Committee of the Teachers' Association,—not, be it remembered, of the Conference, for there the question was not discussed on its merits,—was that no change should be made in the Elementary Examination, but that if any candidate wished to have an examination in Dutch, or any other subject instead, in addition to the Elementary Examination, an opportunity might be given him of so indulging himself, and that he would be told if he had passed, and how he stood in comparison with any others that might make the same choice. This was described as a *concession*. In what respect is it so? The Dutch boy, let us say, complains that, owing to his imperfect knowledge of English, he is placed at a disadvantage as compared with his English fellow-competitor in trying to gain the honour of a good position, or the more substantial reward of a bursary,—and this when both have to take the same number of subjects,—and the answer is, that the grievance may be redressed by letting the English boy remain with his four subjects, while the Dutch boy may burden himself with the preparation of five, four only of which will have any value in the examination referred to. The reasons for declining to make any change in the Elementary Examination may or may not be good,—I shall come to that presently,—but surely no one can be astonished that the Dutch party decline, even with some warmth, to accept the recommendation of the committee as a *concession* to their views. The question at the present moment therefore lies as unsettled as ever, and the longer it lies unsettled the greater is the risk of an open rupture, and of an embittered struggle between the parties, a result which would be disastrous to the education of the Colony for years to come ; so believing it to be the duty of every friend of education to strive by all means in his power to bring about some arrangement that will let the two parties work in harmony, I wish to submit to the Commission the scheme given below as my contribution towards an amicable settlement. First, however, I should like to discuss the reasons given for declining to interfere with the Elementary Examination as it stands. The two generally given are—(1) that any addition would tend to make the work less thorough, and (2) that the addition of any other subject would make the examination cease to be elementary. The first objection, if well founded, would be so serious, indeed almost fatal, that I must ask leave to examine it at some length, more particularly as I am aware that many teachers whose opinions I hold in the highest respect attached so much weight to it, that it, and it only, prevents their agreeing to any change. Now what is the age of the ordinary Elementary Candidate? I think we may say that it seldom is, and hardly ever ought to be, less than about fourteen. The candidates will always be of two kinds—either those who look forward to the School Higher and Matriculation Examinations, or those who mean to leave school immediately after the Elementary Examination. The former class, as they cannot take the third of the three examinations before they are sixteen, will not be wise if they take the first before they are fourteen. The latter consists of two distinct varieties, the town boy and the country boy. The one leaves school for business or a trade, and surely in his case it would be wise, in absence of compulsory education, to use every inducement to keep him at school till he is fourteen ; the other leaves school to go farming. and as he comes to school later, he is nearly always past fourteen when he leaves. I think therefore we cannot go far wrong in arguing on the basis of a standard age of fourteen. If so, can it be maintained that a boy of fourteen will be overworked if he has more than the four elementary subjects to work at, or that as a matter of fact he is even now usually confined to those four subjects, or that if he is learning a fifth subject, it can possibly do him harm to be examined in it (provided, of course, that the examiners are competent). I believe that every one of these questions should be answered in the negative. The first, being perhaps a matter of opinion, I pass over ; with regard to the second, we all know that if a boy is to pass Matriculation at sixteen, he ought by the time he is fourteen to have made some progress in at least Latin and a modern language other than English, while most of those who are to leave school for farming, learn Dutch ; and as for the third, whatever charges may be brought against examinations, it surely cannot be said that, if conducted with even a moderate degree of competency, they tend to make the preparation more slip-shod or less thorough. On the whole, then, I think it may be fairly maintained that the addition of a fifth subject would have, at worst, no ill effect, my own opinion being, for the above and other reasons not so closely connected with the present question, that the examination would thereby be distinctly improved. In one thing however, I agree with those who fear to overburden the Elementary Candidates. The work even as it stands may be made too heavy, owing to the extreme vagueness of the demands in history and geography. If these two subjects were more carefully defined, as might easily be done, it would be possible, even with the addition of an extra subject, to make the preparation for the Elementary Examination at once burdensome and more educative. The second objection,—that the examination would no longer be elementary,—is of comparatively little importance. It matters little what you call it, provided only it is suitable to the age and circumstances of the general run of candidates. Say if you like the School Elementary and School Higher; the University Junior and Senior Locals respectively, you would then remove the objection, if any, and also have names more accurately descriptive of the things. Assuming then that an extra subject may safely be added, what option should candidates be allowed to have? At the age of fourteen; the only specialization of taste that usually shews itself is towards languages on the one side or natural science on the other, mathematical development coming later, and therefore the most natural as well as most useful arrangement that could be made would be to let the candidate take either a modern language or a natural science. In both cases, especially in the second, the work required should be carefully defined, and while restricted to the elementary stages of the various subjects, it should be made as thorough as possible so far as it goes. Elementary Latin might also be allowed, because though not so suitable theoretically for such an Examination, it might be practically convenient in many schools. While this would fit in with the work of boys who meant to go on to the higher University course, it would also suit the case of those who meant to leave school immediately after the Elementary Examination for those who wished, or whose parents wished them, to take Dutch would have an opportunity of doing so, while those who either could not or did not wish to take Dutch or any other modern language, would have in a natural science, even imperfectly taught, one of the most educative courses possible for them in the short time allowed them at school. The scheme of work for the Elementary Examination would then stand as follows :—

Professor Robert Mac-William. Sept. 14th, 1891.

Compulsory Subjects.
1. English.
2. Arithmetic.
3. History } These two subjects to be more carefully limited than at
4. Geography } present.
A third of the marks in these four subjects to enable a candidate to pass as at present.

Optional Subjects.
5. Either (a) Modern Language—Dutch, German, French, Kafir, Sesuto.
   (b) Elementary Latin.
   (c) Natural Science—such as Botany, Geology, Animal Physiology, &c.

The marks made in the subject chosen to be added to the rest to settle the position of the candidate in the combined pass list. I am aware that some of those who agitate in favour of the greater recognition of Dutch take exception to this on the ground that it puts that language too much on the footing of a mere accomplishment. I feel the force of that objection, and sympathise with it. I think, however, it might be met by allowing a failure in English to be made up for by a pass (or a superior pass, as might be arranged) in Dutch—a privilege that could be allowed to it on account of its superior importance in this country, but not to any of the other optional subjects. I do not see that either the Education Department or the University Council could object to this, as they both act on the principle already, the Education Department in the Standard Examinations, and the University Council in the University Examinations proper, where surely, if such a concession is required at all, it is not so much required as in the less advanced School Examinations. The question is also sometimes asked whether candidates should be allowed to answer the history and geography papers in Dutch. Theoretically I do not see the slightest objection. The practical difficulty would be the trouble and cost of making the necessary arrangements, which I imagine it would be hardly worth while incurring, for I do not believe that one candidate in a hundred would avail himself of what even that one would look on as a very doubtful privilege. It is hardly necessary to add that though for convenience I have spoken only of boys, I mean my arguments and suggestions to apply to boys and girls alike. Such is the scheme that I venture to lay before the Commission. I do not claim that it is by any means ideally perfect, but I do think it possesses the following merits. It

Professor
Robert Mac-
William.

Sept. 14th, 1891.

leaves it still possible for the mere pass man to get through with the old subjects, which is all that he was likely to accomplish in any case ; it also makes a reasonable concession to the wishes of the Dutch-speaking population ; and it does so without in turn doing an injustice to the non-Dutch-speaking candidates. I also feel convinced that it would accomplish this without in any way prejudicially affecting the education of the Colony, and I have some reason to believe that it possesses besides, this great practical advantage, that it would be accepted by the leaders of the Dutch party as at least a fair compromise. For all these reasons, therefore, I would earnestly appeal to the University Council to give this or some similar scheme their most favourable consideration, believing as I do that such a conciliatory policy is not only right, but which is of much more importance, also expedient.

6055. *Dean Holmes.*] If you add marks to the general total, do not you in a certain sense make it compulsory for every child to take five subjects instead of four ?—Yes, practically so, unless the candidate thinks he can make more marks out of the four subjects than out of the five.

6056. Do not you then destroy the elementary character of the examination ?—I do not think so. I do not agree that it is more than a boy can do to take the five subjects.

6057. Why do you think that any one of those subjects mentioned ought to be added as a fifth paper in the Elementary examination ?—The question is raised by the admission of Dutch. I believe the Dutch-speaking population have a fair claim to have some value given to that language in the Elementary examination, and at the same time, it is advisable that those who cannot speak or who wish to learn Dutch should have an opportunity of passing the examination upon equal terms.

6058. Do you think that Dutch boys who now go up for the Elementary examination are handicapped in that examination by not having Dutch ?—The rural boys are.

6059. And the town Dutch boys ?—Not in the slightest. If you look over the list you will find that.

6060. Would it do, instead of what you suggest, to have a fifth paper only in Dutch submitted to boys going up as an optional paper, the marks in that counting, but not added to the others, and a bursary given to those distinguishing themselves in the Dutch paper, provided they pass the Elementary examination or attain a certain position in it. Would that encourage Dutch ?—No : quite the reverse.

6061. Why not ?—The wish at present is, that the Dutch-speaking boy should be enabled to make some use of Dutch in the Elementary examination as his mother tongue. As it is, you have four subjects to pass, and the Dutch boy feels that he is put at a disadvantage by being compelled to answer all in English and learn English, and especially so in the case of country boys. That proposal, which was made by the Committee of the Teachers' Conference, amounts to this, that the Dutch-speaking boy would have still to keep the four subjects, and if he wanted to take Dutch, it would be an additional subject. He would have five subjects to learn, and only four of which would count in the Elementary examination.

6062. Do you think your suggestion ought to meet the reasonable wants of the Dutch population, looking at it from their point of view ?—I believe so.

6063. Do you think it is advisable to have separate sets of papers in Dutch and English ?—I do not think the Dutch want that. Theoretically, I do not see the slightest objection to it. In my opinion, the moderate party of the Dutch do not want the English boy to be handicapped because the Dutch happen to be handicapped in satisfying their wants to be examined as they are now in the English language.

6064. Referring to the staff in schools and the utilization of lady teachers more than is the case at present ; are they procurable ?—I believe they could be procurable in much larger numbers than at present, if required.

6065. Are there sufficient certificated teachers ?—They could be encouraged. My belief is, that under the present system, if you want to keep up a good staff of teachers, you must leave room for promotion. A man must look forward in course of time to becoming a head master. The number of assistants must always be immensely larger than the head teachers that you will have.

6066. Are you in favour of having different schools for blacks and white ?—Certainly.

6067. How would you draw the distinction between the two, and frame a rule to define such distinction ?—I believe it must be left to the local Board to say whether they will exclude any one or not, without assigning any cause.

6068. Would you give the managers of schools for blacks power to exclude any-one ?—I would give the Board of Managers of white schools power to exclude those they think should be excluded in the interests of the school. I would not give the managers of schools for blacks power to exclude anyone.

6069. You think that would practically settle the difficulty ?—Yes

6070. *Dr. Berry.*] What is your view as to abolishing the Elementary examination altogether. There are some in favour of wiping the whole thing out?—I do not think it should be abolished.

6071. Are you in favour of letting boys go up for the School Higher Examination without passing the Elementary?—Yes, on the whole I think so, but it should not be encouraged. I have known cases where it might have been advisable, for instance, a boy is perhaps ill when prepared for the Elementary examination, and he is unable to go forward the next year for the School Higher without taking both. In that way he is very severely handicapped.

6072. With reference to the Elementary examination pass list, would you be in favour of the published list of candidates in the order of merit terminating with the honours list, all those passing below that to have their names simply arranged alphabetically?—Yes; that would be a great improvement.

6073. On what ground?—As it is, the nominal order of merit is a pure farce. I know an instance where one of our boys who passed in the Second Class Elementary, when his certificate came, turned out to be three marks below the honours, 522 marks instead of 525, which would have given him a position in the first class; he was 11 or 12 places down the second class.

Rev. N. Abraham examined.

6074. *President.*] I believe you are the Wesleyan Minister at Somerset East?—Yes.

6075. I think you have taken a good deal of interest in educational matters, and are a member of the Public Undenominational School Committee?—Yes; I was a teacher of science and theology in the higher school for girls at Graham's Town, and am also superintendent of the native school in Somerset East.

6076. Have you any suggestions to make with regard to the irregularity of attendance at school?—In large towns I would recommend the appointment of an inspector, the same as under the Board schools in England, but for the country schools, the expense would be very great, and I do not see what can be done beyond the managers themselves encouraging regular attendance by offering special prizes.

6077. Would you put the compulsory system in force at once in towns, or would you make it permissive at the request of any Board that might hereafter be created?—I should make it compulsory, but I should like to know first of all under what conditions compulsory education would be enforced.

6078. Under what conditions do you think it ought to be enforced?—I think that all children who have not passed the fourth standard, or all children who are not of a certain age, if they are found in the streets during school hours, should be sent to school, both black and white.

6079. *Dean Holmes.*] Would you limit it only to children found in the streets?—No; I would apply it to children found anywhere who ought to be in school and are not.

6080. How would you draw a distinction between black and white so as practically to work universally throughout the Colony?—There are the schools for whites, the schools for aborigines, and the schools for coloured people, and as far as my experience goes, those three schools answer every purpose. The children find their own level at those schools.

6081. How would you treat a coloured boy whose parents demanded that he should be admitted into a school for whites?—I think he should be admitted if the parents can pay the fee.

6082. Suppose the managers think that his admission would prejudice the school and cause the white children to leave; would you give them the power to exclude him?—Under present circumstances I think the Board had better have the power to exclude, although that is not my own personal feeling.

6083. But the lower school would not have that power, but would have to receive him?—Yes; there would be no difficulty I imagine. I do not see that it would be right to prevent any native boy in this Colony from rising to a higher state of education if he so wished, and provision should be made for such boys.

6084. Suppose he is excluded, and it is shewn that he is excluded only in the interests of the school, although he is a boy of good character, what remedy would you give that boy?—In some towns there would be no remedy for him at all; in others there would be, because of the higher education carried on in the native schools. I can give you the case of a native boy who has passed the sixth standard, and wishes to carry on his education. He has to go as far as Heald Town to school, and his parents have to pay for him.

Professor Robert Mac-William.

Sept. 14th, 1891

Rev. N. Abraham.

Sept. 14th, 1891.

Rev.
N. Abraham.
Sept. 14th, 1891.

6085. In such a case, would you let the State pay for his education elsewhere at the nearest place where he can get admission to a higher school, or would you let the parents pay?—I think the parents should pay.

6086. Are you in favour of the present system of guarantors?—Yes. I do not see any better system at present.

6087. Do you see any possibility of giving perpetuity to the present Boards of Management?—I have thought about the matter, but I do not see any better arrangement than the present, which is a very good one. People who are guarantors are those who take an interest in the school as a rule.

6088. It has been suggested that a Board should be elected to fill up all the gaps, leaving the present schools untouched so long as they fulfil the conditions under which they exist?—That is a subject I should not like to give an opinion upon. I am very much in favour of the present system.

6089. Is it not a hardship upon a few to have to undertake the duties of the many, and assume their pecuniary responsibility?—It is done now, and if the many were there, I am afraid it would not be done. The men who are guarantors are the men who will work and take an interest in educational matters.

6090. Are not you aware that in England and Scotland the work is done by Boards?—I see no reason why the present guarantors or Boards of Management should not in every way answer to the English School Boards. I am fully in favour of a School Board in each district elected by the ratepayers.

6091. You think they ought to be elected by the ratepayers?—Yes.

6092. And have power over all the public schools in the Colony?—Yes.

6093. Should the property of the public schools be vested in them?—The property of the public schools should be vested in the Education Department. The Department is specially established for educational work, and that work alone, and therefore, when money is raised for the special purpose of building for undenominational school purposes, it should be under the control of and vested in the Education Department.

6094. For general education, or for education in each particular district?—It should be vested in the Education Department for education in the place for which the school is built.

6095. *Dean Holmes.*] Do you think that people would subscribe to build schools and immediately hand them over to the Department?—I do not foresee any great difficulty arising, provided it is purely for educational purposes. I think that many would rather subscribe because of that.

6096. *President.*] What would you do with the present mission school property now vested in denominational and other bodies?—We could not touch that. I should not propose to touch anything except all money that has been raised by the public for the one peculiar and special object of erecting premises for the purposes of education.

6097. You would not put mission schools under this elected Board then?—No, I would let the mission schools stay just as at present.

6098. Would you allow them to come under the Board if they liked, they receiving a grant from Government, which may be fixed upon their being recommended by the Board?—Yes, if they wished.

6099. Would you in such a case allow the denominational body to carry on its own school, if the Board approved of the management?—I do not think that any denominational work except mission schools should receive any help at all from Government; they should be entirely on their own basis. I am very strong upon that.

6100. Does your body receive any aid for its mission schools from Government?—Yes.

6101. Are you in favour of Government refusing to continue that aid?—I exclude mission schools.

6102. Do you mean mission schools for whites?—All mission schools, whether for whites or blacks, should still receive aid.

6103. But you would allow them to come under the Board if they wished?—Yes.

6104. And if the Board approves, you would allow them to retain their management?—Yes, if they so wished.

6105. *Dr. Berry.* What is your reason for saying that other voluntary bodies besides mission schools should not receive aid?—The mission schools are for the poorer classes, and unless some provision were made for them, both white and black, they would not receive any education at all. The churches which take up the work must be helped, or else it could not be done.

6106. Why should not the community take up the education of the poorer Europeans just as well as the education of the rich?—If the community will do it, all well and good, but at present there are denominational mission schools existing all over the country, and they are practically supplying the want in many places, all that is required. Of course if you wish to make national mission schools, there can be no possible objection to that.

6107. Would you have any objection to substitute fourth-class public undenominational schools for mission schools for European children?—I should prefer the mission schools remaining as they are, both for whites and blacks. If you get help from Government for a mission school, you can then give a very cheap education, and the poorer children can avail themselves of it. In the denominational voluntary schools the fees are generally high, and they must be high if they receive no grant from Government, therefore you obtain a class of children who are willing and can afford to pay for the kind of education they receive. Thus, two distinct and quite separate classes of children have their educational wants met. In some cases where there is an undenominational school in a place which is aided by Government, education is made cheap, and all classes of children go to that school, the very poor and those in a better class of society, they are all forced into that one school, but I do not know that it is a very desirable thing that both classes should be obliged to mix together in one school. Where, however, you have a mission school established in which a very cheap education can be given, and you have side by side with that a voluntary denominational school where the fees are high and not receiving Government aid, there is a distinction made at once, and the different educational wants of the two classes are met. I would not do away with the present mission schools, but where there are no mission schools, and it is necessary that some provision should be made for the poorer classes, then certainly establish a Government aided fourth-class school.

6108. You would prefer the mission schools for Europeans that are in existence because they are in existence?—Yes.

6109. As far as new departures are concerned, you are in favour of their being undenominational public schools?—Yes, quite favourable.

6110. *President.*] If a voluntary body were to satisfy the Government or a Board by its low fees, you would give power to the Board to recommend that such voluntary body should establish a school?—Certainly.

6111. But you would reduce the fees to meet the wants of the poorer classes?—Yes.

6112. Would you allow volunteers to be aided, provided they are volunteers, to meet the wants of the poorer classes?—Provided those volunteers are not denominational. There are certain denominational schools now in existence, high class schools, not receiving Government aid. I do not wish them to receive Government aid; let them do their own work. It is a peculiar and very valuable work, which no Government school can do. Let them alone, and do not interfere with them either with grants or anything else. There are mission schools in existence for whites and blacks; some of those are denominational; some I suppose are not. These receive grants, and I would still let them receive grants, and if any elected Board wished to establish such schools because there was a need for them, I should say certainly; let the Board establish them for the benefit of either whites or blacks.

6113. *Dr. Berry.*] Not necessarily mission schools, public undenominational schools as they are called?—Yes.

6114. *President.*] Supposing private schools that are doing good work for the better classes are willing to be inspected on condition that they receive aid, would you allow them to receive it or refuse it?—I would refuse it.

6115. On what principle?—I think they are doing a certain class of work unaided, and they are much better left entirely to themselves. If we begin to aid private volunteer schools I do not know where we should stop, and then there would be a tendency to throw education in many districts too much into sectarian hands, which I should consider a very great grievance.

6116. Then why aid any high class schools?—The only high class schools which are aided are the colleges and the first-class undenominational schools.

6117. Why aid them?—Because they are undenominational. I would aid undenominational schools because they are public schools, voluntary schools are not public schools.

6118. Suppose they are prepared to become public schools, and have a conscience clause?—Provided their Board of Management is elected in the ordinary public way, then I would not mind, but many of these voluntary schools are under a system of ecclesiastical government, which is not according to the consciences of a great many people, and I do not see that under those circumstances they should receive Government aid.

6119. Is not that the case with mission schools too?—Yes, to a certain extent.

6120. Then why draw a distinction?—I draw a distinction, because in the case of mission schools it cannot be helped. They must have Government aid or else they could not be carried on. The poorer classes would actually be starved for want of education, while the rich would not.

Rev.
X. *Abraham.*

S, pt. 14th, 1891.

6121. *Dr. Berry.*] Would you in any case be prepared to give mission schools assistance out of the local rates?—No.

6122. Should the higher public undenominational schools get help from the public rates?—I do not think so; I prefer all the aid to come from the Education Department.

6123. Suppose a deficiency arose in the the funds of a public undenominational school, who should be responsible?—At present the guarantors are responsible for it, and although it presses hardly upon them no doubt, I think it is a very good thing, because it helps the guarantors to look up the schools and see that they are worked properly.

6124. Does not the system rather tend to frighten guarantors on account of their liability?—I have not known it to be so. No doubt it presses heavily at times.

6125. Are you in favour of anything being done generally to raise the quality of education in the country?—I should like to see more technical education given to the natives, and indeed to whites too if they wished it.

6126. Do not you think the standard of attainments of scholars generally in this country is very poor?—I think this, that so far from having the elementary standard done away with, a great deal more attention should be paid to the elementary work in schools. · The boys too often in this colony, as I have known them, have no thorough grounding in the elementary sections of education; they are utterly at sea; and they are frequently taken on to higher work when they ought to be sent right back again almost to the very beginning. I consider that to be one great defect in the educational system of this Colony, too great a desire to push on to·higher standards at the expense of a good ground work.

6127. You say you are in favour of the guarantee system, but is not this a matter in which the public as a whole are interested, and they should therefore take their share of the burden—Would you not be inclined under any circumstances to shift the responsibility from the guarantors who now volunteer, to the ratepayers, who would be compulsorily liable for any deficiency that might arise?—I am afraid it would not work. I think you find that Boards throughout the Colony are always grumbling that they have not money to do their own proper work. It is better to elect bodies to do a special work. If you go to bodies elected for other purposes, and give them some extra work to do, you are not likely to get it done well.

6128. I refer to a body elected specially for school purposes; would you be prepared to remove the responsibility from the guarantors and put it on a Board?—I would rather let the guarantors bear the responsibility, although it may seem hard, and oftentimes is; still, the system has its advantages.

6129. Have you anything to suggest with regard to the system of examinations?—I am entirely in favour of the pass lists being published with the numbers in the order of merit; it is better than having them alphabetically arranged. Schools that do good work ought to be recognized, and this is one of the best ways of publicly recognizing it, by the places that scholars take in the examination lists.

6130. What do you say to the objection raised by some teachers that it is merely the effect of a little extra attention devoted to a few with the neglect of the many?—I say that that is the outcome of the examination system under any circumstances. There is always a great desire among teachers to pass their children well, and it is only fair when certain schools work hard, that they should get some recognition.

6131. *President.*] Would you give these bodies which are carrying on mission schools any help for school buildings at all?—No, I would not.

6132. Would you increase the aid for school teaching?—I would do so if necessary.

6133. Upon a uniform principle?—Yes.

6134. What ought the increase to be?—According to the teaching requirements of the school. There ought to be some arrangement for increasing the staff. For a certain number of children there ought to be a teacher, and for every additional teacher there ought to be a separate and special grant.

6135. Would it not be a good thing to give so much per head for attendance?—I have no objection to that.

6136. What amount do you think would be fair, or would you fix any amount?—I am not prepared to do so.

6137. You said something about technical schools, do you think they ought to be encouraged?—Yes, schools that would teach trades. The youth of this colony ought to understand trades. There are too many boys growing up who are only fit for clerks and are, as it were, a drag upon society, whereas if they knew a trade they would be a great benefit. In view of the rapid opening up of this country, the thing we need is technical education, almost more than anything else.

Rev.
N. Abraham.
——
Sept. 14th, 1891.

6138. Would you have technical education in mission schools too?—Yes, if Government could make the necessary arrangements. I am not losing sight of the necessary expense.

6139. Would you have it for blacks also?—Certainly.

6140. What sort of technical education would you have for the general average black?—I think handicrafts such as masonry, carpentry, brick-making and the like.

6141. Would you have spade work too?—Certainly, though that does not need so much teaching. I am convinced that for many years to come, in view of the development of this country, the education that will help us most is technical education. At present, there is a number of young men with a good education, some of them with University degrees, at the gold fields and elsewhere, who cannot make a living because they know no technical work. A man who does know some technical work is a great help and benefit to society.

6142. Do you think your mission schools for blacks would undertake technical or industrial training in connection with the literary training imparted, and could they do so if they received a little aid?—I am afraid it would have to be a considerable increase of aid in order to carry that work out thoroughly. I think you would have almost to establish technical schools apart from the other schools.

6143. In large towns, where there are three or four mission schools, could not a technical school for teaching the lower class of industries be established, where all the children attending these mission schools could attend, and would be allowed to attend, without any friction on the part of the managers?—It would be impossible for the Government to give a technical department to every school, and therefore some arrangement such as that would have to be made.

6144. What should be done in the case of the girls?—In our mission schools there is a special grant for sewing mistresses, and some of the schools are specially set apart, or nearly so, for training domestic servants. Among the natives I think anything along those lines would be very valuable. We must train the native girls for domestic servants, and I do not think we ought to train them for anything else at present, so far as the benefit of the colony is concerned.

6145. You would not have literary pursuits for them?—No, I do not think so.

6146. Nor for the boys?—Not generally.

6147. You would teach them reading, writing, and arithmetic?—Yes, just the rudiments.

6148. With regard to higher technical schools for whites, what do you suggest; would you have certain centres in towns or would you associate any technical teaching with farm schools?—Unless technical work is done well it is not worth doing at all, and if you begin to give a little help to this and that school for technical training, it will be no good or very little good. I therefore think that some central well-maintained institution should be provided in a town, where all who wished could, under certain conditions, receive benefit, but it must be done well.

6149. You would not force anybody into it?—I do not think so.

6150. Have you any knowledge of the wants of the agricultural population in regard to education?—So far as I know, their wants are as fairly met as we are able to meet them. I think they are being met by farm schools to a great extent.

6151. Do you know anything of circuit schools?—No.

6152. Do people avail themselves of farm schools sufficiently?—So far as my experience goes in this district I should say they do.

6153. If a Board were established, would you let people apply to them for this kind of help?—Yes.

6154. You think it would be a good thing?—Yes, if the Board is thoroughly representative, I thoroughly approve of it; the danger is in getting made up Boards, especially in some districts. If it is thoroughly representative, I quite believe in such a Board.

6155. Would you give the central Government power to make grants even although the Board objects, after it has duly considered the objections?—I would leave the power in their hands, provided their rights are not touched.

6156. Dr. Berry.] Have you a superintendent of native schools here?—I am practically superintendent myself.

6157. Do the natives pay fees?—Yes. There is not much difficulty in getting them in as they are low, ranging from threepence up to a shilling a month.

6158. Do the native parents neglect sending their children to school on the ground that they cannot afford the fees?—Some do. Some have large families, and then it frequently happens. We have something like 160 children in this native school.

6159. Generally speaking, are you in favour of compelling the natives to pay for their education?—Yes, in part.

Rev.
N. Abraham.

Sept. 14th, 1891.

6160. Right through the country, including the Transkei ?—I do not know about the Transkei, I have not had any experience there, and things are different there I think. In the colony proper, everybody should pay something. At the same time, Government might make arrangements for free scholars in mission schools, so that no one should be prevented from getting an education simply because he is poor. '

6161. Are you in favour of compulsory education for native children in towns ?— Yes, but if you compel them, you must adopt some form of free education, because it would be impossible for all the natives to pay for their education.

6162. Would you be in favour of compelling those to pay who can pay ?—Yes.

6163. Whether they send their children or not ?—Not if they do not send their children.

6164. Would you be in favour of a general householders' tax in the location for school purposes ?—No.

6165. *President.*] Why not?—I believe in free education for everybody. Let the State educate everybody as far as it can free ; and where it can help, let it do so.

6166. You do not think it is practicable to levy any tax upon the natives for educational purposes within the location ?—I do not think so. I have no objection to the principle, but in carrying it out there would be a great difficulty. If you have compulsory education, then the State must pay for it. If you like to levy a tax which would go direct to the Education Department, irrespective of where it came from or whose it was, I should have no objection to that, and then it could be distributed by the department as the grants are distributed now.

6167. Have you considered at all the subject of language in this country ?—Yes.

6168. What is your opinion as to the bi-lingual difficulty ?—My opinion is this : I think that Dutch should be taught to those who wish it, but I do not think it should be compulsory for any boy to learn it. Let it be an optional thing, and with regard to the examination, I think the subjects should remain just as they are, but that a Dutch paper should be set, not as an extra subject so much, but for any boy who wishes to take it. Suppose any boy does take it besides the other subjects and passes in it, then a note should be added when his pass is published, to the effect that he has passed his examination in Dutch.

6169. Suppose he passes high, would you give a bursary or some prize for having excelled in it, by way of encouragement I mean ?—No. I would not do that unless I gave the Dutch boys a similar prize for excelling in English. If there are special prizes for the one, I have no objection to prizes for the other.

6170. It is said that as a Dutch boy is handicapped in the Elementary examination by having to use English as the medium throughout the examination, it is but fair to handicap the English boy by making him learn Dutch. Is that your opinion? —I do not hold with that opinion. The Dutch boy may be handicapped to some extent, but it is really to his advantage to know English.

6171. Would it not be to the advantage of the English boy to be handicapped by making him learn Dutch ?—That is doubtful.

6172. Is not any person who lives here the better for knowing Dutch ?—Yes, but the time that an English boy gives to learning Dutch, he might be devoting to learning something else. He would be sure to pick up Dutch in some way.

6173. Would not all the residents in this country be the better if they knew Dutch grammatically ?—I do not see that, because grammatical Dutch is not the language that is spoken here, and it would be lost labour to a great extent to acquire it. If the time comes when high Dutch is spoken in this country as much as the *patois* Dutch is now spoken, it might alter my views about it.

6174. Is it not a good thing for people to be able to communicate readily with each other, which they could do more efficiently if every one knew both English and Dutch ?—That may be so to a certain extent, but I should not like a boy of mine who was at school to be compelled to learn Dutch. I should probably advise him to do so, but I should not like him to be under compulsion. Dutch is very useful, but boys have so many subjects to learn at school.

6175. Are you in favour of Professor MacWilliam's suggestion in regard to this matter ?—I prefer my own suggestion, which I have already stated, to his.

6176. *Dr. Berry.*] Would the system he proposes give a great advantage to some schools and not to others. The subjects he enumerates, might be taught in certain schools, while in others they could not possibly be taught, is not that so ?—I am not at all in favour of it. I should have no objection to it if it were not for the question of language, Dutch being one of them ; but I think Dutch should be taken quite separately by itself, and it would be quite a sufficient reward for a boy if he had a certificate showing that he had passed in Dutch. If he wanted a situation, it might be a great advantage to him.

6177. How would it do to have a Dutch paper and also an English paper and let the boy choose, or let there be a paper partly in Dutch and partly in English, somewhat like the system that prevails in Switzerland?—If a boy likes to take it all in Dutch or all in English, I would not object.

Rev.
 N. Abraham.

 Sept. 14th, 1891.

Somerset East, Tuesday, September 15th, 1891.

PRESENT:

Sir J. D. BARRY (President),

Dr. Berry,	Rev. Moorrees,
Mr. Theron,	Dean Holmes.

Miss Margaret Houliston examined.

6178. *President.*] I believe you are principal of the Bellevue Seminary here?—Yes.

6179. Is it a voluntary school?—It is an undenominational Government aided school for girls.

Miss
 Margaret Houlis-
 ton.

 Sept. 15th, 1891.

6180. How many girls have you there?—About 140.

6181. Is it a first class school?—Yes.

6182. What are your fees?—They range from 10s. up to £2 10s. per quarter.

6183. Do you teach Dutch in the school?—Yes.

6184. But I suppose the medium of instruction is English, is it not?—Yes.

6185. Would there be any difficulty in examining the pupils all round in Dutch: are they all capable?—No. They do not all take Dutch. There are a great many who do not.

6186. How many take it?—I think about 40 take Dutch, we only teach it in the higher department; it is not taught to the little ones.

6187. Why is it not taught to the little ones; would there be some difficulty in making them learn Dutch?—I think there might be an objection on the part of some of the parents. Even in the higher department there is sometimes an objection.

6188. *Mr. Theron.*] Are they Dutch or English parents who object?—Mostly English, but there are some of the Dutch parents who object. I do not think, however, they object to the Dutch, but because it is a difficult language to learn.

6189. *President.*] The Dutch parents do not show any preference for it, do they?—No.

6190. Is there a special teacher for Dutch?—Yes; Miss Hofmeyr.

6191. Do you teach elementary science?—No.

6192. Have you followed the discussion which has been going on in regard to the bi-lingual question?—I have to a certain extent.

6193. What is your opinion about it?—I do not quite see how Dutch could be made the medium of instruction. As far as the Elementary examination goes, it might be made an optional subject and taken in that way, but I do not think it could be made compulsory.

6194. Could it fairly be made an optional subject, the marks counting and being added to the total, or ought it to be kept separate entirely?—It should be kept separate altogether.

6195. Do you think that would encourage Dutch?—I cannot say whether it would.

6196. Do you think if some bursary or prize were given to those who passed well in Dutch, more would take it up?—I do not know. My experience here is that children find Dutch, very difficult, and it was exactly the same in the Western Province. I was at Stellenbosch.

6197. Colonial children, whether they are Dutch or English, find Dutch difficult?—Yes; but I think it ought to be encouraged and well learned.

6198. Do you think a bursary or prize would prove an encouragement?—Yes; a prize at any time encourages pupils.

6199. Do you think a child of Dutch parentage is at all handicapped in the Elementary examination in consequence of English being the medium of instruction?—I do not think so. Their home training may perhaps tell somewhat against them, as they carry on conversation in Dutch, but at school they learn in English.

6200. *Mr. Theron.*] Then to that extent the Dutch child is handicapped?—Yes, as far as home training is concerned.

6201. *President.*] Is the ordinary Dutch girl behind the English girl in learning, do you think?—I cannot say they are on a par.

6202. If the Dutch girl is a little weighted by her home training, do you think it would be fair to handicap the English girl a little by forcing her practically to learn Dutch—that is, making the marks for the Dutch paper count, and tell in the total?—

cc 2

Miss
*Margaret Houlis-
ton.*

Sept. 15th, 1891.

I scarcely think it would be, because although Dutch is spoken, I do not know that it is of such very great advantage to know it. Girls and boys, for instance, learn one kind of Dutch in school and speak another kind out of school, so that it does not seem to improve them.

6203. *Mr. Theron.*] Is it fair to compel Dutch children to learn English?—English is more widely spoken.

6204. Have you seen Professor MacWilliam's proposals on this subject?—Yes, and with those views I very much coincide.

6205. That is to say, you would have a number of alternative subjects?—Yes.

6206. How would you apply the suggested process of helping the boy who is deficient in English over the stile; is not that a weak point on the part of Professor MacWilliam?—I think so. A uniform plan would almost be preferable.

6207. *Rev. Moorrees.*] Is it not fair towards the Dutch boy, who is somewhat weighted, that if he fails in the English paper through the conversation at home not being in English, a pass in Dutch should make up for the failure in English, but no pass in any other subject can make up for failure in English?—It does seem but fair.

6208. *President.*] From an educational point of view, is it an advantage or a disadvantage to have Dutch spoken at home and English the medium of education?—If pure Dutch was spoken it would be an advantage.

6209. Then you do think that having two languages is an advantage from an educational point of view, as it tends to expand the mind?—Certainly.

6210. Does it matter much which is the second language, as long as it is pure, from an educational point of view. Would French, for instance, or any other language answer as well as Dutch?—Yes.

6211. Dutch being so generally used, if you could have it taught and spoken grammatically, would it not be wise to encourage that language in preference to any other, such as French or German, both from an educational and a national point of view?—I think it would.

6212. Therefore it would be wise to have Dutch well taught?—Yes; well taught and well spoken.

6213. If elementary science was made an alternative subject in the Elementary examination, would the children at your school be able to make use of it?—If it was necessary we would teach it. Girls often find science a difficult subject.

6214. What do they generally take up instead of science?—They have taken physical geography instead of chemistry. Of course they do not get the full marks, but they find chemistry rather difficult.

6215. Is it not a good thing to stimulate them to learn elementary science?—It might be if we had them sufficiently long at school, but they do not remain long enough to advance much.

6216. You do not think a mere smattering is of any use?—I do not think so; they just learn names without much else.

6217. From an educational point of view, do you think elementary science is a proper subject to encourage?—If pupils continue their education it is, because it is required in the higher branches.

6218. Is it with that view you would suggest it as one of the alternative subjects?—Yes; because it is advantageous afterwards.

6219. Is Latin taught in your school?—We have just commenced it.

6220. And French?—Yes.

6221. All those alternative subjects could be made use of by some of the children in your school, could they not?—Certainly.

6222. How many children do you generally send up for the Elementary examination?—Last year we sent up eleven. Eight out of the eleven would have taken Dutch in preference to French or Latin if there was an alternative subject. Only three out of the eleven learned French.

6223. Would none have taken up Latin or science?—No; we have only recently commenced to teach Latin. I have not been quite a year here.

6224. Have you been in the Western Province?—Yes; I was at the Bloemhof Seminary at Stellenbosch.

6225. How many pupils there went up for the Elementary examination?—About thirteen as a rule.

6226. Out of those thirteen how many do you think would have taken up Dutch?—Almost all learn Dutch in the Western Province. I do not think we had more than two or three French pupils in the school.

6227. Those who learned French did they also learn Dutch?—No, they learned French instead of Dutch.

6228. Then two or three would have taken French at the examination?—Probably. Far more would have taken Dutch than French.

6229. **Would the great majority even here take up Dutch from choice ?—-Yes.

6230. From an educational point of view, would it be any harm if they all took up Dutch ?—I do not see any harm.

6231. Suppose you started it next year and practically made it compulsory, do you think it would prejudice some of the children unduly ?—I fear it would. I daresay it would take three years. Language is always very difficult for girls to acquire.

6232. *Rev. Moorrees.*] You are aware that in the University examinations certain subjects receive more marks than others; do you think the two languages of the country, English and Dutch, ought to receive more marks than other languages ?—I have hardly thought about that at all.

6233. *Dr. Berry.*] What is your opinion about the pupil teacher system in the colony ?—I do not think we can say that we have a pupil teacher system in the colony.

6234. Can you suggest any way by which it could be improved ?—I certainly think if we go in for pupil teachers, there should be a system whereby they could get regular training in teaching. That is what we require. A girl may pass the teachers' examination and satisfy the Inspector, but for all that her teacher's capabilities may be, and too often are deficient. We do not give sufficient training to teachers.

6235. Do you think the grants for pupil teachers are liberal enough ?—I do not know how they are dispensed. In some schools they have several, and in other schools none at all.

6236. Can you do anything in your school here to train girls as teachers ?—I have tried to do what I can. I have two girls going up for the teacher's examination. We do not look upon them as pupil teachers, as we do not receive any grants for them.

6237. Why not ?—I do not know.

6238. Have you applied ?—Yes ; but we are told there are none to be had.

6239. Will those two girls you speak of become teachers ?—Yes ; I have tried to give them what training I possibly could just as if they were pupil teachers.

6240. How would you propose to increase the number of available teachers in the colony ?—I have not formulated any opinion, but I do think we ought to train teachers properly in the colony. If you want a trained teacher you generally have to send to England.

6241. Would you be in favour of having a special school for training teachers, or would you attach the work to the higher institutions of the country ?—The work ought to be specialised ; but they ought to be somewhere where teaching is going on, and where they can take classes and assist. If you put them in a place where no teaching is going on, they get training without experience.

6242. *Rev. Moorrees.*] You want a Normal College with a school attached ?—Yes.

6243. *Dean Holmes.*] What is called in England a practising school ?—Yes.

6244. *Dr. Berry.*] Would it be a good thing if Government started it ?—It is very much needed in the colony.

6245. Where would be a good centre for such an institution ?—I could hardly give an opinion. I do not know much about the Eastern Province. There is a little more done in the Western Province than here. At Stellenbosch they had a great many pupil teachers, and they carried on the system as well as they could.

6246. *Dean Holmes.*] Do they actually teach them how to teach ?—Yes.

6247. Would it be practicable in this colony to have such a system as you suggest, or are the distances too great ?—I do not know whether it would be practicable, but there ought certainly to be proper training.

6248. Would you have a training college with a practising college in each province ?—I think so.

6249. Could you start one here ?—I think so.

6250. How many pupil teachers can you train efficiently in your school if you had proper inducement ?—I cannot say,

6251. *Dr. Berry.*] In your opinion does the teacher's certificate as now granted necessarily show that the holder of it is adequately trained as a teacher ?—Not in all cases. I know a school at Stellenbosch, for instance, where they did give a good practical training, because they had a trained teacher, and she taught quite on the Home system, but in other schools it was different.

6252. Then the defect in the elementary teachers' certificate system is the want of proper training of the candidate ?—Yes.

6253. *Dean Holmes.*] Is your school here under a Board ?—Yes.

6254. *President.*] Have you an Industrial Department in connection with your school ?—We have at present. It is confined to the boarders.

6255. How many boarders have you ?—23.

6256. When do you have the industrial training, is it after the others have left ?—Yes ; we find it rather interferes with our work, so we are going to discontinue it. You must have four hours a week for it, and that has to come after the five hours schooling, which makes too long a time for the girls.

Miss
*Margaret Houlis-
ton.*

Sept. 15th, 1891.

6257. Could not you have the industrial teaching for less time?—No; it would hardly be worth while.

6258. What kind of industrial training is it?—Chiefly dressmaking and sewing. That was what the grant was for.

6259. Do you get a grant from the Government for it?—Yes; but we are going to discontinue it, as it makes too much inroad on our time.

6260. Do the parents of the children wish it dropped?—They are quite agreeable. It has not been a great success as far as our school is concerned.

6261. In what respect has is not been a success?—I hardly know. The pupils do not seem to have made much progress. Perhaps it may have been in the training. We do not go on any scientific principle for one thing, and in order to make it a success, you must have a thoroughly efficient teacher, which we have not had.

6262. Do you think it wise to drop it?—In our case it was a question whether we would drop this or lose having a teacher to assist with the work of the school. We preferred to have the latter.

6263. Suppose you got both?—If we got both, then we should continue it.

6264. Do not you think it is better for young ladies in after life if they have industrial training?—Yes; if they are thoroughly trained.

6265. The sewing comes in under the ordinary training, I suppose?—Yes.

6266. That is really industrial training, is it not?—Yes.

6267. Do you have that every day?—Yes, for about an hour.

6268. Would you encourage this double grant?—It would not be necessary in all cases, but in our case we were rather short of teachers.

6269. Have you considered the question of night schools: do you think them desirable for girls?—They might be; but the question arises, who is to teach in them?

6270. Would it be expedient to start a night school here?—I do not know Somerset East sufficiently well to say.

6271. Who do you think ought to go to night schools?—Those who wish to continue their education after they are compelled to leave school; but the question is, whether the thirst for education is sufficiently great.

6272. Do you think night schools are necessary for girls?—I do not think so—at any rate, they would require to be well conducted.

Professor MacWilliam further examined.

Professor
MacWilliam.

Sept. 15th, 1891.

6273. *Mr. Theron.*] I understood you to say that in the Elementary examination you would make Dutch optional, and have several alternative subjects, and if a boy was rather low in his marks for English, then Dutch would count, and the marks be added to it?—My proposal is that if he failed in English, a pass in Dutch should make up for it, but not a pass in anything else.

6274. *Dr. Berry.*] Have you anything to say with regard to the pupil teacher system?—Such a system can hardly be said to exist fortunately.

6275. Are you not in favour of developing that system?—Very far from it.

6276. What is your objection?—Having been a pupil teacher myself I can speak feelingly. It may be a cheap system, but it is not good for pupils to be taught by one who necessarily is so little qualified as a pupil teacher must be from his age and experience generally; and it is most mischievous for the pupil teachers, as it keeps them back very much. I know in my own case, by the kindness of the head master of the school, I was released from work for half a day and allowed to do my University preparation at the same time, but in spite of that, I look upon the four years that I was a pupil teacher as the worst spent of my life. I have never ceased to regret that I wasted so much time. I am perfectly sure that any school teaching I got nothing like made up for the waste of time.

6277. What suggestion would you make for increasing the number of teachers in the colony?—There should be an increase in the number of training colleges to provide assistant teachers under Government, and as far as possible lady teachers instead of male teachers should be utilized, even in boys' schools. In the younger classes they produce better work as a rule.

6278. *President.*] Can you get lady teachers more readily?—Yes, and it opens up a useful calling for young ladies. At the same time, you are less likely to overstock the profession. If you get a large number of young men in, they cannot all look forward to becoming headmasters: it is not possible; and if they remain a few years as teachers, what else can they take to. Pupil teachers might be allowed to do a certain amount of the routine work for a very short time every day.

6279. *Dr. Berry.*] Have you read this in Sir Langham Dale's last report:—" The system of day-school training must be at once enlarged. I have used the discretionary powers entrusted to me in attaching a small staff of pupil teachers to each of the following schools, viz., Rhenish Institute for Girls, Stellenbosch; All Saints' Girls'

School, Wynberg; St. Cyprian's Girls' School, Cape Town. Those institutions have exceptional facilities for training, and only by the extension of this plan to all first-class schools for boys and girls that offer such facilities can I hope to keep up a fair supply to fill vacancies as governesses in private farm schools and assistants for the undenominational schools of various grades." Do you agree with that?—1 do not quite agree with that. I think that is carrying it too far. It practically means so many normal schools. I don't quite understand what Sir Langham Dale means by pupil teachers. I should like that point more fully explained. In some correspondence with the Gill College, he speaks of attaching 15 or 20 pupil teachers to one school, but they could not be pupil teachers in the European sense, because you could not employ them; they would be in the way, and instead of being an assistance in a school, they would be a positive hindrance to the work.

Professor
MacWilliam.
——
Sept. 16th, 1891.

6280. *President.*] Would you have the teachers in farm schools inspected?—Yes.

6281. Would there be any means of inspecting the teaching from time to time on the farms?—There is an annual inspection as it is.

6282. Would you have more than that annual inspection?—I do not know whether the cost would not be more than could be afforded.

Mr. Peter Botha examined.

6283. *Mr. Theron.*] What are you?—A farmer, residing at Bruintjes Hoogte.

6284. Have you a school on your farm?—Yes. I had one and it was stopped, and then I started one again. The reason was, that my children grew up, and I had a teacher instead of a governess, and afterwards I thought it more advisable to send my children to the seminary at Somerset East. I think the present schools answer very well. I obtained a certificated governess from Uitenhage. There are similar schools within an hour's ride all round me, and they are largely used except by the very poorest classes who have not the means to send their children to school. The boarding in town is too expensive for them.

Mr.
Peter Botha.
——
Sept. 15th, 1891.

6285. Are you acquainted with the facilities at present offered by the Government?—I have heard of the grant of £3 for each child, but I think that the people generally are not sufficiently conversant with what the Government gives. When it is better known, more advantage will be taken of it. In the direction of Vogelberg, seven or eight miles from Somerset, there is a want of schools. About two years ago, there was a farm school in existence at Commadagga, and it answered well, but it disappeared. Why I cannot tell. Within half an hour's ride of my place there is a white man who has four children, one daughter and three sons, ranging from 12 to 17, none of whom have ever had any teaching. They cannot use my school because it is too far for them as day scholars.

6286. Are you aware that Government gives a grant of £6 a head as a contribution for indigent children as boarders?—No. I would have taken in the children I refer to for £6 a year each, if I had known that I could receive such aid. It is all the better for the school on my place to have more children there.

6287. *President.*] If you get the £6 for boarding and the £3 besides, that is £9 a year, you think for that you would have taken these children?—Yes. About an hour away from Somerset East there is a farm called Grootplaats, where there is a day school attended by 15 or 16 children. There is no boarding there.

6288. *Rev. Moorrees.*] Are there any circuit schools about your neighbourhood?—No; I do not think, near to Somerset, there are children enough in certain centres to establish circuit schools, but at a distance of seven or eight miles from the town there might be.

6289. What is the medium of instruction in your school?—English; but Dutch is also taught. Everything goes in English, and I think myself there is an advantage in knowing English. I never went to a Dutch school, but always learned English, but yet I am not ashamed of Dutch. My parents' impression was that we know Dutch and we do not know English. A couple of days a week learning Dutch is sufficient, seeing that the remainder of the time is required to acquire English. A Dutch child requires three or four times as much time to learn English as Dutch. A Dutch child would learn as much of Dutch in two days as it would of English in four days. In the seminary here Dutch is taught two days in the week, and three days are devoted entirely to English. It is necessary that children should learn Dutch for confirmation.

6290. Are you acquainted with the Dutch people in the district?—Yes; and I think there is a general desire for Dutch.

6291. *President.*] Is there also a general desire to learn English?—Yes.

6292. *Mr. Theron.*] Which is the best, an Englishman who does not know Dutch, or a Dutchman who does not know English?—It is difficult to answer that question. I have seen in Somerset East, Englishmen who do not know Dutch, and they try very hard

Mr.
Peter Botha.

Sept. 15th, 1891.

to learn it. I also know Dutchmen who do not know English, and they also try very hard to learn the language. I think that inasmuch as there are these two languages existing, both should be learned.

6293. *President.*] Do you think that is the general wish of the farming community ?—Yes.

Mr. *J. S. B. Holden* examined.

Mr.
J. S. B. Holden.

Sept. 15th, 1891.

6294. *President.*] I believe you are in business at Somerset East ?—Yes.

6295. Are you a member of the school committee ?—Yes, I am a member of the committee of the girls' seminary and also the Gill college.

6296. Are they under the same management ?—No, under separate management. They are both State aided.

6297. Have you had any experience with native mission schools ?—Yes.

6298. Do you think there ought to be any change with regard to them ?—As far as I can see they work very satisfactorily.

6299. Do you think an industrial department should be attached to them ?—Yes, it is very important on large locations.

6300. What sort of industries would you have ?—Trades, such as blacksmiths' work, shoemaking and carpentering.

6301. Can you teach such trades to large numbers inexpensively ?—I think so, any of those trades I have mentioned.

6302. Would you have spade industry taught ?—Yes, manual labour as well as trades.

6303. Do you think the managers of the present mission schools would undertake that duty ?—Many of them would if they were in a position to do so.

6304. How much would it require to enable them to do so with any degree of efficiency ?—That is a very difficult question to answer.

6305. I suppose you would require additional assistance ?—Yes. I think that in many cases £100 would be a very great assistance.

6306. For how many children ?—From 60 to 100 children. I take it that a great deal of what was produced could be sold at a profit and thus become a source of income to the institution.

6307. Do you think if the Government gave aid at the rate of £1 per head for the average attendance throughout the year it would be acceptable to the managers ?—I quite think so.

6308. It would enable them to work such a school ?—Yes.

6309. Would it be better than the present system ?—Yes.

6310. Do you think the natives would fall in with such a system ?—I think they would be glad. I have been to Lovedale and Heald Town, and there is no trouble about it there.

6311. Were you educated at Lovedale ?—Yes, I was there at school.

6312. Could the Lovedale institution supply the necessary assistant teachers in large numbers ?—Yes.

6313. Are there many teachers being trained who would be competent to aid in such a way ?—I think there is a large number being educated for this work at the two institutions I have named.

6314. In your own experience have not you found that there are too many mission schools belonging to different denominations crowded on one area ?—Yes. In some of the smaller towns it is a great drawback.

6315. Is it advisable by degrees to do away with that and have fewer mission schools within certain areas and rather extend the missions outside those areas ?—With reference to that, it seems to me that in the small towns every denomination has a native cause in connection with its church, and this native cause brings in a certain amount of revenue. That is the position of affairs in Somerset East.

6316. Does not this excessive competition cause them to lose revenue rather than otherwise ?—It is an evil in one sense, but many of the churches would not be able to exist without it.

6317. *Dr. Berry.*] Do the funds derived from the mission schools go towards the church funds ?—Not the church funds, but towards the natives.

6318. *President.*] You think it is desirable not to destroy these mission schools, but not to multiply them ?—Yes.

6319. *Rev. Moorrees.*] Do you mean that the proceeds from the mission schools are sufficient to keep them going and give a balance to the church itself ?—No. With regard to the Wesleyan Church in Somerset East, they have raised a certain amount, and the European minister, till quite recently, has done the native work as well as the English work, so what has been received from the natives has gone towards the minister's stipend. They had no minister of their own.

Mr.
J. S. B. *Holden.*

Sept. 15th, 1891

6320. *President.*] What have they done with the school fees?—They have gone towards the teachers' salaries in the native schools.

6321. Have they been sufficient to maintain those schools?—Not alone; we have had to supplement them.

6322. If the Government gave some aid for industrial purposes, would it be wise to have one industrial school where all the children could assemble from the various mission schools?—Yes; if it could be managed.

6323. Could something of the kind be managed if a Board was brought into existence whose duty it should be to see that there were sufficient schools in existence throughout the district?—Yes; it would be a good thing.

6324. Are you in favour of such a Board?—Yes.

6325. And for native purposes you think the Government ought to contribute at the rate of £1 per head?—Yes.

6326. That £1 you would approve being contributed by the Government upon the Board recommending that it should be given?—Yes.

6327. Do you know anything about the schools in Basutoland?—Yes. I spent four years in Basutoland, and visited most of the French missionaries there constantly, and I found that the industrial departments are a very great success. They do their own printing, and various trades are taught. With their own money they have been able to raise these industrial schools, and they are a very great benefit.

6328. Is the money got from the natives?—Yes. They teach printing, shoe-making, blacksmiths' work, carpentering, the use of agricultural implements, and in fact pretty well everything. I have seen the French missionaries themselves go into the workshops, and they spend so many hours every day assisting and directing the pupils. That is what is wanted here.

6329. Has it a good effect on the natives?—Yes.

6330. Do you think the Basutos are more industrious than other natives?—They are most industrious.

6331. And do you attribute that to some extent to this teaching?—Yes.

6332. *Dr. Berry.*] What do they pay in these schools?—The payment is very small. I forget exactly what it is.

6333. The French Protestant missionaries are aided, are they not, by a large grant from the parent body in Paris?—Yes, they have assistance, but it is gradually decreasing, and at the present time it is but small; the institutions are almost self-supporting.

6334. *President.*] If the Government levied a small tax in the way of a hut or property tax upon the natives for the express purpose of aiding education among them, do you think that would be a wise thing?—I am opposed to that strongly. I think the natives at the present time are not ready for such taxation. Most of the natives as a rule are giving liberally according to their means towards educational and other purposes.

6335. It has been stated by some missionary gentlemen that the so-called school Kafirs alone contribute towards school purposes, and that if a tax were to be imposed upon all the Kafirs within an area and they saw they were getting something for their money, they would send their children to school who otherwise would not go, is that so?—That may be, but I take a different view. Taking Somerset East, it would not answer at all, because the people have not the money. They are paying so much towards school fees and the support of the minister, that they are not able to pay an additional tax.

6336. If instead of paying anything towards the school, a tax were levied and this was handed over in lieu of fees to the managing school body, would it not be an improvement, and would you not know what your income was better?—I am in favour of the fee system. There is so much changing and moving about with these people, that it would be found difficult to levy and collect a tax of that description.

6337. *Dr. Berry.*] Are you in favour of compulsory education for blacks?—Not at the present time.

6338. *President.*] Is it not advisable in towns that children should be sent to school daily for a few hours?—It seems to me that the natives are advancing so rapidly that they are sending their children of their own accord.

6339. Would it not facilitate matters if it was understood that there was a law requiring children to go to school, black children I mean?—It might answer, but many of these people are so poor, that even lads of 13 and 14 are going out to work in order to help support the family.

6340. Is it advisable that they should go out before they are 13?—Perhaps not.

6341. Up to that age you would compel them to go to school?—Yes, I would be in favour of that.

Mr.
J. S. b. *Holden.*

Sept. 15th, 1891.

6342. Have you thought at all of the subject of night schools ?—I do not think in small villages they would answer.

6343. Neither for boys nor girls ?—No.

6344. Do you know anything about farm schools ?—I am strongly in favour of every advantage being given to those.

6345. Would you give further facilities, or are the present facilities sufficient if they were more widely known ?—At present very good work is being done, and I think nothing further is required.

6346. Do you know anything about technical education ?—No.

6347. Have you formed any opinion upon the subject of language ?—Yes ; but not a very decided opinion. I should not like to see the Dutch language made compulsory in our schools.

6348. Would you like to see it practically compulsory, that is to say, make the marks in the Elementary Examination tell in such a way as to make it almost necessary to learn the language ?—I could not express a definite opinion as to that.

6349. *Rev. Moorrees.*] Would you be good enough to state your reasons for preferring the School Board system to the present arrangement ?—On the whole, the working would be more satisfactory in several ways. In many of our institutions at the present time, things do not work as well as they might ; there is a sort of dual committee, and the managers are not sufficiently united. Take for instance the first-class public undenominational girls' school here. There are so many put on the committee by a certain Church, and so many are elected by the public vote, and there are, as it were, two distinct bodies, resulting very often in a certain amount of friction.

6350. Are not the members of the Church members of the public also ?—At the girls' seminary here there are eight members on the Board. Five of those by arrangement are nominated by the Dutch Reformed Church. I understand that the public gave them liberty to do that. The remaining three are elected by the public. The reason of this was that the Church undertook the financial responsibility, and the public gave them the power of nomination on that account.

6351. Is the result unsatisfactory ?—Yes ; it causes a great deal of dissatisfaction among the public. They are continually arguing that they are not sufficiently represented.

6352. *Dr. Berry.*] Are you a member of the Board ?—Yes. I was elected a member by the public.

6353. *Rev. Moorrees.*] Would the public be willing to undertake the financial responsibility ?—I am not in a position to answer that question.

6354. They would like to have the management but not the responsibility ; is that it ?—I do not think they would undertake the responsibility.

6355. *President.*] Ought they to do so, do you think ?—It would be for the welfare of the institution and the community at large if they did.

6356. *Rev. Moorrees.*] I understand you to complain that a certain church exerts perhaps too much power on the School Committee. Now, if you had a Board elected by the ratepayers, would not it very often happen that the great majority of the ratepayers would belong to a certain church, and so the same thing would happen over again ?—I think not. The power would be more evenly distributed.

6356A. What difference would the name of the body make if the body is elected by the same electors. How can the changing of the word " School Committee " into " School Board " make such a difference in regard to any church influence there may be ?—I not do see that the name would make any difference. I think however that it would give more satisfaction if the ratepayers elected.

6357. Whether School Committees or School Boards ? –Yes.

6358. *President.*] Is it better that the ratepayers throughout the whole district should elect one Board to represent that district ?—Yes.

6359. And the school be worked through that Board as the representative body ? —Yes.

6360. *Dr. Berry.*] Should that be supplemented by making the ratepayers responsible for the financial management of the institution under their control ?—I think so.

6361. *Rev. Moorrees.*] Would you prefer the election to be by the ratepayers instead of the householders, or is it immaterial ?—I think an election by the householders is more satisfactory. At present, suppose we wish to have a member elected for the Board of the Seminary or the Gill College, notices are placed in the local papers by the committee to the effect that on such and such a day there will be an election, and any one who is a householder has a right to come that day and vote for his man.

6362. *Dr. Berry.*] Is the invitation to meet addressed to the householders in the district or town, or both ?—The notice is that on such a day there will be an election of members for the committee, and as a rule we have it as nearly as possible on a day that will meet the convenience of country people.

Mr.
J. S. B. Hoffin.

Sept. 15th, 189?.

6363. Do they come up?—Yes.

6364. How many attend these meetings?—The number varies from 10 to 80. It is generally on a Monday or Tuesday.

6365. Who presides?—The chairman of the committee.

6366. Do they sign any guarantee?—No, they simply vote by ballot.

6367. Then no list of guarantors is formed at all?—No, the list of guarantors is already created by the Church.

6368. Suppose a deficiency arose, would you be called upon for your share?—No, I am elected by the public.

6369. *President.* Have you ever seen the document which the Church signed, whereby they undertake the financial responsibility?—I have not seen it.

6370. Have you ever asked to see it?—I cannot say I have.

6371. From any information you have received, do you know what the nature of that document is?—The chairman of the Seminary Committee is the Rev. Mr. Leith. I asked him about the matter, and he told me that a public meeting was called, and the public gave the Dutch Reformed Church certain powers to put five men on the Board and the Church signed a guarantee, and undertook all financial responsibility.

6372. In what form was the document?—I cannot answer that question.

6373. But you believe there is a document of that kind?—The chairman told me so.

6374. The triennial election is only for three of the members?—Yes.

6375. Then apparently one set of householders many years ago have withdrawn from future householders the power of electing the five members?—Yes, you may look at it in that light. It was done many years ago.

6376. Was it with the consent of the Education Department?—That I cannot say. I was not in the town at the time.

6377. *Rev. Moorrees.*] Have the public ever offered to take over the financial responsibility?—I do not think so.

6378. *President.*] Is it Church property on which the seminary stands?—I believe so.

6379. Has the Government contributed anything in money towards the seminary buildings?—That I cannot answer.

6380. All that does not come before you as a member of the Board, does it; I mean the question of expenditure on the buildings and so on?—Recently it has; within the last two years.

6381. How long have you been a member of the Board?—About six years.

6382. Then during four years these matters did not come before the Board?—No.

6383. By whom were they dealt with?—By the guarantors, the Dutch Reformed Church. No financial matters were brought before us.

6384. Why have they recently been brought before you?—I am not in a position to state. I can only say that the chairman and myself felt the position we were in very much, namely, that we had no say with regard to financial matters, and we both resolved to resign, as we were the only two Englishmen on the Board. Shortly afterwards, some correspondence took place between Sir Langham Dale and the chairman, and financial matters were then brought before us. The chairman did not show me that correspondence; he simply told me that it had taken place. Now every financial matter is brought before us.

6385. What you would like is, that at the end of three years the public should elect all the members of the Board?—I take it that the public should undertake the entire responsibility of the institution as they are required to do by law.

6386. *Mr. Theron.*] Did the school suffer in any way in consequence of this state of things?—That is a question which is very difficult to answer.

6387. Were the public called upon to make good any deficiency?—No, all the financial responsibility is undertaken by the Dutch Reformed Church.

6388. So that you as a member of the committee may consider it a favour rather than otherwise that the Church has done such a thing?—I think that unless the Dutch Reformed Church had come forward at that time we should not have had the school.

6389. Then under any circumstances they did a good work?—They did a very good work indeed. Had it not been for the Dutch Reformed Church coming forward and offering to risk so much on the institution, we should never have had it, and it is an institution which is doing a great deal of good in our district. I am not going against the Dutch Reformed Church in any way.

6390. *President.*] Has any Government aid been given for building on that property?—I cannot answer that. I would state in justice to the Dutch Reformed Church, that up to the present the institution has not paid its way, so that they have not made a profit, although they have undertaken this important work.

Mr.
J. S. H. Holden.

Sept. 15th, 1891.

6391. *Dr. Berry.*] Is there any debt?—I believe there is a debt of £2,000 on the buildings alone.

6392. How is the interest paid?—I am not positive on that point.

Mr. A. Louw examined.

Mr.
A. Louw.

Sept. 15th, 1891.

6393. *Mr. Theron.*] I believe you are a farmer residing in the Bedford district?—I live about three hours from here at Ondersloordrift.

6394. Are there many farm schools in your part of the division?—I cannot say there are very many, but there are two or three round me.

6395. Have you a farm school?—I had one, but it is given up, the reason being that my governess took ill.

6396. Is there a great need in your division for such schools?—Yes.

6397. Why do not the farmers make more use of the facilities offered?—Those who can have made use of them; but there are many who cannot.

6398. Why?—Because they are too poor.

6399. Do they know what the Government contributes to such schools?—In my opinion there is considerable ignorance of the Government regulations.

6400. Do the people know what grant the Government gives for these farm schools?—I doubt if they all do.

6401. Do you think the grant would help them to get up such schools?—It was a great help to me, and it would be to others I am sure.

6402. Are the farms pretty close together in your part?—Yes; from 30 to 45 minutes distant.

6403. Are there any circuit schools in that part?—No; not in the part I live in.

6404. Are there many poor people who cannot make use of these farm schools?—Not where I am living. The farmers about there are able to establish farm schools with the Government aid. I do not know about elsewhere.

6405. Do the people know that the Government gives a grant for indigent boarders?—I was not aware of that. I had a poor child for twelve months in my school, and I never applied for such a grant because I did not know about it. I knew that such a grant was given to schools like the Seminary, but not to farmers. A district boarding school in my part would be a great assistance to the farmers. At Middleton there is a good school receiving Government aid. It is attended by the children of railway employés.

6406. Does the school work well?—Yes.

6407. *Rev. Moorrees.*] Have you thought of any plan for reaching the poorer class of children who cannot get to school?—I have often thought about it, but the difficulty is to get the funds. I think there ought to be a poll-tax in order to pay for the boarding of the poorer children attending the farm schools, such a tax being in proportion to the means of the tax-payer. I have one objection to the present system, and that is that to certificated teachers a higher grant is given, and by this means the poor suffer.

Mr. Jan Hendrikus Overman examined.

Mr.
Jan Hendrikus
Overman.

Sept. 15th, 1891.

6408. *President.*] I believe you are at the head of the agricultural department at the Gill College?—Yes.

6409. How many students are there in your department?—At present there are nineteen.

6410. Are they also students at the Gill College?—Most of them.

6411. Do you work into the college system?—It is all separate, but the hours are so arranged that I am able to receive students from the college who are anxious to be educated in my department.

6412. Does that work well?—Yes; but it might work better. I think the boys have too much work for the University examinations, too much literary work, and not enough attention is paid to the agricultural teaching.

6413. What alterations would you suggest?—I could not suggest anything at present, as we have not many boys. If we had a good number we could do more perhaps.

6414. Have you any technical teaching?—Yes. I have a second teacher for chemistry, and I have asked to have a teacher for botany, zoology and such like subjects.

6415. *Dr. Berry.*] What particular teaching do you impart to the pupils?—There is a dairy farm, and they are taught sheep, horse, and cattle-breeding, and also manual agriculture.

6416. Do you teach the use of agricultural implements?—Yes.

6417. Have you any ground for practising on?—Yes, we have nearly two morgen of ground; it belongs to the college. I take as much as I find necessary. The Town Council have also given me a large piece of commonage as pasture ground for cattle. I want to teach the boys how to make butter and cheese. I teach them all about planting and manuring, and so on.

Mr.
Jan Hendrikus
Overman.

Sept. 15th, 1891

6418. Do the boys actually work in the garden?—Very few.

6419. Who does the manual labour?—Black people generally. Mr. Fischer, the Agricultural Secretary, has sent me lately a German labourer.

6420. Then the boys simply come and look on?—Yes, generally; but when there is something special they do it. Last year we had tobacco planting, and in a case of that kind I like them to assist practically, because then they learn how to do the work themselves later on.

9421. Are they the sons of farmers who receive this education, or the sons of townspeople?—Nearly half-and-half.

6422. Which class shows the most interest in the work?—About the same, but the town boys can follow it much better than the others, as they have a superior education.

6423. Have you been sufficiently long a time at this work to enable you to watch the effects of the teaching on the boys' after career?—No. The school was only opened on the 3rd of February, 1890, not two years ago, and no pupil at present has followed the full course.

6424. Have you seen the effect of the system in any other country?—Yes. In Holland and Germany.

· 6425. What is the effect there upon boys after they leave?—They generally go on the large farms. From Holland they are frequently sent to India in connection with forest cultivation and other things.

6426. Does the Government insist that all young men receiving such appointments shall have gone through a previous course of training?—Yes.

6427. Have you a department of forestry here?—No, not at present, but it will come. Mr. Fischer has sent me seeds and trees.

6428. Do you give lectures to the boys?—Yes.

6429. On what subjects?—Various subjects, such as dairy farming, botany, horse and cattle-breeding, and so on.

6430. Did I understand you to say that only boys from the Gill College attend, or do boys come from other schools?—There is one boy at present who was at college in Graham's Town. He passed his Matriculation examination and then came to our agricultural school.

6431. How old is he?—17 or 18; he is a farmer's son.

6432. Is he likely to be a farmer himself?—Yes, I think so.

6433. This class of education can hardly touch the mass of the people, it is too costly, is is not?—The fee is only 10s. a quarter for the agricultural school; but students must have a certain preliminary education. At present, they must have passed the Elementary examination, but that is not enough. It would be better if they had passed a higher examination.

6434. Is there anything to hinder a teacher like yourself being attached to every first-class school in the colony?—There is no objection to it, it would be a very good thing.

6435. Would you advise such a course in the interests of agriculture and for the benefit of farmers' sons?—It would be a good thing to have a teacher for chemistry, botany and natural science.

6436. One teacher for the whole?—Yes, for all the natural sciences. Of course if you can have more than one teacher, so much the better.

6437. How would you propose to make a beginning in that direction?—In Holland and Germany they do not teach classics so much, but more natural science, and I think if the University examinations here could be extended to such subjects as botany, chemistry, and the like, it would have a very good influence. To be really effectual, an agricultural school ought to be on a farm.

6438. *President.*] Then you think you ought to have a farm here, a larger place?—Yes.

6439. *Dr. Berry.*] You think you cannot hope for much if you do not go in for that?—No. You should have the same as they have in Holland in a small way. There the sons of farmers and the poorer class of people work all day on the farm, and come into the village in the evening for two or three hours theoretical work. That works very well.

6440. *President.*] Then the scientific agricultural teaching in Holland is imparted at night principally?—Yes, in the case of the lower classes.

6441. Would you advise something of the kind being done here?—When they can come at night it would be a very good thing.

6442. Do you think it would answer here in Somerset East?—I am afraid the farmers' sons live too far away from the town here.

6443. *Dr. Berry.*] In Holland, who maintains these poor boys while they are being educated?—They go back to their own homes every night.

Mr.
Jon Hendrikus
Overman.
———
Sept. 15th, 1891.

6444. *President.*] Could not you arrange to give evening lectures here ?—Some people have asked me, and I intend starting a class for young farmers. They cannot come very often to town, but I think it will be on the first and third Saturday in every month. They have formed a kind of association for it.

6445. Do you think industrial teaching might be imparted to young native boys for two hours a day on such a farm if you had one here ?—I do not think so. Farm servants must be brought up on a farm, and I doubt if they get much good from what is understood as agricultural training. In Holland there are schools for teaching gardening, and something might be done in that way.

6446. Could you not make use of some of these natives on the farm and in that way teach them ?—It might be done. Gardening schools would be a good thing for the children of poor white people, for they are very ignorant of the commonest things. Some of them I know cannot work with a spade, or plant potatoes, or do anything in fact.

6447. Would you train boys to do this kind of work ?—Yes. In the garden schools in Holland they are all trained to it.

6448. *Mr. Theron.*] In what language do you give your lectures ?—In English.

6449. Are they all English boys ?—Half Dutch and half English.

6450. Do the Dutch boys understand English ?—Yes.

6451. Would you have your lectures that you speak of for farmers' sons also in English ?—Yes.

6452. Can they understand you ?—I think nearly everybody in this district understands English. You could not give lectures to the poorer people in English perhaps.

6453. Would you then divide your classes into Dutch and English ?—Yes, in such a case.

6454. Suppose you had nineteen students understanding Dutch as well as English, and one or two not understanding English, what would you do then ?—When you have only the poorer class you must teach them in Dutch.

6455. Do not you think that may be the reason why these boys do not come to your classes, because they do not understand the language ?—I do not think so.

6456. Do you think that a Dutch boy, at the stage when he is fit for the Elementary examination, is able to understand in English all the technical words you use ?—To pass the Elementary examination he must be pretty well up in English.

6457. Take the case of a farmer's boy whose associations have all been Dutch ?—I tell the pupils if they cannot understand anything, they must let me know, and then I tell them what it is in Dutch.

6458. If it were necessary, would you give the lectures in Dutch ?—I would prefer it very much. When I came here I could not speak a word of English.

6459. Would not the lectures be more attractive in Dutch than in English ?—I do not think so. As a rule, the boys can easily follow me.

6460. Are there many Dutch farmers about here ?—Yes.

6461. And it is your object to train their children, is it not ?—Yes.

6462. Would not you encourage them more to come to your classes if the lectures were in Dutch instead of English ?—I do not think so.

6463. Are there any boys in the class who do not understand English ?—There is only one.

6464. In their daily life is it not desirable that young farmers should understand Dutch as well as English ?—Yes. I think it is a good thing to know both languages.

6465. *Rev. Moorrees.*] Do boys in Holland begin to learn a second language at a very early age, or later on ?—They learn the first language when they are seven or eight years old; then they learn French, German and English when they are very young. A great many boys in Holland understand four languages.

6466. There are some people who think that if you begin a second language early, you destroy the elementary character of your instruction, but according to the experience of Holland it would seem not to be the case, would it ?—No.

6467. *Mr. Theron.*] Do they start with French or Dutch in Holland ?—They learn Dutch when they are 5½ years old very often. They go to school very early there.

6468. *President.*] What language are the examinations in ?—In Dutch.

6469. Do you agree with Professor MacWilliam's proposals with regard to Dutch in the Elementary examination ?—Yes.

6470. Is it about the best proposition you have seen ?—I think so. The English boys, in my opinion, will always have some advantage over the Dutch boys, and therefore I agree with his proposals.

6471. Do you think it would be a good thing to force English boys to learn Dutch ?—No.

6472. Why not ?—It is best to let everyone be free. You must not force either language.

6473. *Rev. Moorrees.*] Do you think it is right to encourage English boys who are living in this country to learn Dutch ?—Yes.

6474. And Dutch boys to learn English ?—Yes.

Mr.
Jan Hendrikus
Overman.

Sept. 16th, 1891.

Rev. J. H. Hofmeyr examined.

6475. *Rev. Moorrees.*] I believe you are minister of the Dutch Reformed Church here ?—Yes.

6476. How long have you been here ?—Since 1867 ; nearly twenty-five years.

Rev.
J. H. Hofmeyr.

Sept. 15th, 1891.

6477. Have you been connected with education for a very long while ?—Yes, to a certain extent. I have never been teaching directly, but I have always taken an interest in it and had a good deal to do with it.

6478. In your opinion, how can the irregularity of attendance of children, especially in the town schools, be prevented or alleviated ?—I think everything should be done in the way of inducement, and children should be encouraged to attend by means of bursaries and prizes.

6479. *President.*] Do you think compulsory education would be a good thing for the waifs and strays in towns ?—Yes, I do not think it would do any harm in town. If it were proved that parents could send their children and were altogether neglectful, they should be compelled, in the interests of the country, but even in that case persuasion should first be tried.

6480. Would you attempt it in some of the more populous centres ?—There might be this difficulty. If it were made a hard and fast rule, it might deter people living in the country moving into town for the purpose of educating their children, for fear of coming under its operation, as they might find it hard to conform to the rule in all respects. If some fair and equitable plan could be hit upon, I do not see much objection.

6481. *Rev. Moorrees.*] Are there any mission schools here ?—Yes ; there are several.

6482. Are they attended by coloured or white children ?—As far as I know by coloured children. There may be a few whites, but I hardly think so.

6483. Do you think the poorer class of white children is provided for in your schools in the town ?—Not altogether ; to a great extent they are. I think the school committees here have been very liberal in affording opportunities to poor children to attend school, both at the college and the seminary. There are a great many admitted as free scholars, even more than we are compelled to admit by law, and several others again are admitted at reduced rates—half, or even less.

6484. Is there any necessity here for some such school as the proposed fourth class public undenominational school ?—I do not think so.

6485. You have a wide acquaintance with the country, do you think these fourth class schools ought to be undenominational, or ought they to be under the same managers as the mission schools ?—No ; I think if fourth class schools are established, it would be better to have them on the undenominational principle.

6486. *Dr. Berry.*] Would you limit your opinion about undenominational schools to such as are necessary for the European population, or would you say that if it is necessary to set up additional schools in towns then these fourth class schools should be for the natives also ?—I am not sufficiently acquainted with mission schools. I cannot say whether they supply all the wants. If they do supply all the wants, it would be as well just to retain that system.

6487. Suppose there are more black children than can be put into the existing mission schools, would you be in favour of providing the required additional school accommodation more in the way of undenominational schools ?—For black children I would extend the mission schools ; it would be cheaper.

6488. Why would you do that ?—The machinery exists, and it would only require an additional teacher and perhaps an additional room. That would be much cheaper for the State than if a separate class of schools altogether had to be established.

6489. *President.*] Would you add an industrial department ?—I certainly think so, if the means can be found. At the same time, I think it would be very expensive for the country.

6490. Do you think the country would save it in the end by having these coloured people trained early in life to habits of industry ?—If they profit by it, there would be a saving in the long run.

6491. *Rev. Moorrees.*] Is not the best industrial training these natives can get to be had on a farm ?—If they go to farms ; but a great many do not go, and if some means can be devised to compel them to go in for some industrial training, I think, although expensive, it would be a good thing.

6492. *Dean Holmes.*] Would you be in favour of their being taught handicrafts as well as spade work ?—I would not go so far as that. It would be too expensive on the

Rev.
J. H. Hofmeyr.

Sept. 15th, 1891.

one hand, and on the other hand you would make them unfit for the station they have to fill in life. In the majority of instances, those who have ability will elevate themselves without such assistance.

6493. *Rev. Moorrees.*] What steps do you think should be taken to give Boards of Management perpetual succession?—I think it is of the greatest importance to have permanency in these Boards, and the best plan in my opinion would be to elect the members of the Board for two years, with this proviso, that half of the number should retire at the end of the first year, so as to have the other half remaining.

6494. Do you think the ratepayers throughout the district should elect?—My idea was that the simplest plan would be to follow the present lines as far as possible. At present, the different committees are elected by the resident householders.

6495. Would it not be better to have the Board chosen by the electors or by the householders for the whole district, and let it have control over all the schools in the district, and start schools wherever they were necessary, there being always an appeal from the local school committees to such Board?—If that were so, you would do away with the functions of the Superintendent-General of Education and his office to a great extent. Rather than have one Board of Management, I would have different committees, each committee promoting the interests of education in that particular district or field-cornetcy or whatever the area is. Then of course the committees would be responsible to the Superintendent-General of Education, receive instructions from him, and send in the returns to him.

6496. Is not there this difficulty, that if there is a deficiency, and a tax has to be levied, there is no machinery to collect it?—You have the necessary machinery in the Divisional Councils for collecting taxes, and they should be empowered by Act of Parliament to pay a certain amount over for the cause of education. If possible, I should say let the tax levied be the same throughout the country, and not separate for each district. My reason for that is this, that there would not be so much occasion for dissatisfaction with the tax as there would be if the different Divisional Councils levied different taxes, because then the inhabitants of one district might say, why should we have to pay a penny in the pound, whereas the inhabitants in other districts only pay a farthing or a half-penny. Then again, if there is a general tax, I think everyone knowing that he has to pay the tax, whether there is a school in his vicinity or not, would be induced to take more interest in education than they otherwise would do. If there happened to be a surplus in one district, it could go to defray the expenses in another district.

6497. Would not that system be very expensive, and would not each Board of Managers try to get from the fund as big a share as possible and embark perhaps on expensive undertakings?—I would lay down a rule that there should be no more than a certain number of schools in each district, according to its size. The wants of the country should be investigated, and then parcelled out into certain districts, and with a view to save expense, there might be one or two smaller elementary schools in each field-cornetcy. If the Divisional Council levies a tax, there is a certain class that would not have to pay, because as it is now, I believe they can only levy on fixed property, so that those who are tenants and derive benefit from mission schools would go free, although their wants would have to be supplied. In their case I think there should be either a tenants' tax or a hut tax.

6498. *Mr. Theron.*] How would you fix the tax, and what district would you select to base your calculation upon?—I do not know whether it would do to select a special district. My idea was, that before levying such a tax or drawing up an Act of Parliament, investigation should take place in each district to see how many schools would supply its needs, so as to bring a school say within two hours' walking of each parent. By this means the expense could be calculated more or less.

6499. Suppose you have in one part a first class school in good order, paying its expenses and something over, and in another district you have a school heavily in debt, the managers having to struggle and make sacrifices in order to keep it going, how would you arrange the division of the funds?—My idea is, that the income should simply be from the rates and from the school fees. If under such circumstances in one district there is a surplus and in another there is a deficiency, I should say let the surplus of the one go towards the expenses of the other. There would be no injustice in that, because the whole population would pay the same tax.

6500. Would you place mission schools under the same Board?—If those benefiting by the mission schools contribute their share of the taxes to the divisional council, otherwise not; it would be unfair.

6501. If you are going to make a general tax for education, that is, tax Europeans as well as natives, would it not in that case be far better that the Government should impose the tax and collect it through their several officers?—If that can be done, by all means. The simpler the machinery the better.

6502. Then you would dispense with the Divisional Councils altogether?—Yes. I only named them because I thought in that way it would be cheaper, but I have no objection to the other plan. It is immaterial to me in what way it is done, as long as those who are immediately interested in the education of a particular district have a voice, and have the means of establishing a school.

Rev. J. H. Hofmeyr. Sept. 15th, 1891.

6503. *Dean Holmes.*] Would it not be more palatable in imposing the tax, if the taxpayers felt that the money was to be spent in their own district, rather than sent off to some unknown part of the colony?—It might look more palatable, but I think that education is a thing of such importance that we must not ask whether it is palatable or not. The time has come when I think we should do all in our power to educate everyone, and whether palatable or not, it is a burden that ought to be borne by every citizen.

6504. *Dr. Berry.* You said that where there was a surplus in one division you would be in favour of applying it to the needs of another division not so well off?— If there is general taxation I do not see that it matters, so long as everyone has his wants supplied.

6505. *President.*] Is it not a fact that under the present system there is no duty imposed on anyone to bring into existence a school where it is wanted?—Yes, and facilities are given to oppose the establishment of schools by irresponsible persons.

6506. And there is also no duty imposed on anyone to continue a school, is there? —None whatever, except a moral duty.

6507. Does not that apply both to denominational and undenominational schools. The mission schools are the creation of the churches, and the undenominational schools are the creation of the guarantors, and the moment they step aside, the schools may fall, may they not?—Exactly.

6508. Would it not be wise to bring into existence a body charged by law with the duty of finding schools to fill up the gaps wherever they find there are no schools throughout the district?—It should be the duty of someone.

6509. If you call upon the ratepayers to pay, is it not also fair to give them a voice in the expenditure of the money which they have contributed?—Yes.

6510. Do you think the ratepayers would be contented if they had not a voice? —Certainly not to such an extent as if they had a voice.

6511. As the State is interested in education, do you think it is a proper thing that it should contribute largely out of the public funds towards its promotion?—Yes.

6512. Where people cannot pay, you think the State ought to come forward liberally and even pay everything if necessary?—Yes.

6513. Are you in favour of substituting for the guarantors a Board created by the Superintendent-General of Education?—No, I would have a Board elected by those interested in each particular school. They would be guided by certain regulations and have certain powers.

6514. Suppose there is a deficiency, upon whom would you come?—The Superintendent-General of Education should have the right to demand a slightly increased rate for the next year. It should be arranged for the school fees to be sent to the Superintendent-General of Education and also the school rate, which ought to be regulated with a view to the necessary expenditure, so that if possible there should be no deficiency.

6515. Suppose the local Board is extravagant, and spends more than is necessary? —I do not see how that can happen if they have got their regulations to guide them. Everything must be defined, and it is known beforehand what the Government will have to give.

6516. But you do not know what fees you will get. Suppose they are less than you anticipate, there is a deficiency at once, is there not?—In such a case, if the fault lies with the committee, the public would find it out, and have reason to be dissatisfied with the managers.

6517. Would it not be a good plan, if there was a deficiency after the Government contribution and the fees had been paid, that it should be made good by a rate levied throughout the whole district?—If different taxes are levied in different places I am afraid it would do harm to the cause of education and bring about discontent. The inhabitants of one district would complain that they had to pay more than their neighbours.

6518. *Dr. Berry.*] We are asked here to recommend to the Government what steps we think should be taken to give Boards of Management perpetual succession. Virtually we are asked to say whether, in our opinion, Boards of Management ought to be abolished or continued, and if continued, how? I understand from you that you are in favour of abolishing the present Boards of Management?—Yes; elected by the guarantors.

6519. You must have some local experience that enables you to come to your opinion. What is your experience as to the working of that system here under the guarantor system?—I have had no experience, simply because before the college took over the first-class boys' school and the Consistory of the Dutch Reformed Church the first-class girls' school, there never was a first-class school in the district, for what reason I do not know—whether they were afraid of the guarantee principle, or whether they were too penurious; but there was nothing of the kind.

6520. In reply to the circular issued to chairmen of Boards of Managers you state: "The rents and profits of the Gill estate stand as a guarantee in lieu of the pledge required from guarantors, and the trustees of the college are *ex officio* members of the Board of Managers." I want to know how this came [about. How does a private body like the trustees of an institution come to be managers *ex officio* of the first class public school?—I came here in March, 1867, and then there was for boys a Government school under the old system—that is to say, the teacher was paid exclusively by the Government, and admission was free. I believe that afterwards a small fee was paid, but it was very little. Then the Gill College was established, but according to the will of Dr. Gill it was to provide only for higher education. We thought there ought to be a first class school to act as a feeder to the college, a kind of preparatory school, because the college was intended originally exclusively for young men preparing for the higher examinations. We held a meeting, but could not get the public to establish a first class school, so we decided to establish a second class school. A certain number put down their names as guarantors, and we got a teacher, but the thing fell through. We had to pay a certain percentage of our guarantee, and then there was no school again for several years. Afterwards, I think about 1882, the trustees of the college felt that something was necessary, and that a preparatory school ought to be established in connection with the college. As the inhabitants did not come forward, one of the trustees spoke to Sir Langham Dale about it, and asked him whether there was not a possibility of connecting a first class school with the college. He was told what the circumstances were, and after some discussion he agreed to accept the trustees in lieu of the guarantors, provided the public agreed to it at a public meeting properly convened, the public to have a right to elect three members, who with the trustees should form the school committee. That was brought forward at a public meeting and accepted.

6521. How many trustees were to be on the Board of Management?—All the trustees. There were ten members of the Board altogether.

6522. Where do these trustees come from?—Five from the district of Somerset and two from the district of Bedford. Dr. Gill, under his will, appointed seven trustees.

6523. Are those alive now?—Only one out of the seven.

6524. Where do the six new ones come from?—He made provision in his will that if anyone should resign or die, the remaining trustees could elect another trustee in his stead.

6525. And that has gone on until six have been elected out of the original seven?—Yes; the trust is perpetuated by self-election.

6526. So that your public school is now managed by a body of ten members, seven of whom are self-elected?—Yes; but it must be borne in mind that the public does not incur a farthing of responsibility.

6527. Do you think it is a good thing for the public thus to shuffle off their responsibility?—Perhaps not altogether, but they ought to have come forward.

6528. I see it also stated in your reply to the circular: "The trustees of the college are the legal holders of the property. By the donor's will the property is vested in a Board permanently. In order to erect a boarding house, application was made to Parliament for £1,000, but it has not yet been received; but the trustees hope to get it soon, and also a loan of £3,500, in terms of Act 11 of 1882." How does that matter stand. Has that £1,000 been received from Parliament, or the £3,500?—I am no longer on the Board of Trustees, so I cannot speak with confidence; but I believe the £1,000 has been paid.

6529. You were on the Board when the application was made, were you not?—Yes.

6530. The £1,000 has been paid and spent on property that is not held by a public body, has it not?—The £1,000 is for the boarding establishment. I do not know what negotiations have taken place.

6531. Has the loan of £3,500 been received or not?—I have been told so.

6532. To whom was it paid?—I suppose to the trustees' treasurer.

6533. Where would the interest payable for that money come from?—From the proceeds of the boarding establishment. It was to supply a want.

6534. Is the trust no longer in funds?—It is not in funds for the boarding establishment; it is in funds for paying the professors.

6535. So the interest on the £3,500 which has been borrowed will be payable out of the school revenue?—Yes; I believe it is borrowed under the Public Loans Act, and will repay itself in twenty-five years.

6536. Do you think your system of management is a good one, and is it carrying out the law under which public undenominational schools exist. Sir Langham Dale says the great boon of these schools is that they are the people's schools, but here we have a school that is not the people's school; it is in the hands of certain men who elect themselves, is it not?—They would not have had any school had it not been so.

6537. Does not this case prove that the system as it at present stands leads to some abuse?—Yes.

6538. *Mr. Theron.*] Are the Victoria College, the South African College, and the Wellington Seminary under the guarantee system, or under the Higher Education Act?—I believe they are under the guarantee system, but I cannot speak positively.

6539. *Rev. Moorrees.*] Do you think the trustees would at any time be willing to forego the privilege of being managers if the public would undertake the responsibilities of a first class school?—I think they would, and even if they did not feel inclined, I think the public is perfectly at liberty to break the engagement and say, we do not wish to have you conducting our first class school; we will conduct it on our own lines. It was simply a case of necessity. It would have been much better if there were a first class school, as then there would have been more funds to raise the college. If there was a properly equipped and effectively working first class school, there would have been so many young men who could go to the college, and the college would have flourished much more than it has done for years past, and the funds that have to be devoted to some extent to the preparatory department could have been devoted to higher education.

6540. So that at any moment the public can step in and make it a public school if they like?—Yes, I believe so. I may say that the Girls' Seminary is somewhat on the same basis, but there the holders of the property are the Dutch Reformed Church. It was established in much the same way. I came here in 1867, and up to 1885 there was not a first class girls school in Somerset East. Once there was an attempt to start one, and the promise of a grant was obtained from the Superintendent-General of Education, but it never really started, and the grant was never drawn. In the interests of the children belonging to our church we started the seminary, and afterwards, when we saw that the general public reaped the benefit of the institution, I spoke to Sir Langham Dale and obtained a grant on certain conditions. The Consistory of the Dutch Reformed Church is responsible, and they appoint five members of the Board of Management and the public three members. We brought the matter before the public at a properly convened meeting, and the public endorsed what had been done, and cordially approved of it. The school has been working very well and harmoniously up to this time. Some time ago, we asked the Superintendent-General of Education for a grant for building purposes, and we got £1,000, but it was with the express stipulation that for twenty years these buildings should be used for a public undenominational school, and if at any time within twenty years they ceased to be so used, the Consistory should bind itself to repay the money, which we did.

6541. *President.*] After the twenty years, to whom do the buildings belong?—I suppose they would fall to the Consistory of the Dutch Reformed Church after they have served the purposes of education.

6542. And in the case of the Gill College, if the undenominational school falls through at the end of three years, which it may do if the guarantors stop, the £1,000 given for the purpose of building will be sunk in property belonging to the Gill College, will it not?—Yes.

6543. So that the Gill College trustees will get the benefit of that £1,000?—Yes, I suppose so.

6544. By what process of law can the Government step in, or anybody else step in, and deprive the Gill College trustees of its right to its own property?—That is more a question for the lawyers. There are several other institutions conducted on the same lines.

6545. Can you name them?—I believe the Cradock school for girls is one; and such arrangements just prove that something else ought to be done.

6546. *Rev. Moorrees.*] With regard to the language question, would you let a pass in Dutch in the Elementary examination make up for failure in English?—Certainly, just the same as it is now in the Matriculation examination. There, English and a modern language are lumped together. There are 500 marks, and 100 marks is a pass in those two subjects, so there is a possibility of a candidate not knowing a single word of English and yet passing, and *vice versâ*.

EE 2

Rev.
J. H. Hofmeyr.

Sept. 15th, 1891.

6547. Do not you think that Dutch and English being the two languages of the country, a higher average of marks ought to be assigned to them than to other foreign languages ?—There may be a good many whose mother tongue is German, French, or Kafir.

6548. But they are not the acknowledged languages of the country like English and Dutch, are they ?—Kafir would be if you are to judge fairly.

6549. Kafir is not spoken in Parliament, is it ?—You could not say it is not a language of the country because it is not spoken in Parliament. I think what you suggest would be rather unfair over against the children of French or German parents.

6550. Is not there unfairness now for Dutch children at the Elementary examination ?—There may be a little unfairness perhaps in the case of country children who have come to school rather late ; they may not have such a command of English as to be able to express themselves with that facility which is required for passing an examination well, and just for that reason I should extend the Elementary examination and add another subject. I think further, that the time has passed now for having the Elementary examination so low. The age is fixed at sixteen at least, but at fourteen or fifteen I think they ought to be far enough advanced to be able to pass an additional examination. One great advantage would be this, that there would not be such a number going up for the Elementary examination, and it is very difficult to examine the papers as they should be examined in the limited time given.

6551. Is there not a danger of Dutch being neglected, or not sufficiently taught rather, in some schools, on account of its not being a subject for the Elementary examination ?—If there is any such danger, I think it is caused more by the indifference of the parents. If children knew that they would have to pass an examination in Dutch, a good many would apply themselves more thoroughly.

6552. And the teachers would take more pains, would they not ?—Yes. There would be better provision for teaching Dutch.

6553. Do you think it would destroy the elementary character of the examination? —I do not think so.

6554. There are people who think that there is a very wide difference between the dialect spoken in the country·and high Dutch, in fact they seem to think they are almost two different languages ; what is your opinion ?—I cannot say I am an authority, but I think such an idea is altogether wrong ; the difference is very much exaggerated. I know it is the general impression that those who speak the so-called Dutch patois could not make anything out of a Dutch book, but that is quite erroneous. It is exactly the same language, only those who speak the Cape Dutch do not know much about the inflections, conjugations, and grammar—that is the chief difference. I may add that I know Dutchmen who have come from Holland and expressed to me their conviction that the Dutch spoken here is more easily understood by Hollanders than many of the dialects spoken in Holland by the people themselves.

6555. *President.*] What additional facilities do you think should be given to meet the wants of the agricultural population ?—At present there are circuit schools and farm schools, and if these could be carried out to their legitimate issue I believe it would prove very expensive. If all the farm schools for instance, were to get grants according to the regulations, I think the whole amount paid in that way would very nearly amount to the half of what good elementary schools in suitable places in different districts would cost, and if it could be done, I certainly would prefer the latter. If more elementary schools under efficient lady teachers could be established, I think those schools would not be very expensive, and in that way much better provision would be made for the wants of the country population than by the present plan.

6556. Have you formed any opinion on the subject of night schools ?—I think in large places they ought to supply a great desideratum ; but I cannot express much opinion about them.

6557. Do you know anything about technical schools ?—I should be certainly in favour of them. One or two technical schools should supply the wants of the colony, but the great thing is cheap board and lodging. That is the great difficulty.

6558. *Dr. Berry.*] At a private farm school now, an indigent child can receive a grant of £9 from Government, £3 for schooling and £6 for boarding : does that throw any additional light on your reply about the establishment of elementary schools as opposed to private farm schools ?—No; the same thing would apply there.

6559. Do you think there would be any chance of getting a moderately well-to-do farmer to take indigent children and have them educated with his own, if he got £9 a year for each ?—A well-to-do farmer would not do it, but he would probably take the child or children of a poor relative with pleasure.

6560. Then something might be done in that way you think ?—Yes.

6561. Is it generally known that such a sum of money is available ?—I do not think it is.

6562. Ought such a grant as £9 to promote education, in your opinion ?—It ought to promote it, but it would not supply the want altogether, because there would be many who would not have the advantage of sending a child to school ou the farm of a relative, and if they are to subsist on £9 it would not pay.

6563. Would such elementary schools as you propose starting be helped by this arrangement ?—I think so.

6564. Would not the attendance be irregular at such schools ?—The benefits would at any rate be much greater than the disadvantages.

6565. What salary would be required for ladies starting such schools ?—I should say £40 to £50 a year.

6566. You would require a house for the teacher and a building to teach in, would you not ?—Yes, that would have to be supplied by the Government.

Mr. Edward A. Brailsford examined.

6567. *President.*] What are you?—Chief clerk to the Civil Commissioner at Somerset East.

6568. Do you take an interest in educational matters ?—Yes.

6569. What is your opinion about the present system of guarantors ?—I think that the School Board system should take the place of the guarantors.

6570. For what reason ?—Under the present arrangement you cannot perpetuate a school. I know an instance in Victoria West, where we had a school with guarantors. The teacher could only bring up the children to a certain standard, as they were drafted away to Cape Town and other places; the guarantors withdrew their names, and the school fell through.

6571. What became of the school property ?—They had the school in a small building attached to the church ; it was a kind of mission school connected with the Church of England. The minister carried it on afterwards just as a kind of charity school, with no support whatever.

6572. Do you think that a permanent School Board should be brought into existence ?—Yes.

6573. How would you constitute it ?—The members should be elected by the rate-payers.

6574. What duties would you vest in that Board ?—The management of the schools.

6575. Would you force it to find schools sufficient for the wants of the people ?—Yes ; and there ought to be a rate levied if necessary.

6576. Should the Government contribute largely out of the general revenue ?—I should say half. The school fees should be taken by the Board, and if there is a deficiency then the rates should pay it.

6577. Was that the opinion of the community in Victoria West where you were ?—It was the opinion of the intelligent part of the community after the experience they had which caused the school to fall to pieces.

6578. Is it the opinion of a large section here ?—I think so.

6579. Has the matter been discussed here frequently ?—Yes.

6580. Have you taken part in the election of members for the Boards of the Seminary and Gill College ?—Yes, both.

6581. Is there any objection to the present system by which the electors choose only three of the members?—Public opinion is against it, and at the election before last there was some ill feeling caused. At the present time, the Dutch Reformed Church has a right to put a certain number of members on the Board and they are altogether in the majority, which creates a great deal of dissatisfaction.

6582. Could that state of things be remedied if there was a School Board as suggested ?—Yes.

6583. *Dr. Berry.*] Is there any outcry on the ground that the public do not have a sufficient voice in the management of the schools?—Yes, and there is another grievance. The ratepayers are called upon to vote for members of the Board, and yet they never know anything about the proceedings of the Board. We have repeatedly spoken about it, but we are always told that Sir Langham Dale has an objection to the proceedings of these Boards being made public. It is different in the case of Divisional Councils and Municipalities. There you elect your members, and you know what they do, as the proceedings are published, but in this case it is not so.

6584. You want more publicity given to the proceedings ?—Yes.

6585. Do you think the public here would be prepared to resume their responsibility and return to the old system, they electing the whole Board of Management ?—If a rate was levied to defray expenses.

6586. You think the two ought to go together ?—Yes.

Mr.
*Edward A.
Brailsford.*

Sept. 15th, 1891.

6587. *President.*] What is your opinion on the subject of language, do you agree with the views expressed by Professor MacWilliam?—Yes.

6588. Do you think they represent the opinion in Somerset East generally?—I think so.

6589. *Dean Holmes.*] When you say generally, are you thinking of the Dutch people as well as the English?—I think it meets the wants of all the people here. The more intelligent portion of the farmers with whom I come in contract do not want Dutch exclusively taught, although some again are all for the *taal.*

Middelburg, Thursday, September 17th, 1891.

PRESENT :

Sir J. D. BARRY (President),

Dr. Berry, | Rev. Coetzee,
Dean Holmes, | Mr. Theron.

Mr. J. Joubert, M.L.A., examined.

Mr.
J. Joubert,
M.L.A.

Sept. 17th, 1891.

6590. *President.*] I believe you are a member of the Legislative Assembly for the district of Albert?—Yes.

6591. And you have been so for many years?—Yes.

6592. Do you reside in that district?—Yes; I am a farmer.

9593. Have you been on any School Board?—No.

6594. I believe you have always taken an interest in educational matters?—Yes.

6595. Can you offer any opinion on the subject of the irregularity of attendance of children in town schools. Do you think the time has arrived when more attention ought to be paid to getting into school all children of a schoolable age?—I have been under the impression for many years since that something ought to be done to force children to go to school, but I have spoken to several people in the district who do not approve of it. I may say that in connection with the Dutch Reformed Church at Burghersdorp, to which I belong, we have a fund out of which we educate poor people's children, and notwithstanding this, we have had great difficulty in getting parents to make application with a view to getting their children sent to school.

6596. You mean to get them to make application for a portion of the funds?—Yes. They can get teaching and boarding as well, but they will not come forward. We have to run after them to get them to send their children, and when they are in school, we have to look after them all the time, as the parents do not trouble themselves to see that they attend properly.

6597. Is this fund for the benefit of farm children or children in town?—It is only for children connected with the Church on farms or in town.

6598. What reason have they given for not sending their children?—They think they ought to be left free to send their children or not, and that no parents should be compelled. The better class of parents, who take an interest in education, send their children; it is the poorer classes who are so neglectful.

6599. Do these parents think that education is a bad thing, or do they merely say it ought to be voluntary?—They say it ought to be voluntary, but I cannot account for their negligence.

6600. Do you think that every parent ought to send his children to school if he can, and if they do not, they ought to be made to?—Yes, every one ought to be made to send their children to school.

6601. Where they will not, do you think the State ought to step in?—Yes; assistance ought to be given by the State. Our Church, as I say, has got a fund for education, but it is only for children connected with that Church. It was originally intended to prepare children to become members of the Church.

6602. What is the amount of the fund?—I cannot say exactly, but the people make so little use of it that it is accumulating.

6603. *Rev. Coetzee.*] What allowance do you give out of the fund?—It all depends upon whether the parents can contribute themselves or not.

6604. What is the maximum amount given by your Church for educating these poor children?—We have paid £1 a month for boarding, and 10s. a month for schooling.

6605. *President.*] You mean to say that in some cases the Church has actually paid £18 a year for a child?—Yes, where necessary.

6606. To what school do you send the children?—To any school where there is a chance of sending them. There is a committee appointed.

6607. *Rev. Coetzee.*] Have any of these children ever attended the public school at Burghersdorp?—No; not the public school.

Mr.
J Joubert,
M.L.A.

Sept. 17th, 1891.

6608. Suppose children from the country attend a school in town, how do they find the rest of the boarding if you allow £1 a month. It requires about £40 a year, does it not ?—They have never applied yet, but I daresay it would be granted if necessary.

6609. Have you explained the thing to the parents ?—Yes, we have tried to get them to come forward and make use of the advantage, but they seem disinclined.

6610. *President.*] Do you think it would be a good thing for the Government to lay down a rule to the effect that every child up to a certain age living in towns should go to school, the State providing such school if the parents cannot pay ?—I think in towns children should be forced to go to school. There are numbers of children running about who ought to be in school.

6611. Would you also apply compulsory education to coloured children, and force them into some school ?—In the case of coloured children and the poorer class of whites, I would suggest that they might be taught in night schools, and during the day be trained to some kind of handicraft.

6612. What sort of industries would you suggest in Burghersdorp for these children ?—The principal work that coloured children ought to learn is to till the soil, but they might also learn certain trades, such as carpentering.

6613. Do you think that would have a good effect on the native population afterwards ?—Yes, my experience is that if children grow up idle it becomes a habit with them not to work.

6614. Would you have two classes of schools, an upper and a lower, into which children of a certain age should be forced, the State helping where the parents are too poor to pay, and in the lower school do you think the training should be chiefly industrial ? —Yes.

6615. *Rev. Coetzee.*] With regard to the rural population, would you be in favour of compulsion in the districts as well ?—Yes ; where necessary.

6616. How would you provide the school accommodation there ?—Provision ought to be made either by the Government or by the churches.

6617. In what way should the Government make provision ?—My idea is, and I stated it at the last general election, that there ought to be one industrial school at least in each district, provided by the Government, and I think to a large extent it would be self-supporting. It may not be so at the commencement, but afterwards it would. Children whose parents are not able to have them taught at their own expense, ought to be sent there to have not only literary teaching, but also industrial work. When they have reached a certain age, they can go on a farm and assist their parents. That has been my idea all along to have schools like that in every district. If Government does not do anything in that direction, then I think that each district ought of its own accord to have a school of that kind.

6618. Where all children should be compelled to go ?—Yes ; children whose parents are neglectful, and who do not themselves send their children to school.

6619. *President.*] You say if the Government will not do this, the several districts should. Do you think the Government ought to contribute largely ?—My idea is that every church should have its own school and provide for it ; but at the same time, it is the duty of the Government to assist and see that all children are being educated.

6620. How would it do for the State to find half the teaching and half the building, and then if after the fees have been paid there is a deficiency, let it be paid out of the rates. Is not that fairer than putting it on the Church which may perhaps not have the means at hand ?—I think that children ought to get religious as well as mental training, and the Government cannot so well see to the former. There are so many different sects.

6621. You think that as things are now, it is better perhaps to work through these agencies ?—Yes. That is my opinion. I do not believe in education where only the mind is trained, and where no religious education accompanies the mental training.

6622. You think the training of the mind, body, and heart all ought to go together ?—Yes. My idea is that the failure to a large extent of the education in this country is due to the fact that moral training has been neglected, and only mental training has been attempted.

6623. Do you think that is the secret why farmers as a rule object to native education ?—Yes ; and the education in the Government schools as well.

6624. You think if the natives got more industrial training combined with moral training, there would not be so much objection ?—I do not believe there would, provided the literary teaching did not go beyond a certain point.

6625. Is your opinion shared by the vast majority of farmers in your district ?—I believe it is.

6626. Have you pretty well gauged their opinion from time to time ?—Yes. It is the same with the poorer class of white children. I do not believe that all children

226

ought to be educated up to the same standard mentally. Very many of them might get their education in night schools, and be taught to work at various trades during the day time. As soon as they are old enough to work, they ought to go out to assist their parents.

6627. Up to a certain age, do not you think it is a good thing to let all school children have mental, moral, and physical training, even in the day time?—Yes, from about eight years of age.

6628. Would you say even before eight?—Yes.

6629. *Mr. Theron.*] As I understand, you would make this industrial institution a denominational school, that is, work it through church agencies?—There cannot be more than one of these schools in each district, and of course that will have to be kept up by the Government and consequently be undenominational. I think the country requires that children should learn to work.

6630. If it was found difficult to work this on denominational principles, you would not mind in that case working it on undenominational principles, would you?—No.

6631. *President.*] You think where the parents can afford it, they ought to send their children to some centre to be taught, and they should be made to do so, and where they cannot afford it, the State and the district should join in helping them?—Yes. Where there is an industrial school, there must be some provision made for boarding the children.

6632. Do not you think that would be rather expensive?—It would; that is the only objection that occurs to me. Under the present circumstances of our finances I see a difficulty.

6633. Apart from the expense, do not you think there would be some degree of unwillingness on the part of the farmers to submit to such a law and take their children from the farms into town?—Yes; they do object. I have spoken to several, and I have found very few who agree with me. They do not think there ought to be any compulsion.

6634. Would it not be a good thing to apply it only to the towns at first as an experiment?—Yes; that could be done.

6635. If you were to force coloured children into industrial schools in town, do you think the parents would take kindly to it, or would they be likely to leave the town and go among the farmers?—I think they will take to it kindly.

6636. If they do go away from the town, it would be all the better for the farmers, would it not?—Yes.

6636A. *Mr. Theron.*] Would such an industrial institution in town be likely to attract many of the servants on farms?—I do not think so, because the parents would not be able, as a rule, to afford to live in the town. It would be only those whose families are not large.

6637. *President.*] If anything, it will have the effect of making them go into the country rather, you think?—Yes.

6638. Altogether, you think it is a thing that ought to be started?—Yes; it is necessary for the country to have something of the kind, so that children who are running about idle may be taught to work.

6639. *Mr. Theron.*] In saying that, do you include both whites and blacks?—I have been thinking more of the interests of the whites, but of course it can be made to apply to the blacks as well.

6640. Would you put up boarding houses for the natives?—It ought to be left in the hands of a Board to make all the necessary arrangements as to what children should be taken in, and for how long, and so on. It is not possible to take all children.

6641. Would you make boarding provision for the blacks as well as for the whites?—I was thinking more of the whites when I spoke of boarding. I think the ratepayers ought to provide for it.

6642. You think that the natives should have industrial training?—They should work in the day, and receive their education at night.

6643. *President.*] Would you start some such schools on native locations?—I thi k so.

6644. *Dr. Berry.*] Take a district like Queen's Town, where you have a native location about 25 miles long by 10 miles wide, containing a population of some 8,000 natives, what would you do there?—Every child could not of course be taken into school. I am afraid it would be too expensive.

6645. Would you add industrial work to the other schooling?—Yes. I am in favour of giving them training in all kinds of industries. My idea is, that a boy when leaving school, ought more or less to know how to begin to work for his living.

6646. *President.*] Do you think it would be a good thing to levy a tax for the education of the natives?—Yes; something of the kind will have to be done in each division for the whites also. Government should contribute largely, but it cannot be expected to do everything.

6647. If a locality contributes, it ought to have a voice in the management of the school, ought it not?—Yes.

Mr. J. Joubert, M.L.A.

Sept. 17th, 1891.

6648. And you think there ought to be a School Board?—Yes. I hardly think the Divisional Council is a suitable body, as men are not elected on that body usually with a view to their interest in educational matters.

6649. Is it not often the case that a Divisional Councillor may be unwilling to do Divisional Council work, who would be a very good man to do educational work?—Yes; it may be possible to combine the two qualities, but I should prefer a separate Board.

6650. How would you elect such a Board?—I think the Divisional Council should have a voice in the matter, as we would have to go to them if a tax was necessary.

6651. Would you let the Divisional Council nominate one or two members?—Yes.

6652. And would you give the Government a voice?—If the Government contributes, it would expect to have a voice, but I think it would be better not so.

6653. Rev. Coetzee.] Would this Board have to provide for the education of the children in the whole district?—Yes. For those who cannot afford to pay. Wherever there is a school wanted they must supply it.

6654. Would it have to include the natives in the district?—Yes.

6655. Dr. Berry.] Take the Queen's Town Divisional Council, would you give them power to levy a tax on the natives for school purposes?—It is only fair that they should contribute.

6656. Would you say that the Divisional Council should hand over the whole of that money to the School Board for native purposes?—Yes, what is collected for their education. They should levy a special tax on Europeans as well.

6657. Mr. Theron.] How would you arrange the rate?—The same as in the case of the Divisional Council rate, where three farthings in the pound is set apart for roads and one farthing for the Divisional Police.

6658. Should the education tax be a separate tax?—Yes, but levied at the same time as the general rate.

6659. You would not levy a heavier tax than is required for the year, would you, and if the schools work well and there is no deficiency, then there would be no tax?—Just so.

6660. You would not give the Board money in hand which it did not require would you?—No.

6661. Do not you think it would be dangerous to leave the Board without any representative from the Divisional Council to act as a check on the expenditure, otherwise they might run into extravagance, and come to the Divisional Council to make good whatever they want?—The Divisional Council ought to be represented.

6662. Rev. Coetzee.] Suppose there are different schools and different Boards, and there is a deficiency in only one of the wards, would you tax the whole district to make up the deficit, or only the ward?—It would be difficult to take a ward: you must stick to the division.

6663. Mr. Theron.] The Board has to provide for the education of the division, has it not?—Yes

6664. If this Board is brought into existence, would you give it any control over the present undenominational schools?—It is difficult for me to say, but a Board like that ought to have control over all the schools in the division.

6665. Would you by degrees bring the present undenominational schools under it?—Yes, I would as soon as possible.

6666. Would you bring them at once under it by force of law?—I am afraid it is almost impossible to do it all at once.

6667. Do you see your way to giving the present Boards of Management perpetual succession?—I am afraid that the two bodies will afterwards come into collision with each other if there is another Board in the same district. I should have thought that after the lapse of three years, the present bodies would work into the new Board.

6668. You think the creation of a new Board is the only way to give perpetual succession?—Yes.

6669. Would you vest the school property in the new Board to be created?—Yes.

6670. Rev. Coetzee.] Then you would abolish the guarantors?—Yes.

6671. President.] If you establish this system, you do not want any contribution from the Divisional Council do you, except in the way you have indicated, namely, the rates?—No.

6672. How far do you think the rates ought to be responsible for building and teaching. If the Government gives half and the fees are collected, should the rates pay the deficiency for building and teaching?—Yes.

6673. How would you prevent extravagance on the part of the Board?—I have not made up my mind how far they ought to go, but still I think there ought to be a limit fixed.

[G. 3—'92.]

FF

Mr.
J. Junhart,
M.L.A.

Sept. 17th, 1891.

6674. Would it be a good thing if it was required that they should come to the Government for advice and for its consent before spending the ratepayers' money beyond a certain amount?—I would rather leave it with the Divisional Council in each division to decide how far they should go. Some districts are rich and others are poor, and every district cannot pay equally.

6675. *Dean Holmes.*] You might have a very extravagant Divisional Council. Would it not therefore be well to give the Education Department some power of veto?—As the Divisional Councils are elected by the ratepayers, it is for the ratepayers to see that there is a check on too much expenditure.

6676. Suppose a School Board wanted to spend say £60 upon the decoration of a building, would you say that was a fit thing to refer to the Central Department, whether they should be allowed to spend so much on mere ornament?—I do not think it likely that a Divisional Council would spend money extravagantly.

6677. Are you averse to giving them any reference to the Education Department?—I think each Board in a division ought to know what is required, and it is for the Divisional Council to know whether the division can afford it.

6678. Is it not right that the Education Department should have a say as to whether expenditure is necessary or not?—If the Government contributes, it should have a voice too perhaps.

6679. *President.*] Can you suggest anything beyond what exists at present to meet the wants of the agricultural population?—I do not see what more can be done than is done at present.

6680. If this Board is started, would it be able to supply any wants?—I think so. The difficulty that farmers labour under now is that in most instances they cannot very well afford to send their children to boarding schools in towns and they are obliged to take teachers on the farm.

6681. *Rev. Coetzee.*] Do not you think if the grant for indigent boarders is increased, the farmers will be able to avail themselves more of the existing institutions?—I do not think it is generally known among the farmers that the grants available are £6 for boarding and £3 besides for education.

6682. Where there is no district boarding school on a farm, would you give more aid than £6 to the parents of indigent children, in order to enable them to be sent to boarding school where the boarding is higher than it would be on farms?—If the finances of the country could afford it they ought to get more, because in most instances you find the farmers for some reason or other cannot have their children taught on the farm; they have to send them to boarding schools in the town, and if there are many children, their education is neglected.

6683. What is the great difficulty with the farmers; is it the school fees or the boarding?—The boarding is the principal thing: the school fees are comparatively nothing. When you send a child to school in town, you have to pay £40 a year as a rule: in very few instances is it £30.

6684. Would you give the Board the power out of the local rates to contribute £6 in addition to the £6 contributed by the Government for boarding?—Yes, that might be done.

6685. In the Albert district and many other parts of the Colony there are many homesteads where the people are unable to find school accommodation for their children; can you suggest anything to meet the wants of these people?—It is difficult to meet the special cases.

6686. *President.*] With regard to these special cases, would you give the Board the power to start a free school in any country locality to meet the wants of indigent children on farms, the Government contributing half and the Board contributing the other half, provided the Education Department fully approves of such a thing?—Yes. I know that all the wants cannot be provided for at once: it must be gradual, and you must not spend too much at a time.

6687. *Mr. Theron.*] Suppose there is no land available for such a school to be put up on a farm, what would you do in that case; or land might be mortgaged and sold, and it would be risky to put up a permanent building, would it not?—I should say where it is possible to get a teacher on a place, a temporary building might be erected.

6688. Then you think you may not only have a circuit teacher, but a circuit teacher's building with a school attached?—Yes; a wooden building that could be moved if necessary. A farmer might not like to allow Government to take a piece of ground about his homestead.

6689. Would you give Boards power to erect such movable buildings?—Yes.

6690. *Mr. Theron.*] What further facilities, in your opinion, can be afforded for giving instruction in both the English and Dutch languages, and how far can that object be attained through the medium of the Elementary and other examinations.

Do you think there is at present sufficient provision made in our schools for teaching Dutch?—I am not not very well acquainted with the matter, but to my idea the teaching of Dutch is too much neglected.

Mr.
J. Joubert,
M.L.A.

Sept. 17th, 1891.

6691. Why do you think it is neglected?—I know that in Burghersdorp it has been neglected. The children have received a Dutch education, but I think not sufficient.

6692. Is there any reason why they do not receive more instruction in Dutch?—No. I really cannot say why it is. I know my children who went to school in Burghersdorp, received very little Dutch education, scarcely any at all, in fact.

6693. *Rev. Coetzee.*] How long ago is that?—Three or four years ago.

6694. *Mr. Theron.*] Are the teachers bound by any rules or regulations?—I know there is a certain amount of Dutch taught; all the children learn a little Dutch, but not sufficient. I do not know whether it takes up too much time, or why it is. Perhaps the teachers who give the lessons are not quite competent; I cannot say.

6695. Is not the cause due to the Elementary examination, no Dutch being required for it?—There was an examination in Dutch at the school, but nevertheless my children learned very little. I have had to teach them Dutch over again when they came home. The farmers cannot do without Dutch; we have it in our Church, and it is required every day. I find that I require my Dutch as much as English.

6696. Could further facilities in your opinion be afforded for giving instruction in Dutch in our schools; have you thought of any way out of the difficulty?—The only thing is, there is not enough attention paid to it.

6697. Would you lay it down as a rule that more Dutch should be taught in the schools?—Yes; I think it should receive more attention.

6698. Suppose you had a son or a daughter intending to go up for the Elementary examination, would not you handicap the child, by having it taught in Dutch, when the examination has to be done in English?—In the higher examinations it might perhaps to some extent handicap the child, but I do not think so in the lower examination. When I was educated, we had only small schools, so I cannot speak as to the higher examinations. As far as my education has gone, I find that it did not interfere with my learning English to learn Dutch as well, in fact I find it advantageous to me. When I know what an English word is in Dutch, I know the meaning of it so much better.

6699. The Elementary is the first examination that a child goes up for, and nearly all children go up for it as a rule, what guarantee would you have that your child knows sufficient Dutch if that examination is only passed in English?—That is why I think in the Elementary examination a child should pass in Dutch as well. Every child ought to be compelled to learn Dutch. If the parents think it is not necessary, or that it is not required, I say it is necessary in this country.

6700. Would you compel an English child to pass the Elementary examination in Dutch?—That was my idea, that every child should be compelled to learn Dutch. It may be that in certain centres where it is not required it would be hard to compel a child to learn Dutch. When I sent my children to school, I was asked whether they were to learn French and German. I said, no, I did not see the necessity for French, as it is not used here in this country. At the same time, if it had been a rule in the school, I would not have had any objection to letting them learn French or German.

6701. Would you compel an English child to pass his examination in Dutch; would not you handicap that child, and put it to great difficulty and inconvenience unnecessarily?—I do not think so. It is necessary for every child in this country to know Dutch to a certain extent, and the only way to be sure that it knows enough is to have it in the Elementary examination.

6702. *Dean Holmes.*] Would not that have the effect of diminishing by more than half the number of candidates going in for the Elementary examination. The parents might say, we do not care a bit about your examination, might they not?—I do not think that would be the case.

6703. If a child has not been taught Dutch, a parent might say, I am not obliged to send it up for examination. I will keep it out altogether and send to England for papers. Is not that so?—I doubt if that would be done.

6704. If there were Boards created, would not a great deal of this difficulty be got over, by their providing for Dutch teaching in accordance with the wishes of the district?—Yes. It would be a good thing.

6705. If there was an optional Dutch paper in the Elementary examination, do not you think that boys throughout the country would take the Dutch paper, and that that would be better than making it compulsory?—I think in most districts the boys would like to go in for it.

6706. Do you think it would be an encouragement if bursaries were given to those who passed well in Dutch?—I think so.

FF 2

Mr.
J. Joubert,
M.L.A.
——
Sept. 17th, 1891.

6707. Is it not better to lead people on voluntarily than compel them, except where it is absolutely necessary ?—Yes.

6708. Would not that meet the difficulty by giving bursaries or prizes, as is done in the case of the Civil Service. There the candidates have a situation to look forward to ?—That might perhaps meet the case in my district, and I think all the districts about here. As far as I know, the young men, with few exceptions, would go in for learning Dutch.

6709. *Mr. Theron.*] Would you like to see English done away with in the Elementary examination ?—No, certainly not.

6710. But you would like to see all children learn Dutch ?—Yes, the two languages are officially required in this country. I admit that English is required more than Dutch, but still we require Dutch.

6711. Do we find any difficulty in Parliament with our Dutch, that we cannot be understood by other members ?—Certainly not. At the commencement, some did not understand well perhaps, but now they do.

6712. *Rev. Coetzee.*] Do the Dutch people look upon it as a grievance that Dutch is not taken up as a subject in the Elementary examination ?—Yes, they do.

Mr. James R. Cuthbert examined.

Mr.
James R. Cuthbert.
——
Sept. 17th, 1891.

6713. *President.*] I believe you are headmaster of the Public Undenominational School at Burghersdorp ?—Yes.

6714. How long have you been so ?—About five years.

6715. Have you had any experience as teacher before in the Colony ?—Yes, I was headmaster at Cradock for three years in the Public Undenominational First Class School, and also first assistant master at the Public School at Graham's Town for three years.

6716. Do the children on the roll attend regularly ?—I have had no difficulty in that respect. The attendance is very good indeed at Burghersdorp, and it also was at Cradock, the percentage of absentees being very small, at the outside not more than about five per cent.

6717. Are there any children outside the reach of the schools who are not on the roll ?—Yes.

6718. Do you think they ought to be brought into school ?—Yes.

6719. What scheme would you propose ?—There are facilities in the way of free scholarships in the case of Burghersdorp. Deserving cases, approved of by the managers, are admitted free. At present we have twenty-two free scholarships in the school.

6720. Are there many who do not avail themselves of this and who ought to do so? —Yes; a good many.

6721. Is there room for them ?—Yes; quite sufficient.

6722. Would you force them into school as they do in Europe ; do you think a compulsory Act should be passed to meet the case of children running about the streets during school hours ?—For large centres it might be advisable, but not in up-country towns I think.

6723. How would you work the compulsory system where it was enforced ?—Pretty much as they do in England, through a Board. There should be a truant officer also.

6724. Are you in favour of bringing School Boards into existence ?—Yes.

6725. How would you constitute them ?—I should like to see an elected School Board, but as far as the country villages are concerned, it would not be suitable ; a nominee Board would be better perhaps.

6726. If you had an elective Board would you have it for the whole district, to include town and country, and let the whole district have the advantage ?—I should be opposed to an elected School Board for the country districts : it means rating power. You cannot always get the best class of men for School Board purposes ; the clergy and professional men are generally the most active in the country districts, and I hardly think those men would seek election on such a Board.

6727. Do not you think if the Board was limited to educational work, men of the class you mention would endeavour to get a seat on it ?—In some towns it would be the case, but not everywhere. In Burghersdorp especially we have exceptional men in that respect. We have men who would seek it, and it would work there.

6728. If the Government contributes half the total expense of teaching and building and then you have the fees added, do not you think it would be fair for the rates to be called upon to make up any deficiency, in the same manner as the guarantors are now. Would it not be better to distribute the amount of the deficiency among all the ratepayers than limit it to the guarantors ?—Yes, it would be certainly, but I hardly think the country population would care for direct taxation.

6729. If they did, it would be the best thing, would it not ?—Yes.

Mr.
James R. Cuthbert.

Sept. 17th, 1891.

6730. Can you suggest any better scheme that would meet the requirements of the country, and be workable ?—There might be a nominee Board, the Divisional Council nominating two members, the municipality two, the Government two, and the school managers two, in each district.

6731. Suppose there was a deficiency after the Government had contributed its half, to what body would you go to make it up ?—In the case of a town school, the municipality might pay half the deficiency, provided the Government paid the other half, on the £ for £ principle.

6732. Then you would still go to the rates for something ?—But it would be indirectly.

6733. Do you think the ratepayers would be satisfied with such an arrangement ? —I think they would.

6734. *Dean Holmes.* In your neighbourhood, would the managers of voluntary schools be willing to work under such a Board ?—Yes, I think so.

6735. Provided they were allowed to manage their own affairs ?—Yes, as a sub-committee, but the Central Board would have full control and could be appealed to.

6736. *Rev. Coetzee.*] Are you in favour of retaining the present guarantee system ? —No. It is too much a fluctuating body.

6737. *President.*] You would prefer to substitute a Board ?—Yes, I think so.

6738. Can you suggest any means for giving perpetual succession under the existing arrangement ?—Not unless you incorporate the Boards of Management by Act of Parliament or have a nominee Board.

6739. In whom would you vest the school property ?—In the new Board. In some cases there are trustees already. In the case of Burghersdorp, the school property is vested in the Civil Commissioner for the time being, the minister of the Dutch Reformed Church, the chairman of the municipality, the chairman of the library, and the eldest Justice of the Peace.

6740. *Rev. Coetzee.*] Would you give the Board rating powers ?—In the case of Cape Town, Port Elizabeth, Kimberley, Graham's Town, and some of the larger towns, I think it might have rating powers, the same as under the School Board system at home. I do not think our Dutch friends would care for direct taxation.

6741. *President.*] You think it a sound principle, and it must ultimately come to that ?—Yes, in time.

6742. *Dr. Berry.*] Have you seen an election of school managers in Burghersdorp ?—Yes.

6743. How is the meeting called together ?—By advertisement in the local papers, and posters about the town. A notice is also put up at the municipality and the court room.

6744. Who gets up the guarantee list ?—Generally the Secretary or the Treasurer of the old Board.

6745. Do the guarantors sign for a specific amount, or for a pro rata share in any deficiency ?—It is generally left to themselves what amount they will give.

6746. And after that, the managers are chosen ?—Yes.

6747. *Mr. Theron.*] Are they only holders of the property for the time being ?— Yes. When the school is wanted for public purposes, the managers have nothing at all to do with it; it is left entirely with the trustees.

6748. Are any of the trustees *ex officio* managers ?—No. They are quite separate.

6749. *Dr. Berry.*] Have you ever had any deficiency in your school ?—I believe there was once a small deficiency.

6750. *Dean Holmes.*] Is the school carried on on a sufficiently liberal scale for all educational purposes ?—Yes.

6751. *President.*] Ought there in many cases to be any deficiency at all if the managers did their duty ?—No.

6752. Then the ratepayers would not have much to fear ?—No.

6753. Would you have the members of the Board paid ?—No.

6754. Would you pay the country members when they come into town anything for travelling expenses on the same scale as members of Divisional Councils are paid ?—I think so.

6755. Need the time occupied by such Board, if it devoted its time wholly to educational matters, be very great ?—No.

6756. In the case of Burghersdorp, how much time would it take for such a Board to do its work thoroughly ?—When once the system is properly organized, it might meet once a quarter. I think that would be sufficient; there might be a special meeting occasionally.

6757. Would you be in favour of the Board doing its work directly, that is to say, starting and working schools under its own management, or would you be in favour of

Mr.
James R. Cuthbert.

Sept. 17th, 1891.

allowing volunteers to work under its supervision, the volunteers in that case getting the Government contribution which otherwise the Board would have, or would you let the two go on side by side, giving the Board power to do what they like?—I would give them power to do what they like.

6758. You think that would really fit more into the circumstances of the country?—Yes, so far as my experience goes.

6759. Would there be much friction between the denominations if such an elastic system were brought into existence?—I think so.

6760. Do you think the present system of educating the natives is the best one that could be devised?—I think they ought to have a great deal more industrial work than they are having.

6761. What sort of industrial work would you recommend?—As far as the girls are concerned, they should be taught sewing and household duties. That is done in the Institutions of the French missionaries in Basutoland which I have visited. They try to make them good domestic servants. The males are taught shoemaking, carpentry, and various trades, as well as ploughing and other agricultural work.

6762. Does it require a very large capital to be invested originally for such industrial education of a simple character?—I think a small capital would suffice.

6763. Do not you think it would be a good thing, wherever you have a native school, to have some industry taught in connection with it?—Yes, especially in towns I would have trades taught.

6764. Do you say that with a view to the future vocation in life of most of these natives; they have to work, and therefore the sooner they begin to learn the better?—Undoubtedly.

6765. Would you teach them to read and write?—The three r's, but nothing beyond standard three or four.

6766. Would you put these schools under the Boards?—I do not think so. The churches are doing good work, and it is a cheaper system.

6767. You would allow the Board to let the churches do the work if they thought it best?—Yes, I hardly think it is advisable to change the present system as far as the natives are concerned. I would leave the Board to deal entirely with the European population.

6768. Would you give more aid to these bodies that work with the natives than they get now, in consideration of their having an industrial department?—I think the present grants are quite sufficient for native schools.

6769. Would not you give them some aid for industrial work?—Yes, to start it.

6770. Would it be a wise thing to levy some sort of tax upon the natives in locations for educational purposes?—Yes.

6771. And hand it over to the Board?—Yes, that could be done very well.

6772. Would that be sufficient to establish the buildings required for industrial purposes?—I believe it would be more than sufficient.

6773. Would you allow the Board to have a free hand entirely, or would you require them to do what the Central Education Department considered an absolute necessity?—They should certainly be under the control of the Education Department.

6774. So they would not be able to screen themselves by saying, we will not do anything; they must supply the wants which are necessary?—Yes, and failing that, the Education Department should compel them.

6775. Would you allow the Education Department to step in and do the work where it was not done?—Yes.

6776. Would such a system work, in your opinion?—Yes, I certainly think it would.

6777. *Rev. Coetzee.*] Suppose the Board finds it necessary to establish a school in a certain locality and the Education Department says no?—I hardly think they would.

6778. But suppose it happens?—The department would want very strong evidence.

6779. *Dean Holmes.*] Would you be satisfied with the decision that the department was convinced there was no need for such a school?—Yes, quite so.

6780. Suppose this Board took charge of the native districts, would you give them power to close any mission schools which overlap one another?—Yes.

6781. They would take into consideration the actual needs of a district, and if they found it over provided for they should take steps to bring it to its proper limit?—Yes.

6782. Would you allow that to be done without the approval of the Education Department?—Yes.

6783. Would you give voluntary bodies this safeguard, that they should never be interfered with unless the Central Department authorized it?—Yes.

6784. *President.*] Suppose a mission school declines to come in under the Board, and prefers to remain going on as it is, what would you do in such a case; would you let it go on as long as it fulfils the conditions?—Yes, as long as it fulfils the present conditions, but I would give it no further aid.

6785. You would only give it further aid after the approval of the Board ?— Yes.

6786. Suppose an undenominational school also refuses to come under the Board, would you allow it to continue until such time as it did want to come in ?—Yes, it was so in England. It is only a matter of time ; they have to come in.

Mr. James R. Cuthbert
Sept. 17th, 1891.

6787. *Dean Holmes.*] Were not those voluntary schools that refused in England ?—Chiefly voluntary schools.

6788. Not public undenominational schools, were they ?—Yes, they were really public schools under the old parochial system.

6789. *Rev. Coetzee.*] What were the objections of the schools you refer to ?—I believe they objected to the rating power.

6790. *Dr. Berry.*] Suppose the Divisional Council or the Municipality failed to nominate their two members, what would you do ?—I presume there would be some Act to compel them to do so if the nominee system were established.

6791. *Dean Holmes.*] With regard to the election of the Board, is it not preferable to give the election to the ratepayers who would come under the Divisional Council franchise, and in addition to that, allow the Divisional Council to have a representative upon the Board ?—I do not think it is advisable, the work is quite different, and the men are not always suited for it.

6792. The ratepayers would proably elect men competent to control educational matters, and then as the rates would come through the Divisional Council, should not that body have power to send one of its members to represent it on the School Board ?—I do not think so.

6793. Have you known the case of any nominee Board in this Colony that has ever worked well ?—I have not known the case of a nominee Board in the Colony.

6794. Have not you heard of objections to the Medical Board in Cape Town ?—Yes ; but in country districts and towns you have a different class of men. I know that in Cradock we had men seeking election on the municipality for the purpose of cutting down the school expenditure. I think it would be better to let the majority of the Board be elected by the ratepayers. The Divisional Council might perhaps be allowed to nominate one member in order to inform the Board of the financial position of the district.

6795. *Dr. Berry.*] How does the present system of Boards of Management affect teachers ?—In the case of Burghersdorp we could not have a better Board ; in the case of Cradock it was slightly different : the men were not the best men to be had. There were one or two uneducated men on the Board, and they were inclined to tamper with the school.

6796. *President.*] Were these men elected by the municipality ?—By the ratepayers and by the municipality.

6797. *Mr. Theron.*] Under the present guarantee system, is there any security of tenure so far as the office of teacher is concerned ?—No, at the end of three years the teacher is liable to be dismissed. They never do so in Burghersdorp, but in many schools I understand they give notice to the head-master and the whole staff.

6798. *President.*] Is that another reason why there should be a Board ?—Yes.

6799. *Mr. Theron.*] Under the present guarantee system, is the new Board, when elected, compelled to take over the teachers and debts, and everything else from the old Board ?—I think they would be compelled to take over the debts, I do not know about the teachers.

6800. The new Board system would have to be constituted under an Act of Parliament, and then although there is a new election every three or five years, there will be permanency in such a body, will there not ?—Yes. I should like to see teachers have a little more security of office, even under such a Board. I think they should have an appeal to the Education Department, so that the case might be thoroughly sifted.

6801. *President.*] How far would you allow the Education Department to interfere ? If they found the man was thoroughly efficient and doing his work well, they might say if he was not retained, the grant would be withdrawn.

6802. *Dr. Berry.*] What was your experience under the Town Council in Cradock ?—I think the system of working a school under the Municipality is really a good one as far as my experience goes in this country. What I object to as a rule is the character of the men on the municipalities ; they are not the best men you can get. That was my experience in Cradock.

6803. If they were elected for educational purposes, it would be a different matter, would it not ?—Yes.

6804. Were the proceedings of the Education Committee of the Town Council published in the papers ?—Yes.

6805. Is that a good or a bad thing ?—I think it is desirable that the public should know what is going on. It should be left in the hands of the Town Clerk to say what were private matters.

234

Mr. James R. Cuthbert.

Sept. 17th, 1891.

6806. Should the proceedings be conducted in public or privately?—I think it better on the whole to have them private. Many things come before the Board of a private character.

6807. *Dean Holmes.*] Is it not better for reporters to be present at the Board meetings; any work of a delicate or private nature could be transacted in committee, could it not?—Yes; that might meet the case.

6808. *Dr. Berry.*] Did you observe any friction at Cradock between the nominee members of the Dutch Reformed Church and the Town Council members?—Yes, there was a slight friction.

6809. *Rev. Coetzee.*] Was there ever a deficiency in the school at Cradock?—No.

6810. *Dr. Berry.*] How was the debt of £1,000 paid?—Out of the school funds.

6811. *President.*] On what ground was the school at Cradock built?—On ground belonging to the Church.

6812. Do you think it advisable in any case in future, that Government money should be given towards any portion of a building not on public school property and vested in a Board?—I should think not.

6813. Therefore if a volunteer body does the work, it must do it on condition that it only receives a grant for teaching and not for building?—Yes.

6814. *Rev. Coetzee.*] Are any Divisional Council or Municipal rates levied on the Burghersdorp school buildings?—The Act exempts school buildings from both Divisional Council and Municipal rates. I think on the school house they have to pay rates. I do not think that is exempt.

6815. *President.*] Have you anything to suggest with regard to meeting the wants of the agricultural population?—The present facilities are I think all that can be desired, they only require to be better known.

6816. Do you think if there were a Board, the knowledge of the present facilities would be more widely diffused?—Yes.

6816A. *Rev. Coetzee.*] Do you think the present grants are sufficient?—In the case of farm schools they are very liberal, but in the case of district boarding schools in outlying districts, where the population is scattered and the farmers are poor, there might be an improvement in the present grants. They give now £100 for the head teacher, £60 for the second, and £6 a head capitation grant. I think it might be £125, £75, and £12 respectively. I have had some experience in country schools of this description, and I find they have very great difficulty in getting along.

6817. Have you had any experience in localities where there are indigent children?—Yes.

6818. *Mr. Theron.*] What was their difficulty in getting along as you say?—The income is not sufficient to meet the expenditure. The poor farmers generally would be more inclined to take advantage of the system if greater facilities were offered.

6819. Would not you carry that out by increasing the capitation grant only?—I think you want a better class of teachers; you cannot get a good teacher for the money. In farm schools, the grants are liberal enough, but in district boarding schools, the work is a little more advanced.

6820. *President.*] Do you think district boarding schools are sufficiently endowed as far as boarding goes?—No. I should increase the allowance from £6 to £12 per head.

6821. In that case would you call upon the Government to pay the whole, or if a Board is brought into existence, would you let the Board look to the rates for half the contribution for indigent children?—I would go to the Government for the £12 capitation allowance.

6822. Would not that have this effect in some cases, that the Board might call upon the Government too readily for this increase?—I do not think so.

6823. Would it not lead to possible abuse?—The Government would have to enquire into the matter and require the fullest information before contributing. It might come too heavy upon the rates, and people might object to it.

6824. *Mr. Theron.*] You say that you have about twenty indigent children in your school; but are there not other poor children in the place?—Yes.

6825. Might there not be an outcry that there was favouritism going on?—I would say then let the Government give half and the School Board half, so as to avoid anything like favouritism or undue pressure.

6826. *Dr. Berry.*] It has been suggested by some witnesses that instead of developing that system which you now propose, efforts should be made rather to establish elementary schools under female teachers much more thickly in the agricultural districts; would that plan work?—Yes; in some districts it would be very necessary, but there are outlying places where it would be impossible to do that; you would have to establish a boarding school.

6827. Suppose you put an elementary school under a female teacher practically within eight or ten miles of almost every householder, might not it be done cheaper than by developing the boarding school system, which would be rather costly ?—You often get a lot of farmers together and you have to start a school and it would be cheaper and better to have a good centre ; you could organise it better and have a larger and better staff.

Mr.
James R. Cuthbert

Sept. 17th, 1691.

6828. *Mr. Theron.*] You spoke about the insufficiency of teachers, do you think the present arrangement for training teachers enough to give a good supply of teachers ? —I do not. I think the pupil-teacher system should be extended, especially in the case of girls, in order to supply the wants of private farm schools. We want a better class of trained teachers for the more advanced public schools. I have worked under the pupil-teacher system in Scotland, and it has its disadvantages, but it is the best thing for the country in my opinion. In Scotland it works well, and it certainly made me a good teacher, if I am one.

6829. Do you consider that our teachers, trained as pupil teachers, when they leave school to undertake their duties, are sufficiently trained for the work they undertake ?—I would remedy the evil by extending the pupil-teacher system only in first class schools under competent teachers.

6830. Would you give a further grant for that purpose ?—I think the grant is quite sufficient. There is one thing in favour of the pupil teacher system in this country, they are very much older when they begin teaching than they are at home. They have not to pass the Teachers' Examination here till they have reached eighteen, with three years' apprenticeship beginning at fifteen.

6831. *Dean Holmes.*] How would you compare the Teachers' Examination here with the Queen's College examination at home ?—It is infinitely easier.

6832. Have not you found in certain cases very elementary people teaching in chools ?—Yes.

6833. And in other cases have not you found teachers who are not good at their work, though they may be fairly instructed themselves ?—Yes, I have found that.

6834. Where you have inspected, what is your experience as to the results of farm schools as compared with public schools ?—In many cases I have found farm schools doing quite as good work as my own, and I have found also the reverse.

6835. *Dr. Berry.*] The average standard is quite as high in these as in other schools, is it not ?—Yes.

6836. *Dean Holmes.*] Does the Government Inspector in your district ever go to these schools ?—No.

6837. He leaves it to you always ?—Yes.

6838. *Dr. Berry.*] Have you seen Sir Langham Dale's recommendation about pupil-teachers ?—Yes, I think that recommendation should be carried out. I find that very often farmers come to me to get teachers for their schools, and I have great difficulty in getting farm school teachers. The supply is not equal to the demand, so I would suggest that we should have a kind of central registry at the Education Department, where we could get the names of eligible candidates. That would be a great facility.

6839. Where anyone open to engagement as a teacher from any part could have his or her name registered ?—Yes, and failing the School Board system being introduced, I think an organising inspector should be sent round the district to see what the educational wants are.

6840. Even with the Boards, would not that be well, so as to be able to let the Government know whether they were doing their work ?—It would be very desirable, but there would not be the same necessity for it.

6841. *Rev. Coetzee.*] Do you think there is any necessity for increasing the staff of Inspectors ?—Certainly.

6842. Is it advisable that they should stay a longer time in a place and acquaint themselves with the style of teaching and other things ?—Yes, I have found it a great advantage in inspecting farm schools, when the inspection is finished, to take the children and teach a certain lesson in the presence of the teacher, and show her how it ought to be taught, particularly in the case of object lessons, and they have been very grateful for it. I think the same thing would be an advantage in the third class schools. Many teachers are very glad of a hint or two, and when the inspector goes round, instead of just leaving after the inspection, he might spend a day in instructing the teacher in this manner.

6843. *President.*] Do you think that elementary science is taught sufficiently ?— It ought to be taught more in all our schools.

6844. What would you suggest for farm schools in that direction ?—Object lessons. There is a suitable series which is very well graduated, and it would be very suitable for farm schools, and even many town schools. I have such a system at my school through all the standards, even the very lowest.

GG

Mr.
James R. Cuthbert.

Sept. 17th, 1891.

6845. Would you suggest anything for the other schools in addition to what they have now?—The pupils should be taught botany, geology, acoustics, the principles of light and heat, &c. They should have a selection of these subjects, and in certain places I would have the principles of agriculture taught. I would almost make that compulsory in the first class school of every district, a part of the school curriculum.

6846. Would not you want some ground?—You could teach the theoretical part without ground.

6847. Could you suggest anything in order to have practical teaching?—I should say that the School Board might offer facilities for the children of farmers to go to a place like Stellenbosch or Somerset East, and bursaries might also be awarded.

6848. Have you considered the subject of free education at all?—Yes, I have taken a great interest in what has been going on at home.

6849. Have you any suggestion to make?—I would like to see it carried out here, but of course there are many obstacles. Money is the chief thing.

6849A. Would you give the Board the power, where there is an indigent class, from whom you can expect no fees whatever, or where the collection of the fees would absorb too much of the master's attention, and be troublesome and irritating, to bring into existence a free school, Government contributing half the expense and the rate-payers the other half?—Yes, I should like to see that.

6850. In no case without the consent of both?—Certainly.

6851. What is the objection to bringing into existence free schools in this country? —The chief stumbling-block is the Government not providing sufficient money.

6852. Have you anything to suggest with reference to night schools?—I should like to see them established. I think a great many young men in towns would be glad to take advantage of them if a proper system was organized.

6853. What system would you organize if you had to start the thing?—I would give a fairly reasonable grant to a teacher if he would undertake the work so many nights a week.

6854. On condition there was a certain attendance?—Yes.

6855. Would you have the school inspected?—Yes.

6856. By the Board?—By the Education Department.

6857. *Dean Holmes.*] You would have it open for a certain number of nights in the year, and each pupil presented for inspection for a grant must have made so many attendances?—Yes.

6858. *Dr. Berry.*] Would you employ the teacher of a Government aided day school for the work?—Yes.

6859. It has been suggested that it is too much for a teacher to teach in the day-time and at night as well?—To a certain extent that is quite true, but I think assistant masters might do it. The headmaster has quite sufficient to attend to without giving his time to night schools. I have known them refuse it on all occasions, and give the assistant master the benefit.

6860. You would not object to your assistant working in a night school, would you?—No; I should be only too delighted.

6861. *Dean Holmes.*] Would you have night schools for young women also?—I do not see why there should not be. I would have a mixed school as far as that goes.

6862. *President.*] Would early morning schools answer?—Yes. We want that. I would say in summer begin at seven and work till half past eight; then break up for breakfast till half past nine, and work on till one. If there is any additional work to be done, the pupils might come back about five o'clock, after the heat of the day is over.

6863. What I meant was, early morning schools in lieu of night schools?—I hardly think that would be practicable.

6864. Have you any knowledge of technical schools?—Not in this country. I have lectured in technical schools at home on magnetism and electricity.

6865. Do you know the Heriot School?—Yes.

6866. Do you think it is advisable to attempt to create technical schools here?— Very advisable.

6867. How many?—Two would be sufficient, one for the East and one for the West, or even one as a start, somewhere near Cape Town, say at Salt River where there are facilities.

6868. What do you mean by lecturing?—Lectures are given on certain subjects and accompanied by experiments, and afterwards examinations are held. Having fixed upon a suitable centre, I would have a well equipped staff, and let candidates from the various public schools have inducements offered in the way of bursaries.

6869. Should such a technical school be supported entirely by the central Government?—I think so.

Mr.
James R. Cuthbert.
Sept. 17th, 1891.

6870. And you would invite pupils from all parts?—Yes.

6871. What do you think would be the cost?—I think £1,500 should cover the expenditure.

6872. Could you work such a school in connection with an agricultural college such as they have at Stellenbosch?—It could be done, but I think that would hardly be a suitable centre.

6873. Do you think our agricultural schools have been a success as far as you have been able to judge?—I am not in a position to reply to that question.

6874. With regard to the facilities for the children of railway employés, have you considered that subject?—Yes. I feel sure when the present facilities are better known, they will be more appreciated and made use of.

6875. Are there any further facilities wanted in your opinion?—I do not think so; they are quite adequate.

6876. It has been suggested that it would be better to have the girls concentrated in certain centres in towns as boarders, a contribution being granted towards the expense; do you think that would answer?—I do not think that is necessary.

6877. Do you think the farm and railway schools could be worked into one?—Yes, at certain places, and they are in fact being worked in that way.

6878. At Molteno, where the junction is to be, is there such a school?—No.

6879. Is there one at Aliwal?—Yes.

6880. Did you organise that?—I did.

6881. How many children attend there?—There are twenty-three on the roll. The time of the trains is very suitable for bringing the children and taking them home—that is, in the direction of Aliwal, not in the direction of Molteno. When the junction is completed, no doubt the facilities in that respect will be all right, and we shall be able to make a very much larger railway centre. I have spoken to the Traffic Manager, and he will do his best to let the trains run so as to accommodate the children going and returning. I daresay there would be fifty or sixty daily.

6882. Do you think farm children should be granted free passes to travel to and from school?—I do not think that is necessary. They have the advantage of farm school grants.

6883. You think it would be rather an unwise thing?—Yes; it might prevent farm schools being a success.

6884. If there are farm schools in the neighbourhood, do not you think it advisable to induce the children of railway employés to attend them?—Many of them do take advantage of the farm schools.

6885. Which in your opinion are the best, the farm schools that are being used in this way, or the schools specially provided for the children of railway employés?—I think that both do equally good work.

6886. *Dean Holmes.*] Is the railway school at Burghersdorp under the management of a committee?—No.

6887. What kind of management is there?—The Stationmaster, Inspector of permanent way, the Rev. Bodington, and myself manage it.

6888. Who elects you?—We elect ourselves.

6889. *Dr. Berry.*] Where is the school held?—In a building at the station.

6890. If there was a Board brought into existence, do you think it would be wise to bring these railway schools under it?—I think so; very desirable.

6891. Would it not be well in multiplying these schools, to take into consideration a place like Molteno?—Yes; that will come, and other places also. There is one at Cyphergat.

6892. Is there one lower down?—There is one below Queenstown, at Tylden.

6893. Is not a school required between Cyphergat and Queenstown?—There is one required, but the trains do not run suitably.

6894. What would you do in that case?—If a farm school exists near the railway, let the ganger's children go there.

6895. *President.*] Would you provide for those parents who are anxious to let their children go to centres for their education?—I do not think that is necessary in the case of these gangers' children.

6896. Would not it be better for them if they mixed with children in town schools? No.

6897. You think they are a lower class?—Yes; I approached my own managers with a view to taking this school under their direct management, and they refused it on that ground.

6898. That it would tend to injure the character of the school?—Yes.

6899. If this Board is started, and it is the opinion that it is necessary to have two schools drawing the same amount of aid from the Government, would you allow

Mr.
James R. Cuthbert.

Sept. 17th, 1891.

those two schools to come into existence on account of the character of the pupils, or is it better to have one?—It is better to have one; you can mould the character of the children better.

6900. Do you think it advisable for the Government to extend its aid and give any contribution to private adventure schools?—Not where a school is managed by a teacher for his own profit, by no means.

6901. Where it is not conducted upon that principle would you aid it?—Yes; I would, if it satisfied the Board—only then. I might say that the regulations are evidently very flexible, inasmuch as a grant is given to a voluntary school at Burghersdorp as a district boarding school. The regulations provide that a district boarding school must be six miles from the nearest public school.

6902. *Dean Holmes.*] If there were a system of compulsion in the larger towns, would you allow inspectors who are properly qualified to visit these private adventure schools, and if they reported that they were inefficient, that should not be counted as an attendance?—No.

6903. Would you allow a number of children in a place to be educated in a quite inefficient school perhaps?—As long as they are attending school.

6904. As an educationalist do you think that would be good?—It would hardly be just to punish these people.

6905. Suppose an inspector in the course of his visit reports that a school has totally insufficient space, inadequate appliances, and that it is altogether unsatisfactory, how would you deal with such a school?—I hardly think if a school is so bad as you describe, it would be in existence. Parents would take their children away, and send them to a better school. Taking the circumstances of this country into consideration, it would be too much interference, and at present I would not do it. With regard to the education of gangers' children, I think it would be a good principle to adopt, that when men are removed from a section near a school, only those with children should be put in their place. I have met with some difficulty in that respect. Gangers with no children should be put far away from educational centres.

6906. *Dr. Berry.*] That would mean that a ganger whose children had grown up beyond a schoolable age, should be taken away and another man sent in his place, in order to keep the school going, would it not?—Yes, I should say so. I do not see why he should have the advantage of staying on in a certain cottage when there is a man with children to be educated wants to come there.

6907. *President.*] Have you thought at all of the bi-lingual difficulty in this country?—Yes. I think that every facility is afforded for instruction in Dutch, and there seems no reason why the views of those who advocate an additional paper in the Dutch language should not be met.

6908. To what extent?—You might have two separate lists, one with four subjects and the other with five subjects, which could be published separately, the candidates' names appearing in the order of merit, (*a*) those taking four subjects, (*b*) those taking five; or you might adopt Professor MacWilliam's scheme, which is a very good one, and give an alternative subject, such as physical science, to those who do not care to take up Dutch.

6909. Would you introduce a clause to the effect that a good paper in Dutch should make up for a bad paper in English?—Yes.

6910. Would not that encourage a want of thoroughness in learning English?—No. I think that the teachers in preparing pupils do their very best. I judge by those I have come in contact with, and we often have a boy who is very weak in English, and it would be an advantage to him to have this outlet or loophole of being able to pass in the examination.

6911. But would not the result be a want of thoroughness in English?—I do not see why we should exact too much from a Dutch child. I would say, let the Dutch and English marks be added together, and if they come up to the pass, let the boy go through.

6912. *Dean Holmes.*] Do you think it is a good principle of education to have two weak subjects instead of one strong one?—No, it is unsound from an educational point of view no doubt.

6913. *President.*] What do you think of having a separate paper in Dutch and giving substantial bursaries if a boy excels in Dutch, provided always that he passes the regular examination?—That would be a very good plan.

6914. Would not that be a better means of encouraging Dutch than any other you can think of?—I think it would.

6915. It can do no harm to anyone, can it?—No.

6916. Do you think bursaries are better than prizes?—Yes. They make future education a condition.

6917. Do you think that plan would meet the wants of the Dutch?—Yes. I think it would be a very fair and reasonable concession to them.

Mr.
James R. Cuthbert.

Sept. 17th, 1891.

6918. *Dr. Berry.*] If that system were adopted, do you think it might be extended to the School Higher Examination as well?—Yes, I think so, and it would be well to do so.

6919. So that a boy who gained a bursary at the Elementary examination might have the means of further studying?—Yes.

6920. And in this way, the Dutch language would be thoroughly well studied, would it not?—Yes.

6921. *Mr. Theron.*] Is not provision already made for Dutch in the higher examinations?—Yes; but if Government gave bursaries it would have a beneficial effect on the language.

6922. *Dean Holmes.*] You see an advantage of bursaries over prizes, inasmuch as it enables boys to carry on their education?—Yes.

6923. *President.*] What do you think of having two papers, one in Dutch and one in English?—I see no objection to that.

6924. Would it not in fact make two systems of education—one in Dutch and the other in English?—Yes, it would to a certain extent.

6925. And it would be to a certain extent revolutionary, would it not?—Yes.

6926. That would not you think be best from a national point of view?—I do not think so. Not to have the whole thing in Dutch, because we have not facilities in the shape of books or teachers.

6927. *Mr. Theron.*] Would you in any case make Dutch compulsory?—No. It would not do. In such places as Graham's Town and King William's Town there are no facilities for acquiring Dutch.

6928. Do you think in the interests of the country it is necessary that all Dutch children should learn English?—Yes.

6929. Have you ever known parents object to that?—No, never; it is rather the other way. There is a growing desire on the part of Dutch people to learn English. A case happened the other day where a farmer applied to me for a teacher, and said he must only know English. Upon my asking him the reason, he said that the English had cheated him in business relationships, and he wanted his children to be educated in English in order that they might return the compliment.

6930. Do not instances like that point to the necessity for some alteration being made in the Elementary examination?—It is highly desirable that there should be an alteration, and Dutch form part of it, but I would not make it a compulsory subject, only optional. I think altogether it would be a good thing if elementary science were added as a fifth alternative paper, with some language, because we are by degrees getting up to a higher standard in the Elementary examination.

6931. Do you hold to the opinion that ultimately English will be the only language spoken in this country?—I do not suppose it will be in our generation, but the day will come. Take Gaelic, for instance; it has existed for a long time, but it is dying out very rapidly.

6932. You think it is desirable that both Dutch and English should be known by every colonist?—Highly desirable.

6933. *President.*] Are you in favour of giving increased grants to mission schools? —Yes. At present the grant is £75 a year whether there are 50 or 500 children. I think the grant should be increased proportionately to the average attendance at the school.

6934. What grant would you give so as to create efficiency and enable a cheap industrial department to be added?—I think £1 or £1 10s. per head should be given over and above 100 children in average attendance. It is a matter of detail however that requires to be thought out after communication with the Education Department.

6935. Would you allow such grant to be made unless the Board approved of it, or would you allow the Central Department to give it only after it has had a full report from the Board?—Only after a full report from the Board.

6936. *Dean Holmes.*] Do you think Sir Langham Dale's proposal for fourth class public undenominational schools a sound one?—I think it would be better to give a capitation allowance; it would be fairer, as the numbers fluctuate so much.

6937. How would you arrange a capitation grant when children are coming and going?—I would pay it on the average attendance for the month.

6938. *President.*] If the Board system is introduced, would you give the same aid from the general revenue to voluntary, that is to say, mission schools, that you would to the Board schools?—Yes, or nearly so.

6939. With this exception, that you would give voluntary schools no grant whatever for building purposes?—No. The churches must undertake that.

Mr.
James R. Cuthbert.

Sept. 17th, 1891.

6940. You would not allow a penny of public money to be put into soil that was not public school property, would you ?—No, that should be a *sine quâ non.*

6941. Would you apply the same principle to mission schools for blacks where they pay a tax ?—Yes.

6942. Where they do not pay a tax, would you have a contribution in the shape of a grant from the Central Government ?—It might remain as it is at present pretty much.

6943. You would not increase the grant, would you, unless they submit to a tax ?—Precisely.

6944. *Dr. Berry.*] You said that you would make the grant to a public school the same as to a voluntary school; I presume you do not wish that to apply to first-class public schools, do you ?—No.

6945. *President.*] How would you draw a distinction between black and white ?—I would have two classes of schools. In the upper school, anyone with a white skin should have a right to go, but I would give the managers or Board power to exclude from the upper school coloured children, if they think that such exclusion is necessary in the interests of the school.

Mr. G. J. Steenekamp examined.

Mr.
G. J. Steenekamp.

Sept. 17th, 1891.

6946. *Rev. Coetzee.*] What are you ?—I am a farmer in the Albert district.

6947.—Where do you reside ?—At Kopfontein.

6948. I believe you belong to the Dutch Reformed Church, and are also a member of the Divisional Council ?—Yes.

6949. Have you had a school close to your farm ?—Yes. Some time ago, it was a private boarding school unaided by Government; it existed two years, and then fell to the ground because we were unable to keep it up by voluntary effort, and also because we were unable to get good teachers. The desire for education has very much increased since then, and if Government were to grant us any aid, we should be able to start several schools. I can mention several places where it is impossible to start schools without the aid of Government. One is in my neighbourhood, where there are six farmers, and there are 42 children receiving no education. Of those six farmers, only two are in a position to afford instruction for a couple of their children. In another place in the neighbourhood there are 45 children also receiving no education. At another place there is a number of bywoners, and altogether 22 children not receiving any education, and there are many other places similarly situated.

6950. What do you think can be done to meet the case of those children ?—I think it would be a good thing if Government would aid in starting a boarding school, where children could be sent to be educated.

6951. How about the building ?—I think the people would be willing to subscribe towards the erection of a building if Government contributed say half.

6952. What would you do about the ground ?—I think in some cases the ground would be given for school purposes, and in others it could easily be bought for a small sum. In my opinion it is better that it should become school property. It might be vested in the Education Department.

6953. Why do not you apply to the Government under the existing rules for aid ?—The difficulty we experience is, that Government will not contribute towards the erection of school buildings. I know in the neighbourhood of Haaspoort there was an effort made to start a school, the arrangement being that some were to contribute bricks and others labour, but it fell through because they could not raise the means.

6954. What do you think Government ought to do ?—I think in the district of Albert, three schools might be started, one in the Stormberg, the other at Haaspoort, and a third at Modderbult. I think in each of those places, fifty children at least, and probably more, would attend.

6955. What contributions do you think can be expected from municipalities or divisional councils ?—I do not think that the ratepayers of the municipality or divisional council could contribute towards these schools, but the inhabitants would no doubt contribute half in the manner I have stated.

6956. *Mr. Theron.*] What is the present divisional council rate ?—Three farthings in the £; bringing in a total revenue of about £2,000.

6957. Might not the divisional council contribute ½d. in the £, and would not that enable you to establish schools for the places you have mentioned ?—The people might be agreeable to a poll tax, but they are opposed to a tax on property. If the rate were small they might not object, but at present the farmers are not prosperous, and any substantial rate would be a serious matter and prove unpopular.

6958. Do you think a Board elected by the ratepayers to look after the interests of education in the district would be desirable ?—Yes, I think it would be, and education would be greatly helped on thereby.

6959. Do you think that all school buildings should be transferred to such a Board ?—Yes.

6960. *President.*] Are there many black children in the towns ?—Yes.

6961. Do your coloured people get religious instruction ? —Yes.

6962. Do you think it would be a good thing if a hut tax were levied upon the natives for educational purposes ?—Yes.

6963. And would you advise adding industrial training to their other teaching ? —I think it would be a good thing if the children of natives living on locations were taught industries; they would then be more useful on farms. Some grown up natives come to my place not knowing how to work at all, and I have to teach them.

6964. *Rev. Coetzee.*] You think they would make better servants if they had such a training ?—Yes. I have had servants who have been taught, and they have proved very useful in consequence, while others again have been no good. It is the nature of one man to profit by his education and another not to do so.

Mr. P. J. Grobler examined.

6965. *Rev. Coetzee.*] What are you ?—A farmer in the Albert district. I reside six miles from Burghersdorp.

6966. Are you a member of the divisional council ?—I was formerly, but not now.

6967. Have you any knowledge of schools ?—A little. I had a private boarding school, unaided by Government, on my place.

6968. How many children were there there ?—About fifty. It fell through some ten years ago ; we were unable to secure a good teacher, as the salary we could pay was so small. At present there is a third class undenominational public school aided by Government, on another farm of mine 18 miles from Burghersdorp. It opened with 13 children. The master gets a salary of £80 a year. The greatest difficulty we have is in erecting buildings for school purposes. If Government would contribute half, we should be able to find the other half for building purposes.

6969. Is the desire for schools among the agricultural population great ?—Yes. They attempt to start schools, but very often fail, because they are unable to get the gurantee made up.

6970. Do you think an elected Board would be a good thing ?—Yes, but it would depend upon the constitution of the Board. I think that any tax for school purposes ought to reach not merely the owners of land but also the occupiers. It must be remembered that many farmers have small holdings in town, and upon these they have to pay not merely town rates but also divisional rates, and they have to pay also divisional rates on the farms, so that the farmers are heavily taxed. I think any tax should reach all round and be fairly distributed.

6971. *Mr. Theron.*] You think it is natural for a man to take an interest in what he pays for ?—If a school is started, and a man contributes towards it, the probability is, that he will make some use of it if possible. People who live far away from centres of population are rather backward, and therefore something should be done to help them and place them in a better position.

6972. Have you anything to say on the subject of education for the children of railway employés ?—I notice that the children of railway employés living near to me go into town daily free to school, while my child who comes home once a fortnight from school has to pay half fare. I do not think that is right. I think that farmers living along the line ought to have the same privilege for their children as railway employés.

Mr. N. Kruger examined.

6973. *Rev. Coetzee.*] What are you ?—A shopkeeper in Burghersdorp.

6974. I believe you are District-Bestuur of the Afrikander Bond ?—Yes.

6975. And you have been living among the Dutch people for a number of years ? —Yes.

6976. What is the great difficulty in starting schools ?—To find the means necessary for buildings. There are a lot of poor people who cannot afford to pay for the boarding of their children.

6977. What would you suggest with regard to buildings ?—I think the Government should pay two-thirds towards the cost of school buildings. At present, what Government contributes for farm schools is sufficient, but not for third class schools.

6978. Suppose the fees came to more than the remaining one-third, what would you do with what was over ?—The Board can pay the school fees of poor children.

6979. Would you be in favour of a Board for a district, elected by the ratepayers to have the management of schools ?—It might answer. The members of the divisional council are not always the right persons to look after education.

6980. Are not the ratepayers sensible men, and able to elect good representatives as they do in the case of members of Parliament ?—Yes; I think the divisional ratepayers might elect a Board.

6981. Do you think it would tend to more interest being taken in education ?—I think so.

,6982. Whenever a deficiency occurs, what contribution would you expect from the divisional council or the municipality to make it up ?—I am not in favour of divisional councils or municipalities giving grants for school purposes.

6983. In what way would you make up the deficit ?—I should prefer voluntary contributions.

6984. Suppose they were not forthcoming ?—Then I think a tax to reach everyone would be a good thing, and I would be in favour of it.

6985. *President.*] What tax would you recommend ?—Either a house tax or a poll tax.

6986. Should such a tax reach the natives too ?—Yes, I think the taxation should reach everyone who can pay, and not merely the owners of land, who are already heavily taxed.

6987. *Rev. Coetzee.*] Would you be in favour of some tax for the natives towards their education ?—Yes, I should be in favour of a hut tax.

6988. Should that money be spent for the education of the natives exclusively ?—Yes.

6989. Is it advisable to teach them industrial as well as literary work, how to handle a spade, and so on ?—Yes.

6990. As far as the white population is concerned, would you be in favour of some industrial branch connected with the schools ?—Yes.

Rev. H. J. Withers examined.

6991. *President.*] I believe you are the Wesleyan minister here ?—Yes.

6992. Have you a school here ?—Yes, a mission school.

6993. Do you teach yourself ?—No. I have a native teacher. I am responsible for the government of the school.

6994. How many children attend ?—There are fifty on the books.

6995. What is the average daily attendance ?—A little over 42.

6996. What aid do you get from Government ?—£37 10s. a year. There are no white children in my mission school.

6997. Do you think it is desirable that there should be white children in mission schools for natives ?—I see no objection ; the white children themselves or their parents do not object.

6998. Suppose they do object ?—Then I suppose they would not come.

6999. Where would they go to ?—In Middelburg there is provision for them at the public school : if not, the suggested fourth-class schools, if carried through, would provide sufficient accommodation for such children.

7000. *Dr. Berry.*] How long have you been here ?—Fifteen months.

7001. Has there been any election of a school committee while you have been here ?—Yes.

7002. Were you present ?—No.

7003. Why ?—I did not know the election was coming off. The notice convening the meeting was posted on the schoolroom door, but as I am not a visitor of the school I did not see it.

7004. *Dean Holmes.*] Was it advertised in any of the papers ?—Not that I am aware of. It would only be published in the Dutch paper, and as I cannot read Dutch, I should not have seen it.

7005. *Dr. Berry.*] How is the school committee elected ?—It is supposed to be elected by the public. A meeting was held, but I did not know anything about it, and several others in town who would have been present did not know anything about it. We considered that not sufficient public notice was given.

7006. *President.*] What sort of notice do you think should be given ?—At least a month's notice should be given in the papers.

7007. *Dr. Berry.*] Have you thought of the question of having School Boards ?—Yes.

7008. What is your view ?—I think if we have compulsory education, School Boards would be an absolute necessity, but just at present I do not think School Boards for districts would be workable ; the population is too scattered, and unless these School Boards had the means of running boarding schools and not merely day schools, I do not think they would be workable in the country districts.

7009. Would it not be a good thing if such a Board was elected to manage and control all the educational interests and provide schools where they were wanted ?—If it had sufficient rating power to run boarding schools it would be a great boon and I should be delighted to see it.

Rev.
H. J. Withers.

Sept. 17th, 1891.

7010. Is the present machinery for starting schools and managing schools sufficiently adequate in your opinion ?—Certainly not ; very far from adequate.

7011. How are the children in the native location educated ?—There are two mission schools, one belonging to the Dutch Reformed Church and my own.

7012. Do you get any fees from the natives ?—Yes.

7013. Are the natives who do not pay taking advantage of these schools ?—Only a few who cannot pay.

7014. Do they get their children into school notwithstanding they cannot pay ?—Yes ; in deserving cases. In the case of my own school, I reserve the right to say whether they shall come in or not. There are a few members of my church for instance, who are invalided and cannot work, and if they have children, they can come to school free.

7015. Is it left to you to say who shall come free to school ?—Yes. I suppose it comes to that practically.

7016. *Mr. Theron.*] You stated that you thought the notice given of the meeting was not sufficient ; are you acquainted with the requirements ?—I am not.

7017. Then it is simply your own idea ?—I think in a small town like this, if sufficient notice were given, everybody would know it. If there is any other meeting to be held in the town, all the people generally know it in plenty of time.

7018. Do you know what the requirements are ?—No.

7019. *Dr. Berry.*] What is your opinion with regard to industrial training in schools ?—I think that it is absolutely necessary that some amount of industrial training should be given to natives.

7020. In what direction would you give it in towns like this for instance : what could you carry out here ?—With our present staff and buildings we could do nothing, but I think some system might be brought into use by which children could be taught useful trades. Of course in our school, as I believe in all mission schools, we teach the girls sewing. We have a sewing mistress, but I should like to see the boys taught to work as well as to read and write.

7021. If the municipality were to lend you a piece of garden ground, could you teach spade husbandry ?—Yes, possibly.

7022. Could you teach the boys brickmaking ?—Not under our present conditions.

7023. Could you if you had a master ?—Yes ; if I had a master. The education given in our school is very elementary. We have two children going in for the fourth standard, and two for the third, but beyond that, there are none above the second.

7024. *Dean Holmes.*] Is it difficult to get means to carry on the school ?—Not at all ; the church gives money, and there are private subscriptions.

7025. *President.*] Do you rate your natives for school purposes ?—For church purposes we do, so much per head.

7026. How many members have you in the church ?—Between 60 and 70. The average subscription comes to about 10s. a year per head ; that is besides all the voluntary contributions such as collections and so on. It is a purely mission church.

7027. Do you have a white congregation as well ?—Yes.

7028. Suppose a tax were levied on the location at so much per hut, and the money was handed to the Board or any other body to distribute for the purpose of expressly contributing to native education in the direction you have indicated, would it be a good thing and bring within reach of education some who avoid the missionary ?—I think it would be a good thing ; but it depends almost entirely upon the organization of the Board. I do not think a Board elected by the ordinary ratepayers for the management of the education of the district would be competent to manage missionary education.

7029. How much would it be fair for the Government to contribute for the natives so as to enable volunteers like yourself to carry on independently of a Board, the educational work, including the industrial department, with some degree of effect ?—I cannot give any idea as to the industrial work, perhaps from £30 to £50 a year.

7030. Suppose a Board were brought into existence whose duty it would be to see that the natives were educated, would it not be to their interest to approach an organization like yours and say, you do the work and you will get the money ?—I think it would be a good thing.

7031. Would not that cause the people in the district to take an interest in educational work ?—I think so. People in the district take very little interest in this kind of work at present.

IIII

Rev.
H. J. *Withers.*

Sept. 17th, 1891.

7032. You think that denominations, that is to say church bodies, ought to be used, whether the Government or a Board has the control, directly for the purpose of education?—I think they are quite necessary. I do not think that any other body could carry on the work of education as the churches are carrying it on now.

7933. You think they could not do it so cheaply and so effectively?—I do not think so.

7034. Would you be in favour of compulsory attendance within limited areas?—Yes. Taking this town for instance, there are many native children who do not attend any school, and many also in the location, and there is absolutely no reason why they should not. It seems to me that it would be a comparatively simple thing to pass a compulsory Act for places of this sort. Under existing circumstances, it would be utterly impossible to compel children on farms 15 or 20 miles away, to attend school, but in towns it could be carried out well, say within a radius of two miles.

7035. Would you take these native children into a mission school where there is industrial as well as literary work?—Yes.

7036. You think it would be a good thing for the natives themselves and also for the country generally?—Yes.

7037. Do you think such a thing would commend itself to the farming population; taking the natives to such schools I mean?—I do not know. I do not think it would, simply because, from my experience, the population is not in sympathy with mission work generally.

7038. Would it not bring them into sympathy with it if more industrial training were given instead of so much literary education?—I think it would tend in that direction.

7039. Is not that one reason why there is not more sympathy between the farming population and the missionaries, because of the difficulty in getting a native to work after he has been educated?—Yes; that is one of the reasons, although it is perhaps somewhat exaggerated.

7040. *Dr. Berry.*] What officer do you think in towns should be charged with the duty of seeing that these children come to school?—In a town like this it would be difficult; a special officer would have to be appointed, but in some towns where there is an inspector of locations, I think that duty could be added to his other duties without any difficulty.

7041. Have you no inspector here?—I think not. The police, who have very little to do, might also be used for the purpose of getting children into school.

Rev. A. F. *Weich* examined.

Rev.
A. F. *Weich.*

Sept. 17th, 1891.

7042. *President.*] What are you?—Dutch Reformed Church missionary for the natives.

7043. How many natives are there in your school?—Eighty-one.

7044. What is the average attendance?—Between seventy and eighty.

7045. What are the ages of the children?—From four years up to sixteen.

7046. What contribution do you get from the Government?—£45 a year.

7047. Do you think it is desirable to have white children in the mission schools?—Not in one like mine.

7048. What education do you give the children?—We go as far as the third standard.

7049. Do you think it is desirable to add industrial training?—Yes, very desirable.

7050. What sort of training would suit best all round and be least inexpensive?—Farm work and trades.

7051. Do you think your church body would aid in that direction?—I hardly think so, they say they are not able.

7052. Do you think you could carry out the system if you had assistance?—Yes, we really require more assistance to do properly our present work with eighty-one children.

7053. How would you set about it?—We would have to get a teacher in the industrial department and another to help in the ordinary school work.

7054. And you would superintend the whole?—Yes, both departments.

7055. Would the outcome be that children would be better trained for their future calling than they are now?—Yes, I think so.

7056. And they would lose in learning what they do now?—They would learn less of some things which they do not require, but they would not learn anything else beyond what they really need.

7057. *Dean Holmes.*] Do you mean that you would want two extra male teachers?—One male and one female would do.

Rev
A. F. Woch.

Sept. 17th, 1891.

7058. *President.*] Do you think if a tax were levied on the natives for educational work solely it would be a good thing?—I do not know whether it would be advisable unless you can levy it on those who have fixed property.

7059. Would you have a poll tax?—No, that is not a fair tax.

7060. *Dr. Berry.*] Is there any reason why there should be two mission schools in Middelburg?—I cannot say. It is a thing which exists in very many towns.

7061. Would one school do the work of educating the natives in this town?—Yes, if there was a proper staff of teachers.

7062. Would not one strong school be better than two weak ones?—Yes.

7063. Are the natives very much interested in our denominational differences?—Some are.

7064. To such an extent as to make amalgamation of the schools impossible do you think?—I do not know about the schools, but the congregations.

7065. Suppose there was a Board created to look after the school interests in the district of Middelburg, would there be any great unfairness if that Board said there should only be one mission school aided?—Yes; I think it would be unfair.

7066. Why?—Unless you make it altogether an undenominational school, it would ultimately end in this, that children trained in the school under whose denomination it stands would all become members of that church.

7067. Suppose you made it an undenominational school?—If you do that, you will have to change the whole system on which grants are given.

7068. Why should we not do so?—Personally, I would not have any objection to it.

7069. *President.*] What is the objection?—As it is now, the objection is this, that children as a rule become members of the Church in which they have been educated. All the mission schools are connected with one or other Church, and as a rule, children educated in a school in connection with the Wesleyans, become Wesleyans, if they are educated in a school connected with the Dutch Reformed Church, they become members of that Church, and the same with the Church of England.

7070. *Rev. Coetzee.*] You said that personally you would have no objection to make all schools entirely undenominational; would you be in favour of secularizing education entirely and leaving religious instruction out altogether?—No.

7071. *Dean Holmes.*] You would not do away with the conscience clause, would you?—No, certainly not.

7072. *President.*] Do not you think the time has arrived when it may be said that the mission influence for school purposes is no longer essential in most of the colonial towns?—I think it is essential at present.

7073. Do you think if mission influence in connection with schools were withdrawn, it would be prejudicial to the natives?—Yes.

7074. If other schools were started, into which native children were brought and educated and received some sort of moral training, would not the effect be equally good?—They would not be got as easily into school as they are now, unless you had a compulsory Act.

7075. Suppose there were a compulsory Act, and you took these children and taught them industries as well as reading, writing, and arithmetic, would not they turn out as good citizens as they are turned out now?—No; I do not think so, because the missionary has an influence over them which others have not. It is desirable that the missionary should have his hands free to devote to purely religious work.

7076. Is it not out of place to ask a missionary to superintend industrial training?—Yes; because it fills his hands with work which really does not belong to him. I would teach industrial work if I had the time, but I have not; there is so much other work.

7077. If you have so much other work, is it not a good thing to take that work away from you?--Yes, certainly, if it can be done in a proper way, but it would not do to take the work away and give it to another man if by that means the cause would suffer.

7078. Could one missionary do all the native work here, secular as well as religious?—No; I do not think so.

7079. *Dr. Berry.*] One missionary could look after the church interests of the natives here, could he not?—No; he could not.

7080. *President.*] Do you go to the farms?—Yes. I go and preach to the natives.

7081. Do you give them secular instruction on the farms at all?—No.

7082. Do they receive any?—No.

7083. Then virtually outside the town, the natives receive no secular instruction?—No; not in this district.

7084. Would one native school for the town suffice?—No. I have 81 children now, and if I had room enough I could get easily 120. The Rev. Mr. Withers has

246

Rev.
A. F. Weich.
Sept. 17th, 1891.

50, that makes 170. If I teach five hours a day, it is utterly impossible to do all the other work conscientiously.

7085. You would not teach unless you were a missionary, would you?—No, it is part of my church work.

7086. Would you work under Government?—Yes. Teaching and doing mission work also is really more than one man can conscientiously do. I only do it because I have to do it; if I gave it up, these children would be running about the streets.

7087. Is it a good thing for a clergyman to be a schoolmaster, or should the clergyman and the schoolmaster each have his respective work?—It would be better if the two were separate, I think.

7088. Do you think better work would be done?—Yes; better religious work and better school work.

Rev. G. Van Niekerk examined.

Rev.
G. Van Niekerk.
Sept. 17th, 1891.

7089. *President.*] I believe you are minister of the Dutch Reformed Church in Middelburg?—Yes.

7090. Are you interested at all in any of the schools here?—Yes; I am chairman of the First-class Public Undenominational School.

7091. How is that school worked; are the buildings on church property?—Yes; the school building is church property. It is let to the committee.

7092. Who built it?—The Dutch Reformed Church; the congregation contributed.

7093. Did the State contribute anything?—No. Our school has become a first-class school since July.

7094. How many children have you at school?—There are 117 on the roll, all white.

7095. What is the average attendance?—The attendance is very good.

7096. Do you think that something more should be done to secure the attendance of children?—No. The attendance on the whole is very good, and the register shows it. Sometimes parents are obliged to keep their children at home because they have no servants; they pay their fees.

7097. Then it is not to avoid the fees that they keep away?—No.

7098. How would you get over that difficulty?—The labour question is the great thing.

7099. Do you think that any child under twelve should be kept away from school under any circumstances during school hours?—No, I do not think so; but circumstances are often such that a parent is obliged to keep children away. For instance, in the course of my pastoral visits, I once came to a farm where there were two children, a little boy and girl, who were herding sheep, the father had the plough, and the mother the whip, and a daughter, seventeen years of age, was leading the oxen. It would be impossible for the parents in that case to send their children to school.

7100. That would not apply to towns, would it?—In towns it is often the same. This man I allude to brings things from the town to the station, and he has a wagon, but he really cannot get a boy. He is obliged to take his son from school to help him in his work.

7101. I suppose he makes money by transport riding; cannot he hire a Kafir?—Very often he cannot get a Kafir.

7102. Is there a deficiency in your school?—No.

7103. The guarantors have had to pay nothing?—No, not in my time. I have been there seven years. Before my time, the school was very unsatisfactory; they could not keep it going; there was always a deficiency.

7104. Why was that?—It was before my time. Now there is a slight profit every year.

7105. What are your fees?—The children pay according to standard.

7106. If there is a profit what do you do with it?—We have a great deal of expense; for instance, rent has to be paid and furniture supplied. It was not long ago that we got some new furniture. We have also given some prizes.

7107. Is there a debt on the school buildings?—Yes, there is still a debt, but that is a debt of the Dutch Reformed Church congregation.

7108. *Mr. Theron.*] Do you use the surplus to pay the debt on the school?—Not a penny.

7109. But you do use it to pay rent, do you not?—Yes.

7110. *President.*] Who fixes the rent?—The Kerkeraad and the school committee. The school committee consists of seven members chosen by the public at a meeting.

7111. Has the Kerkeraad anything to do with the school committee?—Not as the Kerkeraad. A notice is affixed to the court-house door and also to the school building, to the effect that a meeting would be held at such a time, and then at that public meeting the guarantee list is formed and signed, and then from that a committee is chosen.

7112. Among the committee are there a good many members of the Dutch Reformed Church ?—Yes.

7113. They are not elected because they are members of that Church, are they ? —No.

7114. Does an election take place every three years ?—Yes.

7115. Do you think it is a good system that a few men should do the work of the many ?—I do not think it is a wise system, and it is not right. If there is a loss, the school may stop.

7116. Would it be a good thing to bring into existence a School Board, to be elected by the ratepayers ?—I think so.

7117. And make the ratepayers responsible for any deficiency, the Government contributing and the fees contributing ?—I think that would be a better plan than what we have at present.

7118. Would it bring the people more together, and make them feel an interest as citizens in education ?—I think so. If the ratepayers have to pay, they will take more interest and make more use of the school itself, and try to make it pay ; they will also try and get their neighbours and others to make use of it.

7119. Rev. Coetzee.] Do you think this Board should provide for education both in the town and district ?—It would perhaps be well to have one Board for the town and district, else you have to do with different bodies. It is better to have one body, and then there might be sub-committees in different wards, and you could work through them, and also work through voluntary bodies.

7120. Dr. Berry.] Have you raised your school from a second class to a first class school since you were elected ?—When I came here as minister of the Dutch Reformed Church, this school was just forming. It was a first class public undenominational school, but it was a hard struggle to keep it going, and after a couple of years we asked the Superintendent-General of Education to bring it back to a second class school, and it was a second-class school some years. It worked so well that recently we asked Sir Langham Dale to raise it to a first class school again.

7121. After you were elected on the present Board, did you raise the school, or was it before you were elected this last time.?—Before I was elected. I was only elected about a month ago.

7122. Was it the last Board that raised it ?—Yes.

7123. And yet the guarantors who signed three years ago, signed for a second class second class school, did they not ?—Then they signed for a second class school, but this last time they signed for a first.

7124. Meanwhile the character of the school was changed without the consent of the guarantors who signed the time before, was it not ?—Yes.

7125. Rev. Coetzee.] Have the old members of the previous Board been re-elected ? Yes, all of them.

7126. Dr. Berry.] Were the inhabitants generally consulted about changing the character of the school ?—No ; the Board did it.

7127. President.] Do you think there would be any harm if the meetings of the School Board were open ?—The meetings are open.

7128. Would you have any objection to reporters being present ?—No.

7129. Do you think it would be a good thing, and lead the public to take more interest in school matters ?—Yes. Our meetings are held in the Town Hall with open doors.

7130. Then if anybody says they do not know anything about what is going on, it shows they do not take that interest in education that they might, does it not ?— Yes, that is just it.

7131. Do not you think if there was a School Board it would lead the public to take greater interest in education ?—Yes, I really think it would ; it would bring the people more together, and they would understand each other better.

7132. Mr. Theron.] Would you prefer a nominee Board or an elected Board ? —An elected Board.

7133. By whom should it be elected ?—By the Divisional Council ratepayers.

7134. Would you give such a Board rating powers ?—The Divisional Council ought to be the body to provide for any deficiency.

7135. Would you give the Divisional Council any voice in the management of the Board, seeing that it is the body which has to provide the means ?—I think the Divisional Council ought to have a say in the matter if it is responsible for any deficiency.

7136. Dr. Berry.] Did you change the teachers when you raised your school from a second to a first class school ?—No ; the teachers remained.

Rev.
G. Van Niekerk.

Sept. 17th, 1891.

7137. *Mr. Theron.*] With reference to the farming population in your community, is there great necessity for schools among the farmers; are many of their children receiving no education?—I have been taking the Church census, but I cannot say from memory ; there is an improvement in education in the district, and the private schools have been increased since I took the last census three years ago. There are six new private schools in the district, but there is still a great want of schools, and parents do not assist in the matter as they ought.

7138. Do you think the parents are all acquainted with the means provided by the Government or the Education Department to help them ?—I do not think they are. I have tried my utmost to bring to their notice what the Government is willing to do for the children of the farmers. I think they are in great ignorance with regard to the facilities.

7139. Those not attending schools in the district, do you think they are in a minority or a majority ?—In a majority.

7140. Then a great deal can be done in your district ?—Yes, people are getting to appreciate education more.

7141. *Dr. Berry.*] Have you any difficulty in finding teachers for the schools when farmers ask you ?—I have not been unsuccessful in finding teachers.

7142. How do you meet with them ?—I ask my brother ministers, and invite applications.

7143. Are they certificated teachers as a rule that you get, or are they uncertificated ?—A good many of them are uncertificated ; only small salaries are offered in the schools, and, as a rule, the certificated teachers do not apply. It is more uncertificated teachers who apply.

7144. *Dean Holmes.*] Have you any instance within your knowledge of there being an inefficient teacher at your schools ?—I do not speak of aided schools, but at the private farm schools there are some inefficient teachers, and I would rather they were not there.

7145. Do you know cases of old people teaching ?—No.

7146. *Mr. Theron.*] Do you mean that the teachers are not sufficiently trained as such ?—Yes, that is it.

7147. Are they young girls often ?—There are young girls among them. The parents being uneducated themselves as a rule, cannot judge of the capabilites of a teacher, and they often just take one because they get her for £24 or so a year, and then they just struggle on.

7148. *President.*] Have you found that the less parents are instructed the less interest they take in education ?—Yes, that is so.

7149. *Mr. Theron.*] What further facilities do you think can be afforded for giving instruction in the Dutch language. Is Dutch taught in your school ?—Yes.

7150. Do you think it is sufficiently taught ?—No.

7151. Why not ?—We have a teacher who is able to teach Dutch, and he is a friend of the Dutch language, but there is no encouragement for him, because Dutch is not included in the Elementary examination. My opinion is with regard to Dutch, that it ought to be included ; there ought to be a Dutch paper provided.

7152. *Rev Coetzee.*] Would you have it compulsory or optional ?—I would have it optional.

7153. *Mr Theron.*] You would not compel an English child to learn Dutch or pass an examination in Dutch, would you ?—No.

7154. But you would give him a chance if he liked to do so ?—Yes, he should get marks for Dutch, and they should be added to the aggregate. I would like my boy to be well up in both languages, English and Dutch, one just as much as the other.

7155. Do the rest of the people in your congregation think the same with you ? —There are only a few cases in my congregation where the parents have said to me they want their children to learn Dutch only, but that is because they take no interest in education, they are exceptional cases. Speaking generally, I think parents wish to have their children understand both languages.

7156. You think that another optional paper should be added in the Elementary examination, and that that should be a Dutch paper ?—Yes.

7157. Suppose a Dutch child at the examination could not do that Dutch paper but an English child could do it, would you do justice to that child and add his marks to the aggregate ?—Certainly.

7158. And you would expect the same for a Dutch child, would you not ?—Yes.

7159. *President.*] Would it not encourage the learning of Dutch if bursaries were given ?—I think it might to a certain extent ; it is so in the Civil Service examination, where a successful candidate has something to look forward to. I certainly think there ought to be a Dutch paper in the Elementary examination. The only fear is that if bursaries were given, they would not learn Dutch because they wanted to know it, but for the sake of the bursaries. I think something more is wanted. Rev.
G. Van Niekerk.

7160. Is it not better to encourage Dutch by something that so to speak does not punish anybody?—I do not think that it punishes anybody. I have been a minister thirty-one years, and I find when a doctor for instance comes to the village, one of the first things he asks me is for advice as to learning Dutch. I cannot say whether awarding a bursary for Dutch would promote the learning of the language more than what I have suggested; I have not thought enough about the subject. Sept. 17th, 1891

7161. *Rev. Coetzee.*] Do you think that a Dutch boy by having to prepare for his examination in a foreign language, is at some disadvantage over against an English boy?—Yes.

7162. And by introducing Dutch into the Elementary examination and making it compulsory, you place him on an equal footing with the English boy, who also has to take up a language he may not be acquainted with; is that your idea?—Yes.

Middelburg, Friday, September 18th, 1891.

Sir J. D. BARRY (President),

| Dr. Berry, | Mr. Theron, |
| Dean Holmes, | Rev. Coetzee. |

Mr. N. T. de Waal examined.

7163. *President.*] I believe you are Deputy Sheriff and a law agent and auctioneer here?—Yes. Mr.
N. T. de Waal.

7164. How long have you been here?—Ten years.

7165. Are you secretary to the committee of the Public Undenominational School here?—Yes. Sept. 18th, 1891.

7166. Is the attendance at the school regular?—Yes; fairly regular.

7167. Do you think anything ought to be done to promote regularity of attendance?—In the public school I hardly think so. Sometimes children are kept away from school because their parents are poor and want their assistance.

7168. Then the children of poorer parents do not attend so regularly?—No. Sometimes they are obliged to take the children away from school for two or three days to assist them at home, and consequently the school suffers.

7169. Have you any white mission school here?—No.

7170. Do you think anything can be done to improve the attendance?—I have not thought out any plan. The labour question is intimately connected with it.

7171. Are there any children who are not reached by any education in the town?—No white children. All those children who wish to go to school, can go to the public school. Free scholars are taken. There may be a few isolated cases of children not going to school.

7172. Should such children be taken to school by an attendance officer?—Yes, but it depends upon the expense which the country is put to.

7173. Do you think there ought to be compulsory education for towns?—No; I am not in favour of it for this country. We have a number of poor white people who cannot do without their children's assistance. I know myself of one or two masons in this place who live from hand to mouth, and who are obliged to take their children to assist them, as they cannot afford to pay for labour. There is great difficulty in getting labour, and it would be a hardship for those parents if they were compelled to send their children to school.

7174. What wages does a mason get?—Five shillings a day.

7175. Is the system of guarantors a good one in your opinion?—In this district it is. I cannot judge as to other places. It answers very well here. There is a little dissatisfaction perhaps with the existing state of things, but that cannot be obviated. There are some people who misunderstand the meaning of the word undenominational. They believe that in order for a school to be really and thoroughly undenominational, there must be a person of every denomination on the Board, and these people are dissatisfied with the present School committees.

7176. Are you in favour of School Boards elected by the ratepayers?—Very much. I would like to see a permanent Board elected by the ratepayers to take the place of the present arrangement. I would be opposed to nominees.

7177. Would you be opposed to nominees by the Divisional Council?—There might be one or two nominees by the Divisional Council, but not by the Government.

7178. Is there any public school property here?—No; we have a good school, but the property is private.

Mr.
N. T. de Waal.
Sept. 18th, 1891.

7179. How would you do with the property if there was a School Board?—The Board might continue to hire it.

7180. Suppose school buildings are required?—The people ought to pay for them, the ratepayers, conjointly with the Government, on the £ for £ principle. I believe in that.

7181. Would the Board have control of all the schools throughout the district?— The only difficulty is this, that if you have a number of schools to manage in the district, you might want salaried men, paid like the secretary to the Divisional Council, if the work was to be done properly, and that would involve expense and perhaps give dissatisfaction. There would also be an idea perhaps that the country schools were managed by the town, and so there would not be that general co-operation which we all desire. I would suggest that in field-cornetcies there might be sub-committees under the Central Board.

7182. Would you suggest that the Central Board, if they like, should delegate their power to volunteers where they think volunteers would do good educational work?—I see no objection to their doing so.

7183. What contribution under those circumstances do you think ought to be given by the Government?—The Government should continue to give half, exactly as they do now.

7184. *Mr. Theron.*] What do you understand by volunteers?—I understand it in this way. A man comes forward and says that in his immediate field-cornetcy there is a school wanted, and the initiatory work of arranging for such school would be left to this party, the Board delegating to him a general power for the purpose. I do not understand that volunteers could be appointed to take the management of the school permanently.

7185. Suppose in towns you have no voluntary bodies?—I am speaking with regard to the country, not towns.

7186. *President.*] Suppose the School Board thought that a mission school for natives was doing good work, would you allow them to recommend that mission school to receive further aid from Government than what it got already?—I think the Board should only take charge of the present public undenominational schools, not private schools in any way whatever, either in town or country.

7187. *Rev. Coetzee.*] Would the Board have to look after the native education as well in the district?—I think the natives at present manage to get on very well.

7188. *President.*] Would you have the same sort of education as there is now for the natives, or would you make it more of an industrial character?—I object to industrial schools for natives; the best industrial school is the master's farm.

7189. But suppose they are in towns?—They ought to go out of the towns.

7190. You cannot force them. Many of the farmers have to let their own children herd sheep, because they cannot get labour. If you had more industrial training, would it not fit the natives better for their work?—Possibly; but we have two classes in this country, whites and blacks, and we must be just before we are generous. Our first duty is to look after the whites, and many white children are not able to go to school because labour is so scarce. I experience it every day. The native boys will not work as long as they have a few shillings in their pockets; they will stay in the town and not go to the country, and white farmers have to let their children herd sheep instead of going to school. If we have industrial schools for the natives, I believe the state of things with regard to the blacks will become worse and worse. The farms are now being sub-divided to a large extent. A farmer bequeaths his property to his children in plots of 700 or 800 morgen, which is not sufficient for them, and consequently they will have to turn their attention to something else and become masons and carpenters, but if those positions are filled by natives, there will be no chance for the children of farmers who are growing up, and they will have to leave the country.

7191. But might you not teach the native children gardening and so on; industrial training does not necessarily mean trades?—My experience of the educated native has not been fortunate; he is generally worse than the uneducated native.

7192. That being so, is it not the fault of the education?—Possibly.

7193. Would not you correct that defect by introducing the industrial element. Do you think it would be a good thing to have industrial education for all classes, both white and black?—No.

7194. In the upper schools would you have technical education for whites?—Yes.

7195. And in the lower schools industrial education of a lower character?—Yes; but I still hold that a native can best learn his proper business on a farm.

7196. *Mr. Theron.*] I understood you to say that there was some dissatisfaction about the present school committee; what is the cause of it?—Some ten years ago there was very little interest taken in schools in this district. The Dutch Reformed

Church, which is a powerful organisation in the district, and to which a number of people belong, took the matter in hand, and by means of private subscriptions raised sufficient money to build a school, costing about £2,000. Application was then made for the formation of a public undenominational school in the town ; a public meeting was held, and everything done according to law. The Civil Commissioner presided, and those persons who intended to send their children came and selected the committee. It so happens that out of the 120 children who go to the public undenominational school, 110 belong to the Dutch Reformed Church, and 10 to other denominations in the district. The committee does not include other denominations, but the members belong to the Dutch Reformed Church, but it was properly elected, and it was a case of the majority having an advantage over the minority. That minority is naturally dissatisfied with things as they exist at present, and they would like to be represented, but that is not the law. If it were, it would kill our public school system.

Mr.
N. T. de Waal.

Sept. 18th, 1891

7197. *President.*] Was the meeting convened according to the regulations?— Most decidedly. If it had not been, those who objected would have put the law in motion and upset the committee. All the requirements of the law have been complied with.

7198. Was it well notified?—It was not notified in the paper, but that was merely an accident. Formerly it was. I edit the paper myself, and I generally had some local notice put in, but the school committee did not think it worth while to advertise as it was not required, and we had no money to waste. A notice was affixed to the schoolroom door and also to the door of the magistrate's court. . I saw it myself repeatedly.

7199. Who was the chairman of the meeting?—Mr. Friedlander was the chairman. He is a Jew. He would not have been there if I had not met him and taken him over; he did not know anything about it he said.

7200. Is he a guarantor?—Yes.

7201. Is he on the committee?—No.

7202. Is there anyone on the committee who does not belong to the Dutch Reformed Church?—No, they all belong to the Dutch Reformed Church.

7203. Is the complaint that the public undenominational school here is virtually a Dutch Reformed Church school?—No ; that the committee all belong to the Dutch Reformed Church.

7204. And that in fact the school is conducted on Dutch Reformed Church lines, is it not?—No, that cannot be proved. The complaint is that all the members of the committee belong to the Dutch Reformed Church ; and they think that they should be liberal enough to place upon the committee men of a different opinion and different views to their own.

7205. Is it not a good thing for minorities to be represented on public Boards?— It depends on the minority ; some men can do a great deal of harm in the way of obstruction.

7206. But he can be outvoted?—But he could keep the rest sitting all day long ; we have not got the *cloture*. He can put hindrances in the way, and prevent harmonious working, and the result might be that parents would take their children away from the school.

7207. Is Mr. Postma a member of the Board?—No.

7208. Is he not at the head of a large section of the Dutch Reformed Church?— Yes.

7209. Has he been asked to join the Board?—No.

7210. Why not?—I wanted him to become a member, and my own opinion and that of the Rev. Mr. Niekerk was that he would certainly accept.

7211. Has he been here many years?—No ; he only came about twelve months ago. I went to him and offered to resign on the school committee, so that he could take my place, but he would not accept it. I thought he ought to be there, as he was a very good man.. If there is another election he will get in

7212. *Rev. Coetzee.*] Did not Mr. Postma say he would be on the Board, but not as a favour ; he wanted to come in in the regular way, and stand on his own merits?— I know he did not join.

7213. *Mr. Theron.*] At the election, could you have prevented this committee being elected?—No ; there were 60 or 70 guarantors there, and they were unanimous in their choice.

7214. So that whatever may be said about it, the committee was elected by the guarantors according to the regulations?—Yes ; otherwise it would have been upset.

7215. *Dr. Berry.*] Should the election be by the guarantors?—In this case it would have made no difference, because everyone present at the meeting signed the guarantee. We called two meetings, one at nine and one at ten o'clock. At the latter

Mr.
N. T. de Waal.

Sept. 18th, 1891.

meeting the public were convened, and everyone who came
is nobody in Middelburg who takes an interest in education
willing to sign the guarantee list. In practice, we have rep
gentlemen who are to appoint the managers, although I nov
the meeting that should do it. In our case, the notice conve
given, and everybody who attended became a guarantor, w
ever, otherwise it would not have been legal.

7216. *President.*] Has the question as to who is a hous
ever been raised ?—No, we would like to have it defined.

7216a. Would there be any objection to a hut-holde
because it says householder, not hut-holder.

7217. Suppose it is the case of a native who lives in a
room, would you let him vote ?—No.

7218. What do you call a householder ?—It is defined
No. 9 of 1836, as amended by section 7 of Act No. 13 of 1
this municipality. It says the occupier of any dwelling-h
not less than £10. The only difficulty as to the municipal
a yearly value of £10.

7219. What have you decided ?—We decided that a
valued at £100 or who pays £10 a year rent is a household
7220. The Divisional Council franchise is £75 and the
franchise would you adopt in the election of members for the
as the Divisional Council would be called upon for any de
fair that their franchise should be taken.

7221. But suppose they had not to meet any deficiency
objection to the Parliamentary franchise, although I like
high in educational matters. If you put it low, you get 1
able to judge as to the capacity of the members. I pre
qualification, because you are more likely to get intelligent :

7222. *Dr. Berry.*] If this Board is called into existence
an office, and secretary, the members would have to be paid
and there would be various other expenses to be incurred
money from ?—I suppose the Divisional Council would ha
the rates.

7223. *President.*] Could not the offices and the machine
generally be used for the purposes of the School Board ?—Y
the Divisional Council could very well be Secretary of the
additional pay, or a very slight addition. I am secretary of
and there is very little to do. As treasurer, I have a grea
difficulty at all in the Secretary of the Divisional Council
Central School Board.

7224. In Sir Langham Dale's report of last year, your
class school, does it not ?—We changed it from a second to

7225. How was it done ?—The managers wrote to Sir
for permission, and he granted it.

7226. Did you call the public together when the c
changed ?—No ; it was not necessary, Sir Langham Dale sa
we would have to do would be to sign an additional guaran
teacher.

7227. Were the same teachers continued ?—Yes, at in
there was no difference in the work. We had been doi
school really.

7228. Do not you think it would practically work
public meeting came through the Civil Commissioner ?—I
if the regulations required the notice to be published in the
has over been made about notice not having been given
objection was that there was not sufficient publicity by pu
at the court-room and one or two other places.

7229. What do you think would be the best way of p
to a notice of this kind ?—I think the notice should be pub
in a paper circulating in the district.

7230. By whom should it be signed ?—By the chairm
sioner, I should say. I think the Civil Commissioner migl
it ought to be notified in the local paper.

7231. *Rev. Coetzee.*] Did you ever have any deficiency
7232. *Dr. Berry.*] Is the rent of the buildings paid o
Yes, out of the fees. The buildings are worth £10 a mont

year; but they are worth £120. The Dutch Reformed Church let them to us at a very reasonable rental. There is no debt on the buildings. I find in my answer to the circular sent out by the Commission I stated that the managers of the school were elected by the general body of guarantors; I should have said by the householders, not the guarantors.

Mr.
N. T. de Waal.
Sept. 18th, 1891.

7233. *President.*] Do you think there is a general misapprehension about the matter of electing managers?—There is evidently a general misapprehension about the matter, and I was labouring under it.

7234. *Rev. Coetzee.*] In the case of a deficiency occurring, would you have it made up by the local body, or should the Government contribute something towards it?—I think the Government should give half the salaries, as it does at present. The Central Board, after having approved of the deficiency, should get it paid through the Divisional Council out of the rates.

7235. *President.* Do you think the ratepayers here would be averse to anything of the kind?—I do not think so, but it all depends upon how the matter is explained to them. I think if the Government paid the deficiency, local men would not pay so much attention to educational matters, and they might become extravagant.

7236. *Dr. Berry.*] Would you in any way limit the responsibility of the local body?—Yes. The rate should not exceed say a farthing or one eighth of a penny in any one year; it would depend on what the expenses are.

7237. *President.*] Would you allow a rate to be levied before an account showing the deficiency had been audited by the Central Government?—No; certainly not.

7238. *Dr. Berry.*] Would you allow the members of the Board any expenses?—No, only travelling expenses, just as in the case of the Divisional Councils. I do not believe in paid men for posts of that kind. The secretary might be paid if he has to do the work, but as I said before, I think the Secretary of the Divisional Council might be got to do it for a nominal sum.

7239. How often does your Divisional Council meet here?—Once every two months.

7240. Does the Civil Commissioner attend the Divisional Council meetings?—Yes; he always attends here and presides.

7241. *Rev. Coetzee.*] What contributions would you expect from municipalities towards making up any deficiency?—None. Municipalities, as a rule, are very poor, and require all the money they can get. In the district of Middelburg, the Divisional Council levies a farthing and the Municipality a penny, but they cannot come out with that, but we always come out with a farthing rate.

7242. *Dr. Berry.*] Would you be in favour or otherwise of the Municipality separating itself from the Divisional Council for school purposes?—Yes, I would not give the Municipality anything to do with the school system. I speak of the country districts. You would have to make a different arrangement for large centres.

7243. Would you in any case allow a municipal area to constitute itself as a school district with its own Board and machinery?—No; not unless it were a large centre like Cape Town, Port Elizabeth, or Graham's Town. It would require separate legislation. It would not do for small places.

7244. *President.*] Are the educational wants of the farmers pretty well met in this district?—I think that something might be added in the way of giving more railway facilities. I have made several applications for farmers living very close to the line of railway.

7245. Do you think the Government should allow farmers' children to travel free in such cases?—Yes, in fact all children who are near to a school and can use the railway ought to be able to travel free, because the trains run in any case.

7246. You would give them the same facilities as are given to the children of railway employés?—Yes. Railway children ought not to have any more facilities than farm children; the railway belongs to the public. Of course these facilities ought to be limited to children going to a school very close to the line in the district; a child should not be able to go to Graham's Town free. I also think that at places like Middelburg Road, and wherever there is a junction, it would be a good thing to establish a school.

7247. Would you give the School Board any voice in the setting up or management of farm schools in the division?—Yes. I should have no objection to have a central Board, and then have minor Boards working their own schools, but for the purposes of general education you must give the central Board some sort of power over the others with regard to finances, and so on.

7248. Would you bring private farm schools under the Board?—No. They should be allowed to remain as they are, with a Government grant issued direct.

7249. Would it not be an advantage to let private farm schools also work through the Board, because sometimes there might be an application for such a school, and the

Board might see from its local knowledge that there was really no necessity for it or they might suggest something better?—The Board might have a final vote as to whether a grant should be allowed to a private farm school or not, but I would not interfere with the internal working; it would give too much trouble to a Board sitting perhaps once or twice a month. I am very much in favour of aid to private farm schools.

7250. Should the application for aid go through the Board?—I should have no objection if it were an elected Board. If it were a nominated Board, I should seriously object.

7251. *Dean Holmes.*] In towns would you have any objection to existing mission schools being brought under this Board?—I think altogether that the Board should not have anything to do with mission schools, inasmuch as the rates are not to be responsible for any deficiency.

7252. Suppose these mission schools were to come under the Board under their own managers, rendering accounts to the Board, which should pay any deficiency that might arise; would that answer?—I should object to that.

7253. Would you not in very many cases do away with existing mission schools?—No, I would not. I am quite prepared to leave them what they have, but I would not give them more.

7254. Do you think a grant of £75 a year is enough for a school educating 200 children for instance?—In some cases I think the education of the natives is overdone. In our town you will see natives of 19, 20, and 21, grown up men and women, going to school with a slate under their arm, and it is impossible to find servants in the town. The ladies all complain that they cannot get domestic servants. Under these circumstances there should be a line drawn with regard to the education of the natives. I do not think a native of 18 or 19 should be on a school bench, he ought to be out working for his living. I speak of places like Middelburg. I would do more for the education of the whites than the blacks.

7255. Would you like these mission schools to be brought under the scheme of the fourth class public undenominational schools?—In some instances, but in Middelburg, if we had a fourth class school it would kill the first-class public school. It would take all our younger children away from us, and if it existed in a place like this, we might close our doors.

7256. But the Board would not sanction a fourth class public undenominational school to come into existence in such a case as that, would it?—In some places it might work well, in other places it might do great injury. A mission school composed of whites exclusively, should be brought under the fourth class school system and come under the Board. The taxpayers of the district should pay for those children just as much as for any others, as long as they were white, but I draw the line between white and black.

7257. *Dr. Berry.*] Is it not almost absolutely necessary when you come to consider that the Divisional Council would be liable for the money spent on the public schools, that white mission schools should come under the Board, otherwise they might absorb all the children at their own scale of payment?—Yes, but I draw the line as to colour. If this country were in a better condition as to labour, I would be in favour of a compulsory system of education. In Holland we have it, and it is very satisfactory, but in this country it would not do. I know instances where farmers cannot even get servants to look after their sheep, and so they have to keep their children out of school.

7258. With regard to white mission schools, it would be a very arbitrary proceeding at present to say to the managers, you must give up your school and become a public aided school; do not you see any plan by which mission schools for whites could be continued under the Board system without endangering it?—I see no plan, it would be a dangerous precedent.

7259. *President.*] Suppose they can only come under the Board where the Board consents to it, would not that answer?—There ought to be one system of education as much as possible I think.

7260. *Dean Holmes.*] Can you conceive of the case of a School Board being called into existence where there are two white mission schools; how would you deal with that? —I would transfer them into fourth class public undenominational schools.

7261. But you cannot take their property away, can you?—I would buy it.

7262. Suppose they would not sell, and would not let you rent it, what then?—If they were so obstinate as all that, I would get a school somewhere else and leave them out in the cold.

7263. Would not that be a very arbitrary proceeding?—I do not think so. This property here, which cost £2,000, belongs to the Dutch Reformed Church; suppose it so happened that this district was populated solely by Jews, and Jews composed the

Board of Management, there is no doubt about it the Dutch Reformed Church would let them the property, and why cannot mission schools do the same ?

Mr.
N. T. de Waal.
Pro- Sept. 18th, 1891

7264. Would you allow them to remain under the existing management?—Provided they came under the regulations of the Government ; then I would pay any deficiencies, but not otherwise. If you pay their deficiencies, they must come under the one system of the Colony, otherwise we open the door to all denominations, and the taxpayers will have to pay the deficiencies of private schools.

7265. *Rev. Coetzee.*] Would you retain the conscience clause if such a Board is created ?—Yes. I do not think it works badly. We have half an hour's religious instruction every day. The Bible is read, and there is prayer, and nobody can object to that. No doctrinal subjects are ever discussed in our school, nor do we try to make proselytes of the children.

7266. *President.*] Have you formed any opinion as to the language question ?—I think that great injustice is done to a Dutch child in regard to the Elementary examination. For instance, a Dutch child goes up for the Elementary examination at 14, it has been reared in a Dutch household, and has heard that language spoken daily. It goes to school when it is eight or nine years of age, and has to learn English, which is a foreign language. I admit that every Dutch child should learn English, but at the same time, in regard to the Elementary examination, that child is certainly handicapped. I know two or three children who have failed for want of understanding the questions. If you examine a child in mathematics, we do not want to ascertain whether it knows English or Dutch, but whether it has obtained a knowledge of mathematics. I do not see therefore, why in the examination papers the Dutch translation could not be put immediately below the English. Then, if a Dutch child did not understand what a certain word was in English, it would not be at a loss. I can see no objection to that, and it would involve no appreciable extra expense. Then again, I would give a Dutch child, if he wishes, the right of answering in his own language. This would show to the Dutch people that their language was to a certain extent recognized over German, French, or Kafir. There is no doubt that the Dutch form a large proportion of the population, and I think such a concession, after all, a minor concession, might very well be made. I have known instances where Dutch children have misunderstood the English question in the Elementary examination, and they have consequently failed, although they were perfectly able to answer it. The question was not brought clearly to their minds.

7267. That being so, would you be in favour of having two sets of papers, one in Dutch and one in English ?—I think one set of papers would do, with a Dutch translation underneath the English.

7268. Would you have the answers given in English or Dutch ?—Just as the child likes.

7269. Would it not be convenient to have the papers one side in Dutch and the other in English, and let the candidate choose ?—I think for the Dutch child it would be more just if the questions were printed in the two languages, one underneath the other. If we are examining a child in science or mathematics, we do not want to find out his knowledge of language at that particular moment.

7270. But when a candidate adopts a language in answering, he must stick to that throughout, must he not ?—Yes.

7271. *Rev. Coetzee.*] Would not what you suggest lead to confusion ?—I do not think so. The questions could be printed in the same manner as you sometimes see songs set to music printed, one language underneath the other. It assists to catch the sense to a great extent. When a child is asked a question, it must first understand the question before it can answer ; it must be put clearly before it, and as I say, a Dutch child is often handicapped by not understanding the question.

7272. Is all the teaching done through the medium of English ?—Yes ; and that is why I think a Dutch child should be assisted in the way I suggest. If he is at a loss for a word, he would at once see what it was. The same thing might apply to Italians, or Germans, or Kafirs. We want to find out whether they can answer a certain question put to them on science, arithmetic, or whatever it may be. You are not testing their knowledge of language.

7273. If a candidate is up to the standard required for the Elementary examination, do not you think he would be able to understand the questions in English ?—He might and he might not. There are some Dutch children who would be flurried at the examination time, while others again are quick and can express their thoughts easily. If the right were conceded for a child to answer in Dutch, any apparent injustice could be remedied at a very small cost, and it would give a recognition to the Dutch language, which I think the people would like.

7274. As a matter of fact, are not people very anxious to have their children examined in English ?—Yes, but I do not know that parents would prefer to have their children examined in English, say on arithmetic.

Mr.
N. T. de Waal.

S pt. 18th, 1891.

7275. But they are taught arithmetic in English at school, are they not?—The medium of instruction is left free to us as a School Committee; we can teach in Dutch if we like. I think it is unfair to the Dutch-speaking community that in the School Higher and Matriculation Examinations a Dutch paper is introduced, while it is not in the Elementary examination. I see no reason why an easy Dutch paper should not be given in the Elementary examination. I would not make it compulsory. There might be an alternative subject, although I believe where people intend to make this country their home, they should make a point of learning both English and Dutch. They are always useful. I certainly think a Dutch child is somewhat handicapped through the Dutch language being ignored in the Elementary examination, and seventy-five per cent. of the Dutch children do not go beyond the Elementary examination. To them it is the final educational stage.

7276. How would you count the marks if Dutch was optional?—I would put French or elementary science as alternative optional subjects with Dutch, and let the marks count for both. That would be perfectly fair. It could be an easy paper, and the marks need not be high, but it would be a recognition of the Dutch language.

7277. Do you think that would meet the supposed sentiment about English boys not wishing to learn Dutch?—I believe there are very few English boys who would learn Dutch. In the Civil Service it is required, and it is a semi-official language.

7278. From an educational point of view, which is the best, a second language or elementary science?—I speak two or three foreign languages, but they are of no use to me whatever here.

7279. Then you think that elementary science ought to be encouraged in every way?—Yes.

7280. Would you introduce Latin also?—No, not in the Elementary examination, unless it was very easy. As I said just now, seventy-five per cent. of the Dutch children do not go further than the Elementary examination. Dutch might be optional, with a little Latin.

7281. Do you think it would destroy the elementary character of the Elementary examination if Dutch was introduced?—I do not think so. I would sooner see a child go up for the examination six months later than not have Dutch introduced.

7282. It has been suggested, among other things, that there might be two classes of papers, one with the present four subjects, and another with five subjects, of which Dutch should form one, would that answer?—I see no advantage in it.

7283. You think it is better to have four subjects compulsory, and a fifth alternative optional paper?—Yes, which should count.

7284. You think that would better encourage the learning of Dutch?—Yes.

7285. You think that practically Dutch would be taken up?—Yes; by English as well as by Dutch boys.

7286. Would it encourage it still further if you gave a prize or a bursary to those passing well in Dutch?—I have no objection to that; it would tend still further to encourage it, but I would not put that in lieu of what I have suggested.

7287. In such a case you would make it compulsory for a boy to pass in the four subjects, would you not, to show that he has been educated?—Yes, decidedly. If we got what I propose, and bursaries in addition, it would be a great concession.

7288. And you think it would really tend to promote education?—Yes; and it would also tend to make some people who object to their children learning Dutch, forego such objection, if they saw that bursaries could be obtained by successful candidates.

7289. Would you be in favour of extending the Elementary examination still further and having say six papers?—I think that might destroy the elementary character of the examination.

Rev. M. Postma examined.

Rev.
M. Postma.

Sept. 18th, 1891.

7290. *Rev. Coetzee.*] I believe you are minister of the Reformed Church here?—Yes.

7291. Are you connected with several schools in the division?—Yes; three.

7292. Are they boarding schools?—Yes; two are aided by Government.

7293. What do you call them?—District boarding schools.

7294. Have you anything to complain of in regard to the attendance?—No; the attendance at all the schools is very regular.

7295. What is about the percentage of attendance compared with the number of children on the roll?—I should say about 75 per cent., perhaps rather more than less.

7296. Have you any difficulty in starting schools in the district?—I have not experienced any difficulty since I have been here.

Rev.
M. Postma.

Sept. 18th, 1891.

7297. Do you always get people to come forward willingly to sign the guarantee list ?—Yes ; we have a guarantee list on this principle : The guarantee is £2 10s. per annum, and it must be signed by each person for three years, whether or not he has a child at school. The boarding fees are paid quarterly.

7298. What do they amount to ?—£20 a year, either in money or kind. At the Wolvekop School, which has been in existence nine months, and is attended at present by 63 children, the boarding fees per quarter are : Three sheep, 75 lbs. of sifted meal, 4 lbs. of salt, 5 lbs. of coffee, 5 lbs. of sugar, 5 lbs. of rice, 1 lb. of tea, some vegetables, 9s. boarding fee, and one load of fuel or £1 per annum from each boarder. At the other school, Wolvefontein, it is rather more, but the payment is also in kind. I think the charge is too low, and I do not see how the teacher can make it pay, but it is the only means of starting a school and keeping it going. We give the teacher an allowance of £15 additional per annum, to make up for whatever may be deficient.

7299. Do you get any capitation grant from Government ?—Yes, £6 a year for the boarders.

7300. Do you think that is sufficient ?—No. The parents we find are unable to keep the children on with such small aid as that.

7301. What would you suggest so as to enable the parents to keep on their children at school ?—I would suggest that the amount should be doubled, make it £12 instead of £6. I would state that we have a fund started by the congregation and all who are interested in education, which we call a supporting or aiding fund. Each person contributes sixpence a week to it ,and from this fund, grants are given to poor children, which go to supplement the £6 given by Government. If it were not for this, we could not keep the children at school.

7302. Do you get sufficient to enable you to give the teachers a good salary and procure competent, well qualified men ?—We pay at present £155 a year for the principal teacher.

7303. Is that sufficient to procure a good man ?—Not altogether ; I think £200 a year should be the minimum. I would suggest that Government should give a larger grant to District Boarding Schools. Instead of £100, they should give £125 or £130 to the principal teacher.

7304. And the assistants ?—You might get a single man who would be able to undertake the duties for £100 a year. It must be borne in mind that farmers' children have to pay for boarding, which children residing in town do not, and, therefore, a good allowance should be made. The fees in our District Boarding Schools are too low altogether, indeed, if they were not supplemented in some other way the schools could not be kept going.

7305. Dr. Berry.] Do the schools you have mentioned appear in the returns of the Education Department for 1890 ?—No ; they have only recently been started. There are 63 children at Wolvekop school, 40 at Wolvefontein, and 28 at the other, which is unaided. Wolvekop is about an hour and a half from here, near Sherborne siding ; Wolvefontein is a ward, four hours from here ; that is not near the line ; the other school is about an hour from here in another ward.

7306. President.] How are the schools worked ?—By a committee.

7307. Are all those who attend these schools members of your Church ?—Yes.

7308. Are there any children belonging to the Dutch Reformed Church ?—Yes ; we have in the Government aided schools some Dutch Reformed Church children, but our children are in a very large majority at present. In the unaided school there are no children belonging to the Dutch Reformed Church, but there is no objection to take them. The management of all three schools is practically in our hands. When the guarantee list was formed, it was left open, and the public were invited to sign. It was well notified, and circulars were sent throughout the whole district.

7309. Do you work harmoniously ?—Yes.

7310. Are there any other Government aided schools formed by other church bodies near to you ?—No, in fact there are none in this district. There are no Government aided district schools except those formed by members of my congregation.

7311. And initiated by you to a great extent ?—Yes.

7312. Rev. Coetzee.] What is your opinion about the guarantee system ?—I have not found any difficulty with regard to it. It is a question I have studied a good deal. At Aliwal North, I was headmaster of the Public School for five years, and I found the guarantors had a good deal of difficulty, and in some cases they had to pay to the amount of £20 to £25 each out of their own pockets to make up the deficiency. At Burghersdorp, there never was any deficiency. I do not see how the matter can be remedied, or how any other body could be substituted for the guarantee system. On the whole it is a very good and wholesome principle that men who evince the most interest in the schools should take the initiative, and in every respect also support them. Of course it comes very hard when through untoward circumstances they have to put their hands in their pockets to a large extent, but I see great difficulty in Municipalities or Divisional Councils taking over the schools as is done in some cases. I feel that you do not get the proper men to conduct the school.

7313. Do you see an objection to Municipalities or Divisional Councils becoming guarantors?—Yes. In many cases local questions would arise. Persons would try to get in for merely party purposes, to effect a certain reduction, or from some feeling either for or against the teacher, and so on. On the whole, I should be disposed to keep the guarantee system.

7314. Had you any school property at Aliwal North?—Yes.

7315. In whom was it vested?—In certain trustees. I think the chairman of the Municipality and the chairman of the Divisional Council were trustees.

7316. President.] Did it become public school property?—Yes.

7317. Not under the control of members of your Church?—No.

7318. Rev. Coetzee.] It has been suggested that School Boards should be created to manage all the schools in a certain area; what is your opinion as to that?—I have considered that question, and I think there would be a good deal to commend such a plan, but the difficulty is that an over Board would not be sufficiently acquainted with local wants in a particular ward, and would not meet those wants adequately. I find in my own experience, for instance, that though the two schools, Wolvekop and Wolvefontein are not more than five hours apart, in many cases I have to proceed on quite different lines even in those two wards. I think an over Board might clash with the local Board.

7319. Could not the over Boards acquaint themselves with the peculiar circumstances of each ward?—It would not be impossible.

7320. President.] Could not such an over Board work through sub-committees?— Yes. I would not be against that, but I would not let the over Board interfere in all minor matters.

7321. Rev. Coetzee.] Would you retain the present managers as sub-committees? —Yes, the over Board giving help and advice where necessary.

7322. And recommending schools for aid where they thought it was needed?— Yes.

7323. What contributions should be expected from Municipalities or Divisional Councils in cases where there is a deficiency?—Towards erecting school buildings, I think some aid should be given, £30 to £50. I may state for the information of the Commission, that at Wolvekop we had to erect all the buildings ourselves; the Government could not give any aid, as they were built on the property of the proprietor of the farm, so we had to raise the money by means of contributions and collections, and we have succeeded in paying off nearly all the cost. If we could have got some assistance from the Divisional Council or Municipality, it would have been a great boon and enabled us to make larger extensions.

7324. These schools have been started for a period of three years, have they not? —Yes.

7325. What provision have you made with regard to retaining the buildings for school purposes?—At the end of three years, all the buildings are the property of the proprietor of the farm, and he repays the amount of £40 to the committee. In addition to that, he allows free grazing for three years for all the cattle, sheep, and horses sent to the farm.

7326. President.] Suppose at the end of three years he repays the money and turns the school off, what would you do?—We should have to go to the expense of erecting new buildings. There is no likelihood of such a thing, but of course he has the power to do so.

7327. How would you stop it. Do you think it is advisable to vest such property for public school purposes for over?—Yes, but we should have to get a certain piece of ground, one or two morgen attached specially for school purposes. The difficulty in this case was, that if the school was not placed on a certain farm, there would be no means of boarding all the children, we could not at once have erected sufficient buildings. If we had had to get a certain piece of ground and erect school buildings and a master's residence, I do not think we should have mustered the number of children we have at present. It is by reason of the teacher taking some children, say twenty, and two farmers boarding another twenty, that the school has been a success.

7328. Has the teacher a house that has been built?—It was a house which we had altered to accommodate the teacher.

7329. Do you think the farmer would be willing to part with the land for Public School purposes, so as to perpetuate the school?—I do not think he would have any objection, and it would be a good thing. Whether we should have the same number of children I question, because easier terms are sometimes made for poor children by farmers living on a farm than teachers can make.

Rev.
M. Postma.

Sept. 18th, 1891.

7330. Could not these farmers still accommodate the poor children ?—If the school is not too far.

7331. *Rev. Coetzee.*] Is there anything objectionable or difficult in the way of securing a piece of ground, say a morgen or half a morgen, and erecting a building thereon for school purposes, and vesting it in a School Board or over Board, and so keep the school going ?—I do not see any difficulty.

7332. *Mr. Theron.*] Is it not better to pay rent for a building in such a case ?— That might be a good thing. The question has engaged my attention a good deal, and I felt the difficulty. In all possible cases, I think a certain piece of ground should be bought for school purposes where it is likely to become perpetual, and vested in the Board, and towards that the Government must contribute.

7333. *Rev. Coetzee.*] In what proportion ; on the £ for the £ principle would you say ?—Yes, I think so. If we could get that, we should be satisfied. Where the school is not certain to be perpetual, you might have a movable structure.

7334. *President.*] At what expense could such a structure be erected ?—At Wolvefontein we have a movable structure. It cost about £60. It was a second hand building.

7335. How large is it ?—It is 40 by 20 feet. We had to alter certain buildings on the farm for the accommodation of the teacher, and all those alterations of course are for the benefit of the proprietor of the farm. We have to pay at the end of the three years £10 ; the rest we get free.

7336. Can you remove the structure ?—Yes.

7337. How many children are there there ?—Forty at present. It would accommodate a good many more.

7338. *Dr. Berry.*] Would you have a movable structure also for the teacher as well as for the school-house ?—It is not advisable ; in winter time it is rather cold. Of course you might do that if you cannot do better.

7339. *Rev. Coetzee.*] What contribution would you expect from the ratepayors ?— I should say 50 per cent. If the deficiency is £50, £25 should be contributed by the Municipality or Divisional Council and £25 by the Government.

7340. Does the undenominational public school system work in the town of Middelburg in a satisfactory way ?—I think not.

7341. Why ?—It is not representative, because all the members of the School Committee belong to the Dutch Reformed Church. I have been here one year and nine months. Shortly after I came here, I saw there was a grievance in regard to the constitution of the School Committee, which was composed only of members of the Dutch Reformed Church. The election is arranged so as to be within the letter of the regulation, but certainly not within its spirit. The meeting is called by notice affixed in prominent places, as required by the regulation, but it is not sufficiently made known either in the town or district, certainly not in the district, and the result is that only the members of the Dutch Reformed Church are elected as members of the committee.

7342. What further publicity would you suggest should be given ?—I would suggest that as required by the former Government regulations five years ago, there should be a notice in the newspapers.

7343. There was no notice in the local paper here in this case, was there ?—No ; but it should be required in the interests of education. I was away at the Synod just at the time of the election. In compliance with the regulation, there was a notice affixed to the school-room door and the door of the court-room, I believe, but I never saw it, nor was it brought to my attention. Had it been, I should certainly have been at the public meeting and required that more publicity should be given, in order that a fairly representative body should have been elected as the School Committee.

7344. You know that householders are called upon to attend at the meeting ; what is the general idea as to who householders are. Do you know of any case in which the question has arisen as to what constitutes a householder ?—Yes ; it arose at the election for the Municipal Council. I believe it was stated that a householder was anyone who resides in a house to the value of about £50. I think the Magistrate ruled that for the particular occasion. With regard to the election in question, it is a matter of great grievance in the district and also in the town, especially among my congregation. As a matter of principle, it is fair that all public bodies and all classes of the community should be represented in these undenominational schools. It is not that I think the children of my congregation would attend largely the public school, because I am strongly in favour of district boarding schools for our agricultural population. I believe from my own experience, that the children make more progress in such schools, and that the supervision is better than can be given in town schools. If you can place children under proper supervision in town, it is all right, but in many cases it is not done, and what progress they make is not nearly

260

Rev.
M. Postma.

Sept. 18th, 1891.

as rapid as they make in district boarding schools. I am not anxious to be on the committee, because I have my hands full; and have more than I can do, but I certainly think, as a matter of principle, that more publicity should have been given to the meeting.

7345. *Mr. Theron.*] I understood you to say that if you had been at the meeting, you would have moved that it be adjourned and more publicity given. Do you mean that they were outside the regulations?—No, they were inside the law.

7346. By what right would you have objected to the meeting?— I would have had no legal right to object, but I think I should have appealed to the meeting as to whether it was fair to get one body of men returned on so many occasions, especially when it could be proved by evidence that not sufficient publicity was given throughout the whole district in the matter of the election. I believe in a district like this, the more publicity the better, and I may state that before starting the Wolvekop and Wolvefontein schools, I sent letters and printed circulars throughout the whole district. The more these matters are done on a thoroughly public basis, the better for the school.

7347. Do you mean that the regulations as laid down are faulty?—Yes, more publicity should be given.

7348. Were not those who convened the meeting within the limits prescribed by the regulations?—Yes; but the committee knowing that a grievance had existed for so many years, should have done all in their power to obviate it by giving more publicity.

7349. *President.*] Did they know there was a grievance?—Yes; at least I should think so.

7350. You say that you did not know about the meeting, and that practically there was ignorance about it in various quarters throughout the district?—Yes.

7351. Do you consider this meeting in connection with the first class public undenominational school is for the whole district or only for the town?—For the whole district.

7352. Is that generally known?—I think so.

7353. You say that practically the school seems to be worked for one denomination?—Yes.

7354. And you think that ought to be remedied if possible?—Yes. If sufficient publicity had been given and only Dutch Reformed Church members were returned, I should not have complained, but have taken matters as they came.

7355. *Mr. Theron.*] Were there a good many people that day in town?—It was my Nachtmaal.

7356. Was not all done that was required by law?—Yes; but I think a notice should be inserted in the newspapers.

7357. Do you wish to infer that that was not done with some object?—I would not like to criticise it, but I think the object is to do everything possible to keep the school under the Dutch Reformed Church.

7358. Do you know who was the chairman of the public meeting?—Mr. Friedlander. He was elected on the spot. I told him he should have used his influence to get a representative meeting.

7359. *Dr. Berry.*] Were the functions of the general public also ignored when the school was raised from the second to the first class?—I do not know how that was done; no public meeting was called. I merely heard that it had been raised from a second to a first class school.

7360. Should not the public have had a voice there?—Yes, certainly. No meeting was called, and no notice was given, unless it was affixed to the doors.

7361. *Rev. Coetzee.*] What has been the practice in the schools with which you have been connected as to the election of managers; are they elected by the guarantors or the householders?—In one case by the guarantors and in another by the householders. Sir Langham Dale supported the last.

7362. Where was that?—At Aliwal North. There was a dispute upon the subject, and Sir Langham Dale decided in favour of the householders, but of course the committee members must be guarantors. In all places I have been acquainted with when school committees have been formed, not only has a notice appeared in the newspaper, but a bellman has been sent round summoning the meeting for a certain day. If I am here when another election takes place, I shall certainly move in the matter as far as I can, so that the meeting shall be more representative.

7363. *President.*] You think that in the interests of the public it ought to be, the object of the Government being to make the school a public one?—Yes.

7364. *Mr. Theron.*] How long is it since Sir Langham Dale expressed that opinion about householders electing?—About twelve years ago. I was in Cape Town, and he explained it to me in his office. There was a dispute at Aliwal North, and he subsequently wrote and told me that he had expressed that opinion.

Rev.
M. Postma,

Sept. 18th, 1891.

7365. *President.*] Suppose public notice is given and thorough publicity given, and then there is a meeting; do you think it would be wise to continue the system of guarantors in the interests of the public, or would you allow any deficiency which arose after the Board has been elected, to be paid out of the rates?—I think the rates should contribute.

7366. Who do you think ought to attend the meeting?—All the public; the householders.

7367. What should the qualification for a voter be?—Every man who owns a house or every man who occupies a house and is in receipt of a salary should be able to vote.

7368. *Dean Holmes.*] Would you allow a man a vote for each property he possesses?—Yes. For the tenants, I would go upon some scale of salary, making the basis as broad as possible.

7369. *President.*] Would you take the Parliamentary franchise?—Yes.

7370. Would you impose upon the Board the duty of filling up gaps and supervising the educational needs of the district?—Yes, and the public undenominational schools should come under the Board.

7371. How much do you think the Government ought to contribute?—Half the expenses of buildings and teaching.

7372. And after the fees have been collected in addition, you would come upon the ratepayers for any deficiency?—Yes. The Divisional Council should collect the money and pay it over to the Board. In the case of agricultural schools, I should recommend that more than half be contributed by the Government. I think also the over Board should not in any way clash or interfere with the country school committees, but only have a general oversight and supply what is necessary.

7373. *Rev. Coetzee.*] Should the local managers of a school in any district be responsible to the over Board?—Yes.

7374. *President.*] In the case of mission schools, should they come under the Board?—Not necessarily, but if they liked. I would also give country school committees the right to refuse to come under the Board if they did not choose to do so, because they might find that it hampered them in many respects; the over Board might make certain stipulations with which a ward could not comply. I would also always require a report from the Board.

7375. *Mr. Theron.*] With reference to the qualification of voters for this Board, suppose you accept the Parliamentary franchise; would you be able to rate salaried men and others who were not owners of property, through the Divisional Council?— No; unless you had a poll tax, or something like that. I would not be in favour of any direct taxation. I think the Divisional Council should give a certain sum from its funds, and they would try possibly to retrench, so that no rates should be levied.

7376. Under the present Divisional Council Act there are two special rates that can be levied for main roads and divisional roads, so that the money cannot be used for other purposes as the law stands, and if you want to introduce the principle that they should contribute out of their funds for any school deficiencies, you must make provision for it. The deficiency you say is to be made up by the Divisional Council; is it fair that the Board should be elected by the Parliamentary voters, and the Divisional Council voters be taxed?—I see a difficulty, but I do not know how it could be obviated in the interests of education. Very often persons who are not proprietors of landed property are the men who work most zealously for the school, and perhaps contribute from their salaries or otherwise.

7377. *President.*] Could you obviate the difficulty by giving the Board power to work through volunteers who would be responsible for the balance?—That might meet the case.

7378. Do you think men interested in education would often work with the Board in that way?—Yes.

7379. *Dean Holmes.*] Would you introduce any property qualification for members of the Board?—No. I might state that the people who have assisted me most in the matter of education are certainly not the wealthiest farmers.

7380. *President.*] I believe you have taken great interest in industrial education, have you not?—Yes. We have resolved to endeavour to establish an industrial department in connection with the Wolvefontein district school, and I have also the promise from Sir Langham Dale of a grant of £50 a year. We intend to get a man at a salary of say £75 or £100 a year, to which the Government will contribute £50, and the parents whose children go in for trade classes will pay a certain extra school fee. The articles which are made will be sold in the ward or district, which would perhaps bring in another £30 or £40 a year. Instead of orders being sent to carpenters in town, they will be sent to the school by the people living in the

Rev.
M. Postma.

Sept. 18th, 1891.

neighbourhood. By this means I think that instead of there being a deficiency we shall always have a surplus.

7381. How about the building?—The building would be erected out of the profits.

7382. Would you have it a shifting building in the first instance?—Yes.

7383. Do you think it is a good thing for white children to learn some handicraft?—Certainly. It has engaged my attention, and among very many of our population there seems to be a latent talent to some extent.

7384. Do you think that talent has been neglected?—Very much.

7385. In what way?—Because there has been no opportunity for learning trades.

7386. Have the people rather gone back in that way?—Yes; in former times when there were not so many carpenters' shops and so on, most of our elderly people had to do everything themselves in that way, and a workshop with an anvil and other things were to be found at a good many farms, but now they seem to have all disappeared. Farmers were able to make their own chairs and tables, or repair their wagons, but that could not be done by their children, simply because they have had no occasion to do it. I think therefore, if an hour a day from play time was devoted to the workshop, the lads would find a real pleasure in the employment. There would be emulation, and good practical results would follow. The difficulty I find is to fill up the time after school hours, there is so much spare time on hand, and the taste for reading is not sufficiently cultivated, indeed you could hardly expect that boys coming to-day from a farm would take to reading books readily to-morrow; it must be gradual, but I think it would be an excellent thing if when a carpenter was constructing a building, the boys helped him, and also if they tried to make some article out of wood. There is a clear indication, not only in the Middelburg district, but all over South Africa, that industrial schools should be established. I am confirmed in this view by my visit to Griqualand West last week, where a great many people are going from all parts of the Colony. It is new ground, and houses are required, but in some of the districts, carpenters are not to be got, and even if they could be got, people cannot afford the expense after trekking a long distance. If these people understood carpentering, and so on, it would be a great saving, and it would help to make them more self-reliant.

7387. Have you found in your experience that physical exercise, if not excessive, promotes mental activity rather?—Yes, certainly.

7388. You would encourage industrial training for white children?—Yes.

7389. With regard to coloured children, are you opposed to their receiving any education?—No.

7390. What is the nature of the education that you would think best for coloured children?—Strictly elementary and religious teaching.

7391. Would you have industrial training of some sort?—I do not think so, except manual labour perhaps. If you look at the condition of matters, it is evident that most of the coloured people all over South Africa are destined to be the labouring classes, and we should therefore adapt all the education of the natives accordingly.

7392. How would you do it inexpensively and so as not to let it clash with the industrial education which you have indicated for the whites?—I would not teach them any of the trades which the whites have to practise.

7393. Would you allow them to take the trades if they were prepared to pay for it?—Yes.

7394. What is the industrial education you would principally prescribe for the natives?—It is difficult to say. I think labour itself is the best practice for them. I would train the girls for domestic servants, and make the boys work in the field and garden.

7395. How would you train domestic servants unless you had a large house?—The difficulty would be to do it practically. If circumstances permitted, I would make them in rotation go through domestic duties, and teach them to make soap, candles, and such things, so that the white people could get better servants than they have at present. The boys should be made to go through farming operations, and do everything that a farm servant has to do. I would require them to be punctual in the performance of their duties and train them generally. The labour question is a very serious one, and is intimately connected with the question of education. During my visit to Griqualand West, I found to my regret that many of the sons of white farmers had to herd the sheep themselves, and on two of the farms the daughters had to do this duty. The labour difficulty is one which stands in urgent need of a remedy; it is well nigh impossible to get servants.

7396. If you had industrial education on the location, do you think the natives would go out among the farmers?—I do not know whether they would, but they ought to go out.

7397. Would not industrial training such as you have indicated, rather have a tendency to cause parents and children to say, I will go away from these schools and get among the farmers?—I do not know that it would; they would prefer to stay at the schools, which are more attractive. I find that the native has an objection to work.

(right margin: Rev. M. Postma. Sept. 18th, 1891)

7398. If they went away from the locations, they would have to go among the farmers and work, would they not?—You would have to make it compulsory in some way I think.

7399. Would you make it compulsory for them to attend the industrial teaching?—Yes, but I have not seen much good from industrial training even at Lovedale. We do not find many native carpenters or blacksmiths about.

7400. Would you like to have them?—No.

7401. Is not that the reason perhaps that they do not come, because you do not employ them?—You will find that in the country where there is a native carpenter he gets work.

7402. *Dr. Berry.*] I understand you to say that you want to train the natives to be labourers, and you want the farmers' sons to be taught trades; where are the tradesmen to find work if every farmer does his own?—I would not make them professed tradesmen, but teach them sufficient to help themselves in case of necessity. I make a distinction. I do not see why a farmer, for instance, should always have to send to the town for a carpenter, when he might do the work himself. If he has a house to be built, of course he could not do all that. As I said just now, in many parts of the country, carpenters are not to be found, so that I think all would find work who understood their trade. Apart from that, employment of this kind helps to fill up a boy's time, the eye is trained, and they become more useful citizens. I would not, as I say, make them all carpenters and masons, and so leave no room for tradesmen, but I would give them sufficient instruction, so that if necessary they could do what was required about their houses, and so on.

7403. You have about a million and a quarter of the native population; what is to become of them; can you suggest any practicable scheme for the education, amelioration, and usefulness of these people?—That is a great difficulty, but I do not think the imparting of higher education which is being done in some quarters will ameliorate their condition. I should be in favour of elementary and religious instruction for the natives, and limit it to that, and in all possible cases teach them to labour with their hands.

7404. Would it not be a good thing if you were to differentiate these people among themselves, and train some to be artizans, some to be printers, some to be shoemakers, and some carpenters. Do you think they will ever get on if they are all on one uniform dead level?—Then you do away with the labouring classes of the whites.

7405. *President.*] Is not the labour difficulty in the Free State as great as it is here?—It is greater.

7406. Has not a farmer there in many cases to give up one-third of his farm to natives, so that he may have some sort of location where he can go for labour?—Yes; he is obliged to have huts on his farm.

7407. Then in the Free State they have not surmounted the labour difficulty, have they?—No.

7408. Can you suggest some practical industries which you could apply universally to coloured children at school?—Not beyond what I have already suggested. The girls should be trained for domestic service, and the boys taught manual labour. The best training school for a native is on a farm, where he is obliged to put his hand to anything that he is told, and where he does not come in contact much with town servants. Such natives are generally most obedient, and can put their hand to anything and everything. You would require very expensive machinery if you are going to teach the natives agricultural work from a technical point of view, a model farm would be wanted in fact, and after all, I doubt very much whether you would turn them out as well as if they had been actually trained by the farmers themselves in the ordinary way. If there is any system whereby they could be put under a certain contract with farmers for so many years, that would be the very best thing, far better even than industrial training.

7409. *Dr. Berry.*] Would you be prepared to advise a system of apprenticing these people to European masters, so that they could get literary as well as industrial training?—I think that some such plan would answer. Some reward or inducement might be held out to parents placing their children in such a way for a certain number of years.

7410. *President.*] Who is to offer the inducement?—It might proceed from the Government.

264

Rev.
M. Postma.

Sept. 18th, 1891.

7411. If it lay between attendance at an industrial school or apprenticeship, which do you think would be preferred?—They would prefer the industrial school because they would think there was less work to be done.

7412. *Dr. Berry.*] It is impossible to provide education for a million and a quarter of natives; and if we go on neglecting things and allowing these people to take their own course, that million and a quarter will become two and a half millions; and are we as the rulers of this country to let them grow up and swamp us. Would it not be a wise thing to establish a labour bureau for these people, through which a certain number of the children could be taken and apprenticed to masters, either Europeans or superior natives, so that they could be trained for a certain number of years in their early life. To what extent would you be prepared to go in recommending a system of that kind?—I would go to a great length, but I would never advocate anything in the form of slavery either directly or indirectly. I quite admit that something must be done with regard to this large mass of natives, and whatever can be done to fit them for their proper sphere, namely, labourers and tillers of the soil, should be encouraged and supported.

7413. Do you think anything should be attempted in the direction of a labour bureau?—Yes; I would have no objection to that. I think the Government should take the initiative in any question with regard to the natives, and if they did so, such a bureau could be started at different places, and servants might be got in that way. In the Middelburg district we are worse off than almost any other district, I think.

7414. Have you seen the working of the Juvenile Offenders Act, under which small boys caught thieving or doing mischief can be apprenticed for a certain number of years to a master?—I have not seen the working of that. I think the apprentice system would give better results than industrial schools, and also give us better servants.

7415. *Rev. Coetzee.*] What is your opinion with regard to the teaching of Dutch? —I think that more facilities should be given for it; at present they are not sufficient. Dutch ought to be made compulsory in the Elementary examination all over the Colony, and at inspection in all the standards, the Inspector should require the children to read in Dutch and be qualified in the language. The Inspectors themselves should also be acquainted with both languages, English and Dutch. I could bring forward instances that have come to my knowledge where they have not been so qualified. Then again, certain prizes should be offered for boys knowing both languages. In school libraries, the committees should see that the books are not only English, but Dutch also; there should be Dutch literature as well as English supplied. I cannot myself see any reason for the objection one hears urged sometimes that it retards a child's education to take two languages. In Holland, four modern languages are taught; not every one learns four, but very many do, especially those destined for commercial life. I have noticed during my experience of fifteen years' teaching, that our Afrikander children have a special talent for languages, and as the majority of the European population is Dutch, that language should receive far more attention than it does.

7416. Would it not put an English child at a disadvantage if you made Dutch compulsory?—No, because an English child never knows where his future is to be in South Africa, and for educational purposes alone, it is all the better for him to know both languages. We all know that in many respects they are branches of the same stem, and the one throws light on the other. The simultaneous study of the two languages is most beneficial to the English child, and if it is a disadvantage, as is said, to such child, it is a far greater disadvantage to a child with Dutch surroundings, to have to pass an examination in English. I think we should go further and not only extend Dutch to schools, but to Government offices, stations, and other places. There should be a general competency in both languages, so that a farmer say who had to travel from Middelburg to Kimberley could address the stationmaster in Dutch and receive a reply in the same language. In the examinations I see it is suggested that Dutch should be optional, but I would like to have it compulsory in all, and as many marks given for Dutch as for English. At present, the English paper in the matriculation numbers 300 marks, and Dutch 200, I believe, but that is an injustice to the Dutch; each should be 300, and so all through, from the lowest to the highest. In the appointment of teachers, school committees should have evidence before them that they are qualified in Dutch as well as in English in all our colonial schools, even in English centres, inasmuch as a child trained in Graham's Town may have to spend his future life in Griqualand West, the Free State, or the Transvaal. In the appointment of the University Council, the voters should bear that point in view. There is no doubt that the matter of Dutch has received injustice at the hands of the University Council, and as one taking an interest in University elections, I should like to put a councillor through the same footing almost as a member of Parliament is put through, and ascertain his views on Dutch, and if he hesitated to give equal rights to the language with English, that alone would be sufficient ground for my not recording my vote in his favour, but for another equally competent man, who would support both languages.

7417. *President.*] Have you anything to suggest with regard to the education of the children of the agricultural population ?—I would start as many district boarding schools as possible, and the Government allowance should extend beyond the £ for £ principle. I think the capitation grants should be doubled for indigent boarders. Where a school is situated on the line, farm children as well as railway children should travel gratis to and fro, and an organising inspector should be appointed with the special object of starting schools in a district.

7418. *Dr. Berry.*] Would he be employed and paid by the Board or by the Government ?—By the Government.

7419. Under whose direction ?—Under the direction of the Government.

7420. But if you had a Board in the district to manage the education of that district, would it not be necessary for him to be under that ?—He could act in harmony with the Board. During my experience as a minister, I have not found so much difficulty in starting schools, but people are not acquainted with the conditions of aid and the facilities provided, and it should therefore be the duty of the organising inspector where people are ready and willing to start schools, to show them the way how to do it. I think if that were so, a good many more schools would be started. It simply depends very often upon people putting their heads together and getting others to co-operate. It is already made a provision by the Government in district boarding schools where the committee finds it advisable only to teach in Dutch, and that the children should not be forced to learn English, that their hands should be left free. I am not against the teaching of English for a moment ; I think it is absolutely necessary for people in the country as well as in the towns, but I find from experience, that a child whose surroundings are entirely Dutch, will learn more in two years in Dutch than if he or she has to acquire all that knowledge through the medium of English, which is a foreign tongue to such child. At the Wolvekop school, the history and geography of South Africa are taught entirely through the medium of Dutch, and they learn it very much quicker than if they had to plod through a manual in English. Let English of course be taught as a language as well. The University should set the papers in the Elementary examination in Dutch as well as in English, so that if there is any country school where only Dutch is taught, the children would have an opportunity of passing the same standard in the examination as English children.

Mr. Nicholas Durenage examined.

7421. *President.*] I believe you are a farmer, and reside at Wolvekop in this district ?—Yes, where the boarding school is.

7422. Have you anything to say with regard to the educational wants of the agricultural population ?—I think there is a necessity for more schools in this district.

7423. Have you any trouble in getting schools ?—Yes, we have not sufficient support for the purpose of building. The children of the railway employés near us are anxious to come to our school, but it is inconvenient for them, as the trains do not suit.

7424. Do you take any boarders on your farm ?—Yes.

7425. How much do you receive for them ?—£20 a piece. I consider it very cheap. Out of that, Government contributes £6 a year, which is not sufficient. I think the Government ought to contribute £12 a year, and the remainder might be paid by the Divisional Council.

Mr. Stephanus Buis examined.

7426. *President.*] I believe you are a farmer in Middelburg ?—Yes, I am a member of Mr. Postma's congregation, and live in the town. I was formerly a member of the Divisional Council.

7427. *Rev. Coetzee.*] Have you anything to say with reference more especially to the educational wants of the agricultural population ?—The farmers live as a rule a long distance apart, and when they want to send their children to school, the great difficulty is the expense of boarding.

7428. What would you recommend ?—An increase of the grants.

7429. Are you satisfied with the present guarantee system ?—No. In my opinion, instead of imposing upon a few the obligation of becoming guarantors, it would be better to have something like a Board started. It would be fairer.

7430. Do you think that children of parents living along the line should be allowed to travel free by rail to and from school ?—Yes.

7431. Do you think the Government should contribute a little more for the boarding of children at farm schools ?—Yes, £6 a year is too little ; I should say it ought to be £9 or £12 in the case of indigent children.

Mr.
Stephanus Buis.
———
Sept. 18th, 1891.

7432. What is your opinion about the teaching of Dutch?—I think it would be a good thing to teach all children both languages up to the stage of the Elementary examination.

7433. Do you think the Government inspectors should be well acquainted with both languages?—Yes.

7434. Are you in favour of industrial training for the coloured people?—Yes. I do not see any necessity for giving them so much literary teaching; it would be a good thing for native children to receive some industrial training.

Mr. D. H. Theron examined.

Mr.
D. H. Theron.
———
Sept. 18th, 1891.

7435. *Mr. Theron.*] What are you?—Headmaster of the First-class Public Undenominational school in Middelburg.

7436. Is the attendance in your school regular?—Pretty regular.

7437. Are there many children in town here who ought to be in school but are not at present?—There are some, but not very many.

7438. Can you give any reason why they are not at school?—Sometimes on account of poverty, and sometimes neglect on the parents' part.

7439. What means would you suggest in order to provide for the education of those children?—I think that an allowance might be made for taking free scholars; Government might give an extra grant, and let a justice of the peace, the magistrate, or the Divisional Council be entrusted with the payment of the school fees for these children, otherwise the school might be swamped with too many free scholars.

7440. Suppose these children were all brought to your school, would you have sufficient room?—At present we should not. We have more children than we can accommodate at present, and the school committee is about making some provision.

7441. *Rev. Coetzee.*] How many free scholars have you?—I cannot say; there are a good many.

7442. *Mr. Theron.*] Is the school conducted on the guarantor system?—Yes.

7443. Do you approve of that system; do you for instance consider your position permanent under it?—I know the school might lapse at the end of three years. I get notice at the end of that time, and then another arrangement has to be entered into with the incoming committee.

7444. Do you think that is satisfactory?—I do not think it is at all.

7445. What would you suggest as an improvement?—There are two ways which suggested themselves to my mind. The first is, that instead of the School Committee coming to an abrupt termination at the end of three years, so many members might retire by rotation, the same as on the Boards of Insurance and other companies; the next plan is, to abolish the guarantee system altogether, and substitute a body like the Divisional Council for the guarantors.

7446. You mean a kind of Board?—Yes, I would like to have an elected Board.

7447. What do you think should be the qualification for the voters?—I think those who are entitled to vote for members of the Divisional Council.

7448. Would you be favourable to making the franchise broader, say for instance on the Parliamentary basis?—Then you would, I fear, have persons voting for members of the School Board who have no interest in education at all.

7449. You would prefer rather the Divisional Council franchise?—Yes.

7450. Would you vest all school property in such a Board?—Yes, because then there would be permanency, an element which is wanting at present.

7451. Under a Board, would you consider your position as a teacher more secure than under the existing system?—Yes, certainly.

7452. Do you know anything about farm schools?—Yes, I generally go out and inspect private farm schools in the district.

7453. Are there many about here?—Yes, a good many now; I think about eight or nine. They have all sprung up lately.

7454. Do you think that all the educational requirements of the district are met by these schools that are now in existence?—I do not think so. I think there are very many children in the district who are not attending school.

7455. What would you do to reach those children?—I scarcely know what can be done, because I am under the impression that Government has granted already all the facilities it possibly can, but very many of the farmers do not make proper use of their opportunities. Very often it is through ignorance of their existence. I think bodies like Divisional Councils should be exhorted to acquaint farmers with the facilities that already exist, and then no doubt they would make more use of them. There is also a good deal of misunderstanding sometimes. I have known for instance a farmer thinks that because he used a room in his house for a school, that he would not be able to get the Government grant for private farm schools.

7456. Did that farmer get the grant?—Yes.

Mr.
D. H. Theron.

Sept. 18th, 1891.

7457. So far as the Government is concerned, it is willing even to forego some of the regulations if education can be promoted is it not?—I do not think there is a regulation saying that there must be a distinct room for private farm schools. I put it in the report that this school was held in a room.

7458. Do you know to what extent Government is disposed to help indigent boarders?—Yes, the grant is £6 a year, and then there is £3 in addition for the teaching. That makes £9 a year for every child, as far as indigent boarders are concerned.

7459. Is that generally known among the farming population, do you think?—I do not think so.

7460. Are there many poor bijwoners in this district?—I think so.

7461. Do you think their children are reached by the present system?—They can be reached, but I do not think they are.

7462. *Rev. Coetzee.*] With regard to the Board, in what way would it make up a deficiency when it occurs in a school?—The Divisional Council might be empowered to levy a tax on the ratepayers to wipe out the deficiency.

7463. Do you expect any contribution from the Government to make up the deficiency, or should it be done by the Divisional Council?—The Government should give a grant as they do at present, and then the deficiency should be met by a Divisional Council rate.

7464. Do you teach Dutch in your school?—Yes.

7465. Is the medium of instruction Dutch or English?—Both; mostly English, but frequently I use Dutch as the medium to make myself understood by the pupils.

7466. You do not do that as a general rule, do you?—No.

7467. Which is taught most in your school, English or Dutch?—English.

7468. Have you many English boys in your school?—I think there are three.

7469. Do they learn Dutch also?—Yes.

7470. Do the parents object?—No. One is a little boy; he does not learn Dutch, but he will by and bye.

7471. Do you teach Dutch with the object of afterwards passing the children through any examination; suppose there was a Dutch paper in the Elementary examination, would your children be able to take it?—Yes.

7472. Would an English child taught in your school find any difficulty in such an elementary paper?—I do not think so. Most of the English boys I have in my school learn Dutch with the others; they are in the same class and they get on as well as the others.

7473. Did you send up any children for the Elementary examination last year?—Yes.

7474. How many?—I think I sent up seven.

7475. *Dean Holmes.*] How many out of the seven passed?—Six.

7476. *Mr. Theron.*] Do you think there is any necessity for making more provision for teaching Dutch than there is at present?—Yes, certainly, I think there ought to be more provision. I would like to see it one of the subjects in the Elementary examination.

7477. How would you like to have it introduced into the Elementary examination?—I would like to have it as it is in the School Higher Examination, and as Greek is in the Matriculation at present. Let it be an optional subject, but the marks should count, and be added to the aggregate.

7478. Would not that handicap an English boy?—I have mostly Dutch boys in my school, and very frequently they are sharp and clever, and stand a good chance at the Elementary examination, but they are beaten by the others who do the examination in their mother tongue.

7479. Suppose you had two papers with all the subjects, one in Dutch and the other in English, would that be satisfactory?—I have never thought about that, but it seems rather a clumsy way of doing it. I would have Dutch introduced into the examination, because every English boy as well as every Dutch boy requires Dutch in after life, so that it will not do him any harm if he takes it up; those who do not take up Dutch have more time to devote to the other four subjects solely.

7480. Would you be in favour of giving a bursary to those boys who passed an optional Dutch paper satisfactorily, provided they were proficient in the other subjects, would it be an encouragement, do you think?—I certainly think it would.

7481. Would that satisfy you?—I would sooner have the marks count and added to the aggregate. You may have two boys, one of whom passes the Elementary examination, but not in honours; he simply passes, but he does the Dutch paper well, and then he gets a bursary, while the other boy who passes the Elementary examination in the other subjects, passes as well in honours, but he does not do so well in Dutch, and does not get the bursary; I do not think that is fair, and it will not encourage boys to take up Dutch.

M
D. H. Theron.

Sept. 18th, 1891.

7482. Would you compel an English boy to pass the examination in Dutch?—Certainly not.

7483. Another idea has been suggested, that the questions should be printed in English and Dutch, one underneath the other, do you think from your own experience that that would help the Dutch boy to form a better idea of what he is required to answer?—Yes, certainly: I find that myself; if you see the thing in the two languages, you are able to grasp it better.

7484. *Rev. Coetzee.*] Take Euclid and arithmetic, would it not lead to confusion if you translate the terms used in those subjects?—When they go up for the School Higher Examination I think they understand enough English to have the questions in English alone, but in the Elementary examination I do not think it would lead to confusion at all. In arithmetic, if the medium was Dutch, they would look at the Dutch question, and if it was English they would look at the English question.

7485. *Mr. Theron.*] If the Dutch was put underneath, would it not help them to understand the English question?—I think so, especially in the Elementary examination.

7486. Do many of your scholars proceed much further than the Elementary examination?—Not very many.

7487. That is finality with them?—Yes, with the majority.

7488. *President.*] Do you teach elementary science in your school?—Animal physiology and natural physiology are required for the sixth standard. I scarcely go beyond that at present.

7489. Is it a good thing to teach elementary science?—Certainly.

7490. Do not you think in many ways elementary science, as far as the value of education in after life goes, is quite as good as language?—I think so.

7491. And therefore quite as desirable for elementary education?—Yes.

7492. Would it be a good thing to have an elementary science paper in the Elementary examination; would many of your boys take it up?—I think so.

7493. So that at present they are not examined in a subject which they know something about?—That is so, so far as the Elementary examination is concerned.

7494. Would you make Dutch and elementary science optional in the Elementary examination as a fifth paper, and let the candidate choose between the two?—It would be better to have another language, and make it optional between Dutch, German, and elementary science. That is what I suggested at the Teachers' Conference.

7495. Do you think it would be a good thing to have Dutch, German, French, and elementary science, and let the candidate choose between the four?—Yes, that would be a good thing.

7496. Would it be a good thing from an educational point of view?—Yes.

7497. *Rev. Coetzee.*] Do you teach the two languages at the same time in your school?—Yes.

7498. As far as your experience goes, does that retard the progress of the children?—No; I think it rather accelerates it. At present I am bound to teach in two languages. If I taught in English alone, they would not understand it.

7499. *Dean Holmes.*] When you have examined farm schools, in what condition have you found Dutch education, is it high?—In many of the farm schools nothing but English is taught; they are English farmers. The others take up Dutch just as I do more or less, and one school teaches nothing but Dutch; no English is taught there at all. There are about 26 pupils in that school.

7500. *Rev. Coetzee.*] Is there a strong desire on the part of the Dutch farmers to have their children taught English?—Yes, English as well as Dutch, they are beginning to teach English more. I have recommended them to do so.

7501. *Dean Holmes.*] Is there much difficulty in getting good text-books in the Dutch language?—Yes, there is.

7502. How is that to be accounted for?—I suppose it is because the medium of instruction is English in this country. If you want text-books, you must write to Holland for them. I got a few from Holland lately.

7503. Are they expensive?—Not when you get them direct, but they are not altogether suitable.

7504. *President.*] Is it not a good thing to know a language thoroughly so that you are able to express your thoughts clearly in it?—If you learn two languages, as far as my experience goes, the mind becomes more developed.

7505. Have you thought at all of the subject of night schools?—I think it would be a good thing where the necessity exists, if the Government was to subsidize night schools.

7506. Could you start one here effectively do you think?—I think we might get a few pupils, not a large number.

7507. Have you the time to work it yourself?—I do not think so, but I should like any night school to be under the management of the School Board, if Government gives any aid.

Mr.
D. H. Theron.

Sept. 18th, 1891

7508. Are there many who cannot attend a day school who would make use of a night school?—No. There are not many here, perhaps four or five. I have taken a few pupils myself out of charity at night. Of course if there was a regularly organised night school, and fees were charged, they would get a better education. I cannot always attend now.

7509. Would you expect a contribution from the Government after the school had been examined and found satisfactory?—Yes, let the inspector examine the school and then give aid the same as in the case of farm schools.

7510. *Dean Holmes.*] Might there be some difficulty in the inspector timing his visits when the night school term was on?—Yes; that is a difficulty.

7511. Could the examination be done through the head teacher of the first-class school?—I think they have too much to do, and they require their evenings to themselves.

Rev. W. B. Wallace examined.

7512. I believe you are a Clerk in Holy Orders and reside at Graham's Town?—Yes.

Rev.
W. B. Wallace.

ept. 18th, 1891.

7513. Could you furnish the Commission with any information in regard to the educational requirements of the children of railway employés?—I may say that my experience was gained in two years' work amongst the platelayers on the northern part of the Eastern system. On that system, the number of children is about one per mile, nearly 300 in all. There are no special schools, or means of using the public schools along the line; their education is entirely neglected. Some scheme is absolutely necessary which will give these isolated people their own schools, or facilities for making use of those in the towns along the line. By persons who have had some experience of railway employés' needs, two schemes have been suggested, but they do not commend themselves. I will take them separately, and state my objections to them. First, an itinerant master, who would spend an hour or two at each cottage. Let us suppose this plan in operation. He could hardly begin his work before 9 a.m., the children would not be ready. He spends two hours at Cottage No. 1; leaves at 11 a.m. on a trolly for Cottage No. 2, where he arrives at 12, if the line has been fairly level. He gets through one hour's work, when dinner intervenes, after that, he puts in the other hour, and leaves at 3 p.m. for cottage No. 3, where he arrives at 4 p.m., and two hours' work here finishes the day. He has spent six hours in teaching, two in travelling and one on dinner. At this rate, if there be a master for every 100 miles of line, that is for every 25 cottages, it will take him nine days to visit the whole of his length, and there will be an interval of nine days between each lesson at each cottage; so the children, in most cases, will have forgotten what they learned in the previous lesson, and will have constantly to begin all over again. This plan would probably result in nothing but a waste of time, money, and energy. The second scheme seems quite impracticable, but I believe it has been attempted. It is this: to procure the use of a saloon carriage from the Railway Department, and station it on a siding fifty miles, say, from Cape Town. Then by some means, unexplained, all the children from the cottages 50 miles north and south of this siding are to be located close to the saloon carriage for a space of six months, the master living and holding school in the carriage. It does not appear how the children are to be boarded and lodged during the six months. At the end of this time, the carriage is moved on 100 miles, and the process repeated. If this plan could be carried out and there were two carriages working simultaneously, one for each 300 miles of line between Cape Town and Kimberley, there must be an interval of a year between the school terms on each section of 100 miles. These two schemes being open to such very obvious objections, I shall say no more about them, but proceed to lay before you two other schemes which seem thoroughly practicable, and moreover fall in with the rules and regulations of the Education Department as regards farm and district schools. 1. Boarding Schools.—I would suggest that Government provide a school for every 300 miles of line, that is, if my calculations are correct, for every 300 children; this does not mean that accommodation will be required for 300 pupils, as not more than a third of these will be of an age to go to school at one time. This school should be placed as nearly as possible in the centre of the 300 miles, as among the Railway employés there exists a very general dislike to sending their children far away. With the help of the two Inspectors of Permanent Way, I obtained the opinions of all the men between Aliwal North and Queen's Town on this subject; as to the desirability of a boarding school, there was but one opinion, all wished for it; and as to fees, it seems to be pretty generally agreed that £2 10s. a child per quarter would bring the

Rev.
W. B. Wallace.

Sept. 18th, 1891.

school within reach of all. I consulted with the late Mr. Samuel, Inspector of Schools, who after going carefully into the figures and all the details of practical working, came to the conclusion that with the Government grant on the £ for £ principle, it should be possible to maintain a very good school. The principal, and perhaps the only difficulty would be at the outset. The numbers for the first two years would probably not be large enough to keep the school going without extra help; until parents had seen some practical good results, I suspect they would not be so ready to send their children, as we may have been led to expect. In that case I would suggest that Government should give a special grant each year, sufficient to keep the school going until the number of pupils is large enough to make it self-supporting with the usual £ for £ grant. As an alternative scheme, arrangements might be made for the boarding out of the children in the towns along the line, and for their attendance at the public schools at reduced fees up to a certain standard. This plan seems to be preferable to the last, in that it would be more easily carried into effect, and at less cost, no special building being required and no master or mistress having to be paid.

Vryburg, Monday, September 21st, 1891.

PRESENT :

Sir J. D. BARRY (President),

Dr. Berry.

Mr. H. W. Howarth examined.

Mr.
H. W. Howarth.

Sept. 21st, 1891.

7514. *President.*] What are you?—I am general foreman at the Railway Station, Vryburg.

7515. How many children have you?—Six.

7516. What are the school facilities here?—In connection with others, we are anxious to have a station school. I have already made application about it to Mr. Howell, but have received no reply.

7517. Have you seen the circular issued by the Department relative to the railway schools?—No. After having seen it now, I think the terms and conditions would be very suitable for this place.

7518. Would there be any difficulty in forming a Board of Managers or providing a suitable teacher?—No. We have a very suitable female teacher. The requisite number of pupils would be forthcoming at once.

7519. *Dr. Berry.*] Do any of the children of the railway employés attend the public school?—Inspector Medworth has two or three girls and two boys attending the public school in the town, but it is very awkward for the children to go there in rainy weather. He would gladly avail himself of a station school, and others also. The school in Vryburg is two miles away from the station, and very difficult of access. It is practically of no use to railway children.

7520. *President.*] Do the trains serve to bring to school here the children of platelayers or others along the line?—No. The first train arrives here at half-past eleven in the morning. I might add that when the line is continued to Mafeking, this will be an important depôt, and there will be a good many railway employés here probably.

Mrs. Mary Chiddy examined.

Mrs.
Mary Chiddy.

Sept. 21st, 1891.

7521. *President.*] What are you?—I am a teacher here. I was brought up in Graham's Town.

7522. Are you a certificated teacher?—No, but I have been a governess for several years. I have been teaching here for five months, since May last.

7523. How many pupils have you?—Thirteen, including two of my own children. Nine of the pupils belong to railway employés.

7524. Are there any children of railway employés not attending school?—Yes. I know of six.

7525. Could they attend?—Yes, if the arrangements were satisfactory.

7526. Where do you carry on your school?—At present in a tent. I should very much like a school building to be placed at my disposal.

7527. Is there any building you know of which could be utilized for the purpose?—No. It would have to be erected.

7528. What fees do you charge?—Ten shillings a month for children over ten, and five shillings a month for children under ten years of age.

7529. How many months in the year do you have school?—I intended to give a month's holiday at Christmas, and a month in June that is all.

7530. Are you aware of the regulations governing schools for the children of railway employés, issued by the Railway department?—No. I have not seen them.

Mrs.
Mary Chiddy.

7531. Having seen them now (a copy having bo handed to the witness), do you think they would be suitable for this place?—Yes. I should be quite contented with the terms.

Sept. 21st, 1891.

7532. How much do you make out of your school now?—£72 a year. I have to find my own board and lodging.

Kimberley, Tuesday, September 22nd, 1891.

PRESENT:

Sir J. D. BARRY (President),

Dean Holmes,   Dr. Berry,
Mr. Theron,   Rev. Moorrees.

Ven. Archdeacon Gaul examined.

7533. *President.*] You are, I believe, Archdeacon of Kimberley?—Yes.

7534. And you have been so for some time?—Yes, I have been a resident here for eleven years.

Ven.
Archdeacon Gaul.
Sept. 22nd, 1891.

7535 During all that time, and indeed previously, have you always taken an interest in education?—Yes.

7536. Are there many children outside all education here, children of the poorer classes, who either receive no education at all or a very imperfect education?—There is a large number of what I should call vagrant children about the locations and in the poorer parts of the town who do not go to school.

7537. What do you think ought to be done with them? If some system of compulsion could be adopted, it would be a very good thing, without actually calling it compulsion. I think that any Board which may be appointed should have a paid inspector, who should inspect all the schools within the area, and collect information from various ministers of religion and others about all the children found not going to school. The parents should I think first of all be visited by the minister or teacher, and an effort should be made in encouraging them to send their children to school. If they are too poor to pay, then the children should be taken free, but if they refuse to send their children, then I consider they should be treated as parents who have deserted their children, on the same principle that if a man deserts his child and refuses to give it food, the State steps in at once; and if the parent is destitute and cannot feed and clothe his child, the magistrate takes possession of it. So I think we are bound to educate every child that comes into the world as far as we can, and where a parent refuses to do his duty, the State should come forward *in loco parentis* and see that the child is properly trained.

7538. What sort of schools would you suggest for such children?—I think there should be more industrial training. There should be in a colony like this, so many technical schools established on broad and generous principles. Perhaps the best plan would be to start and organise one thoroughly at first, and then having made that one a success, you might establish more in other large centres. Besides that, I would suggest that under the existing system, or any modification, expansion, or extension of it, there should be facilities granted for teaching elementary trade. I have an instance in my own mind where a carpenter in England spends two afternoons a week in teaching elementary carpentry, and I think something of that sort might be done here in connection with some of our schools. Then I think that cookery should certainly be taught in all our girls' schools, and in the case of destitute children who are taken possession of by the State, the girls should be apprenticed as domestic servants, on the condition that they attend the elementary schools so many hours a day, and in those schools they should be taught plain cookery.

7539. Would you apply this to both black and white?—Certainly.

7540. Do you think there would be any serious objection to treating white children in this way?—Not poor white children.

7541. Do you think that a sufficient number of masters and mistresses would be found willing to undertake the duties?—I think masters and mistresses would be found if they were encouraged by a little extra grant to take an interest in the work.

7542. I take it from what you say that you are in favour of industrial schools for the poorer classes?—Certainly.

7543. Would you make them free?—Not necessarily. In the case of compulsory children they would be free.

7544. Would you have a fee, and where the parents refused to pay or were totally unable to pay, would you consider they had virtually abandoned their children, and let the principle of apprenticeship come into force?—Yes. In the case of persons abandon-

Ven.
Archdeacon Gaul.

Sept. 22nd, 1891.

ing the proper charge of their children, the State, I consider has a right to step in *in loco parentis*, and do the best it can.

7545. *Dean Holmes.*] Would you make the parent contribute in that case towards the cost of the education?—In the case of parents who desert their children and can pay, I would make them pay. There are such cases.

7546. Where parents can pay and will not, instead of using the law against them, you would rather let the State step in; take possession of the children and indenture them?—I would first of all force them to pay, and if it is a clear case of desertion, then the State should step in.

7547. Do you apprehend that industrial schools would be so expensive as to be beyond the power of the State to undertake them?—As I have said already, I should begin by having one good technical or industrial school, whatever you like to call it, established at some centre, and work that thoroughly; then I would use the existing schools with adaptations, perhaps by adding to the staff or by giving an extra grant to those teachers who would take in hand the teaching of so much industrial work as could be fairly expected.

7548. How many Church of England mission schools have you here in Kimberley and Beaconsfield?—Three; St. Matthew's and St. Cyprian's, at Kimberley, and All Saints, Beaconsfield.

7549. Are they for white or black children?—Both; they are for anybody who comes, but the children are principally coloured.

7550. Are they mixed boys and girls?—Yes.

7551. What fees do they pay?—They vary very much. There is a very large variation made on purpose, in fact, I have gone on the principle in my mission schools of getting the parents to pay as much as they can, as it is right for them to do so. The fees vary from threepence a week, which is our smallest contribution here, to one shilling and sixpence a week.

7552. Do you think if some further aid was to be given to these mission schools, they would be able to have an industrial department in connection with them; would your Church be able to establish it?—Yes, if too much was not expected I certainly think so.

7553. What aid do you think it would be necessary to contribue in order to enable them to start such an industrial department for the children who are at school already?—The rate of wages is high here, and I should think a grant of £50 a year for each school would give us material aid, although it might not give such perfect results as we could wish.

7554. What are the present school hours?—Four and a half hours.

7555. Would you introduce industrial training during those hours?—I would use a part of the time for industrial training—finish off with it.

7556. Can you speak for other mission schools outside your Church?—I cannot speak for other schools, but I should say they would be very glad of something of the kind.

7557. Do you consider that these mission schools give all the education that is necessary for the children?—For the class of children which attends them certainly.

7558. Are you in favour of Board Schools?—Yes. I think in a community like ours, a public Board would probably do the secular work of education better almost than purely denominational agencies.

7559. Do not you think a public Board like that might also manage an industrial department better or equally well?—I should be glad to see an elected Board in every fiscal division; I would make every large town into a county practically, as they make London into a county. There should be a Board publicly elected by the divisional ratepayers, and they should have a general sort of control over all the schools in the division. They should appoint themselves their own inspectors, a visiting Board in fact, whose duty it should be to visit every school from time to time, so as to aid the Government inspector in his annual inspection and visits. That is about my idea.

7560. Suppose that Board finds there is an educational want in certain parts, would you impose upon it the duty of supplying it?—I should say a meeting of the ratepayers should be called, and the matter put before them, and if they think it necessary, a school should be established.

7561. Would not you give the Board power without calling the ratepayers together, to start a school of that kind or induce some volunteer body to do the work?—I should have no objection to that.

7562. Then you would in fact make the Board take the place of the guarantors under the present system, only you would let it include the poorer classes which the present guarantors do not deal with?—I would not in the least abolish the mission schools, but I would develop them.

Ven.
Archdeacon Gaul.

Sept. 22nd, 1891

7563. Would you let the mission schools work through the Board, the Board inspecting them and recommending them for further aid if they found it necessary?—Quite so.

7564. What would you do with regard to the buildings of the mission schools?—I should leave the property of the mission schools entirely in the hands of voluntary bodies.

7565. The volunteers must find the buildings, you think?—Yes; but the School Board of the district should be empowered to see that the secular education given is of the best and most liberal kind.

7566. And the Board should recommend them to the Government for aid where necessary?—Yes.

7567. Should the rates be responsible for any deficiency in the case of mission schools?—I think the division itself should support its own schools from its own rates. There should be a school rate for the aid of all schools in the division. My feeling is that the present annual Government grant should cease, and that each division should find its own school rate, and then with regard to buildings, that Government should give a grant apportioned according to the recommendation of the Board.

7568. Would it not be better to give aid to mission schools on condition that they did the work, and leave them to find their own buildings?—I would not object to that.

7569. Dr. Berry. Would you abolish all the grants in aid to public schools and let them trust to the local rates for support beyond the fees?—For all current deficiencies.

7570. President.] Have you considered the recommendation of Sir Langham Dale with regard to fourth-class public undenominational schools?—I have, and I think that if the recommendations of Sir Langham Dale with regard to fourth-class schools are just simply transferred to mission schools, we should be able to work our mission schools under the Board I suggest with perfect efficiency and without loss.

7571. If a Board were brought into existence, should not one of its first duties be to start such schools and work them through denominational bodies if they can?—That is my idea. The Board should have power, where there is need for a school, to establish that school, supposing no voluntary body takes the matter up, but where a voluntary school does exist, the suggestion of Sir Langham Dale with regard to fourth-class schools should be applied to existing mission schools.

7572. I see it stated in one of the local papers that there is a large number of private schools in Kimberley for the lowest classes, which are very inferior. Is that so?—Yes, many of them are very inferior.

7573. How would you deal with them?—My idea is this, that no school should be recognized at all by the Board that is suggested, or be inspected, unless the teacher of that school is registered as efficient.

7574. And certificated would you say?—That would be a little difficult sometimes; certificated or registered.

7575. If an incompetent master is registered, what virtue is there in that?—The inspector when he visits the school finds out the inefficiency.

7576. How would he deal with such a private school?—You can hardly stop a private school, but a teacher would not be registered unless he or she were properly efficient.

7577. Supposing a school refuses to register?—Then you must leave it.

7578. And suppose the children persist in going to the school?—The only way is to try and educate public opinion. The parents would surely listen to the statement of a Board that such and such school was inefficient. If it were known to the public that no unregistered schools were acknowledged by the Board, I should say that parents would have the sense to send their children to a school that was registered.

7579. Suppose you have compulsory education brought into existence, which means that the vagrant children can be forced into the schools that are created, and a parent shews that a child is in one of these private schools which is inefficient, how would you deal with such a child?—If you had the compulsory system, you would have to insist upon their attending a registered school.

7580. Then virtually you would take the child out of that private school and put it into an efficient school?—Yes.

7581. You would not recognize as efficient any school that was not registered?—No.

7582. And the Board should only register those schools the masters of which they found to be efficient?—There is a certain number of schools in this country presided over by uncertificated masters and mistresses, who are very fairly efficient, and the Board would exercise its discretion and wisdom in patronising and helping those schools as far as it could.

Ven.
Archdeacon Gaul.

Sept. 22nd, 1891.

7583. Do you approve of the system of guarantors?—I would much rather see the system of guarantors abolished and a Board elected by the ratepayers. I should prefer the divisional ratepayers myself.

7584. Do you think that any deficiency should be paid out of the rates instead of by the guarantors?—Yes.

7585. Is there anything which would prevent the present undenominational school property being vested in such a Board?—You can go to the High Court and have the matter settled.

7586. Is there anything which might create a difficulty in transferring the property from the present holders to an elected Board?—I see none.

7587. That would give permanence would it not?—Yes.

7588. *Rev. Moorrees.*] How is the school property here vested?—There are public trustees here, but there is no difficulty in transferring the trust.

7589. *Dr. Berry.*] Has there been any deficiency in the management of the Kimberley school?—I do not think so.

7590. *President.*] The public undenominational school has superseded the private church school, has it not?—Yes, we closed our church boys' school which had been for some time very successful and done very good work, but manifestly, when the public undenominational school was started with large Government aid, we were very much handicapped, and I myself thought it better in the interests of the children to close our school and throw our influence and interest into the other.

7591. Has the effect been prejudicial from any point of view?—As far as secular education is concerned, I do not think so at all.

7592. Is it better?—No, I do not think it is better; it is quite as good, and the Board has the right and the privilege of allowing religious instruction or disapproving of it.

7593. On the whole, you think it works well?—As a secular school it works very well.

7594. Is there any objection to the school that you can see?—No.

7595. *Dr. Berry.*] Have you any difficulty in getting up the list of guarantors?—No, not the least.

7596. Are the managers chosen at a meeting of householders?—The guarantors are elected by the householders, and then there is a meeting of guarantors to elect from themselves a Board I think.

7597. *President.*] Are there any besides the householders at the public meeting who guarantee?—I think not.

7598. *Dr. Berry.*] Would you let the School Board of the division have any school under its own direct control, or would you prefer that the School Board should delegate that duty of control to sub-committees?—I think the Public School Board should have control over all the schools in its division, and then that they should appoint a visiting committee from their number, whose duty it should be to visit the schools in rotation from time to time, and work with the Government Inspector during the year. My point is this, that the Government Inspector only makes an annual visit in the case of the present mission schools. In my own case, for instance, I visit my mission schools if I find anything loose, and come down on the teacher at once. When the Public Board takes control over all the schools, it would be very advisable that this visiting Committee should make say monthly or weekly visits to those schools, "surprise visits," for the sake of encouraging and helping the general work of the school, without of course interfering in the management of the school, but in order to supplement the annual inspection by the Government Inspector, just as at the hospital there is a visiting Board.

7599. *President.*] Suppose, after all, it is found that a school is wanted which no mission body supplies, would you give the Board power to start such a school and work it directly?—Certainly.

7600. And pay any deficiency out of the rates, after receiving the fees and the Government grant?—Yes.

7601. Would you put on the Board a nominee of the Divisional Council?—I hardly think that is necessary, as the Divisional Council ratepayers elect the Board.

7602. *Dr. Berry.*] How would the financial management of each school be conducted on this plan. Suppose you had second or third or fourth class schools in the district, the fees would have to be collected and paid to some over Board, the teachers would have to be paid, the Government grant received and the deficiency accounted for; how would all this be done?—There would have to be a proper financial return by each school on a form supplied by the Board.

7603. Who would make it?—In the case of voluntary schools, the religious body which ran the school, or otherwise the Board itself would have to do it.

Ven.
Archdeacon Gaul.

Sept. 22nd, 1891.

7604. Who would be on the spot to see that it was done properly ?—In the case of Kimberley, it would be a county, or division by itself.

7605. But take some of the divisions of the Colony, they comprise enormous areas, and there might be a considerable number of schools started in outlying parts of the area: who is to manage it all in that case ?— I imagine that where the divisional ratepayers elected all the committee, they would take care that each district was well represented.

7606. Would it not be better that there should be small sub-committees working under the School Board ?—It is always in the power of the Board to appoint sub-committees.

7607. You would have no objection to carry on local schools, would you ?— No. I should leave that to them.

7608. And they would see to the collection of fees and the general superintendence of each individual school ?—Yes. It is of great importance to introduce as much local interest as possible in the matter.

7609. In that way the School Board proper need have no particular school under its control at all ?—No, only the general management of all the schools.

7610. *President.*] What objection is there to the Central Government finding all the schools and working the whole thing ?—I think it is better to have local interest aroused and local responsibility developed as much as possible in the interests of education ; home rule within certain limits in fact.

7611. *Dr. Berry.*] What would be the relation of this School Board to what are called the private farm schools ?—My idea is that all the farm schools should certainly be under this Board.

7612. Should the Board have a voice in the setting up of such private farm schools ?—Yes.

7613. A voice, that is to say, with the Department ?—Yes.

7614. *President.*] Should it be such a voice as to debar a school from being set up if they veto it, or would you merely compel the Department to have a report from the Board, and consider their report before they act ?—You cannot take away the control from the Board. If it is to find the money, it must have the control, and the power of setting up a school.

7615. Would you make the Board pay for these farm schools or any proportion of them ?—Every farmer would have to pay his share of the school rate ; there is no doubt about that. I do not think he would feel it, as the amount would be very small, and it would give him a direct interest and feeling of responsibility for seeing that as many schools as were needed in the district were set up. I think with regard to these farm and smaller schools, that they should only be allowed to go up to a certain standard, and after that, the children should be drafted to some central school in the district, and the Railway Department might fairly be asked to grant free passes to children along the line so as to attend any central school conveniently near. I feel sure they would co-operate with the Board. I do not think myself that it is advisable to encourage the long attendance of children at farm schools ; it is better that they should be drafted to a larger central school after passing the second standard.

7616. *Rev. Moorrees.*] How would you provide for the boarding, that is the difficulty, is it not ?—I should leave that matter to solve itself. I have just concluded a ten days' cart journey, and I came across a Dutch boy who said he had gone a good many miles from his father's farm to attend a school that a private schoolmaster kept ; and he was paying a farmer £1 a month for his board. That was the case of a very poor farmer, and I think if one farmer will allow a boy to board for £1 a month, probably a great many others would do the same, and take in children in this way.

7617. The boarding seems to be the chief difficulty. A farmer might manage to send one child, but if there are more the expense is a consideration. I do not see how you can make any hard and fast rule ?—Quite so. In the case of all these farm schools, I would be against any hide bound principle at all. I would certainly insist upon all children passing a certain standard, say the second standard, and then that they should attend as far as possible for six months or a year some 'district school. The inspectors themselves should have the same latitude that they have now, that is to say, they do what they can for every child that comes under their notice, or every school that comes under their notice, they make allowance for the difficulties of distance and local circumstances, and so on. I think if a sensible plan of that kind were carried out in some way, there would not be any difficulty that could not be overcome by generous treatment. Of course I would not allow any teachers to teach on these farm schools unless they were registered. I do not say certificated.

7618. *President.*] At present the Government contributes in the case of indigent boarders £6 a year towards the boarding and £3 a year towards the teaching : do you think that is liberal ?—I think it is, but I would group these farm schools together,

Ven.
Archdeacon Gaul.

Sept. 22nd, 1891.

and have one district school, and I would transfer the boarding grant to the district school. I would put the district school on some farm where there were facilities for boarding.

7619. Would you encourage district instead of farm schools?—I would not discourage farm schools, but I would extend the system.

7620. Have you anything to say on the subject of night schools here?—There certainly ought to be provision made for a night school grant. We have got a small night school at present, which we work in connection with our mission school, and the Education Department gives a couple of pounds' worth of books now and then for it, but I think if there was a regular grant for night schools, proportionate to the numbers attending, it would be a good thing. In large towns generally there is a large number of boys who go out and assist their parents; they have a certain amount of education perhaps, but they would be greatly benefited by further instruction at night.

7621. Are those boys over the age of fifteen as a rule?—I should say their age is from twelve upwards.

7622. And in the interests of their parents they could not attend a day school?—No.

7623. Are there many such boys?—There is a good number here; and they earn high wages many of them.

7624. Have they had some education?—A little.

7625. Are there boys who at the age of twelve get high wages?—Yes. There are some boys who at twelve years of age get 10s. a week.

7626. Are they employed all day?—Yes.

7627. Would you interfere with those boys in regard to their employment?—I certainly would.

7628. Up to what age?—In this country I think boys should not go out to work before they are thirteen.

7629. *Dean Holmes.*] If they passed a certain standard, would you object to their going out at an earlier age?—No, say if they have passed the fourth standard.

7630. *President.*] Would you send all boys up to that age who have not passed the fourth standard into some school?—Yes.

7631. *Dean Holmes.*] Would you allow attendance at a certified night school to count?—Yes, after twelve years of age.

7632. *Dr. Berry.*] Do you think teachers in day schools might be made available for teaching in night schools?—Yes.

7633. Would you have night schools for both sexes?—No.

7634. *Dean Holmes.*] Would you have them inspected by the Government?—Certainly.

7635. *President.*] Have any night schools been started here?—Yes; it is difficult in the summer time to make them a success. We have got one under a lady which is doing very good work. I think it has been in existence over two years. The late Mr. Samuel visited it, and was very pleased with it.

7636. *Dean Holmes*] Would you require a certain number of attendances before a boy was presented for examination?—Yes.

7637. And then allow a Government grant if he passed?—I would prefer the grant as a whole being given or withheld according to the report of the Inspector on the working of the school.

7638. You would abolish payment by individual results?—Yes. I do not myself think that plan answers best.

7639. *Dr. Berry.*] Do you think there is any need of night schools for girls?—I think not. I think among the poorer classes especially they attend school long enough to get as much instruction as is necessary for them, and then they either take domestic service or go to their homes, and when girls reach thirteen or fourteen they are better at home at night.

7640. *President.*] How would it do for the Government to fix a certain sum per head to be paid in proportion to the number of the poorer class in average attendance at any mission or other school; could anything of that kind be devised?—Practically under the present system, unless a school has a certain number of children in attendance, it does not get a grant, and after getting a certain number, it does not get an increased grant unless it has increased the attendance. In fact, the present system is almost upon the principle of average attendances. Of course the Government consider local circumstances as generously as they can.

7641. Do you know anything about schools for the children of railway employés?—I think a paid inspector or inspectors should certainly visit railway and farm schools as frequently as possible, and give advice and so on. The inspector should be a practical teacher, one who has had experience in the Colony, and who is able to converse both in Dutch and English. An itinerant inspector of that sort would be very valuable.

Ven.
Archdeacon Gaul.
Sept. 22nd, 1891.

7642. Sister Cecile, of St. Peter's Home, Graham's Town, has offered to take the daughters of railway employés and board and educate them for £12 a year, do you think any one here would do the same?—I dare say any of the religious bodies would take up such a work.

7643. Would you encourage it?—Yes; but the town of Kimberley is not favourable for boarding schools, according to my idea.

7644. If boarding schools for female children are started, you would sooner they were started elsewhere?—Yes. I imagine that the children of railway employés go to the public school.

7645. Are there any special wants in connection with education here which you have not mentioned, that might be dealt with by the Government?—A technical School of Mines might be started. I think it should be worked in connection with the University system as far as possible.

7646. *Dean Holmes.*] Suppose we could introduce compulsory education into large towns, would the people object do you think to the visit of an attendance officer whose business it would be to enquire whether the children were being educated, and report accordingly?—I do not think generally they would. I think if the matter is talked of, and people's common sense appealed to, the great majority of them would not object.

7647. *President.*] What stamp of man would you appoint as attendance officer?—You must be careful as to that; you must have a man I should say who has been engaged in practical education himself, and who knows how to get on with the people, give them advice, and encourage them to send their children to school as much as possible; you do not want a police officer.

7648. To some extent you would enlist the sympathy of the clergy, would you not?—Yes, the attendance officer should work with the clergy and the school teachers generally, and the right sort of man would not find much difficulty in putting his power into force I think.

7649. *Dean Holmes.*] It has been suggested that the police should be employed; would you object to that?—Yes.

7650. Do you think it would be an objection even in the case of truant children, inasmuch as it would rather make it appear that they were criminals?—The population is not large enough to go into that question. If you take up the truants you must have a truant school established as they have in America on an island or somewhere or other where they cannot run away, and send them off there bodily.

7651. Do you understand the compound system here?—Yes, I think it would be a very excellent thing to compound a good many people.

7652. *Mr. Theron.*] Do you come in contact with many farmers in your travels?—Yes.

7653. Are the farmers mostly Dutch?—Yes.

7654. Are there many schools established at the places you visit about here?—Very few. Sometimes when travelling about, I come across a farmer with three, four, or five children being taught by one of these itinerant teachers, and I question the children and encourage them, and occasionally manage to get them a grant of some books, but I must say that in most cases the master is not the kind of man who would be registered.

7655. Are there among these farms many of the bywoner class, white servants who assist the farmers?—I do not think there are very many.

7656. Do you think the reason why the farmers do not make more use of the Government aid is because they are ignorant of the facilities offered?—Yes; to a large extent. It is also due to the want of proper teachers.

7657. Would farmers always be able to get a room for the teacher?—Yes; I think generally some sort of room. If the itinerant inspector was the right stamp of man, he would be able to encourage the farmer and give him advice.

7658. Are there any clusters of farms where you could establish district boarding schools?—The farms are scattered about a good deal, but there are a few places where they could manage it, but the principle of a district school and then carefully arranged farm schools, teaching up to a certain standard under registered teachers, would be the most practicable system, and the farmers would be very glad, I believe, to work with it.

7659. *President.*] As to the teachers being in many cases inefficient on farms, is there any means of establishing a normal school here with the object of getting good teachers; are you in favour of the pupil teachers as distinct from assistant teachers?—I think they should be supplementary to the assistants, for this reason: There is a certain number of promising pupils always in the school who have teaching powers, but unless they are paid slightly, they would be taken away and sent to service, but if after passing the fourth or fifth standard they were made pupil teachers, and a grant

Ven.
Archdeacon Gaul.
___
Sept. 22nd, 1891.

given, and they received supplementary instruction as they do now, they would come on as assistant teachers afterwards, and be able to take their certificates. Pupil teachers as supplementary to assistant teachers are very valuable.

7660. Have you considered the question of language at all?—I have my own opinions on the subject. I think that as far as the encouragement of education throughout the colony goes, especially in the country districts (of course here we are different), teachers should certainly have a knowledge of Dutch as well as English, and that the farmers and others should have their rights, so to speak, in regard to language, preserved to them as far as possible, but the actual education of the children should be through the medium of the English language. It should be a matter of accommodation as much as possible. The teacher himself should have a knowledge of the Dutch language, and should be able to teach English; in fact, you cannot teach English to a Dutch child unless you have some knowledge of Dutch. I do not think, myself, that we should in any way enforce the teaching of Dutch in every school; there must be an accommodating principle. My experience is, that a Dutch farmer wants his children to learn English; he has some sort of notion that the child will profit more in his education by learning English. It may not be very clearly defined in his own mind, but there is such a feeling.

7661. With regard to the Elementary examination, have you considered the question in connection with that?—I would not alter the existing arrangements.

7662. Would you be in favour of adding a fifth paper in Dutch, and letting the marks count?—My feeling is that it is impracticable in the country districts; you cannot get the Dutch language taught in the country sufficiently to make it a subject of examination.

7663. *Mr. Theron.*] Are you aware that children on farms generally have only a limited time for their schooling?—Yes.

7664. Would you in view of that, have them instructed in their own language or in a different language?—I should teach them the language in which they learn most.

7665. Which would that be?—I am not quite sure; it would vary in various families. Sometimes you get a man and his wife—the man speaks English, and he wants his children to learn English; he gets English books and so on, and I think it would do them more good in the long run. In a case where nothing else but Dutch is spoken, I would educate the children in Dutch, because the time of the children is limited.

7666. If they have to take up two languages they will probably know a little of each, but know neither well?—Yes; at the same time, I think you will find that practically most farmers prefer their children, even in a limited time, to be taught as much English as possible. They may learn their catechism in Dutch, and learn to read the Bible in Dutch.

7667. We want proper grammatical Dutch taught, not the *taal*; do not you think in a country like this it is very much better for people to know both languages?—Yes; I think so, as far as possible, but you must make exceptions. I have already recommended that the inspector should be a man who knows Dutch as well as English.

7668. *President.*] Is it desirable in the Kimberley schools that Dutch should be universally taught?—I do not think so.

7669. Why not?—I think the ordinary medium of instruction will necessarily be English, as well as the ordinary medium of communication with the world and one another.

7670. Do children in schools here generally know Dutch or desire to know it?—I should say not.

7671. Could they be examined in that language?—No; in Kimberley you would have to teach Dutch as a foreign language, as you teach Latin in fact, if the pupils are to be examined in it.

7672. Is Latin taught in the higher schools?—Yes.

7673. Is elementary science taught?—Yes.

7674. Is it desirable, in your opinion, that in the Elementary examination, candidates should be examined either in Latin or elementary science, or both?—In both, I should say.

7675. *Rev. Moorrees.*] Do I understand you to say that in a bi-lingual country it is no advantage for a boy to know both languages?—No; I do not say that.

7676. Would it be an advantage for boys at Kimberley to learn Dutch?—If they are going to live in the country districts it would be very valuable for them to know the *taal* at all events.

7677. Suppose they go to the Free State?—If they go to the Free State, Dutch would be necessary.

7678. *Mr. Theron.*] Is not Dutch requisite in the Cape Civil Service ?—Yes. If boys are compelled in certain walks of life to know Dutch, there ought to be a professor of Dutch, and it ought to be thoroughly taught, but I would not make it compulsory.

7679. You say that it is desirable, but you would not make it compulsory ?—It is desirable for those who need it in after life.

7680. But you would not make it compulsory ?—No.

7681. *Rev. Moorrees.*] Do you think a very great proportion of our population need the two languages ?—You get into the question there as to whether it is right and advisable to improve the *taal* and make it a thorough language.

7682. I speak of proper grammatical Dutch ?—In the ordinary walks of life in which two-thirds of our population are engaged, apart from the Civil Service and apart from the professions, the *taal* is what would be useful, and it is very useful to know it, but I should be very sorry to have to learn the *taal*.

7683. Will you explain the difference between the *taal* and proper Dutch ?—I think that in the majority of cases you would find that the time spent in learning technical Dutch in school, where a pupil has so many subjects, would not prove the advantage to the country that is anticipated. That is my feeling.

7684. Why not ?—It would take up too much time, and a boy's time is limited at school; you cannot introduce ever so many languages. There is one language which the commercial world has accepted as the medium of communication, and that language happens to be English, and therefore I think we must certainly see that all our boys who are destined for the struggle of life should be well grounded in that language, whether they are Dutch boys or German boys or French boys or English boys. In this country a very large section of the community speak Dutch, and as a rule boys pick up enough Dutch in their ordinary course of life to get along with. If I had been born in this country I am perfectly certain I should have been able to converse in Dutch, and if I were even now to stay six months on a farm, I should be able to converse in Dutch; so that I do not think myself, considering the time that a boy has to spend at school is limited, it is wise to insist upon a technical knowledge of Dutch, when he will pick up as much as he wants to get along with in an ordinary way.

7685 What I want to know is this, is it not a greater advantage for a boy living in this bi-lingual country to know the two languages of the country than to know a foreign language ?—In this country probably a boy would get as much good from a technical knowledge of Dutch as of French, but I do not think he would thank you for it in after years if he continued his studies. I do not think, for instance, that the literature open to him in the Dutch language would be so pleasant, agreeable, or profitable, as the literature open to him in the French language.

7686. Are you acquainted with the Dutch literature at all ?—No; only by reputation.

7687. *Mr. Theron.*] As far as the picking up of a language is concerned, do not you notice in your travels among the Dutch farmers that they pick up English also ?—Yes.

7688. And is it not abominable English which they pick up; would not you sooner see them learn English properly, as it ought to be learned ?—Yes; but that is not practicable when the time at school is so limited.

7689. You object to the picking up on one side, and we object to the picking up on the other. We do not like our Dutch boys to pick up English; we want them to be taught properly, and therefore we say, would it not be well on the other side if Dutch was taught well ?—There is the practical difficulty about the time in school. Personally I should have no objection, if there were time, to boys learning Dutch as a technical language, but my feeling is that they must learn English somehow or other sooner or later, and if they are going to mingle in the various walks of life, it seems better that they should have the English language taught them. In the meantime you must let the other matter solve itself.

7690. *Rev. Moorrees.*] We all agree that English is more advantageous, but if you can have both, is it not better still ?—No doubt, but I do not think you can: that is the point.

7691. We have it in evidence that in countries like Holland, France, and Germany, boys take to learning a second language at their seventh year, and by the time they are about the same age as our boys who go up for the Elementary examination, twelve or fourteen, they know more or less three languages, their mother tongue that is to say, and two besides. If a boy of seven years of age in Holland can do that, could not boys here learn a second language, and that one of the languages of the country ?—In Holland, in the country districts, I doubt if they really do learn a second language. In Belgium I found people only speaking Flemish.

Ven.
Archdeacon Gaul.

Sept. 22nd, 1891.

7692. The poorer farmers perhaps, but I am speaking of the general system. As a matter of fact, if boys take up French in their examinations, ninety per cent. would drop French after some years, would they not ?—I am afraid so, and German too.

7693. But Dutch would be useful in the practical walks of life, in the professions, and in the Civil Service, would it not ?—Yes ; there is that of course.

7694. *Mr. Theron.*] Is it not a fact that 90 per cent. of our boys never go farther than the Elementary examination ; that is their final stage, is it not ?—Yes ; I am afraid so.

7695. *Dr. Berry.*] Have you a Dutch teacher in the first class boys' school here ? —Yes.

7696. And in the mission school also ?—No.

Mr. *William Norrie* examined.

Mr.
William Norrie.

Sept. 22nd, 1891.

7697. *President.*] I believe you are head master of the public undenominational school here ?—Yes.

7698. How long have you been so ?—Three years and six months.

7699. Were you engaged in educational work previously ?—For thirty-five years altogether, in England, Scotland, and New Zealand.

7700. Do you understand the system of public elementary education in those countries ?—Pretty fairly. It has been altered since I left England, but I have read the discussions that have been going on.

7701. When did you leave England ?—Finally in 1882.

7702. Do you think that education reaches all the children here ?—I do not think so.

7703. What proportion in your opinion is unreached ?—A very small proportion of the children are in efficient schools. A large number is educated in private schools, but the statistics I am not able to give.

7704. What do you call efficient schools ?—Schools conducted by teachers who are certificated, or who have had experience in teaching, and have been recognised by the Government.

7705. Do you consider mission schools efficient ?—So far as the education in those schools is concerned, they are generally conducted by certificated teachers, or teachers recognised by the Government.

7706. I see it stated in one of the local papers : " The Commission might be asked to be conducted through some of the slums of our town, to shanties where crowds of children are sweltering in stifling rooms under the charge of teachers who have no other qualification for the title than the fact that they receive fees from the children." Is that a correct statement ?—I believe so far it is correct. In some of the outlying places here, a female will sometimes open a school and collect together a number of children, from thirty to sixty perhaps, in one room, built of iron. I have myself seen children taught in a place not fit for keeping horses in. This was by a girl who afterwards came to the public school, and was not qualified to go into the fourth standard.

7707. What fees would such children pay ?—I am not aware ; I think from 5s. to 10s. a month.

7708. Are they white or black children ?—White, as well as coloured. In connection with our own schools we opened a branch at Newton, and on the roll there are forty-four pupils ; but on the other side of the road, in a private house, I am told there is a school conducted by a woman. What her qualifications are I do not know, but she has about double the number of pupils in her school.

7709. How does she attract them ?—The children seem to prefer her school.

7710. Are the fees lower ?—They may be ; I do not know.

7711. Is it desirable, do you think, that other education should be supplied to these children ?—I think it is most desirable.

7712. Are there also children who are totally outside all education here ?—There must be many in Kimberley who are not in any school at all, both white and coloured children.

7713. Are there school buildings actually in existence here sufficient to supply their wants ?—No.

7714. How would you bring them into existence ?—It is a question of funds. I would propose that the Government should still contribute a certain amount towards the education of the country, and that the municipalities in towns like this, for example, should levy a rate for education. The divisional councils also should levy a rate on all householders under their jurisdiction.

7715. Who should be charged with the duty of bringing these schools into existence ?—A School Board should be elected for the purpose.

7716. *Mr. Theron.*] Do you hold the opinion that divisional councils should only go as far as their jurisdiction extends outside the municipality ?—Outside the municipality, but they should also have jurisdiction within the municipality in regard to levying rates. I do not speak of the management of schools.

7717. Should the municipality levy a rate for all the schools in their area; is that your opinion?—I think perhaps if a Board were elected by the ratepayers throughout the district, they might formulate a scheme by which an education rate might be fixed and collected through the machinery of the divisional council as well as through the machinery of the municipality, and paid into the Board, or it might be collected by the School Board, whichever is the most economical.

7718. What do you think should be the duty of the School Board?—To establish schools where they were found to be necessary; to decide where compulsory education should be introduced in the district over which they had jurisdiction; and take the general management and control of the schools, leaving it to Government to appoint their inspectors and report to the Government on the efficiency of the schools.

7719. Would you have local inspectors appointed by the Board?—In a large town like this, if there were many schools, it would be an advantage to have local inspectors.

7720. Would you let this Board establish schools directly, or should it have the option of working through volunteers, the Government contributing?—Where the Board sees that sufficient provision is made by voluntary aid, it might of its own accord allow voluntary schools to remain if they are efficient. It might be more economical and advantageous, I think, that the Board should have the whole control of the schools.

7721. In case it had the whole control it would have to bring into existence new schools, would not that be expensive?—They might use the buildings of voluntary bodies if the owners of such buildings were willing to put them into their hands.

7722. Suppose they were not willing, what would you do, work through the volunteers?—If the volunteers would permit the Board so to work.

7723. How would you deal with mission schools; do you class them among the volunteers?—Yes; I should keep the present mission schools going as long as they are efficient.

7724. Would you make them in any way responsible to the Board for their efficiency?—I would make them responsible to the Board for their efficiency in regard to secular education at all events.

7725. Would you have the Board Inspectors visit these mission schools and report to the Superintendent-General of Education?—Yes; that would be an advantage.

7726. Suppose they are efficient, do you think you would allow an increased Government contribution to be made if the Board approves?—Yes.

7727. But only if the Board approves?—Yes.

7728. Would you tie the hands of the Government in regard to giving them further aid, even if the Board does not approve, but the Government thinks fit to give it them?—I do not think I would tie their hands.

7729. Is it desirable that before any further aid is given, a report from the Board should be issued?—I think the Government would act wisely in giving power to receive the report of the Board, and let them act as they chose.

7730. What do you think would be the effect of such a system?—I think the effect would be to extend the advantages of education and make them more available than they are at present.

7731. What advantage has such a system over a system by which the central Government undertakes the education?—There is this advantage, that everyone is made to take an interest in the education of his own particular district. If the whole matter of education is centralized in the Government, and the Government Department is at a distance from the district, wants are not sufficiently known, and perhaps one district may be assisted more than it deserves, while another is neglected. I think when a locality is interested in the matter of choosing School Boards and the matter of managing schools, the educational feeling grows in that district, and the children become better educated altogether.

7732. How would it do if a local Board were nominated by the Government, and all applications for aid were to be made to the Government?—I should not approve of that. There might be nominees of the Government on the Board, or nominees of public bodies such as municipalities or divisional councils, or the Government might have an *ex officio* member of the Board, but I would not approve of having the Board made up entirely of nominees.

7733. Would you prefer all the members to be elected?—I do not say that. The majority of the Board might be elected, and there might be representatives of public bodies as well.

7734. How would it do to make the Government liable for all deficiencies instead of making the rates liable?—I look on municipalities as to a certain extent having the right to educate the children within their area, and the Government, as the chief

Mr.
William Norrie.

Sept. 22nd, 1891.

police force, should also see that every child within its jurisdiction is educated; as the divisions would be benefited by the education of the children, it is but right they should bear a share of the expense, and as the Government generally is benefited, it is but right it should share the expense

7735. Do you think if the rates were not made liable in some way, local bodies would be more extravagant with the money of the central Government than they otherwise would be?—If the rates were exonerated altogether and the Government were to provide entirely for the education, then I should approve of a nominated Board.

7736. Would the effect of that be to increase the Government expenditure, and perhaps make it a little more lavish?—I think that is likely.

7737. What do you think would be the effect of relieving the shareholders from their responsibility for any deficiencies?—I think it would immensely increase the Government expenditure.

7738. You think it is desirable that the ratepayers should have a voice, and having a voice, that they should also be charged with some part of the expenditure?—Yes, especially for elementary education. I think in Germany, for example, the Government bears the larger proportion of the expenditure for higher education, and the municipalities bear the larger proportion for elementary education.

7739. How much do you think the Government ought to contribute?—I am not prepared to say what proportion either the Government or the local bodies ought to contribute, but each should bear a share I think.

7740. Suppose the Government contributed half towards education and half towards construction, if a deficiency existed, should the rates be responsible for that?—If the Government bears half, the rest of the deficiency should come from the ratepayers.

7741. Are you in favour of the present system of guarantors?—No. I am certain that the present system, if continued, will not supply the educational wants of this colony, because it is left entirely in the hands of the people whether they shall establish a school in a district or not. Kimberley, for example, was not provided with a proper school for years, and the education of the place was entirely left in the hands of volunteers. I think, where necessary, schools should be brought into existence.

7742. Suppose the Board refuses to bring schools into existence, should there be power to force them, if they are actually wanted?—I think so. If representations were made to the Government that a school was wanted and the Board did not do its duty, then the Government ought to start the school.

7743. *Rev. Moorrees.*] Is not a Board, which is in some way liable for the deficiency, the best judge as to whether a school should be established in a certain locality?—I should say so. If the Board did not establish a school, and representations were made that such a school was necessary, the Government might be asked to make enquiry, and they would then ascertain whether it was necessary or not.

7744. Then you think there must be a very clear case made out against the Board before the Government interferes?—Yes; but I do not think it would be likely.

7745. *President.*] Would it not be a wise thing to have the power vested so that they might know how to act in a certain case?—Yes.

7746. Can you suggest any possible means of continuing the present system of guarantors and giving perpetuity unless through this Board?—No; I do not think it would be necessary to continue the guarantors if you appointed a School Board.

7747. Would you vest the school property in the Board?—Yes.

7748. Should this Board be invested with the duty of saying whether outside towns are sufficiently provided with schools?—I think in large towns such as Cape Town and Kimberley it would be advisable to have separate School Boards, apart from the country districts.

7749. Do you think for the country districts the Board could work through sub-committees?—Yes; if men sufficiently representative of the division were chosen, local committees might be appointed.

7750. Do you think that every application for aid for starting a school in the country should be made to the Government through these committees, so that they could report to the Government?—Application should be made in the first instance to the Board; they refer it to the committee, and then it goes to the Government.

7751. You think the Government should not start a school unless it first had a report?—No.

7752. *Rev. Moorrees.*] Would you tell us the advantage of such a Board over the present system of local committees?—There would still be local committees if the Board system were carried out, only the local committees would be responsible to a higher committee, and there would be this advantage, that school teachers would not be subject to the irritation which local committees sometimes cause them, and they would come under a fairer tribunal. If any differences arose out of local causes unconnected with teaching at all, they could refer the matter to a larger and more responsible committee. The present committees expire at the end of three years.

7753. If a scheme could be devised to make these bodies permanent, and to provide a substitute for the present guarantee system, would there be any objection to have the present committees instead of a general Board?—So long as the committees were elected by the ratepayers of the town, I do not think there could be any objection.

7754. The great objection to the present system as far as you can see is the want of permanence, is it not?—Yes; there is no objection to the guarantee system if it were to take hold of all those who are of a school-going age and provide for all the wants of education, but I do not think it is able to cope with all the wants of education in the colony.

7755. *Dr. Berry.*] Is not the great objection to the present system this, that there is no elasticity; men feel hampered by the guarantee, knowing that any losses will come upon their own pockets?—Yes; people are unwilling to become guarantors, especially in a place where there is not a paying population sufficient to support a school.

7756. Is it not another great objection to the present system that there is no sure ground of belief that it is in sympathy with the vast bulk of the people of a district. Is not its tendency to vest the management of the public schools in the hands of a few instead of in the hands of the mass of the people of a division?—I think so; I have not had much experience of the working of the system in the country, but I think there is such a feeling. I have heard of it, but there is no such feeling in existence in Kimberley. The provision made in Kimberley is sufficient for the upper and middle classes, but it is not sufficient for the general education of the community.

7757. The guarantors cannot bring into existence new schools, can they; they can only provide for themselves?—That is a defect.

7758. Do you think the time has arrived when the system must be changed on account of these drawbacks?—Yes; I think decidedly the time has arrived. I have, for example, suggested to our own committee here that they might make provision for coloured children who desire to go further than the mission school education provides for, but the committee is hampered, it has no further funds beyond what their own school fees and the Government contribute.

7759. In fact, the guarantors as they at present stand, are just for a particular school, and not for education in general?—In villages, I understand, that is so. The guarantors here might if they chose provide for education outside of their own school, and they have done so. They opened a branch school, but there has been a deficiency, and I think if there were not the funds of the main school to fall back upon, that branch school would collapse.

7760. *President.*] Do you think the guarantors are timid?—Yes; after they have been bitten once they will not become guarantors again.

7761. *Rev. Moorrees.*] If a School Board were established in this district, would not you practically have the same men on it as you have on your committee now?—I think it would be very desirable that we should have.

7762. That would be the practical outcome, you think. You do not anticipate any great change in the constitution of the Board, do you?—I do not think so. It might happen that the ratepayers desired to choose other men, but I think in the matter of School Boards they would very likely rely on the class of men who had been appointed.

7763. Do not you think the practical outcome in almost every district of the colony would be more or less the re-election of the same men?—Yes.

7764. *President.*] But if they were re-elected, and had the rates at their back to start new schools, they would not be so timid, but would do their duty, would they not, whereas now they only care to help themselves?—Yes.

7765. *Dr. Berry.*] If you parcelled out a division into wards, each ward electing its own representative, would not that of itself secure a little variety in the constitution of the Board?—Yes.

7766. Practically now the managers of schools are townsmen, are they not?—Yes.

7767. By means of this new machinery, you would get country farmers on the Board, would you not?—Yes; similar to the Divisional Council members.

7768. *Rev. Moorrees.*] Is it a fact that practically now the managers of schools are townsmen?—Managers of town schools.

7769. Do not you think it is for the interest of a school that all the members of the division should be represented on the school committee?—It is not the fact that the village members of the school committee are all townsmen, farmers are also members.

7770 *Dr. Berry.*] The present system gives a preponderance to towns in the Boards of Management, does it not?—There are some towns, I think, in the colony where the guarantors are chiefly members of the Dutch Reformed Church, and they do not provide for the wants of all the population in the town, but chiefly for members of the church. In that case, farmers belonging to the church are members of the School Board.

7771. *Rer. Moorrees.*] Do you mean that they have church schools?—They are not church schools; they are Government schools—public undenominational schools; but they are very largely under the control of the same body as manages church affairs.

7772. Would that exclude from the school any other denominations?—Not theoretically, but practically.

7773. Would not that be the practical outcome whatever scheme you may devise? Take, for instance, districts like Richmond, Victoria West, or Fraserburg, and many others where the great majority of ratepayers belong to the Dutch Reformed Church; whatever scheme you propose, whether you have a Board elected by the district or elected by the towns, would not the result be that the great majority of the Board would be Dutch Reformed Church?—I should think so. If the majority of the people belong to the Dutch Reformed Church, they would still be the majority on the School Board.

7774. And is it not fair that as long as they do not elect as members of the Dutch Reformed Church but as ratepayers, that the largest class of ratepayers should be most largely represented on the Board?—Certainly.

7775. *Dr. Berry.*] But is it fair that minorities should be excluded?—No.

7776. In order to get the representation of minorities, would you adopt some other method such as the cumulative vote?—Yes.

7777. *President.*] Does that exist in Scotland?—Yes, in the election of School Boards; or it did when I was in Scotland. I do not think any change has taken place.

7778. *Mr. Theron.*] How does it work?—If there are fifteen members to be elected for the School Board, each voter has fifteen votes, and in this way the Roman Catholics were able, in a town like Edinburgh, to put in their member at the head of the poll by combining all their votes and giving them to one man; every voter gave his fifteen votes to one man. In the actual working of, the system they had no advantage, only they were represented on the Board.

7779. *President.*] Do you know anything about the educational wants of the agricultural population?—In visiting the outlying districts I have seen the wants of the schools in several places.

7780. Have you gone to examine any schools yourself?—No; there are very few schools about here, and they are all under inspection. There have been two farm schools established lately, chiefly at my suggestion. I quite agree with what has been said as to ignorance on the part of the farmers as to what the facilities offered by Government are. That is a great drawback to the establishment of farm schools; farmers do not know what is required or what has been done for education. I went to a place called Riverton, and found several houses, some farms, and an hotel, and I suggested that they should apply for a farm school grant, and they did so, and got it, and they now have twelve or thirteen children under a teacher as the result. At Modder River there is another farm school established in the same way. I think if a School Board were established, and they made enquiries, they might start schools at convenient distances without having very expensive buildings, and provide teachers; and where the farmers live near the railway, passes should be given to the children to go to school. Schools might be started near the railway if possible, and then they would supply both the wants of the railway employés as well as the farmers in the neighbourhood.

7781. The local knowledge of these Boards would enable them to discover what the wants were and supply them, would it not?—Yes.

7782. Have you given any attention to the subject of night schools?—Yes. My experience is this: that in schools such as ours in Kimberley, boys leave in large numbers after they have passed the fourth standard, being tempted by the pay they get in offices and elsewhere. Sometimes they get as much as £1 or £2 a week while their education is not half completed. I think that some provision should be made for them in night schools. You cannot compel them to attend day schools after they have passed the fourth standard, but they might desire to continue their studies to the fifth standard or the Elementary examination.

7783. Do you think the Boards would be the proper body to deal with these schools also?—Yes. Night schools should be under the same management as day schools, and the same course of education should be followed, but they should be restricted to boys after they have reached a certain age. I should not give boys of twelve years of age the advantage of attending night schools rather than day schools.

Mr.
William Norrie.

Sept. 22nd. 1891.

7784. At what age should they begin to go to night schools?—It is better to decide that by the standard they have reached; perhaps after they have passed the third, or possibly the fourth standard.

7785. Suppose a big boy of sixteen has not passed the required standard, and has some occupation, would not you give him an opportunity of going out?—Yes; the age and the standard might be combined.

7786. Boys after they have reached a certain age would be admissible without regard to standard, but before that age they would be admissible if they have passed the standard?—Yes.

7787. What is the age you would fix?—I should fix it about fourteen, and I would say the third standard.

7788. Have you any knowledge of technical schools?—I have no practical knowledge.

7789. What is your opinion with regard to technical schools?—There are two kinds of technical schools; there are industrial schools, in which carpentry and different trades are learned, and there are higher technical schools in which instruction is given in arts and sciences with their adaptation to commercial life, manufactures, or agriculture. Such schools require the presence of pupils who are able to take advantage of the higher instruction, and the best kind of schools of that class exist in Germany. I believe they have been commenced in England, but the experience of many of them there has been that the pupils have had to be taught in the elements before they could go on to the necessary subjects, such as the Owens College in Manchester. Although there are distinguished professors there, many of the pupils who applied for admission had to be instructed in elementary science.

7790. These higher schools presuppose a knowledge of elementary science together with some literary education, do they not?—Yes.

7791. Which must be acquired in other schools?—Yes. I approve as far as possible of attaching some industrial department to every school. I think it would be an advantage in our public school here to have a carpentry class, where the boys could be taught how to use tools.

7792. Would not you also attach to the lowest class of schools for blacks and whites some industrial department?—Yes.

7793. Industries of what nature would you say?—There might be a variety.

7794. What would you propose for blacks?—I should establish a school where carpentry could be taught.

7795. You would not make every boy a carpenter, would you?—Some might learn blacksmiths' work, shoemaking, or gardening.

7796. Do you think that our coloured population would be all the better for some industrial training?—Decidedly, and the white population too.

7797. Would you mix the colours in this place, or draw any line of demarcation?—If you established but one industrial school in a place like Kimberley, there would be a feeling of aversion between whites and blacks, and it would prejudice the school.

7798. Then you would draw a distinction?—Yes.

7799. How would you practically set about it in order to prevent any possible injustice to boys who may be ambitious; how would you exclude a black boy from a white school?—In the same way as we exclude them at present; we do not admit coloured children now into our school.

7800. Do you use the word "coloured," or do you say, we will not admit such children as will prejudice the school?—The School Board has the power to refuse any child, but practically they apply that power to coloured children.

7801. Those refused by your school you would give a right to be admitted to the other school, would you not?—They must be admitted to the other school.

7802. Do you think that would work?—Yes.

7803. *Mr. Theron.*] Under what regulation is there power to exclude any child?—I think it is in the Education Manual, and as a matter of fact, the opinion of the Superintendent-General of Education has been taken on that point. His opinion was, that if sufficient provision is made for coloured children, we are not compelled to admit them.

7804. *Rev. Moorrees.*] Have you tried to start an industrial department in connection with your first class public school?—Not yet. We have no funds for extending the work, and any suggestions that have been made for extension do not meet with approval.

7805. *Dean Holmes*]. Are you aware that you can get a grant of £50 for trade instruction?—No application has been made for it.

7806. Then you have not utilized the existing advantages?—No.

NN 2

Mr.
William Norris.

Sept. 22nd, 1891.

7807. *President.*] Is it desirable in your opinion to give the Board the power to bring into existence a higher class school than your school here?—I think not. The public schools work sufficiently well.

7808. Are there not many who do not come to your school, not because they are dissatisfied with your teaching, but because they are dissatisfied with the mixed classes there?—I cannot say that. I think we have the best social classes attending this school. There are other schools in existence which they say are more select.

7809. Would you advocate the Government contributing towards any voluntary school building on private property?—Yes, if the voluntary body undertakes to carry on a school in perpetuity, and to use the building for school purposes.

7810. Suppose that such voluntary body fails in carrying on that school, what would become of the Government money spent on private property?—I should say that the Government ought to hold a bond over the school to the extent of the money contributed.

7811. The Gill College is a private corporation, and on the college property a first class public undenominational school has been built, towards which the Government has contributed in money. I may add that with the consent of Sir Langham Dale, seven out of the ten members forming the committee of management are nominated by the Gill College, and three are elected by the householders every three years, the result being that the householders are always in a minority, and they can always be outvoted by the seven members who are nominated by the corporation. There are some who think the effect of that is simply to destroy the present system, because instead of being a public school it is really the school of the Gill College. A public meeting was called, and the public elected the Gill College to be the public school of the town, and the public agreed that a certain number of the trustees of the college should in perpetuity form the committee. How would you deal with such a case as that under your scheme?—It seems to me that a resolution of that kind was contrary to the spirit of the Education Act, and might be considered illegal.

7812. Being contrary to the spirit of the Act, how ought it to be dealt with under your scheme, which proposes to vest all the property in this Board?—I would look out for a school building sufficient to accommodate the pupils, and would apply to the Gill College trustees, as the building is there, for the use of their building, which might still be vested in the trustees and used for a public school with the consent of the trustees.

7813. And suppose they did not consent?—If they did not consent, then they can do what they like with their building.

7814. In cases of that kind what you would suggest is, that the money having been given, the gift cannot be withdrawn, but that the future public school should try and hire the building?—Just so.

7815. And if they cannot do so, find a school elsewhere?—Yes. I would not for the sake of the Gill College trustees make an exception in the election of the School Boards. I would not allow that to continue, as I think it is a bad principle. The public element should control the management as in other districts.

7816. *Rev. Moorrees.*] If the public elect the managers, you would require the public to take over the liabilities of the school, would you not?—Certainly.

7817. *Dr. Berry.*] Why should they, seeing they do not have a voice in the creation of the liabilities?—It was by their own act they did not have a voice, although practically it was the voice of a previous public.

7818. *President.*] Say there is a debt of £3,000, should that be taken over?—Yes, because it is a liability which almost every School Board would have to undertake if they erected other buildings. Perhaps an Act of Parliament would require to be passed divesting the trustees of the property, and vesting it in the new School Board. The Government would have a voice in that, having contributed the money. If the Government has contributed £3,000 towards the erection of the buildings, an Act of Parliament might be passed, or the Government might step in and say: Pay us this £3,000; if you do not, we divest you of the building and vest it in other trustees; because the Government would have to contribute at any rate to the building of another school.

7819 What further facilities do you think can be afforded for giving instruction in both the English and Dutch languages, and in how far can that object be attained through the medium of the Elementary and other examinations?—I think it fair to the Dutch population here that they should be put on an equal footing with the English in regard to the Elementary examination. I think some scheme might be formulated by which the Elementary examination should continue as it is at present as a pass examination, but there might be an honours subject added, which should be selected by the pupil himself. There might be two languages or three languages, Dutch, German, and French, and also a scientific subject, and equal marks should be given for

287

each of those subjects. If a pupil preferred to take Dutch, he would have his marks and his position regarded equally with the pupil who preferred to take science; but I do not think it is at all necessary to alter the system of education so far as the teaching of Dutch is concerned. Something was said just now about the short time for education on a farm, and I think it would be quite fair that the inspector should take cognizance of a child being taught in Dutch, and should inspect him in Dutch and pass him in the standards so far as he has gone; but I do not think if the children of a farmer wish to go up for the Elementary examination, they will at all grudge the time spent in learning English. The inspector might take notice that these children had been taught in Dutch, and they might be examined in Dutch as far as they have gone. I quite agree with Archdeacon Gaul that Dutch parents are anxious for their children to learn English as a rule.

Mr William Norrie.
Sept. 22nd, 1891.

7820. *Rev. Moorrees.*] Do not you consider that a Dutch child is handicapped in the Elementary examination at present?—I do not consider there is any necessity for a change in the Elementary examination. I think a Dutch boy, if he is educated up to the standard of the Elementary examination, will be able to take as many marks as an English boy if he has been educated through the medium of English.

7821. Is it not desirable in your opinion to have a paper in Dutch, so as to practically force all boys to learn it in their own interest?—I would not force the teaching of Dutch on all boys, because I should not force the teaching of any modern language on all boys. You might as well enforce the teaching of French or German. I would encourage the teaching of Dutch, and in the way I mention, by giving an extra paper with extra marks in the Elementary examination, leaving the Pass examination as it stands. Then there need not be any position given to the Pass examination, all pass alike.

7822. You would make those who go in for the extra paper go in for the honours subject, and in the honours list the marks for the four subjects would count, and also the fifth paper?— Yes.

7823. Would you make Dutch the sole subject?—No; I would have alternative subjects—Dutch, French, German, or science.

7824. Is it not a wise thing almost to force boys to learn Dutch in this country? —I think parents themselves will best see what is to the advantage of the boys, and I would no more enforce the teaching of Dutch than the teaching of Latin.

7825. *President.*] Do you agree with Professor MacWilliam's scheme on this subject?—Yes.

7826. In view of the fact that the object of education is to teach a thing thoroughly, do not you think that his idea of letting a good Dutch paper make up for a weak English paper and *vice versa,* rather tends to a want of thoroughness?—Yes, I do not quite agree with him there. I would make it absolute that the Dutch boy must pass on the same grounds as the English boy.

7827. *Rev. Moorrees.*] Is not Professor MacWilliam's idea more to show the equality of the two languages?—The Elementary examination is not a compulsory examination, which every pupil must enter; it is an examination by which children in the Colony are tested, and so far as it goes, it is perfectly fair for those who wish to enter. If a boy fails, he does not get the University pass certificate; that is all it amounts to. At the same time, as I said just now, in farm schools or small village schools, where there is a purely Dutch community, recognition should be made by the Government inspector of the work done in Dutch, and then the Dutch population would be perfectly fairly treated.

7828. Is it fair that the test you speak of should take no cognizance whatever of one of the two languages of the country?—I think so. As we are at present, Dutch is not a recognized language of the country, and it is not the legal language of the country, although it is necessary for entrance into the civil service. I do not see that there is any unfairness in the present arrangement of the Elementary examination.

7829. Is not Dutch spoken by the majority of the people in this colony?—What I say is that it is not the legal language of the country any more than English was in the time of William the Conqueror in England.

7830. Is not Dutch recognized in Parliament and in the courts of justice?—Yes.

7831. *President.*] Ought not the teaching of Dutch to be encouraged in this country?—Most decidedly.

7832. And if Dutch is taught, should it not be well taught?—Most decidedly; it should not be taught at all unless it is well taught.

7833. In view of that, would it not be a good thing to give bursaries to those who do well in Dutch?—Yes, I think that would be a very good plan, for this reason, that I think the grammatical Dutch would be as difficult for a Dutch boy as it would be for an English boy.

7834. In view of that, would not this take place, that English boys would also go in for that examination in Dutch?—Yes.

Mr.
William Norris.

Sept. 22nd, 1891.

7835. Would it not be a good thing if they did?—Yes.

7836. Can you see any possible objection to it?—None whatever; but I would extend the system and give bursaries for other subjects as well.

7837. In view of the fact that it is desirable to have Dutch well spoken, you would give bursaries for it, whether you create bursaries for other subjects or not?—Yes, I quite agree that it is a commendable thing to encourage Dutch ; I only object to enforcing it.

7838. If there were bursaries given, would not the effect be to make boys pay more attention to Dutch?—We pay sufficient attention to it, but possibly boys might be more inclined to learn it, with the knowledge that they would get a bursary.

7839. Can you see any objection from an educational point of view to giving bursaries to those who pass well in Dutch?—No further than giving a bursary for any other subject.

7840. Do you think any time would be lost by encouraging the learning of Dutch?—It might distract the boys' attention from subjects which would be of more use to them practically.

7841. Can there be anything more useful than knowing Dutch thoroughly in this country?—It is an advantage for every boy to know Dutch, but it is not an all essential thing.

7842. From an educational point of view, is it not a good thing for boys to know two languages?—Most decidedly.

7843. Is it not better to know two than one?—Yes.

7844. Would it not be an advantage to boys, from an educational point of view, if the system of encouraging the learning of good Dutch were started?—It would be a greater advantage for boys in this colony to know good Dutch than to know good French or good German. Dutch is a very valuable language for any boy in this colony, and I would encourage the teaching of it.

7845. You think it is a good thing for every boy to know a second language?—Yes. I would certainly encourage the teaching of Dutch.

Mr. E. A. Judge examined.

Mr.
E. A. Judge.

Sept. 22nd, 1891.

7846. *President.*] I believe you are Civil Commissioner at Kimberley?—Yes.

7847. Are you a member of the committee of the first class public undenominational school?—Yes.

7848. And a guarantor?—Yes.

7849. Is the attendance of children at school regular as far as you know in Kimberley?—As far as I know it is fairly regular.

7850. Are there many children outside education altogether at present?—I should think so.

7851. Do you think it is desirable to bring them under the influence of education?—Certainly.

7852. What in your opinion is the best means of doing so?—Perhaps free education would be the best means. Possibly the children do not attend as they ought because the parents cannot afford the fees, although they are small.

7853. Do you think it arises from neglect on the part of the parents?—Possibly.

7854. Where the parents can pay for their children's education, do not you think they ought to do so?—Yes.

7855. *Dr. Berry.*] Do you think the question of fees is a serious factor in the case here?—Where a parent does not value education very much, he does not even care to pay a small fee. I am inclined to think you would find a good deal of difficulty with compulsory education in this country.

7856. In towns would there be any difficulty as apart from the country?—You would have to increase the education grant very much indeed. A great many children do not go to school, and you would have to provide for them somehow or other. The number of schools must be increased in the first place. I doubt also whether the fees would be sufficient to pay for the teaching; Government would have to increase the grant.

7857. Would it do if the Government paid half, and then if, after the fees were paid, there was a deficiency, the municipal or divisional rates were called upon for the balance?—I have not given that question much consideration.

7858. Do you think the guarantor system is a sound one?—I think it works very well as far as I have known it.

7859. Have you been a guarantor yourself elsewhere than here?—Yes ; at Worcester, and I think at Queen's Town.

7860. Under the guarantor system, can you reach the poorest classes—will volunteers come forward and find schools for them, and pay any deficiency?—I do not ink they will come forward unless pretty certain there would be no loss. I have ever had to pay up for any deficiency as yet.

7861. If they find schools for the lowest classes there would be no fees, and there ould therefore be a loss, so you must either have free schools or go to the rates ; is ot that so ?—I think the present system of mission schools is best as regards free Jucation.

7862. Can missionary bodies find schools for nothing ?—If they are assisted by he Government.

7863. Can you suggest any steps to give the present Boards of Management erpetual succession ?—There might be official trustees under the Trustees Act, to hold ll property on behalf of the Boards of Management.

7864. Who would you suggest as official trustees ?—Usually in country towns the Mayor and the Civil Commissioner are trustees of most public institutions.

7865. Would you let the official trustees pay any debt that existed ?—They would old the property.

7866. But who is to pay the debt ?—Under the present system, the guarantors.

7867. If you put trustees in the place of the guarantors, what would be the consequence ?—I take it that if there is any deficiency in the management of the school, he guarantors would have to pay it.

7868. You would leave the property in the hands of the official trustees, and let he guarantors pay the liabilities of the school, whether for building purposes or not ? —Not for building purposes. There should be a bond on the property, and the interest hould be paid from the ordinary school revenue.

7869. And you would vest the property in the Mayor and the Civil Commissioner ?—I think that would be quite sufficient ; any two trustees who may be fixed 1pon.

7870. You said that there were children outside all education for whom schools would have to be found ; if so, at whose expense ought they to be built in towns ?— Either by public subscription or by the municipal council, but I think the municipal council before using its funds for building schools, should have the consent of the rate-payers.

7871. Suppose the ratepayers decline ?—Then I suppose the town would have to go without a school, unless you have compulsory education.

7872. If you have compulsory education, who is to find the schools ?—Government must find the money if you have compulsory education. My opinion is, that every child is entitled to education up to a certain point—reading, writing and arithmetic— at the expense of the State.

7873. Suppose a parent can pay, ought he not to do so ?—Not for elementary subjects. My own opinion is, that every child is entitled to elementary education. If a parent requires more, then that parent must pay.

7874. Do you speak of black children as well ?—Yes ; but of course it would be too expensive to carry that out in practice. I only speak theoretically.

7875. Then there is no alternative between free education and no education ?—I would not say that. You must do the best you can with mission schools and first, second and third class schools.

7876. But are there not many children outside education altogether, who are not reached by mission schools or undenominational schools ?—Yes.

7877. Can you state what contribution should be expected from divisional councils and municipalities in support of schools or for the erection of school buildings ?— I do not think it ought to be compulsory on divisional councils or municipalities to make contributions, but I would give them an opportunity if they wished.

7878. Why do you say that ?—The divisional council rates are derived from the whole division, and it is not fair to use those rates to set up schools in the towns ; the farmers would derive no benefit from schools established in the towns, and they pay the divisional council rates principally. I think it should be optional with public bodies to contribute.

7879. What optional contribution do you think should be expected ?—They would have to fix the amount, I take it, if it is optional.

7880. Have you anything to suggest as to the wants of the children of the farming population ?—No. I have not seen the working of the farm schools.

7881. Have you considered the subject of night schools at all ?—I have seen them in towns, and they are successful sometimes. I have not formed any opinion about them.

7882. Have you any experience as to technical schools ?—No.

7883. Have you followed the discussion which has been going on relative to instruction in the Dutch language ?—No. I should prefer not to say anything on that subject.

Rev. D. D. Fraser examined.

7884. *President.*] What are you?—Deputy Inspector of Schools. I am in Kimberley on official business just now, but I reside at Port Elizabeth.

7885. Have you visited the various schools in the Eastern Province ?—During this year I have already inspected schools in the division of Herschel, Albert, Wodehouse, Tarkastad, Cradock, Bedford, Somerset, Graaff-Reinet, some in Middelburg, some in Colesberg, and some in Kimberley.

7886. Are they all undenominational schools ?—Mission schools as well ; they all receive Government aid. In some instances, I have inspected private schools which have invited inspection.

7887. In towns or on farms ?—It does not matter, whether in towns or on farms, but in this case they have been in towns, on mission stations, and at the seat of magistracy.

7888. Have you done so for the Education Department ?—Yes. I am their officer.

7889. Have you formed any sort of opinion as to the relative proportion of children on the school rolls throughout the colony and those who actually ought to be in school ?—That would be a very difficult point to arrive at without making some statistical calculations, which are outside my province, but I am quite satisfied from personal observation, that there are a great many children outside the sphere of the operation of our present schools.

7890. Are you of opinion that they ought to be brought within it ?— Certainly. Every child ought to be educated, our first duty lying with the European children, and then with the natives as far as possible.

7891. Whose duty do you consider it to be ?—The primary duty of educating a child lies necessarily and essentially in my opinion with the parents, but failing that, the State is bound for its own preservation to instruct the children.

7892. How should the State act, from the centre or from localities ?—I am of opinion that the general principles should be conducted from the centre and the details from the locality.

7893. What do you mean by the details ?—The actual conduct of the schools and their adaptability to the requirements of the place and so on.

7894. Are you in favour of a School Board ?—Decidedly.

7895. How ought these School Boards to be created ?—In my opinion, education is a matter of such importance, that School Boards should be elected by the ratepayers for school purposes simply.

7896. What should be their duty ?—Their duty should be to act in accordance with the instructions of the central Educational Department, to appoint teachers, regulate the affairs of the school, and see that the funds are raised in sufficient quantity and properly disposed of.

7897. And bring into existence schools where they are required ?—My idea is that there should be schools everywhere in sufficient number to educate the population.

7898. How would you provide funds for carrying on these schools ?—The German system is after all as good a one as we can get ; and if I understand it, it amounts to this, that the fees are fixed at such a moderate rate, that the bulk of the parents at least can pay them. It is not intended that the fees should cover the whole of the expense, and in the elementary schools the State itself directly pays two-thirds of the deficiency, leaving one-third to fall on the local bodies.

7899. How are you to arrive at the deficiency till you have built your school and worked it ?—In the first place, schools would be built by the local parties, with aid from the State. I speak of carrying on the school after it has been started.

7900. You think the buildings should be erected by a local Board ?—I think so.

7901. Out of what fund ?—The liability should be on the local parties, and the funds provided by the Government, and paid off by means of a sinking fund.

7902. Would you make it a charge on the local rates ?—Yes.

7903. Government lending the money ?—Yes.

7904. You would have the local Board acting for the ratepayers and bringing into existence these schools, built by money borrowed from the State, to be charged on the rates ?--Yes.

7905. How would the expense of carrying on the school be provided for ?—In this way. The School Board would consider the number of children they had to educate and the extent of ground that their education would cover, and they would then arrive at some estimate of the amount of funds required to pay the teachers and keep up the school building. Having adopted a scale of fees, they would get as large an income as was convenient from the pupils, and then at the end of the year the Board would find what was the deficiency to be made up, that is to say the difference between the expenditure and the amount of the school fees and the Government grant, and the local rates should be come upon for the deficiency, after a precept has been issued.

Rev.
D. D. Fraser.

Sept. 22nd, 1891

7906. Are you in favour of the English system of School Boards?—I prefer the German system. The English system is now in a transition state; it is hardly one thing or the other. They have just made a change from paying education to free or almost free education. I am decidedly of opinion that a School Board should be elected for school purposes purely and be responsible to the ratepayers.

7907. The fees should be fixed at a very low rate, you think?—Yes.

7908. How would you get children into these schools when they were started?—There we are brought face to face with a difficulty. Such a system as I propose would not meet our country population altogether, but our hands would be much less tied in the towns. We could, I think, and ought to have compulsory education in a town like this. It is a danger to the inhabitants that thousands of young children of all colours should be allowed to grow up without any fear of God before their eyes, or regard for man.

7909. How would you set about it?—The first thing is to find out what number of children of a school-going age there are and what provision there is. If new schools are required, they should be erected. There is a very large provision for educating children in this town if it was taken advantage of. It is no uncommon thing for me to go to a school where there are upwards of 200 names on the roll and only 110 present.

7910. Is that a good percentage?—No. I mention that as showing how ridiculous it is to take merely the number on the school roll as a guarantee of how many children are being educated.

7911. You mean to say that the percentage of attendance is very small compared with the number on the roll nominally?—Yes.

7912. How is that?—There is a system of paying fees weekly, and if a child is away on Monday it will perhaps stay away the whole week. It is astonishing how great the irregularity is, especially in mission schools.

7913. Besides that, is there a number of children outside the roll altogether who ought to be at school?—I have only been a few days in Kimberley, but it is my opinion that there are a good many children here who are not on the roll of any school.

7914. How are you to get those children into school?—I should, in towns like this, advocate compulsion, through a truant officer and an attendance officer, to visit the houses.

7915. What class of man would you appoint for the duty?—The man who picks up the children in the street would be a kind of policeman, as a rule, and he would not be exactly the class of person with sufficient tact to visit the houses of the parents.

7916. Who would you appoint?—I would leave that to the Board, I think.

7917. The police might take up the children in the street, might they not?—Yes; but the attendance officer should be a man of some tact, as far as possible. The British citizen believes that his house is his castle, and resents interference.

7918. You stated that this system of compulsion ought to be started at once; what do you think would be the most effective means of doing so under existing circumstances?—Of course compulsion must go along with having suitable provision for the children. You cannot compel a child to go to a school that does not exist.

7919. How would you work the present system with compulsion?—I do not see how the present system can be worked with compulsion, because if you compel all the children of a school-going age at Kimberley to attend, the buildings would not hold them. You would land yourself in a great difficulty.

7920. Have you considered Sir Langham Dale's proposition of fourth class public undenominatial schools?—Yes. I have seen what he said.

7921. What do you take that to be?—My idea is, that Sir Langham Dale wishes to meet the case of European children who are not on the school roll. The only objection I have to fourth class schools is, that while they are called public schools, they are really left under denominational management. I thoroughly believe in what Matthew Arnold says in his work on education, and that is that whenever people are compelled to go to school, they insist on undenominational schools.

7922. Do you think that a Board elected by the ratepayers of the division could work these fourth class public undenominational schools?—Yes.

7923. Is the best means of working them through a Board?—Yes.

7924. If there is a deficiency, would you call upon the ratepayers to pay one-third and the State two-thirds?—Yes.

7925. And would you force the Board to borrow money to erect buildings?—I would not propose that in the country at present, but in towns I would do so.

Rev.
D. D. Fraser.

Sept. 22nd, 1891.

7926. Under the present system. is it impossible to start a Board to fill up the gaps ? -I have not considered that question fully.

7927. Do you like the present guarantor system?—Certainly not. In the first place, the teacher does not know who is his master, whether it is the school committee, or the inspector, or the parents, or those men who have guaranteed. In a small country village sometimes, if a teacher happens to give offence to some one on the guarantee list, he might soon find himself in a bad way. I am decidedly opposed to the guarantor system.

7928. What other defect is there in the system?—Another defect is, that the system to a large extent helps those who are well able to help themselves. That is why we have such a large proportion of the population who would be left helpless but for the kindly offices of various ministers of religion who get up mission schools.

7929. How would it do to help this Board to the extent that it is helped now by the Government in the way of buildings, and in the way of teaching for the fourth class schools, and then have very low fees, and let the ratepayers pay any deficiency through the Board?—I think the ratepayers would be very unwilling to have these fourth class schools as the only class of schools that are to be aided in that way.

7930. Suppose all the schools are to be helped in the same way?—That is pretty much the system I have been speaking of. I know many schools that have not got a half-penny from the Government for building.

7931. Do not you think that if the Government contributes as they do now to schools that are in existence and to schools which are to be created, and then you bring into existence an elected Board with the power to go to the ratepayers if there is a deficiency, such a system might work?—I think it might, but the whole thing is tentative, and whatever change is brought about, it must come gradually. We cannot go and alter the system all at once.

7932. Are you in favour of supporting mission schools?—Certainly not.

7933. Can they be utilized by the Board?—My experience carries me back to the time when there were denominational schools throughout Scotland, and I remember being in Scotland at the time when the School Boards came into operation, and I know that so anxious were the Scotch people to have a thorough system of education, that in the majority of instances many of the bodies gave up their schools, and made a present of them to the State, in order that the work of education might be properly carried on.

7934. Is there any reason to suppose that the religious bodies here will not do the same?—I have no reason to suppose that they would object. I have never entered into conversation with any representative man belonging to these religious bodies on the point, and I would not like to commit myself one way or the other. I have no great reason to believe it would be different here.

7935. Would there be any objection to letting mission schools which are in existence work under their present conditions as long as they fulfil their contract with the Government, letting the Board fill up any gaps which may arise from time to time, and giving the mission schools an opportunity of getting through the Board, where it approves, a larger grant from Government than they do now?—The objection is simply this, that, instead of having a homogeneous scheme we would have a system of patchwork. I have the highest testimony personally to bear in favour of mission schools.

7936. If they do good work, why should a crochet stand in the way?—Some mission schools I have visited do very efficient work, but others I fear are doing very little good.

7937. Would you give the Board power, with the consent of the State, where it saw that a mission body was not doing good work, to have the grant withdrawn ?—Yes ; in any case the grant would be withdrawn on my recommendation.

7938. If there is that power in existence, where is the harm ?—The only difficulty, as I said just now is, that you have a system of shreds and patches.

7939. What advice would you give, taking all the circumstances into consideration ?—That is a very large question. I think for a time at least, the State must work in harmony with the work that is going on at present, and perhaps what you suggest is after all the better plan, that for some time the mission bodies might be allowed to work the schools already in existence if they are found to be working well, but if a new system were introduced, I would not open any fresh mission schools on the present basis.

7940. Would you be in favour of bringing into existence a Board at once ?—Yes ; especially if you have these fourth class schools.

7941. Would you transfer to the Board the public school property ?—That is a very large question. In this country it is the property of private individuals as a rule.

7942. Can you give us any instance of property used by a public school which is not public property ?- In Adelaide it is the property of the Dutch Reformed Church, and the school committee rent it, and there are many other similar cases. At Graham's Town the property belongs to the Government.

Rev.
D. D. Fraser.
Sept. 22nd, 1891.

7943. To whom would you transfer that property?—To the Board decidedly. Whatever is Government property, that the public has a right to, should be transferred at once into the hands of those acting for the public.

7944. Has Government money been put into the school building at Adelaide?—I do not believe Government has given a penny towards it.

7945. That not being public property in any way, you would not expect it to be vested in a Board, would you?—Not unless the Dutch Reformed Church chose to make a gift of it to the Board.

7946. Can you name any case where Government money has been spent upon private property?—I think the Bellevue Seminary at Somerset East was put up largely out of funds subscribed by the Dutch Reformed Church on their own ground, and they have got aid from Government, which has gone into the buildings. So far as I understand, after a certain number of years, that becomes the property of the Dutch Reformed Church.

7947. Would you do anything towards placing that property in the hands of the proposed School Board?—It would not be fair to go behind a bargain.

7948. How would you approach that body which has brought into existence through its voluntary effort these buildings, towards which Government has contributed upon condition that if the church performs its part of the contract, the Government has no claim on the property at the end of twenty years?—The bargain should be carried out, and Government should be prepared to do so to the full, but a little persuasion with the Dutch Reformed Church might be used, to see if they would not give up the property in whole or in part. It was in order to get a good school that the Dutch Reformed Church started this Seminary, and I daresay they are amenable to reason.

7949. You think if the property could be got, it would be wise to get it?—Yes, it would save expense in building other schools.

7950. Do you know the Gill College at Somerset East?—Yes, I have inspected it.

7951. With regard to the property there, is the building in course of erection an undenominational public school?—What is being erected is for a boarding department. The college was erected out of money left by the will of Dr. Gill. That is why it is called the Gill College.

7952. Towards that building many thousand pounds have been contributed, and money has also been borrowed under the Public Loans Act; how would you deal with that, suppose a School Board is brought into existence?—If the money has been contributed wholly by the Government for school purposes, it is only fair that it should remain in the hands of the public.

7953. But how is it public property if it has been spent in building on private property?—You must go according to law. I am not a lawyer.

7954. Mr. Theron.] Are you positive that it is on private property?—Yes; it is on the Gill College grounds, there is no doubt about that. Mr. Leith, one of the members of the Board of the Gill College is here, and he can give you information about it. You cannot interfere with people's legal rights.

7955. How would you approach the Gill College in this matter, or would you leave that school there and have special legislation?—You must understand that the Gill College is not now simply a first class public undenominational school, it is under the Higher Education Act. A portion of it is a first class public school; it enjoys a double benefit.

7956. How would you act in regard to the undenominational school?—As far as I know the members of the Gill College trust, I do not think there would be any difficulty in arranging for a transfer of the property so far as the trust will permit.

7957. Have you considered the case of the Grey Institute at Port Elizabeth?—I believe the Grey Institute is under an Act of its own.

7958. You know the Government contributes largely there?—Yes.

7959. How would you work the Grey Institute side by side with a Board such as is suggested?—We should have to consider that largely in the light of what has been done at home. There are many schools there that had endowments and grants and special Acts of their own, but in many instances these have been interfered with, when it was found by the Commissioners that they were not acting pro bono publico.

7960. Have you any proposition to make?—No; my information as to the Grey Institute is of the most fragmentary description, and I should not like to make any proposition.

7961. Do you know of any other place where Government money has been put into buildings on private or corporate property?—I cannot say. This matter of what contributions Government has made to schools for building purposes does not come officially within my cognizance.

7962. I understand you to say broadly that you would vest in this Board the property now known as public school property ?—In so far as you can interfere with private rights, where it is public property.

7963. And you would try to get the other in without violating any contract ?—Yes ; my experience of schools shows that where people are interested in education—and I hope it is so here—private property has been given to Government in order to further the national system.

7964. With regard to the management of those schools, do you know the system of management in existence with regard to the Gill College ?—Only from outside. I should not like to go into the matter.

7965. If we find the undenominational school of the Gill College is managed by a committee of ten, seven of whom are elected every three years by the householders assembled at a meeting, what would you say about that system of management ?—I should say that that has arisen from circumstances peculiar to the Gill College, and it has been the best way the Superintendent-General of Education could see of getting out of a difficulty, when it was proposed to bring it under the public school system, but it is not advisable that public schools should be managed by any body but a public School Board.

7966. And the members must be elected periodically, must they not ?—Yes.

7967. Then you think that this system of importing into the management a majority nominated by a corporation is not to be imitated ?—It is not commendable I think.

7968. How would you get rid of that ?—That is a legal question which I should not like to face.

7969. *Dr. Berry.*] Would you like the proposed School Board to be elected by the ratepayers ?—Yes.

7970. By the Divisional Council ratepayers ?—By the Municipal ratepayers. If it is for the benefit of the division, then by the Divisional Council.

7971. Would you have as voters, those on the Parliamentary roll or those on the Divisional roll ?—I would have the Parliamentary franchise. Every person is interested more or less in education.

7972. Would you have any qualification for a member of a School Board ?—It would be ridiculous to put on a man who was not to some extent at least educated, and I think that the ratepayers as far as my observation goes, unless they are influenced by wire pullers or log rollers, will as a rule, elect the best men. There is too much log rolling and wire pulling at elections, but if people are left to themselves, their common sense generally leads them to make the right choice.

7973. If you take the divisional roll, would you have them vote in wards for members, or should they vote in a lump ?—They should vote for a division in a lump, but I do not profess to speak with any authority on the matter. It lies outside my particular sphere.

7974. Would you give the Board power to elect its own chairman ?—Yes ; certainly.

7975. Would it be fair to give the Divisional Council the right to nominate two members or the Municipality the right to nominate two members ?—I would give the ratepayers a right to elect the School Board, and let the Board appoint a chairman from one of their number. There should also be a paid secretary who should not be one of the number.

7976. Inasmuch as the Municipality or Divisional Council is responsible for the funds, is it advisable to give either body a direct voice in the administration of the funds ?—The system has worked well elsewhere.

7977. Would you give the Board a right to delegate any of its functions to sub-committees of its own members or others ? —The ratepayers having elected the Board to do the work, I think that they should do it and accept the responsibility.

7978. And have no power of delegation ?—Not outside themselves.

7979. *President.*] Why should not they delegate and accept the responsibility ?—On the whole, I am not in favour of the principle of delegation.

7980. Would you place any limit upon the demand that a School Board might make on the Divisional Council in any one year, or would you give them unlimited control to send a precept for any unknown amount ?—They have had that at home.

7981. How would you do here ?—If you go and put a limit upon them, you may find that if the limit is expressed in actual quantity, they may be brought face to face with the difficulty that they cannot carry on. You must put some trust in the persons you elect. As a rule, persons who have to pay, will take care what they do. In a small town in this colony it is difficult to get a farthing rate for anything, however necessary; the whole body of householders objects at once. They would rather let the streets remain covered with filth than pay a small rate to keep them clean very often.

7982. Are you aware that the rating powers are limited here?—If that is the custom, it would be hard to break through it for schools, and in that case it might be wise to accept a compromise.

7983. I understand you to say that you would be quite prepared to give the Board power to accept the mission schools for the present as workers under it?—Yes; with the distinct understanding that no new ones are to be started.

7984. Would it also be on this understanding, that there should be power to revise the conjoint action at some future time?—The object in view, I take it, is eventually to bring all schools directly under the control of the Board; I have no wish to see a patchwork of schools, and while we might be obliged to accept a compromise for some or perhaps many years to come, the aim should be to get a uniform system throughout. Hence I would certainly keep in view the idea that eventually mission schools are to be worked out of the present management and brought under the Board.

7985. What is your view about mixing the white and coloured children in schools? —I think that is a difficulty that practically solves itself, because the upper class of white children will never associate with coloured children, however nice those coloured children may appear to be in dress and so on. The lower class of whites manifest no objection to sit side by side with the coloured children, and the whites are not always the cleverest in the mission schools.

7986. Do you think it is objectionable from a national point of view to mix the two races, or otherwise?—I think it is objectionable to make a hard and fast rule that coloured and white children must sit on the same benches; you would go quite contrary to the current of popular opinion.

7987. Is it not objectionable to make a hard and fast rule that they shall not?—I think so.

7988. What would your rule be if you had to lay it down in black and white; would you have two public schools, one for one class and the other for the other class?—You cannot double your schools; you cannot have a first class school for the whites and a first class school for the coloured children.

7989. Cannot you have fourth class public undenominational schools?—Yes. I inspect schools at present which are called Dutch Church Native and Dutch Church European mission schools.

7990. Would you have fourth class schools Native and fourth class schools European?—Yes. I have no objection to that.

7991. Suppose a coloured parent comes and claims that his child shall be in the European school, how would you act?—In the fourth class schools, if they are filled with the class of children that usually go to mission schools, you would not find much difficulty.

7992. What do you mean by mission schools. They are as I understand, intended for blacks, but in Cape Town the blacks have all been pushed out, and there are only whites; is not that so?—I have inspected mission schools in which there are both whites and blacks. I would not like to formulate any rule on the subject.

7993. Would you give the upper fourth class school power to exclude anyone that might prejudice it, and then lay down a rule that the other school of the lower class should receive all excluded from the upper?—I should not like to make a rule like that. There ought to be some reason for distinctly excluding a child from a school, either its manners or morals.

7994. Suppose a coloured parent wants to send a black boy to the upper school where there is a number of whites, and the other pupils say they will leave the school if he comes?—In the South African College school in Cape Town, which is a first class school, there is one Malay at least. I believe there are more. That carries out the principle I have enunciated. The managers of that school thought it would not prejudice it by admitting this boy, and he was admitted. When I was a teacher in the first class school at Bedford, I have had more than one native boy.

7995. If you found that the others would leave if such a boy came, would you not place it in the power of the managers to exclude him?—Something of that sort would have to be done I suppose, where the presence of a boy would distinctly prejudice the school and do it harm.

7996. With whom would you leave the ultimate decision?—It should rest with the Board.

7997. Dr. Berry.] You have travelled about the country a great deal, do you think this proposal to give school boards a lien upon the rates in respect of public schools would be very unpopular?—The question has never arisen in my experience, but speaking on general grounds, I do not think it would be very unpopular. I believe

Rev.
D. D. Fraser.

Sept. 22nd, 1891.

that in towns where you have as a rule a number of earnest people, and people who look at education from a broad point of view, you might have less difficulty than in the country, because this is a land in which people are accustomed to expect a great deal of freedom, and the idea that they are forced to do anything, does not go down at all.

7998. This proposal has been a good deal talked about lately; surely if it was very unpopular, you would have heard some mutterings of opinion against it, would you not?—As to the opinions of individuals, I have heard opinions expressed both for and against, but never in the manner that we are accustomed to gauge public opinion by in the way of public meetings held and resolutions carried. That is the way we generally estimate the current of public opinion at home.

7999. *President.*] With regard to your proposal that the buildings should be entirely found by the ratepayers, do not you think that the Government might contribute half?—What I said, I did not lay down as a hard and fast rule.

8000. Would it not be a wise thing if the Government actually undertook to find half the cost of buildings, on the £ for £ principle?—Of course if the Government finds half, it would be so much easier for the ratepayers. Perhaps it would be the best way.

8001. If that were so, might not the ratepayers be called upon to pay the whole of any deficiency after collecting the fees?—I have not thought that out. I proposed the other because it was familiar to me as the German system, but if the Government is willing to pay half the buildings and half the working, the ratepayers I think might find the other half, after getting the benefit of the fees.

8002. *Dean Holmes.*] What are your views regarding the cumulative vote for members of the School Board?—My experience of cumulative voting is not such as to prejudice me in favour of it.

8003. Does it not give minorities a chance?—I am not in favour of it. It opens the door for wire pulling. Two or three people lay their heads together, and a very few people by manipulating their votes can put in a majority of the parties wanted.

8004. Is it not a good thing that the views of the minority should sometimes have weight in elections?—Yes. It is right that they should have, but they should not have it to the extent that a cumulative vote gives them, in my opinion. That gives them more than their share. From my knowledge of the working of the cumulative vote at home, I am decidedly opposed to it, on the ground that it gives to the minority more than its real representation. Minorities get to know their own power by means of the cumulative vote, and they work on a system, and on such a system the majority is sent into a very small corner at times.

8005. Can you illustrate that?—Suppose there are seven members to be elected and there are fifteen candidates, every man has seven votes. The minority may club together to give all their votes to one man and so put him at the head of the poll. My experience is based on practical knowledge of what takes place in Glasgow.

8006. *Rev. Moorrees.*] Do you find majorities working together as a rule?—If the majority is very large, they have minor differences among themselves as a rule.

8007. Would you exclude the minority altogether?—They must just take their chance.

8008. *President.*] Can you suggest any additional facilities to meet the wants of the children of the agricultural population?—I think if members of the various bodies did their duty, the facilities at present afforded would be more largely taken advantage of.

8009. What do you mean by duty?—It is the duty of a minister of religion to explain to those over whom he has the oversight, what the Government facilities for education are. The Rev. Mr Postma, of Middelburg, does this. He has enlightened the farmers, and got up quite recently several boarding schools. I think ministers have a great deal of influence over people in educational as well as other matters.

8010. *Dr. Berry.*] What do you propose should be the relationship between the School Boards and the private farm schools?—I think it would be better to let them be worked as they are at present. The farmers will stand no interference of the Board with their private arrangements. The farm schools are not public schools, and the teacher on the farm school is not recognised as a teacher in connection with the Education Department, but simply as the servant of the farmer. The money is given to the farmer as a contribution from the State to enable education to be carried on and diffused. If a teacher on a farm school does good work, he does not thereby receive the advantages that a public school teacher would receive. The only thing is, that such a teacher would be more likely to get a public school if he applied for it, but he is as much the farmer's servant as the groom.

8011. *President.*] Do you think the farm schools ought to stand outside the Board?—I should be slow to advise the interference of the Board with private farm schools.

8012. Might not the Board be approached in the case of applications for grants to farm schools, so that the Government might ascertain whether such applications ought to be granted?—The Government might ask the Board whether a school was outside the radius of six miles which is at present laid down, and that sort of thing.

8013. Might not the Government also ascertain through the Board whether a district school did not already provide the [necessary requirements, when there was an application for a farm school grant?—That is fair enough. The Government lays it down as a rule that farm schools are given to aid the farmers who are situated far away from any school, and it is quite right that before giving any grant, the School Board should be approached and asked whether it is outside the radius. I would not however put farm schools under the Board so that the Board can interfere with them in any way.

8014. Would you bind the Government by the action of the Board?—If the farm school was outside the radius, the Government would act on the report. The question as to whether it was necessary or not might be put to the Board by the Government and settled definitely, but after the Government has once accepted a farm school, I think they are best managed as they are now.

8015. Would you have the inspection of farm schools continued?—Yes. The farmers do not object to it.

8016. Dr. Berry.] Do you think it is a good plan to make an inspection of public school teachers?—I should not like to offer any very strong opinion, especially seeing that as a school teacher I was inspector of farm schools for seven years myself. It might be supposed that my evidence was prejudiced.

8017. Do you agree with those who say that it leads to a want of uniformity in the results of the inspection?—I have heard that said, but the result of my own experience is that children who pass standard 3 or 4 before the inspection at a farm school, are very often unfit to pass the same standard when they come before me in the town school. To obviate that, I have in several instances given cards of arithmetical questions and questions in geography, grammar, and so on to teachers as a guide, to show them what is expected.

8018. Rev. Moorrees.] It is in the interests of the teachers not to be too lenient, is it not?—Yes; if they could only see it so. I may say that some of the best teachers have come to me and asked to have specimens of my cards to see exactly what the standard I require is.

8019. Dean Holmes.] Are the results in these farm schools lower than in town schools or third class schools?—The statement is generally made, although I cannot vouch for the truth of it, that a child who passes standard 3 in a farm school before the inspection, would not necessarily pass standard 3 with me at a town or mission school. I as much as possible make the standard the same in every school, because you cannot quote a child as having passed a certain standard unless you make it tolerably uniform.

8020. President.] Is it not better to have one officer to do all the work?—Yes, I suppose it would be; but you would require to increase your inspectors by half, if they had to inspect farm schools.

8021. Is the class of teachers instructing at farm schools of an average character? —In my own experience there has been a very great increase in the capabilities and character of teachers in farm schools within the last ten years I am glad to say. Formerly the class of men acting as teachers on farms was anything but desirable.

8022. Mr. Theron.] Do you approve of the present system of training pupil teachers?—Yes. I was a pupil teacher myself for five years in Scotland, and I think it is the best training a man can get for the profession, but of course it depends altogether on the school at which he is apprenticed, and the facilities afforded for getting a proper training. Only yesterday, application was made to me about two pupil teachers, and my answer was, that as the school making the application offered very unusual facilities for the training of pupil teachers I had no hesitation in recommending. There are schools I would not say that of.

8023. Dean Holmes.] In the interests of education, do you think it is a good thing that children who have not completed their own education should be put to teach other children in the school?—It depends altogether on the class of children they are set to teach and the class of work they are asked to do. A pupil teacher in this country is not as a rule of the same standing, intellectually, as a pupil teacher at home. A pupil teacher can hear a child say arithmetical tables, correct dictation and do mechanical work of that description just as well as the head master, but the head master, if he is not sufficiently alive to his responsibility, may set a pupil teacher to do work beyond the scope of a child. For instance, any man who set a child of thirteen or fourteen to explain the principles of physical geography, the principles of fractions, or the principles of language to a class, is certainly making a great error.

298

Rev.
D. B. Fraser.
Sept. 22nd, 1891

8024. In the interests of the pupil teachers themselves, do you think it is a good thing that they should give up so much time to teaching instead of studying?—My experience goes to show that pupil teachers here do not study so much as they do in the old country. I know one large institution where the pupil teachers study just as much as the other children, and give an hour or two a week to practice.

8025. You prefer to have teachers properly trained?—Yes. I have seen men sent into a school, and they never saw the work of a school going on till they had charge of it.

8026. Would you like to see a system of training colleges introduced, with practising schools attached, so as to instruct teachers how to teach?—We have that in the Normal College in Cape Town; there is All Saints' school at Wynberg, and a school at Wellington for girls.

8027. Is there any normal school in the Eastern Province?—No. I have no information before me to show how far the number of teachers provided corresponds with the number required. I would have no objection to an increase in the number of training schools if more teachers are required.

8028. Is it difficult to find competent teachers now?—If you are willing to pay men, they will come out from Europe.

8029. Why must we depend on teachers from Europe?—Of course it is advisable if we can do it, to train and educate our own teachers.

8030. Mr. Theron.] Can you point out the way to do that?—I have not thought sufficiently over the matter.

8031. President.] Have you considered the subject of night schools at all?—I should have no objection to night schools being introduced for the purpose of enabling young people to keep up their education to at least the point at which they were when they left school.

8032. What age would you limit that to?—It would depend on the scheme of education that was introduced, and whether you made education compulsory up to a certain age. As a rule, it is not advisable that children under fourteen or fifteen should be out in the street at night.

8033. Would you advocate night schools for girls?—I am rather opposed to that.

8034. Do you know anything about technical schools?—I do not think that in this country we are ripe for technical schools properly so called, that is to say, we have neither the facilities nor the demand that would justify any very large provision being made for a first class technical school.

8035. What would be included in the curriculum of a first class technical school?—If it were in a place like Manchester, it would take up very largely cotton manufacture, the best means of preparing cotton, and the best system of machinery for dealing with it. If it were in Yorkshire, it would take up the woollen industry, and in Newcastle, coal mining.

8036. What does the Heriot school go in for?—Largely for applied mathematics. I may say that I saw a good description of the Heriot school in the blue book on the Scotch educational system for last year; the last one issued.

8037. How would you apply such a school at Kimberley?—I have not any local knowledge of Kimberley.

8038. What subjects would you introduce here under any circumstances?—I do not think the circumstances of the colony justify us in having a first class technical school or college, but I think we might do something towards it. I wrote a prize essay on industrial education for the Graham's Town exhibition. We could make provision in all our schools for drawing, not so much freehand drawing, although that is advisable, as drawing to scale. It is a great help to any child entering life, if he is able to draw to scale with the use of instruments. That is a faculty which can be brought out in children to an extent that freehand drawing cannot develope, because freehand drawing is a gift which some have and some have not. Drawing to scale should be encouraged and cultivated in most if not in all our schools.

8039. You would not want a technical school for that, would you?—No.

8040. Would you have drawing to scale taught in every school?—Yes, where possible, and where the children are old enough to handle the instruments, a straight edge and a pair of compasses. We might have also something like what they have at the Science and Arts department in South Kensington. There you have 24 or 25 sciences ranging from plane and solid geometry up to navigation. Of course here the scheme would have to be modified so as to meet local wants. For instance, we could have in some schools, facilities for teaching the principle of the steam engine, practical assaying, chemistry, and things of that sort. These might be taught in connection with a Government examination held on the lines of the Science and Arts Examination in London in May, every year. I was a science teacher myself for many years in connection with the Science and Arts department, and the classes were taught in the evening, for the benefit of children who had left school, so that they might do in the best way possible the work in which they happened to be engaged. Mining for instance, was one of the subjects. A pupil must get at least 25 lessons in mining. He is given a text book, but it is always understood that it is practical work which counts, and not book work; the teacher is supposed not only to give lessons out of a book, but to take the pupils down a mine and explain the practical working, and at the end of the instruction, the class is examined, and prizes and certificates given to those who pass. In another centre perhaps, geology would be taught. That was largely gone in for in Glasgow. In other centres, there would be chemistry, mechanics, and so on.

Rev.
D. D. Fraser.
Sept. 22nd, 1891.

8041. What is the objection to having all these subjects taught at one centre?— There is no objection to a large centre. There could be preparation in various schools for a first-class technical institution.

8042. Could there be preparation in connection with night schools?—Yes.

8043. Would the ordinary pupil you would suggest for a night school be fit to take up this work, or would you have another class of pupil?—In Glasgow, there were lads of seventeen and men of thirty at the classes. They were engaged at their work all the day and studied in the evening.

8044. Would you recommend such technical instruction being associated with night schools?—Yes. Agriculture was one of the subjects taught at home, and I do not see why agricultural schools here could not be made the basis of some slight technical instruction.

8045. It has been suggested that there should be lecturers appointed who should go about the country with their apparatus and lecture for a month at a time in a place, and at the end of the course, an examination should be held, those students passing satisfactorily to get a certificate entitling them to admission into the Government workshops: do you think that would be a good thing?—To the idea of having a lecturer going about, I would be rather favourable, if it can be shown that there is any work for him to do.

8046. Could not young men be educated here as telegraphists instead of importing them?—I think the best telegraphists must be imported for some time to come, but the rank and file might be educated here.

8047. Do you think it is desirable that in the schools for natives there should be some industrial training?—European artisans and others seem to think that teaching the natives industries might clash with their interests; for my own part I think the gospel of work is a very good gospel for the natives.

8048. Would not the schools be more useful if there was simple industrial training of some sort?—I believe that the industrial training given at Lovedale, which is the institution I am best acquainted with, is a very useful factor in the development of the native question.

8049. Could industrial training be given in an inexpensive manner?—I am not in a position to say.

8050. If the natives were taught gardening for a short time when at school, would not they be better after they leave school for it, and be more fitted for their future calling?—I think they would.

8051. Can you devise some inexpensive way of starting industrial training for these people?—That is rather out of my experience. It would be a good thing to start it if it can be done cheaply.

8052. Mr. Theron.] Is that system carried on in Basutoland at the present time? —I have no knowledge of what is done in Basutoland. I have never been there. I have met a few French missionaries who have schools in the Herschel Division, bordering on Basutoland, but I would not like to give any opinion on the subject.

8053. Have they industrial training there?—Yes; there is carpentry and a little out-door work in the fields. At the Bensonville Institution for training native teachers, I was shown tables, chairs and window frames that had been made; also some brickwork, and something was done in the way of agriculture. A note of it appears in my report.

8054. President.] Can you suggest any practical means of dealing with native education outside towns or farms?—I have not thought it out.

8055. Do you know anything about railway schools?—I have inspected a number of these schools. As a rule, they are doing very efficient work. The great drawback to railway schools as at present conducted, is, that children are not allowed to travel free by passenger train, they are only allowed to take advantage of such goods trains as may suit, and this sometimes puts them to very great inconvenience. I think we might do something for railway children if we allowed them to attend schools in towns. At Cradock there is no railway school. I do not think there should be any objection to allowing children bonâ fide going to Cradock, to travel free as they do to railway schools, the same also with regard to Kimberley.

8056. Is it the case that they can only travel by goods train ?—I think so. I know the complaint is made in various schools. When I was in Burghersdorp as a teacher in the Academy, I influenced the local parties to allow the children to come, but Mr. Price, the Traffic Manager, sent word that they were only to travel by goods train.

8057. Are you acquainted with the Eastern line ?—Yes. From Sterkstroom up to Aliwal North.

8058. Are there any schools there ?—Yes, at Cyphergat and Burghersdorp.

8059. Do you see any reason why the Government should not assist railway children in the way of boarding, on the same principle as they assist country boarding schools ?—No.

8060. *Dean Holmes.*] Mr. Howell suggested that the train service should be utilised as far as possible, and the trains stopped at the various platelayers' cottages, taking the children to the various centres free of charge, and bringing them home again ; would that answer ?—My experience is that the Railway Department does not want the children in the passenger trains. Complaints have been made to me by teachers that difficulties arise, from the fact that children are only allowed to travel by goods train.

8061. Mr. Elliott, the General Manager, was asked, " What facilities does the Railway Department offer for children residing at a distance from the stations ; do they travel free ?" and his reply was, " We allow them to travel free by rail to the nearest available school ; we are rather averse to let them go on a trolly, because there have been several accidents in connection with trollies. The children are apt to be careless, and their clothes might get caught in the wheels, and so on. The children travel free where there are no facilities in the neighbourhood " ?—At Burghersdorp, I understand, the people complained of the delay to the trains, and Mr. Price sent up a notice distinctly stating that children were to travel only by goods train. I was there at the time.

8062. *President.*] Have you formed any opinion on the bi-lingual question ?—My experience is that Dutch children are only too glad to learn English when they get the chance.

8063. Have you read the discussion which has been going on with regard to this subject ?—Yes.

8064. Do you think there ought to be a fifth paper in Dutch in the Elementary examination ?—No ; I do not agree with that.

8065. What do you think ought to be done ?—My impression is this, that if the agitation is genuine, the promoters of it should insist upon there being two examinations, one entirely in Dutch and one entirely in English, but that they will not do. They never proposed it. The Elementary examination is the only examination in which Dutch is not included in this colony. If the candidates choose to take it, it is put on the same footing as any other modern language in the School Higher, Matriculation and other examinations.

8066. Do you think that is all that is advisable ?—So far as my experience has gone in dealing with Dutchmen, I have found that the great majority, practically all, who have spoken to me, have come to the conclusion that it is no use teaching Dutch in school, but I think that children are better for being instructed in their own language. I am surprised at the want of grammatical knowledge on the part of children in Dutch ; and sometimes the simplest words they cannot translate correctly. I was inspecting a school at Wonderhoek, and the lesson was about the *spoorweg*, but although the children were living within four miles of a railway, they did not know what *spoorweg* was. Many Dutchmen have said that they do not want instruction in Dutch ; that *Hollandsch komt zelf.*

8067. *Rev. Moorrees.*] You did not understand that they did not want Dutch, did you ; it comes of itself they think ?—There is a good deal of Dutch taught, and when taught grammatically as it ought to be, it is taught by a foreigner. There are only one or two schools in my district in which Dutch is taught grammatically by Dutch people, but when it is taught it is taught well.

8068. Do you think there would be any difficulty in getting good Dutch teachers ? —I have seen some very good teachers. It would be difficult to get good teachers if Dutch was taught in every school.

8069. *President.*] Do you think it would answer to have a separate Dutch paper in the Elementary examination and put a bursary at the end of it for those who passed well ?—It would be a very fair thing to have a separate examination in Dutch by itself. I would not have it connected with the Elementary examination, but to encourage Dutch, there might be a bursary attached.

Kimberley, Wednesday, September 23rd, 1891.

PRESENT:

Sir J. D. BARRY (President),

Dr. Berry,　　　　　　　　　　Rev. Moorrees,
Dean Holmes.　　　　　　　　　Mr. Theron.

Mr. Arthur H. Bleksley examined.

8070. *President.*] I believe you are Sanitary Inspector in Kimberley?—Yes.

8071. And as such you come in contact with every part of the town?—Yes.

8072. Are there many children in Kimberley who do not attend any school at all?—Yes; a very large number.

8073. Where are they principally?—Throughout the town.

8074. Both black and white?—Yes. Chiefly white I am afraid.

8075. Whose children are they principally?—Children of miners of the lower class.

8076. How is it these children do not attend the mission schools?—The parents complain that in the mission schools they do not care about the coloured children, and as regards the higher schools, they complain of the high fees.

8077. Then the mission schools are almost entirely attended by coloured children?—Yes.

8078. Have you formed any opinion as to what is best to be done with regard to these children?—I am afraid they will never be sent to school unless there is compulsion.

8079. If they were compelled, is there sufficient room for them in the schools in the town?—Yes, the accommodation is adequate. I have drawn up a list of the various schools here which I will hand in. [See Appendix].

8080. You say that there is a number of children who do not attend any of those schools?—Yes.

8081. And they attend no school at all?—No.

8082. Is there also a large number attending private schools?—A very large number.

8083. Are those private schools good or bad?—There are good, bad, and indifferent schools.

8084. Are there some very bad?—Yes, very bad indeed; in fact, some of them I do not think should be permitted to exist, if only for sanitary reasons, they are too crowded, and they are perfect hovels some of them.

8085. How do the children find their way to these schools?—I presume it is owing to the parents getting education at a cheaper rate.

8086. Is the teaching also bad in this class of schools?—Yes; I should say so, judging from the people who keep them. They appear to be very illiterate people most of them.

8087. If you had a system of compulsion, how would you work it without unnecessarily offending anyone; would you have an attendance officer to visit the houses?—Yes. I might point out that a large number of these children who are not going to school, are children who are working. I cannot say whether it is so now, but a short time ago, it used to be a very common thing for young children to work the points on the floors at the mines, children of from ten to sixteen years of age. In the tobacco and cigarette factories, and also at the various printing offices here, you will also find a number of young children.

8088. Are they employed all day?—Yes.

8089. What are the hours?—The average hours would be from about seven till six.

8090. Do you think those children ought to go school?—Yes; although perhaps it would inflict a hardship upon the parents. I could quote cases in which some of these children are the only support of their parents, very often of the mother where the father is dead. I know one case of a woman who has four little children, all at work, and they keep her, although she is a drunken disreputable creature.

8091. As far as those children are concerned, they would be better away from the mother, would they not?—Undoubtedly. In many cases children have to be sent out where there is a large family.

8092. Even at the age of ten?—Yes, and even younger.

8093. Those children receive no education whatever, do they?—No.

8094. Are they white children?—Yes.

8095. If some system of compulsion were established, should an attendance officer visit the parents and tell them their duty?—Not only tell them their duty, but enforce it.

PP 2

Mr.
Arthur H.
Bleksley.

Sept. 23rd, 1891.

8096. With regard to children running about in the streets, would you have a truant officer for them?—Yes; that ought to be left in the hands of the police.

8097. You see no objection to having such children taken up by the police?—1 think not. We have Government police and Borough police.

8098. Which would you employ for the purpose?—Both. I can quote a case which came under my notice a little time ago, where we found a regular den of boys, ranging from about ten to sixteen. There were eight or nine of them in an old stable near the Market Square. They lived apparently only by thieving, and one or two of them were the children of respectable parents who had been compelled to give them up as simply incorrigible.

8099. Waifs and strays, in fact?—Yes. We took drastic measures to put a stop to it. I do not know what has become of them all, but we compelled those who had parents to return to them.

8100. Was any attempt made to indenture these children?—No.

8101. Why not?—We sent some of them to their homes and the others disappeared, where I cannot say.

8102. Before you could do anything they disappeared?—Yes.

8103. Are they still about somewhere do you think?—Undoubtedly.

8104. Do you think there will be any difficulty when you get these children to indenture them?—I do. I am afraid you would find great difficulty in indenturing that class of children to anyone. People would simply not have them, as they know they are incorrigible; they would rather get a good honest boy.

8105. What would be the best thing to do with these children?—There are only two courses open, either to send them to school compulsorily and give them some technical education, or else send them to a reformatory.

8106. Suppose they have no home?—That difficulty has not presented itself to my mind.

8107. Are there no homes for destitute children in Kimberley?—Yes; there is Nazareth House: that is an orphanage; they accept children of all denominations. It is a Roman Catholic institution I believe; they do not impart religious instruction there. It is a home for the destitute.

8108. Do they receive aid from the State?—I cannot say; I believe not. As far as I know, it is kept up by the Roman Catholic community.

8109. Are industries taught there?—Not at present.

8110. Do you think these waifs and strays might be taken into such a school as that?—Yes, but the question is whether these people would receive them unless they got some aid.

8111. You think it is proper that some institution should be provided to which these children should be taken?—Undoubtedly.

8112. And where they could receive industrial training as well?—Yes. No child, I think, should be allowed to run about the street without being able to give a good account of itself.

8113. Up to what age?—Up to the age of sixteen, I should say. After that, it would come under the Vagrancy Act.

8114. Are there children running about after that age, against whom the Vagrancy Act is brought into force?—Yes.

8115. Is it actually enforced?—I will not say that it is enforced against children, but it is against grown-up people.

8116. From what you know of mission schools here, do you think there is any possibility of getting mission schools to take in these children upon certain conditions of aid?—I have no doubt the mission schools would be quite willing to take them in if the children would go.

8117. Suppose they are brought there?—Then some system must be introduced in order to keep them there.

8118. Have any of the mission schools industrial training?—No.

8119. Do you think any of them could undertake industrial training, and would they do so?—I have hardly any doubt that both the English and Dutch Reformed Churches would be willing to undertake it if they received aid.

8120. Do you think it is desirable to separate the white and black children?—I think it is very desirable.

8121. They mix together now in the mission schools, do they not?—Yes.

8122. How would you separate them?—By having aided mission schools to which white children only would be admitted.

8123. And also aided mission schools to which blacks only would be admitted?—Yes. It is a great mistake for young white girls to be brought up with coloured boys in the same school, as is now the case. There is too much familiarity.

8124. You spoke of certain industries existing here, such as cigarette making and so on ; are there any other industries that might be taught in the schools?—I think tailoring might be taught, and also saddle making and carpentry.

8125. If these things were taught, do you think the schools would to some extent receive support from the results?—I think that the sale of the articles would bring in a certain revenue. Of course as regards technical schools, the great objection is the floating character of the population. The children would never remain long enough at school, I am afraid, to master the work.

8126. From what you know of Kimberley, do you think there would be any feeling against such articles being sold, or such training imparted?—On the contrary, I think it would receive support from the public.

8127. Is that statement applicable both to whites and blacks?—Yes.

8128. You spoke of mission schools doing this work ; if they are not prepared to do it, what would you suggest as a means of educating the poorer classes?—I would suggest some system of technical schools, with aid from the Divisional Council and Municipality under the direction of the Borough Council or Board to be nominated by those bodies.

8129. Do you think a School Board ought to be brought into existence?—I do.

8130. Would you have it nominated by the Divisional Council, the Municipality and the Government in equal proportions?—No, it should be *pro rata*, according to the amount which those different bodies contribute.

8131. Should it be the duty of the Board to provide schools in order to fill up gaps?—Yes.

8132. Do you think that is the only means of really effectually filling them up?—I think so.

8133. Do you think that mission schools would be unable to do so effectively?—I am afraid so. The great difficulty that mission schools would have would be to compel the children to attend.

8134. If you force the children into these mission schools, might not they be able to undertake the work?—Under the present regime, if you do force them into the mission schools, you have no means of keeping them there.

8135. What means would you suggest for keeping them there?—The only way of doing it would be to bring in a Compulsory Education Act.

8136. Suppose you do that, and the mission schools open their doors wide to all under some scheme of aid, would the mission schools be as good as the Board schools or not?—Not as good, because I do not think the mission schools at present have the proper amount of supervision they should have, nor the means.

8137. If this Board is brought into existence, would you try and put an end to mission schools, or would you allow the Board to work through mission schools if they thought fit?—I would allow them to work through mission schools. The Board should be appointed to supervise every school and the whole of the education within its local limits.

8138. Including private schools would you say?—Yes, there should be the right of entry and inspection, and qualified teachers only should be allowed to impart education.

8139. What would be the measure of the qualification?—The third class Elementary teacher's certificate.

8140. You think there would be no difficulty in getting sufficient teachers with that certificate to supply the wants?—None whatever.

8141. Do you speak of females?—Both males and females. At Wellington I know there is a number who pass every year and obtain certificates, and they would be willing to go out teaching.

8142. At what salary?—In the case of females, from about £96 to £120 a year, and in the case of males, from about £100 to £144 a year. I know from my personal knowledge that there is a number of competent teachers willing to go out, but at the present moment they cannot do so because they cannot obtain situations.

8143. Do you know anything about the facilities for the education of railway employés' children?—I may say that I am an old railway officer, and I know that we always found a very great difficulty. The only way of overcoming it, as far as I can see, is to have schools at different stations, and allow certain trains to stop and put down or pick up children. There is no doubt that a large number of these children are growing up without education simply because they have no means of getting it.

8144. Are there any schools between here and the Vaal River?—Yes.

8145. Where would you have a school northward from this place?—I would have one at Fourteen Streams.

8146. Are there many children there?—Yes. There is quite a settlement there. There is no school there at present.

8147. Would you have one school for both sexes?—Yes, in such cases.

Mr. *Arthur H. Blaksley*

Sept. 23rd, 1891.

8148. From what you know of the country, are there many farmers or others living near the line who could also make use of that school?—Yes; and they would use it.

8149. Do you think they would use it whether they had to pay the railway fares or not?—I do not think they would use it if they had to pay railway fares. In the case of the smaller class of farmers, they could not afford to do so.

8150. What contribution from Government would enable such schools to be worked effectively?—I am afraid the railway schools would have to be supported or maintained entirely by Government or by the Divisional Council.

8151. Would you put such schools under the Board if it was created?—Yes.

8152. *Dr. Berry.*] In the case of a school at Fourteen Streams, would not they be able to get the Government grant of £30, if the local people found £10 and board for the teacher?—I am afraid that would hardly suffice. You could scarcely get a competent teacher for so small a sum in the first place, and secondly, it would fall very hard on a certain few, if they had to provide board and lodging and £10 a year for a teacher.

8153. *Mr. Theron.*] Is not there a public school at Warrenton?—I believe there is one there.

8154. Is it too far away?—Yes; it is about four miles from the station, and the children could not manage to go that distance.

8155. Do you think the school ought to be on the line?—Yes; at the station, It is too far to expect young children to walk, and there is a certain amount of danger in their travelling by themselves backwards and forwards on the railway. I think if the board and lodging of the teacher could be provided for, there would be no difficulty in obtaining one, but I am afraid you would not be able to find anyone to give board and lodging at Fourteen Streams gratis, as it is a very expensive place to live at.

8156. *Dr. Berry.*] Is there a railway station school at Kimberley?—No.

8157. Why is that?—I cannot say.

8158. *President.*] Is there any building that might be utilised at Fourteen Streams for a school?—I cannot say.

8159. How many children would there be in attendance there?—I could not say. I only quoted it as an example.

8160. Do you see any objection to the passenger trains being used to take children to and from school?—None whatever.

8161. *Mr. Theron.*] Are they not used now?—I cannot say whether they are now. They were not in my time.

8162. Were the other trains used?—No; no trains were allowed to stop to take up or put down children; the conveyance was by trolly.

8163. Do you think that objectionable?—Yes; it is dangerous in the first place, and it is also very tedious and onerous, as men have to push the trolly sometimes 15 or 20 miles perhaps. Two men would have to be told off for it, as the children could not be trusted with a trolly alone on the railway line.

Rev. W. Leith examined.

8164. *President.*] I believe you reside at Somerset East?—Yes; I am minister of the Presbyterian church there.

8165. Are you connected with any schools there?—I am chairman of the committee of the Bellevue Seminary, and one of the trustees of the Gill College, and am on the Board of Management.

8166. Can you suggest to the Commission any means for giving Boards of Management perpetual succession?—In the case of the Gill College, it was created under the will of the late Dr. Gill, who left a large sum of money for the endowment of an institution to be formed as far as possible on the model of the Glasgow University. It was felt desirable that there should be a preparatory school to act as a feeder ᴖ the college, and fit pupils for going in for higher work. There was a public school ᴀ Somerset, a Government public school, and under the Herschel system the principal teacher had his salary direct from the Government. After he had retired, it was necessary to provide education for those who were not fit to join the preparatory class, and accordingly a public meeting was called, and a number of the people in the town guaranteed so much, and the guarantors elected a committee to carry on the second class school. A room was rented and a teacher appointed, and the school went on very favourably for some time.

8167. Are you one of the guarantors?—Yes; there was a deficiency the first quarter, but it was allowed to slide, thinking it would be made good the next quarter.

8168. How did you find a building?—We rented one. It was the Wesleyan Church building. The next quarter the deficiency was considerably greater, and there was a call made upon the guarantors to make it up. A number of the guarantors paid and many refused to pay. They never expected a call and thought it was only a formal thing when they signed, in order to secure the Government grant. The committee then had to consider what they should do. I was secretary, but no one liked to prosecute the defaulting guarantors, thinking it would cause unpleasantness in a small place like Somerset, so the committee paid the deficiency out of their own pockets and closed the school.

Rev.
W. Leith.
——
Sept. 23rd, 1881

8169. Was the matter brought before the notice of any public meeting before you closed the school?—I cannot say.

8170. Was it brought to the notice of the Superintendent-General of Education?—Yes, I think so. After that, there was no other provision for the children, and most of them applied to be received at the preparatory class of the Gill College.

8171. Was there at that time a preparatory class of the Gill College in existence?—Yes; worked by the college.

8172. Did the institution provide any salary out of its own funds for that preparatory school?—I think they guaranteed the teacher's salary. It was a private venture of Mr. Woodroffe's in the first place, and then the college received him with his class. They had allowed him a room in connection with the college for doing his teaching, so that he was actually on the spot.

8173. But Government aid was not then contributed, was it?—No. The aid that was contributed was out of the funds of the Gill College.

8174. What was the date of this?—About 1876. The children, as I say, most of them went to this preparatory class. It was found that there was more work than one teacher could manage, so an assistant was appointed, and that went on for some two or three years, the additional teacher being paid partly from the fees, and the Gill College trustees providing the rest. At that time, the college was not in receipt of any Government money, and after this had gone on for a number of years, a correspondence arose between Sir Langham Dale and the trustees—my impression is that it originated with Sir Langham Dale—as to the desirability of having the college recognised as a public undenominational school. It was felt that other districts in the colony were getting aid from the Government and as the Gill College trustees were doing the work of a public school and getting no grant, an arrangement was made, either at Sir Langham Dale's suggestion, or with his approval, that a public meeting should be called and some statement put forward to the effect that Sir Langham Dale would recognise the Gill College as the first class public school of the district and give the usual grant for such a school, on condition that three individuals from the public were elected: the trustees of the college and these three individuals constituting a board of management for the first class public school.

8175. How many trustees were there?—I think seven under the will. The public provided nothing and they had no responsibility: the trustees were guarantors for the whole amount, and they provided the buildings for carrying on the work. I think when we started we got somewhere about £300 from the public funds through Sir Langham Dale as aid for the public school, and the trustees contributed about £900 towards carrying on the work, keeping the buildings in repair, and all other necessary expenses.

8176. The buildings being the Gill College property?—Yes.

8177. Was this scheme submitted to a public meeting?—Yes. After it was drafted in writing, a public meeting was called.

8178. By whom was the public meeting called?—I think by the chairman of the Gill College corporation, at that time I believe, Mr. Solomon of Bedford. It was fully considered and adopted, and the resolutions that were carried were sent to Sir Langham Dale. My impression is that it was really Sir Langham Dale's suggestion, but of that I am not positive.

8179. What time was it when it started?—Perhaps 1877 or 1878, and it has continued pretty much on that basis ever since.

8180. Has there been a re-election every three years?—Every three years there has been a meeting of householders called. The usual notice in connection with elections for public school committees has been given, and the meeting held in the Town Hall generally.

8181. Have you always been yourself a member of that Board?—I have been for a number of years. I think when these changes were introduced, I was not a member of the trust. Before that, they had themselves elected one or two who took an interest in education, to form what they called a senate. I was one of those.

8182. Who elected the senate?—The trustees themselves. The senate undertook the work of administering the school, but they had nothing to do with the funds; only with the educational arrangements.

8183. Afterwards you came on the Board, did you not?—Yes.

8184. Have you been re-elected from time to time?—I am acting still on the Board.

8185. Have you had any further contribution from the Government?—We have had the usual contributions from the Government that are given to first class public schools, until last session, when the Gill College was recognised as one of the teaching colleges of the colony, and was put under the Higher Education Act.

8186. Have they got any aid for building a boarding house?—They received a grant of £1,000 towards the erection of a boarding establishment in connection with the college.

8187. Not the public undenominational school?—No. It is in connection with higher education. The Board of the public undenominational school have no pecuniary responsibility. It is upon the property of the trustees that the boarding establishment is erected, and it was given distinctly to the trustees.

8188. Are these boys going to the public undenominational school or to the college?—I suppose some go to one and some to the other. It is open to both.

8189. Is the education conducted all in one establishment?—Yes; and virtually all under one management. The college matters, strictly speaking, are matters relating to the Gill estate, and they are under the Board of Trustees; matters relating to the first class public school are under the control and administration of the Board of Management.

8190. But the school itself is worked as though it were all one, is it not?—Yes.

8191. Are the masters separately employed; some by the college trustees for higher education, and some by the Board of Management?—The two who are doing college work were appointed by the trustees; those who are doing the ordinary school work are appointed by the Board of Management. There are two professors; one for classics and the other for mathematics.

8192. Does the whole thing work harmoniously?—Yes. There was a meeting of the trustees the day I left Somerset, and I hardly know what the final arrangement is. There required to be some re-arrangement, in consequence of the college being put under the Higher Education Act. I drafted a scheme before leaving, and it was to the effect that Professor MacWilliam should be principal of the college and Mr. Mason head of the public undenominational school. There were also certain other details as to discipline and so on.

8193. Then Professor MacWilliam was not to be the head of the public undenominational school?—Mr. Mason is in one sense the head, but in the matter of discipline, text books, and so on, there is one head over the whole.

8194. You mean that Professor MacWilliam was to be head of the college and head also of the public undenominational school, Mr. Mason working under him?—Yes; of course he would have more power being head of the first class school than he would have simply as one of the assistants.

8195. Was Mr. Mason treated as receiving the grant from Government for the public undenominational school, or Professor MacWilliam?—Mr. Mason receives the grant as the head master of the public undenominational school, and Professor MacWilliam the grant under the Higher Education Act as professor.

8196. Is not there some friction going on about the boarding department?—Yes.

8197. What is it?—The friction is this, that Professor MacWilliam expected to have the management of it, and the Board of Trustees have not seen their way to agree to his terms.

8198. Is the friction continuing?—I suppose so.

8199. Is there an election of three members every three years?—Yes; whatever friction there may be, is purely with regard to the matter of boarding, it has nothing to do with the working of the school or the working of the college under one head.

8200. Professor MacWilliam is supposed to be a sort of general head?—I think that would be the arrangement, but I left before the matter was considered.

8201. Can you suggest any scheme for giving Boards of Management perpetual succession?—I have not thought of that. Two of the trustees since I was connected with the college, have been non-residents, so that in point of fact we could never count on more than five working trustees on the Board of Management. Two live out of the division, a long distance away, and attend very rarely.

8202. *Mr. Theron.*] How would you give a Board of Management of ten members say, perpetual succession?—The only way would be to elect them as life members.

8203. *President.*] Is the present system satisfactory, or is there anything that does not wholly meet with your approval?—I think on the whole it works very well in Somerset, and I do not see why in the future it should not work quite as successfully as it has done in the past. I do not think that we could very well have a satisfactory first class public undenominational school apart from the Gill College. There would be a difficulty in providing the buildings and in getting the guarantors. As it is, nothing is required from the public, and they have no responsibility. All they have to do is simply to elect the most suitable men every three years to fill the vacancies.

8204. This Board of Management consists of ten men, seven of whom are trustees; how are the trustees elected?—They are elected under the late Dr. Gill's will. He appointed seven trustees, and directed that in case of a vacancy arising, the remaining trustees were to elect a successor.

8205. Then they elect themselves in fact?—Yes; it is a close corporation.

8206. And the public, with the exception of three members, are shut out?—Yes.

8207. Do you think it satisfactory that a public school should in perpetuity remain virtually in the hands of a self-elected body?—If you put it on general grounds I should say not, but if you look at it in regard to the circumstances of Somerset, I do not think there is any hardship arising. I think the men who have been elected as trustees have generally served for a longer or a shorter time either on the Senate or on the Board of Management.

8208. Are you in favour of the system of guarantors continuing?—Certainly not, judging by our experience at Somerset.

8209. What do you consider are the defects of the system?—One of the defects is that sometimes individuals refuse to pay, and if you have to prosecute them, it causes a great deal of unpleasant feeling in a small place like Somerset.

8210. Where there is no Gill College to assist with funds, what would you suggest?—I think the better way would be instead of guarantors to have an educational rate.

8211. *Mr. Theron.*] What security did the Gill College give for the money it borrowed?—The buildings and the school fees.

8212. Who is liable for the repayment of the money?—Only the trustees.

8213. Not the three members elected by the public?—No.

8214. The whole of the Gill College is responsible for it?—Yes. The whole property and revenue of the Gill College is responsible for the repayment.

8215. I believe you got a grant of £1,000 and you borrowed £3,500?—Yes.

8216. Under the Act, the corporation is bound to provide boarding accommodation, it is not?—Yes. This £3,500 we have borrowed is borrowed distinctly for that particular purpose.

8217. *President.*] The trustees borrowed this money under the Public Loans Act, did they not?—Yes.

8218. And besides that, they got £1,000 grant which they put into building?—Yes; and which is to cost about £4,000.

8219. *Dr. Berry.*] Does the interest on the loan come out of the revenue of the school and college?—The trustees provide for the payment of the interest, and they are responsible for all money connected with the institution. The board of managers are responsible for nothing.

8220. *President.*] The trustees have a revenue outside the school fees, have they not?—They have revenue from the Gill estate.

8221. Do they pay this interest out of the Gill estate?—I presume it would be paid out of the Gill estate. The school fees in the first place go towards the payment of the salaries of the teachers, and then whatever is deficient in the revenue arising from school fees is made up out of the revenues of the Gill estate.

8222. Then if the school fees are sufficient to keep the school going, and also to pay the interest, the Gill estate would not be called upon at all, would it?—No, but such a supposition is not likely to be realised.

8223. *Dr. Berry.*] What is the private revenue of the Gill estate?—I believe at one time it was supposed that about £20,000 was left. From what I can gather, the interest would be from £900 to £1,000 a year. I speak from memory.

8224. Do you charge the school for rent of the premises?—No.

8225. The public school is rent free?—Yes.

8226. *President.*] Suppose the public school, in consequence of the large number attending, were worked at a profit, where would the profit go to?—Such a contingency has never arisen. I hardly know how it would be disposed of.

8227. Would not the trustees devote such profit to paying the interest on the loan?—Possibly, or it might go towards improvements about the establishment or increasing the teaching power, so as to render the institution more efficient.

8228. *Dr. Berry.*] As a matter of fact, the funds were left for the establishment of a college, were they not?—Yes.

8229. But owing to circumstances, you have been obliged to use a large portion of the funds to establish a public school?—Yes; I suppose it comes to that. It started as a college, and was very successful for some years, and then it went down considerably. It enjoyed in earlier days the grant for colleges, but because the number of those taking higher work diminished, that was withdrawn, and in point of fact, for a number of years it was simply doing the work of an ordinary school, but latterly it

308

Rev.
W. Leith.

Sept. 23rd, 1891.

has been growing, and a number of pupils take higher education ; very many more than formerly.

8230. *President.*] By taking advantage of the Public Undenominational School Act, it has managed to work its way and do good work ?—It has done good work ; but I do not know that it is through taking advantage of that Act. I think the credit is largely due to the teachers we have had. Professor MacWilliam has devoted a great deal of time and labour.

8231. Do you think the public school could be worked independently of the college if the premises were hired ?—I do not see how you could very well work it under the same roof ; you would require to have other premises quite apart, otherwise there would be constant danger of little collisions and irritations.

8232. You think that a public undenominational school would have to be worked under a different roof in Somerset ?—Yes ; if you wish to have the public school entirely separate from the college, then I think it would be better for it to be under another roof, and quite apart.

8233. *Dr. Berry.*] Can you suggest any way by which the public can recover their right of electing the managers of the first class school and at the same time the rights of the trustees be safeguarded ?—I do not see how it can be done unless the public are willing to take the responsibility.

8234. Suppose the responsibility is forced upon them by a School Board being brought into existence, which has a lien upon the rates, how could the public recover their right to elect the managing body of the first class school and the interests of the trustees be at the same time protected ?—If the rates were responsible for the first class school, that might relieve the trustees, and they could then devote all their time and all their revenue to higher education.

8235. *President.*] How could you work a public school there if that was done ; could the school be carried on in the building on the Gill College estate ?—I think that is doubtful ; you would have two ruling powers there.

8236. Then in fact if the public wanted to recover their right to appoint all the managers, they would have to bring into existence a school elsewhere or hire a school elsewhere ?—That is my impression.

8237. Would the effect of doing so be to prejudice the college ?—It might be injurious to the interests of the college in some ways. It is a somewhat difficult thing to define where the higher education begins and the school education ends. Most of the first class schools carry their pupils up to matriculation. In connection with the colleges again, all the matriculation work is done in the colleges, and often where they have preparatory schools, boys are moved out of the preparatory schools and put under the masters of the college to do college work. Preparation for the matriculation is always considered part of the college work.

8238. Where in your opinion ought higher education to begin ?—I should say, strictly speaking, it would be after matriculation, but as things are in this country after the School Higher examination. After they have passed the School Higher examination, they should pass into the college classes to prepare for matriculation.

8239. Then properly speaking, the Gill College ought only to take boys after they have passed the School Higher examination ?—I think that is the arrangement that will be carried out. The work of Mr. Mason, who will now become head of the first class school, will be Elementary and School Higher, and as soon as the boys have passed the School Higher, they will come under the professors and prepare for matriculation.

8240. If the Gill College limits itself to that work, and the public start a public undenominational school, educating up to that point and no higher, then you think it would have to be in another building ?—I think for the comfort of all it would be better to have another building. I do not say that it is absolutely necessary.

8241. If they did have another building, would the boarding establishment be used for the Gill College proper or for the boys in connection with the public undenominational school ?—In the erection of the boarding establishment, they contemplate making provision for the boys attending the college and also the school ; the proposition of having another school entirely separate I do not think has been considered by any of those connected with the Gill College.

8242. Suppose it had been ?—If there was accommodation, there would be no objection to using the boarding establishment and mixing the students with the boys. The students at the college would have the preference, but supposing there were any vacancies, I do not think there would be any objection to the boys attending the school having accommodation there.

8243. The primary object of the Gill College you say is for the purposes of higher education ?—Yes.

8244. What would you substitute for the guarantors if they were abolished ?—A public rate.

8245. But if the public are rated, ought they not to have a voice in the management?—Certainly.

8246. How would you elect the managers?—The ratepayers would elect them.

8247. For the district or for the municipality?—I think the ratepayers throughout the district ought to elect the Board. It would hardly be fair simply to rate the inhabitants of the town, when a large proportion of the children living in the district are also getting the benefit.

8248. *Rev. Moorrees.*] Are you in favour of the Board superintending all the schools, or would you have a Board for every separate school elected by the ratepayers?—There should be a general Board having supervision of the whole of the schools.

8249. *President.*] And acting through sub-committees?—Yes; for the separate districts.

8250. The rates being responsible for any deficiency?—Yes.

8251. What do you think ought to be the contribution of the central Government?—About half.

8252. Both for educational and building purposes?—Yes; and the other half should be contributed from the rates.

8253. Ought there to be some universal system of fees throughout the district?—I should as far as possible have the rate of fees uniform, but I would not make a hard and fast rule, because in some places you might have a very much poorer district than in others.

8254. *Dr. Berry.*] Would you allow the Government to contribute one-half of the other expenses, such as the salary of the secretary and treasurer, office rent and so on, or should that be a charge on the rates solely?—I have not thought of that.

8255. Is there any advantage in having the election for all the School Boards of the colony at one and the same time of the year?—I think it is desirable to have them about the same time, but not all on one day.

8256. *President.*] Who in your opinion ought to be voters for the Board; would you take the Parliamentary or the Divisional Council franchise?—The Parliamentary franchise. The Divisional Council franchise is considerably higher, but I think it is desirable in this case that all who are interested in education and who contribute, should have the right to exercise their privilege of voting.

8257. Would not the effect of having the lower franchise be to relieve some of the voters from contributing to the rates?—I do not think so.

8258. What would be the lowest number of members for the Board that you would suggest?—Perhaps ten or twelve for the whole district.

8259. *Dr. Berry.*] Should the voters elect members for particular field-cornetcies, or should they vote in a lump?—I think the latter plan would be the best.

8260. Would there not be some advantage in getting local representatives?—I do not know whether that would be so or not. I think under the other arrangement you are more likely generally to get good men. If you make the voting local, it is just possible a local man might be put in because he has friends and is liked in the district, although he has no special qualification for sitting on a School Board.

8261. What is your opinion about the cumulative vote as it is called?—I am not in favour of that.

8262. Would it be necessary to take any steps to protect the interests of the minority on the Board?—I do not think the interests of the minority would require protection. If you have a general vote, it is pretty likely that the interests of the minority would be fairly represented.

8263. *President.*] It has been suggested that an organisation could work the cumulative vote so as to get in a particular candidate; if such an organisation existed and they were the majority, could not they work the thing so as to exclude anyone but members of such organisation from having a seat on the Board?—Perhaps so, but those are details I do not like to pronounce any confident opinion about.

8264. *Rev. Moorrees.*] I understood you to say that you are against elections in field-cornetcies; but if one general Board is to manage the schools of the whole district, do you think it very likely that such a Board would know the wants of the different field-cornetcies unless the wards are represented on it?—The districts are not so very large but what the men are likely to have a pretty good idea of the general wants.

8265. Are you acquainted with the Midland Districts?—No; I speak more of the Somerset district.

8266. With regard to the elections, you wish to make the franchise wider than the Divisional Council franchise, do you not?—Yes. I would take the Parliamentary franchise.

8267. Do you think that is fair. If the Divisional Council has to provide the deficiency, is it not fair that the electors should be the same as for that body, and do not you bring a certain number of electors in who are not touched by the Divisional

Rev.
W. Leith.

Sept. 23rd, 1891.

Council rates ; they would have a voice but would not contribute anything ?—I suppose that would refer only to those living in towns ; but they would be liable for municipal rates.

8268. *Mr. Theron.*] Would you entitle people who can never be reached by Divisional Council taxation to have a say in the matter of electing the School Board ?—They might be reached by municipal taxation.

8269. *President.*] Are you of opinion that every one who is a voter ought to be reached by taxes ?—Yes.

8270. Would you vest public school property in the Board so elected ?—Yes.

8271. Can you suggest any further facilities to meet the educational wants of the farmers ?—I think that so far as the Somerset district goes, they are fairly provided for. If it was necessary to make further provision, you might make the number of children entitling to a grant four instead of five. That is about the only thing I can think of.

8272. Do you think the present facilities should be more widely known ?—Yes. I think the clergy of the Dutch Reformed Church might do a good deal in that way. I believe in our districts the facilities offered are very largely taken advantage of, but it is not so in other districts. There are many places where a farmer has not five children, but he might get one or two from a neighbour to come to his farm for school purposes and they could return home every week.

8273. I think you said you thought it desirable to have white children separate from the black ?—Yes.

8274. Do you think the kind of education for the lower classes is entirely satisfactory ?—If you teach the blacks the three r's, that is about as much as you can do.

8275. Would you add anything else ?—If you could train them to manual labour it would be a very good thing, but it appears to me that it would involve a good deal of expense if you had an industrial department in connection with every school.

8276. Do you think the mission bodies might have some sort of manual training in connection with their schools, provided they received a little further aid ?—If they have a large number of children in a large centre, but at many of the out-stations it would be quite impossible.

8277. In these large centres would it be better to give the mission bodies a further grant on condition that they added industrial education, or would it be more expedient for the Board to start some industrial centre where all children could meet for industrial teaching ?—There would be a difficulty in carrying that out. It would mean separate buildings and separate teachers for the industrial institution. I do not know whether that would work. The mission bodies might prefer to keep the children rather than let them go to an industrial institution. In towns, perhaps, you might have two hours' industrial teaching in the afternoon when the usual school instruction is finished, the literary work being taken in the morning. That might be a good thing for boys, and fit them perhaps for some future calling.

8278. What additional facilities can be provided to meet the wants of children of persons employed on the lines of railway ?—I have had a little experience with regard to the railway school at Cookhouse, and I think the Government might do somewhat more than they do. We have had a great deal of difficulty in connection with that school. It began with about twelve children in a small room, not more than 12 or 15, and it went on till there where between 30 and 40 in a small wooden place. It was a third class school, but nobody seemed to take any interest in it. When I went to Cookhouse to hold divine service, I enquired into the matter, and subsequently wrote to Mr. Elliott, the General Manager of Railways, putting the facts of the case before him, and I also wrote to Sir Langham Dale, who replied at once, but it was some months before there was any answer from the Railway Department. It was favourable when it came, but many months more elapsed before anything was done. They brought a wooden house from another part of the railway system, but after it arrived, it lay some months before they put it up.

8279. You think that prompt action and the prompt performance of promises of aid ought to go hand in hand ?—Yes. There is also a difficulty about the guarantee. Nobody at Cookhouse has any particular interest in the matter, as they are birds of passage, constantly going and coming, and they do not care to take any responsibility, the result being that the school suffers in many ways. I think the Railway Department might take the place of guarantors.

8280. Would you also put these railway schools under the proposed Board ?—Yes.

8281. Have you formed any opinion about the teaching of the Dutch language ? —No very pronounced opinion. I have been the commissioner for the University examinations in Somerset ever since they started, and taking the Elementary examination as a test, I should say that the Dutch children do not suffer any disadvantage from having instruction imparted in English. I think, taking them as a whole, that the Dutch children show as favourably in the examination as the English children do.

8282. Would you be in favour of adding another paper in Dutch to the Elementary examination and letting the marks count?—There could be no objection to having another paper in Dutch : either make it a special paper for which Dutch children can go in if they like, or give one or two alternative subjects, so that a boy might take mathematics or some other subject, that is to say, if the results of the Dutch paper were to count in the Elementary examination. I think Dutch should be a separate subject.

8283. Would you add the marks for the Dutch paper to the general marks, and have it a fifth paper?—I should let the present Elementary examination stand. I would not interfere with that at all; but you might have another alternative paper, and let the answers for that count, so that children having a knowledge of Dutch should have full opportunity of showing it.

8284. In view of the fact that Dutch is so generally spoken, is it not a good thing that it should be well learned?—It is desirable to have it well learned.

8285. In order to promote that, would it be a good thing to offer bursaries for those passing well in Dutch?—I would not give special bursaries for Dutch.

8286. Would not the effect be to induce many to go in for it who otherwise would not?—So far as I know, I think the number of those taking up Dutch is more than was the case a few years ago, without any attraction of bursaries. I judge that in connection with the college and other schools I know something about. Where formerly French used to be taken as a modern language, Dutch is now learned almost exclusively.

Rev. W. Leith.
Sept. 23rd, 1891.

Mr. J. S. Cowie examined.

8287. *President.*] I believe you are the Mayor of Beaconsfield?—Yes.

8288. Are there many children there who are not at school but who ought to be?—I think there is a large number.

8289. Do they belong to the poorer classes?—Yes.

Mr. J. S. Cowie.
Sept. 23rd, 1891.

8290. Why are they not at school?—In many cases because the parents cannot afford to send them to school.

8291. And in other cases?—That is about the only reason I can give for the majority not being at school.

8292. How would you provide schools for them?—My opinion is that the control of the matter ought to rest with the municipality.

8293. As it is constituted now?—Yes, with a little additional power given.

8294. You think the municipality ought to be a Board of Management, taking the place of the guarantors?—Yes.

8295. Have you a public undenominational school at Beaconsfield?—Yes.

8296. Would you admit all these children to that school free of charge?—It all depends. If we could get a grant of £300 a year from the Government, and the municipality provided another £300, I think we could make provision for a large number of the children who cannot afford to pay.

8297. And give free education in the existing public undenominational school?—Yes.

8298. Are there buildings enough for that?—Not quite.

8299. Then you would have to erect buildings, would you not?—Yes.

8300. Who would pay for them if you did?—Under the present arrangement, the Government would be willing to grant up to £1,000 on the £ for £ principle, and the municipality might give the rest.

8301. Would you force the municipality to do this work for the poorer children?—At the present time, our municipality could not afford to contribute anything towards buildings, and I would not like to advocate it with our present revenue. I would, however, advocate their borrowing the money for the purpose.

8302. Could they hire buildings?—They have a hired building now.

8303. Could not they hire further?—Yes, that could be done.

8304. Would you oblige them to find school accommodation and education for all the children of the poorer class?—Yes.

8305. Have you many mission schools at Beaconsfield?—At the present time we have two.

8306. Are they doing the principal work for the poorer classes?—They mostly teach the coloured population. The public undenominational school and All Saints school are the only schools of any consequence.

8307. Suppose the mission schools gave up the work, would you impose on the municipality the duty of finding schools for the poorer classes?—Yes, with the aid of the Government; it is not more than right.

8308. Which do you think is the best, for the municipality, or the mission schools to do the work?—I should say while they can do it, the mission schools are the best to

Mr.
J. S. Cowie.

Sept 23rd, 1891.

work schools for the coloured classes, but I would not like to see a poor man's children sent to a mission school and mixed up with blacks because he cannot afford to pay.

8309. Would you give the municipality any control over mission schools?—Not unless they gave any aid. If they gave aid at all, they would have to have control.

8310. Would you advise a system by which the municipality should have the power to recommend mission schools to receive further aid to do this work, if it was not prepared itself to give it?—Yes, I am certainly in favour of the municipality having that power or authority to recommend aid on behalf of the Government, if it is not willing to undertake it itself.

8311. Do you think the present education given in mission schools is entirely satisfactory for the natives or the poorer Europeans?—I think for the natives the education given is quite satisfactory.

8312. Do you think that industrial education for the poorer whites and the coloured children is desirable?—Most certainly.

8313. How would you work it?—Let the Government give additional aid for white children as well as to mission schools. I would say for the industrial training of white children the Government might give £150 grant, so as to enable the means to be provided, and for the coloured children £100, where the number exceeds one hundred.

8314. *Dr. Berry.*] Do you think it would be acceptable to your body of ratepayers that the municipality should contribute towards the schools?—Yes, I certainly think so. My opinion is that the ratepayers who pay the rates would not object to a small part being expended in that way.

8315. Do you come here representing the municipality?—I have been elected by the municipality, together with one of my colleagues, to give evidence here.

8316. May we take your opinion as the opinion of the body you represent?—I am here giving my own opinion, but I have advocated in the Council repeatedly that they should give aid even to the present school we have.

8317. *President.*] Have the municipality asked you to come here and represent their views?—Yes, and give my opinion.

8318. May we take it that the ratepayers are not opposed to being rated for the purpose?—I do not advocate an additional rate.

8319. You think if it is necessary and if the Government gives further aid, the municipality will come in and from the rates supply any deficiency, is that so?—My opinion is that they ought to.

8320. Have you formed any opinion with regard to the language question?—Being an Afrikander myself, I am very much in favour of the Dutch language being brought prominently forward, but at the same time I do not think it ought to be made compulsory. I am of opinion that bursaries or other encouragements to learn Dutch, which is very essential in this country, should be offered by the Government, so as to stimulate children to take it up. This year the boy in our public undenominational school who took the gold medal awarded by the municipality annually, for passing highest in the Elementary examination, was a Dutch boy. I think the Dutch language ought to be encouraged.

8321. Do you think your municipality might give a Dutch prize also?—I have not the least doubt they would do it.

8322. Are you in favour of levying an education tax on the natives?—Under the present law, a shilling is paid by natives when they obtain a pass, and that shilling goes to the hospital. As they do not contribute to the revenue of the country, I do not think it would be any hardship if another sixpence were charged when they take out a pass, and in that manner you could tax them in order to help the mission schools.

Mr. C. A. Blackbeard examined.

Mr.
A. Blackbeard.

Sept. 23rd, 1891.

8323. *President.*] I believe you are one of the municipal councillors at Beaconsfield?—Yes.

8324. Have you been deputed to come here and state your opinion?—Yes.

8325. Do you agree with the last witness that a number of the children requiring education at Beaconsfield is not reached by the present system?—A great many are not reached.

8326. The poorer class of whites and coloured children?—Yes. I am one of the committee of All Saints' School, and we have many children there whom we educate free, as the parents are unable to provide their education.

8327. Besides these children, are there others?—Yes, a number of others who do not go to any school.

8328. Why is that?—The parents are unable to pay.

8329. Do you think your school could receive them if they came, or would you require further accommodation?—We could provide for a great many more.

8330. Would you do so if you received further aid ?—We receive no aid from the Government at all. The Church of England members generally make up the deficiency.

Mr.
C. A. *Blackbeard*
Sept. 23rd, 1891.

8331. Do you think you are entitled to aid ?—Certainly.

8332. If you received aid, would you take all these poorer children who were brought to you ?—I would not say all, but we would take a great many. We do so now without aid.

8333. And the church finds the funds ?—Not the church ; the members.

8334. Are you in favour of compulsory education for these children ?—Yes.

8335. How would you get them to come, by means of the police ?—I have not thought of that.

8336. Do you think the municipality ought to be the controlling body in the matter of education ?—I think there might be the magistrate and one or two members from the Divisional Council and the municipality.

8337. Beaconsfield is within the district of Kimberley is it not ?--Yes.

8338. How would it do to have a Board elected by all the ratepayers for the whole district, which should be able to delegate its powers to a sub-committee at Beaconsfield, so as to work the schools there ?—I think that would be a feasible plan.

8339. Do you think the denominations there would work under that Board, if the condition was that they were to be inspected and receive aid ?—I certainly think so. The Roman Catholics have a mission school, and there is another one. I do not think either of those receive aid from the Government.

8340. Do you think they might receive aid on condition of being inspected, and proving that they were doing good work ?—Yes. There is a distinction between All Saints' mission school, which does get a grant, and All Saints' school, of which I am a member.

8341. You think the Board might wisely give aid to those schools, the Government contributing also ?—Certainly.

8342. How many children are there in All Saints' school proper, which receives no grant ?—I think we have about 60 or 70 at present.

8343. *Rev. Moorrees.*] What class of children are they ?—The better class. The parents can pay, although not all of them do.

8344. *Dean Holmes.*] Do you give a higher class of education there than in the mission school ?—Yes.

8345. What standard would the pupils reach ?—I cannot say.

8346. Do you know whether the pupils go up for the Teachers or Elementary examination ?—Only the Elementary.

8347. Who is the teacher ?—Miss Johnson.

8348. What fees do they charge ?—From five shillings to ten shillings a month.

8349. Have you a Dutch teacher ?—No.

8350. *Dr. Berry.*] Are you personally opposed to any grant from the municipal rates in support of schools ?—I am in favour of it.

8351. Generally, would a proposal of that sort be acceptable to your Board, do you think ?—I believe so.

8352. *President.*] Do you think industrial education could be added with advantage in the case of the poorer classes ?—Yes.

8353. Do you think there is a feeling among the people generally that it ought to be added ?--Yes. I think the £ for £ principle is scarcely enough to expect from the Government ; they ought to provide about two-thirds of the deficiency after the fees have been paid.

8354. *Rev. Moorrees.*] For all schools ?—Yes.

8355. *President.*] And the buildings ?—We have provided our own buildings.

8356. Do you think you would be prepared to hand over your buildings to a School Board if it was established ?—I should scarcely think so. As members of the church, we take an active interest in the school, whereas if it was left to the public, it is possible there would not be so much zeal manifested.

Rev. W. *Yule* examined.

8357. *President.*] What are you ?—Presbyterian minister at Beaconsfield.

8358. Are you a member of any School Committee ?—I am a member of the committee of the second class public undenominational school at Beaconsfield.

Rev
H. *Yule.*
Sept. 23rd, 1891.

8359. Having heard the evidence of the last two witnesses, do you agree with them with regard to the rates being liable for any deficiency in the school revenue ?—Yes, certainly ; but I should like to see all the scholars brought into one large undenominational school.

8360. Controlled by the electors ?—Yes ; either through the Council or a School Board elected by the ratepayers.

Rev.
B. Yule.

Sept. 23rd, 1891.

8361. Would you be in favour of a School Board for the whole district, delegating its power to a Board at Beaconsfield?—Yes, I would.

8362. Do you think that would work satisfactorily?—I speak from personal experience when I say that in Scotland the system works admirably.

8363. Do you think this Board might utilize volunteers, such as mission bodies, to do school work where they find themselves unable to do it?—I am not so sure about that; we have nothing of that sort in Scotland. I have only been out here a little over a year.

8364. Would you suppress the mission schools at once?—No. I would leave them just as they are; they do very well.

8365. Would you allow the School Board to work through them?—Yes.

8366. And recommend them to receive Government aid if they deserve it?—Yes.

8367. Rev. Moorrees.] How long have you been out here?—It is just fifteen months since I left London.

8368. President.] Is there free education in Scotland?—Yes; and it works very well.

8369. How does it work into the Board system?—There is one School Board for the centre, and they depute their power to committees to manage certain schools in the district.

8370. Virtually every child is compelled to go to school?—Yes.

8371. Do you think that a good thing?—Yes. It is very essential in Beaconsfield.

8372. Suppose every child receives free education, is it not a tax on the community?—I think it is about one of the best ways possible of spending money. I do not think it is ever regretted. I know that people at first find fault with it, but they gradually get to see it in another light.

8373. If they are taxed all round, it is very much the same as paying all round, is it not?—Yes; only in the one case the strong help the weak.

8374. How would you deal with the coloured population?—I do not know very much about that.

8375. Would your community be prepared to give free education all round to the blacks?—I do not know. I am not clear on that point.

8376. Should the principle of strong and weak apply there also?—I do not know.

8377. Is it not the fact that the blacks earn good wages as a rule, and yet they are not taxpayers?—That is so.

8378. That being so, do not they escape their share of the burden, which is all thrown on the whites?—Yes. I see no reason why all should not be taxed equally, if you include their children.

8379. How would you tax them if they are not reached by the present municipal rates?—I do not see any difficulty in levying a tax which would cover them.

8380. Do you think the present system is the best for the natives?—It is doing very well.

8381. Would you add industrial education?—Not unless it was made applicable to the whites as well.

8382. Do you think the whites require it too?—Yes. I may say that subject has been talked over pretty well in our committee in connection with the Beaconsfield school, and we are just on the point of asking the Government to give us a grant for the purpose of industrial training.

8383. What sort of industrial training?—Carpentry, joinery and blacksmith work.

8384. What grant will you ask for?—£50.

8385. What would you propose to do with that in the way of industrial training; would you start buildings?—We must have an additional building.

8386. What would that cost you?—About £200.

8387. How many boys would you propose to have in it?—As many as the place would hold. The instruction should be given for about two hours a day.

8388. Would you employ an additional master?—Yes. We must have a competent teacher.

Rev. George Mitchell examined.

Rev.
George Mitchell.

Sept. 23rd, 1891.

8389. President.] I believe you are a clerk in holy orders at Kimberley, and Church of England missionary at the native compound?—Yes.

8390. Have you any schools?—Yes; two.

8391. Who teaches there?—Myself. Adult natives are in the schools; they come down to work in the mines. They can only get time to come to school which they spare from their sleeping hours. It is entirely voluntary on their part. I used to have a night school, but that has been discontinued for several reasons. I have my school

315

Rev.
George Mitchell.
—
Sept. 2nd, 1891.

at De Beer's mine from 7 till 9 in the morning, and at the Central mine from half past 2 till 4 in the afternoon. The men work night and day shifts, and it is only when they are working in the night shift that they are able to come to school.

8392. *Dean Holmes.*] Do you get any aid from Government?—No; those who come to school pay a shilling a week.

8393. *President:*] What number have you in the schools?—For the present quarter, the number at the Central mine is 18, and at De Beer's 17. They attend very irregularly, and the schools are not very flourishing. If I get as many as eight, I think I have a good school.

8394. Who supplies the building?—The De Beer's Consolidated Mines, and I give my services. Last year the number that attended was 75 at De Beer's and 53 at the Central. Sometimes they come only for a week, and sometimes they will go on seven or eight weeks.

8395. Why has there been a falling off?—Sometimes the men get ill, or they leave the compounds.

8396. What natives are they?—Basutos principally; they come down to work in the mines.

8397. *Rev. Moorrees.*] Are there any other schools in the compounds?—Yes; the Lutherans have a school and the Wesleyans had one, but it has been discontinued some time. The Lutherans have a school in the morning at the Central; I do not know what their hour is at De Beer's.

8398. *Mr. Theron.*] Are those all schools for natives?—Yes; for secular instruction.

8399. Are there any schools for the children of Europeans employed at the mines?—There is a school at Kenilworth for European children at the present time.

8400. *Dean Holmes.*] Are there any native boys employed by the company who ought to be at school; too young to be at work in fact?—Yes; there are some.

8401. *President.*] How would you deal with them?—It is very difficult, as they only remain for a month or two perhaps.

8402. Are you acquainted with the mission school here?—Yes.

8403. Do you think it would be wise to add some industrial education for these children?—I have a theory of my own about that. I think that the colony ought to have central industrial institutions in different parts, where a large number of children could be taught. It is a waste of money and energy to have a number of little institutions of the kind.

8404. Would you have one in Kimberley?—Yes.

8405. Would you bring all the coloured children to one of these centres and give them industrial combined with a certain amount of literary training?—I think it should only be voluntary, except in the case of orphans with no home, who might perhaps be boarded there.

8406. Do you consider that industrial is better than literary teaching for these children?—I think they want a little of both.

8407. Are you in favour of compulsory education?—Yes; I wish we had that system.

8408. If you force them into literary schools, could not you also force them into industrial schools?—Yes; I think the State ought to provide in some way for the education of all children, otherwise they grow up to be a dangerous element. There are hundreds of children here growing up without education.

8409. What industries would you give instruction in?—Shoemaking, carpentry, tailoring and such trades as are useful for the natives. I know the case of one native who has gone down from here to Cape Town to learn shoemaking. He is one of Khama's people.

8410. Do you think that most of these natives would be able to pay something for their teaching?—I do not think so.

8411. Have they no means of paying?—They might if they took care of their money, but unfortunately they have not been taught the habit of thrift. They do not know the value of money, and they spend it as soon as they get it.

8412. Suppose the parents cannot pay or will not pay for their children's education, what would you do. Would you take the children away from the parents entirely?—I do not think that under the British Government we can act so despotically as to compulsorily take children away from their parents. There is no law that would support that.

8413. Do you think it is expedient to run these children into some school?—Yes, certainly.

8414. *Dean Holmes.*] Are there young white boys employed at the mines to attend to the points?—Yes; there are some white boys who do that work. It would be far better if they were still at school, but I suppose the parents are poor, and glad

Rev.
George Mitchell.

Sept. 23rd, 1891.

for the children to earn a little money. Morally speaking, I should say it was very undesirable for them.

8415. What is the age of these children?—About twelve or thirteen.

8416. *President.*] Is there a growing desire for education here in Kimberley?—I cannot speak generally. I can speak particularly as to the natives, and among the Basuto tribes there is a tremendous desire for education. Those natives at the compounds who come to school do so under very great difficulties, and at great self-denial.

8417. To what do you attribute that; is it due to the system of schools in existence in Basutoland?—They are anxious to improve themselves, and be able to read and write. You would be surprised at the number of letters they write to their countrymen, though some of them are not very legible.

8418. Are they also anxious for industrial education?—Yes, but it is impracticable, because they attend only for a short time.

Dr. Arnold Watkins examined.

Dr.
Arnold Watkins.

Sept. 23rd, 1891.

8419. *Dr. Berry.*] I believe you are a medical practitioner residing in Kimberley?—Yes.

8420. Have you been a long time in the colony?—Sixteen years in the colony and six years in Kimberley.

8421. I believe before residing here you lived at Alice?—I was at Boshof, in the Free State, for eight years, and at Alice two years.

8422. Have you any practical knowledge of the working of our educational system in the colony?—I have been a member of the School Board here for five years, and I was a member of the School Board at Boshof, in the Free State, for five or six years.

8423. Do you know anything about the irregularity of attendance of children at school here?—I have not paid much attention to it.

8424. What steps do you think should be taken to give Boards of Management perpetual succession, and provide for the tenure of public school property. You are aware of the present method of electing Boards of Management for public schools, are you not?—Yes. The present system of guarantors is not very satisfactory. At the expiration of three years, it amounts to the old committee forming themselves into a public meeting and re-electing themselves. There is practically no competition.

8425. Consequently there is very little interest taken in the matter except by the guarantors?—Quite so. I complained of it at the last annual meeting here.

8426. What do you think that arises from?—I think it is because the public do not feel that there is any question at issue. If there were any special question at issue, either political, religious or otherwise, they would turn up, but as long as the school goes on smoothly they do not trouble.

8427. Suppose the question of rating for school purposes was to come up, would that evoke more interest, do you think?—I imagine it would, but it is hard to say.

8428. Would you propose any amendment on the present plan?—I have no proposition to make.

8429. You are aware that the guarantors are responsible for any deficiency that may arise in the management of the school, are you not?—Yes, but deficiencies do not arise after the schools are once started; it is only at starting.

8430. They have arisen in some instances. Do you think it is fair that the guarantors should be saddled with the deficiency?—No; I do not think it is. A deficiency may arise through the outbreak of an epidemic, necessitating the closing of the schools. The burden ought to fall on the whole body of the public, not simply on those who choose to make themselves responsible.

8431. Is it not a defect of the present system that there is nobody charged with the duty of bringing schools into existence where they are needed?—Yes; when we started our school here, it was left entirely to the energy of three or four men to work it up. Mr. Samuel had failed before to get a public school started.

8432. Would not a Board be a good thing, upon whom the Government could call to provide such schools as were needed by the community?—Yes; I think it would certainly.

8433. Do you think it would be right that such Board should be elected by the ratepayers of the district?—Yes, I think so, certainly. It should not be a Government nominee Board.

8434. You would be in favour of a Board having the right to call upon the Divisional Council, say for any deficiency that might arise in the school revenue?—Yes, provided they could show good cause for the deficiency.

8435. How much do you think the local body ought to be called upon to contribute; would you put any limit on it, or would you make them liable for any *bonâ fide* deficiency. Assuming there is a Government grant, and the fees are paid, and over and above that

a deficiency arises in the school management, who should be called upon to pay it?— Dr.
Arnold Watkins.
The local rates.

Sept. 23rd, 1891.

8436. Would you limit that amount in any case, or would you say that they should be called upon to pay whatever deficiency arose?—I would not limit the amount, provided it could be shewn that the deficiency had arisen, *bona fide*, through circumstances which were unavoidable.

8437. I believe you have resided for some considerable time in a district largely inhabited by natives?—Yes. I was for two years at Alice among the native population.

8438. What do you think ought to be done in the way of educating the children of these natives?—I think that you should give every facility for education to those who desire it. I doubt whether the time has arrived when you should have compulsory education for native children.

8439. Would not you be in favour of compulsion in the case of all children living in towns, both whites and blacks?—I would, certainly, for whites and for Cape coloured people, and perhaps Kafirs residing in towns. It rather depends upon what you mean by living in towns. If you had a large location adjacent to a town, I should not call that residing in a town. I am not sure that I would compel the children of a man living in a straw hut outside a town to attend school. I would afford them every facility.

8440. What would you do with a child if the authorities reported that it was growing up idle and dissolute; would you not force such a child into school?—I do not think so.

8441. Would you force it to go to work?—I imagine if he wants work he will seek it, or his parents will send him.

8442. Take a child between seven and fourteen; would not you be in favour of some steps being taken to prevent that child and other children of a similar class, growing up in habits of idleness and vice?—I object to the system of apprenticing to masters on a large scale; on a small scale it may be a valuable way of disposing of some of the waifs and strays. On a large scale I think it would be a very dangerous proceeding.

8443. Would you be in favour of levying an educational tax on these natives to help pay for the cost of their schooling?—I think so. It is fair that they should contribute to whatever they enjoy the benefits of.

8444. Do not you think it would be the means of encouraging or stimulating them to go to school if they were made to pay for it, whether they went to school or not?—Perhaps.

8445. Have you studied at all the colonial method of educating the natives?—I have not; I have seen something of it at Lovedale. I lived close to Lovedale for some time, and I saw a good deal of it there.

8446. Do you think the system adopted at Lovedale could be extended throughout the whole of the colony?—I think it might be very largely extended. I see no reason why it should not.

8447. Is it not a very costly system?—I could not say. I think each native contributes £5 a year towards the expense.

8448. Can you suggest any method by which some industrial training can be given to the natives on a less costly or extravagant scale; are you in favour, for instance, of manual industry being added to the ordinary curriculum in a native school, such as carpentry, brickmaking, and gardening?—I do not think there is any difficulty about their learning trades; whenever their parents like, they can get them taught some trade by apprenticing them. The apprenticeship must be left to the parent and not to the Government, if he wishes a boy to learn a trade. You do not want them all to learn trades, there must be some labourers in the country.

8449. Are you in favour of teaching them to labour?—I do not think a man wants teaching how to dig a piece of ground.

8450. The census returns show that there must be over a quarter of a million of native children now in this colony who cannot be accounted for in the schools at all, and who cannot be accounted for in the labour supply of the country, and the unavoidable inference is that they are growing up in habits of idleness and bad conduct, and it is part of the duty of this Commission to see if it cannot make some recommendation under that head which the Government can carry out; have you anything to suggest so as to help us to come to a reasonable conclusion in the matter?—Anything in that direction must be a matter of time; you cannot expect in the course of one generation to effect a complete change in the native habits, and deal with the question *en bloc* so to speak.

8451. What do you think should be done by way of a beginning?—You must give all the facilities you can for education, and make it cheap and practical.

RR 2

Dr.
Arnold Watkins.

Sept. 23rd, 1891.

8452. How would you be in favour of making it cheap; by giving large Government grants or taxing the natives themselves?—Perhaps both. I would certainly be in favour of adding industrial training where it can be done.

8453. Would you put the management of that system into the hands of a local Board elected in the division in which it is to be carried out, or would you keep it in the hands of the Education Department in Cape Town?—You must keep it in the hands of the Department in Cape Town. I do not think you must place the education of the Kafirs in the hands of white men who happen to live in their neighbourhood.

8454. Why not?—Because I do not think from my experience of the colony, that as a rule the white man is keenly anxious about the interests of the native. I do not mean that he would do what is grossly unfair in any way, but the average farmer will not certainly take a keen interest in the civilization and education of the natives in his neighbourhood.

8455. Do not you think he might do so more than he has done if it was understood that the native had to pay a good deal towards it?—He does not feel that he has a duty towards the native; and if he does not feel that, why should he go out of his way to look after the schools in which they are to be educated.

8456. Suppose Parliament says it is a duty which must be discharged, how would it be then?—A duty which a man discharges because Parliament tells him is badly discharged as a rule.

8457. Would you prefer leaving all this to the Central Department in Cape Town?—The education of the natives, certainly.

8458. Do you think anything can be done here in the matter of night schools?—I am afraid not much. We tried it in our undenominational schools, and started classes to enable young men to pass their B.A. or Matriculation examination in Cape Town, but it fell through for want of attendance. There was an opportunity given, but they did not come. It is very difficult, unless they have got to pass an examination or have some other object in view, to get them to attend these schools. I think nevertheless they should have an opportunity if possible.

8459. Do you know anything about technical education?—Very little. It would be difficult to introduce it here on anything like the scale on which it is provided for in some English Board Schools.

8460. Would you be in favour of adding a trade class to our public schools, and let a master tradesman attend for two or three hours a week to give instruction in the use of tools and so on, to the boys attending the school?—I think that might be done with advantage. It would not be really adding to their school duties; it would be a sort of play hour to them.

8461. Have you any such department in connection with your school?—No.

8462. Have you anything else to suggest?—With regard to our schools here, I think the Government should give in places like Kimberley a local allowance in the case of school teachers, as is done in so many other branches of the civil service. The salaries paid are inadequate for a place like Kimberley. We do not get aid on the £ for £ principle; we get a certain Government allowance, and we have to give the larger share ourselves towards the payment of the teacher.

8463. *President.*] Are you in favour of starting a normal school here?—No; I do not think it would be a good training place for teachers, but we ought to get a higher allowance, because living is more expensive. We have to pay our native teachers £150 a year; they cannot live decently on less, and the Government only give £60, so that we have to pay £90 ourselves out of the school funds.

Mr. Gardner F. Williams examined.

Mr.
Gardner F. Williams.

Sept. 23rd, 1891.

8464. *President.*] I believe you are general manager at the De Beer's Consolidated Mines?—Yes.

8465. What are you by profession?—A mining engineer.

8466. You have a technical knowledge of the work?—Yes.

8467. Would you advise starting a technical school in Kimberley?—That is a very difficult question to answer, for the reason that living is very expensive here, and if boys have to come from other localities, it is a question whether the school would be well patronised, as it would be costly for parents to send children here to be educated. It is a very serious matter with those who have to educate their children.

8468. Have you any knowledge of the special working of any technical schools in Europe or America?—I was for three years in a school of mines in Saxony. It was a purely mining and metallurgical school.

8469. Are you in favour of starting a technical school on such lines here?—You would require to have it on a very modified plan, owing to the expense of tuition and getting proper professors.

Mr.
Gardner F
Williams.

Sept. 23rd, 1891.

8470. What scheme would you suggest?—You must have all the necessary technical apparatus for learning mining. as it is necessary to get a practical as well as a theoretical knowledge. You must have professors properly trained and educated, and all that becomes expensive unless the attendance is very large. After thinking the matter over, the conclusion I came to is this, that those who could afford to send their boys here might just as well send them to England or elsewhere and put them at a mining or mechanical engineering school, where the facilities are better than we can expect to have for many years. I doubt if the attendance would be very great, owing to the cost of living here ; and it would cost very much more than the education of a boy at home.

8471. Do not you think we ought to make a beginning?—Yes, you might make a beginning.

8472. What sort of a beginning would you make?—I am a comparative stranger here. I have only been at Kimberley about four years, and therefore cannot speak very authoritatively, but I should advise starting a small school, if it could be done, in connection with some other institution, such as a public undenominational school.

8473. Would you have the technical and literary education going on simultaneously, or would you first complete the literary education before starting the technical?—As a rule, the ordinary education goes on till a boy is 17 or 18, and then he goes to a technical school. I have a boy 17 years of age, and I am going to send him to the Massachusetts School of Technology, where he will have a three or four years' course.

8474. Is he not training now in some sort of way?—He is in California at a private school, and is being educated with a view to going to an institution where they teach mechanics, mining, metallurgy, engineering and so on.

8475. Which of those branches do you think could be started with the best hope of success here?—I should say mechanics and mining. We have not any metallurgical works of any magnitude : that could be added later on. Mechanics and mining offer the best employment here for labour.

8476. Could a department where these subjects were taught be tacked on to any school in existence here?—I should think not.

8477. Then you would not recommend starting anything of the kind in Kimberley?—It would cost a great deal of money to make a commencement, and Kimberley is a very expensive place.

8478. With regard to your son, in preparation for his future career, what sort of a training has he been undergoing?—In the United States there are schools outside of the public schools where you can send a boy, and he is educated upon certain lines laid down in the regulations. If he is going to enter upon a classical course at the university, he has tuition accordingly, or perhaps he has a mathematical or a scientific training. In America, there are different universities, and he enters that for which he has been educated. There is a mechanical department, a metallurgical department, and so on, connected with all our universities. Then again, in connection with our public schools, there are workshops where boys become familiar with the use of tools, and they get sufficient knowledge to go to work about a house and do almost anything. That is really more play than study for them. Such departments have been introduced very successfully in schools answering to your public undenominational schools here. Many of these boys take up mechanical studies afterwards.

8479. Is drawing taught?—Yes.

8480. Have you heard of the Heriot School?—Yes. Such schools have grown up from a small beginning, and so you must grow here. In some of the United States, technical education is given free, and the cost of maintaining the universities is met in two ways, one is by State aid, through the sale of public lands, and the other by means of private contributions. Large donations are sometimes made, and the interest on this money goes to pay for professors ; but of course all this is greater than the needs of South Africa demand.

8481. It has been suggested to have an itinerant lecturer, who should go about from place to place with his apparatus and lecture upon technical matters, those attending undergoing an examination at the end of the time, and receiving a certificate if they pass, which would entitle them to admission into the Government workshops at Uitenhage or Salt River. Are you in favour of that?—It would no doubt induce many to turn their minds in that direction, but you cannot gain much knowledge simply from lectures. The pupils must study and take up the thing in earnest.

8482. Could not the mines here be utilized in some way?—After the students had received a certain amount of technical education, they could come here in charge of a professor and have access to the mines, or they could go to Johannesburg, where they would see very good mining going on, or they might, as far as mechanical work is concerned, go to Uitenhage or Salt River, the Government granting them facilities for practical education there. They would then see how work was done and get a thorough

Mr.
Gardner F.
Williams.
———
Sept. 23rd, 1891.

insight into the matter. When I was in Cape Town, I saw Dr. Hahn, who is very anxious to attach a technical department to the South African College, and he urged me to see Mr. Rhodes about it and see if something could not be done, but Mr. Rhodes was too busy at the time to go into it. I know Dr. Hahn wishes to make a beginning in Cape Town, and I think the idea is a very good one, to connect such a department with the South African College. I should be very glad to urge the same sort of thing at Kimberley if I could see my way clear, but it is really a question of expense.

8483. Is not the cost of living here much less than formerly?—It is cheaper, but it is still much greater than in other places.

8484. *Mr. Theron.*] You think that the theoretical part of the instruction might be given at college, and then the students could come to Kimberley or Johannesburg to prosecute the practical part?—Yes.

8485. And those who wanted to go in for engineering could go to the Government workshops?—Yes. They would get an insight into the work there.

8486. Are there any schools at Kenilworth?—Yes, we have a school for the children there.

8487. Is it an undenominational school?—No. Those who live at Kenilworth and send their children contribute so much towards the expense, and the company give aid on the £ for £ principle.

8488. Is it a free school?—Yes; for any well behaved child residing in the village.

8489. Is it limited to the employés of the company?—Yes; we have not a regular school house, but we have taken half of one of the new houses as school rooms, and they are just debating, as the school has increased to such an extent, about increasing the teaching staff.

8490. Then as far as Kenilworth is concerned, you have provided for that?—Yes; there has been some talk about coming under Government control, but nothing has been decided. Mr. Norrie asked why we did not come under the Government, but I do not know why the Government should take us over; it would only be an expense, and if the De Beer's Company is willing to contribute, why should the Government be anxious to step in. There are only 21 houses altogether at Kenilworth, but some of the families are very large. In one case, eight children from one family attend the school.

8491. Inside your compounds do you allow teachers for those men who wish to receive instruction?—Yes; all denominations who have asked have been accorded permission to go into the compounds. Mr. Morris and Mr. Mitchell come frequently, but the others I do not meet as often. Those two are constantly going to the compounds, and they hold service there as well as school. A number of the boys attend when they are off work. I have not gone into the details of the thing, but I should say it was more religious teaching than anything else.

8492. So that although these natives are in the compounds, they are not altogether neglected as far as that goes?—They are not neglected. Most of them are grown up men and rather beyond book learning I should say.

8493. But there are facilities for them, you say?—Yes; it rests entirely with the various denominations.

8494. *President.*] Have you any night schools in the compounds?—I think the school is generally held in the day time.

8495. If there was any necessity for night schools, I suppose the chances are that they would be started on the same principle, would they not?—It all rests with the teachers; they have full liberty to do what they think best within reason. Our only object is to retain our labour.

8496. Do you think it is a good thing in this country to have literary training supplemented in its early stages by some sort of industrial training for both whites and blacks?—I think it would be very useful. My idea about the blacks is that they are the tillers of the soil, and they should be treated somewhat as we treat our native races in America, allow them to retain large areas of country, and furnish them with every facility to cultivate that. We call it a reserve, and certain people are obliged to live on these reserves. In this country you allow these natives to go and seek for labour. So far as industrial training is concerned, I should confine it more to the white population. You have a very large white population, which it is difficult to provide for, and the better skilled their labour is, the better chance will they have of making a living for themselves. In the native reserves in America, Government furnishes them with a large amount of supplies in the shape of agricultural implements and seeds, and they are under supervision. Someone is appointed to look after them, and they are assisted as much as possible to carry on agricultural pursuits.

8497. Are those agricultural pursuits limited to that reserve?—As far as the natives are concerned, that is only for their own maintenance.

8498. Are not they allowed to go abroad if they like ?—No. If they go abroad, they become rather difficult people to handle. They are put on these locations, and we try to keep them there. It is not a small tract of land, but hundreds of thousands of acres; almost a State. In this country I think it would be better for natives if something of the kind was done.

8499. Do those men whom you place over them teach them agricultural pursuits and so on ?—They are taught to a certain extent to dig and use agricultural implements.

8500. Do they get any sort of literary training ?—I think so, and some of the tribes become very well educated. A tribe called the Cherokees are well educated, and they learn to raise crops, build huts, and work for themselves in every way.

8501. Are not they allowed to come out of the reserves to sell their produce ?—Buyers go to them if they have anything to sell. I do not know exactly how it is done, but facilities are offered for the sale of produce if there is an over supply. There are stations all round about.

8502. You do not want the native labour supply outside these areas, do you ?—Our native supply is different to what it is in this country. An Indian never works outside the reserve; he raises his own mealies and so on. In this country you can train the natives to work. I say, first do all you can for the white man, because the native can make a living if you give him a piece of land to till. It is the white man who suffers in this country. The native people can provide for themselves far better than the whites can.

8503. Do you think the natives could as a rule till the ground here to advantage ?—It depends on the season of course. We had a good crop of mealies last year at Kenilworth, twelve or fifteen acres.

8504. What would you suggest to induce the children of the lower class of whites to go in for labour; what sort of training would you give them ?—That is very difficult to say. I do not know that we have got anything that you can put children into the same as in older countries; there are no manufactures for instance.

8505. Have you any industries that you could employ them on ?—I do not know of anything. The conditions of this country are very different from what they are in Europe or America. There the white man has to work, but here the white man wants the native to work for him.

8506. Would you encourage industrial training for native children to fit them for agricultural work ?—The natives should be the tillers of the soil, and the white population should be taught higher industrial pursuits.

8507. What would the farmers do for shepherds here if the natives were kept in their locations ?—In England that work is all done by white people, and I have seen the same thing in California, and I do not see why it should be different in this country, except it is that white men could not stand the climate.

8508. Do you think it is rather a good thing for the poorer class of whites on farms to take to herding among other things ?—It is better for them to take to anything they can to make an honest living, rather than grow up in idleness. The trouble with a large percentage of our population is that they have really no calling; mechanics, miners, and people of that class are nearly all employed; but the people among whom distress exists are very often the sons of Cape farmers, who come up here without education of any kind, and get to be overseers perhaps, which is really no trade at all, as they have only to sit and watch the natives. Owing to the underground working, that occupation has pretty well gone out of fashion, and as these men are fit for nothing else and have never been trained for anything else, they feel it.

8509. Do you think a large industrial school in Kimberley for the children of whites would be a good thing to start ?—I think it would be a help. I do not know whether you can carry it out or not, but perhaps in connection with the schools here it might be tried as an experiment. I think something should be done for the white population in the way of industrtrial training. For instance, in this country you can raise an enormous quantity of fruit, and yet a great deal of canned fruit is imported from elsewhere. Here, it seems to me, is a good opening, which should lead to the employment of a number of people.

8510. Should we not begin with industrial schools for whites, and take the matter in hand thoroughly, instead of sending our sons to England ? —It would be a very good thing if you could manage it, and no doubt a small commencement might lead to large results.

Rev. W. Pescod examined.

8511. *President.*] I believe you are in charge of the Wesleyan mission school at Beam-street, Kimberley ?—Yes.

8512. How many children have you ?—There are 187 on the books.

Mr
Gardner F.
Williams.

Sept. 23rd, 1891.

Rev.
W. Pescod.

Sept. 23rd, 1891.

Rev.
n. *Pescod.*

Sept. 23·d, 1891.

8513. What is the average attendance ?—150.

8514. Do you consider that fairly regular ?—Yes.

8515. What contribution do you get from Government ?—£75 a year.

8516. How many assistants have you ?—Three assistants besides the principal teacher.

8517. Are there any white children in the school ?—Two or three.

8518. Are there many children outside of any education in this place ?--I think there are.

8519. Do you think it is desirable for the Government to step in and bring them all under education ?—Yes. I think it is very desirable.

8520. How would you do it ?—By compelling people to send their children to school.

8521. How would you operate upon them ; would you fine those who did not send their children, and take up those children found about the street ?—Yes, and I would enforce regularity of attendance on those coming to school.

8522. If that were done, would there be room enough in the existing schools here ?—No.

8523. How would you manage then ?—We should have to fall back on people for contributions for new buildings, and get subscriptions and donations.

8524. Would that be sufficient do you think ?—In all probability we should have to come to the Government for a little assistance. I should use all my influence first to get as much as I could from the people, and then from the Government.

8525. Do you think it would be a good thing to a have a School Board ?—Not in connection with mission schools.

8526. Would volunteers be found willing to do the work ?—In a place like Kimberley, people are very liberal in supporting education.

8527. How is it then there are so many outside of any education ?—I think one reason is that the people have not been educated themselves, and they do not see the advantage of educating their children. Another reason is, that some of the people are very poor.

8528 If there was compulsory education, would you want enlarged buildings ?—Yes ; and an additional grant for carrying on the work of teaching.

8529. You think if that were supplied it would be enough ?—I think so.

8530. As you are not bound to do this work, would it not be a good thing for the electors in a district to appoint a Board to see where education is wanted, and supply the want either through the medium of mission schools, by giving them contributions, or else find schools themselves ?—It would be a very good thing for Divisional Councils to contribute something towards the support of public schools, but I should be sorry to see such a body stepping in to govern mission schools.

8531. Why ?—Some of the members do not know very much about the working of schools.

8532. Do you think mission schools are necessary ?—Yes ; the mission bodies are the only bodies to supply schools for the poor.

8533. Is not that because there has been no other body charged with the duty ?—Yes.

8534. Is it not advisable to have another body ?—Perhaps so.

8535. *Dr. Berry.*] Is there anything special about mission schools that could not be overtaken by a Board having the power to get funds by the assistance of the rates ?—Of course, if such a Board were elected, there would no longer be mission schools.

8536. Is there any special reason why there should be mission schools in preference to public schools ?—I do not know that there is.

8537. Is there any particular work done in mission schools that could not be done by public schools ?—No.

8538. That being so, is it not the first duty of the community to see that these schools are provided ?—Yes.

8539. Has the community any right to leave the burden to a few individuals here and there ?—No, I do not think it has.

8540. *Mr. Theron.*] In the case of mission schools, are they burdens ?—As regards my school, the town has not been burdened with the support of it. I have worked it up to the present without asking any outside aid.

8541. If your school was changed into a public school it would become an unde-nominational school, and would lose its denominational character, and the religious teaching would perhaps be limited to an hour or half-an-hour a day, as the case may be ; would you object to that ?—I think I should. I should prefer to teach the children, as I have the responsibility of finding the funds to a very large extent, and have worked the school up.

Rev.
W. Pescod.

Sept. 23rd, 1891.

8542. *Rev. Moorrees.*] Would you object to change your school into an undenominational school if a public Board undertook the responsibility?—As regards my own school, I should be sorry to turn it into a public school. I have worked it up myself from the beginning. I commenced with about six children.

8543. *Dean Holmes.*] Would you be willing to work it under the supervision of a Board if you were allowed all the management and internal discipline arrangements?—I do not think so. I would not like it.

8544. *Rev. Moorrees.*] Is your school attended chiefly by coloured or white children?—Chiefly by coloured children. It is a school for coloured children; we have a few whites; but as a rule, I discourage them; I do not care for their coming.

8545. *Dean Holmes.*] You do not approve of mixing the colours, do you?—No; and more than that, the influence of coloured children is not good always for white children, and the influence of the white children is not good for the coloured children. The white children coming to our mission schools seem to think they can do pretty much as they like.

8546. *President.*] Do you think it would be wise to start night schools here?—Yes.

8547. Have you ever started one?—Not myself, but I have encouraged my teacher to do so.

8548. Has he started one?—He had one last winter, but it was not a very successful school, simply because he had to work all day himself and at it's close all his energy was spent. I do not approve of a man working in the day time and at night also.

8549. If there was a Government grant which would enable him to have an assistant at the night school, and he simply supervised the work, would that help?—I should not care for that exactly. I think that a night school should be officered by someone who can give his whole energies to it, and it should be worked as efficiently as a day school.

8550. Do you think there is an opening for such a school here?—I think so.

8551. *Rev. Moorrees.*] Would you get a regular attendance at such a school?—I think so. There are night schools during the winter months in pretty nearly every part of the Camp.

8552. *Dr. Berry.*] What class of lads would come?—Lads working in shops and offices.

8553. What would you say would be the most practicable method of starting such a school here?—I think the Government should be approached for some assistance, and the teacher should devote himself solely to the night school work. Regular fees should also be charged, as in the day schools.

8554. What conditions would you attach to the issue of a public grant: what should Government demand from the managers of a night school?—The school should be under inspection, and a certain number should attend in order to secure the grant.

8555. What salary would the teacher require?—If that was his only work, he would require £3 or £4 a week, say £150 a year.

8556. Would not that be rather high for the colony generally?—In some parts so much would not be required.

8557. *Dean Holmes.*] Would you keep such a school open all the year round?—No.

8558. Would you object to its being placed under a public board if it were established?—No.

8559. *President.*] What age would the children attending the night school be?—It would vary from twelve to twenty.

8560. Would you have night schools for boys at twelve years old?—There are boys in shops and offices at that age.

8561. Ought they not to be in a day school?—Yes, no doubt.

8562. If you provide a day school for them they would not require a night school, would they?—No.

8563. Is not a night school rather for boys who have left school, after they have reached sixteen, say?—That is my idea of a night school, but in Kimberley the children are sent out to work as soon as they can earn anything.

8564. Do you think that is a misfortune and ought to be stopped?—Yes, decidedly.

8565. What are these young boys employed at?—As errand boys, and so on.

8566. Have you thought of industrial schools in connection with your native schools?—No.

8567. Do not you think it would be a good thing to associate some industry with the literary teaching if you got an additional grant?—I do, if the conveniences and accommodation are available.

8568. What would you do if you had an additional grant?—I would teach the boys a little carpentering work, shoemaking, tinsmiths' work, and so on.

Rev.
W. Pescod

Sept. 23rd, 1891.

8569. Could you work that sort of thing here in the town?— It would be very difficult to work it here, but it is a very desirable thing.

8570. What aid would you require to work such a school with fair efficiency?—I could not say.

8571. If you got £100 a year, could you do it well?—I am scarcely prepared to say. Men who teach these trades demand high wages.

8572. Do you think it is necessary for the blacks to learn trades; is it not better for the general run of them to learn how to use a spade and to use their hands?—Yes; they ought to have same manual labour. I should be in favour of teaching them trades.

8573. If a boy has been taught to dig, cannot he always get work. There is not much digging in a place like Kimberley.

8574. If you taught the natives trades, would it not interfere with the Europeans, a good many of whom are out of employ?—I do not think so.

8575. It seems there is a number of poor European boys here who do not find their way to school; what do you think ought to be done with them?—I do not know. I think where the parents are not able to pay for their education, additional grants might be given to schools that received them.

8576. Would you have industrial schools for them?—I should be very glad to see them.

8577. Do not they want industrial training more than the black boys?—I do not know that they want it more. If they are willing to work in the garden, or on the farm, there is always something for them to do.

8578. Is it within your experience that coloured boys like literary training and are fond of it?—I do not think so as a rule. I think they are fonder of trades.

8579. Are your boys the sons of Basutos?—Cape people; half castes. With regard to mission schools, I am of opinion that we scarcely receive an adequate grant for the amount of work that is done. For instance, I have 187 children on the books, and there are other schools in town just as well attended as mine. We only receive a grant of £75 a year. When the attendance was only about 120, I received the same amount of grant, and my school is far more efficient now than it was twelve months ago. There is a better attendance, and the children come more regularly, but although I require more assistance in teaching, the grant remains the same.

8580. What grant ought you to get in order to do the work thoroughly?—I have three assistants and a principal teacher. I also teach myself in order to get the children forward, and to keep the school out of debt. I think we should receive something similar to what a third class school does, that is £60 a year for the principal teacher and £30 for each assistant.

8581. You think you ought to get about £150 a year?—I think when a school has attained a certain standing, and can pass a certain number of children in the different standards, an additional grant should be made.

8582. Would it do if the Government paid you so much per head, according to the average attendance, where you pass the children in a certain standard; would that system do?—No, I think it tends to pushing children on so as to get a larger grant.

8583. Suppose you got so much a head upon the average attendance, and upon approval after inspection?—Yes, that would do.

8584. How much per head do you think would be fair?—I think £1 per head.

8585. If you got that, would you include industrial training?—I am afraid it would be very difficult for us in Kimberley to do that; we have not the accommodation.

8586. *Dean Holmes.*] Would you be satisfied with the scale of payment proposed by Sir Langham Dale in regard to fourth class public undenominational schools? —Yes; that would suit me. Why I referred to this is, that we see of course the reports of the third class public schools, and we are really doing the same work. I do not refer to my school alone, but also to schools in connection with other churches, who do the same amount of work, and yet our grant is only about half what is given to a third class public school.

8587. Why do not you offer to do third class public school work and get their pay?—I should require to have a Board of guarantors.

8588. If a Board were brought into existence, all you would have to do would be to go to them and satisfy them you are doing the work, and ask them to recommend you to Government for a grant; would not you like that?—I should prefer working through the Government Inspector himself. I think he is better qualified to report on the school than any outside body.

8589. The Government would not give any grant without first sending an Inspector to ascertain whether the Board's recommendation is verified; do you think you are likely to be unfairly treated by that system?—I should not care for the school to be under a School Board.

8590. Is it because you are afraid of it?—No; but you may not always get the right men on the Board.

8591. *Rev. Moorrees.*] You would prefer an increased grant, but you would like it to come direct from the Superintendent-General of Education?—I should not like to say because I receive the grant I am to have the governing of the school; far from it. I should prefer the grant to depend on the numbers attending the school and the efficiency.

8592. Taking your school as it is, you think you ought fairly to get a larger grant, but you would prefer that grant to come from the Superintendent-General of Education?—Yes.

The Most Rev. Bishop Gaughran examined.

8593. *President.*] I believe you are Roman Catholic Bishop at Kimberley, and have been here some time?—Five years.

8594. And you take great interest in school work?—Considerable interest.

8595. Have you several schools?—We have two mission schools, and there is the Convent high school besides. There is the high school for boys, and the high school for girls, near the church in the Du Toit's Pan Road. One of the mission or parochial schools is in Currie-street, and another of the same sort in Beaconsfield.

8596. Do you receive any aid from the Government?—No; we have never received anything in any way, either for building, furniture, or teaching. The old Griqualand West Government promised £200 towards building a school, but it was only a verbal promise, and the Cape Government decided not to keep it.

8597. How many children are there in those schools?—373.

8598. Are they boys and girls mixed?—In the two parochial schools they are mixed, and then there is the Convent High School for boys, and the Convent High School for girls.

8599. Are they all white children?—Yes.

8600. Are there many children of your denomination who are outside any education at all?—Very few. There are some Roman Catholic children not coming to our schools, but who go to private schools; they are some of the smaller ones, and it is because of the distance they live from our schools. I do not know of more than twenty Roman Catholic children who are not attending school.

8601. *Mr. Theron.*] Are there children of other denominations attending your schools?—Yes, there are 159 children of other denominations.

8602. Why do they attend your schools?—I suppose because they find them better than their own.

8603. What are the fees?—They vary. They are supposed to be 10s. a month, but in most cases that amount is not charged, because the parents, especially of late, are not able to pay it; but we make no reduction for children who do not belong to our denomination, because it is not to our interest in any way.

8604. Are there many children outside your denomination who do not attend school at all?—I cannot answer that.

8605. Do you think some method ought to be adopted for securing better attendance?—I do not think we have anything to complain of in the way of attendance. Our children attend very well.

8606. Do you give any industrial training?—Not here.

8607. Do you approve of it?—Certainly, very much.

8608. Why do not you introduce it into your schools here?—It is rather expensive as regards industries for boys. The girls are taught to sew. It is not easy to get tradesmen here to teach; they are much more expensive than a schoolmaster.

8609. It has been suggested that a Board should be brought into existence, elected by the ratepayers, whose duty it should be to fill up gaps where there are no schools, and if they like, have the opportunity of working through volunteers already in existence, recommending them for aid to the Government where they find the volunteers do the work as efficiently as they could do it themselves?—I do not think that would be very acceptable to us.

8610. Why not?—If they had any control, they might interfere with our principles of teaching, and we certainly could not admit that at all. We require Catholic teaching in our schools for those who are Catholics, and the others are not taught religion in any way. We require also that in the books used there should be nothing against our religion. If such a Board had any control over the school management, we certainly should object to it.

8611. Suppose the Board did not control your system of education so far as religion was concerned, but required inspection, in order to see that the secular results were satisfactory?—I do not think a Board of that kind would be likely to give general satisfaction, and I should much prefer dealing with a central educational authority.

326

Most Rev.
Bishop Gaughran.

Sept. 23rd, 1891.

At the same time, we are quite prepared to have the fullest inspection as regards our secular instruction.

8612. *Dr. Berry.*] Are your parochial schools mission schools?—The same thing.

8613. Why do not you get aid?—Perhaps it is because we have not made application in the proper way. The schools have paid for themselves, and there has been no necessity up to the present time. Lately, of course, we have felt the pressure of the times, but there has been no need to apply for aid.

8614. *Dean Holmes.*] Have you ever invited inspection?—There is frequent inspection of our schools. Sir Langham Dale, in fact, was rather anxious that the schools should be placed under Government.

8615. *Dr. Berry.*] Would there be any difference between the parochial schools here and the school we saw at Port Elizabeth, managed by the Marist Brothers?—There would be no difference in reality, the class of education is about the same; only the name differs. As a rule, the boys in the parochial schools are juniors.

8616. Is there the same kind of teacher?—Not the same order of Marist Brothers. Where I have been able, I have tried to send boys to the boarding school at Uitenhage. They have a better chance of being educated away from Kimberley.

8617. *President.*] Are you in favour of compulsory education?—As a general rule I am, but I do not think there is very great necessity for it as regards our denomination, and I do not know that it would be wise to establish it. Many of the parents would resent it here I think, as they have a keen sense of liberty.

8618. What would you do with the waifs and strays about the streets?—In that case, compulsory education is a good thing. It has been a great help to the schools in England. At the same time, it is rather an expensive system, and unless it is carried out properly it is better not to do it at all. You require a sufficient staff to see that the children are looked after. At present, we do that ourselves. The teachers take a walk after school hours, and visit the parents of the children who are absent during the day.

8619. They are virtually attendance officers, are they not?—Yes. I believe in the system myself, and think it is a very good one.

8620. Have you thought of the subject of night schools at all?—No. We have a night school for a certain number of boys who have left school, generally boys whose parents are not in good circumstances, and who have to go to work at an earlier age than they would otherwise.

8621. Is it kept up throughout the year?—Yes, the whole year round. There are not many pupils, not more than seven or eight.

8622. Should anything be done in your opinion to encourage more night schools?—I think it would be difficult to get boys to come; the amusements in Kimberley are too many, and so far as my experience goes, it is not easy to get boys to come. I should like to see more night schools, as I think they would be a benefit to a great many lads and young men after their day's work.

8623. Have you any knowledge of technical education?—Not very much.

8624. Have you formed any opinion with regard to the introduction of a system of technical schools either in Kimberley or any other part of the colony?—It would be an expensive thing to establish them.

8625. Do you think you would get the attendance?—I cannot say.

8626. *Dr. Berry.*] Have you any criticism to offer on the colonial system of education generally?—I have not studied it sufficiently to be able to criticize it. Our schools are altogether apart, so to speak.

8627. Can you tell us how your schools in Basutoland are managed?—The principal school there is a boarding school at our central mission, Roma. There we have an industrial school, and it is necessary to have the boys as boarders in order to carry it on properly.

8628. Do the boys pay?—Nothing. Occasionally the parents will give a present, perhaps something towards clothing the boys, but it is impossible to have a fixed permanent payment.

8629. What industries do you teach?—Nearly all the trades; carpentry, building, shoemaking, tailoring and turning.

8630. Has that system been long enough in practice for you to be able to say what is the effect on the boys in after life?—It has only been established three years. Already there is a certain number of the older boys who have left the school and are able to make a living for themselves in the Transvaal or the Free State by means of the trade they have learned, although they may have learned it only imperfectly. You cannot have much control over the pupils there.

8631. Are the reports from that mission favourable as to the industry and intelligence of the boys?—There is no fault to find with their intelligence; they are perfectly well able to learn almost any trade, but it is impossible to fix any trade for a boy; you must leave him to choose. If he takes a fancy to any special trade, he will be able to learn it in a very short time. Their industry is not very highly commended, but they have great intelligence and learn very quickly. Most Rev.
Bishop Gaughran,
Sept. 23rd, 1891.

8632. Do you educate them with a view to their being engaged in trades among their own people, or that they shall come out into the colony?—It is principally for their own benefit, so as to encourage civilization among the people. Sir Marshall Clarke has promised me that he will provide work for all children who learn trades there.

8633. Do you teach them garden industry?—Yes; farming, gardening, and so on. As a rule, the Basutos are very good at anything in the way of agriculture.

8634. Is the mission supported entirely by your Church?—There is a grant of £250 a year from the Government there for the different schools, but as there are ten schools, it does not amount to much each. For the foundation of the industrial school we have received £1,450. From time to time also, Sir Marshall Clarke makes a special grant for books or furniture for the schools, a small amount.

8635. Is the same system carried out in connection with the Protestant missions in Basutoland?—Yes; in the French mission they have the same system; they also have an industrial school, but they teach only a few trades.

8636. Have they been longer in the country than you?—Yes; twice as long as we have been.

8637. *President.*] Do they teach industries in the ordinary schools also?—No, except that girls are taught to spin and weave and make their own clothes; there is no industrial training for boys in the ordinary schools. They generally send on boys who have shown any aptitude for trades to the central mission.

8638. Seeing that you have started at Roma this industrial training, and made it a permanent feature, is it owing to the fact that you think the future calling of the natives requires them to have industrial rather than literary training?—When I started the school I felt that the natives were increasing very much in Basutoland, and that they could not all live upon the land; they must either fight with their neighbours or find a livelihood for themselves, and therefore the wisest thing to do would be to provide them with the means of making a livelihood either within or outside their own country.

8639. Are they industrious on their land?—Yes.

8640. Are they fond of spade work?—Yes; the Basutos are exceptions to the ordinary native; they do not leave all the work to the women as they do elsewhere.

8641. Is it necessary to train the Basutos to use the spade?—As a general rule, the Basutos have ploughs and so on, and they grow mealies and wheat, but they do not care so much for gardening and the cultivation of vegetables. It is necessary to teach them that.

8642. In view of the fact that the natives are destined to be the tillers of the soil, should they not know how to use the spade among other things, and should not there be some sort of industrial training in this direction as an adjunct to every school, making trades rather a higher sort of teaching?—We have a very large garden, and all the boys are taught to work in it, whether they learn a trade or not. There are certain times when they go and work in the garden; they are also taught how to plant trees and so on.

8643. Have you any coloured children in your schools at Kimberley?—We have a school for Indians, but none for Kafirs.

8644. *Mr. Theron.*] Is the school for Indians separate from the others?—Yes; there are about forty Indian children in that school. There are very few Roman Catholics among the Kafirs, and they are in the compounds. We do not encourage our own people in Basutoland to come here to work, as they stand a chance of losing any good they have got. When they get back to their own people, they are worse than before they left, so we try to help them at home as far as possible.

8645. *President.*] In view of the enormous increase of these people, is it not a good thing to give them industrial training?—Yes; and it is for that purpose that we have established industrial schools.

Kimberley, Thursday, September 24, 1891.

PRESENT:

Sir J. D. BARRY (President),

Dr. Berry,	Dean Holmes.
Rev. Moorrees,	Mr. Theron.

Mr. F. L. Dwyer examined.

8646. *Dr. Berry.*] I believe you are Railway Maintenance Engineer at Kimberley?—Yes. Mr.
F. L. Dwyer.

Sept 24th, 1891.

Mr.
F. L. Dwyer.
Sept. 24th, 1891.

8647. How long have you been here?—I have been in charge of this district since December last.

8648. We are asked to recommend to Government what additional facilities can be given to meet the wants of persons employed on the lines of railway in the matter of school accommodation and provision for education generally. Can you offer any suggestion on the subject?—The train service does not always suit to take children to school and bring them home again. If a school were established at Taungs, it would serve the gangs between there and Vryburg. That would be eight gangs in all.

8649. Are there any gangers there with children?—Yes, most of the gangers are married, and all the gangers north of Kimberley are white men. The gangers between Kimberley and De Aar are mostly coloured men.

8650. Would you recommend placing at Taungs what the department calls a station school?—Yes, I would.

8651. Could a committee be got together?—At Taungs station there would only be the Stationmaster, the night stationmaster, and one ganger. Those are all the men required at Taungs.

8652. Are they married men?—Yes; many of them are.

8653. Have you seen the circular issued by the General Manager of Railways about station schools?—I saw it some time ago when it was first issued.

8654. Would it be within the power of these men at Taungs to comply with the conditions of the circular, do you think?—When the circular was issued I was at De Aar: we tried to get a school at Victoria West on these terms, but we could not raise the guarantee from the men.

8655. Would it be advisable for the department in some cases to give the guarantee, do you think?—It would be the surest way of getting a school established. The men do not like to render themselves liable.

8656. Is there a difficulty in the way of finding a guarantee, owing to the men being liable to be moved about suddenly from one place to another?—I do not think so. I have never heard that advanced as a reason by any of the men.

8657. Would it be objectionable if the department was to give a guarantee in respect of the children attending the school and make stoppages from the men's wages?—I think that would be a good plan.

8658. Is there a building at Taungs suitable for a school?—No.

8659. Would you recommend that a wooden house be set up temporarily?—Yes.

8660. Have you any idea of the number of children who could be got there?—No; but if a school was established there, I would shift my gangers in such a way as to give men with families an opportunity of sending their children to school.

8661. Would you advise the establishment of a railway station school at Kimberley?—It is hardly required. There are plenty of schools in Kimberley.

8662. Do the children avail themselves of the public school?—Yes; I think so. I may say that I moved up one of my inspectors so that he should be able to send his children to school at Kimberley, as he had a large family.

8663. Have you anything to say about the wants of the men in any other parts as regards education for their children?—No; a school was established at Naauwpoort, which has been extremely successful. The children were brought to and fro by train. It was established while I was stationed at Cradock, in the beginning of 1886 I think.

8664. Is it a fact that there is some difficulty about giving children free passes by the ordinary passenger trains?—I do not think there is any difficulty. I have never heard of it.

8665. Some of the witnesses have said that there was a difficulty, and that the railway department rather objected to children travelling by the ordinary passenger trains, and insisted on their coming by the goods trains; is that so?—I never heard of any complaint along the lengths between Naauwpoort and Colesberg, and Naauwpoort and De Aar. The children used to come in from along the Colesberg line by the ordinary passenger trains.

8666. As far as you know, no order has been issued to the contrary, has there?—No.

8667. Do you think it would be safe for children to travel by trollies?—Certainly not; in fact it is doubtful whether it is safe for very young children to travel by themselves even in the train.

8668. You think that schools ought to be brought as near to the children as possible?—Yes.

8669. Would you be in favour of a plan for taking the girls belonging to the maintenance men to some centre like Graham's Town or Cradock, and putting them at some boarding school, or would it be beyond the means of the men?—It all depends upon what it would cost. The white men along the Midland Section get about 8s. a day, and the coloured men 6s.

8670. Suppose it could be arranged that the girls were taken at a cost of about £6 to £8 a year to the parents for board and education?—I think that would be very reasonable, and the men probably would be willing to pay that, and I think they could afford it.

Mr. *F. L. Dreyer.* Sept. 24th, 1891

8671. Are the gangers along the line anxious to have education for their children?—I know they are along the Midland line. The men here are rather unsettled as yet, it is a new district, and a lot of the men who have been old construction hands are just waiting to get on construction again. I think some of them have left already. After a while, the men in the regular gangs will get settled down and stop in the district, but I have not had any applications from the gangers about the facilities for education; they have not spoken to me in any way on the subject.

8672. Suppose more station schools were established, would officers like yourself be able to visit them at frequent intervals and report to the Education Department how they were getting on?—Yes. I could visit them, and the medical officer also; we are both of us constantly passing up and down the line.

8673. One great difficulty seems to be that these men are unable to initiate or conduct any correspondence between themselves and the Education Department; they do not know how to set about it apparently. Would it not be well if an officer like yourself made it his business to see the men, report occasionally how things are getting on, and conduct any correspondence with the head of the Education Department on their behalf?—Yes, I think it would be a good thing.

8674. Suppose School Boards were established in various districts throughout the colony, do you see any objection to bringing these railway station schools under the management and control of such Boards?—No.

Mr. Evan H. Jones examined.

8675. *President.*] I believe you are Mayor of Kimberley?—Yes.

Mr. *Evan H. Jones.* Sept. 24th, 1891.

8676. Have you been so for some time?—I am Mayor this year, and I was formerly Mayor in 1888.

8677. Are you a member of the School Board?—Yes; since it has been in existence.

8678. Are you in a position to say whether there are many children in Kimberley outside all education?—I think so. It seems to me that the question of irregularity of attendance is a very important matter, and I am very glad that attention has been directed to it. What I would suggest is that in each town some sort of permanent Government Board should be formed, so that the members should not go out of office periodically as they do now. Where the people take an interest in education, School Boards work very well. We find that to be the case with our School Board, but when the public are careless and indifferent, I can imagine there would be considerable difficulty. There must be some constituted authority to see that education is carried on on a proper footing. We have a number of private schools in Kimberley, which would astonish the members of the Commission if they visited and inspected them.

8679. In what respect?—They are conducted in such a loose and careless manner. In some places here, the parents only pay sixpence a week for a child's education. The teachers in many cases are not at all fit for the work; and I think there should be some proper system of inspection of these schools. I do not see why a Government School Board should not be appointed, consisting say of the Civil Commissioner, the Resident Magistrate, the Mayor, and the Chairman of the Divisional Council, with special power to deal with cases of irregular attendance and other matters connected with education.

8680. *Dean Holmes.*] Do you mean that under the existing system such matters cannot be properly dealt with?—Yes; there are a great many children in Kimberley who, owing to the neglect of their parents and other causes, are growing up without education, both white and coloured, and there seems to be no machinery for getting them into school. In addition to that, many of the little private schools require to be under some system of control, both in regard to the accommodation and the teaching.

8681. *President.*] Do you know anything about the facilities for the education of railway children?—I think the railway authorities should give facilities to the people living along the line for getting their children to convenient centres where they could be taught. I think however there are others who could give better evidence on this point than I can.

8682. What steps should be taken to give the Boards of Management perpetual succession, and provide for the tenure of public school property?—I would say that where there is no Board of Management in existence, or where a Board does not carry out its duties efficiently, the Government should appoint a Board to act. There are

Mr.
Evan H. Jones.
——
Sept. 24th, 1891.

places where the public take no interest in forming Boards of Management, and I know that we had a great difficulty here in forming a school on undenominational lines. The Borough Council wished to assist the cause of education, and we have authority under our Act to vote a certain sum of money in aid of schools. We accordingly put down on the estimates a sum of £1,200 to assist in opening a public undenominational school The public here, however, were interested in denominational schools, and Archdeacon Gaul, Mr. Goch, Mr. J. B. Currie, and several others spoke against the undenominational system, and the result was, that at the public meeting there were only two in favour of an undenominational school, and it was thought that the Council should divide the money among the existing schools which had already borne the heat and burden of the day, and incurred expenses in the way of school buildings, teachers, and so on. The Council however decided after the public meeting, not to divide the money among the existing schools, and the result was, that since then they have done nothing towards education. Although we have the power, we have left the matter of education to the public. Since then, a public school has been established, which has the support of all the denominations except the Roman Catholics. We have ministers of different denominations on the School Board, and we find that this school is thoroughly successful, proving that the principle of undenominationalism is a sound one as far as we in Kimberley are concerned. With regard to school property, I am of opinion that it should be vested in two trustees, say the Civil Commissioner and the Mayor, with a Government auditor to go through the accounts once every year; that is, where you have these authorities already existing. In our own case there is a debt of about £2,000 still on the school property, advanced by the Government as a loan, on which we pay interest. Eventually we hope to pay that off.

8683. What further facilities do you think can be afforded for giving instruction in the English and Dutch languages?—I think the present facilities in the public schools are ample as regards the teaching of English. With regard to Dutch, I think that further provision might be made. There are more facilities for children to learn English than there are for them to learn Dutch, and there are many schools where, if the teachers were required to teach Dutch, they would not be able to do so with the same ease and freedom that they teach English. I think that teachers should be required to qualify themselves in Dutch, so that any parents requiring their children to learn both languages in a thoroughly efficient manner could have their needs met.

8684. What contributions should be expected from local bodies, such as Divisional Councils and Municipalities, in support of schools and for the erection of buildings?—I would suggest that municipalities be required to contribute an equal sum to that given by the Government towards school buildings in a town, whenever such buildings require to be erected. If there was a Board elected, they would be able to report to the Government from time to time as to the attendance at schools and as to the necessity for erecting further buildings to provide for the education of children who otherwise would not go to school at all. In such cases, it is only right that the ratepayers should assist in erecting the buildings, the Government coming forward with an equal amount. Government should also contribute half the teacher's salary, the remainder being made up by the fees. The difficulty now is, that the outside private schools do not come up to the standard, and therefore they get no support whatever, unless the minister of some denomination makes it his business to examine the school and suggest that aid should be applied for; but very often they do not care to do this, because they are not quite sure whether the teacher is a person who can be relied upon. There are many itinerant teachers who are here to-day and gone to-morrow. I think that the Divisional Councils should be called upon to contribute in the districts, and the municipalities in the towns, and there ought to be so many free scholars provided for.

8685. What additional facilities can be provided to meet the wants of the children of the agricultural population?—I do not think I am prepared to give any answer as to that. I think Government should require all children to attend some school, and inaugurate some system of inspection over all private schools. I am strongly in favour of compulsory education, as far as the rudiments of learning are concerned, and upon this basis you might build a certain amount of technical education.

8686. What is your opinion as to night schools?—I think they are very much needed, especially in mining centres such as we have here. It is only of late years that Kimberley has been supplied with schools to reach almost all classes, and as a result, there are many young men who would gladly attend night schools if they could be made to fit in with their daily avocations. As to technical schools, I am strongly in favour of their establishment in all the principal centres like Kimberley, subject of course to Government supervision.

Hon. Mr. Justice Solomon examined.

Hon. Mr
Justice Solomon.

Sept. 21th, 1891.

8687. *President.*] You are one of the judges of the High Court at Kimberley?—Yes.

8688. Have you taken an interest in education?—Yes.

8689. Are you at present chairman of the public undenominational school here?—Yes

8690. I suppose you are acquainted with the guarantee system?—Yes.

8691. Do you approve of it?—I think it is an unsatisfactory system in some respects. In the first place, it is an objection that the guarantee should last only for a period of three years. It is a great nuisance at the end of that time having to elect a new body of guarantors. I do not see why if a man is willing to guarantee he should not do so for an indefinite time, until he removes his name from the list of guarantors. I do not care about the system myself, and see no reason why the ratepayers should not be responsible for the deficiency in case any arises, but I think it is rarely that it does arise.

8692. Is that in consequence of the liberal grants given by Government?—Yes.

8693. Would you extend those grants as far as buildings are concerned?—I think the Government ought to give on the £ for £ principle. On our schools here we have spent nearly £8,000, over £4,000 of which has been collected from the public of Kimberley. Government has only given us £2,000. We have asked for more, and we ought to have more I think.

8694. Does the £8,000 you have spent include that £2,000?—Yes. The schools have cost nearly £8,000.

8695. If the rates are made liable for any deficiency, do you think the ratepayers should have a voice in the control of the schools?—Yes; they ought to have the appointment of the Board of Managers. Practically, they have that now, as the householders elect the Board.

8696. Would it be better to have a Board for the town or for the whole district?—A Board for the whole district would have too much to do. I do not see how they could very well exercise supervision over the whole district; it would be rather a difficult matter.

8697. Might not the Board act through sub-committees?—Yes; they might appoint sub-committees in the district, and make them responsible. I know in connection with our own school, we have a good deal to do, and if the Board of Managers was responsible for the education of the whole district, it would be rather a difficulty.

8698. Here in Kimberley the work is heavy, but in the district it is comparatively small, is it not?—Yes.

8699. If you acted through sub-committees, the district work would not be nearly so great as in town would it?—No. I think not.

8700. Would you vest all public undenominational school property in the Board?—Yes, certainly.

8701. Suppose such Board is not elected, do you see any way of giving perpetuity of succession under the present system?—I do not see why instead of the whole Board going out of office at the end of three years, a certain number should not go out every year, say one-third.

8702. If they are guarantors who go out, would you perpetuate their liability for ever?—I am talking of the managers themselves, not the guarantors.

8703. The managers must be guarantors, must they not?—Yes. At present the whole body ceases to exist at the end of three years, and a new body of managers has to be appointed. If one-third of the number went out every three years, there would be constant succession.

8704. Would the liability of those going out cease?—No; they would be still guarantors, but they would cease to be managers.

8705. But they guarantee only for three years, do they not?—I would not have them guarantee for only three years. I would have it understood that a man who becomes a guarantor for a certain amount, does so until he withdraws his name from the list. I think the majority of people would be willing to be guarantors as long as they remained in the place.

8706. Should the guarantee be for so much a year?—The limit of the guarantee here is £10 for three years.

8707. Do you think there are men who would guarantee for life?—Yes. They would simply give a guarantee without limiting their liability in point of time, unless they left the place, or for some other good reason chose to withdraw their name, but very few would do so I believe.

8708. Suppose there was a deficiency, and they wanted to withdraw then?—If there is a deficiency, the amount ought to be collected from the guarantors as soon as possible. I would not allow anyone to withdraw his name while there was a deficiency.

Hon. Mr.
Justice Solomon.
——
Sept. 24th, 1891

8709. Suppose one man wants to withdraw at the end of four years and another at the end of five, how are you to ascertain the deficiency and make up the accounts?—You find out what the deficiency is at the end of the year, and collect it from the guarantors.

8710. Would it not be very inconvenient?—I think it would be better to make the ratepayers liable.

8711. Does not the present system invite men to become guarantors in order to carry on a school for the rich and not for the poor?—I have not noticed that. I think the Boards of Managers as a rule are very ready to assist the poor. I know that here we have a number of free scholars in the school. If we find that people cannot afford to pay the fees, we are very willing to assist them to a certain extent, either by reducing the fees or admitting them as free scholars.

8712. At present there is not anybody charged with the duty of initiating schools either for the rich or the poor, is there?—No.

8713. Is not that a great defect?—Yes, I think so.

8714. Can that defect best be remedied by a Board?—Yes.

8715. Who would you make the voters?—The ratepayers. I would adopt the Divisional Council franchise.

8716. Would you oblige the Board to find schools where they were wanted?—It would be their duty to look after the educational wants of the district, and provide a sufficient number of schools.

8717. Would they have to supply the wants of the coloured people also?—That would be a difficulty. I think industrial rather than literary schools are wanted for the coloured class. In Kimberley, there is not a very large number of coloured children, so it is not such a serious matter.

8718. Can their parents afford to pay?—I am not in a position to say.

8719. Would you limit industrial schools to natives, or would you include the poorer class of Europeans?—It is desirable to have them for the poorer class of Europeans also, but you must have separate schools I think; the two classes would never mix together.

8720. Is it desirable to draw a distinction?—I think so. It would interfere, I think, with the efficiency of a white school if natives were allowed to go there.

8721. How would you draw the distinction between the white and black?—I think the question settles itself pretty satisfactorily in actual experience.

8722. If you made any hard and fast rule, would you exclude coloured children who might not be objectionable from the higher school?—That we have to do now. We had an application from a native of Mauritius, a most respectable and well educated man, whose son had been at college in Mauritius; we were very anxious to assist him, but we could not get him into the school, as there was such an outcry from a number of the parents, and it would have injured the school.

8723. If it would not have injured the school, would you have admitted him?—Yes.

8724. Would not you leave it in the discretion of the managers to admit or exclude in the case of schools for whites?—You would find that all managers would act on the same principle; they would find it necessary to do so in the interests of the school. It is unpleasant to have to refuse any one undoubtedly, especially in such cases as the one I have mentioned, where very respectable people apply. It would be much better if the odium were not thrown on the managers I think.

8725. Do you know anything about the circumstances connected with the Gill College?—No; I only know there is such an institution.

8726. In that case it is found that the householders have consented to an arrangement of this kind, that the public undenominational school should be carried on on the Gill College property and in the Gill College premises, the committee of the college becoming guarantors. There are ten members on the Board of Management, three of whom are elected, but they have no responsibility; they only sit on the Board. The Government, knowing the circumstances, has contributed £1,000 towards the erection of a boarding house on the Gill College land. How would you deal with a case like that, if a Board such as has been indicated were brought into existence?—It is a very exceptional case, and rather difficult to deal with. I think a case of that sort would have to be dealt with by special legislation, as it is so different from any ordinary case.

8727. Suppose you had to draft an Act to deal with it, how would you set about it?—It would take some time to consider. You would have to meet the trustees of the Gill College and find out what they were willing to accept.

8728. Would you try to get possession of the land and work the school through the system you have indicated; or would you in that case set aside the general rule and invest the Gill College with all the powers of the Board?—If they are prepared to

333

accept the responsibilities of the Board, and do their work satisfactorily, I do not see why the matter should not be left as it is.

Hon. Mr. Justice Solomon.
Sept. 24th, 1891.

8729. Does it not take from the public for ever the power of controlling the school, seeing that seven members of the Board are the Gill College trustees, and the public are only represented by three members, so that they are always in a minority?—Perhaps, on the whole, it would be better to bring it under the general rule; but they should try and see how far the trustees would be willing to meet the public, so as not to injure either the public or the institution.

8730. *Dean Holmes.*] Suppose such a Board as you have indicated were brought into existence, how would you deal with existing mission schools in towns that belong to different church bodies?—I should be disposed to bring them under the authority of the Board. I do not see why the churches should not be compensated for any money they have spent on the schools.

8731. Would you be in favour of allowing them to continue, provided they did good work, subject to visits from the School Board Inspector, and then let them be recommended by the Board to the Government for aid from time to time?—Yes.

8732. They have been doing good work all this time, and you would not destroy them, would you?—No; if they wished to come under the Board, I should let them do so voluntarily.

8733. *President.*] How would you deal with those bodies that refused to come under the Board, although they were doing good work?—If they are doing good work, I should not interfere with them.

8734. If they get aid now, you would continue it?—As long as they do their work well I would.

8735. But the tendency should be to bring them all under the Board as far as possible, should it not?—Yes.

8736. Would you give bodies doing good work that came under the Board aid for the construction of buildings on their own land, or would you make it a condition that whenever public money is spent on buildings, it must become public school property?—It should become public school property where public money is spent.

8737. Would you allow the Government to contribute to mission schools as at present, or would you give them a further contribution if the Government is satisfied, even though the Board might not be satisfied?—Not until they actually came under the School Board I think.

8738. You would not give increased aid from the Government unless these schools were recommended by the School Board, would you?—If the Government wished to give increased aid, I do not know that I should care to interfere if I were on the Board.

8739. Would you require the Government first to secure a report from the Board before giving aid?—I suppose naturally the Government would consult the Board.

8740. Would you bind them to do so, whatever resolution they came to ultimately?—They ought to consult the Board, but they would not be bound by the decision.

8741. Would you bind the Government to consult the Board, and not to act till they got its consent?—No, I would not do that. I would let the Government consult the Board and then act as they pleased.

8742. What contributions should be expected from local bodies, such as divisional councils and municipalities, in support of schools and for the erection of buildings?—I think the Board ought to come in. That is my answer to that.

8743. Have you any suggestion to make about night schools?—I think they are very desirable in a place like this. We have had to consider the matter, as there is a number of young fellows here who would like to attend, but the difficulty is the expense. We found we could not establish such a thing in connection with our school, because the masters have their time fully occupied during the day, and they could not very well work at night also. We should have to employ new masters altogether.

8744. Would night schools be for the purpose of enabling these young fellows to continue their education?—Chiefly.

8745. Do you think the Government ought to contribute?—I think so.

8746. What contribution would you expect from the Government towards night schools?—The same as they give at present towards day schools, on the same principle.

8747. And for buildings?—There would not be any difficulty about that, as the same buildings could be used.

8748. Have you paid any attention to the subject of technical education?—I think it is a very desirable thing; the only difficulty is the expense.

8749. Do you think the Government ought to embark upon such expenditure?—I think they ought to begin in a small way and gradually extend.

8750. Would you have schools in several places or only in one?—I should begin in the chief towns of the colony; say Cape Town, Port Elizabeth, Kimberley, and

TT 2

Hon. Mr.
Justice Solomon.

Sept. 24th, 1891.

Graham's Town. I think the more we can promote technical education the better; it is chiefly the matter of expense that stands in the way.

8751. What sort of technical education would you start here?—I have not considered the question sufficiently.

8752. As to industrial schools for the lower classes, do you think the principle a sound one?—Decidedly.

8753. Suppose a parent refuses to send his child to school, or is totally unable to do so, not having the means, do you think in such cases a system of apprenticeship might be adopted?—I think every child ought to be educated, but it is difficult to see how you can make it compulsory unless you make it free at the same time.

8754. Are you in favour of compulsory education?—Yes, if you make it free.

8755. If you had schools initiated and kept up partly by the Government, partly by fees, and partly by the rates, could you not force into them all children, whether they paid or not?—There is the difficulty of enquiring into each separate case.

8756. Cannot it be overcome?—To a certain extent; but the difficulty is to find out whether a parent can pay or not. If you are satisfied that he can pay and is wilfully keeping his child away, then of course he ought to be made to pay.

8757. Where he cannot pay, you think education ought to be free for that child?—I think so.

8758. If it is found that the parent can pay but will not, do you think instead of imposing a fine, there might be some system of apprenticeship adopted?—I do not like the system of taking children away from their parents compulsorily. The parent is the best guardian of the child in the majority of cases. Moreover, it would be very difficult to find masters to take children on the condition that they were to educate them.

INDEX AND ANALYSIS

OF

MINUTES OF EVIDENCE.

INDEX AND ANALYSIS

OF

MINUTES OF EVIDENCE.

[NOTE:—The figures in the Index refer to the Pages of Evidence. The analysis merely gives the chief results of the examination of each witness, and the gist of his evidence, in as condensed a form as possible, for purposes of reference.]

A

Abraham, Rev. N., Wesleyan Minister at Somerset East, 199; Irregularity of attendance, 199; Compulsory education, 199; Mixture of races, 199; Guarantor system, 200, 202; School Boards, 200; Mission schools, 200, 201, 202; Fourth-class schools, 201; Technical schools, 202, 203; Industrial training, 203; Native education, 203, 204; Bi-lingual question, 204.

B

Bishop of Grahamstown, Most Rev., 19; Existing appliances should be better utilised rather than inaugurate new principles, 19; School inspection deficient, 19; More attention should be paid to the qualifications of teachers, 19; Proper accommodation should be required and a thoroughly effective conscience clause insisted on 19; Not favourable to Boards or taxation for school purposes, 20; Training colleges, 20; Private adventure schools should be aided, 20; Pupils should be allowed option of being examined in Dutch or English, 21; Industrial schools, 21.

Berghegge, Rev. Father, Dutch teacher at St. Aidan's College, 84; Teaching of Dutch language, 85.

Brooke, Rev. S., Rector of St. Paul's, Port Elizabeth, 141; Mission schools, 141; Fourth class schools, 142; School Boards, 142; Night schools, 142.

Buckley, J., Inspector of Police at Port Elizabeth, 177; Native education, 177, 178.

Brister, J., Merchant at Port Elizabeth, 180; Divisional Councils should supervise education, 180, 181; Native education, 181; Industrial training, 181; Mixture of races, 182.

Botha, P., farmer, 209; Grants for indigent children as boarders, 209; English and Dutch teaching, 209; Farm schools, 209.

Brailsford, E. A., chief clerk to C. C., Somerset East, 223; Guarantee system, 223; School Boards, 223; Language question, 224.

Buis, S., farmer, 265; Educational wants of agricultural population, 265; Facilities for travelling by rail, 265; Boarding grant too small, 265; Language question, 266; Industrial training, 266.

Bleksley, A. H., Sanitary Inspector, at Kimberley, 301; Children not attending school, 301; Inferior character of many private schools at Kimberley, 301; Compulsory education, 301, 302; Mission schools, 302; Industrial training, 303; School Boards, 303; Education of children of railway employés, 303, 304.

Blackbeard, C. A., Municipal Councillor, at Beaconsfield, 312; Education of poor children; 312; Compulsory education, 313; Municipalities and schools, 313; Industrial training, 313.

C

Chubb, Rev. T, Wesleyan Minister, 11; School attendance, 12; not favourable to Boards elected by ratepayers, 12, 13; Mission schools 12; Fourth-class schools, 14; Dutch teaching; facilities sufficient, 16; Bursaries, 17; Compulsion might be applied to towns, 17; Industrial education, 18; Night schools, 18.

Cecile, Sister, St. Peter's Home, Graham's Town, 32; Advocates more industrial training, 32, 34; Mission schools, 33; Girls of Railway employés would be received at very low rate, 33, 35; Difficulty in getting qualified Dutch teachers, 34; Question of colour, 34.

G

Grobler, P. J., Farmer, 241; Educational facilities for agricultural population, 241; Children travelling by rail to school, 241.

Gaul, Archdeacon, Kimberley, 271; Compulsory education, 271, 277; Industrial training, 271, 272; Mission schools, 272; School Boards, 272, 273, 274, 275; Fourth class schools, 273; Inferior character of certain private schools at Kimberley, 273; Guarantee system, 274; Facilities for boarding, 275; Night schools, 276; Schools for children of railway employés, 276, 277; Farm schools, 277; Normal schools, 277; Language question, 278, 279, 280.

Gaughran, Bishop, Most Rev. Kimberley, 325; Roman Catholic schools, 325; Industrial training, 325, 326, 327; School Boards, 325; Compulsory education, 326; Night schools, 326; Missions in Basutoland, 326, 327.

H.

Hijst, F. M. de Vries, Dutch Master, St. Andrew's College, Graham's Town, 40; Growing desire to learn Dutch, 40; Dutch in the Elementary examination, 41, 42.

Hecnan, R. H H., District Railway Engineer, Port Elizabeth, 125; Railway schools, 125, 126, 127; Technical education, 127, 128; Night schools, 129.

Hall, A. T. M., Headmaster, Diocesan Grammar School, Port Elizabeth, 135; Establishment of public undenominational schools, 135; Local Boards, 136; Separation of whites and blacks, 136; Language question, 137, 138; Elementary examination, 137, 138.

Hewitt, Rev. Dr., Incumbent of Trinity Church, Port Elizabeth, 154; Mission schools, 154, 156; Compulsory Education, 154, 158; Mixture of races, 154, 155; Boards, 157; Government contribution to buildings, 159, 160; Guarantee system, 159; Wants of agricultural population, 160; Schools for railway children, 160; Dutch language and the Elementary examination, 160, 161; Technical schools, 161; Industrial teaching for blacks, 161, 162.

Houliston, M., Miss, Principal of Bellevue Seminary, Somerset East, 205; Dutch teaching, 205, 206, 207; Normal schools, 207; Industrial training, 207, 208; Night schools, 208.

Holden, J. S. B., Somerset East, 210; Native mission schools, 210; Industrial training, 211; School tax for natives, 211; Dutch language, 212; School Boards, 212, 213; School committee, Somerset East, 213.

Hofmeyr, Rev. J. H., Dutch Reformed Church Minister, Somerset East, 217; Compulsory education, 217; Fourth-class schools, 217; Industrial training, 217; School Boards, 218, 219; Rating powers, 218, 219; Guarantee system, 220; Management of Gill College, 220, 221; Dutch teaching, 221; Elementary examination, 222; Wants of the agricultural population, 222; Night schools, 222; Technical schools, 222; Boarding for indigent children, 222; Elementary schools in suitable centres, 222, 223.

Howarth, H. W., Railway Foreman at Vryburg, 270; Station schools, 270.

J

Joubert, J., M.L.A., 224; Irregularity of attendance, 224; Compulsory education, 225; 226; Industrial training, 226; Tax for native education, 226, 227; School Boards, 227, 228; Guarantee system, 227; Facilities for boarding should be increased, 228; English and Dutch language, 228, 229; Elementary examination, 229, 230.

Judge, E. A., Civil Commissioner at Kimberley, 288; Free education, 288; Guarantor system, 288, 289; Rating for school purposes, 289.

Jones, E. H., Mayor of Kimberley, 329; Irregularity of attendance, 329; Private Schools at Kimberley, 329; Railway employés' children, 329; Boards of Management, 330; School property, 330; English and Dutch Teaching, 330; Night schools and technical schools, 330.

K

Kakaza, Rev. G., Native Wesleyan Minister, 56; Industrial schools for Natives, 56; Tax on Natives for Education, 56.

Kruger, N., Shopkeeper at Burghersdorp, 241; School buildings, 241; Boards, 241, 242; Taxation for School purposes, 242; Native education, 242.

L

M

N

O

P.

R

S

T

GENERAL CIRCULAR AND REPLIES

EDUCATION COMMISSION.

GENERAL CIRCULAR.

The following are additional replies received to the General Circular of Questions issued by the Commission :—

1. What suggestions have you to offer for remedying the irregularity of attendance ?
    (*a*) In Town Schools.
    (*b*) In Country Districts.

Molteno Town Council as Managers of Second Class U. P. School.—Printed circulars, explaining the importance of regular attendance should be given to parents at the time a scholar enters, and also at the end of each vacation.

J. H. Brady, Esq.—Education should be compulsory. In the country, due regard should be given to the parents' right to the services of their children in urgent farming operations, and the law should be made applicable only to those living within a certain distance, say three miles, of a public school. Managers might be allowed to appoint thirteen weeks holiday every year, according to local requirements.

F. Beswick, Esq., High School, Queen's Town.—Irregularity of attendance cannot be complained of in the public European schools which have come under his notice.

W. Milne, Esq., Stellenbosch—Recommends compulsion in some form or other, especially in larger towns. During school hours, children might be accosted in the streets by the proper officers, and parents summoned before School Attendance Committees, or taken before the Magistrate. Employers of labour would also have to be prohibited from employing children till they had passed a certain standard. Compulsion could not be enforced in country districts, but some good might be done by granting "leaving certificates" to all who had passed a certain standard. An improvement also might result from giving school committees the right of making enquiry and reporting such cases to the Church or Mission Authorities ; but beyond a general attempt to quicken public interest, much cannot be done as yet, to remedy the evil in country districts.

Rev. Cormack, Burghersdorp.—A note from parents should be insisted upon, and enquiry should be made as to the cause of absence. Marks should be given for regular attendance.

H. T. Elliott, Esq., Queen's Town.—Notice of absence should be immediately sent to parents. If it continues, there should be a personal visit. Wilful absence should be severely punished. Regular attendance should be encouraged by reward cards, with punctual attendances marked in red ink. Paid visitors should be appointed to bring into school and keep there the lower classes of white, coloured, and mixed races. Attendance must vary with the weather. It should be compulsory for the amount of work set for the week to be done in child's own time if he or she be absent. Prizes and medals should be given for punctual attendance. Interesting object lessons should be given occasionally. These methods were pursued in a school in London, where the average attendance was over 95 per cent., about the best in England. Generally speaking, the best test of the value of a teacher is the regularity or otherwise of the attendance.

Rev. T. G. Jones, Hackney.—There should be a school rate, and direct compulsion in town schools. In the country, there should be a school rate and a little indirect compulsion. such as not allowing children under twelve to be apprenticed or do any remunerative work, unless they have satisfied the Inspector in, say Standard IV. The Act might name a minimum standard.

F. H. Ely, Esq., School Inspector.—Chief cause of irregularity of attendance, a matter which has not been brought prominently to his notice, is the necessity under which European parents of the poorer class find themselves of employing their children in domestic work. Compulsory education could not be enforced without pressing unduly on this class. In the case of natives, a better attendance would be secured, if they were made to pay a fixed proportion of the teacher's salary. This would be an indirect mode of compulsion, and would be attended with good resu ts.

J. Lamont, Esq., Adelaide.—The great evil of irregularity of attendance diminishes in proportion as parents realize the high value of education. Compulsory attendance, however, is the only complete remedy.

J. McLaren, Esq., Blytheswood.—In the native territories, the abolition of the Easter and Spring holidays, and the lengthening of the summer and winter holidays would have a good effect. A certain number of attendances might also be required as a condition of examination for the standards. Small prizes given for regularity would stimulate attendance, and show that it was looked upon as a matter of importance.

H. J. McClure, Esq., Mossel Bay.—Compulsory education is the only remedy. The only way to remedy the irregularity of attendance in third class schools is to introduce free education. The necessity for parents to employ their own children through the want of labour, interferes with regular attendance.

T. R. Price, Esq., East London.—It must be definitely accepted that it is the duty of the State to see that children are educated. So long as it is left for private individuals to volunteer to undertake the responsibilities of organizing schools and administering school funds at their own risk, and largely at their own discretion, and at the same time Government grants are continued to be made under existing conditions, it seems difficult to devise any acceptable means of improvement likely to be attended with permanent, if any, success.

W. E. Clarke, Esq., St. Andrew's College, Graham's Town.—There seems to be no reason why the same methods for enforcing attendance at schools that are employed in England, should not be adopted in this country, if the control of education in districts were entrusted to Boards elected by and responsible to the ratepayers. Regularity of attendance might also be made one of the conditions of the payment of the Government grant.

Professor MacWilliam, Gill College, Somerset East.—So far as experience goes, the attendance is not so irregular as to require legislative interference, but even if it were, it would be impossible to compel children to attend school regularly, so long as it is impossible to compel them to attend at all. Where attendance is irregular, the only means to improve it would be for the teachers and others interested in education to bring their personal influence to bear on the heads of the irregular families, always few in number. The question as regards country districts can apply only to farm schools. The average farmer when he employs a teacher, sees that, as regards time at least, he gets the worth of his money.

Rev. J. H. Hofmeyr, Somerset East.—In so far as I am acquainted with the town and country schools in this district, I do not think there is any reason to complain of irregular attendance.

Miss Redford, Kimberley Girls' School.—Special prizes or certificates should be offered for regular attendance; but no prize should be given for distinction in any subject to a scholar who does not make up say nine-tenths of the regular attendances. In the case of children between the ages of six and twelve years, pressure should be brought to bear upon the parents.

F. W. Bampton, Esq., Humansdorp.—In town schools, parents should be subjected to a fine, increasing in amount for each offence. Such fine might be added to the fees. In country schools, much of the irregularity of attendance might be stopped by giving school committees power to close public and farm schools during certain seasons, when farming operations such as ploughing and harvesting are in operation.

E. Noaks, Esq., Port Elizabeth.—Under the present system, fair results seem to be attainable. To take the Grey Institute, I find the percentage of attendance to have been on an average for last year—at the Hill School 94 per cent., at the North End Branch 85 per cent., and at the South End Branch 86 per cent. The percentage for schools under the School Board for London was—

In 1880	..	..	..	80 per cent.
In 1886	..	..	..	78 per cent.
In 1889	..	..	..	78 per cent.

In schools which are fed from a poorer stratum of society, the percentage must be considerably lower. So far as irregularity is due to children being kept at home to mind younger children, the establishment of infant schools and crèches should prove useful. Something too might be hoped from an improvement in our school curricula in the direction of greater attractiveness and greater practical utility. As a matter of school discipline, *written* excuses for any absence (however short) should be brought by the pupil on his return to school, if such are obtainable. In superior schools, a teacher whose position is sufficiently influential, can bring parents to recognise a distinction between valid and trifling excuses. The experience of the School Board for London seems to show that not much can be expected from administrative interference.

As the educational system widens its sphere of influence and secures a larger proportion of children from the lower classes, the percentage of attendance is harder to maintain.

Rev. J. D. Don, King William's Town.—In the free school intended for the poorest class of the white population, the irregularity of attendance is serious. It is owing chiefly to the fact that parents keep their children at home when they require their help—sometimes also on account of their clothing.

2. In your opinion could a system of compulsory attendance in town schools be enforced?

If so, can you make any suggestions for the practical working of such a system?

Molteno Town Council as Managers of Second Class U. P. School.—The time has not arrived when compulsory education could be wisely enforced in the colony.

J. H. Brady, Esq.—Compulsory education is feasible, not only in towns, but also in the country. In the case of towns, a necessary preliminary to the establishment of a system of compulsory education would be the putting of the whole aided education of the town in the hands of one body, either the Municipality, or preferably, a School Board elected by the ratepayers. Proper safeguards should be given by law to the rights of the various religious bodies which have already established mission or other schools reaching a defined standard of suitability in staff, lighting, ventilation and air space of class-rooms, furniture and apparatus, and in sanitary arrangements, to carry on their denominational work without undue municipal or school board interference, and to have a certain just proportion of whatever State or municipal aid is given. It would be necessary to start entirely free ragged schools for the waifs and strays, and to make provision for giving free education in all the lower grade schools, as far as the compulsory standard or age, to all such as can make out an *a priori* case for claiming it. If education were made compulsory, provision should be made as far as possible for the separate instruction of those of pure European race from those of African or mixed stock. It is far better for both that they should be kept separate. The age limits might be over 7 and under 12. The attainment limit might be Standard III (with Bills of Parcels added); the attainment of the standard over-ruling the age limit, and the attainment of Standard II permitting one child in a family to be a half-timer. A disciplinary home or reformatory for children who are incorrigible truants, or who have entered on vicious courses, would be necessary in towns.

F. Beswick, Esq., High School, Queenstown.—Compulsory attendance of European children might be carried out in our town schools; but if so, the fees at present payable would have to be greatly reduced. Hardly thinks free schools are needed. If in the towns of any considerable size there were two or three classes of schools, with fees regulated accordingly, inability to pay the fees need never be urged by parents. Scholarships could be reserved in the higher class school for the most deserving pupils in the lower class school, and thus no child of merit would be debarred through poverty from obtaining the best possible education within reach. In villages with one school, scholarships could be available in cases of real necessity. No children should be allowed to be employed in daily labour until they have at least passed III Standard.

W. Milne, Esq., Stellenbosch.—Yes. It would have to be done on the lines of the compulsory powers granted to School Attendance Committees in England. The Town Council might safely be entrusted with the duty and control of the necessary officers.

Rev. W. Cormack, Burghersdorp.—Compulsory attendance might be practicable in large towns, but hardly necessary in small towns or villages. In these, teachers, school committees, or local managers, might accomplish much by using their influence with neglectful parents. To meet cases of poverty, the Education Department should insist on local managers giving free education to poor children to the full extent of the Government grant requirement.

H. T. Elliott, Esq., Queenstown.—Unless a very expensive system of paid visitors, &c., were to be introduced, compulsory attendance would be a failure. What is wanted is (1) a law compelling every person to send his or her child to school, under penalty; (2) sharp and summary punishment for infringing the law. Unless you make education very much cheaper than it is now, it will be difficult to make it compulsory. Free and compulsory education should be synonymous.

Rev. T. G. Jones, Hackney.—Yes; by enacting that all children between say 7 and 14 shall be under instruction in some way or another to the satisfaction of the Education Department. Each Municipality should have a School Board, and each Divisional Council should be divided according to circumstances into two, three, or more Boards, but at the same time making the Divisional Council the rating authority for the whole district.

J. Lamont, Esq., Adelaide.—Compulsory attendance should be enforced in towns. Where a Government school is established, the children of a certain age within a radius of five or six miles must attend that school, if not receiving education elsewhere. Should the parents be unable to pay the fees, Municipalities and Divisional Councils should provide the necessary funds through the levying of a small rate.

T. R. Price, Esq., East London.—Under existing conditions, no, and possibly not in any case till we reach the stage of free education. A considerable step in the direction of compulsory education can be taken when the educational arrangements are entrusted to duly elected representatives, such as the School Boards of Great Britain or America. Such local authorities, when elected, could be entrusted with power to enforce attendance, the exercise of the same being left to their discretion. As an inducement to secure attendance, among other things, the Government grants should be made more largely dependent on the number of scholars on the register, and the average attendance.

W. E. Clarke, Esq., St. Andrew's College, Grahamstown.—Yes. Compulsory attendance at some school, either authorized by or acceptable to such a Board, could be enforced by the Board's appointing an officer whose duty it should be to enquire into and report to them cases of non-attendance, which, if persisted in, might at the instance of the Board be brought before the local magistrate.

P. Warren, Esq., St. Andrew's College, Grahamstown.—A system of compulsory attendance in town schools could be enforced. Similar machinery to that adopted by School Boards in England, with remission of fees (partial or total) in extreme cases of undoubted hardship.

Professor MacWilliam, Gill College, Somerset East.—I believe that in the larger towns such a system could not, and that in the smaller it neither could nor should, be enforced. A compulsory clause must apply to the *whole* population of the place. I do not believe that public opinion would sanction the compulsory education of the coloured population, say of Cape Town, largely at Government expense, while so many white children in other parts of the country would have to go uneducated. If the clause were to apply to white children only, who is to draw the line between white and coloured? Such a law applied in the smaller up-country towns would tend to keep the farmers from coming to reside in them for the education of their children, and this would tend not to further but to retard the spread of education.

H. J. McClure, Esq., Mossel Bay.—As the Government allows the establishing of third class schools in towns and villages, there is no occasion to establish fourth class schools. It will interfere with the routine of the present system. In Cape Town and other large centres it is no difficult matter to find out who are absenting themselves from school.

Rev. J. H. Hofmeyr, Somerset East.—I do not think, however desirable the objects of a system of compulsory education may be, that it would work well. Comparatively high fees must be charged on account of the present system of aided schools, which compels the managers, in order to secure the existence of the school and to save the sub-guarantors from making good a deficiency at the end of the year, to guard against low school fees, and this places the school beyond the reach of many. Rather than spend a certain sum of money on the necessary machinery for compulsory attendance, I would use that money for holding out inducements, in some shape or other, to parents for sending their children to school.

Miss Redford, Kimberley Girls' School.—Compulsory attendance should be enforced in the same manner as in England. In case of poverty, free scholarships might be granted.

F. W. Bampton, Esq., Humansdorp.—Compulsory attendance should be enforced both in town and country. In towns, the chief constable might have power to take the names of all children not attending school, and authority to summon the parents. In the country, the members of the Cape Police, field-cornets, and justices of the peace might be empowered to do the same.

E. Noaks, Esq., Port Elizabeth.—Yes, provided that free schools (1) for the white, (2) for the coloured pupils were established, with sufficient accommodation for those requiring compulsion (*i.e.*, for those who do not as yet attend any school). I do not think that it would be advantageous, certainly not at present, to remit school fees generally in this colony upon the lines now proposed in England. It would be enough, I think, to have in the larger towns, free schools set apart for waifs and loafers. It would never answer to draft this class of children as "free" scholars into existing schools. The police could be requisitioned to take in charge children running the streets during school hours, and the Magistrate be empowered to compel parents to send such children to the "free" schools.

Rev. J. D. Don, King William's Town.—Unnecessary here. Every class seems desirous of education.

3. Can you suggest any improvement on the present system of Managers?

(*a*) As to constitution.
(*b*) As to mode of election.

Molteno Town Council as managers of second-class U. P. School.—There seems to be no alternative (in small towns especially) but to place the management of Government aided schools in the hands of the Town Council whose members retire periodically. This system exists in many places already and seems to work satisfactorily. In larger towns, a Committee of Management is preferable, subject to the Town Council administering the funds and making appointments.

J. H. Brady, Esq.—For schools on farms and in small hamlets, the present condition and method of election of managers is the most practicable, as long as there is no central body such as the Divisional Council (or District School Board) to take over the general management of a division or district. In the case of a town or village, if the management be undertaken by the Municipal Council or Management Board, or a committee specially appointed by the ratepayers, the present systems of constitution and election would naturally be superseded. In other cases, the present systems might in the main be adhered to, the principal alterations being:—The addition of Government nominees, not necessarily guarantors, to the committees: an alteration in the rule regarding election, providing that one-third of the committee retire every year, thus giving the committee a more continuous existence: the admission of all who have paid school fees for the preceding year to the privilege of voting for members of committee.

F. Beswick, Esq., High School, Queenstown.—The present system of managers should be abolished; and there should be for every fiscal division a School Board, with local committees, to look after the educational interests of that district. This Board should be chosen by the ratepayers, have perpetual succession, be a corporate body, holding all school property in the district, and with the power to levy an educational rate. The money thus raised should be for the purpose of erecting and keeping in repair school buildings and making up the deficiency which occasionally occurs between the ordinary revenue and expenditure of any school through unforeseen circumstances, such as the fluctuation of population, severe drought, &c.

H. J. McClure, Esq., Mossel Bay.—School Boards should be constituted in every district. The mode of election should be the same as that followed in the election of members for Divisional Councils.

W. Milne, Esq., Stellenbosch.—Teachers always like the most intelligent men of the community on their School Committees, and as a rule they are on them, but there are many places where committees are not particularly intelligent, and the school sometimes suffers. It would be well in such places if committees could be taught to understand that teachers are not their servants but the servants of the public, just as the civil servants are. It would free small communities from much unnecessary friction and local school difficulties. A school cannot be maintained in a village if the teacher's authority is not above question by all.

Rev. W. Cormack, Burghersdorp.—The present system of election of managers by the guarantors has answered well here. The same right of election might be extended to parents who have children attending the school.

H. T. Elliott, Esq., Queenstown.—I have not been in the colony long enough to judge of this question. My impression is that unless the guarantee system be abolished, no alteration can be effected. Every manager should visit the school once a week to (*a*) check registers, (*b*) consult with the teacher. A rota could easily be arranged so that the work would be light.

Rev. T. G. Jones, Hackney.—School Boards should be established, and the members should be elected in municipalities by the payers of town rates, and in country school districts by payers of road rates, but in order to meet the case of squatters in native locations and people living on communal properties, the school rate in their case should be tacked on to the hut taxes and collected in the usual way, or it might be levied the same as on title-holders and collected by the Divisional Council, as if it were road rate.

F. H. Ely, Esq., School Inspector.—Instead of Boards of Managers, elected as at present by guarantors, and holding office for a period of three years, I would recommend the formation of school districts. The inhabitants of each school district should elect its School Board, which should be a corporate body capable of holding property, and empowered to levy a rate to make up any deficiency, should the Government grant and school fees (which should be as low as possible) together fail to cover the necessary expenses of the school. The School Boards should also have the power of levying a rate for the erection and repairing of school buildings and property, to supplement the Government grant for these purposes, such grant to be made on the £ for £ principle; but the amount of any school rate should be limited by Act of Parliament. The rate might be collected by the Divisional Council on the application of the School Board.

J. Lamont, Esq., Adelaide.—Can suggest no improvement.

Professor MacWilliam, Gill College, Somerset East.—If a national system of education is to be established, the guarantor system must be abolished. This is *urgently required*. The School Board might then be elected in various ways, *e.g.*, it might consist, like the University Council, partly of Government nominees and partly of members popularly elected, but I am afraid this might lead to friction, so I think it would be better to have the whole Board popularly elected. Such a plan, however, would require some effective check to prevent extravagance in spending public money and to prevent arbitrary treatment of teachers, perhaps also to prevent the school from becoming denominational in everything but the name.

Rev. J. H. Hofmeyr, Somerset East.—With a view to what I say below, I think that Boards of Management should:

(a) Consist partly of *ex officio* members, named in the Act of Parliament that requires to be framed, and partly of representatives of the public;

(b) The non-official members should be chosen, as at present, by resident householders: for the elementary schools, by those in the immediate neighbourhood in town or country; for the higher classes of schools, by the householders in town and country. It should be expressly stipulated that the meeting for electing members for a Board of Management shall be held at such time and place as would be most convenient to all parties interested in the school over which the Board has to preside. If the present system remains in force, I would give the right of electing managers *only* to the guarantors.

T. R. Price, Esq., East London.—The first steps to take to secure the object indicated are (a) to alter the principle of electing the local authorities to whom the duty of organizing and managing the schools is to be entrusted, and (b) the method of according Government grants. The latter should be made to depend in a greater measure on average attendance and results. The towns and districts should be required to contribute their quota towards the provision and support of schools, and their representatives, duly elected as in the case of municipal, Divisional Council, and Parliamentary, representatives, either with or without Government nominees, should be entrusted, under Government supervision, with the duty of the provision of school accommodation, management, administration of funds, and other matters appertaining thereto.

W. E. Clarke, Esq., St. Andrew's College, Grahamstown.—A Board of Governors or Managers, elected by the whole body of the ratepayers of a district, and having a more or less direct control over education generally and over all schools within the district that are in receipt of Government aid, including the right of recommending the giving or withholding of Government aid, would have a more representative character than the present system of managers, and would also have a more authoritative and responsible position. Such Boards ought, like Divisional Councils and Municipalities, to be empowered to levy rates for educational purposes.

P. Warren, Esq., St. Andrew's College, Grahamstown.—School Boards for towns and divisions, to be elected by the same voters as for Divisional and Town Councils; a certain proportion (say one-third of the Board) to retire annually, but to be eligible for re-election ; they should have the right to levy rates, if necessary, to supplement the fees, and to provide buildings, furniture, &c., such rates not to interfere with the present system of Government grants, which should remain much as at present, on the £ for £ principle. The public school property should be vested in such Boards, and any voluntary, denominational or private school, sanctioned by such Board, and accepting Government inspection and a suitable conscience clause, should be eligible to receive the Government grant in the same way as public schools. Such sanction once given not to be withdrawn without the permission of the Education Department after reason assigned in writing to the Education Department by the local Boards.

Miss Redford, Kimberley Girls' School.—Managers should not have the power to dismiss teachers without the consent of the Education Department. All ratepayers and parents should have a voice in the election, whether guarantors or not.

F. W. Bampton, Esq., Humansdorp.—The managers of public schools in villages and towns should be the members of the Divisional Council, with the Civil Commissioner at their head. The managers should not be compelled to become guarantors. The Government should collect the school fees, and pay the teachers a fair wage. The £ for £ principle is bad, as it leads to a great deal of equivocation, false declarations, and so on.

E. Noaks, Esq., Port Elizabeth.—The system adopted at the Port Elizabeth public school, under an Act of Incorporation (4th June, 1856), subsequently amended in 1888, presents features which it might be found possible to extend to the colony generally. The Board of Managers consists of 15 members, two of whom—the Civil Commissioner and the Mayor—are members *ex officio*. Of the remaining 13, six are elected by the Town Councillors from their own number, and 7 by subscribers and donors of £5 within the twelve months preceding the election ; school fees for this purpose being considered subscriptions. [To place this system upon a more popular basis, all voters possessing the Municipal or Divisional franchise might be given a voice in the election. The advantage would be in giving electors an opportunity to choose representatives with educational qualifications and interests. The representatives of the Town Council would combine financial with other qualifications.] A standing committee is appointed, consisting of 5 members (3 being a quorum) to which important questions are for the most part referred for consideration. The meetings of the Board are public, reporters being present ; but not those of the committee. One of the bye-laws gives to the rector a seat at the Board and in the Committee, for purposes of consultation, but not with the power of voting. This serves to give a certain continuity to the system, and perhaps possesses other advantages.

Rev. J. D. Don, King William's Town.—The constitution and election, as at present existing, seem suited to the present system viewed as a whole. Representatives of Government might be introduced in consideration of the extent to which Government support is provided. Any change in the incidence of financial responsibility, as for example, by the imposition of a school rate, would necessarily imply that the management should be lodged in a School Board elected by the ratepayers ; but I am not in favour of such a change, which would be, I believe, detrimental to the interests of education.

---

4. What steps should be taken to give Boards of Management perpetual succession, and to provide for the tenure of public school property ?

Molteno Town Council as Managers of second class undenominational public school.— See answer to question 3.—With reference to the tenure of public school property, it should be held in trust for the towns by the Town Council, supposing they are the managers of the school.

J. H. Brady, Esq.—In the cases in which the education of a town or village or division (or school district) is undertaken by the Municipality or management Board or Council, the perpetual succession is already provided. Where, however, this is not the case (that is in the very great majority of public schools), the matter is one which presents some difficulties. In many villages the buildings have been put up, or bought, or are being maintained nominally by a constantly changing and sometimes suddenly ending body called the school committtee, but in reality, by a church corporation, or even by a private individual. In some of these cases, a large and often extravagant outlay has been made, interest to a considerable amount has to be paid ; and in some, money has been advanced as a free gift by Government. Some of these buildings are badly designed, badly built, and often put up at a ruinous cost, but still it would hardly be expected that private corporations would give up property without being in part at least remunerated for their outlay, or without retaining some control over it ; nor could a School Board or the Government be expected to pay even for suitable buildings more than they were worth. Any legislation on this subject should be thoughtfully and cautiously devised and judiciously applied. In one case, a debt which was still in existence last year, was incurred on school buildings many years ago on the security of the individual members of the then existing committee, the majority of whom have since died or become insolvent, while the remainder have left the place. In another case, a building which, I am told, was erected by public subscription for school purposes, has been taken possession of by a church, and is now regarded as church property. I am strongly of opinion that no Government aid, either by free grant or under Act 11 of 1884, should be given to school buildings unless they are vested in a Municipality or Village Management Board, or Divisional (or school district) Council, or failing these, in the Civil Commissioner, except of course in the case of such a Board as that of the Grey Institute. In rural schools, there is no need for any change. The school is generally held in a private house or farm building. In some instances, however, laudable attempts have been made to erect a worthy and permanent separate school building ; and I even know of one case in which a farmer gave land for the purpose of erecting thereon a school and master's house. Good might be done, if Government encouraged such liberality as this by giving to the building and furniture on the £ for £ principle, the property of course being vested as mentioned above.

F. Beswick, Esq., High School, Queenstown.—The current expenses of each school should be borne at present by the fees and the Government grant. The rate levied by the School Board could be collected by the Divisional Council.

H. J. McClure, Esq., Mossel Bay.—The establishment of School Boards would remedy the present defect in this respect, and one result would be that teachers would have more fixity of tenure than under the guarantee system.

W. Milne, Esq., Stellenbosch.—There should be a considerable proportion of Government nominees on every School Council. The Councils should be for a larger area ; they should have very much enlarged powers ; and they should be Corporate bodies. The members should retire by rotation. (See Stell. Coll. Act : No. 11, 1882 :—The Council of which works admirably.)

Rev. W. Cormack, Burghersdorp.—Here the school property is vested in a body of Trustees, consisting of the Magistrate, the minister of the Dutch Reformed Church, the Chairman of the Municipality, the Chairman of the Public Library, and the oldest Justice of the Peace, and their successors in office. But an Act of Parliament would be the best means of producing uniformity with regard to all school property.

H. T. Elliott, Esq., Queenstown.—The only way to effect this desirable object is to : (1) appoint a Divisional Board with power to make a rate, or ; (2) to affiliate the management of our public schools with the present Town Councils and other public bodies.

Rev. T. G. Jones, Hackney.—The School Board should be made a body corporate, with perpetual succession and a common seal, with power to acquire and hold property. The present school rooms could be utilised by selling or leasing to the Board.

J. Lamont, Esq., Adelaide.—The same law should be applied as in the case of Municipalities or Divisional Councils, the property being vested in such bodies.

T. R. Price, Esq., East London.—The present arrangement is unfair to teachers, apart from the feeling of constant uncertainty created. All public school property should be vested in trustees, of whom one or more should be Government officers ; preferably the representative of the Education Department and the Civil Commissioner for the district.

W. E. Clarke, Esq., M.A., St. Andrew's College, Grahamstown.—The present undenominational public schools might be transferred to these Boards to be completely under their supervision and control, and to be held by each successive Board in trust for the community within the district.

Professor MacWilliam, Gill College, Somerset East,—There should be a statutory School Board say in in every division, which should have the same rights to hold property as Municipal Councils and other public bodies.

Rev. J. H. Hofmeyr, Somerset East.—To secure perpetual succession, the Boards of Managers should have one-half of their non-official members retire at the end of each year, each member being elected for *two* years, except the one half that retires at the end of the first year.

H. Lardner Burke, Esq., Grahamstown.—Under the earlier Education Act (No. 14 of 1858), which was repealed by the present Education Act (No. 15, 1865), regular succession in school commissioners was provided for by section 14, while section 30 dealt with the tenure of property. The various Acts dealing with special colleges or schools, *e.g.*, Graaff-Reinet College (Act 29, 1860, section 17), and Stellenbosch College and Schools (Act 9, 1881, section 17), contain provisions relative to the tenure of property; *vide* also as regards the S. A. College, Act 15, 1878, section 7. The matter is perhaps most completely dealt with in the Port Elizabeth Public Schools Act (No. 6, 1856), in section 3 (which gives the Board of Managers its name or style and clothes it with perpetual succession) and in section 15 (which deals with the tenure of property). The Act 13 of 1865 provides machinery whereby grants-in-aid shall be given by the Government on certain conditions to certain schools to be established in the various towns or villages, etc., in the colony. These schools are known as "public schools," apparently because they receive Government aid and are subject to Government inspection, but as regards formation and establishment, management and control they are dependent on local arrangements. No proper provision, however, is made for the choice or election of local managers. The schedule deals with them as existing, but contains no provision for calling them into existence. It is desirable that the Act should be amended in this matter, and the whole question of the qualifications of managers, the nature of their constituencies, and the mode of election, should be dealt with. To these provisions dealing with the constitution of the Boards of Management should be added others which should give these Boards perpetual succession, and provide for the tenure of them by school funds and property. These provisions might be generally in accordance with sections 3 and 15 of the Port Elizabeth Public Schools Act, referred to above. I am not acquainted with the particular circumstances under which Act 13 of 1865 was passed, nor have I seen any report of the discussions which took place in Parliament; but it seems not improbable that Municipal and Divisional Councils were then expected to undertake the duties of school management (*vide* Act 13, 1865, Schedule, School Regulations Order A, Class 1, section 13), to a much larger extent than has hitherto been the case (*vide* par. 6, Report of Superintendent-General of Education, 1889).

Miss Redford, Kimberley Girls' School.—It is not advisable to give Boards of Management perpetual succession, as it would place too much power in their hands.

F. W. Bampton, Esq., Humansdorp.—Objects to this entirely in Boards of Management.

Rev. W. J. Snijman, Venterstad.—Guarantors should be obliged to remain in office, when they tender their resignation, until the newly-appointed guarantors actually take their place, and their successors should take over all the obligations of those who have resigned.

E. Noaks, Esq., Port Elizabeth.—The Act quoted in the previous answer contains the following provisions:—"The Board of Managers aforesaid shall stand and be possessed of all lands which may be granted to the said Board by Her Majesty the Queen, or by any private person, for the use and benefit of the public schools aforesaid and of all lands and buildings which may be purchased, erected, or in any manner acquired by the said Board for the purposes of the said schools; and of all funds and moneys granted to the said Board from and out of the public revenue of this colony, or given, subscribed, bequeathed, paid, or in any manner coming to the said Board for the use and benefit of the said schools; and generally of all property, movable or immovable, belonging to the said schools. It shall be lawful for the said Board, with the sanction of the Governor of this colony for the time being, first had and obtained, but not otherwise, to sell by public sale, but not otherwise, any portion or portions of any land which may have been granted to the said Board by Her Majesty the Queen, which land it may be found expedient to alienate; and the said Board may, in case the sanction aforesaid shall have been obtained, lease any of the said last-mentioned lands at the best rent that can be obtained, without any fine or foregift, for any term not exceeding thirty-three years from the time when such lease shall be made. All transfers, leases, contracts, or other instruments to be executed by the said Board, for any of the purposes of this

Act, or of the said schools, shall be executed by three members of the said Board, acting for and on behalf of the Board, of which three members the Chairman of the said Board for the time being shall be one. It shall be lawful for the said Board to purchase or rent all such lands or buildings as shall be necessary for the purpose of the said schools; and when it shall be desirable so to do, to sell again by public sale, but not otherwise, any lands or buildings which the said Board shall have *purchased*, and shall no longer require; and the said Board may also contract for the building of any buildings, or the supply of any furniture or apparatus which shall be required for such schools: Provided that no contract for any purpose which shall require an expenditure above £20 shall be entered into, unless tenders for the same shall have been called for by a notice, written or printed, and posted at the office of the Resident Magistrate of Port Elizabeth for not less than 8 days, as also by an advertisement to be published in some one or more of the newspapers of Port Elizabeth for not less than 8 days. The Board of Managers aforesaid shall cause detailed accounts, in writing, of all sums of money received by them for any of the purposes of this Act, and of all sums expended by them for any purpose thereof, to be made up to the 31st December in every year; and the said Board shall also frame a full report of the state and proceedings of the schools up to the same day in each year, and shall cause a copy of such accounts and of such report to be transmitted to the Governor of the colony, not later than the 1st of March in the next succeeding year; and the said Governor shall lay a copy of such accounts and of such report before each House of Parliament, should Parliament be sitting at the time.of the receipt of such accounts by such Governor, and in case Parliament should not then be sitting, the Governor shall lay the copies aforesaid before the said Houses respectively at the then next ensuing session of Parliament. And the said Governor shall also cause the said accounts and report, or an abstract of them, to be published in the *Government Gazette.*"

Rev. J. D. Don, King William's Town.—The addition of official representatives of Government to the existing Board as suggested above would, I presume, provide the element of permanence necessary.

5. To what extent should contributions be expected from local bodies such as Divisional Councils and Municipalities?

> (*a*) For school buildings;
> (*b*) In support of schools;
> (*c*) If so, how should contributions be collected?

Molteno Town Council as managers of second class undenominational public school.—Contributions might be made for school buildings from Divisional Councils to such an extent as the merits of each individual case commends itself to the Superintendent-General of Education, and from Municipalities to such an extent as the Town Council may decide; subject, however, to the approval of the ratepayers. Beyond the present aid received from Government towards the teachers' stipends, no further assistance is necessary in support of schools. Contributions should be collected by rates; in the case of Municipalities by special rates.

J. H. Brady, Esq. — If a local body undertook, or were compelled by law to undertake, the administration of the educational grant in a municipality or division or district, I think that, as far as regards the support of the schools in its charge, it would naturally be in exactly the same position as the existing school committees, *i.e.*, it would have to make up any deficiency. In the matter of school buildings, it is difficult to say, apart from a completely formulated scheme of School Boards, what the local bodies should do. I may here mention that my experience of schools managed by Municipalities or Divisional Councils has been most satisfactory. The school committees at Knysna, six years ago, paid £86 per annum for rent of miserably bad school rooms and for teachers' house allowances. The Municipality was then persuaded to take over the management of the schools. They borrowed money from the Government, and built excellent schools and a good master's house. The schools were well furnished and provided with everything needful, and the annual amount paid for the whole in interest and redemption fund was less than £71. To do this, and to materially reduce the fees, a rate of ½d. in the £ had to be levied, which I am told causes no dissatisfaction. A special grant of £750 has just been made, so that the total debt is less than £400, which will render a rate unnecessary or allow of a still further reduction the school fees. Though no dissatisfaction exists, still there has been perpetrated here an injustice which should be guarded against in any legislation on the matter. The whole of the population within the Municipality is taxed, but the only part that benefits is the better class, who send their children to the public school. The mission school, to which alone the poorer and the coloured people can send their children, receives no part of the rate. At Uitenhage, three years ago, the boys' school appeared to be in a moribund state. It had been declining in numbers and efficiency for years past, and there were then about 40 pupils. The Divisional Council, after some hesitation, consented to take it over. There are now two thoroughly efficient departments—a boys' higher school with 153 pupils, and a lower grade mixed school with 115 pupils. The boys' school has been put into a state of complete repair at great cost, and has been furnished throughout with excellent furniture. And all this out of current receipts, without costing the Council one penny.

W. Milne, Esq., Stellenbosch.—They might fairly be expected to provide school buildings, and make up just and lawful deficiencies after the income from fees and grants is exhausted. Government Inspectors would have to certify as to deficiencies. Such contributions should be collected along with the local rate, and paid to the Education Department on receipt of demand.

Rev. W. Cormack, Burghersdorp.—These bodies are not usually composed of those who take the greatest and most intelligent interest in educational matters, and little pecuniary aid can be expected from them. The cost of buildings should be defrayed by Government.

H. T. Elliott, Esq., Queenstown.—The Divisional Council or Municipality should bear half the initial expense of building, and the Government the other. First class schools should be self-supporting, with the aid of the present Government grant; second class schools should be aided one-fourth by the Divisional Council; third class and other schools should be fully supported, i.e., all deficiencies made up by the Council. The amount of the contributions might be found by adding to the road or other tax.

Rev. T. G. Jones, Hackney.—For school buildings none. Let the Board, under authority of an Act of Parliament, borrow the money and repay it in 50 years. In support of schools, a sum which when added to the school fees will make up one-third of the current expenses. The collection could be made thus : When money has been borrowed from the Government for building purposes, the whole should be locally repaid with interest in 50 years, on a sliding scale arrangement; the total sum needed to satisfy the sliding scale and current expenses of the school or schools to be collected as one rate by the Municipalities and Divisional Councils respectively. The Government ought to pay two-thirds of the current expenses. The tendency of the age is towards free education.

J. Lamont, Esq., Adelaide.—To erect new buildings and for maintenance of the school, Municipalities or Divisional Councils should provide one-half the necessary funds, and the Government the other half. The contributions might be collected in the same way as other rates.

H. J. McClure, Esq., Mossel Bay.—A school rate should be levied to meet deficiencies.

J. McLaren, Esq., Blytheswood.—A Divisional Council rate would be the best method of supporting schools.

T. R. Price, Esq., East London.—One-third should be contributed by local bodies, and two-thirds by Government. The public contribution should be collected by a rate, either as an independent school rate, or included in the general rate, or added in the same way as water rates are now usually added. The method of requiring a definite and regular contribution through local authorities is far preferable to expecting the districts to make up any shortfall after the expenditure has been incurred, while by making the Government grant dependent on local contributions, a sense of responsibility is created.

W. E. Clarke, Esq., St. Andrew's College, Grahamstown. — No contributions would be required from these bodies if the suggestions in answer to No. 3 were adopted.

P. Warren, Esq., St. Andrew's College, Grahamstown.—See answer to question 3. The contributions should be collected by the same machinery as for Divisional Councils and Municipalities.

Professor MacWilliam, Gill College, Somerset East.—The necessary funds both for the erection of school buildings and for the support of schools should be supplied in equal shares by the Government grant and by the local Board. The share of the latter would be raised partly in all probability by fees, the balance if any, being provided by a rate collected through say the Divisional Council.

Rev. J. H. Hofmeyr, Somerset East.—In consequence of the opinion expressed under No. 8, and based upon observation for many years, I think it absolutely necessary that (a) school buildings should be supplied by the country. The expense of their erection might be covered by grants under the Public Loans Act, one-half of the interest being paid by Government and one-half by the Board of Managers. (b) For the purpose of providing for their share of interest and of supporting the school, the Boards should have at their disposal, in addition to the school fees, such a share of the rates levied by the Divisional Councils, as shall be fixed by law, after consideration of the probable income of the schools and of the probable expense of working them efficiently. (c) If the Divisional Councils levy the rate, no extra provision need be made for collecting the contributions.

F. W. Bampton, Esq., Humansdorp.—Divisional Councils, Village Boards of Management, or Municipalities, should contribute a share of the erection and repair of school buildings, and the cost of furniture, &c., and the Government also a share. An educational rate might be levied by Divisional Councils.

Rev. W. J. Snyman, Venterstad.—It is not at all desirable that these bodies should have any connection with schools. Opposed to a tax for education as too burdensome.

E. Noaks, Esq., Port Elizabeth.—Grants for *School Buildings*, on the joint recommendation of the Superintendent-General of Education, and of some such representative School Board as above indicated, might be required from Municipal and Divisional Councils, Government contributing upon the £ for £ principle. Grants to supplement deficiencies in the school revenue should be borne entirely by the Municipality or Division, subject to the above-mentioned general conditions. Contributions should be collected by means of a Municipal or Divisional rate (included amongst the other rates), upon the issue of a precept from the Education Department.

Rev. J. D. Don, King William's Town.—Some change in the existing system is desirable. It imposes too heavy a burden and responsibility on the small part of the community willing to assess themselves for educational purposes. The general community should be made to bear the burden, but it should not be transferred to local bodies, as the interests of education would thereby suffer. The Parliamentary grant available for educational purposes should be largely increased, the necessary funds being provided by a general instead of a local rate. The school buildings should be provided and owned by the Government. With increased grants, it would be possible to lessen the fees, but the need of a local guarantee would remain, at once furnishing a check on expenditure, and providing for a local Board of Managers modified as already suggested.

---

6. What provision is made in the schools with which you are acquainted for instruction in the English and Dutch languages?

    (a) Can you suggest any further facilities?

    (b) How far do you think that object can be attained through the medium of the Elementary and other examinations?

Molteno Town Council as Managers of second class undenominational public school.— The qualifications of the head teacher embrace the teaching of both English and Dutch; but teachers are not numerous enough to make this requirement indispensable at all times. With regard to the second clause, the object should be fully attained where the system is carried out thoroughly.

J. H. Brady, Esq.—English is taught in all the schools (excepting one) with which I am acquainted. In some mission and third class schools, however, there are pupils who do not learn English. Some of these are big boys and girls who are sent to schools for 6 or 12 months to prepare for confirmation; and some are young children who are beginning their education with the more familiar language, intending to take English later, while some again, though young, are not allowed by their parents to learn English. Dutch is taught in the majority of the schools situated among the Dutch-speaking population. Full statistics on these points will be found in the last of my triennial reports laid before the Parliament in 1889. In the lower class schools, nothing is attempted in Dutch beyond reading and dictation; and these as a rule are about as well taught as the corresponding subjects in English. Translation, too, is often taught, but not as a rule well. In the higher class schools, grammar is added, and sometimes, though rarely, an attempt is made to teach composition. As far as the Education Office is concerned, I cannot see what further facilities could be given. As it is at present, the inhabitants of a locality have the power, through the committee which they elect, of deciding whether their children shall learn English or Dutch or both languages; and even in schools where the medium of instruction is professedly English. and where the majority of the pupils take little or no Dutch, the desires or prejudices of those who wish their children to be taught Dutch only are as a rule regarded. In most of the elementary schools in Dutch-speaking districts, the teachers are themselves Dutch-speaking. With regard to the School Elementary examination, if arrangements were made to have the examination or any part of it in Dutch or English at the option of the candidate (and this is the only just method of admitting Dutch into the examination). I am convinced that not one candidate in a hundred would take Dutch. If, as has been proposed by some, an additional (though not a compulsory) paper be set in the Dutch language and grammar, the examination as far as regards pupils in the non-Dutch-speaking parts of the Colony would cease to be an Elementary one, unless they were content to handicap themselves by taking only 4 papers out of 5, and to resign all chance of a good place in the list. The School Elementary examination might in this way be made an instrument for compelling a few English-speaking people to give an unwilling consent to their children learning a smattering of Dutch, and would certainly make many Dutch-speaking people who do not now see any use in it, have their children taught Dutch on account of the advantage which it would give them in the examination; but I fail to see what help it would give to the Dutch-speaking population, who can, as things now are, have as much Dutch taught as they like.

F. Beswick, Esq., High School, Queenstown.—English is the medium of instruction in Queenstown Public School; and in all the farm schools in the district except one, English is also the medium used, though several of these schools are only attended by Dutch children. Dutch is now taught in the Queenstown Public School owing to the fact that the language is required for the Civil Service examination. There was no demand previously for Dutch. During thirty years experience as a colonial teacher, has had a large number of Dutch pupils, and the great desire of all their parents has been that they should learn English ; they had enough Dutch at home, and many times he has had special injunctions from parents, " Don't let my children speak Dutch ; not even in the playground."

H. J. McClure, Esq., Mossel Bay.—The present system is quite adequate. The English language should be cultivated. The majority of Dutch farmers require their children to speak English as much as possible. and pride themselves on hearing their children converse in that language. This opinion is the result of 18 years experience.

W. Milne, Esq., Stellenbosch.—English is the medium of instruction for all, except in the higher classes for Dutch. A separate teacher has always been employed for Dutch. All pupils are taught Dutch except in the two lowest classes of the preparatory school. As soon as they have a few ideas of English grammar, Dutch is commenced. Can suggest no further facilities. Several pupils have been removed because too much Dutch was taught, but not one because too little was taught. Examinations, if conducted in fairness to all, that is, if all subjects are free and unfettered, and no advantage is given by the selection of subjects, would make no difference. Dutch is taught and will be taught where people require it for their children for practical use in after life, and not for any other reason. If candidates wish to be examined in the Dutch language for any of the examinations, provision should at once be made for such examinations, but there should be no confusion ; where English is the medium of instruction, English must be the language of examination, and the same with Dutch.

Rev. W. Cormack, Burghersdorp.—Dutch is taught in all the standards. Only a very few are exempted from learning it for special reasons at the request of the parents. The medium of tuition is, however, English. Parents generally display a greater desire that their children should learn Dutch now than formerly, but very few pupils, if any, would at present take the Elementary examination in Dutch.

J. H. Brady, Esq., M.A.—I hardly think that Government can do much more than it already does in the matter of offering educational facilities to the rural population, except in the way of providing secondary or technical education. The present booms of free scholarships in all aided public and mission schools, of private farm schools circuit schools, and grants for indigent boarders, will, when they are fully taken advantage of, leave scarcely any white children in the country who need go without education, except by the apathy or selfishness of the parents. The help of all ministers of religion and civil servants in explaining to farmers the extremely easy conditions on which aid can be obtained. Any further multiplication of small schools, or legislation providing increased facilities in obtaining aid, would however be by no means an unmixed benefit. The establishment of aided private farm schools has already caused the employment of a very inferior type of teacher, and in many cases nearly ruined the fairly efficient village schools, by withdrawing the country pupils from whom they used to derive a considerable part of their support; and the latter would result in aid being given even more than at present to a class of persons not contemplated by the originators of such legislation. I think the Government might act a little more liberally than at present to the third class public schools by increasing the grant, without requiring a corresponding increase on the part of the managers, to such as have a satisfactory school building and a certificated teacher. Larger provision should I think be made for giving country schools free grants of reading and copy books, slates and other school materials, and in cases where a satisfactory building, with boarded floor, is provided, and where there is a reasonable prospect of permanency, free grants of desks, blackboards, maps, &c. Wherever the inhabitants desire to build a suitable school and master's house, and are willing to provide a piece of freehold land, and to subscribe half the cost or give their services in making bricks, quarrying stone, cutting and riding poles, rushes, &c., I think it would be an excellent thing to make a free grant of the other half of the cost, or of such amount as would be necessary to procure such materials as the people could not well provide for themselves, viz., window and door frames, ceiling and floor boards, ironware, &c. Such a building would of course be vested in the Civil Commissioner, and would do good in many ways, besides ensuring proper school accommodation. I would recommend also that capitation allowances for indigent boarders be not for the most part restricted to private farm schools, circuit schools, and boarding departments, but be liberally given to poor pupils coming from a distance of more than six miles to any public school, at or near which they can be boarded.

H. T. Elliott, Queenstown.—In the High School, Queenstown, Dutch has been taught simply for the examination purposes of the University. A Hollander has been engaged to teach reading and translation. The grammar is attended to by the ordinary masters. No further facilities can be suggested, unless Dutch is either made compulsory or a means of raising pupils in a class. There might be inserted with the Elementary examination an easy colloquial paper in Dutch, with the object of leading up to the Civil Service examination. Generally speaking, the attainment of high Dutch is quite as difficult to Dutch marks boys as English. The marks for this paper could be added to the aggregate earned; not to raise the pupil a class, but to raise his or her position in a class.

F. H. Ely, Esq., School Inspector.—Dutch as well as English is taught in the undenominational public schools at King William's Town (Boys), East London, Queenstown, Komgha, Stutterheim, and Sterkstroom. Dutch should be a compulsory subject for all candidates for employment in the Civil Service, but making it compulsory for the school Elementary examination which could no longer be correctly called elementary, would have the effect of deterring candidates from the Eastern Districts from presenting themselves, as they would feel that they were too heavily handicapped to compete with any reasonable chance of success against candidates from the Western Districts in which Dutch is more or less generally spoken. Another effect would be, that teachers in the Eastern Districts, finding their pupils excluded from their own University by what all consider an unnecessary and some an irritating addition to the syllabus, would recommend them to offer themselves for the Oxford and Cambridge local examinations, in which they would not labour under any serious disadvantage.

J. Lamont, Esq., Adelaide.—Provision is made in all when required. Can suggest no further facilities. From his experience, instruction in Dutch is only desired and given to fit young people for their place in the Church, and in his opinion it would hinder rather than help forward the work of education to have Dutch introduced into the Elementary examination.

J. McLaren, Esq., Blytheswood.—Dutch is not taught in the native schools in the Transkei, as it would be useless. English is taught in all the schools. Children ought to be got to speak and write English, and translate from their Kafir reading books. Only a few native teachers do this. The study of the English language is well promoted by the school Elementary and other examinations at present, and it is difficult to see how Dutch could be introduced into the former without great injustice to the great majority of children who do not speak Dutch.

T. R. Price, Esq., East London.—English is the usual medium, and is always preferred, with exceedingly few exceptions. The learning of both English and Dutch is encouraged, and sufficient provision made for the purpose. Local authorities can safely be entrusted to judge of the local requirements, and any undue forcing can only result in impairing the usefulness of the school and retarding the education of the children. If the experience of the University Examiners and Government Inspectors is that the examination papers should be printed in English and Dutch, and replies be accepted in either language, I would defer to their opinion, but two things should be borne in mind, viz., the high place at present accorded to Cape University Certificates outside the Colony, and the fact that the children of colonists have now, and may be expected in the future still more, to come in contact and competition with those who, as children, have been educated in countries where education is compulsory, more advanced, and under more favourable conditions than is possible at present in South Africa. If any considerable portion of the school time is occupied in the enforced learning of any language not likely to be of special and general use to them in after life, the children would suffer.

W. E. Clarke, Esq., St. Andrew's College, Grahamstown.—From 2½ to 3 hours a week is given to the study of Dutch, just as French or any other foreign language. From 3 to 5 hours a week is given to English in all classes. Dutch could not be added to the subjects at present prescribed for the Elementary examination without completely altering the character of the examination, as Dutch would be to a large number of the candidates as much a foreign language as French or Latin. If the Boards in some districts choose to make Dutch the medium of instruction to suit the majority of the pupils in those particular districts, they might in this way give additional importance to the study of Dutch. In the Elementary examination, the papers in geography, history and arithmetic might be given both in Dutch and in English, and parallel papers set in English and in Dutch, to be selected by the candidates according as they have entered for the English or the Dutch side, so to speak, of the examination. The character of such a Dutch paper would have to be precisely similar to that of the English. Such a scheme would at least place Dutch and English on an equality as regards the Elementary examination, and its practical working would show whether there exists the necessity claimed for the increased recognition of Dutch.

P. Warren, Esq., St. Andrew's College, Grahamstown.—Both are provided for at St. Andrew's College and school. The only feasible alternative, to the recommendation of the Teachers' Conference is to have two distinct Elementary examinations, one in English and one in Dutch throughout, with a separate class list for each. For the other examinations (above the Elementary), Dutch teachers or parents generally do not, I think, feel that there is any serious grievance as they stand.

Professor MacWilliam, Gill College, Somerset East.—In all schools I know, at least where there is any demand for it, provision is made for teaching Dutch as well as English, and further facilities are not required. There would be more learning of Dutch if it were allowed any weight in the Elementary examination.

Rev. J. H. Hofmeyr, Somerset East.—In the aided schools with which I am acquainted, provision is made for instruction in both languages, i.e., where the teaching of Dutch is desired by the parents. I am, however, afraid that as a rule, sufficient attention is not given to Dutch. This, I believe, is not to be attributed to a desire to act unjustly by this language, but to the difficulty experienced in procuring a good Dutch teacher. (a) At present provision is made for the teaching of Dutch either by one of the masters of a school or by a special teacher. It strikes me difficulties may present themselves in connection with either plan. In the first case, the principal, though competent to teach Dutch, may find it impossible to set apart sufficient time for imparting instruction in this language; and the assistant having several subjects to teach in addition to Dutch, may be appointed with a view to his general efficiency more than to his special qualification for teaching Dutch. In the other case, the inability of the managers to provide the equal amount at present necessary to supplement the Government grant may, and I believe often does, make it impossible to ·appoint a special teacher of Dutch. To avoid these difficulties I would suggest if the system of aided schools remains in force, the application of the principle now admitted with regard to the Industrial Departments of some schools, and to the aid given to "children on farms," so that an amount might be paid by Government for the teaching of Dutch, for which no equivalent is expected from the managers, but only a moiety, say one-half, of the Government grant. (b) Dutch should in my opinion, be added, as a fifth subject to the Elementary examination, in lieu of which candidates should be at liberty to take German, French, Kafir or Sesuto.

Hon. Abercrombie Smith, M.A., Controller and Auditor-General.—The University Council has in my opinion been unfairly blamed for its attitude towards certain proposals which have been made for the purpose of encouraging instruction in the Dutch language, through the medium of the University examinations. In considering this question I shall confine my attention to the case of the School Elementary examinations. The proposals·relating to this examination are best expressed in the following resolutions of the Synod of the Dutch Reformed Church :—

" (a) That the Dutch language should be added to the subjects now prescribed
" for the School Elementary examination, in such manner, however,
" that no candidate shall be compelled to take that subject, *but that any*
" *candidate taking it shall thereby be entitled to obtain higher marks.*
" (d) That in the School Elementary examination candidates should have the
" opportunity of being examined in Dutch in those subjects which they
" have learned through the medium of the Dutch language."

Now I am quite sure that the University Council is desirous of acting with the most perfect fairness, and of meeting the wishes of those who desire to encourage the study of the Dutch language, in any way which is not unfair to a large section of the candidates. Were it not for the last clause of the above resolution marked (a) (in italics), I have no doubt but that the wishes of the Synod would have been met, and the only question would have been to ascertain in what way effect could best be given to the proposals. The Council has, however, hitherto failed to find any course acceptable to the representatives of the Dutch speaking candidates, and at the same time not unfair to English speaking candidates.

The difficulty of arriving at a satisfactory solution is increased by other considerations. In the first place great weight must be attached to the opinions of many practical teachers, that the number of the subjects of examination should not be increased, because in their opinion any increase in the present strain on the candidates would be physically and mentally injurious to them.

In the second place, the proposal that every paper should be prepared in both languages, and that the answers of candidates may be given in either language, presents several practical difficulties, of which by far the most important is that of obtaining a sufficient number of persons competent to examine papers set and answered in both languages, while, if one examiner is employed for the same paper when set in the Dutch language, and another when it is set in the English language, it is almost or altogether impossible to maintain that equality of standard essential to a fair treatment of candidates. This latter difficulty already exists to a certain limited extent wherever alternative papers are allowed, and to that limited extent perfect fairness is not now and never has been secured in those examinations where any choice is allowed. It would be a very serious matter if such unfairness extended to every subject in the whole examination. The task of finding examiners able to examine in both languages is rendered all the more difficult by the consideration, that owing to the enormous increase in the number of candidates, it will be necessary in future (even if no other change is made) to double the number of examiners, giving each only half a paper. If, however, the above difficulties can be satisfactorily overcome, the others are not of sufficient importance to prevent the proposal from being carried out.

Assuming that the candidates are put on a perfectly equal footing by the preparation of papers in both languages, and by being allowed to answer in either language, it would be grossly unfair to English speaking candidates to rank them below candidates, in other respects, equal or even much inferior to them, merely because they are not acquainted with the Dutch language. There may be something to be said in favour of compelling an English speaking boy, especially in the Western Districts of the colony, to know something of colloquial Dutch, but to my mind nothing can warrant compelling an English speaking girl to learn the Dutch language, under the penalty (should she prefer French or German) of ranking her far below her true position in the examination lists. This unfairness would be more especially felt in Port Elizabeth, Graham's Town, King William's Town, and other important centres in the Eastern Districts where a knowledge of Dutch is not required in ordinary life, while competent instruction in that language can scarcely if at all be obtained.

A number of suggestions have been made by which any unfairness may be avoided, and though these are not equally free from objection, some one of them, or some similar* proposal, would no doubt have been adopted by the University Council, but for the fact that no one of them appears to be acceptable to the representatives of the Dutch speaking candidates. Some of these suggestions are as follows :—

(a) That a paper be set on the Dutch language and that in addition to the list shewing the position of the candidates in other subjects, a second list be issued shewing the relative position as regards the Dutch language of those passed candidates who have obtained marks for that language.

(b) That candidates be examined at their option either on the Dutch or English language, the same number of marks being assigned to either subject. This is objected to by the representatives of the Dutch speaking candidates on the ground that every candidate should be examined on the English language.

(c) That in addition to the existing paper on the English language, a second paper be set either on the English or on the Dutch language at the option of the candidate.

(d) That in addition to the existing paper on the English language, a paper be set on Dutch, French, or German at the option of the candidate. This is objected to on the ground that it treats Dutch as a foreign language.

(e) That candidates be allowed to take either English or Dutch, or both English and Dutch, but that for the purpose of placing them in order of merit, their marks in but one of the languages (Dutch or English) be taken into account, whichever is most to the advantage of each candidate.

(f) That candidates be allowed to take either a paper on the English language or one on the Dutch language, or one which is half on the English and half on the Dutch language.

(g) That candidates who take a paper on the Dutch language in addition to a paper on the English language be ranked in an entirely separate list.

(h) That a paper be set on the Dutch language, and that the fact of having passed in Dutch be stated in the candidate's certificate, but that the marks obtained in Dutch be not counted for the purpose of position in the lists.

(i) That the resolution of the Synod marked (a) be adopted, subject to the understanding, that the aggregate marks obtained by each candidate be published, but that the candidates should be arranged in order of merit according to the aggregate marks obtained by them in other subjects.

In considering the attitude hitherto taken by the University Council it must not be forgotten that the leading advocates of the proposals have admitted in Parliament that the grievance is a sentimental one. Had it been a substantial grievance a remedy would certainly have been applied at once, but under the circumstances the University naturally hesitates to adopt one out of a number of courses (which although fair are all more or less open to objection on other grounds) so long as it appears that not one of them is accepted by the advocates of the movement. It may be added that in endeavouring to arrive at a solution which will really satisfy the "Taal" Congress, the fact must not be lost sight of, that that body was apparently by no means unanimous on one important point. For if the reports in the newspapers may be relied on, the Congress avoided any decision on a question which was raised, whether the subject of examination should be classical Dutch or the "Taal," and the impression was conveyed to my mind that many members of the Congress understood, that the "Taal" is meant wherever the word "Dutch" is used in the resolutions. The statement in the second part of the first resolution of the Congress that the examination in Dutch shall include "some questions on ordinary declensions and conjugations" doubtless indicates that the

NOTE.—A resolution on the subject, almost identical with one of those here given, has since been adopted by the University Council.

framers of the resolutions meant grammatical Dutch, and the members of the deputation which waited on the University Council some months ago stated most clearly that classical Dutch was meant. It would, however, be very unsatisfactory if it should be found that any solution accepted as fair and reasonable failed after all to satisfy a large number of members of the Congress, through a misunderstanding as to what is meant by "Dutch." On this point I may say that I draw a wide distinction between the University and Civil Service examinations. In the case of University examinations, I entirely agree with the deputation above referred to that classical Dutch alone can be recognised. On the other hand, in view of the fact that the chief object to be secured in the case of a Civil Servant "is ability to converse in Dutch, "sufficient for the ordinary business of a Magistrate's Court or Civil Com- "missioner's Office," I would personally be satisfied for Civil Service purposes, if the candidates possessed a knowledge of the "Taal" only.

Miss Redford, Kimberley Girls' School.—Cannot suggest any further facilities. Pro- vision is made in this school for all scholars in the fourth standard and above who may learn either German or Dutch free of charge. German is invariably chosen.

F. W. Bampton, Esq., Humansdorp.—The parents (all Dutch) in this school object to the Dutch language being taught, as they say it spoils the pronunciation of the children when speaking English.

Rev. W. J. Snijman, Venterstad.—English receives its fair share of attention, but not Dutch. The latter should be made compulsory in the Elementary examination.

E. Noaks, Esq., Port Elizabeth.—In Port Elizabeth there is |very little demand for Dutch as a subject of instruction. The general feeling is that those who need to acquire the language for commercial purposes can easily do so by a short residence up-country, and that the grammatical study of the language with this object is superfluous. A teacher of Dutch has recently been engaged at the Grey Institute (for the upper classes), and it is proposed in this school to replace the study of French by the study of Dutch, as being of more immediate and practical moment to the majority of the pupils, who cannot be expected to carry either language to the pitch of scholarly precision and critical nicety. The resolution adopted at the Conference of Teachers, which was recently held in Kimberley, upon the question of the advisability of introducing the Dutch language into the "Elementary" examination, embodies a very widely diffused conviction, viz., that the Elementary examination should be kept as at present to strictly Elementary subjects; but that if Dutch is to be introduced, it should be only in conjunction with other strictly optional subjects (of which candidates may or may not take one, at their discretion). If this course be adopted, it is, I believe, the general wish of teachers, and I should hope of the public, that the optional subjects should be kept entirely distinct from the strictly Elementary subjects, and relegated to separate class lists. On the general question of fostering or promoting subjects of study by including them in schemes of examination, I can only say that I do not regard it as one of the legitimate functions which examinations may be made to serve. A subject of study should not lean for support upon examinations as an adventitious aid, but should claim to be included in an examination scheme because of its intrinsic merits. If students are not desirous of learning the Dutch language for its own sake, it seems a pity that they should be exposed to the temptation of taking it up simply as a means for scoring marks in an examination. A language so studied can have but little subsequent significance.

Rev. J. D. Don, King William's Town.—No further facilities needed in this district.

---

7. What additional facilities, if any, can be provided to meet the wants of the children in agricultural districts?

Molteno Town Council, as Managers of second class undenominational public school. —The great and serious want in agricultural districts is the establishment of boarding houses in connection with the schools. The want of this provision in this district, and we think in others also, prevents the majority of farmers sending their children in to the town school. The cost of board and lodging, even where such can be obtained, is beyond the means of farmers who have a number of children to educate. This would in our opinion be a most desirable object, to which the contributions of Divisional Councils and Municipalities could be applied.

F. Boswick, Esq., High School, Queenstown.—The pupil teacher system should be extended, especially in second and third class schools. Perhaps not many young lads would become pupil teachers, but no doubt many young girls, on reaching the age of 15 years, would be glad to qualify themselves. One of the greatest difficulties experienced by farmers at present is to obtain properly qualified governesses for their farm schools. The pupil teacher system, carried out on much the same lines as in the Board Schools in England and Scotland, would supply this much felt want.

W. Milne, Esq., Stellenbosch.—The wants of agricultural districts are amply provided for at present by the Farm School regulations.

Rev. W. Cormack, Burghersdorp.—Aid might be given on the £ for £ principle for the erection of suitable school buildings. In other respects, the system of "Farm Schools" affords excellent facilities for country children. The difficulty is to prevail on farmers to take sufficient advantage of them.

H. T. Elliott, Esq., Queenstown.—A number of farms might be grouped together, and an iron and wood building constructed where the children could be taught during the day by a properly certificated teacher, who should be adequately remunerated. This would obviate the necessity of employing governesses, so often incompetent. If necessary, a dormitory could be added where the children could sleep, going home on Friday afternoons. This is the method employed in Queensland—a colony where education is free and compulsory, and as far advanced as any.

Rev. T. G. Jones, Hackney.—The present organisation including "Circuit Teachers," "Farm Schools," and third class public schools amongst a cluster of farms seems to nearly reach all classes. The amount granted under the "Farm School" is too low. The average grant when the teacher is certificated is about £16 and when uncertificated about £10, much lower than paid for circuit teachers or for third class schools ; amongst "Clustered Farms" payment should be for each child present on day of inspection :

If under certificated teacher	£3
If under uncertificated teacher ..	£2

That would bring the possibilities of farm schools to a level with the other schools mentioned.

J. Lamont, Esq., Adelaide.—By the establishment of schools in their midst. Only a fractional part of the children in the country districts is being educated. Teachers are difficult to get or the parents are too poor. Where ten or twelve children can be got together, a school should be established, half the teacher's salary being paid by the Government and half by the managers. When a deficiency occurs, it should be made up by a small rate.

Professor MacWilliam, Gill College, Somerset East.—Government cannot do more than it now does, unless perhaps by gradually withdrawing grants from farm schools taught by uncertificated teachers. The progress made by the pupils in these schools would in many cases be more rapid if the teachers, most of whom understand colloquial Dutch, made more use of it in explaining the English reading books, &c.

T. R. Price, Esq., East London.—An elective body, such as proposed, would be likely to be best able to devise the most suitable means of providing additional facilities in agricultural districts that would best meet local requirements, and at the same time encourage the increase and minimise the cost of farm schools.

Rev. J. H. Hofmeyr, Somerset East.—The provision made for aiding the instruction of children in agricultural districts by the circuit schools and the grants in aid to farm schools is very liberal. It might be made still more complete by the offer of a capitation allowance for each child, to parents who cannot afford to employ a private tutor, or to avail themselves of existing boarding schools, as an inducement to send their children to the nearest farm school. At the same time, I do not think that the wants of the children in agricultural districts will be fully met, except by a sufficient number of elementary schools scattered over the country and provided by the State.

W. B. Stanford, Esq., Chief Magistrate, East Griqualand.—The Education Act has not been extended to East Griqualand, and farmers are placed at a great disadvantage in comparison with those in Colonial districts, but they are anxious to secure similar advantages.

F. W. Bampton, Esq., Humansdorp.—The school hours in agricultural districts should be from 9 a.m. to 12 noon, and from 12·30 p.m., to 2·30 p.m.

Rev. W. J. Snijman, Ventorstad.—A more liberal allowance should be made by Government. In cases where a committee of farmers provides for buildings, Government should not be confined to the £ for £ system in awarding grants.

E. Noaks, Esq., Port Elizabeth.—No attempt seems to have been made as yet to promote, through Government contributions, higher class Boarding schools for
boys and girls. Such institutions, if managed with due economy upon the
Hostel system, should help somewhat to supplement the farm school system.
Suitable buildings would be the great desideratum.

Rev. J. D. Don, King William's Town.—Farm schools do not suffice for the satisfactory education of children in the country. Existing boarding schools must
be self supporting, therefore the scale of fees is too high to meet the case of
many farmers and traders. Boarding schools giving a plain, sound education,
with comfortable but frugal board, and at a reasonable fee, are a real want.
Schools of the kind exist in India for the poorer Europeans, and they depend
in part upon public subscriptions, but in this country Government aid might
be substituted.

8. Can you suggest any way in which fuller use might be made of the opportunities
afforded for education ?

Moltano Town Council, as Managers of second class undenominational public school.—
In country districts the limits of Government aided schools should be ten
miles instead of six as at present. The existing Government arrangements
admit of the grant being given to farm schools situated almost on the
borders of the town commonage to the great .disadvantage of the town
schools.

F. Beswick, Esq., High School, Queenstown.—Attached to all schools of any size there
should be a properly qualified drawing master and a science teacher. Besides
giving instruction in the public schools, these teachers should hold classes for
those who have recently left school. Evening classes during at least six
months of the year should be fostered in connection with the public schools.
Drawing and science taught in these classes would go far to make them
attractive. The present school standards, on the basis of which each school is
now annually inspected by a deputy inspector, need revision. The school
examinations conducted by the Cape University should receive fuller recognition from the Education Department than at present.

W. Milne, Esq., Stellenbosch.—Pupils might be encouraged by Government offering
prizes, certificates, or other rewards to pupils who made a certain number of
attendances, say during three years, and passed a certain standard before the
age of twelve, say. Under similar conditions, a pupil in the country might
have a free scholarship, ensuring free tuition at school for a year, as a reward
of merit. Further use might be made of the distribution of funds by larger
councils already referred to—the Inspector becoming more of School Superintendent (see J. G. Fitch's notes on American schools and training colleges),
but with civil service appointment. No competent party would take charge
of a large district without reasonable tenure of office. He would not put
himself to the trouble and expense of qualifying himself properly.

Rev. W. Cormack, Burghersdorp.—Country parents often send their children too late
to school, and withdraw them too soon again. In farm schools, the grant for
pupils under *certificated* teachers might be increased say one-half, and books,
maps, &c., supplied to such schools at half-price.

H. T. Elliott, Esq., Queenstown.—*The Elements of Agriculture* should be made a
subject of examination in the Higher Standards, and the first principles of
book-keeping ought easily to be taught. All Standards above III should
read three sets of Reading Books. Sufficient attention is not given in the
curriculum for Standard VI to Literature. A play of Shakespeare well
learnt ; with derivations, analysis, learning by heart say 300 lines, might
well take the place of one of the other subjects.

J. Lamont, Esq., Adelaide.—Compulsory education.

J. McLaren, Esq., Blytheswood.—Compulsory attendance for a limited number of
years in town and country.

T. R. Price, Esq., East London.—By making the Government grants dependent in a
large measure on attendance and proficiency, and further by directing the
education to a greater extent to what will be of most use in after life to the
majority of the pupils taught. Bearing in mind the comparatively isolated
lives to be led by so many of the pupils, and the difficulty there is in getting
any handicraft even decently taught, special and liberal grants should be
made by Government to schools, and so announced, in aid of such teaching
(as additional subjects), conditionally upon efficiency.

W. E. Clarke, Esq., St. Andrew's College, Graham's Town.—A better
graduation of schools into Elementary and Secondary is desirable, the former

confining themselves to the Standard work, and the latter leading up to the
Government aided colleges. Some system of Exhibitions or Scholarships, to the
extent, say of the remission of fees, might be instituted as a means of attract-
ing scholars from the Elementary to the Secondary Schools, and from the
latter to the Government aided colleges.

P. Warren, Esq., St. Andrew's College, Grahamstown.—A more complete
grading of schools, with liberal arrangements for bursaries to carry on
deserving scholars from lower to higher grade; or provision for a certain
proportion of free or partially free scholars at higher grade schools to be
selected from the lower grade schools in the same connected group.

Professor MacWilliam, Gill College, Somerset East.—I think Government could induce
many more young men to make fuller use of the opportunities afforded for
education, if in making appointments in the public service much more
weight were given to the University examinations.

Rev. J. H. Hofmeyr, Somerset East.—My suggestion would be to multiply the number
of schools, and the only plan I know of that will provide a sufficient number
is some system of national education. The aided schools have done excellent
work, but this system will not supply all the educational wants of the country;
nor does it seem to meet with general favour. Sometimes necessary schools
are not established on account of the unwillingness of the majority in a community to make any sacrifices for the sake of education, and those who establish a
school are burdened by liabilities and often made to pay deficiencies, which the
non-guarantor who profits as much by the school as the guarantors, entirely
escapes. If schools are established on conditions and under provisions laid
down by law, there will be no chance for the penurious and indifferent to
shirk their duty, and the educational burdens of the country will be borne by
all interested parties who, either directly or indirectly, profit by the
facilities offered to education.

Miss Redford, Kimberley Girls' School.—Bursaries should be offered to enable girls to
study for teachers, nurses, or doctors.

W. B. Stanford, Esq., Chief Magistrate, East Griqualand.—People often fail to make
full use of the opportunities from ignorance of the necessary steps to be taken
in order to secure them. The provisions of the Education Act, if applied to
East Griqualand, and the rules for the establishment and management of
schools, should be circulated as widely as possible.

Rev. P. L. Hunter, Missionary Superintendent, Griqualand East.—Paucity and irregularity of attendance are a great barrier to a full use of the opportunities for
Education. Would suggest as a remedy that:—

(a) Where the headman and people of a location ask for a teacher, that payment be made compulsory on all men who pay hut tax in that location.
When compelled to pay, whether sending children or not, the parents
would soon seek to get a return for their money.

(b) At the beginning of a session, the names of children offered as scholars
should be furnished to the teacher by the parents, and then the attendance of those thus enrolled should be enforced.

F. W. Bampton, Esq., Humansdorp.—There should be compulsory education, and no
free scholars, except in the case of extreme poverty.

E. Noaks, Esq., Port Elizabeth.—The establishment of scholarships in schools of a
lower grade, tenable at schools of higher grade. The remission of fees
(eventually) in higher class schools for Standard V. and upwards, and in
lower class schools for Standard IV. The establishment eventually of a single
teaching University or College. The total number of students at all our
colleges according to the published returns for 1890 was 197 (excluding a
dozen survey students), and of these, 146 were below the stage of matriculation. A single college could very well undertake the charge of at least 50
undergraduates, and much professional talent would thus be set free for
public-school work (e. g., the preparation of students for matriculation) in
some of the institutions which are now coping under great difficulties with
collegiate work. A large number of bursaries should be attached to such a
University College, and students might be granted free passes, or fares at
very reduced rates, to and from the college.

Rev. J. D. Don, King William's Town.—The present government grant is inadequate.

9. What is your experience of the working of the present systems of—

(a) Undenominational Education.
(b) Schools under the voluntary system.
(c) Mission Schools?

Molteno Town Council, as Managers of second class undenominational public school.—
On the whole the present systems adopted in the various schools mentioned
work satisfactorily.

F. Beswick, Esq., High School, Queenstown.—The present undenominational system
has worked well and shown itself well suited to the wants of the people. No
religious catechism or religious formulary distinctive of any particular
denomination has been taught. In some, lessons on scripture history have
been given at a set hour with the conscience clause; but this teaching of the
oldest and sublimest of histories has not been general, hence the occasional
outcry that our public schools are irreligious. Scripture history—*i.e.*, the
historical parts of the Old and New Testaments—should be taught regularly
in our public schools, of course with the conscience clause. Otherwise, the
greater number of the rising generation will grow up totally ignorant of the
most precious legacy given to the human race. The voluntary schools which
have been started in these parts have not been very successful: they have
seldom been able to stand long against the competition of the public school.
If public schools of different grades were opened in the large towns, to suit, in
the matter of fees, the several classes of the community, and if Scripture
history, which is all that most parents mean by religious teaching, was made
a fixed part of the instruction given in them, I believe the objection now
urged by the supporters of voluntary schools against the public undenominational schools would be greatly lessened.

W. Milne Esq., Stellenbosch.—My colonial experience has been in an undenominational school. I think that is the system which should be fostered and
extended. There is no other system likely to meet the wants and adapt itself
to the peculiarities of this country, and it is the system which takes the deepest
hold on all free communities. It is the American, the Scotch, and rapidly
becoming the English system of schools under public management In 1875
the Board Schools of England taught few pupils; now the number in them
is enormous. I had a short experience of a voluntary school in Scotland, and
I vastly prefer the undenominational. No experience of mission schools.

Rev. W. Cormack, Burghersdorp.—Experience has been mainly with undenominational schools, which is the only system suitable to the circumstances of this
country. Were the voluntary system adopted, the result would be that where
in villages there is now a well equipped first class school, there would soon be
three or four weak and ill equipped third class schools, unable to support well
qualified and efficient teachers.

H. T. Elliott, Esq., Queenstown.—There are great anomalies in the work set for the
different standards.
(1) Mental arithmetic is required in the IV and VI Standards, but in *no
    other*. Mental arithmetic is required more in the lower standards than
    the upper, and should always be of the nature of sums in the *next higher
    standard*.
(2) Grammar is required in the *IV* Standard and *not in the V or VI*. This
    is surely illogical, as so much grammar is required in the Elementary
    examination.
(3) Dictation (very simple) is required in the IV Standard and not in the V,
    and is again required in Standard VI (very difficult.)
(4) Reading is not required in Standard V. The time set for the completion
    of Standard VI renders it very difficult for any pupil to get the public
    schools certificate.
Of course an able conscientious teacher would supply these deficiencies himself; but no credit would be given him, and there is a sore temptation to let
work slide which is not required by the Government. Could not the Department introduce the system of pupil teachers; to serve a number of years; to
be annually examined: and only on the successful completion of their apprenticeship to be given a teacher's certificate. We should then have the nucleus
of a body of practical, experienced teachers.

Rev. T. G. Jones, Hackney.—The undenominational system works well. Schools
under the voluntary system should get no grant. Mission schools could be
turned into public or board schools, should rates be levied in aid of schools.
There is no other reason for their existence than the difficulties in raising the
fees. Present mission schools might be allowed to continue receiving grants
in aid.

F. H. Ely, Esq., School Inspector.—With reference to undenominational education, I
consider that the present system has done excellent work, and if its principal
defect—the guarantee—were removed, I think it would be admirably suited

to the wants of such a mixed population as our own. I would, however, suggest

(1) That, to avoid invidious distinctions, all schools should be called public schools, without any division into classes. The present third class school might be taken as the unit from which the grants should start. For every extra subject taught, an additional grant might be made, until the grants, fees, and rates together, amount to what is now given to a first class school. The only difference between the schools then would be in the range of subjects, which would be wider in the larger schools :

(2) That the clause on religious education should be made compulsory instead of permissive, so as to afford the clergy of the different denominations every facility for meeting pupils for the purposes of religious instruction :

(3) That the time devoted to that subject should be definitely fixed by Act of Parliament, and this for two reasons :

(a) That religious instruction might be wholly neglected in no school ;

(b) That an undue portion of the school time might not be given to it.

The conscience clause should be left as it is. Mission schools among the natives should also be placed under Boards, of which the missionaries of the different denominations should be *ex-officio* members. A rate of half-a-crown on every hut would go far towards compelling the natives to send their children to school. At present, the fees paid by them are in many cases nominal, while the demand for new schools goes on increasing. The consequence is, that schools, for which competent teachers cannot be provided, are needlessly multiplied, and missionaries are driven to employ such as are incompetent or careless in the discharge of their duties.

J. Lamont, Esq., Adelaide.—

(a) The present system is working well.

(b) Voluntary schools ought to be inspected in the same manner as undenominational public schools.

(c) Compulsory attendance should be enforced.

J. McLaren, Esq., Blythswood.—

(c) My experience is confined to native schools and institutions in the Transkei. These have generally improved, in the qualifications of the teachers, the standard of attainment, and the attendance for scholars within the last nine years. What is required to make them strictly successful is a local rate of 1s. per hut, to be collected by the Magistrates at the same time as the hut-tax, and expended on the support of the schools in the district where it was collected. This would save the teachers the annoyance of having to collect the fees, with consequent lawsuits, bad feeling, and interruptions to the proper work. Unqualified teachers should be gradually weeded out and their places supplied by certificated teachers.

T. R. Price, Esq., East London,—

(a) Undenominational education is undoubtedly the best suited to the needs of the colony and is the only form that should receive Government or other public pecuniary support.

(b) Voluntary schools have served a useful purpose as "spurs" to Government aided schools. They have on the other hand, by the withdrawal of many pupils, impaired the usefulness of the public schools, by reducing the number of teachers and the better classifying of scholars at the latter.

(c) My direct personal knowledge of mission schools is limited to two such schools, but I have availed myself of the many opportunities that have come in my way of ascertaining what is being done.

The impressions I have formed are :

(1) That while mission schools are rendering a service to the colony which is not sufficiently realised, the service would be still further increased by less attention being devoted to mere book learning and more to the advantage and necessities of the first stages of civilization and habits, including the boys being taught and regularly practising the simpler handicrafts, and the girls cooking, plain sewing and household work. Government grants should be made largely dependent upon proof by inspection, &c., not only of such teaching, but constant practice of same.

(2) That this is done at some mission stations with the best results.

(3) That the mission schools can be made the means of materially helping to solve, in a satisfactory manner, the question of native labour which is occasioning so much perplexity.

(4) I have been much struck by the self-denial practised by many town natives to provide the means for sending their sons to native institutions such as Lovedale and others to be educated and trained.

W. E. Clarke, Esq., St. Andrew's College, Grahamstown.—

(a) Undenominational schools can be much better adjusted to meet the requirements of general education than schools under the voluntary system. Their whole scheme of work is free to be arranged in the manner best adapted to suit the time, say, of the various University examinations or whatever may be the goal of the year's work.

(b) Voluntary schools may suffer very serious detriment to what may be the most desirable plan of general education, unless the means for specific religious instruction or the requirements of church festivals, etc., are studiously arranged so as not to conflict with the general scheme of the school work.

Professor MacWilliam, Gill College, Somerset East.—

(a) (b) Having been connected with an undenominational institution during all my residence in the colony, I can speak only from observation of the working of voluntary schools, but I have seen nothing to induce me to change the opinion I formed before coming to this country—that the voluntary system tends to be more expensive, or less effective, or both, than a public undenominational system, and that the sparser the system the more marked this tendency is.

(c) Mission schools I believe should as soon as possible come under the Public School Boards I have already suggested, but I do not know enough about them to say whether I could recommend such a change at once.

Rev. J. H. Hofmeyr, Somerset East.—With regard to undenominational education, the plan originated by the Superintendent-General of Education and hitherto followed, is the best adapted to the circumstances of the country.

Miss Redford, Kimberley Girls' School.—I consider that the present system works well, only that the work from one standard to another is too much to get through in a year. The generality of parents (except among purely Dutch communities) do not care for religious teaching. I have taught in schools where a great deal of religious instruction was given, and have not found the moral tone one bit higher than in this school. We teach the children to be truthful, honest, kindly in thought in deed, and honourable in their work, because it is right to be so and pleasing to God; because wrong doing is harmful to themselves and to others, and will render them unhappy both in this life and in the next. We can teach this, though there is not a doctrine of any sort introduced, and it applies to Jews and Christians of all denominations.

W. B. Stanford, Esq., Chief Magistrate, East Griqualand.—The undenominational school is working well. Mission Schools among the natives are becoming more and more appreciated, and are doing much good.

Rev. P. L. Hunter, Missionary Superintendent, Griqualand East.—

(a) The present system of Mission Schools seems adapted to the requirements of purely (or nearly so) heathen locations or districts. Much depends on the personal efforts of the Missionary as to the progress of the school, as the red people take little or no interest in it.

(b) In the absence of compulsory measures, attendance is often thin or irregular, the children being withdrawn on the slightest pretext of doing work, which their parents ought to do.

(c) Headmen and leading men interested in the school often fail to understand what amount of authority they have in the control or dismissal or appointment of a teacher, yet Government instructs them to see that the teacher does his work.

(d) There is a danger of work overlapping or of districts being neglected where different denominations are working in the same or neighbouring districts.

F. W. Bampton, Esq., Humansdorp.—Undenominational education is the best form, as it proves an effective bar to creed jealousies and bigotry. Mission schools should not have the minister for manager, but a chairman and committee elected by the congregation.

Rev. W. J. Snijman, Venterstad.—Provided Dutch receives its due, the present system is very efficient. The name of "public" schools should be substituted for "undenominational."

E. Noaks, Esq., Port Elizabeth.—The standards of instruction in Elementary subjects are under the present system the same for all classes of school. The result of this is that children in our first class public schools are compelled to go through almost precisely the same course up to the age of 14 or 15 as children in schools of a presumably lower type. The standards to be reached from year to year are sufficiently exacting, and the tests applied are of a very mechanical description. The result is, that in higher class schools the more formative and humanising subjects are in constant danger of being crowded out, and the treatment of the prescribed subjects is apt to be modelled on the uniform requirements (necessarily very inelastic) of the inspector. In higher class schools, at any rate, far more latitude seems to be desirable in the arrangement of school curricula. It is not indispensable as a safeguard for efficiency that all these schools should be of one pattern, however convenient it may be for the purposes of inspection and for the tabulation of "returns." The fact that mission schools are not entitled to receive any grant from Government for building purposes, and that the maximum grant available for any one school (even though there are over 200 children in attendance) is £75 per annum, will account for the inadequate building accommodation and staffing in some of the best of these schools in such a town as Port Elizabeth. The proposed scheme of fourth class undenominational schools should do much to remedy these evils.

Rev. J. D. Don, King William's Town.—
(a) In regard to undenominational education it would be impossible to provide anything more than Elementary schools in most places throughout the country on any other system.
(b) The prejudice which exists in many minds is due to the fact that undenominational education is practically looked upon as *secular* education. Of course this is not the case; but my inference is (1) That everything should be done that can be done to avoid giving a shadow of justice to the charge that undenominational schools are necessarily secular; (2) That every encouragement should be given to school committees and headmasters or mistresses, to maintain the Christian stamp of the education given in the schools, while avoiding the semblance of denominational teaching. There may be a theoretical difficulty in formulating this distinction, but in practice there is no difficulty at all. It is said of Dr. Arnold, "His education, in short, was not based upon religion, but was itself religious." This is better than dogmatic or denominational teaching. It is all that is needed, and is probably all that most of those who advocate denominational schools really want. If it were well understood that such education can be had and should be aimed at in our schools, the prejudice against them as secular would disappear.
(c) There can be no doubt that these are often too thickly planted in the same district. Missions overlap each other. Two missionaries plant schools, each for his own people, but too near for either to prosper. It is high time something were done to put a stop to this. There are practical difficulties, for the need of the missionary inspector is so real that his opposition cannot be made light of. He is necessary in order to make any system work at all. But the conviction that a change is necessary is spreading among missionaries themselves.

———

10. Have you any suggestions to make with regard to Industrial and Night schools?

J. Lamont, Esq., Adelaide.—Night schools should be established in every town, and aided upon the same system as Farm schools.

J. McLaren, Esq., Blytheswood.—The industrial departments attached to training institutions in the colony and the Transkei are very popular and successful. At Blytheswood, apprentices to carpentry are indentured for five years, receiving a small wage, from 8s. to 18s. a month and board. Any system of industrial teaching, to be successful, must be thorough-going, and should include a period of indenture to some particular trade for a period of three to five years. Apprentices and servants here attend a night school, but after the fatigue of the day, their progress is not very great.

Professor MacWilliam, Gill College, Somerset East.—I think it of great importance that boys should be taught the use of tools, and girls cookery and needlework The difficulty would be the cost, but I should like to see the experiment tried at a few suitable centres, and it might then be found possible to extend it if sufficient support were given or interest shown. I am afraid no great demand exists for night schools. I believe the method that would produce the best results would be to have short courses—not more than three months—of lessons on practical or scientific subjects, something on the lines of the Science and Art Department Examinations in England.

W. B. Stanford, Esq., Chief Magistrate, East Griqualand.—That it would be a wise step.

Rev. P. L. Hunter, Missionary Superintendent, Griqualand East.—Night schools are impracticable in the country. Industrial education under proper management is necessary to true education. In small mission schools it could only be attempted in a limited or private way.

F. B. Bampton, Esq., Humansdorp.—They should be encouraged and receive aid.

APPENDIX

TO

REPORT AND PROCEEDINGS

OF THE

EDUCATION COMMISSION.

[G. 3—'92.]

EDUCATION COMMISSION.

(APPENDIX A.)

RETURN OF SCHOOLS IN BOROUGH OF KIMBERLEY, furnished by the Sanitary Department, at the request of the Education Commission.

Where Located.	Teacher in Charge.	Public, Private, or Mission.	Attendance.		Sex.	Race.	Remarks.
			On Books.	Average.			
Recorder-street	W. Norrie	Public Und.	468	466	Mixed	E.	
Dutch Market	A. Cyle	do.	44	38	do.	E.	
Morris-street	P. Williams	Gov. Aided	150	130	do.	Mixed	Semi Mission.
Malay Camp	P. Mayega	do.	83	78	do.	N.	
Lanyon Terrace	St Michael Sis.	do.	80	79	do.	E.	
Du Toit's Pan Road	Rev. Twite	Private	36	34	Boys	E.	
St. Augustine's	Miss Marriot	Gov. Aided	21	20	Mixed	E.	Roman Catholic.
George-street	Mrs. T. Smith	Private	50	44	do.	E.	
Clarence-street	Miss Murphy	do.	20	20	do.	E.	
De Beer's Road	,, Manuel	do.	55	54	do.	E.	
Crescent-street	Mrs. Grandon	do.	53	40	do.	Col.	
Ross-street	,, Arapilly	do.	20	12	do.	N.	
Woodley-street	Miss Gorman	do.	35	30	do.	E.	
,,	,, Con	do.	68	50	do.	E.	
,,	,, Atkinson	do.	115	87	do.	E.	
Curry-street	Convent Sisters	do.	140	130	do.	E.	
Halkett Road	Mr. Friekerk	do.	71	68	do.	E.	
Newton	Miss Hendricks	do.	12	12	do.	E.	
Scholtz-street	Mrs. Wesley	do.	20	19	do.	Mixed	
Bultfontein Road	,, Van Abo	do.	30	25	do.	do.	
,,	,, K. Murray	do.	16	16	do.	E.	
Tyburn-street	,, Gassoman	do.	24	24	do.	E.	
Hampden-street	Miss Dunstan	do.	74	59	do.	E.	
Gladstone	Miss Campbell	do.	16	15	do.	E.	
,,	,, Bevan	do.	40	36	do.	E.	
De Beer's Road	,, Busell	do.	13	13	do.	E.	
Long-street	,, Hyam	do.	18	15	do.	E.	
Green-street	,, Cock	do.	18	18	do.	E.	
,,	,, Hall	do.	12	12	Girls	E.	
,,	,, Maritz	do.	22	20	Mixed	E.	
Clarence-street	Mrs. Teychcee	Mission	177	125	do.	Mixed	Episcopalian.
Cricket-street	,, Gordon	do.	181	150	do.	do.	Wesleyan.
Curry-street	Convent Sisters	do.	120	115	do.	Col.	Romanist.
Transvaal Road	Miss Webster	do.	40	35	do.	Mixed	Episcopalian.
Barkly Road	,, Foxwell	do.	100	75	do.	do.	do.
			about	about			
No. 1 Location	Rev. Grury	do.	50	40	do.	N.	Congregationalist.
No. 2 ,,	B. Joseph	do.	50	40	do.	N.	Episcopalian.
,, ,,	Rev. O'Rooyen	do.	50	40	do.	N.	do.
No. 3 ,,	,, Mayer	do.	50	40	do.	N.	Wesleyan.
No. 4 ,,	Mr. David	do.	50	40	do.	N.	Episcopalian.
Malay Camp	A. B. Effendi	Arabic	125	60	Mixed	Moh.	Mohamedan.
Total			2809	2424			

MEMO.—Re Races:—E., i.e., European; Col., i.e., Colonial races; N., i.e., Aboriginal Natives; Moh., i.e., Mohamedan; Mixed, i.e., White and Coloured children.

Some of the schools classed as "private" may be in receipt of Government aid.

PARTICULARS AS TO PUBLIC UNDENOMINATIONAL SCHOOLS.

EDUCATION COMMISSION.

Cape Town,
March 3rd, 1891.

SIR,

I have the honour, by direction of the President of the Education Commission,
to request that you will be good enough, at the earliest possible date, to furnish the
following information with reference to the school under the management of your
Board :—

A. (1.) Who are the guarantors of the school under your management, how are
the members chosen, and of what other bodies, if any, are members
wholly or partly, *ex officio* managers of the school ?

(2.) On what occasions, if any, have deficiencies arisen in the finances of the
school under your management, and how have any such deficiencies
been made good ?

B. In the case of property acquired for the purposes of the school :

(1.) Who are the legal holders ?

(2.) What provision is made for the tenure of the property ?

(3.) On what conditions is the property allowed to be used for school purposes
by managers who are not the legal holders ? Are the holders prepared
to allow this property to be vested in a Board permanently ? if so, state
views as to the constitution of such Board.

(4.) What amount, if any, has from time to time, or at any time, been
contributed by Government for the erection, purchase, or repairs of the
buildings used for the school under your management, and subject to
what conditions have such contributions been made ?

(5.) What money burdens are on the property, how have they arisen, what
amount is annually payable as interest or sinking fund, and from what
fund is it paid ?

C. In the case of property rented for school purposes :

(1.) What is the amount of rent paid ?

(2.) By whom is it paid ?

(3.) Out of what fund is it paid ?

I am, Sir,

Your obedient Servant,
W. S. FLETCHER,
Secretary.

To
the Chairman of the Board
of Managers of the.........Class
Undenominational Public School at......................

The following are further replies received to the above circular :—

REPLIES, &c.

Name of School.	Particulars as to management, &c.	Particulars as to Property.
Wynberg Second Class Boys'.	Fourteen guarantors, residents in the village, who are liable for £5 each. Managers are chosen by the general body of guarantors only. No ex officio managers. No deficiencies.	Messrs. J. H. Hofmeyr, F. J. Broers, and G. de Kock are Trustees of the property. The conditions are the free use of the school building, for which the managers have to pay interest on £300 debt, repairs, insurance, &c. The trustees are not prepared to have the property vested in a Board permanently. No Government contributions.
Prince Alfred's Hamlet's (Tulbagh) Second Class School.	The guarantors are the Managers chosen. The Managers are chosen from a body of subscribers by those who have bound themselves to pay for a certain number of children. Three of the present Board of Managers are churchwardens of the Dutch Reformed Church, but the school is quite undenominational. An annual deficiency of about £50, caused by low school fees, and the interest to be paid on a bond for £200, is made good by voluntary contributions.	The Board of Managers are legal holders of the property. No Government contribution. A bond of £200 exists, on which six per cent. interest is paid.
Untata Second Class School.	Twenty-two guarantors, and managers are elected from their number. No ex officio Managers. Once during first year there was a call of 5s. in the £ on guarantors to meet expenditure for extra school furniture. No deficiency.	Rent £16 per annum, paid by managers out of school fees.
Jansenville Third Class School.	The guarantors are nearly all parents of the children at school, and from these the Managers are chosen for three years, according to Government regulations. No ex officio Managers. No deficiency.	Property granted for school purposes by the D. R. Church, without rent, managers effecting repairs.
Cradock First Class School for Girls.	There are thirteen guarantors. Managers chosen in accordance with regulations. The Minister of the Dutch Reformed Church is an ex officio Manager. No deficiency.	The Rocklands Seminary stands registered in the name of the trustees for the time being of the Opvoedings Instituit, Cradock, by deed of transfer, there being a provision that it is to be used for school purposes. The Committee are bound to maintain and repair the property out of school funds. It

Name of School.	Particulars as to management, &c.	Particulars as to Property.
Uitenhage First Class (Branch) School.	There are no guarantors, the school being aided by subsidies from Divisional and Town Councils. The Managers are the Mayor, two members of the Municipal Council, three members of the Divisional Council, and two members of the Public School Board. (Boys). No deficiency.	is not proposed to vest the property in any other Board. Government has granted £500, and the School Committee, in conjunction with the Church authorities, have expended over £6,000. Balance bond £300, and £700 due to D. R. Church. Interest at 6 per cent on £300 paid out of school funds. No interest on the £700. No rent paid. Rent £24 per annum, paid by the managers out of school funds.
Mossel Bay First Class School for Girls.	Managers elected according to regulations. No deficiency.	Rent £24 per annum, paid by the managers out of school income.
Mossel Bay Second Class School for Boys.	Managers elected according to regulations. No ex officio Managers. For some time there was a yearly deficiency, met by a collection among the inhabitants.	Strictly speaking, there are no legal holders, the nominal holders being the Board of Managers, who have sold and acquired property, which has been transferred by and to them. No special provision has been made for the tenure of property. Property is allowed to be used for school purposes on condition that it is undenominational. Managers would probably be quite willing to have the property vested in a body comprising the Civil Commissioner and Ministers of the English and D. R. Church, for the time being. Government has contributed £750, the condition being that the building shall be used for the purposes of an undenominational school. £206 is the amount of the debt, caused by purchasing property and building. The yearly interest is £12, paid out of school income.
Middelburg Second Class School.	Managers are elected by the general body of guarantors triennially. Committee members only manage the school. No deficiency.	Rent £60 per annum, paid by managers out of school funds.

Name of School.	Particulars as to management, &c.	Particulars as to Property.
Umzimkulu Third Class School.	Board of Management are the recognized guarantors, and are chosen at the annual meeting of parents and others. No ex officio Managers. There have been regular deficiencies, made good by proceeds from entertainments, &c.	Government has granted two erven, on which it is proposed to build a school house and residence. Ground rent is £3 per annum, and rent of building £12, paid by the managers out of general funds.
Kimberley First Class Boys' and Girls' Schools.	These are presided over by one Board of Management, although conducted in different sections of the same building. The guarantors of both schools, sixty-three in number, are residents in Kimberley, and each is bound, in writing, to pay a sum of £10 a year for three years, or such lesser sum, as may be necessary to supplement the income, when exceeded by the cost of maintenance. The Managers are elected by the guarantors. No ex officio Managers. No deficiencies.	The school buildings were erected for school purposes out of funds collected by the managers from the public of Kimberley, augmented by a Parliamentary grant of £2,000. All school property, movable and immovable, is vested in the Board of Management for the time being. No special provisions exist relating to the tenure of the property, the managers being the legal holders for educational purposes. The buildings cost about £8,000. Of this sum, £4,000 was raised by public subscription, and £2,000 was granted by Parliament, leaving a debt of £2,000 advanced by the Standard Bank. The obligation to the Standard Bank has since been extinguished, with the assistance of a loan from Government. The Colonial Government now holds a mortgage bond on the buildings, passed by the board under the provisions of the "Public Bodies Loan Act," for an advance of £2,000, with which the original debt of £2,000 to the Standard Bank has been paid. The Board pays Government £116 13s. 4d. per annum on the above loan as interest and sinking fund. There are no other money burdens. No property is rented for school purposes. There is a branch school in a part of the town called "Newton," held in premises belonging to the Dutch Reformed Church, but for the use of these no rent is charged.

www.ingramcontent.com/pod-product-compliance
Lightning Source LLC
Chambersburg PA
CBHW030902270326
41929CB00008B/532